Multimedia System

Multimedia System

Editor:

Harinirina Randrianarisoa, Ph.D.

ArclerPress

www.arclerpress.com

Multimedia System

Editor: Harinirina Randrianarisoa, Ph.D.

© 2017 Arcler Press LLC
708 3rd Avenue, 6th Floor
New York
NY 10017
United States of America
www.arclerpress.com

ISBN: 978-1-68094-460-0

Library of Congress Control Number: 2016951401

About the Editor

Harinirina Randrianarisoa, Ph.D.

Hari Randrianarisoa obtained is Ph.D from Institute of Electronics, Microelectronics and Nanotechnology (IEMN) of the University of Science and Technology – Lille (France). His thesis focused for designing and manufacturing of thermal micro sensors. His interests span from on renewable energy especially solar energy. He has a strong knowledge in technology transfer field. He is currently working as a Business advisor for economic development organization in Québec City and as a consultant Scientist advisor.

Contents

List of Contributors

Chiheb Ben **Ameur**
Orange Labs, Rennes, France

Emmanuel Mory
Orange Labs, Rennes, France

Bernard Cousin
IRISA, University of Rennes 1, Rennes, France

Marcella Mandanici
Department of Information Engineering, University of Padova, Via G. Gradenigo 6/b, 35131 Padua, Italy

Antonio Rodà
Department of Information Engineering, University of Padova, Via G. Gradenigo 6/b, 35131 Padua, Italy

Sergio Canazza
Department of Information Engineering, University of Padova, Via G. Gradenigo 6/b, 35131 Padua, Italy

Lilac Al-Safadi
Department of Information Technology, College of Computer and Information Sciences, King Saud University, Saudi Arabia

Lujie Zhong
Information Engineering College, Capital Normal University, Beijing 100048, China

Shijie Jia
Central Plains Economic Zone Wisdom Tourism Cooperative Innovation Center, Luoyang Normal University, Luoyang, Henan 471934, China
Academy of Information Technology, Luoyang Normal University, Luoyang, Henan 471934, China

Youzhong Ma
Central Plains Economic Zone Wisdom Tourism Cooperative Innovation Center, Luoyang Normal University, Luoyang, Henan 471934, China
Academy of Information Technology, Luoyang Normal University, Luoyang, Henan 471934, China

Yongxin Zhang
Central Plains Economic Zone Wisdom Tourism Cooperative Innovation Center, Luoyang Normal University, Luoyang, Henan 471934, China
Academy of Information Technology, Luoyang Normal University, Luoyang, Henan 471934, China

Soumen Kanrar
Vehere Interactive Pvt. Ltd., Calcutta, West Bengal 700053, India
Vidyasagar University, West Bengal 721102, India

Niranjan Kumar Mandal
Vidyasagar University, West Bengal 721102, India

Ivaylo Atanasov
Technical University of Sofia, 8 Kliment Ohridski Boulevard, 1000 Sofia, Bulgaria

Evelina Pencheva
Technical University of Sofia, 8 Kliment Ohridski Boulevard, 1000 Sofia, Bulgaria

Minseok Song
School of Computer and Information Engineering, Inha University, Incheon 22212, Republic of Korea

Jinhan Park
School of Computer and Information Engineering, Inha University, Incheon 22212, Republic of Korea

Vikas Bhandary
Deenbandhu Chhotu Ram University of Science and Technology, Murthal, Sonepat 131039, India

Amita Malik
Deenbandhu Chhotu Ram University of Science and Technology, Murthal, Sonepat 131039, India

Sanjay Kumar
SRM University Haryana, Sonepat 131029, India

Soumen Kanrar
Vehere Interactive Pvt. Ltd., Calcutta, West Bengal 700053, India
Vidyasagar University, West Bengal 721102, India

Niranjan Kumar Mandal
Vidyasagar University, West Bengal 721102, India

Diego José Luis Botia Valderrama
Engineering Department, Universidad de Antioquia, Medellín, Colombia

Natalia Gaviria Gómez
Engineering Department, Universidad de Antioquia, Medellín, Colombia

Chih-Hsiao Tsai
Department of Information Technology, Takming University of Science and Technology, No. 56 Huangshan Road, Section 1, Neihu District, Taipei City 11451, Taiwan

Yin-Hao Kuo
Department of Tourism and Hospitality, Taipei Chengshih University of Science and Technology, No. 2 Xueyuan Road, Beitou District, Taipei City 11202, Taiwan

Kuo-Chung Chu
Department of Information Management, National Taipei University of Nursing and Health Sciences, No. 365 Ming-Te Road, Beitou District, Taipei City 11219, Taiwan

Jung-Chuan Yen
Department of Mathematics and Information Education, National Taipei University of Education, No. 134 Heping E. Road, Section 2, Da'an District, Taipei City 10671, Taiwan

Julio Proaño Orellana
Computing Systems Department, University of Castilla-La Mancha, Campus Universitario s/n, 02071 Albacete, Spain

Blanca Caminero
Computing Systems Department, University of Castilla-La Mancha, Campus Universitario s/n, 02071 Albacete, Spain

Carmen Carrión
Computing Systems Department, University of Castilla-La Mancha, Campus Universitario s/n, 02071 Albacete, Spain

Luis Tomas
Department of Computing Science, Umeå University, 901 87 Umeå, Sweden

Selome Kostentinos Tesfatsion
Department of Computing Science, Umeå University, 901 87 Umeå, Sweden

Johan Tordsson
Department of Computing Science, Umeå University, 901 87 Umeå, Sweden

Tianhua Liu
Software collegeShenyang Normal University

Shoulin Yin
Software collegeShenyang Normal University

Claudiu Cobarzan
Klagenfurt University

Klaus Schoeffmann
Klagenfurt University

Werner Bailer
DIGITAL - Institute of Information and Communication TechnologiesJoanneum research

Wolfgang Hurst
Information and Computing SciencesUtrecht University

Adam Blazek
SIRET research group, Department of Software Engineering, Faculty of Mathematics and PhysicsCharles University in Prague

Jakub Lokoc
SIRET research group, Department of Software Engineering, Faculty of Mathematics and PhysicsCharles University in Prague

Stefanos Vrochidis
Centre for Research and Technology Hellas*Information Technologies Institute*

Kai Uwe Barthel
Internationaler Studiengang Medieninformatik*Hochschule für Technik und Wirtschaft*

Luca Rossetto
Department of Mathematics and Computer Science*University of Basel*

Wen-Ching Liao
Department of Computer Science and Information Engineering, National Taiwan University, Taipei, Taiwan R.O.C.

Han-Hong Lin
Department of Computer Science and Information Engineering, National Taiwan University, Taipei, Taiwan R.O.C.

He-Lin Ruo
Department of Computer Science and Information Engineering, National Taiwan University, Taipei, Taiwan R.O.C.

Po-Hsiang Hsu
Department of Computer Science and Information Engineering, National Taiwan University, Taipei, Taiwan R.O.C.

Abhilash Sreeramaneni
Department of Computer Science and Engineering, Seoul National University of Science and Technology, Seoul 139-743, Korea

Hyungjin Im
Department of Computer Science and Engineering, Seoul National University of Science and Technology, Seoul 139-743, Korea

Won Min Kang
Department of Computer Science and Engineering, Seoul National University of Science and Technology, Seoul 139-743, Korea

Chan Koh
Department of Computer Science and Engineering, Seoul National University of Science and Technology, Seoul 139-743, Korea

Jong Hyuk Park
Department of Computer Science and Engineering, Seoul National University of Science and Technology, Seoul 139-743, Korea
Department of Interdisciplinary Bio IT Materials, Seoul National University of Science and Technology, Seoul 139-743, Korea

Laith Al-Jobouri
School of Computer Science and Electronic Engineering, University of Essex, Wivenhoe Park, Colchester CO4 3SQ, UK

Ismail A. Ali
Department of Electrical and Computer Engineering, University of Duhok, 1006 AJ Duhok, Iraq

Martin Fleury
School of Computer Science and Electronic Engineering, University of Essex, Wivenhoe Park, Colchester CO4 3SQ, UK

Mohammed Ghanbari
School of Computer Science and Electronic Engineering, University of Essex, Wivenhoe Park, Colchester CO4 3SQ, UK

Preface

A Multimedia System is a system capable of processing multimedia data and applications. A Multimedia System is characterized by the processing, storage, generation, manipulation and rendition of Multimedia information. The aim of multimedia system is to provide a creative and effective way of producing, storing and communicating information. The application areas of multimedia are marketing, training, education, entertainment, etc. Multimedia is not a product literally of the term, neither a technology sector as such, but a hybrid, resulting from the merger of technologies until then largely independent. Multimedia is the use of a computer to present and combine text, graphics, audio, and video with links and tools that let the user navigate, interact, create, and communicate. This definition contains four components essential to multimedia. First, there must be a computer to coordinate what you see and hear, and to interact with. Second, there must be links that connect the information. Third, there must be navigational tools that let you traverse the web of connected information. Finally, because multimedia is not a spectator sport, there must be ways for you to gather, process, and communicate your own information and ideas. If one of these components is missing, you do not have multimedia. The multimedia is realized in dynamic way and daily through forms of communications carried out by the individuals on different web spaces. Furthermore, all sectors of economic and social activity (including health, education and training, entertainment, commerce and communications) are transformed by the multimedia. With regard to multimedia system, this book discussed details innovative research ideas, emerging technologies, state-of-the-art methods and tools in all aspects and applications. The literature explored method of processing to increase processor power, optimization of power consumption, storage structures, video management, traffic method routing in real time and transportation. Modeling and simulation of novel algorithm to improve speed execution getting a better interactive session are also described.

Editor
Harinirina Randrianarisoa, Ph.D.

INTRODUCTION

Multimedia is a technology which stores data as text, photo, pictures, music, sounds, graphic, film and animation and gives the methods to collect and modify the data as desired.

A Multimedia System is a system capable of processing multimedia data and applications. A Multimedia System is characterized by the processing, storage, generation, manipulation and rendition of Multimedia information. A computer system with the capabilities to capture, digitize, compress, store, decompress and present information is called multimedia system. The aim of multimedia system is to provide a creative and effective way of producing, storing and communicating information. The application areas of multimedia are marketing, training, education, entertainment, etc.

The multimedia computer generally contains the following components.

1) Computer
2) Multimedia Software
3) Sound card
4) CD-Drive
5) Micro-Phone
6) CD-ROM Disk
7) Multimedia speakers/Head-Phones
8) Digital Camera and many other components.

Application of multimedia

- **Multimedia presentation:** Multimedia presentation can be used to better explain a subject matter to the students because it enhance the comprehension capability of students. It is extremely effective in getting across new ideas and concepts.

- **Entertainment:** Multimedia technology is used by entertainment industry as in games, films, cartoons, animation, sound effects etc.

- **Software:** Multimedia is used for training purpose or guide. So users can operate software without help of trainers.
- **Business communication:** Multimedia is very powerful tool for enhancing the quality of business communication.
- **Multimedia web pages:** Multimedia feature in web pages make more attractive, user friendly.

Different Types of Multimedia Systems

There are many different types of multimedia systems, which are usually developed or designed to meet a particular purpose or for use in a certain environment. Home systems, for example, are intended for enjoyment by a relatively small group of people and for use in a fairly small space. There are systems designed for use in the workplace, which may be intended for somewhat small groups and are used in offices for presentations or employee training. Larger systems are developed for use at trade shows and conferences, and are designed to reach a potentially massive audience. The modular nature of multimedia systems allows many of the same pieces of technology to be used in a variety of settings. A multimedia system is basically a combination of hardware and software used for viewing or displaying different types of media, such as audio and video. Home systems, for example, are usually designed to allow for one or a few people to view programs in a home environment. These often include a television screen or similar monitor, which may be fairly large, and speaker setups that may utilize surround sound and are typically centrally located.

Multimedia systems for use in an office, on the other hand, might utilize multiple monitors and computer terminals, as well as different speaker systems. Depending on the size of the presentation being made, or the materials being covered, a single screen might display an image that is also visible at separate computer terminals. Rather than using a monitor or television screen, this type of system often uses a projector and a screen to produce a large image. For training purposes, systems can be used that allow a single presentation to be made for an entire group, while each individual is at a computer and able to interact with a personal version of the presentation.

There are also multimedia systems that can be used in much larger venues, such as trade shows, conferences, and speaking engagements. These systems use a number of different displays all showing the same images simultaneously. This allows a single speaker to have one large display that he or she refers to while making a presentation, with smaller displays throughout a room that can be more clearly seen by those farther from the main screen. Multiple speakers can also be used in such systems to allow those in a large space to all clearly hear the speaker.

Components of Multimedia

Multimedia applications can include many types of media. The primary characteristic of a multimedia system is the use of more than one kind of media to deliver content and functionality. Web and desktop computing programs can both involve multimedia components. As well as different media items, a multimedia application will normally involve programming code and enhanced user interaction. Multimedia items generally fall into one of five main categories and use varied techniques for digital formatting.

Text

It may be an easy content type to forget when considering multimedia systems, but text content is by far the most common media type in computing applications. Most multimedia systems use a combination of text and other media to deliver functionality. Text in multimedia systems can express specific information, or it can act as reinforcement for information contained in other media items. This is a common practice in applications with accessibility requirements. For example, when Web pages include image elements, they can also include a short amount of text for the user's browser to include as an alternative, in case the digital image item is not available.

Images

Digital image files appear in many multimedia applications. Digital photographs can display application content or can alternatively form part of a user interface. Interactive elements, such as buttons, often use custom images created by the designers and developers involved in an application. Digital image files use a variety of formats and file extensions. Among the most common are JPEGs and PNGs. Both of these often appear on websites, as the formats allow developers to minimize on file size while maximizing on picture quality. Graphic design software programs such as Photoshop and Paint.NET allow developers to create complex visual effects with digital images.

Audio

Audio files and streams play a major role in some multimedia systems. Audio files appear as part of application content and also to aid interaction. When they appear within Web applications and sites, audio files sometimes need to be deployed using plug-in media players. Audio formats include MP3, WMA, Wave, MIDI and RealAudio. When developers include audio within a website, they will generally use a compressed format to minimize on download times. Web services can also stream audio, so that users can begin playback before the entire file is downloaded.

Video

Digital video appears in many multimedia applications, particularly on the Web. As with audio, websites can stream digital video to increase the speed and availability of playback. Common digital video formats include Flash, MPEG, AVI, WMV and QuickTime. Most digital video requires use of browser plug-ins to play within Web pages, but in many cases the user's browser will already have the required resources installed.

Animation

Animated components are common within both Web and desktop multimedia applications. Animations can also include interactive effects, allowing users to engage with the animation action using their mouse and keyboard. The most common tool for creating animations on the Web is Adobe Flash, which also facilitates desktop applications. Using Flash, developers can author FLV files, exporting them as SWF movies for deployment to users. Flash also uses Action Script code to achieve animated and interactive effects.

Challenges for Multimedia Systems

Multimedia systems may have to render a variety of media at the same instant -- a distinction from normal applications. There is a temporal relationship between many forms of media (e.g. Video and Audio. There 2 are forms of problems here

- Sequencing within the media -- ***playing frames in correct order/time frame in video***
- ***Synchronisation*** -- inter-media scheduling (*e.g.* Video and Audio). Lip synchronisation is clearly important for humans to watch playback of video and audio and even animation and audio. Ever tried watching an out of (lip) sync film for a long time?

The key issues multimedia systems need to deal with here are:

- How to represent and store temporal information.
- How to strictly maintain the temporal relationships on play back/retrieval
- What process are involved in the above.

Data has to represented digitally so many initial source of data needs to be digitise translated from analog source to digital representation. The will involve scanning (graphics, still images), sampling (audio/video) although digital cameras now exist for direct scene to digital capture of images and video.

The data is large several Mb easily for audio and video therefore storage, transfer (bandwidth) and processing overheads are high. Data compression techniques very common.

Advantages of Multimedia

We have already mentioned various advantages of using multimedia. We can still specifically list out following points that explains the advantages of the multimedia.

- It can be used to help students and teacher to teach as well as learn the given topics easily.
- It can be used to spread the knowledge easily all over the world wide in the cheap cost.
- It is easy to take the multimedia files from one to other places as it can be stored in the cheap and light storage devices like CD-ROM.

- It can be used for any subject and for anyone.
- It can be used in Television, Films Industries and for personal entertainments.
- It is highly used to realize the concept of Open University, Distance Education System, and Video Conferencing.
- It is also used in Internet to make up the interactive web-page contents.
- We can give the everlasting impression to the intended audiences on a specific topic by the use of multimedia.
- Colored pictures, Motion pictures and other graphics could be shown in monitors and other big screens so that many people could view it and make out the impression about it.
- Multimedia systems are generally very interactive so it is interesting to use.

Disadvantages of Multimedia

In comparison to the enormous advantages we have very little disadvantages of multimedia. These disadvantages could be listed out as:

- It is expensive to produce multimedia contents.
- It is expensive to set up the multimedia systems.
- It needs well trained manpower to create and use it.
- Multimedia files are too large so, it is time consuming to transfer across the Internet and Intranet.

CHAPTER 1

COMBINING TRAFFIC-SHAPING METHODS WITH CONGESTION CONTROL VARIANTS FOR HTTP ADAPTIVE STREAMING

Chiheb Ben Ameur, Emmanuel Mory, Bernard Cousin

Keywords: Traffic shaping, Congestion control, Quality of experience, HTTP adaptive streaming, Bandwidth management

INTRODUCTION

HTTP Adaptive Streaming (HAS) is a streaming video technique based on downloading video segments of short duration. These segments are called chunks, and they are streamed from a HAS server to a HAS client through the network. Each chunk is encoded at multiple quality levels. After requesting a chunk by an HTTP GET request message, when the chunk is received, the player on the client side stores it in a playback buffer. The HAS player operates in one of two states: a buffering state and a steady state. During the first state, the player requests a new chunk as soon as a previous chunk has been downloaded, until the playback buffer is filled. However, during the steady state, the player requests chunks periodically in order to maintain a constant playback buffer size. The steady state includes periods of activity (ON periods) followed by periods of inactivity (OFF periods) [9, 11].

The Quality of Experience (QoE) of an HTTP-adaptive stream depends primarily on three criteria:

1. Video quality level stability [1, 11]: a frequent change of video quality level bothers the user. Therefore, quality level fluctuation should be avoided to improve the QoE.
2. Fidelity to optimal quality level selection: the user prefers to watch the best video quality level, when possible. Therefore, the HAS player should select the optimal quality level, which is the highest feasible quality level allowed by the available bandwidth.
3. Convergence speed: the user prefers to view the optimal quality level as soon as possible. Accordingly, the HAS player should rapidly select the optimal quality level. The delay that the player requires before the optimal quality level has been attained is called the convergence speed [1].

We studied a general use case in which several HAS clients are located in the same home network. In this use case, QoE degradations can be grouped into two main causes:

- Congestion events: video packets sent from the server to the client pass through many network devices. Each device has one or many queues that use a queuing discipline to schedule network packets. The implemented algorithm decides whether to route or drop incoming packets in order to avoid network congestion. The main bottleneck occurs near the home gateway, and more precisely, in the link between DSLAM and home gateway [12]. In fact, the DSLAM may considerably reduce the bandwidth offered to the home network, and it is more likely to drop packets than any other network device. To minimize network effects on the delivery, the TCP protocol implements a "congestion control

Citation: Chiheb Ben Ameur, Emmanuel Mory, Bernard Cousin, Combining traffic-shaping methods with congestion control variants for HTTP adaptive streaming, DOI: 10.1007/s00530-016-0522-9.

algorithm" on the sender side, which reduces the bitrate of packets sent to the receiver when a packet is lost. However, this bitrate reduction may degrade QoE. In addition, there are many congestion control variants with different methods of managing the congestion window size, cwnd, and detecting congestion events. These differences may change the QoE between variants.

- Concurrence with other streams—OFF periods issue: the HAS player estimates the available bandwidth by computing the download bitrate for each chunk when it has finished downloading; this is done by dividing the chunk size by its download duration. As a consequence, the player cannot estimate the available bandwidth during OFF periods, because no data are being received. When a HAS stream concurs with other streams in the same home network, accurate bandwidth estimation becomes more difficult. For example, when two HAS streams are competing for bandwidth and the ON period of the first player coincides with the OFF period of the second player, the first player will overestimate its available bandwidth. This overestimation may lead the player to select a higher quality level for the next chunk. This selection may lead to a congestion event and a resulting fluctuation of quality levels between the two players. Research has demonstrated that traffic shaping can considerably limit this problem [1, 2, 11, 21, 25]. Traffic shaping consists of selecting a target bitrate for each HAS session in the home network based on bitrates of the available quality levels and the available bandwidth. It then shapes the outgoing traffic to each HAS client based on the selected target bitrate.
- The objective of our study is to combine two solution categories, TCP congestion control variants to reduce the negative effects of congestion events, and traffic-shaping methods, to restrict the drawbacks of the concurrence between HAS streams in the home gateway. The optimal combination will have the highest grade of QoE, i.e., the best possible video quality level stability, best fidelity to optimal quality level selection, and best convergence speed.
- We note that there are many implementations of HAS that are currently deployed, such as Dynamic Adaptive Streaming over HTTP (MPEG-DASH), Microsoft Smooth Streaming (MSS), Apple HTTP Live Streaming (HLS), and Adobe HTTP Dynamic Streaming (HDS). For this reason, we wish to emphasize that in this paper we only choose HAS traffic-shaping methods that do not change the HAS implementation either in the player or in the server. This choice provides adaptability to any HAS client or server implementations and thus offers a larger scope of application of our presented work.
- The remainder of this paper is organized as follows. In Sect. 2, we describe the background and related works. In Sect. 3, we detail our methodology and experimental implementation. Section 4 presents the results and discussion. In Sect. 5, we conclude the paper and suggest future directions for our work.

BACKGROUND AND RELATED WORK

In this section, we describe the TCP congestion control variants and the HAS traffic-shaping methods used in this work, and explain the distinctions between them.

TCP congestion control variants

All TCP congestion control variants have two common phases: a slow start phase and a congestion avoidance phase. The slow start phase consists of increasing cwnd rapidly by one maximum segment size (MSS) for each received acknowledgment (ACK), i.e., the cwnd value is doubled for each round trip time (RTT). This rapidity has an objective of reaching a high bitrate within a short duration. When the cwnd size exceeds a threshold called ssthresh, the TCP congestion control algorithm switches to the second phase: the congestion avoidance phase. This phase slowly increases the cwnd until a congestion event is detected.

TCP congestion control variants are classified according to two main criteria [13]:

1. The first criterion is the increase of cwnd during the congestion avoidance phase and the decrease of cwnd immediately following congestion detection. Generally, the increase is additive, and the cwnd size increases by one MSS for each RTT. For decreasing cwnd, the standard variants employ multiplicative decreasing, i.e., thecwnd size is weighted by a multiplicative decrease factor $(1-\beta)$, where $0 < \beta < 1$. This category is called the Additive Increase Multiplicative Decrease (AIMD) approach. Other variants using different techniques are classified as non-AIMD approaches.
2. The second criterion is the method by which the algorithm detects congestion. We distinguish three modes: loss-based, delay-based, and loss–delay-based modes. The loss-based mode considers any detection of packet loss as a congestion event. A majority of TCP congestion control variants that use the loss-based mode consider receiving three duplicated ACKs from the receiver as an indication of a packet loss and, as a consequence, as an indication of a congestion event. However, the delay-based mode considers a significant increase in the RTT value as the only indication of a congestion event. The third mode, the hybrid mode, combines the delay-based and loss-based modes to improve congestion detection.

In order to facilitate our study, we chose four well-known congestion control variants, and we classify them according to the two criteria cited above:

NewReno [3]: this variant is designed as the standard TCP congestion control approach. It uses the AIMD approach with the loss-based mode. Two mechanisms are employed immediately following congestion detection: fast retransmit and fast recovery [14]. Fast retransmit consists of performing a retransmission of what appears to be the missing packet (i.e., when receiving three duplicate ACKs), without waiting for the retransmission timer to expire. After the fast retransmit algorithm sends this packet, the fast recovery algorithm governs the transmission of new data until a non-duplicate ACK arrives. The reason for using fast recovery is to allow the continual sending of packets when the receiver is still receiving packets, even if some packets are lost.

Vegas [4]: this non-AIMD variant is an Additive Increase Additive Decrease (AIAD) variant. It is a delay-based variant that accurately estimates RTT for every sent packet and adjustscwnd size based on actual throughput and expected throughput. If RTT increases, cwnddecreases by one MSS, and vice versa. Vegas is the smoothest TCP congestion control variant [15]; it is able to allocate a fair share of bandwidth with minimal packet loss events.

Illinois [5]: This is a TCP loss-delay-based congestion variant that employs a particular classification of the AIMD approach, C-AIMD, which involves a concave window size curve. Packet loss is used for primary congestion inference to determine the direction (increase or decrease) of cwnd, with a delay for secondary congestion inference to adjust the value of the window size change. More precisely, when the average queueing delay is small (small increase of RTT), the sender supposes that the congestion is not imminent and specifies a large additive increase α and small multiplicative decrease β. In the opposite case, when the average queuing delay is large (large increase of RTT), the sender supposes that the congestion is imminent and selects a small α and large β. Illinois measures RTT for each received ACK to update α and β. Moreover, it retains the same fast recovery and fast retransmit phases as NewReno. Illinois was designed for high-speed and high-latency networks, where the bandwidth-delay product is relatively high. Consequently, it enables higher throughput than NewReno.

Cubic [6]: this variant is loss-based, but it uses a non-AIMD approach. A cubic function is used to increase the cwnd in the congestion avoidance phase immediately after the fast recovery phase, and a multiplicative decrease approach is used to update the cwnd after congestion event detection. The cubic function has a concave region followed by a convex region. The plateau between the two regions, or the inflection point (denoted by W_{max}), corresponds to the window size just before the last congestion event. The cubic function enables a slow growth around W_{max} to enhance the stability of the bandwidth, and enables a fast growth away from W_{max} to improve scalability of the protocol. Upon receiving an ACK during the congestion avoidance phase at time t, Cubic computes the new value of cwndcorresponding to the cubic function at time t. As a consequence, Cubic uses the time instead of the RTT to increase the cwnd. Cubic employs a new slow-start algorithm called HyStart [8] (hybrid slow start), which finds a safe exit point to the slow start, the ssthresh value, at which the slow start can finish and safely move to congestion avoidance before cwnd overshoot occurs. HyStart employs the RTT delay increase and the inter-arrival time between consecutive ACKs to identify the safe exit point, and to modify the ssthresh value [8]. This variant does not make any change to the fast recovery and fast retransmit of standard NewReno. Cubic is the smoothest loss-based congestion control variant [15]: it is characterized by a congestion window that falls less abruptly and that remains constant over a wide range of elapsed time. It is also designed for high-speed and high-latency networks. Cubic is implemented and used by default in Linux kernels since version 2.6.19.

For precise analysis, based on the descriptions of congestion control algorithm variants and their source code, we describe below the update of the congestion window size, cwnd, and the slow start threshold value, ssthresh, for different events:

- Congestion events: there are two cases
- When a congestion event is detected, the Fast Recovery/ Fast Retransmit (FR/FR) phase reduces the ssthresh value and sets the cwnd value to ssthresh+3, for the purpose of remaining in the congestion avoidance phase. The ssthresh value after a congestion event is updated as follows:

Algorithm 1 *ssthresh* update after a congestion event

```
NewReno: ssthresh = max(cwnd/2, 2 MSS)
Vegas:   ssthresh = min(ssthresh, cwnd - 1)
Illinois: ssthresh = max(cwnd.(1-β), 2 MSS)
Cubic:   ssthresh = max(cwnd.(1-β), 2 MSS)
```

where MSS is the maximum segment size, and β is the multiplicative decrease factor.

- When the retransmission timeout expires before receiving any ACK of the retransmitted packet, ssthresh is reduced as indicated in Algorithm 1, and cwnd is set to a small value and restarts from the slow start phase.
- Idle period: when the server sends a packet after an idle period that exceeds the retransmission timeout (RTO), cwnd and ssthresh are computed for the four congestion control variants as in Algorithm 2:

Algorithm 2 *cwnd* and *ssthresh* updates after idle period

```
ssthresh = max(ssthresh, ¾ cwnd)
for i=1 to int(idle/RTO) do
  cwnd = max ( min ( cwnd , rwnd )/2, 1 MSS )
end for
```

In the HAS context, an idle period coincides with an OFF period between two consecutive chunks. An OFF period whose duration exceeds RTO is denoted by OFF*.

Furthermore, we additionally want to emphasize that the rate of a TCP connection can be approximated, if we assume that transients due to slow start and fast recovery can be neglected, by min(cwnd,rwnd)/RTTmin(cwnd,rwnd)/RTT

[26], where rwnd is the TCP receive window indicated by the receiver and RTT is the round trip time between the sender and the receiver. Obviously, this approximation is valid for the four TCP congestion control variants described above. As we have shown, these variants employ different algorithms to modify the congestion window, cwnd, during the congestion avoidance phase and after congestion detection. Accordingly, the generated rate as well as its variation over time is different from one variant to another.

Traffic-shaping methods

Many studies have been conducted to improve HAS performance for cases in which several HAS clients are located in the same home network. The ON–OFF periods characterizing the HAS player in its steady state involve three substantial problems when HAS players are competing: player instability, unfairness between players, and bandwidth underutilization [9]. The cause of these problems is the inability to estimate the available bandwidth during the OFF period, because no data are being received.

Three types of solutions are proposed to improve HAS user experience: client-based, server-based, and gateway-based solutions. They differ with respect to the device in which the shaping solution is implemented. Below, we cite relevant methods for each type of solution:

- The client-based solution involves only the HAS client in order to reduce its OFF period durations. One of the recent client-based methods is proposed in the FESTIVE method [7]. It randomizes the events of chunk requests inside the player in order to reduce the periodicity of ON periods. Consequently, most of the incorrect estimations of bandwidth could be avoided when several HAS clients compete for bandwidth. However, this method is not efficient enough to prevent all incorrect estimations. In addition, it modifies the HAS player implementation, which is contradictory to our specifications described in Sect. 1. Moreover, the client-based solution does not provide the coordination between HAS clients that is required to further improve bandwidth estimations and QoE.
- The server-based solution involves only the HAS server. It proceeds according to two steps: first, finding the optimal quality level for each provided HAS flow, and second, shaping the sending rate of the HAS server according to the encoding rate of this level. In [25], the authors propose a server-based method: it consists in detecting the oscillations between quality levels on the server side and deciding which optimal quality level must be selected. Although this method improves the QoE, it cannot conveniently respond to the typical use cases of several concurrent HAS clients that do not share the same HAS server: the shared link is on the HAS client side. Moreover, this server-based solution requires an additional processing task, which becomes burdensome and costly when many HAS clients are demanding video contents from the same HAS server. In addition, the server-based solution is unable to acquire information about the other competing flows with their corresponding HAS clients. Hence, the selection of the optimal quality level at the server is a vague estimation. This estimation is less accurate than a quality level selection based on a sufficient knowledge about the access network of the corresponding HAS client(s).
- The gateway-based solution that consists of applying the HAS traffic shaping in the gateway is more convenient than client-based and server-based solutions; in fact, the gateway can acquire information about the HAS traffic of all clients of the same home network, which is not possible either at the server or at the client. In addition, the gateway-based solution is able to perform traffic shaping without inducing any modification of HAS implementation code either in the server or the client. Hence, in this paper, our evaluations only consider the gateway-based shaping solution. For the gateway-based solution, the authors assumed that the home gateway can intercept the manifest file during the HAS session initialization and can obtain the characteristics of the available video quality levels of every session. This solution introduces a bandwidth manager in the gateway that defines a shaping rate for each connected active HAS client in the home network. The bandwidth manager should be able to update the number of active connected HAS clients in the home gateway by sniffing the SYN and FIN flags in TCP packets. Therefore, the difference between the gateway-based methods is the manner in which they shape the bandwidth for each HAS session. The two main gateway-based methods found in the literature and used in our comparative study are HTBM [1] and RWTM [2]. They are briefly described in the following.

HTBM

HTBM uses the Hierarchical Token Bucket (HTB) queuing discipline to shape the HTTP-adaptive streams. HTB is integrated in Linux with the traffic controller tool of the iproutes2utility package. It uses one link, designated as the parent class, to emulate several slower links, designated as the children classes. Different types of traffic may be served by the emulated links. HTB is exploited by the bandwidth manager of HTBM in order to define a child class for each HAS session. HTB also employs the tokens and buckets concept, combined with the class-based system for better control over traffic and for shaping in particular [16]. A fundamental component of the HTB queuing discipline is the borrowing mechanism: children classes borrow tokens from their parent once they have exceeded the shaping rate. A child class will continue to try to borrow until it reaches a defined threshold of shaping, at which point it will begin to queue packets that will be transmitted when more tokens become available.

Accordingly, using HTBM enables the shaping of the HTTP-adaptive streams for each HAS session in the gateway, as indicated by the bandwidth manager, by merely delaying packets that are received from the HAS server. The authors of [1] indicate that HTBM improves the user's QoE; it improves the stability of video quality level, the fidelity to optimal quality level, and the convergence speed.

RWTM

The second shaping method, Receive Window Tuning Method (RWTM), is a gateway-based shaping method that was proposed in [2]. It is implemented in the TCP layer and is based on TCP flow control at the receiver side. Indeed, during a TCP session, each receiver specifies the maximum number of bytes that it is able to buffer. This value is called the receiver's advertised window, denoted by rwnd, and its size is specified in the rwnd field in the header of each TCP packet sent from the receiver to the sender. The sender receives the rwnd size from the receiver and limits its sending window, W, so that the number of packets sent in each RTT does not exceed rwnd; W = min(rwnd, cwnd).

The RWTM method consists of modifying, in the gateway, the rwnd field of each TCP ACK packet sent from a HAS client C to its HAS server S in order to limit the sending rate of the HAS server to rwnd/$RTT_{C\text{-}S}$. RWTM uses the defined shaping rate of the bandwidth manager for each connected active HAS client, and estimates the $RTT_{C\text{-}S}$ value to compute the next value ofrwnd. We note that the estimation of $RTT_{C\text{-}S}$ is accomplished using only TCP ACK packets sent from HAS clients to the HAS server by using passive estimation. The rwnd is computed once for each ON period. RWTM was tested in [2] and [21], and results indicated that RWTM enhances the user's QoE: it improves the stability, the fidelity, and the convergence speed.

In [21], we showed that RWTM outperforms HTBM when using the Cubic variant as congestion control on the server side. However, due to the dissimilarity of TCP variants, an extended evaluation using other variants and additional scenarios will give us a better understanding of the interaction between shaping methods and TCP variants.

METHODOLOGY AND EXPERIMENTAL IMPLEMENTATION

In this section, we provide a description of the metrics used to measure performance, the scenarios that cover many operating conditions, and the framework that has been developed to emulate our use case.

Performance metrics

We define three metrics in this section that we use to evaluate the QoE and to understand how each combination behaves. To do so, we present in Table 1 the main parameters that are used to define the metrics.

Table 1 Description of parameters

Parameter	**Description**
I	Discrete time index
$L_C(i)$	Video quality level index of client C at time i
$L_{C,opt}(i)$	Theoretical optimal value of $L_C(i)$
$Q_C(i)$	Video encoding bitrate of client C at time i

We note that the optimal quality level value, $L_{C,opt}(i)$, corresponds to the quality level that the client C should select at time i under the shaping rate defined by the bandwidth manager. This shaping rate is chosen in a manner that ensures the fairest share of the available home bandwidth between clients with prioritization to achieve the maximum use of the available home bandwidth. This entails that some clients could have a higher quality level than others when their fair share of available home bandwidth is not sufficient to maximize the use of the available home bandwidth. Below, we define analytically three performance metrics that describe the three criteria of QoE mentioned in Sect. 1.

Video quality-level stability

Many research studies indicate that HAS users are likely to be sensitive to frequent and significant quality-level switches [22, 23]. We use the instability metric, ISC(K)ISC(K), which measures the instability for client C for a K-second test duration in conformity with its description in [7] as the following equation:

$$IS_C(K) = \frac{\sum_{i=0}^{K-1} |Q_C(K-i) - Q_C(K-i-1)| \times w(i)}{\sum_{i=1}^{K} Q_C(K-i) \times w(i)} \tag{1}$$

where $IS_C(K)$ is the weighted sum of all encoding bitrate switching steps observed within the last K seconds divided by the weighted sum of the encoding bitrates selected in the last Kseconds. The lower the $IS_C(K)$ value is, the higher the stability of the video quality level is.

More precisely, this formula uses the encoding bitrates of the selected quality levels over time, QC(i), instead of the quality level index over time, $L_C(i)$. In fact, the absolute difference between two encoding bitrates that are displayed on the client side during two successive seconds, K−i−1and K−i, and denoted by $|Q_C(K-i)-Q_C(K-i-1)|$, gives more significant indication of the observed video quality change than when using the absolute difference between the quality level indexes. Hence, we can offer an adequate representation of the user expectation.

Moreover, in this formula, the authors of [7] use the weight function w(i)=K−iw in order to add a linear penalty to more recent quality level switches. In fact, their justification is that the switching of quality level is becoming more disturbing for users' experience when the video playback position is far from the beginning of the video stream.

Fidelity to optimal quality level

In [7], the authors define two additional goals to achieve within our use case: (1) fairness between players: players should be able to converge to an equitable allocation of network resources; (2) efficiency among players: players should choose the highest feasible quality levels to maximize the user's experience. Furthermore, in [9], the authors address the bandwidth underutilization issue that may prevent the possible improvement of QoE. So, maximizing the use of bandwidth can be considered as a QoE criterion. Accordingly, in order to provide one formula that satisfies these three criteria, we define our metric called infidelity to optimal quality level.

The infidelity metric, IFC(K)IFC(K), of client C for a K-second test duration, measures the duration of time over which the HAS client C requests optimal quality:

$$IF_C(K) = \left\{ \sum_{i=1}^{K} \theta_C(i) \middle| \theta_C(i) = \begin{cases} 1, \text{if } L_C(i) \neq L_{C,opt}(i) \\ 0, \text{else} \end{cases} \right\}$$

(2)

The lower the IFC(K) value is, the higher the fidelity to optimal quality is.

Here, we note that the theoretical optimal quality level LC,opt(i) aims to resolve the dilemma between the two criteria of maximum use and fair share of bandwidth between HAS players. In fact, considering that only the fair share of bandwidth may cause bandwidth underutilization, in some cases it may leave some residual bandwidth allocated to nobody. Hence, based on the optimal quality level, the value of the infidelity metric is representative of user expectation.

Convergence speed

The convergence speed metric was previously defined in [1]. We provide an analytical definition as follows:

$$V_{C,T}(K) = \left\{ \min_{d \in \{1,...k\}}(d) \middle| L_C(i) = L_{C,opt}(i) \forall i \in [d, d+T] \right\}$$

(3)

This metric is the time that the player of HAS client C takes to reach and remain at the optimal quality level for at least T seconds during a K-second test duration. The reason of selecting this criterion for evaluating the QoE in our use case is observations made in [1, 2, 9, 21]: they show that when HAS players compete for bandwidth, the convergence to optimal quality level may take several seconds or may be very difficult to be achieved. Accordingly, the speed of this convergence is a valuable QoE criterion for our evaluations. The lower the VC,T(K) value is, the faster the convergence to the optimal quality level is.

Additionally, we define two other metrics (CNG and fr_{OFF*}, described below) that enable us to measure the reaction of home gateway and HAS players.

Congestion rate

The congestion detection events influence to an extreme degree both the QoS and QoE of HAS because the server decreases its sending rate after each congestion detection. Hence, by analyzing the code description of the four TCP congestion control algorithms (NewReno, Vegas, Illinois, and Cubic), we found that the congestion event appears when the value of parameterslow start threshold (ssthresh) decreases (see Algorithm 1). Hence, we define a metric calledcongestion rate, denoted by CNGC−S(K), that computes the rate of congestion events that are detected on the server side, corresponding to the HAS flow between client C and server S during a K-second test duration as shown in Eq. (4):

$$CNG_{C-S}(K) = \frac{D_{C-S}^{ssthresh}(K)}{K} \times 100,$$

(4)

Where $D_{C-S}^{ssthresh}(K)$ is the number of times the ssthresh has been decreased for the C–S HAS session during the K-second test duration.

Frequency of OFF* periods per chunk

This metric is important to measure the frequency of OFF* periods. An OFF period whose duration exceeds RTO is denoted by OFF* (as indicated in Sect. 2.1). This frequency is equal to the total number of OFF* periods divided by the total number of downloaded chunks. This metric is denoted by fr_{OFF*}.

For result analysis, we use the QoE metrics to quantitatively discuss the user's experience, and use CNG and fr_{OFF*} metrics to explain the performance of each combination of traffic method and congestion variant.

Scenarios

We define five scenarios that are typical of concurrence between HAS clients in the same home network (scenarios 1, 2, and 3), and how the HAS client reacts when some changes occur (scenarios 4 and 5):

1. Both clients start to play simultaneously and continue for 3 min. This scenario illustrates how clients compete.
2. Client 1 starts to play, the second client starts after 30 s, and both continue together for 150 s. This scenario shows how the transition from one client to two clients occurs.
3. Both clients start to play simultaneously, client 2 stops after 30 s, and client 1 continues alone for 150 s. This scenario shows how a transition from two clients to one takes place.
4. Only one client starts to play and continues for 3 min. At 30 s, we simulate a heavy congestion event with a provoked packet loss of 50 % of the received packets at the server over a 1-s period. This scenario shows the

robustness of each combination against the congestions that are induced by external factors, such as by other concurrent flows in the home network.

5. Only one client is playing alone for 3 min. We vary the standard deviation value of RTT_{C-S} (round trip time between the client and the server) for each set of tests. This scenario investigates the robustness against RTT_{C-S} instability.

The test duration was selected to be 3 min to offer sufficient delay for players to stabilize.

General framework

We propose a testbed architecture presented in Fig. 1 that emulates our use case described in Sect. 1. The choice of only two clients is sufficient to show the behavior of concurrence between many HAS flows in the same home network.

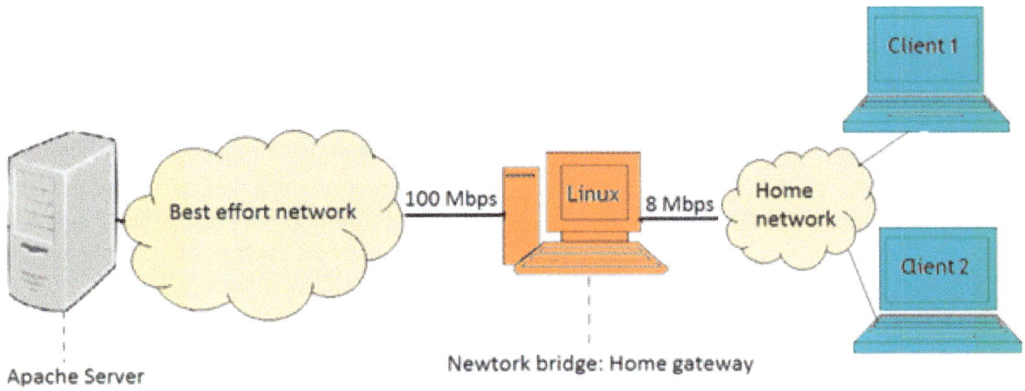

Figure 1 Architecture of the testbed

In this section, we describe the configurations of each component presented in Fig. 1.

HAS clients

We used two Linux machines as HAS clients. We developed an emulated player in each client that reproduces the behavior of the HAS player without decoding and displaying a video stream. The playback buffer size is specified to be 15 chunks, and the chunk duration is 2 s. In [18], the authors indicate that the bitrate adaptation algorithm depends on bandwidth estimation and playback buffer occupancy. Furthermore, players also define an aggressiveness level, as described in a previous study [19]. For example, the Netflix player is more aggressive than the Smooth Streaming player [19]. An aggressive player enables the user to ask for a video quality level that is slightly higher than the estimated available bandwidth. Moreover, aggressiveness is important for minimizing the "downward spiral effect" phenomenon [20]. This phenomenon consists of underestimating the available bandwidth, which leads to a lower video quality level selection. Accordingly, taking into consideration [18, 19], and [20], we used a bitrate adaptation algorithm based on bandwidth estimation in which we define an aggressiveness$\rho_C(t)$ at time t that depends on playback buffer occupancy as follows:

$$\rho_C(t) = \sigma \times R_C(t)/B_C \tag{5}$$

where RC(t)RC(t) is the filling level of the playback buffer at time t, B_C is the size of the playback buffer of client C, and σ is the aggressiveness constant. The fuller the playback buffer is, the closer to σ the aggressiveness is.

All tests use a HAS player with an aggressiveness constant of σ = 0.2. This enables the HAS player to add a maximum of 20 % to its available BW estimation.

Home network

In the modeled home network, the clients are connected directly to the gateway. The total download bitrate, or home available bandwidth, is limited to 8 Mbps. We choose this value because it is lower than twice the video encoding bitrate of the highest quality level. Accordingly, two clients in the home network cannot select the highest quality level at the same time. In this case, one client should select quality level no 4 and the other should select the quality level no 3 as optimal qualities. We do not test a use case in which two clients have the same optimal quality level, because this is a very specific case, and dissimilarity between optimal quality levels is more general.

Home gateway

The emulated home gateway consists of a Linux machine configured as a network bridge to forward packets between the home network and the best effort network.

We emulate the queuing discipline of the home gateway by using the Stochastic Fairness Queueing discipline (SFQ) [24]. SFQ is a classless queuing discipline that we configured using the Traffic Controller emulation tool (tc). SFQ schedules packets based on flow identification (the source and destination IP addresses and the source port) and injects them into hash buckets during the enqueuing process. Each bucket represents a unique flow. Additionally, SFQ employs Round Robin fashion for dequeuing packets by taking into consideration the bucket classification. The goal of using buckets for enqueuing and Round Robin for dequeuing is to ensure fairness between flows so that the queue is able to forward data in turn and prevents any single flow from drowning out the remaining flows. We also configured SFQ in order to support the Drop Tail queue management algorithm when the queue becomes full. Hence, this configuration of the queuing discipline is classified as a Drop Tail class. The queue length of SFQ, which is indicated by parameter limit within the tc tool, is set to the bandwidth-delay product.

In the gateway, we implemented a bandwidth manager that selects a shaping rate for each connected active HAS client in a manner such that each client should attain its optimal quality level described in Sect. 3.1. The shaping rate for each client was chosen as indicated in [1] and [2]; it is 10 % higher than the encoding bitrate of the optimal quality level for each client. The two shaping methods HTBM and RWTM are implemented in the gateway, and they shape bandwidth in accordance with the decisions of the bandwidth manager.

Best effort network

The best effort network is characterized by the presence of network devices to route packets. The round trip time $RTT_{C-S}(t)$ in a best effort network is modeled as follows [10]:

$$RTT_{C-S}(t) = a_{C-S} + q(t)/\varsigma; \tag{6}$$

where a_{C-S} is a fixed propagation delay between client C and server S, q(t) is the queue length of a single congested router (the home gateway in our use case), and ς is the transmission capacity of the router. q(t)/ς models the queuing processing delay. To comply with Eq. (6), we used the normal distribution with a mean value a_{C-S} and a standard deviation equal to 0.07. a_{C-S}. The standard deviation emulates the queuing processing delay q(t)/ς. This emulation is accomplished by using the "netem delay" parameter of the traffic controller tool in the gateway machine interface.

HAS server

The HAS server is modeled by an HTTP Apache Server installed on a Linux machine operating on Debian version 3.2. We can change the congestion control variant of the server by varying the parameter net.ipv4.tcp_congestion_control. All tests use five video quality levels denoted by 0, 1, 2, 3, and 4. Their encoding bitrates are constant and equal to 248, 456, 928, 1632, and 4256 kbps, respectively. HTTP version 1.1 is used to enable a persistent connection.

RESULTS

In this section, we compare the different combinations of TCP congestion control variants in the server and shaping methods in the gateway in the five scenarios. Altogether, we evaluate eight combinations: four TCP congestion control variants combined with two shaping methods. We evaluate QoE by discussing the QoE metrics IS, IF, and V. We also use the CNG and fr_{OFF}. metrics to observe how each combination reacts. For each scenario, we repeated each test 60 times and we computed an average value of each metric. The number of 60 runs is justified by the fact that the difference of the average results obtained after 40 and 60 runs are lower than 6 %. This observation was verified for all scenarios. Accordingly, 60 runs are sufficient to achieve statistically significant results.

This section is organized as follows. First, we begin by evaluating performance in scenario 1, and we analyze the variation of cwnd for each combination. Second, we evaluate the performance of scenarios 2 and 3 to study the effect of transition from one to two clients (and vice versa) on the performance of each studied combination. Third, we present the performance of scenario 4 to measure the robustness of the combinations against induced congestions. Fourth, we study scenario 5 to measure the robustness against the instability of RTT_{C-S} for each combination. Finally, we discuss all results by presenting a summary of observations and defining the combination that is suitable for each particular case.

Scenario 1

In this scenario, two clients are competing for BW and are playing simultaneously. The available home bandwidth permits only one client to have the highest quality level, no 4. We make the assumption that the client who gets the highest quality level no 4 is identified as client 1. Optimally, the first player in our use case should obtain quality level no 4 with an encoding bitrate of 4256 kbps, and the second player should have quality level no 3 with an encoding bitrate of 1632 kbps.

In this section, we present our evaluation results and discuss them. Then, we analyze the cwndvariation for each combination in order to understand the reason for the observed results.

Measurements of performance metrics

The average values of QoE metric measurements for client 1 and client 2 are listed in Tables 2, 3, respectively.

Table 2 QoE for client 1 in scenario 1

Performance metric	Shaping method	TCP congestion control variant			
		NewReno	Vegas	Illinois	Cubic
Instability (%) $IS_1(180)$	W/o*	4.95	2.15	8.35	7.47
	HTBM	1.89	1.08	1.56	1.86
	RWTM	1.69	4.10	1.88	1.63
Infidelity (%) $IF_1(180)$	W/o	41.33	52.31	74.14	50.46
	HTBM	49.57	47.81	7.75	20.45
	RWTM	45.87	32.24	6.17	5.02

Convergence speed (s) V1,60(180)	W/o	100.93	102.11	174.13	145.03
	HTBM	101.83	87.11	21.10	52.06
	RWTM	94.51	104.00	24.22	19.55

Table 3 QoE for client 2 in scenario 1

Performance metrics	Shaping methods	TCP congestion control variants			
		NewReno	Vegas	Illinois	Cubic
Instability (%) $IS_2(180)$	W/o	5.82	3.06	7.85	5.82
	HTBM	1.17	0.95	1.05	1.15
	RWTM	1.09	0.95	1.03	1.13
Infidelity (%) $IF_2(180)$	W/o	26.64	70.77	39.27	36.33
	HTBM	4.72	3.62	4.21	4.47
	RWTM	2.49	2.30	2.47	2.61
Convergence speed (s) $V_{2,60}(180)$	W/o	96.25	137.01	126.33	92.81
	HTBM	12.41	6.95	9.73	13.26
	RWTM	6.73	5.03	6.54	8.95

Our first overall observation is the large dissimilarity between QoE measurements of the different combinations. This observation is a valuable result that confirms that each combination induces a change of HAS player behavior. Consequently, using HAS traffic shaping without taking into consideration the TCP congestion control employed in the HAS server cannot guarantee a good user experience; hence, the prominence of our proposed work.

The results show that traffic shaping considerably improves the QoE metric measurements for a majority of cases, especially for instability, which is largely reduced (e.g., a reduction of instability rate by a factor of 2.6 from 4.95 to 1.89 % when employing HTBM with NewReno, and a reduction by a factor of 4.5 from 7.47 to 1.63 % when employing RWTM with Cubic, as shown in Table 2). Furthermore, RWTM shows better performance than HTBM in the majority of cases. Moreover, client 2 always has better performance than client 1 with both shaping methods: the reason is that the optimal quality level of client 2 (i.e., quality level no 3) is lower than that of client 1 (i.e., quality level no 4): obviously, the quality level no 3 is easier to achieve. In addition, the gap between the QoE metric measurements of the two shaping methods is higher for client 1 than client 2: for example, when considering the Cubic variant, the gap of infidelity rate of client 1 between RWTM and HTBM is 15.43 % (5.02 vs 20.45 %); this is higher than that of client 2, which is equal to 1.86 % (2.61 vs 4.47 %). Consequently, the dissimilarity of performance between different combinations is more visible for client 1. For this reason, we limit our observation to client 1 in the remaining text of this subsection.

Concerning the QoE measurements, based on Table 2, we present the most important observations related to client 1:

- Combining NewReno or Vegas variants with HTBM or RWTM does not improve the QoE. Additionally, these four combinations have high infidelity value (near 50 %) and very high congestion speed value (around 90–100 ms), but a low value of instability. These values indicate that the player was stable at a low quality level during the first half of the test duration and has difficulties converging to its optimal quality level.
- HTBM has better QoE with Illinois than with Cubic: it is slightly more stable, 16 % more faithful to optimal quality, and converges 2.4 times faster.
- RWTM has better QoE with Cubic than with Illinois: it is slightly more stable, slightly more faithful to optimal quality level, and converges 1.24 times faster.

In order to be more accurate in our analysis, we use the two defined metrics: the frequency ofOFF* periods per chunk, fr_{OFF^*}, and the congestion rate, CNG. In Table 4, we present the average value over 60 runs for each metric and for each combination, related to client 1 and scenario 1.

Table 4 fr_{OFF^*} and CNG for client 1 in scenario 1

Metric	Shaping method	TCP congestion control variant			
		NewReno	Vegas	Illinois	Cubic
CNG	W/o	46.13	43.00	66.11	85.65
	HTBM	44.06	40.50	58.68	191.72
	RWTM	0.10	8.26	0.76	1.11
fr_{OFF^*}	W/o	0.42	0.35	0.27	0.40
	HTBM	0.31	0.32	0.06	0.16
	RWTM	0.32	0.41	0.24	0.24

RWTM presents a negligible congestion rate, while HTBM has a very high rate of congestion, especially when the Cubic variant is used. Moreover, HTBM reduces the frequency fr_{OFF^*} better than RWTM, mainly with Illinois and Cubic. These results have a direct relationship to the shaping methods described in Sect. 2.2:

- HTBM was designed to delay incoming packets, which causes an additional queuing delay. In all of the tests, we verified that HTBM induces a queueing delay of around 100 ms in scenario 1 for client 1. On one hand, this delay causes an increase of congestion rate because it increases the risks of queue overflow in the gateway, even when the QoE is good, such as with Cubic or Illinois variants. The dissimilarity of congestion rate between congestion controls variants is investigated in the next Sect. 4.1.2. On the other hand, the RTT_{C-S} value also jumps from 100 to 200 ms, which increases the retransmission timeout value, RTO, to approximately 400 ms, hence reducing OFF* periods. The fr_{OFF^*} of HTBM is noticeably lower than RWTM and the case without shaping (W/o). In addition, the assertion "the higher the QoE metric measurement, the lower the fr_{OFF^*} value" seems to be valid; for example, HTBM presents better QoE with Illinois than with Cubic, and fr_{OFF^*} is lower with Illinois than with Cubic.
- Nevertheless, RWTM was designed to limit the value of the receiver's advertised window,rwnd, of each client. Therefore, no additional queuing delay is induced by RWTM. Hence, the congestion rate is very low. Additionally, the RTT_{C-S} estimation is performed only once per chunk. So, the cwnd value is constant during the ON period, even if RTT_{C-S} varies. In our configuration, the standard deviation of RTT_{C-S} is equal to 7 ms, i.e., $0.07.a_{C-S}$, as described in Sect. 3.3. Consequently, eliminating OFF* periods will not be possible. Instead, the fr_{OFF^*}value will be bounded to a minimum value that characterizes RWTM when the QoE measurements are the most favorable. When testing with the four congestion control variants, this fr_{OFF^*} value is equal to 0.24 for the selected standard deviation. This means that RWTM can guarantee, in the best case, one OFF* period every 4.17 chunks. This frequency is useful, and will be discussed in the next subsection and in further detail in scenario 5.

Analysis of cwnd variation

To explain the results of scenario 1, we used the tcp_probe module in the HAS server. This module shows the evolution of the congestion window, cwnd, and the slow start threshold,ssthresh, during each run. For each combination, we selected a run the performance values of which are the nearest to its average values of Tables 2, 4, i.e., instability IS, infidelity IF, convergence speed V, frequency of OFF* periods per chunk fr_{OFF^*}, and congestion rate CNG. Then, we present their cwnd and ssthresh evolution in Figs. 2, 3, 4, 5, 6, 7, 8, 9. We also indicate the moment of convergence by a vertical bold dotted line. We observed that this moment corresponds to the second from which the TCP congestion control is often processing under the congestion avoidance phase; i.e., when cwnd > ssthresh. In addition, from the moment of convergence, we observe that ssthresh becomes more stable and is practically close to a constant value.

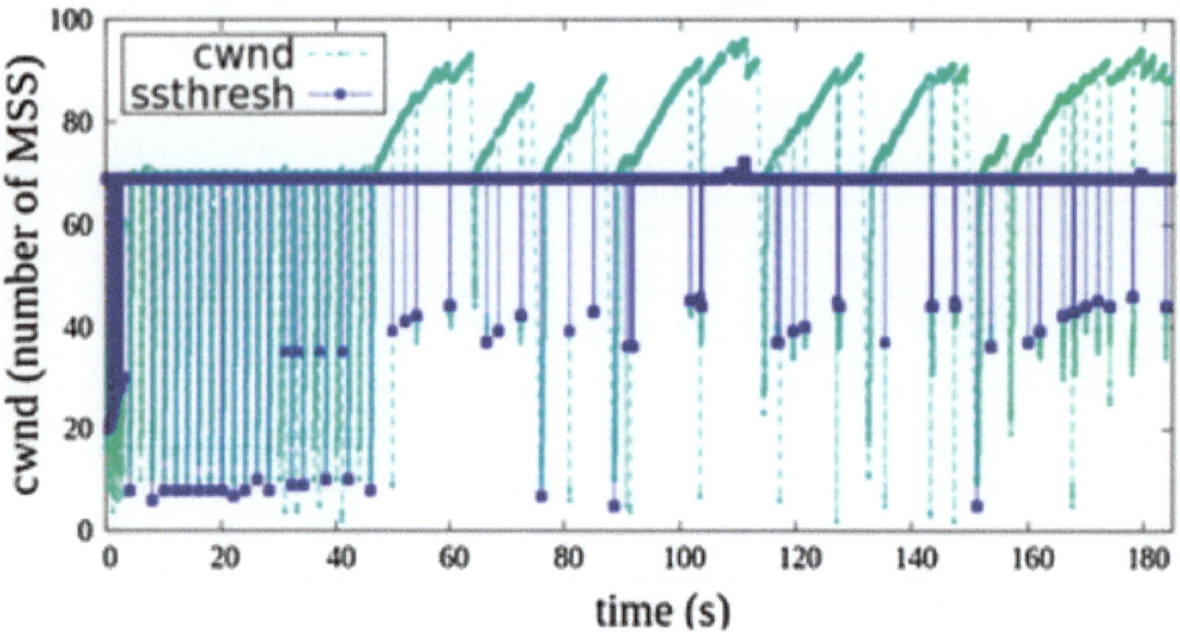

Figure 2 Cwnd variation of {NewReno HTBM} IS = 5.48 %, IF = 35.68 %, V = 180 s, fr_{OFF^*} = 0.2,CNG = 43.33

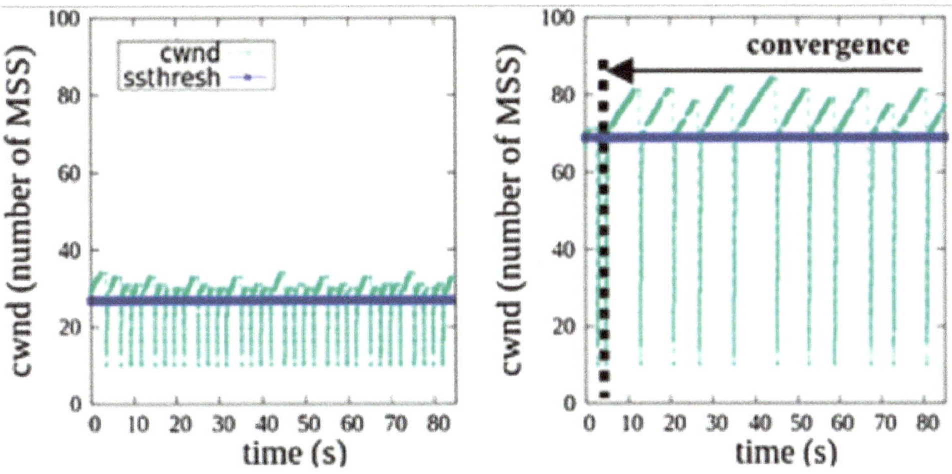

(a) *IS*=0.95%, *IF*=100%, *V*=180 $fr_{OFF^{\bullet}}$=0.68, *CNG*= 0

(b) *IS*=2.62%, *IF*=4.92%, *V*=4 s $fr_{OFF^{\bullet}}$=0.23, *CNG*=0

Figure 3 Cwnd variation of {NewReno RWTM}

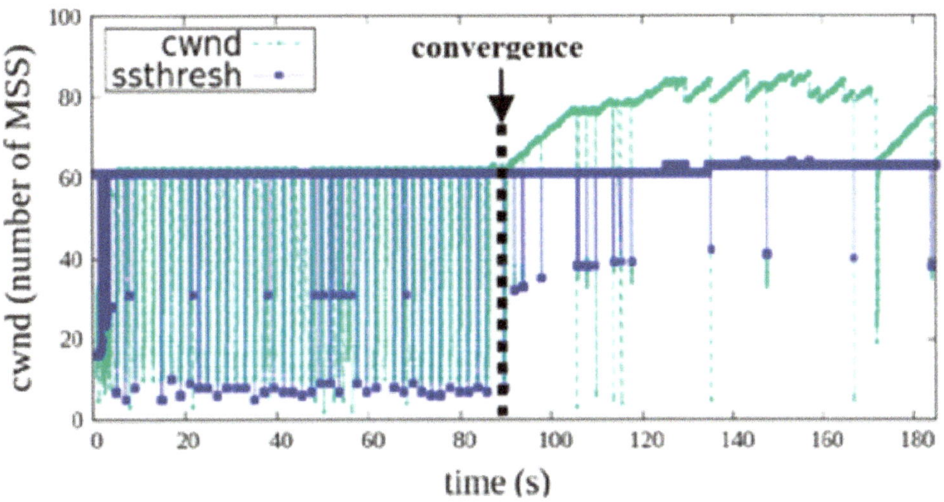

Figure 4 Cwnd variation of {Vegas HTBM} IS = 1.31 %, IF = 46.74 %, V = 87 s, $fr_{OFF^{\bullet}}$ = 0.4,CNG = 46.11

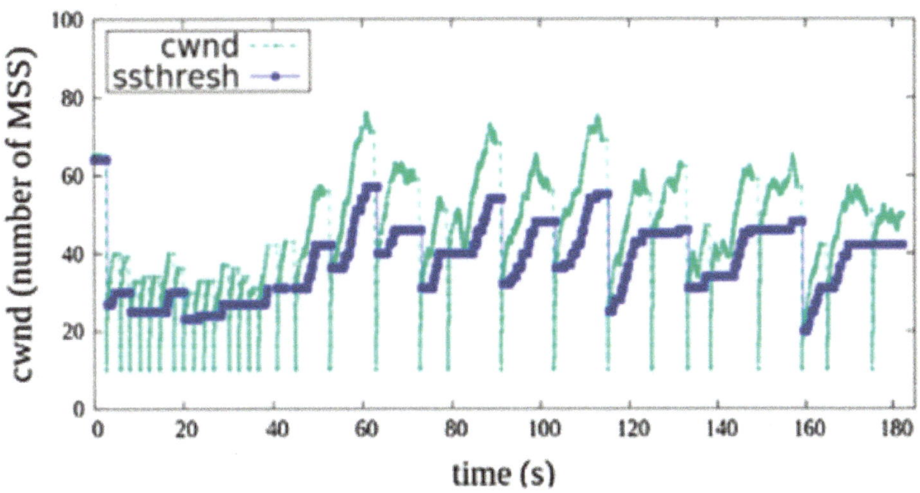

Figure 5 Cwnd variation of {Vegas, RWTM} IS = 5.32 %, IF = 31.15 %, V = 180 s, $fr_{OFF^{\bullet}}$ = 0.29,CNG = 6.11

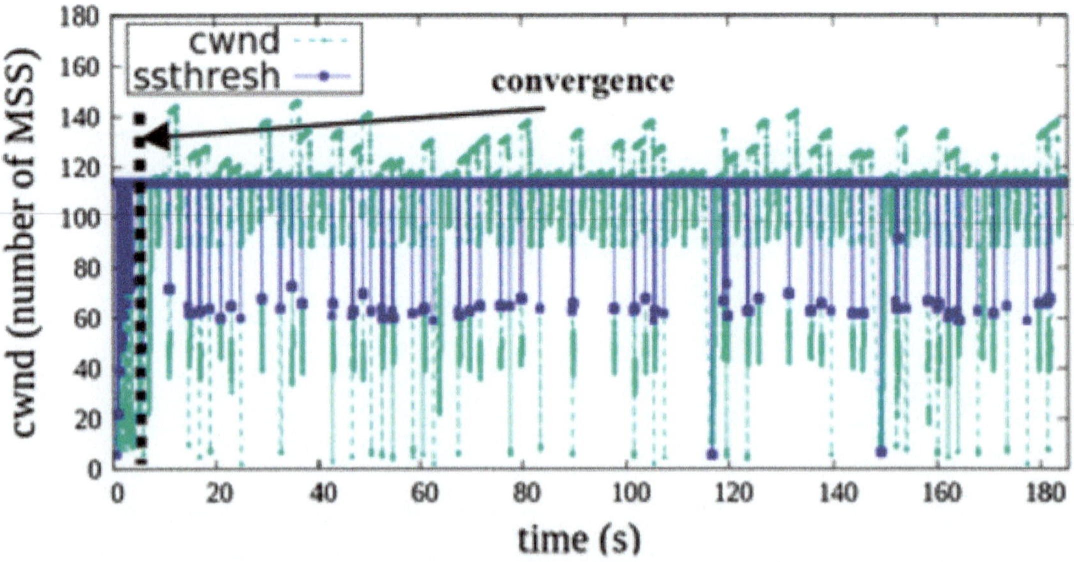

Figure 6 Cwnd variation of {Illinois, HTBM} IS = 2.00 %, IF = 7.66 %, V = 5 s, fr_{OFF^*} = 0.03,CNG = 51.11

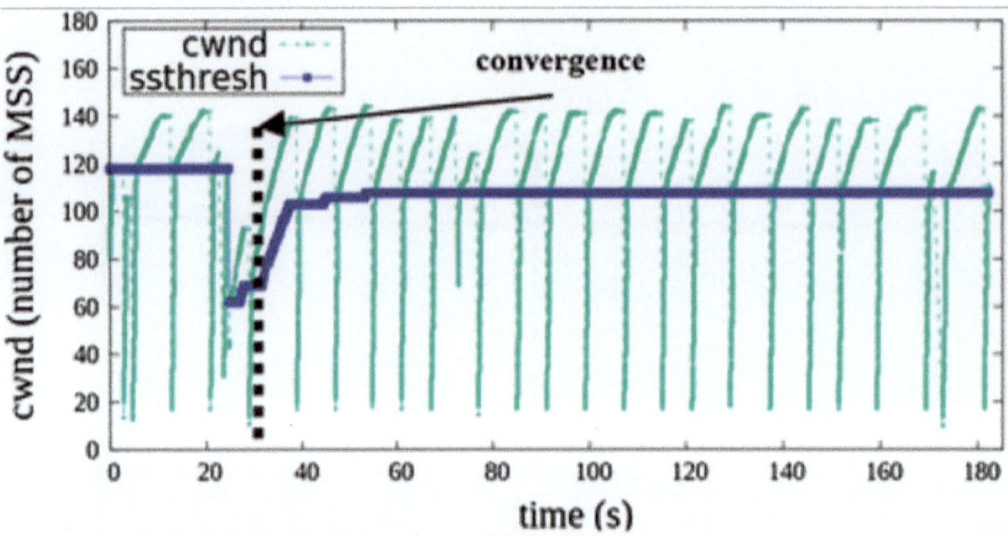

Figure 7 Cwnd variation of {Illinois RWTM}, IS = 2.40 %, IF = 5.47 %, V = 27 s, fr_{OFF^*} = 0.22,CNG = 0.55

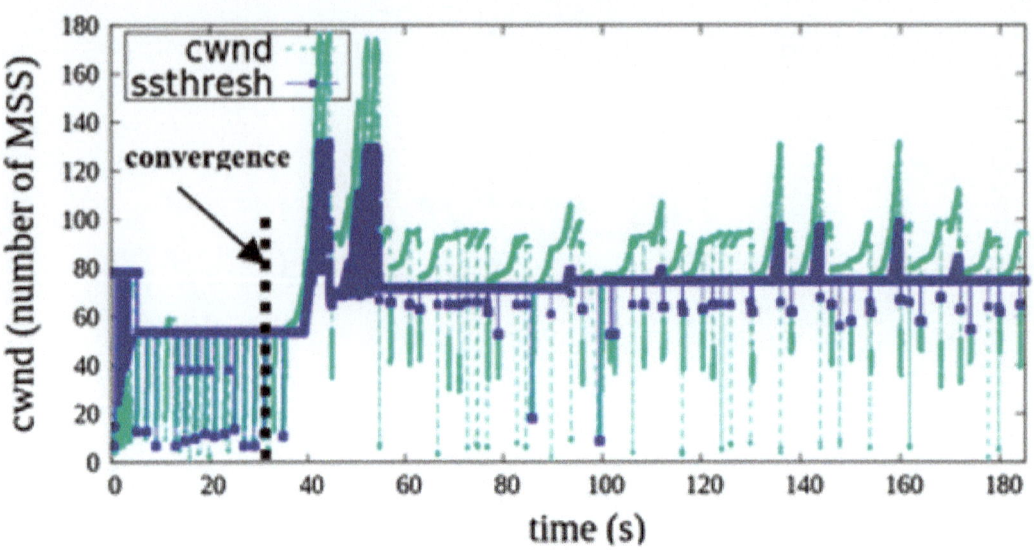

Figure 8 Cwnd variation of {Cubic HTBM}, IS = 1.98 %, IF = 19.03 %, V = 33 s, fr_{OFF}^* = 0.16,CNG = 186.11

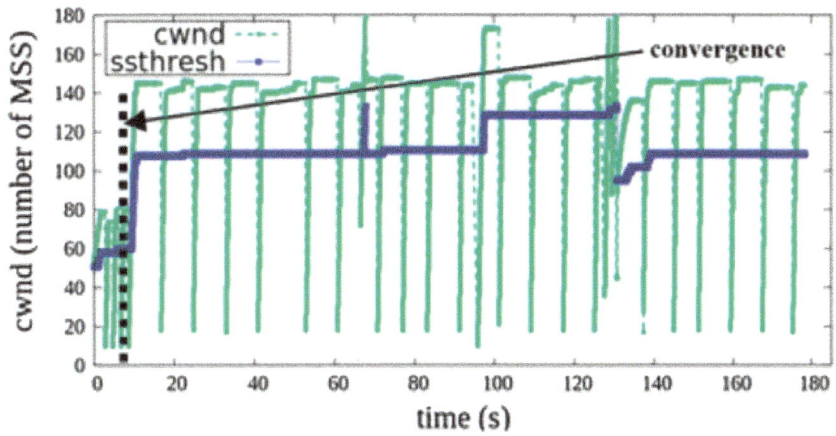

Figure 9 Cwnd variation of {Cubic RWTM}, IS = 1.78 %, IF = 5.5 %, V = 8 s, fr_{OFF^*} = 0.22,CNG = 1.66

Figure 2 shows that the combination NewReno with HTBM cannot guarantee convergence to the optimal quality level. The congestion rate is not very high compared with other TCP congestion variants. After 50 s, cwnd was able to reach the congestion avoidance phase for short durations, but the continuous increase of cwnd with the additive increase approach caused the detection of congestion. Moreover, the multiplicative decrease approach after congestions employed by NewReno was very aggressive; in effect, as described in Sect. 2.2, the new cwndvalue will be reduced by half (more precisely, to cwnd/2 + 3 MSS following the FR/FR phase) and ssthresh will also be reduced to cwnd/2. This aggressive decrease prevents the server from rapidly reaching a desirable cwnd value and, as a consequence, prevents the player from correctly estimating the available bandwidth and causes a lower quality level selection. Furthermore, the fr_{OFF^*} value was relatively high (around 0.3 OFF* period per chunk), which is more than twice that of the Illinois and Cubic variants. This value is also caused by the multiplicative decrease approach that generates a lower quality level selection. Due to the shaping rate that adapts the download bitrate of the client to its optimal quality level, the chunk with a lower quality level will be downloaded more rapidly, which results in causing more frequent OFF* periods. For this reason, the player was not able to stabilize on the optimal quality level, resulting in a poor QoE.

When combining NewReno with RWTM, we observed that test results diverged and could be classified into two categories: those with an infidelity value of 100 % and that do not converge (Fig. 3a), and those with a low value of infidelity and that converge rapidly (Fig. 3b). In both figures, ssthresh is always invariable. Both figures have no congestion events, which is due to the use of RWTM.

The OFF* periods are more frequent in Fig. 3a (fr_{OFF^*} = 0.68) than in Fig. 3b (fr_{OFF^*} = 0.23). Although both figures present a constant value of ssthresh, we observe that the only difference between them is the initial value of ssthresh. Figure 3a has a lower value of ssthresh than Fig. 3b: 27 MSS vs 69 MSS. The additive increase approach of NewReno during the congestion avoidance phase prevents the server from rapidly increasing the cwnd value during ON periods. Therefore, the player was not able to reach the optimal quality level no 4 at any time. The cause of the dissimilarity between the initial values of ssthresh in the two figures is explained in [17]. Some implementations of NewReno use the size of the receiver's advertised window, rwnd, to define the initial value of ssthresh, but in fact, this value may be arbitrarily chosen. Accordingly, the combination of NewReno with RWTM could have high QoE if the initial value of ssthresh is well-chosen.

When combining Vegas with HTBM, we obtain a cwnd variation, as shown in Fig. 4. The convergence moment (at 87 s in Fig. 4) occurs when cwnd becomes often set higher thanssthresh (i.e., TCP congestion control is often processing under the congestion avoidance phase) and ssthresh is often set at the same value. We can observe the additive increase and additive decrease aspect of cwnd in the congestion avoidance phase after convergence. The additive decrease of cwnd involved in Vegas is caused by the queuing delay increases resulting from HTBM. This additive decrease has the advantage of maintaining a high throughput and reducing the dropping of packets in the gateway. Therefore, the congestion rate, CNG, is relatively low because it is reduced in Fig. 4 from around 75 congestion events per 100 s to only 15. The additive decrease also has the advantage of promoting convergence to the optimal quality level, unlike multiplicative decrease. As a result, the delay-based aspect with the additive decrease approach improves the stability of the HAS player after convergence. In contrast, Vegas uses a slightly low value of ssthresh (60 MSS) and employs the additive increase approach for cwnd updates during the congestion avoidance phase. As a consequence, the server cannot rapidly increase the cwnd value during the ON period, which results in slow convergence. Therefore, the player was not able to reach the optimal quality level no 4 at any time before the moment of convergence. Consequently, the frequency of the OFF* period increases before the convergence moment; hence, the high value of fr_{OFF^*}.

The performance worsens when Vegas is combined with RWTM. As presented in Fig. 5, the player was not able to converge. Instead, we observed many timeout retransmissions characterized by ssthresh reduction and cwnd restarting from slow start. The timeout retransmissions are generated by Vegas when only a duplicate ACK is received and the timeout period of the oldest unacknowledged packet has expired [4]. Because of that, Vegas generates more timeout retransmissions than NewReno. Hence, the CNG value is worse than in the other combinations of RWTM. Moreover, OFF* periods are frequent during the first 45 s, because the player requests quality level no 3. Subsequently, OFF* periods become less frequent (they occur only at 79, 125, 138, 150, 165, and 175 s) because the player was able to switch to an optimal quality level (no 4). Hence fr_{OFF*} related to the whole test duration is equal to an acceptable value (0.29 OFF* period per chunk). The player becomes able to request the optimal quality level no 4 predominantly in the second period (after 45 s), but it is incapable of being stable for more than 60 s because of the retransmission timeout events.

When we use the loss-delay-based variant Illinois, significant improvement of performance is observed with the two shaping methods.

In Fig. 6, despite the rapid convergence, a high rate of congestions (that reduces the ssthreshand cwnd values but maintains the cwnd higher than ssthresh, as described in Algorithm 1) and timeout retransmissions (that reduces ssthresh, drops cwnd, and begins from the slow start phase) was recorded. Consequently, the frequent reduction of ssthresh was the cause of the high rate of CNG: in this example, CNG is equal to 51.11. CNG is higher than that recorded for NewReno. The cause is the high value of ssthresh of approximately 115 MSS. The variablessthresh was able to rapidly return to a fixed value after retransmissions, due to the update of α and β using accurate RTT_{C-S} estimation (see Sect. 2.1). As a consequence, cwnd restarts from the slow start phase after timeout detection and rapidly reaches the high value of ssthresh. Hence, the HAS player converges despite high congestion. In addition, OFF* periods were negligible, with only two periods after congestion. This is why fr_{OFF*} was very low (0.03). In the congestion avoidance phase, cwnd was able to increase and reach high values, even during short timeslots. This was due to the concave curve of cwnd generated by Illinois, which is more aggressive than NewReno. As a consequence, the player could be stabilized with optimal quality level no 4.

When using RWTM with Illinois, the player converges, as presented in Fig. 7. The congestion rate is very low (CNG = 0.55), but congestions are caused by the aggressiveness of Illinois (the concave curve of cwnd in the C-AIMD approach) and its high ssthresh value (120 MSS). Congestions slow down the convergence speed and slightly reduce the QoE due to the multiplicative decrease approach of Illinois. As shown in Fig. 7, one congestion event delayed the convergence time to 27 s. In addition, Illinois has the ability to select the suitable ssthreshvalue (110 MSS in Fig. 7) that minimizes congestion events in the future, in spite of the sensitivity of RWTM to congestions. OFF* periods still exist, but with low frequency(fr_{OFF*} = 0.22).

The Cubic variant yielded good performances with both shaping methods. The variations ofcwnd when Cubic is combined with HTBM and RWTM are presented in Figs. 8, 9, respectively.

In Fig. 8, the player converges tardily after a delay of 33 s. The cause is mainly the low value ofssthresh that is selected by the Cubic algorithm. As explained in Sect. 2.1, the HyStart algorithm, implemented in Cubic, defines this ssthresh in order to have a less aggressive increase of cwnd. The ssthresh becomes lower when the RTT_{C-S} increases. Knowing that HTBM increases RTT_{C-S} by introducing an additional queuing delay, HyStart decreases ssthresh to be approximately 57 MSS. This is why the player cannot upgrade to its optimal quality level no. 4 before convergence. The second cause is the multiplicative decrease approach of Cubic and the high rate of congestions caused by HTBM. This second cause makes the convergence to optimal quality level more difficult because the server is not able to increase its reduced congestion window cwnd during the ON period, as it should be increased.

After convergence, many congestions were recorded, and OFF* periods were negligible. Thessthresh becomes more stable around 75 MSS: this is well-set by the HyStart algorithm. This enhances stability in the congestion avoidance phase with a more uniform increase of cwnd, as shown between 60 and 80 s in Fig. 8. Furthermore, there is a set of large cubic curves with inflection points close to the ssthresh value. The variable cwnd is more present in the convex region, which is more aggressive when moving away from the inflection point.

In Fig. 9, the player converges rapidly in only 8 s. The ssthresh begins with a low value (60MSS) for a few seconds during the buffering state, and then the HyStart algorithm implemented in Cubic rapidly adjusts the ssthresh value and enables the server to be more aggressive. Comparing with Fig. 7, selecting a lower initial value of ssthresh is better for accelerating convergence, because otherwise there are more risks of congestion that slow down the convergence speed.

Congestions are infrequent: only two congestions are visible in Fig. 9 at seconds 70 and 130, and they are resolved by fast retransmission in accordance with Algorithm 1 and by using Hystart. As a consequence, separated congestion events do not dramatically affect the performance, as when Illinois is used with RWTM (Fig. 9). The Cubic algorithm chooses the inflection point to be around 140 MSS, which is much higher than the ssthresh value, so that the concave region becomes more aggressive than the convex region. The OFF* periods persist, even with Cubic, but with a low frequency: fr_{OFF*} = 0.22.

Accordingly, the Cubic variant is able to adjust its congestion window curve in different situations. When many congestions occur, the cubic curve becomes rather convex to carefully increase cwnd. When many OFF* periods occur, the cubic curve becomes rather concave, and is thus more aggressive than the concave curve of Illinois in order to rapidly achieve the desired send bitrate and compensate for the reduction of the cwnd value. However, Cubic begins by estimating a low value of ssthresh that is adjusted over time by the HyStart algorithm, which is beneficial only when using RWTM as a shaping method. Using HTBM slows down convergence considerably and affects the infidelity metric.

Scenarios 2 and 3

In this section, we present the five performance measurements of client 1 for the first three scenarios described in Sect. 3.2. We make the assumption that the optimal quality level of client 1 is no. 4. We do not present NewReno and Vegas variants because they demonstrated low performance. The average values of QoE metrics for client 1 in the first three scenarios are listed in Table 5, and the average values of CNG and fr_{OFF*} in the first three scenarios are listed in Table 6. Both tables show the total mean values (denoted by MV) over the three scenarios. MVs are the global performance values proposed for consideration to compare between different combinations.

Table 5 QoE for client 1 in scenarios 1, 2, and 3

TCP variant	Scenario	Performance metric					
		Instability (%)		Infidelity (%)		Convergence speed (s)	
		HTBM	RWTM	HTBM	RWTM	HTBM	RWTM
Cubic	1	1.86	1.63	20.45	5.02	52.06	19.55
	2	3.44	1.43	32.90	3.42	64.13	10.98
	3	2.19	1.63	18.49	4.81	34.65	14.34
	MV*	2.49	1.56	23.95	4.42	50.28	14.96
Illinois	1	1.56	1.88	7.75	6.17	21.10	24.22
	2	3.20	1.56	29.75	4.42	59.58	13.28
	3	1.85	1.76	7.92	5.66	21.03	18.80
	MV	2.20	1.73	15.14	5.42	33.90	18.56

Table 6 fr_{OFF^*} and for client 1 in scenario 1, 2 and 3

Metric	Scenario	Cubic		Illinois	
		HTBM	RWTM	HTBM	RWTM
CNG	1	191.72	1.11	58.68	0.76
	2	375.62	0.82	33.11	0.68
	3	173.48	0.66	56.27	0.76
	MV	246.92	0.86	49.35	0.73
fr_{OFF^*}	1	0.16	0.24	0.06	0.24
	2	0.23	0.24	0.21	0.24
	3	0.13	0.26	0.05	0.26
	MV	0.17	0.25	0.10	0.25

Both tables indicate two valuable points:

On one hand, RWTM has better QoE metric measurements than HTBM with both Cubic and Illinois variants. Moreover, RWTM not only has a lower congestion rate, CNG, than HTBM, but it also has a negligible CNG with the two TCP variants for all three scenarios. RWTM also preserves a constant value of fr_{OFF^*}. Consequently, even the transition from one to two clients and vice versa (i.e., scenarios 2 and 3, respectively) does not disturb RWTM, which preserves its inherit characteristics of negligible congestion rate and its fr_{OFF^*} rate around 0.25. This preservation has positive consequences for the user's QoE. Although the gap between the QoE metrics measurements of {Cubic RWTM} and {Illinois RWTM} is not very significant, {Cubic RWTM} yields better values. Accordingly, we can say that the use of Cubic or even Illinois is beneficial for improving the user's experience, with a slight preference for Illinois.

On the other hand, HTBM presents better QoE with Illinois than with the Cubic variant. In conjunction, it has a fivefold lower congestion rate (49.35 vs 246.92) and lower OFF* period frequency fr_{OFF^*}. This observation is valid not only for total mean values, MV, but also with every scenario (1, 2, and 3). Therefore, Illinois is distinctly better than Cubic for the HTBM shaping method, even when the number of active HAS clients in the home gateway changes between one and two clients. Accordingly, the loss-delay-based variant with the C-AIMD approach used by Illinois has more favorable impacts on QoE, CNG, and fr_{OFF*} than the loss-based variant with the AIAD approach using the HyStart algorithm employed by Cubic.

Scenario 4

The objective of this section is to evaluate the robustness of each combination against the congestions that are induced by other flows. Therefore, we employed scenario 4, as described in Sect. 3.2, in which a heavy congestion is induced. To be able to compare performances correctly, a reference scenario, denoted by WL, consisting of a HAS client working alone in the home network, is used. No loss is observed in the reference scenario. We do not present the NewReno and Vegas variants because they showed poor performance. Altogether, we have four combinations to evaluate: Cubic and Illinois combined with two shaping methods, HTBM and RWTM. The average values of the QoE metrics of the client in scenario 4 are provided in Table 7, and the average values of CNG and fr_{OFF*} are listed in Table 8.

Table 7 QoE for client 1 in scenario 4

TCP variant	Scenario	Performance metric					
		Instability (%)		Infidelity (%)		Convergence speed (s)	
		HTBM	RWTM	HTBM	RWTM	HTBM	RWTM
Cubic	WL[a]	1.08	1.07	3.71	1.79	7.61	4.10
	4	4.86	6.40	48.2	46.14	120.3	129.3
Illinois	WL	1.08	1.07	2.23	1.66	5.37	4.01
	4	2.7	2.92	15.6	17.81	35.48	42.75

[a]Without loss

Table 8 fr_{OFF*} and CNG for client 1 in scenarios 1, 2, and 3

Metric	Scenario	Cubic		Illinois	
		HTBM	RWTM	HTBM	RWTM
CNG	WL	34.2	0.98	38.51	0.79
	4	216.19	120.36	146.68	143.54
fr_{OFF*}	WL	0.03	0.36	0.03	0.43
	4	0.40	0.41	0.09	0.31

The measurements in the two tables indicate three major observations:

- The lowest QoE metric measurements are recorded for the Cubic variant for both shaping methods: their instability is around 5–6 %, their infidelity is near 50 %, and their convergence speed is approximately 125 ms. We also notice that the congestion rate, CNG, is very high, between 120 and 220, and the frequency fr_{OFF*} is important around 0.4 (i.e., one OFF* period occurs for every 2.5 chunks, on average). We observe not only lower measurements, but also a higher degradation rate in performance: the gap of QoE metric measurements, CNG andfr_{OFF*}, is clearly large between scenario WL and scenario 4. Accordingly, Cubic is not suitable as a TCP congestion control variant of the HAS server for both shaping methods when heavy congestion occurs. This result can be verified by examining Figs. 8 and 9 in Sect. 4.1.2, where Cubic has difficulties with rapidly defining the suitable ssthresh value before convergence and after congestion, respectively.
- The RWTM shaping method presents higher degradation in QoE metric measurements than HTBM when we compare scenario WL to scenario 4 for both TCP congestion variants, Cubic and Illinois. The cause is mainly related to the fact that HTBM is used to generate congestion events and maintain high QoE under normal circumstances, which is not the case with RWTM. Accordingly, we can say that RWTM is more sensitive to induced congestions than HTBM. This result can be verified when examining Figs. 7 and 9 in Sect. 4.1.2, in which a single congestion event instantaneously degrades performance.

From the first and the second observations, we can deduce that the best combination that maintains optimal QoE metric measurements with low degradation and has the lowest frequency of OFF* periods, fr_{OFF*}, is ensured by the combination {Illinois HTBM}.

- The second-best combination is {Illinois RWTM}. Here, the QoE metric measurements are acceptable, but the degradation rate is higher than the best combination {Illinois HTBM}. This degradation indicates that {Illinois RWTM} cannot adequately resist against induced congestions, especially when we have a highly congested link between client and server. However, this combination could successfully be used with a link under less frequent congestions.

Scenario 5

In this section, we present the performance metric measurements when the standard variation of RTT_{C-S} varies. The behavior of the resulting curves will indicate how performance degrades when the standard deviation of RTT_{C-S} increases. The variation of QoE (instability, infidelity, and convergence speed) is presented in Fig. 10, and the variation of CNG and fr_{OFF^*} is listed in Fig. 11. We have two major observations:

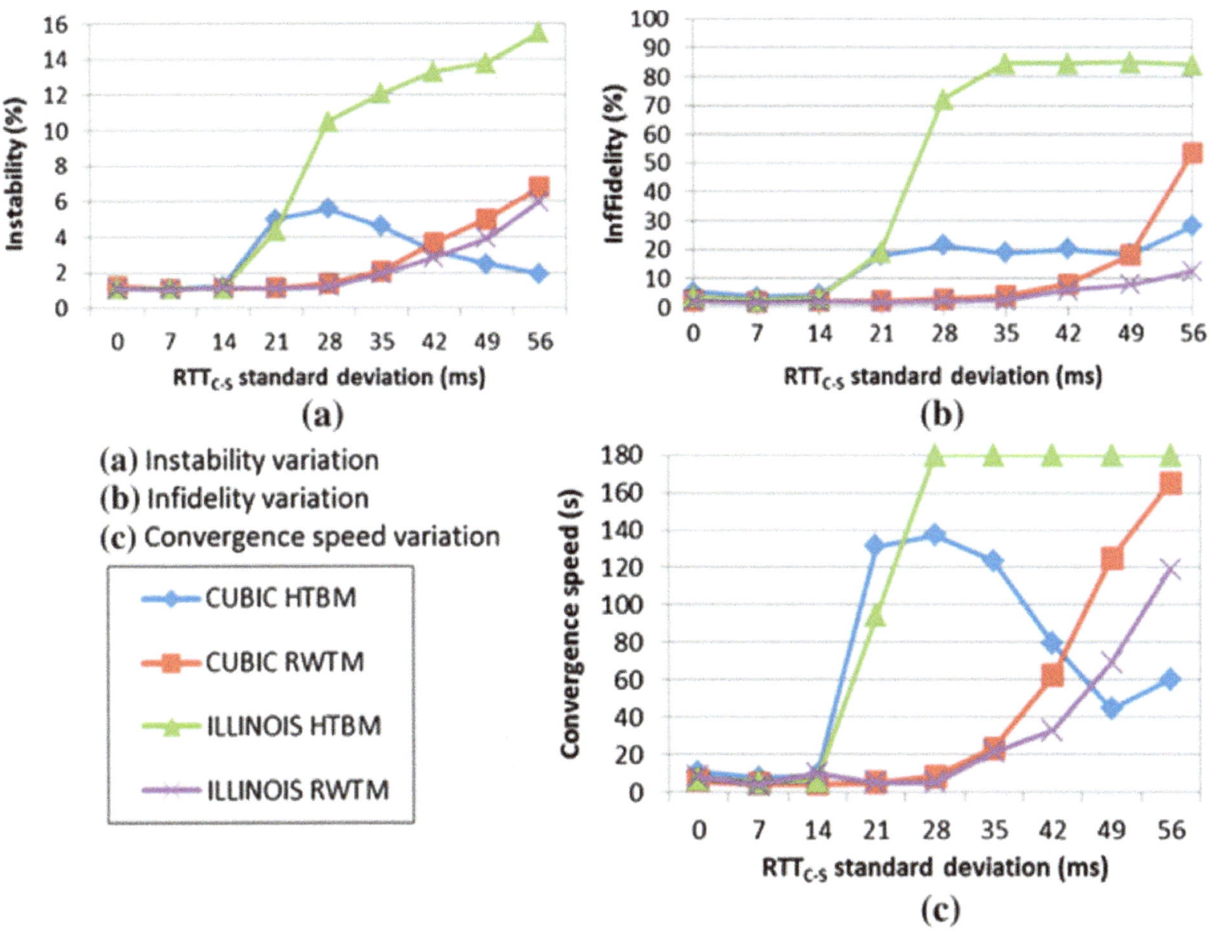

Figure 10 QoE variation

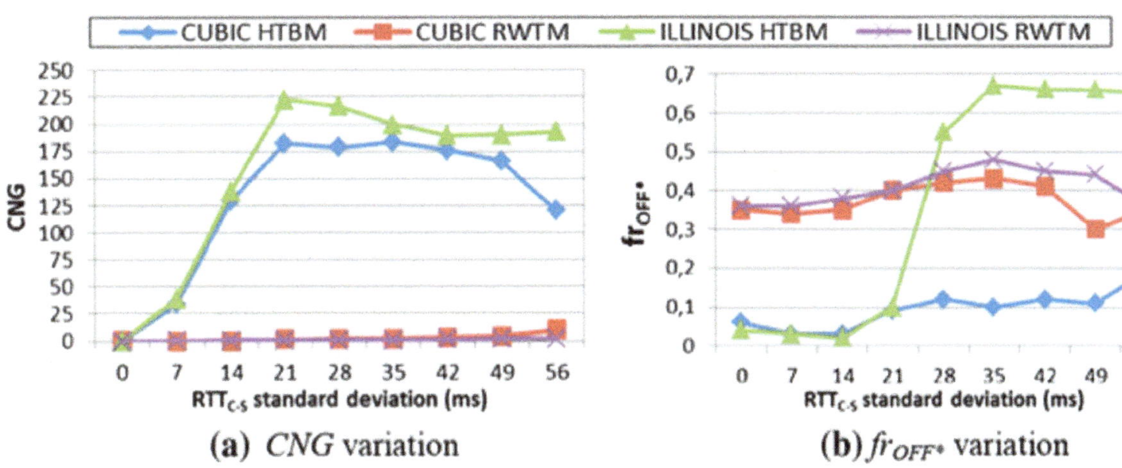

Figure 11 Variation of CNG and fr_{OFF^*}

On the one hand, the {Illinois RWTM} (purple cross) and the {Cubic RWTM} (red square) curves are convex and close to each other and are predominantly below the other curves. The three QoE metric values are good until an $RTT_{C\text{-}S}$ standard deviation of around 40 ms, where performance degradation begins to be visible. Moreover, the combination {Illinois RWTM} preserves its performance better and has a less aggressive degradation rate for higher $RTT_{C\text{-}S}$standard deviation, especially from 35 ms. Accordingly, we can say that using RWTM with Illinois is safer when $RTT_{C\text{-}S}$ is very unstable. Otherwise, {RWTM Cubic} can also be used, most usefully when the standard deviation of $RTT_{C\text{-}S}$ is lower than 35 ms. We also observe in Fig. 11that both combinations have a similarly low congestion rate, CNG, and similar frequency ofOFF* periods, fr_{OFF*}. Based on this observation, we can deduce that RWTM preserves its inherent characteristics with Cubic and Illinois variants, and that the degradation of QoE metric measurements for highly unstable $RTT_{C\text{-}S}$ is mainly caused by the congestion control algorithms used by Cubic and Illinois variants. Since RWTM seems to be more adequate with Illinois, we can say that the loss-delay-based and C-AIMD approach of Illinois helps more than the loss-based and cubic RTT-independent approach of Cubic to preserve good performance for highly unstable $RTT_{C\text{-}S}$ values.

On the other hand, HTBM is less robust against $RTT_{C\text{-}S}$ instability. The green and the blue curves that present the combination of HTBM with Illinois and Cubic, respectively, show a significant degradation of QoE metric measurements when the standard deviation of $RTT_{C\text{-}S}$ is above 14 ms. However, {HTBM Illinois} is more sensitive to $RTT_{C\text{-}S}$ instability than {HTBM Cubic}. This means that combining the loss-delay-based congestion control variant Illinois with the HTBM shaping method that increases the queuing delay, entails harmful drawbacks for QoE when the $RTT_{C\text{-}S}$ is unstable. We can also validate this observation in Fig. 11: the congestion rate CNG of {HTBM Illinois} and {HTBM Cubic} are predominantly close to each other, but the frequency of OFF* periods explodes with {HTBM Illinois} for $RTT_{C\text{-}S}$ standard deviation higher than 20 ms. This implies that the additional delay caused by HTBM is practically the same for both congestion control variants Cubic and Illinois, but the effects on fr_{OFF*} and QoE are quite different and involve more drawbacks for the Illinois variant. In contrast, HTBM with Cubic has fewer drawbacks and presents QoE metrics measurements that are relatively constant for instability and infidelity from $RTT_{C\text{-}S}$ standard deviations around 20 ms. This results can be explained by the fact that the Cubic variant does not use $RTT_{C\text{-}S}$ to compute its congestion window cwnd during the congestion avoidance phase, as explained in Sect. 2.1.

DISCUSSION

After comparing the results of five scenarios, we have made numerous observations, but in this subsection, we want to summarize the most important observations. First, NewReno and Vegas variants do not provide good performance in the HAS context, excepting the combination {NewReno RWTM} that could perform well if the initial value of ssthresh is well-chosen. Second, we summarize the observations of the five scenarios for the four combinations in Table 9. Thus, we assign a score for each combination that ranges between "–" and "++": – (bad), - (insufficient), ± (average), + (good), and ++ (excellent). This score is based on the analysis of results for each scenario.

Table 9 The final score for each combination

Scenario	Combination			
	RWTM		HTBM	
	Cubic	Illinois	Cubic	Illinois
{1, 2, 3}	++	++	±	+
4	–	+	–	++
5	+	++	±	–

The best combination is {Illinois RWTM}: it yields good performance when two clients compete for bandwidth and is robust against high $RTT_{C\text{-}S}$ variation, but it is somewhat vulnerable to heavy congestions that could be caused by external factors. In the second position, we have two combinations:

- {Cubic RWTM}: Unfortunately, it is very vulnerable to congestions and slightly sensitive to high $RTT_{C\text{-}S}$ variation.
- {Illinois HTBM}: It has the advantage of being robust against heavy congestions. However, it is very sensitive to $RTT_{C\text{-}S}$ variation. Furthermore, it causes a high rate of congestion in the gateway that could disturb other sessions in concurrence with HAS sessions.

CONCLUSION AND FUTURE WORK

A comparative evaluation has been developed in order to study the effect of combining two well-known traffic-shaping methods (HTBM and RWTM) in the gateway with four very common TCP congestion algorithms (NewReno, Vegas, Illinois, and Cubic) in the server in the context of HTTP adaptive streaming technique. We examined the user's QoE by applying objective metrics. Furthermore, we observed the evolution of the congestion window on the server side in order to explain the behavior of each combination and its relationship with QoE metrics. We also used the congestion rate and the frequency of OFF periods that exceeds retransmission timeout as indicators. We have addressed many scenarios: two HAS clients competing for the home bandwidth simultaneously, adding or removing a HAS client, inducing a heavy congestion in the gateway, and increasing the instability of the round trip time, RTT, between the HAS server and the HAS client. The results show that there is a significant discordance in performance between combinations. The best combination that improves the QoE, reduces the congestion rate, and reduces the OFF periods in the majority of scenarios is when combining the loss-delay-based congestion control variant, Illinois, which uses the C-AIMD approach, with the TCP flow control-based method, RWTM. The characteristics of Illinois and RWTM seem to be similarly robust against high RTT instability. This combination does not disturb other real-time streams in the home network because it does not induce additional queueing delay and it considerably reduces the congestion rate. However, this combination is slightly vulnerable to heavy congestions that could be caused by external factors such as other concurrent streams.

Having extended our knowledge about the combination of TCP congestion control variants with shaping methods in this work, we intend as future work to design a new TCP congestion control variant that is compatible with all specifications of HAS and shaping methods.

REFERENCES

1. Houdaille, R., Gouache, S.: Shaping HTTP adaptive streams for a better user experience. In: 3rd Multimedia Systems Conference, pp. 1–9. ACM (2012)
2. Ameur, C.B., Mory, E., Cousin, B.: Shaping HTTP adaptive streams using receive window tuning method in home gateway. In: 33rd Performance Computing and Communications Conference, pp. 1–2. IEEE (2014)
3. Floyd, S., Henderson, T., et al.: The NewReno modification to TCP fast recovery algorithm. RFC 3782 (2012)
4. Brakmo, L.S., O'Malley, S.W., Peterson, L.L.: TCP Vegas: new techniques for congestion detection and avoidance. ACM SIGCOMM Computer Commun. Rev. 24(4), 24–35 (1994)
5. Liu, S., Başar, T., Srikant, R.: TCP-Illinois: a loss-and delay-based congestion control algorithm for high-speed networks. Perform. Eval. J. 65(6–7), 417–440 (2008). (ScienceDirect)
6. Liu, S., Başar, T., Srikant, R.: CUBIC: a new TCP-friendly high-speed TCP variant. ACM SIGOPS Oper. Syst. Rev. 42(5), 64–74 (2008). (ACM)
7. Jiang, J., Sekar, V., Zhang, H.: Improving fairness, efficiency, and stability in HTTP-based adaptive video streaming with festive. In: 8th International Conference on Emerging Networking Experiments and Technologies, pp. 97–108. ACM (2012)
8. Ha, S., Rhee, I.: Taming the elephants: new TCP slow start. Computer. Netw. J. 55(9), 2092–2110 (2011). (ScienceDirect)
9. Akhshabi, S., Anantakrishnan, L., et al.: What happens when HTTP adaptive streaming players compete for bandwidth? In: 22nd International Workshop on Network and Operating System Support for Digital Audio and Video, pp. 9–14. ACM (2012)
10. Misra, V., Gong, W.B., Towsley, D.: Fluid-based analysis of a network of AQM routers supporting TCP flows with an application to RED. ACM SIGCOMM Computer. Commun. Rev. 30(4), 151–160 (2000). (ACM)
11. Villa, B.J., Heegaard, P.E.: Group based traffic shaping for adaptive HTTP video streaming by segment duration control. In: 27th International Conference on Advanced Information Networking and Applications, pp. 830–837. IEEE (2013)
12. Stewart, L., Hayes, D., et al.: Multimedia-unfriendly TCP congestion control and home gateway queue management. In: 2nd ACM Conference on Multimedia Systems, pp. 35–44. ACM (2011)
13. David, H., Armitage, G.: Improved coexistence and loss tolerance for delay based TCP congestion control. In 35th Conference on Local Computer Networks, pp. 24–31. IEEE (2010)
14. Ho, C.Y., Chen, Y.C., et al.: Fast retransmit and fast recovery schemes of transport protocols: a survey and taxonomy. Computer. Netw. J. 52(6), 1308–1327 (2008). (ScienceDirect)MATH
15. Jamal, H., Sultan, K.: Performance analysis of TCP congestion control algorithms. Int. J. Computer. Commun. 2(1), 18–24 (2008)
16. Brown, M.A.: Traffic Control HOWTO. Guide to IP Layer Network (2006)
17. Allam, M., Paxson, V., Stevens, W.R.: TCP congestion control. RFC 2581 (1999)
18. Yin, X., Sekar, V., Sinopoli, B.: Toward a principled framework to design dynamic adaptive streaming algorithms over HTTP. In: 13th ACM Workshop on Hot Topics in Networks, pp. 1–9. ACM (2014)
19. Akhshabi, S., Narayanaswamy, S., et al.: An experimental evaluation of rate-adaptive video players over HTTP. Signal. Process. Image. Commun. 27(4), 271–287 (2012)
20. Huang, T.Y., Handigol, N., et al.: Confused, timid, and unstable: picking a video streaming rate is hard. In: The Internet Measurement Conference, pp. 225–238. ACM (2012)
21. Ameur, C.B., Mory, E., Cousin, B.: Evaluation of gateway-based shaping methods for HTTP adaptive streaming. In: Quality of Experience-based Management for Future Internet Applications and Services Workshop (QoE-FI), pp. 1777–1782. IEEE International Conference on Communications (2015)
22. Cranley, N., Perry, P., Murphy, L.: User perception of adapting video quality. In: International Journal of Human-Computer Studies, pp. 637–647 (2006)
23. Mok, R.K.P., Chan, E., et al.: Inferring the QoE of HTTP video streaming from user-viewing activities. In: 1st ACM SIGCOMM Workshop on Measurements Up the Stack, pp. 31–36. ACM (2011)
24. Dumazet, E.: Stochastic Fairness Queuing Discipline.

http://manpages.ubuntu.com/manpages/trusty/man8/tc-sfq.8.html. Ubuntu Manuals (2010)

25. Akhshabi, S., Anantakrishnan, L., et al.: Server-based traffic shaping for stabilizing oscillating adaptive streaming players. In: 23rd ACM Workshop on Network and Operating Systems Support for Digital Audio and Video, pp. 19–24. ACM (2013)

26. Le Boudec, J.Y.: Rate Adaptation, Congestion Control and Fairness: A Tutorial, pp. 1–44. Ecole Polytechnique Federale de Lausanne (EPFL) (2014)

CHAPTER 2

THE HARMONIC WALK: AN INTERACTIVE PHYSICAL ENVIRONMENT TO LEARN TONAL MELODY ACCOMPANIMENT

Marcella Mandanici, Antonio Rodà, and Sergio Canazza

INTRODUCTION

Listeners perceive the surface of a tonal composition as a sequence of discrete pitch-events [1] and can extract the underlying harmonic background only thanks to complex cognitive processes which involve discontinuity and similarity perception, musical entities categorization, and events temporal organization. It is probably the reason why harmony has always been considered a difficult matter to understand, also among professionals. Nevertheless, harmony occupies a very steady place in human perception. A lot of research in the field of music psychology has offered evidence that unlearned adults and children from the very early age of 4-5 years [2] have wide implicit harmonic knowledge comprehending elementary chord functions detection and the perception of regularities in chord occurrences. As tonal music is ubiquitous in our music culture's environment, all these features are learned from mere passive exposition [3] and can so be considered as a cognitive heritage common to every unskilled user. Thus, the main goal of the Harmonic Walk[1] is to offer to people the possibility of experiencing such important musical knowledge in an easy and handy way, contributing to make users aware of tonal musical features (see Figure 1). The application, taking advantage of the large potentialities of a body moving in space, can provide the opportunity to understand the structure of a tonal melody, to explore the harmonic space, and to experiment chordal progressions. Moreover, it can return to users a physical feedback of the spatial relationships which govern the music chords domain, thus helping them to build their personal cognitive map of tonal harmony. The Harmonic Walk, matched with floor projections, can be used for edutainment purposes in demonstration setups as well as in sound and image installations. In schools it can be seen as a didactic tool to support music education programs.

The aim of this paper is to illustrate the Harmonic Walk system and to provide an initial assessment which can outline some interesting points of discussion about the application and its utilization in a didactic context. The paper is organized as follows: Section 2 reports and discusses some similar applications. Section 3 introduces the two theoretical principles upon which the application is based, namely, the fundamental process of tonal melody segmentation (Section 3.1), and the six roots' harmonic space by which it is possible to harmonize a one-key tonal melody (Section 3.2). Section 4 addresses the core question of the Harmonic Walk application: the cross-domain mapping between the theoretical representations of musical features and their rendering in the physical space through a geometric interpretation. Section 5 presents the system architecture, describing the Zone Tracker application and masks for space subdivision, the Max/MSP modules for sound production, and the current implementation

Citation: Marcella Mandanici, Antonio Rodà, and Sergio Canazza, "The Harmonic Walk: An Interactive Physical Environment to Learn Tonal Melody Accompaniment," Advances in Multimedia, vol. 2016, Article ID 4027164, 16 pages, 2016. doi:10.1155/2016/4027164.

of application's interactive interface. Then Section 6 follows where the three phases of the assessment tests are thoroughly described and in Section 6.6 quantitative and qualitative results are discussed. Conclusions and further work are outlined in Section 7.

Figure 1: The Harmonic Walk while being tested by three high school students at the Catholic Institute "Barbarigo," Padova (Italy).

RELATED WORK

The idea of interacting with harmonies through spatial representations is not new. It has been widely developed in the Harmony Space project at the Music Computing Lab of the University of Stanford in 1994 [4]. TheHarmony Space interface shows a desktop bidimensional matrix of pitches ordered by major thirds on the horizontal axis and by minor thirds on the vertical axis. Choosing a key area, a chord size, and a chord mapping, when a note is selected, the chord built on it will sound. The interface has been used to simplify the study of harmony, to analyze musical pieces, and to compose new ones. The environment is very rich and complex as it allows many option possibilities (the number of pitches used for the chord, the chord type, the key, etc.): so the interaction actually depends on a preselected series of options, which rather fits an expert user level. More recent systems like Isochords [5] or Mapping Tonal Harmony [6] are aimed at helping the understanding of the harmonic structure through a visualization of the space of musical chords or highlighting preselected harmonization possibilities. Again, these are very complex environments which improve musical structure consciousness at a high degree of knowledge.

All the interfaces till now described employ some visuospatial schemata of the harmonic space, but these are always reproduced on the computer traditional bidimensional screen. Nevertheless, Holland himself in 2009 tried a physical space extension of his Harmony Space employing a floor projection and a camera tracking system [7]. A GPS system to navigate a wide tonnetz[2] area has also been proposed by Behringer and Elliott [8], where the authors suggest some musical games about composition and harmony features knowledge. ThePaperTonnetz [9] presents a more intuitive approach, where chord progressions are obtained through a pencil navigation on an interactive paper plotted tonnetz. A more recent experience of interaction with Holland'sHarmony Space has also been experimented using a 3D graphical representation of the tonnetz. The user interacts with the interface through colored controllers which are used to select the pitches and to produce the chordal audio feedback [10]. Also in the Harmony Navigator [11] the chord selection, supported by a corpus-based statistical model, is operated by hand gestures in the 3D space around the user. All these experiences show that the role of the physical space in the tonnetz navigation is not irrelevant. "Deeper engagement and directness, rich physical cues for memory and reflection, embodied engagement with rhythmic time constraints,hands which are free for other simultaneous activities (such as playing a traditional instrument) and qualitatively new possibilities for collaborative use" are the benefits of physical interaction outlined by [7]. Others (Bigo et al. [9] and Manaris et al. [11]) emphasize the role of gestures as the preferred interaction style in the chords navigation, because they can help with the engagement of nonacademic musicians or amateurs with the world of harmony (Hedges and McPherson [10]). Lastly, the link between physical motion and the exploration of proximities in chord areas is the main point of Behringer and Elliott [8]. This is also the relevant point of theHarmonic Walk application, which has an immediate predecessor in the Stanza Logo-motoria [12], where the child has to use her/his spatial memory to match sounds with a spoken text. Some preparatory studies about orientation and wayfinding in the Harmonic Walk's environment have been presented in [13], where assessment tests, carried out with a sample of children from 7 to 11 years old, showed that the majority of them was able to find a valid path to perform a harmonic progression. The Harmonic Walk presents a very simple harmonic palette restricted to only six roots without any further option. This aspect is much simpler than Holland's Harmony Space. The roots spatial disposition on the actual surface, derived from a geometrical interpretation of their relationships, allows the user to interact with the roots simply moving on the surface, bypassing so any technical approach. By involving the whole body in the musical interaction the user has to activate harmonic perception, spatial memory, enactive route finding, and rhythmic skills in a measure much greater than interacting with a bidimensional computer screen. Moreover, this very basic setup projects its computational content in the real world, helping to bring the user nearer to complex musical concepts, like tonal harmony.

THEORETICAL BACKGROUND

The Harmonic Walk is a theory-based application concerning the tonal music domain. Hence, the definition of the tonal music's main features is fundamental to shape decisions about the system's architecture and user interaction design. In Section 3.1 the processing of a tonal melody is analyzed in order to outline its schematic representation and to focus on its main components: the melodic segmentation and its underlying harmonic frame. Furthermore, in Section 3.2 the harmonic space of a one-key tonal melody is presented.

The Tonal Melody Representation

As soon as a listener is presented to a tonal melody, s/he first tries to interpret the sequence of notes, grouping them after a metrical and harmonic frame [14]. This produces a segmentation of the composition into different harmonic regions which, in case of one-key melody, shall all belong to the same tonality.

The example in Figure 2 shows an excerpt of a popular melody written in the tonality of F major. The gray units correspond to the tonic regions (T), while the violet ones correspond to the dominant regions (D). In the lower part of the figure, a one-line staff shows the durations of the units, which represent the harmonic rhythm of the composition. As can be seen, it is not regular even in such a simple piece of music. The perceptual, cognitive procedures which lie under this musical representation have been studied and formalized by Lerdahl and Jackendoff [15], who also showed how a tonal piece perception is organized at various levels, starting from the most superficial (grouping structure) to arrive to the deepest (prolongation reduction). Some of these level are shown in the upper part of Figure 2, where, from the 1st level to the 2nd level, a time span reduction is operated, based on the fact that the first dominant unit arrives on the weak part of the first bar. So, it can be incorporated at the upper level, creating a larger tonic unit which occupies two bars. This fosters the idea of the great importance of metrical accents, which rule the changes of harmony in a recursive way. Summarizing, a tonal piece may be seen as a sequence of musical units, segmented on the basis of their perceived underlying harmonic functions. The sequence has a metrical timing organization, which means that the region's length is always a multiple of a basic time unit. Moreover, the chord sequence is also biased by the importance of primary chords and by the supportive role of their parallels. It has a strong recursive nature which leads mostly to prefer the tonic and dominant chords.

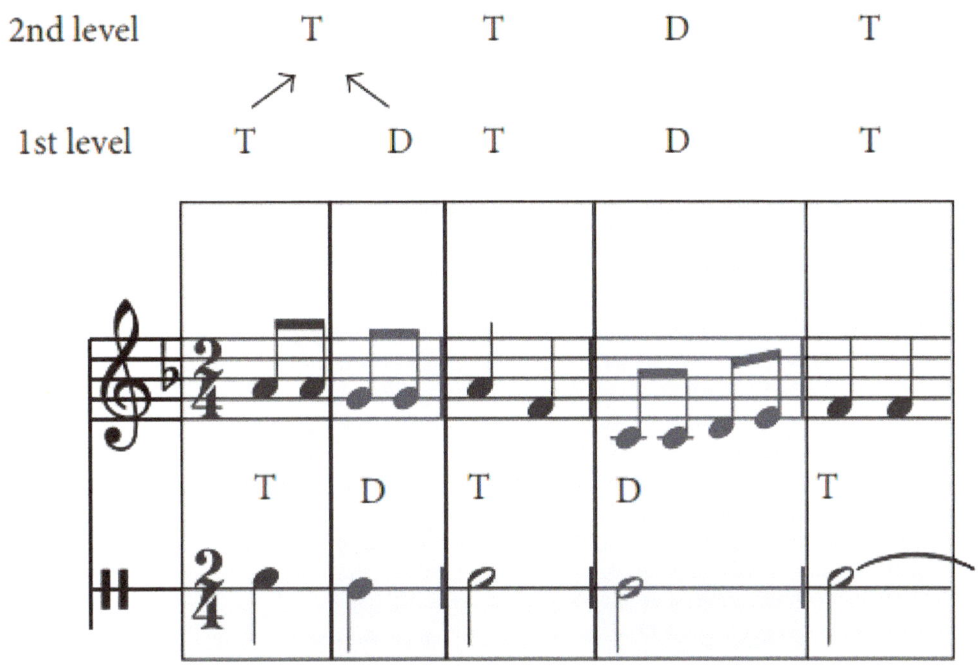

Figure 2: A popular melody's harmonic rhythm and levels of grouping structure.

The Harmonic Walk's Chord Space

The tonal language is a highly hierarchical system based on the prevalence of the tonic chord matched by the dominant (V degree, one fifth above the tonic) and the subdominant (IV degree, one fifth below the tonic). These three chords are said to be primary because they represent the fundamental tonal functions in a given key [16]. Although every one-key melody can be accompanied using only primary chords, also parallel chords, built one third below primary chords, can be used as supportive harmonies. Hence, the complete table of musical chords used by the Harmonic Walk application consists of six chords, corresponding to the first six degrees of the key[3], as showed in Figure 4.

The tonal harmonic space has been historically represented by the tonnetz. In this representation, pitch is disposed in horizontal and diagonal lines. As shown in Figure 3, the horizontal lines connect the circle of fifths. On the diagonal axis SE-NW lays the major third circle while the diagonal axis SW-NE bears the minor third circle. The chord is represented by the triangular area resulting from the crossing of the three axes. The tonnetzrepresentation shows the strict connections among the chords belonging to the same key. If we consider the whole chord progression comprehending the six C major chords from the left to the right (D minor-F major-A minor-C major-E minor-G major), we can see that they all are originated by the so-called edge transformation. The edge transformation is an inversion of the triangle along one of its edges, which means that two chords sharing the same edge have two pitches in common. Particularly, this relationship links each primary chord with its parallel (same color in Figure 3), while primary chords (F major-C major-G major) are originated by a vertex transformation, which expresses the commonality of only one pitch. All these observations can explain why the tonnetz representation of the harmonic relationships is so popular and meaningful also from the perceptual point of view. We shall discuss the six primary and parallel chords' spatial disposition in Section 4.2.

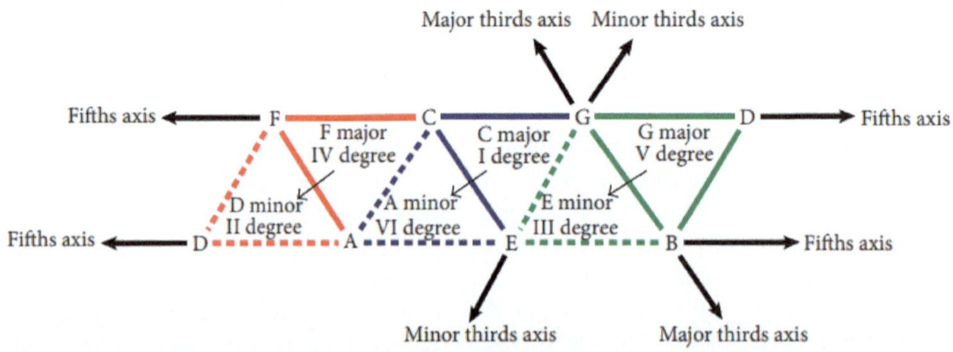

Figure 3: The Riemannian tonnetz representation of the three primary and parallel chords (linked with the thin black arrows) in the C major key. On the horizontal lines (x-axis) lie the circles of fifths, while on the two diagonal axes the circle of major and minor thirds lies.

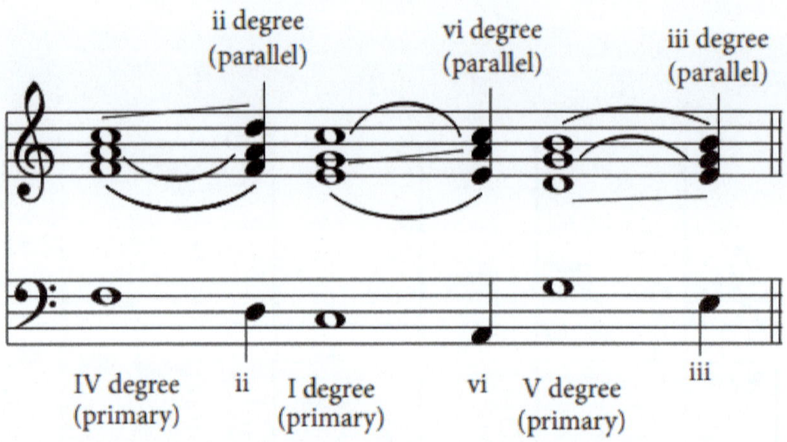

Figure 4: Table of the six primary and parallel chords in the key of C major used in theHarmonic Walk application. The common notes between a primary and its parallel chord are tied, while the changing notes are linked with a straight line.

FROM THEORETICAL REPRESENTATIONS TO THE PHYSICAL SPACE: A CROSS-DOMAIN MAPPING

Music is often said to be the "art of time," as we have just seen that a tonal composition unfolds musical units in sequence along a timeline. Moreover, the concept of time involves musical memory, through which we perceive pattern recursion and formal organization. Nonetheless, the internal structure of musical elements has also a very strong spatial dimension. When we discuss one of the most basic musical structures, the scale, we commonly involve such terms like "ascending" and "descending," which are obvious spatial metaphors. In expert speech as well as in common people's language, melodies "go up or down" or "jump" or "arrive" to a particular point. Tones can proceed by "skip" or by "step," keys can be "near" or "far," harmonies make "turnarounds," and bass lines are sometimes defined as "walking." Music metaphorical schemas relating to embodied cognition and movement have been widely analyzed by Brower [17], Saslaw [18], and Cook [19]. Indeed, even in musical notation a single tone is represented as a point (a square "punctus" in Gregorian music or a circle, a "note" in the modern notation). However, we all know that every tone is not composed of a single element, but, rather, it is the result of the summation of a weighted number of overtones. So, every harmonic sound's inner nature is a manifold whose single elements are organized after a precise spatial relationship: that of the harmonic overtones, to which the tonnetz, discussed in Section 3.2, owes a lot of its theoretical foundations[4].

Now, to represent all this apparatus into a physical space, we need to provide a geometric interpretation of the tonal composition's main features, which are(1)the musical regions sequence,(2)the six root progressions.

A Geometric Interpretation of the Musical Regions Sequence

The time proceeding of the various musical units is led by the melody, whose metaphoric scheme is expressed by the so-called "source-path-goal" schema [20][5]. So, the description of a melody could include a starting point (the source), a series of intermediate steps (all the subsequent musical units), and the end of the musical phrase, usually a cadence to the tonic or to the dominant (goal). Following this metaphor and imagining the simplest motion in space a human can do, the walk, we could represent the tonal composition as in Figure 5, where each step corresponds to the next musical unit.

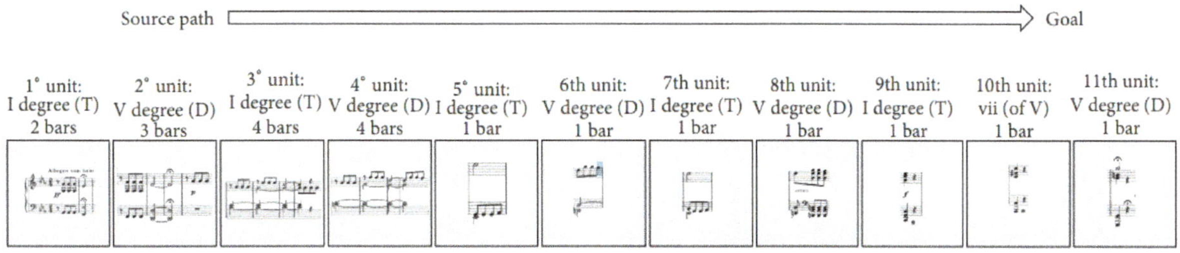

Figure 5: A geometric interpretation of the first 21 bars of Beethoven's Symphony Number 5 segmented in 11 units corresponding to the harmonic changes.

Hence, the geometrical interpretation of the "source-path-goal" schema is a sequence of units disposed along a straight line after which the user can perform the unit sequence till the cadence. To rebuild the piece's correct time sequence, her/his pace has to follow the harmonic rhythm of the composition.

A Geometric Interpretation of the Six Root Progressions

As far as concerns the second musical feature, we need a geometrical interpretation of the harmonic space already defined by the tonnetz along the red, blue and green axes of Figure 3. If we look at Table 1, we see that all the chords, but the problematic vii degree, can be linked with more or less probability with all the others.

Table 1: The table summarizes the most used root progressions in tonal harmony [27]. Note that the vii-degree chord is not represented in root position, but in its first inversion, as it appears most of the times.

From	Often to	Sometimes to	Less often to
I	IV or V	vi	ii or iii
ii	V	IV or vi	I or iii
iii	vi	IV	I, ii, or V
IV	V	I or ii	iii or vi
V	I	IV or vi	ii or iii
vi	ii or V	iii or IV	I
vii^6	I or iii		

This means that, in spite of all its expressive power, the tonnetz is not the best spatial schema to be transferred to the application's actual surface, because it does not allow moving from one chord to the other without touching some other chord. Instead, a user must be able to connect all the chords to realize all the possible harmonic progressions.

For this reason we interpret the geometrical form of the six available musical chords, expanding the originaltonnetz grid to obtain an inner empty zone, which can allow the transition to the other remaining five chords. The proposed geometrical representation, depicted in Figure 6, is a circular ring sliced in six parts corresponding to the six chords. To clarify the relationship between this geometrical form and the tonnetz, we superimpose the tonnetz chord displacement on the upper part of the ring. The bigger thin lined triangles are the primary chords, while the squeezed ones are the parallel chords. To obtain the required linking space, we project the parallel chords in the lower part of the ring. The ii degree is overturned along the F-D axis and is placed just under the IV (following the dashed arrows). The iii degree is overturned along the E-B axis and is placed just under the V degree. The vi degree is overturned along the A-E axis and is placed in front of the I degree. This new displacement provides a logical chord disposition, where from every chord it is possible to reach each of the remaining five chords without touching the others.

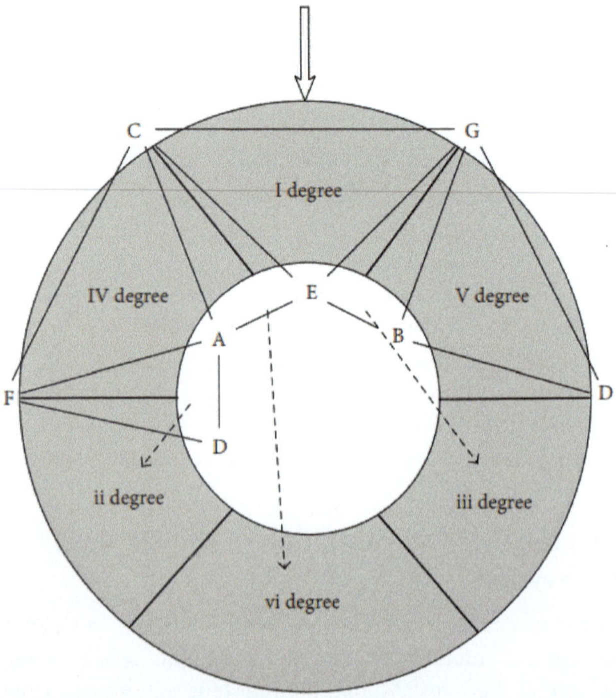

Figure 6: The "stretched" tonnetz with the parallel harmonies overturned in the lower part of the circular ring. The white arrow indicates the position of the tonic, which is in most cases the beginning of a tonal composition.

Summarizing, the geometrical interpretation of the outstanding tonal melodies features to be used in theHarmonic Walk application is a straight line and a circular ring.

SYSTEM ARCHITECTURE

In this section we describe the Harmonic Walk architecture which is composed of two software modules, aimed at video analysis and sound production, respectively.

In Section 5.1 we describe the Zone Tracker application with its video analysis algorithms and masks for surface division. In Section 5.2 also the Max/MSP[6] patch, responsible for the audio output, is presented. The two software modules communicate through the OSC protocol[7]. The application's interface is explained in Section5.3, where the spatial displacement of the musical features' geometrical interpretation is introduced.

The Zone Tracker Application

A ceiling mounted video camera, oriented perpendicularly to the floor, captures the users movements inside a rectangular area, whose dimensions depend on both the distance from camera to floor and the field of view of the lens (see Figure 7). As the system is designed for carrying out educational activities inside a classroom, the camera lens is chosen in order to view a rectangle of about 3 × 4 meters when the camera is mounted on a 2.8/3-meter-high ceiling. The video application, called Zone Tracker, tracks the user's position employing a series of masks. These subdivide the active surface, allowing detecting the portion of space occupied by the user. The video analysis algorithm analyzes the input images in three steps, as shown in Figure 8.

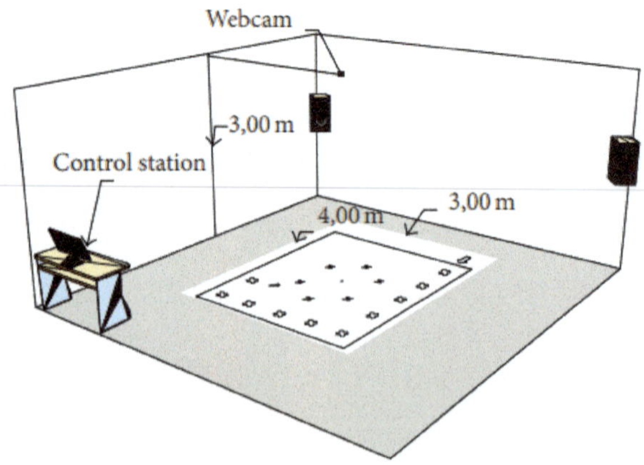

Figure 7: The Harmonic Walk's physical environment with camera placement, audio monitors, and control station.

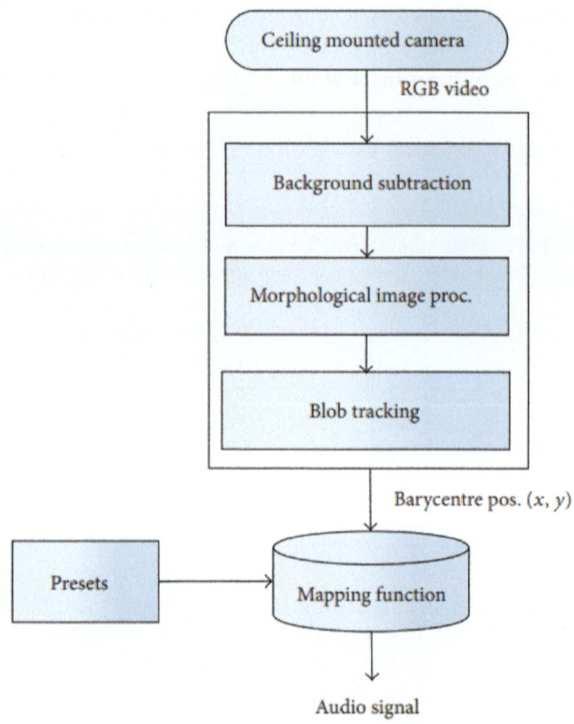

Figure 8: The Harmonic Walk's system architecture.

(1) Background Subtraction. The background is subtracted following the averaging background method proposed by Jabri et al. [21]. The method used is based on statistical modeling of the background for each channel color and detection with adaptive threshold. The background model is obtained by calculating for each channel the average and the standard deviation of each pixel in the course of a certain number of frames acquired from static shots of the background, following the formula:

$$\mu_t = \alpha x_t + (1 - \alpha)\mu_{t-1}, \tag{1}$$

where μ_t is the average calculated up to frame t, α is the learning coefficient of the model and xt is the pixel value at the frame t. After building a statistical model of the background, the new frames are compared with it, thus producing what is called a confiance image, that is, a grayscale image, where the value of each pixel represents the probability that it forms part of a region of the image not belonging to the background.

(2) Morphological Image Processing. These images are processed by means of morphological transformations [22]. Dilation and erosion are the two basic mathematical operations which correspond, respectively, to the expansion and thinning of the black region. A combination of the two leads to opening and closure of morphological operations, aiming at defining well shaped silhouettes blobs. When the value of confiance does not allow deciding for sure whether a region is part of the figure of interest or background, a threshold algorithm can be used. This threshold function was implemented through an operation of nonlinear convolution between the confiance image and a mask (kernel), following the formula:

$$\mathrm{dst}(x,y) = \begin{cases} 1 & \text{if } \mathrm{src}(x,y) \neq 0 \wedge \exists (u,v) \\ & : \mathrm{src}(u,v) = 1, \quad (u,v) \in K_{x,y} \\ 0 & \text{otherwise,} \end{cases} \qquad (2)$$

where src(x, y) represents a pixel of the source image and dst(x, y) a pixel of the image to which the transformation was applied. An uncertain pixel (with nonzero value) is not part of the background if there is at least one pixel equal to 1 in a neighborhood K.

(3) Blob Tracking. The blobs moves are tracked and the twodimensional barycenter of each blob is calculated. For this purpose, the OpenCV addon on openFrameworks provides the classes ofxCvContourFinder and ofxCvBlob. In particular, the findContours method in ofxCvContourFinder, given an input binary image, employs some features of OpenCV to detect blob and store the information in data structures of type ofxCvBlob. Although the video analysis module can track more users simultaneously, this first implementation of the Harmonic Walk is designed to be used by a single user at a time. 5.2. The Zone Tracker's Masks and the Audio Rendering. The users barycenter coordinates are employed by the Zone Tracker application to compute the occupied zone depending on the different masks stored in the application's memory. In this implementation of the Harmonic Walk, we use two different masks corresponding to the two geometric representations discussed in Section 4. The first mask subdivides the tracked zone in 25 squares, whose dimensions, after empirical observations, have been found to correspond approximately to the distance of a human step. This mask is employed to project the straight path of the musical unit sequence. The circular ring mask is subdivided into six zones. The radius of the outer and inner circles is defined accordingly to the same principles as the dimension of the squares. This mask is employed to project the circle of the six chords of the harmonic space. Zone Tracker sends via OSC the numbers corresponding to the various regions to the Max/MSP patch. Here, for each tonal composition two kinds of audio files are stored: one kind is the music audio file segmented following the principles illustrated in Section 3.1; the second kind is a group of audio files which reproduce the chords which belong to the song's key chord space and among which there are the chords employed in the song. The chords are played using a MIDI synthesizer with the same rhythm and timbre of the original composition.

The Harmonic Walk Interactive Interface.

The Harmonic Walk user interface consists of a rectangular area whose dimension changes depending on the ceiling height. To help the user's perception of the active area, we put the straight line of the musical unit sequence along the borders, while we put the center of the circular ring at the center of the rectangle[8]. The user's paths are identified through visual tags which are positioned at the center of each zone. There are two employed paths: the first is the one corresponding to the straight line and is marked with the white crosses, while the second is the circular one, marked with the black crosses (see Figure 9). The beginning of each path is marked with an arrow. In this way the user has a visual cue of the center of the various regions and is guided through them by his inner feeling of the music structure9

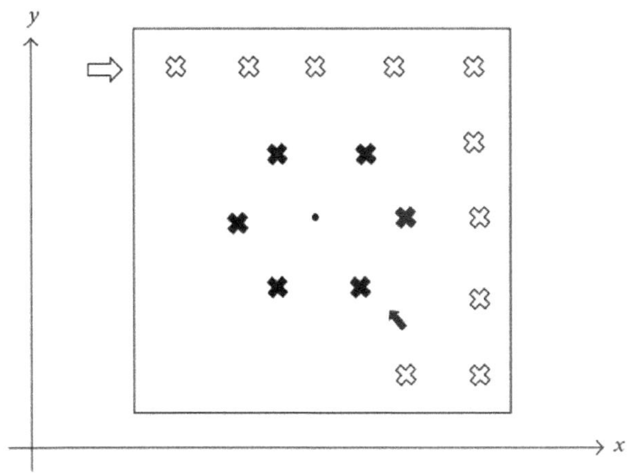

Figure 9: Visual tags of the straight and circular path of the Harmonic Walk. The straight path (white crosses) follows the interface perimeter and displays an 11-unit musical sequence, while the circular path (black crosses), centered with respect to the application's surface, displays the six harmonic space chords distribution. The x- axis corresponds to the interface width; the y-axis is the interface depth.

THE HARMONIC WALK'S ASSESSMENT

The Harmonic Walk's assessment tests were organized at the Catholic Institute "Barbarigo" in Padova during the first decade of December 2014. We wanted to gauge at what extent the application's design is successful in introducing the user to the tonal music features without any previous information about the application's task and materials. To do so, we quoted the subjects' success in the melody segmentation recognition and in the melody harmonization tasks. Moreover, to weight the manifold musical contents of the Harmonic Walk, we prepared a questionnaire to be fulfilled by the subjects (see Section 6.5) for both quantitative and qualitative assessments. In particular, we were interested in evaluating if, after the experience of the test, the subjects could gain some musical knowledge and consciousness about the musical features employed.

Subjects

A total number of 22 high school students between 16 and 20 years old took part in the test. The students were equally subdivided into two different groups: one musically trained and the other not. The first group was taken from classes belonging to the music high school, with specific instrumental and music theory programs. The second was chosen from classes belonging to various kinds of high schools with no music programs in their curricula. Among these we asked for students with no musical practice at all. For preserving clarity in the test's results, we excluded from the test only subjects with a declared state of disability.

Materials

The choice of the music genre and of the music piece which could fit better our student's sample was not trivial. We choose the song as one of the most popular genres of music. Moreover the sung words can help learning, memorization, localization of melodic qualities, and performance. Then we decided to bypass the most up-to-date young people major hits for at least two reasons: these songs' sample could be too restricted for our needs (i.e., it could not offer enough options regarding chords complexity, harmonic rhythm, and so on); moreover, as not all young people listen to the same kind of music, the choice could not guarantee that all the students know the same song.

So, we started with defining the ideal features of our song:(i)The chords employed must belong all to the same key, to fit the six roots' harmonic space explained in Section 3.2.(ii) The song's harmonic progression should include, beyond two or three primary chords, at least one, but not more than two, parallel chords, to offer a medium level of harmonic complexity.(iii)The chord's change (i.e., the harmonic rhythm) must be not too fast to allow easy body movements in the physical space.(iv)The song must be very popular, clear, and easy with the melodic structure.After an accurate search, we choose Adriano Celentano's Il ragazzo della via Gluck[10], whose musical structure is summarized in Table 2. The first musical phrase of the song is composed of 11 segments built upon 3 chords (two primary and one parallel). The column of the "syllables of change" shows the syllables of the text corresponding to the harmonic changes, that is, the points where the melodic segmentation occurs. The table shows that the points of segmentation are 10, as well as the number of chord changes. The column "Duration" outlines the number of bars occupied by the different song's units. As can be seen, the harmonic rhythm is not constant; that is, the song's units do not all have the same duration.

Table 2: Table of musical segments, syllables of change, chords and harmonic rhythm of Adriano Celentano's Il ragazzo della via Gluck.

Number of Seg.	Syll. of change	Chord	Duration
1	—	I	1
2	Gluck	V	2
3	me	I	2
4	ttà	V	2
5	ge	I	2
6	ten	V	2
7	ttà	I	1
8	vrai	VI	3
9	qui	I	3
10	var	VI	3
11	ti	I	3

Scenario

In Section 4 we discussed about two musical features (melodic segmentation and harmonic space), with the two related geometrical interpretations and masks (the straight line and the circular ring). At the present research stage, for the Harmonic Walk's test, we planned a three-phase approach to the tonal melody accompaniment, as showed in Figure 10.

Figure 10: Assessment phases and tasks.

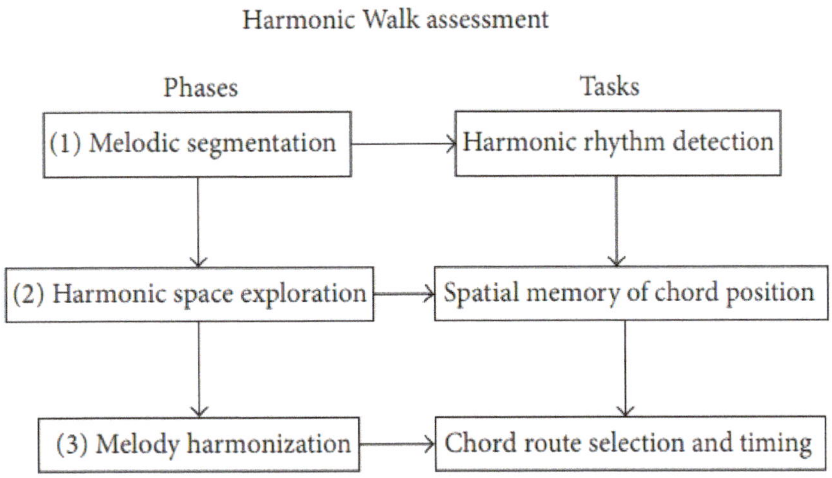

In the first phase the user is presented to the straight path along the borders of the active area, corresponding to the source-path-goal schema shown in Figure 5. Every step through the mapped regions produces the sound of the portion of the audio file corresponding to the segmentation described in Section 3.1. If the user fails to step to the next zone in time (i.e., if s/he is not aware of the song's harmonic rhythm), the audio file ends and the performance is interrupted. In the second phase the user enters the circular ring containing the six roots discussed in Section 3.2, with the aim to explore the harmonic space and to couple the spatial position to the chords sound and function. In the third and last phase, starting from the melodic segmentation knowledge acquired in the first phase and from the experience of the harmonic space acquired in the second phase, the user can now try to find the chords useful for the melody accompaniment of the composition. As usually there is not a unique solution to the melody harmonization, the user can experiment various chord sequences and choose the one s/he prefers. We consider the experience complete and successful as soon as the user harmonizes the whole given melodic excerpt without interruptions and in a way s/he considers valid.

Method

The high school students were tested individually in private sessions where only the test conductor and the music teacher were present. No previous information about the song used during the test was provided to the subjects. Each student was presented with some written instructions about the tasks s/he had to accomplish, while a short demonstration about the environment and its interaction modalities was provided by the test conductor. After this, the student undergoes the first phase of the test, during which s/he listens to the song, trying to understand where the units sectioning points are and trying to link them through an appropriate pace timing. The student is given a maximum of 5 minutes' time to conclude the first phase of the test. In the second phase the student enters the circle of the song's harmonic space and explores it in a free way. S/he has 3 minutes to listen to the chords and to remember their position in space. In the third phase the student is given the text of the song and, with the help of the teacher who sings the melody, tries to find the chords which can fit the song. As soon as s/he feels that the chord is not correct, the song begins again and continues till the end or till the next mistake. The student is given 5 minutes to complete this task. After the time expires or the last task is accomplished, the student is presented to a questionnaire for both quantitative and qualitative feedback about the test. The test conductor fulfills also a form of qualitative assessment and further observations. Moreover, for each of the three phases of the test, the system records the hit zones and the overall time employed by the subject.

The Questionnaire

The questionnaire prepared for the test subjects contains open-ended interviews, true-false and multiple choice questions, Likert-scale surveys[11], and participant observations, as shown in Table 3. It focuses on the first and third phase of the test and it is designed to collect both quantitative and qualitative data from the test subjects.

Table 3: Table of assessment tools utilized in the test's questionnaire. The information required concerning the 1st and 3rd test's phases and the subjects' opinions. The tools are open-ended interviews, true-false and multiple choice questions, and Likert-scale reviews.

	Quantitative assessment				Qual. ass.
	Int.	True-false	Mult.	Lik.	Op. quest.
1st phase	1	1	1	—	1
3rd phase	3	—	—	—	—
Sub. op.	—	—	—	2	2

For the first phase, we prepared an interview about the detection of the song's syllables where a harmonic change occurs, a true-false question about the duration of the song's units, and a multiple choice question about the principle upon which the unit's had been determined and asked for an opinion about the difficulty of linking correctly the various song's units.

We put no question about the second phase of the test, whose data are collected through direct observation and subjects' movement logs.

For the third phase, we put two open-ended interviews about how many times the subject did a chord change and how many overall chords s/he used. After this, we asked to draw on a plotted schema of the six chord circular ring, the route the subject did for harmonizing the melody.

At last, to collect the subjects' application's evaluation, we propose two Likert-scale surveys about the test experience's pleasantness and utility. Both surveys have 5 items. The first survey includes the following items: Very disagreeable (1). Disagreeable (2). Indifferent (3). Pleasant (4). Very Pleasant (5).The second survey includes the following items: Incomprehensible (1). Useless (2). Indifferent (3). Useful (4). Very Useful (5).As this is the first rigorous assessment test we conduct for the Harmonic Walk application, we could not base the item's definition upon previously collected users' statements. So, we opted for rather neutral items. The questionnaire ends with two opinion questions about the subjects' feeling and musical principles employed in the test.

Results and Discussion

In this subsection we gather information obtained by questionnaires, direct observations, and movement logs and organize our results in quantitative (Section 6.6.1) and qualitative assessment (Section 6.6.2).

To help fluency and clarity of reading, we discuss the obtained results from time to time, summarizing them and adding any further consideration in Section 6.6.3.

Quantitative Assessment

The aim of the Harmonic Walk quantitative assessment is firstly to verify at what extent subjects have been successful in identifying the harmonic changes and in harmonizing the melody. Secondly, we gather and discuss the information obtained during the exploratory second phase of the test. The analysis of the subjects movements and behavior is not only quantitative (the logs recorded by the system during the test), but also qualitative (the test conductor observations); nevertheless, we report them together. Thirdly, we want to quote how much musical knowledge has been acquired by the tested subjects during the experience with theHarmonic Walk and what the tested subjects think of the experience with the application.

The harmonic changes perception is the first cognitive result we expect after the test proposed in the first phase. The user had to wait the end of the song's harmonic unit before linking the next with his step. In this way s/he should have reinforced his/her perception of the harmonic changes. To verify if this knowledge has actually been realized by the test participants, we ask them to underline the song syllables where they felt a harmony change occurred. The answers results are shown in the column "Syllables" of Table 7.

As expected, the results of nonmusicians are beyond those of musicians. The best record of hits over 10 syllables to detect is 6 for nonmusicians and 9 for musicians. The worst is 0 for nonmusicians and 2 for musicians. The hits' average changes significantly also depending on the song's harmonic unit as can be seen in Figure 11. As a matter of fact the hits' average drops dramatically among nonmusicians (but also, less dramatically, among musicians) as soon as the song enters the last 4 harmonic changes, those involving the parallel harmony (vi degree), while it is rather high at the beginning of the song.

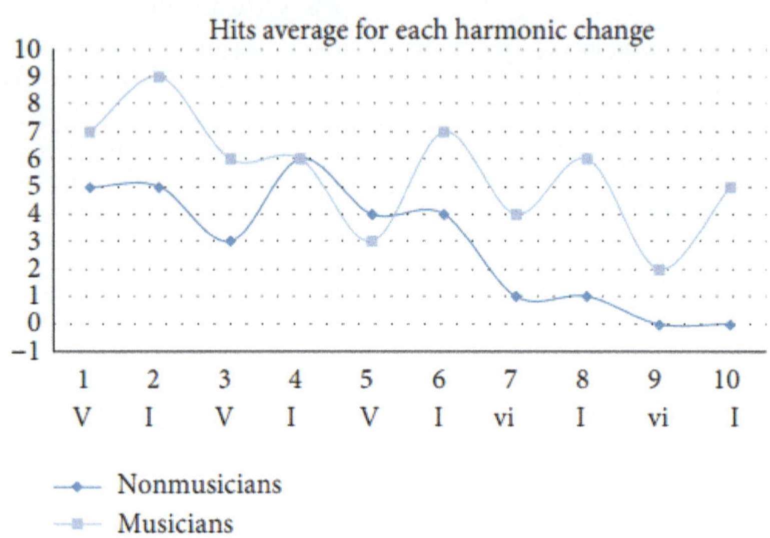

Figure 11: Hits' average over 10 harmonic changes obtained by nonmusicians (blue line) and musicians (azure line).

The melody harmonization is the conclusive main task of the third phase of the application's test. The test conductor reports a complete successful harmonization when the subject can find the chord sequence that s/he considers a good harmonic solution for the song and that s/he is able to repeat. No one of the complete or partial successful harmonization differs from the model proposed in the original song. Again, the results show the difficulty in the perception of the minor parallel harmonic areas. As can be seen in Table 4, among the 6 harmonization only 2 were complete, while the other 4 could accompany the song only in its simplest part, the one involving the tonic and dominant chords.

Table 4: Table of complete and partially successful harmonization over 11 subjects. The partial harmonization happens when the subject succeeds in harmonizing only the first 7 units of the song, involving only the tonic and dominant chords. These subjects failed to identify and/or to find the vi-degree minor parallel chord.

Harmonization	Nonmusicians	Musicians
Complete harm.	1	1
Partial harm.	0	4
Total	1 (9%)	5 (9% + 36%)

Moreover, we asked the subjects to draw the path they performed during the harmonization test on the circular ring, marking it with arrows or numbers. We divide the records in groups depending on the number of right chord sequences identified by the subjects. The results are shown in Table 5.

Table 5: Table of chord sequences identified by the subjects during the harmonization task.

Sequences	Nonmusicians	Musicians
No answer	1 (9%)	0
No sequence	3 (27%)	0
First 2 chords	5 (45%)	5 (45%)
First 3 chords	2 (18%)	0
More than 3 chords	0	2 (18%)
More than 6 chords	0	4 (36%)

In the first row we reported the number of not answered questions and in the second row the number of answers where only the first chord was right and the second was wrong. This means that the subjects failed to identify even the first chord progression of the song, which was instead identified by the subjects of the third row. The fourth-row subjects show to have understood that the sequence returned on the first degree at least once, while the fifths row subjects caught that the sequence was repeated more than once. At least, identifying more than 6 right chords means that the subject has found also the vi degree progression. Nonetheless, there is never a full correspondence between the right or partially right melody harmonization subject and the identification of the right sequence as can be seen in Table 6. Whereas the correct chord sequence is

$$1\ 6\ 1\ 6\ 1\ 6\ 1\ 4\ 1\ 4\ 1 \tag{3}$$

in Table 6 we see that in all the sequences there is always some mistake, or any missing chord (like in subject number 6 where there are only the last two chords missing). In the phase of the harmonic space exploration the subject has the possibility to explore the circular ring where the chords are laid. This experience is crucial for the success of the next required task, the melody harmonization, because it is here where the subject builds her/his spatial map of the harmonic relationships. Therefore, it is important to analyze what kind of movements subjects did while exploring the circular ring. From direct observation and from the analysis of movements recorded by the system during the test, two different approaches to the circular ring exploration were found. In the first approach the subject follows the shape of the circle starting from the left or from the right side. S/he

Table 6: Table of chord sequences identified by the complete and partial successful subjects during the harmonization task.

Subject	CH or PH	Recorded sequence
Number 4 (NM)	CH	1-2-1-2-4-1
Number 1 (M)	PH	1-6-1-6-1-6-4-3-1
Number 2 (M)	PH	1-6-1-6-1-4-3-4-3-5-6-1
Number 4 (M)	PH	1-6-1-6-1-6-1-4-1
Number 6 (M)	CH	1-6-1-6-1-6-1-6-1-4-1-4
Number 9 (M)	PH	1-6

Table 7: Table of the number of syllables of harmonic changes, the number of chord changes, and the number of employed chords recorded by nonmusician and musician subjects. The subjects with the asterisk are those completely successful in the harmonization task, while the subjects with the double asterisk are those partially successful in the harmonization task.

Nonmusicians	Syllables	Changes	Emp. ch.
1	6	7	5
2	—	—	—
3	6	4	2
4*	2	—	4
5	—	—	—
6	0	—	6
7	5	—	4
8	7	4	2
9	0	—	—
10	3	6	2
11	—	3	3
Averages	**3.6 (10)**	**4.8 (10)**	**3.5 (3)**
Number of correct ans.	**0 (11)**	**0 (11)**	**1 (11)**
Musicians	Syllables	Changes	Emp. ch.
1**	—	9	4
2**	8	10	12
3	6	7.5	3.5
4	4	5	4
5**	7	9	3
6*	4	7	3
7	10	10	5
8	7	10	4
9**	4	4	2
10	3	4	4
11	2	—	2.5
Averages	**5.5 (10)**	**7.5 (10)**	**4.2 (3)**
Number of correct ans.	**1 (11)**	**3 (11)**	**2 (11)**

In the phase of the harmonic space exploration the subject has the possibility to explore the circular ring where the chords are laid. This experience is crucial for the success of the next required task, the melody harmonization, because it is here where the subject builds her/his spatial map of the harmonic relationships. Therefore, it is important to analyze what kind of movements subjects did while exploring the circular ring. From direct observation and from the analysis of movements recorded by the system during the test, two different approaches to the circular ring exploration were found. In the first approach the subject follows the shape of the circle starting from the left or from the right side. S/he touches all the six zones in sequence, obtaining the following harmonic progressions:

$$\text{I-V-III-VI-II-IV or}$$
$$\text{I-IV-II-VI-III-V} \tag{4}$$

which are very long progressions without the repetition of the tonic chord. The latter is a fundamental perceptual anchorage point for tonal progressions and if it fails to appear for a certain time, the harmonic progressions lose their direction. Thus the experience does not reinforce tonal chords localization as expected.

The second approach emphasizes movements where the frequent return to the tonic chord is present. This exploration approach is nearer to the actual tonal composition's structure, where the tonic frequently occurs and where chordal progressions are often repeated. Returning to the tonic chord helps to distinguish harmonic functions; furthermore, the repetition of the movement among two well identified space regions trains the body to perform simple and strong harmonic progressions. As demonstrated by the recorded paths (see some examples in Figure 12) and by direct observation of the subjects' movements, the exploratory phase has been only seldom characterized by recursive movements on the tonic chord. Sometimes we registered and observed such movements like 1-6-1 (tonic, dominant, and tonic) or 1-2-1 (tonic, subdominant, and tonic), but never movements like 1-4-1 (tonic, minor parallel, and tonic) or 1-5-1 (tonic, mediant, and tonic), nor perceptually strongest progressions like 1-2-6-1 (tonic, subdominant, dominant, and tonic). The exploratory phase was apparently left free of any biasing element, in the sense that no hint was given to the subjects about the task to accomplish. It seems that, in such conditions, the shape of the projection (the circular ring) has been the most important cue to follow for the subject. Indeed, in nearly all the recorded paths we found at least one circular path while in not all the recorded paths we found the recursive path. Moreover, many of the subjects could not fully understand the difference between the straight path and the circular one and, consequently, showed a clear tendency in using them in the same way, that is, following the shape's contour. On the other hand, the straight logic of this behavior must be recognized and seriously considered in the future work of refinement of the application design. As already outlined, when following passively the ring, many subjects missed the possibility of building a perceptual and a sensorimotor map of the strongest tonality harmonic progressions, thus compromising the possibility of success in the third phase of the test. The search of a satisfactory harmonization path has nothing to do with a random search but follows very clear, perceptually strong, recursive tracks. Of course, we did not expect to find test subjects perfectly aware of these musical structures, but, rather, our aim was to encourage them to discover such features through a perceptual and movement practice.

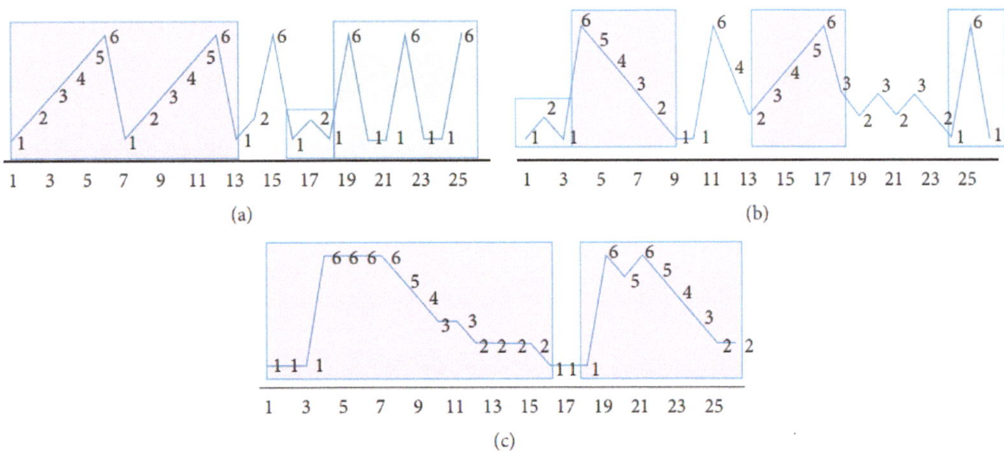

Figure 12: Some exploratory paths recorded during the second phase of the test of theHarmonic Walk. The gray areas correspond to the recursive movements, 1-6-1 or 1-2-1, while the violet areas correspond to the circular paths.

To find out if the tested subjects have gained some knowledge about the song they worked on during the test, we asked them some questions about the musical features employed for accomplishing the test's tasks. The first question concerned the song's harmonic rhythm, and particularly if the song's harmonic units had all the same duration. Nearly the 100% of the subjects answered correctly (i.e., that the song's units do not all have the same duration as showed in the last column of Table 2).

The second question was about the principle upon which the units had been determined. The great majority of subjects (9 nonmusicians and 10 musicians) checked the chord change against rhythm repetition and melody repetition, showing thus to have understood the segmentation principle.

Other less simple questions were about how many times the subject changed the chord and how many different chords s/he employed during the third phase of the test (the melody harmonization), respectively, column of "Changes" and of "Emp. ch." (number of employed chords) in Table 7.

The interpretation of these results is not immediate and can be discussed mainly when they are compared with the results of the first and third phase of the test. For instance, the question on the number of chord changes (column of "Syllables") is directly related to the detection of the syllables of harmonic changes (column of "Changes" in Table 7), as the number of changes is exactly corresponding to the number of syllables detected. Basically the question is the same but is put in a different perspective. It seems that the subjects did not realize the similarity of the two questions, as the answers from the same subject differ in all the cases but one.

Only subject number 7 among the musicians group gave both correct answers, while subject number 9 gave the most coherent answer having detected only 4 syllables of change but also 4 chord changes. Also, if we compare the records of the successful or partially successful subjects in the melody harmonization task (starred and double starred subjects) we see that the correlation is scarce or null. Only subject number 2 among the group of musicians achieved a good record in the number of chord changes, while all the others made a number more or less great of mistakes. Similarly, comparing the number of different employed chords (3 in total, I, V, and vi degree) we see that there is a good match only with subjects 5 and 6 of the musicians group, while the other four starred subjects declared all the wrong number of chords.

In the questionnaire we prepared two Likert-scale surveys. In the first survey we asked to express a judgement about the application's pleasantness and in the second we asked about the utility of the experience made during the test. The results are, respectively, shown in Figures 13 and 14 and discussed in Section 6.6.3.

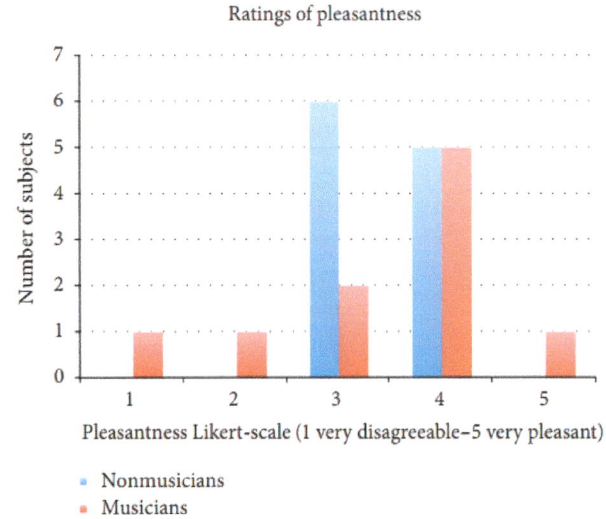

Figure 13: Chart of ratings of application's pleasantness (average of ratings 3.4 for nonmusicians and 2.9 for musicians).

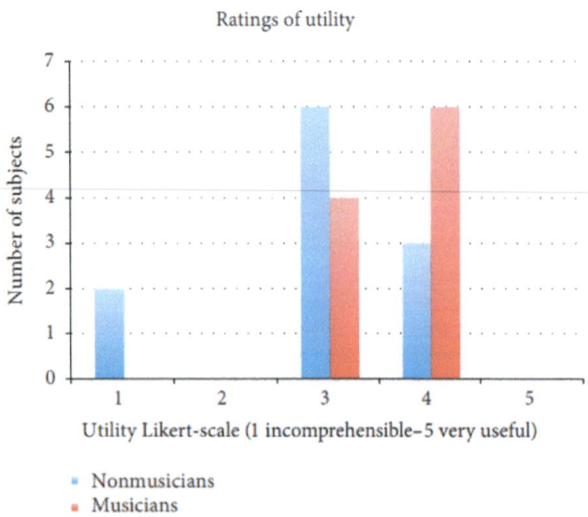

Figure 14: Chart of ratings of experience utility (average of ratings 2.9 for nonmusicians and 3.6 for musicians).

Qualitative Assessment

Data about qualitative assessment come from the three participants' opinion questions contained in the questionnaire. The first opinion question concerned the difficulty the subjects found in linking the different song's units in the test first phase, the second the subject's perception of the application, and the third what musical principles they thought were involved in the test.

Four nonmusicians subjects and 2 musicians reported difficulties in understanding the right moment when it was necessary to move on to change the song's unit. Three subjects from the nonmusicians group reported difficulties in understanding the harmonic structure of the song, pointing out so that the question had not completely been understood but rather that there was some confusion about the first-phase and the third-phase tasks. Only one subject blamed the lack of previous knowledge of the song used in the test.

Some subjects judgements, ideas, impressions, and feelings about the application and its use are partially reported in Table 8.

Table 8: Table of the subjects' ideas about the application.

Judgements	Nonmusicians	Musicians
Useful	3	4
Interesting	3	1
Difficult	2	1
Amusing	1	2
Useless	2	0

Other judgements, expressed only by one subject, were strange, incomprehensible, frustrating, complicated, indifferent, engaging, nice, and beautiful. It is also interesting to look at the reasons why such judgements were expressed. The application was considered "useful" by nonmusicians:(i) To develop the memory of listening.(ii)To evaluate the understanding of musical features.(iii)To understand the musical experience.And the application was considered "useful" by musicians:(i)To keep in time while playing with others.(ii)To work with children.(iii)To keep coordination and precision in music performance.(iv)To learn harmony changes not in theory, but in practice.(v)To develop aural skills.(vi)To test your own musical skills.

It was considered "interesting" by nonmusicians:(i)For discovering how complex a popular song may be.(ii)For seeing how the body reacts to music.And it was considered "beautiful" by 1 musician subject because it can introduce people to music. As can be seen, subjects reported a great number of cues and a variety of ideas about the experience during the test.

We asked the test subjects to point out the main principles upon which the application was designed.

As can be seen in Table 9, musical memory and rhythmic skills are the strongest perceived musical features employed in the design of the Harmonic Walk.

Table 9: Table of perceived principles upon which the application was designed.

Principles	Nonmusicians	Musicians
Musical memory	4	2
Rhythmic skills	1	3
Body reaction to music	2	1
Song segmentation	2	1
Aural skills	1	1
Connections between melody and chords	0	1

Summary of Results

To make a rigorous test of the Harmonic Walk application, we set very hard and strict assessment conditions:(i)High level of musical features involved in the application design.(ii)No previous hints about the application cognitive contents, nor about the song employed during the test.(iii)Strict test protocol and time constraints.

The recognition of the syllables where the song changed its harmonies and where the subject had to make a step to continue the song performance hits an average of 3.6 for nonmusicians and of 4.8 for musicians, over 10 syllables. The average is rather low, but we saw from Figure 11 that it decreases a lot depending on the song's harmonic area (minor parallel area), demonstrating a difficulty in parallel harmonies perception. Nonetheless, as this area arrives in the second part of the song excerpt, the reason of the drop of the number of detected syllables could be also a lack of memorization. The full harmonization task was accomplished only by 1 nonmusician and by 1 musician subject. The other 4 musician subjects accomplished the task only in the first part of the song, involving only the tonic and the dominant chord. So, among 22 tested subjects we recorded a complete and partially successful accomplishment task for 6 subjects, a rate of 26% of the total of the sample.

Nearly the complete sample of nonmusicians and musicians subjects at the end of the test was conscious that the song's harmonic units do not all have the same duration and that the principle upon which the song's unit had been determined was the chord change. But when asked how many chord changes had occurred in the song excerpt, the number of changes drops at 4.8 for musicians and at 7.5 for nonmusicians, over 10 chord changes, with 3 correct answers. The question about how many overall chords were employed in the song (3) shows an average of 3.5 among nonmusicians with 1 correct answer and an average of 4.2 among musicians, with 2 correct answers. This question is crucial for the tonal language musical knowledge, because it shows the difference between the chord changes (10 in eleven harmonic units in the straight path) and the number of places to reach in the circular ring (3, corresponding to the tonic, dominant, and minor parallel chord). This difference is exactly the effect of the recurrence of the tonic-dominant and tonic-minor parallel progressions. In general, we observed a scarce correlation between the partial or total success of the subjects in the harmonization task and the correctness of their answers in the questionnaire, as can be seen in Table 10, where the asterisks outline the correct answers. The explanation of such results is not simple. The results of the column of the syllables of change, mainly for the complete successful subjects, are particularly touching and need further investigations. How can a successful harmonizer miss detecting the syllables of the song where he actually searched and successfully found the right chord? It seems that consciousness lays far away from the embodied knowledge employed by these successful subjects. On the other hand, subject number 7 of the group of musicians detects perfectly all the syllables of change (10) and the number of harmonic changes (10) but misses finding the number of employed chords (5 instead of 3); nevertheless he fails to harmonize the melody in the given time.

Table 10: Table of answers to questions about the syllables of change, the number of harmonic changes, and the number of employed chords obtained by partially (PH) or complete (CH) successful subjects in the harmonization task. The asterisks show the correct answers.

Subject	Harm.	Syll.	Changes	Emp. ch.
Number 4 (NM)	CH	2	—	4
Number 1 (M)	PH	—	9	4
Number 2 (M)	PH	8	10*	12
Number 4 (M)	PH	7	9	3*
Number 6 (M)	CH	4	7	3*
Number 9 (M)	PH	4	4	2

The psychological and cognitive weight of the test's experience is witnessed by the rich and complex output we obtained from the participants. It seems that, independently of the explicit knowledge they succeed to realize at the end of the experience, the Harmonic Walk is able to offer to the users a deeper insight of what a musical experience is. The application's use is not fatigue, as the average of ratings about its pleasantness is 3.15, while the average of ratings about its utility is 3.25, both a little above "indifferent" (see the pleasantness and utility item list in 6.5). In general, the main perceived features upon which the application is built are musical memory, rhythmic skills, and sensorimotor reactions. Not to be ignored, a total of 3 subjects (13% of the sample) labeled the application as "difficult." This result can be interpreted as the other side of the coin of richness of musical contents, because, in spite of its simple interaction modality, the application actually conveys in short a lot of information about complex compositional processes. On the other hand, this is just the field where a proper didactic approach and careful training can help. Moreover, most insightful address to theHarmonic Walk could also highlight the great potential of creative use, which is implicit in its design and which nobody among the tested subjects did even mention.

In general, in the quantitative assessment's records, musicians obtained better results than nonmusicians, as can be seen at glance in Table 7 and as reported in Table 11.

Table 11: Table of records and correct answers differences between musicians and nonmusicians.

Musicians	Syllables	Changes	Emp. ch.
Records	+21%	+29%	−34%
Correct answers	+11%	+33%	+11%

The number of successful harmonizers was 1 among musicians as well as among nonmusicians, while no partially successful harmonizer was found among nonmusicians. If we look at Table 5 we see that musicians were much better than nonmusicians in identifying the right song chord sequence, as the majority of them (54%) could identify a right sequence of more than three chords, while all the sample of nonmusicians equals or remains above this number. In general, in Likert-scale surveys, musicians quoted better the application's utility while nonmusicians quoted better its pleasantness. In particular, in the application's perception opinion question, 2 nonmusicians judged it as "useless," showing that the mere test's experience cannot be considered self-explanatory for all the subjects.

CONCLUSIONS

In this paper we introduced the Harmonic Walk application, designed for practicing and studying the tonal melody accompaniment. To verify the application's utility as a didactic tool, we organized an assessment test involving 22 high school students, subdivided into two groups: one from a music high school and the other from other high schools. This second group was composed of subjects with no musical practice at all. Below we summarize the most important results:(1)The 26% of the tested subjects could accomplish the final application's task: the melody harmonization. Among these only the 9% could harmonize the complete song, while the remaining 17% harmonized only the song's first part, characterized by a very simple chord progression.(2)The harmonic changes perception, expressed by the detection of the song's syllables of change, hits an average of 3.6 detected syllables for nonmusicians and of 4.8 for musicians over 10. The number of detected syllables decreases in the second part of the song's excerpt, characterized by a parallel chord progression.(3)Some musical knowledge about the employed musical features is confirmed by the assessment results, but the consciousness of musical concepts does not coincide with the subjects who actually accomplished the application's main task.(4)In the qualitative part of the assessment, we got a very rich and various feedback from the test subjects, who in general reported a lot of interesting musical cues from the experience.

So, we can conclude that the Harmonic Walk is a strong, enactive tool which can provide a fully immersive and embodied experience of complex and fundamental musical concepts. It can convey a lot of implicit information about the employed musical features which can be considered as a rich basis for music learning programs, whose aim is to help all the implicit knowledge to emerge. Its use is simple and not uncomfortable for the user. Conversely, it has been considered useful, amusing, and interesting by the majority of the test subjects.

Further Work

The future development of the Harmonic Walk concerns essentially two domains. The first is the music didactics domain where a lot of work is necessary to build training programs to work with the students in the application's physical interactive environment. After having tested the great potentialities of the Harmonic Walkin the music field, it is important to focus on some critical cues emerging during the test:(i)The difficulty in the perception of the parallel chords, reported more than once when discussing the results(ii)The confusion aroused by the different use of the two geometrical projections: the straight line, which had to be followed step by step, and the circular ring which instead had to be explored and used employing some recursive harmonic pattern.It is clear that something must be done to suggest to the user that s/he has to change the interaction modality when entering the circular ring mask. Nonetheless, we do not believe that corpus-based statistical tools algorithms, already employed in other similar applications, will help, as the Harmonic Walk's aim is not to give to the user information about the melody accompaniment solution, but to help them to find their solution through a perceptual exploration based on body movements.

The second domain is the study of the application's features from the point of view of its novelty in the human-computer interaction field. The Harmonic Walk, as a motion-based application, belongs to a new generation of human-computer interfaces where the interaction style evolves toward the physical world rather than remaining confined in the computer screen [23]. This means that the user's environment awareness and body skills become the basis of the interaction with the digital world, bringing with them all their expressive power and efficiency. Considering the application from this point of view, other computational, cognitive, and psychological cues emerge, like implicit and tacit knowledge [24], the extended mind [25], and situated cognition [26].

Conflict of Interests

The authors declare that there is no conflict of interests regarding the publication of this paper.

ACKNOWLEDGMENTS

The authors want to thank Leonardo Amico for his support in programming the Zone Tracker application, Cesare Contarini, Dean of the Catholic Institute "Barbarigo" of Padova, and, particularly, Giuseppe Viaro, Music Technology Teacher, for their cooperation during the assessment tests.

ENDNOTES

1. A video showing some tests with the Harmonic Walk can be found at https://www.youtube.com/watch?v=OjwXfzq_CkU.
2. Literally "web of tones": the tonnetz appeared for the first time in a harmony treatise written by Euler in 1739. In the 19th century the tonnetz was reviewed and discussed by the German music theorist Hugo Riemann.
3. With respect to the fundamental, the first interval introducing a new pitch is the fifth, followed by the major and the minor third. A chain for each of these intervals is spread on the three axes of the tonnetz, where each triangular area represents the consonant major and minor triads.
4. With respect to the fundamental, the first interval introducing a new pitch is the fifth, followed by the major and the minor third. A chain for each of these intervals is spread on the three axes of the tonnetz, where each triangular area represents the consonant major and minor triads.
5. After George Lakoff's and Mark Johnson's theory, we can understand abstract concepts through image schemas which are stored in our body cognition and which come from bodily interactions.
6. Max/MSP (https://cycling74.com/) is a visual programming language for audio and video production, algorithmic composition, and signal processing, written by Miller Puckette in 1980.
7. OSC, acronym of Open Sound Control [28], is a communication protocol based on modern network technology (http://opensoundcontrol.org/introduction-osc) which was developed and continues to be a subject of ongoing research at UC Berkeley Center for New Music and Audio Technology (CNMAT). Originally intended for sharing music performance data, it is commonly used to exchange information between computers, applications, and various multimedia

devices.

8. We represent the masks as square and circular ring also if, due to camera pixel shape, the actual masks are, respectively, distorted in a rectangle and in an oval ring.
9. The tags both in the straight line and in the circular ring are not descriptive; that is, they are not marked with the syllables of change or with the chord names, but they have the function to indicate to the user the right position to be occupied on the application's surface.
10. Celentano [29] is a popular Italian singer, very known also abroad. He has begun his career in the sixties.Il ragazzo della via Gluck, written in 1966, was one of his greatest hits.
11. The Likert-scale is a technique used to scale responses in survey research. It employs at least 5 items ranging from negative to positive statements, allowing so an easy and fast computation of the test's results.

REFERENCES

1. R. Jackendoff, Consciousness and the Computational Mind, Explorations in Cognitive Science Series no. 3, The MIT Press, Cambridge, Mass, USA, 1987.
2. K. A. Corrigall and L. J. Trainor, "Musical enculturation in preschool children: acquisition of key and harmonic knowledge," Music Perception, vol. 28, no. 2, pp. 195–200, 2010.
3. B. Tillmann, J. J. Bharucha, and E. Bigand, "Implicit learning of tonality: a self-organizing approach,"Psychological Review, vol. 107, no. 4, pp. 885–913, 2000. ·
4. S. Holland, Learning about Harmony with Harmony Space: An Overview, Springer, Berlin, Germany, 1994.
5. T. Bergstrom, K. Karahalios, and J. C. Hart, "Isochords: visualizing structure in music," in Proceedings of the Graphics Interface, pp. 297–304, ACM, Montreal, Canada, May 2007.
6. mDecks Music, "Mapping Tonal Harmony," 2012, http://mdecks.com/mapharmony.html.
7. S. Holland, P. Marshall, J. Bird et al., "Running up blueberry hill: prototyping whole body interaction in harmony space," in Proceedings of the 3rd International Conference on Tangible and Embedded Interaction, pp. 93–98, ACM, February 2009.
8. R. Behringer and J. Elliott, "Linking physical space with the Riemann Tonnetz for exploration of western tonality," Music Education, pp. 131–144, 2011.
9. L. Bigo, J. Garcia, A. Spicher, and W. E. Mackay, "Papertonnetz: music composition with interactive paper," in Proceedings of the 9th Sound and Music Computing Conference, pp. 219–225, Copenhagen, Denmark, 2012.
10. T. W. Hedges and A. P. McPherson, "3D gestural interaction with harmonic pitch space," in Proceedings of the International Choice Modelling Conference and the Sound and Music Computing Conference (ICMC-SMC ‹13), Stockholm, Sweden, July 2013.
11. B. Manaris, D. Johnson, and Y. Vassilandonakis, "Harmonic navigator: a gesture-driven, corpus-based approach to music analysis, composition, and performance," in Proceedings of the 9th Artificial Intelligence and Interactive Digital Entertainment Conference, Boston, Mass, USA, October 2013.
12. S. Zanolla, S. Canazza, A. Rodà, A. Camurri, and G. Volpe, "Entertaining listening by means of thestanza logo-motoria: an interactive multimodal environment," Entertainment Computing, vol. 4, no. 3, pp. 213–220, 2013.
13. M. Mandanici, A. Rodà, and S. Canazza, "The 'Harmonic Walk': an interactive educational environment to discover musical chords," in Proceedings of the 2014 ICMC-SMC Conference, Athens, Greece, September 2014.
14. D.-J. Povel and E. Jansen, "Harmonic factors in the perception of tonal melodies," Music Perception, vol. 20, no. 1, pp. 51–85, 2002.
15. F. Lerdahl and R. Jackendoff, A Generative Theory of Tonal Music, MIT Press, Cambridge, Mass, USA, 1985.
16. J. Bharucha and C. L. Krumhansl, "The representation of harmonic structure in music: hierarchies of stability as a function of context," Cognition, vol. 13, no. 1, pp. 63–102, 1983.
17. C. Brower, "A cognitive theory of musical meaning," Journal of Music Theory, vol. 44, no. 2, pp. 323–379, 2000.
18. J. Saslaw, "Forces, containers, and paths: the role of body-derived image schemas in the conceptualization of music," Journal of Music Theory, vol. 40, no. 2, pp. 217–243, 1996.
19. N. Cook, "Theorizing musical meaning," Music Theory Spectrum, vol. 23, no. 2, pp. 170–195, 2001.
20. G. Lakoff and M. Johnson, Metaphors We Live By, University of Chicago Press, Chicago, Ill, USA, 2008.
21. S. Jabri, Z. Duric, H. Wechsler, and A. Rosenfeld, "Detection and location of people in video images using adaptive fusion of color and edge information," in Proceedings of the 15th International Conference on Pattern Recognition, vol. 4, pp. 627–630, Barcelona, Spain, September 2000.
22. L. Vincent, "Morphological area openings and closings for grey-scale images," in Shape in Picture, Y. L. O, A. Toet, D. Foster, H. A. M. Heijmans, and P. Meer, Eds., vol. 126 of NATO ASI Series, pp. 197–208, Springer, Berlin, Germany, 1994.
23. R. J. Jacob, A. Girouard, L. M. Hirshfield et al., "Reality-based interaction: a framework for post-WIMP interfaces," in Proceedings of the SIGCHI Conference on Human Factors in Computing Systems, pp. 201–210, ACM, Florence, Italy, April 2008.
24. A. S. Reber, "Implicit learning and tacit knowledge," Journal of Experimental Psychology: General, vol. 118, no. 3, pp. 219–235, 1989.
25. A. Clark and D. Chalmers, "The extended mind," Analysis, vol. 58, no. 1, pp. 7–19, 1998.
26. J. S. Brown, A. Collins, and P. Duguid, "Situated cognition and the culture of learning," Educational Researcher, vol. 18, no. 1, pp. 32–42, 1989.

27. W. Piston, M. DeVoto, and A. Jannery, Harmony, Gollancz, London, UK, 1978.
28. M. Wright, "Open sound control-a new protocol for communicationg with sound synthesizers," inProceedings of the International Computer Music Conference (ICMC ‹97), pp. 101–104, San Francisco, Calif, USA, 1997.
29. A. Celentano, http://www.ilmondodiadriano.it/index.php/it/.

CHAPTER 3

INTERACTIVE MULTIMEDIA TELERADIOLOGY SYSTEM

Lilac Al-Safadi

INTRODUCTION

Communication is an important component in healthcare. Parker and Coiera [1], Coiera [2], and Sutcliffe et al. [3] indicated that poor communication in healthcare results in high costs and undesirable clinical outcomes. Coiera [2], Coiera and Tombs [4], and Fitzpatrick et al. [5] indicated that communication between healthcare professionals is characterised as interactive, instant, and synchronous; and Varpio et al. [6] and Bezemer et al. [7] indicated that the communication between healthcare professionals is characterised as interdisciplinary and interprofessional.

Telemedicine is the use of electronic communication and information technologies to provide or support clinical care at a distance [8]. There are various medical specialties in which telemedicine can be used, and teleradiology is one of the most important. Teleradiology is the ability to transmit radiographic images, such as X-rays, computed tomographic images (CT) and magnetic resonance imaging (MRI) from a remote location to a radiologist's location to facilitate accurate diagnosis. The importance of teleradiology lies in the improvement of medical services and in the availability of quality medicine, mostly in distant areas [9]. In comparison with medical online communities, teleradiology currently has a slow image transfer, lacks a feedback mechanism, and is limited to a certain number of participants [10–14]. In addition, clinicians find that teleradiology demonstrates a fragmented and interrupted experience because text, images, and speech are delivered on different channels and modes.

Research on multimedia shows that humans use both text and images to construct coherent mental knowledge representations [15–19]. This can be achieved by presenting words and images together and in a well-designed and integrated manner. The construction of coherent mental representations supports learning and decision-making [18, 19]. Hence, although medical images play an important role in making good decisions on the diagnosis of particular case, medical consultation between physicians and radiologists would become more meaningful if tools were available that not only displayed medical images on their consoles but also supported the integration of written words, spoken words, and images.

Advances in multimedia technologies and applications and the availability of high-speed bandwidth internet have increased the utilisation of multimedia in healthcare such as supplementary materials to demonstrate the ideal practice of procedures [20, 21] and resources to help students prepare for the clinical examinations [22,23] and to orient residents and students to the operations of hospital departments, and it has also been integrated into electronic medical records [24]. A number of works extended existing teleradiology systems with multimedia components to support interaction [25, 26], collaboration [27], or advanced visualisation [28]. However, the multimedia components have not been efficiently integrated into a single healthcare system [29], and the value of integration for effective interaction and knowledge exchange between referring physicians and radiologists has not been tested.

In this paper we present a real-time multimedia interactive teleradiology management system (MTMS) to support physicians' diagnoses. MTMS provides real-time interaction using several modes (video, audio, and text), and offers a display of radiographic images, image annotation tools, an archiving and retrieving system, real-time interaction, and an audio reporting feature. This is achieved through full integration and

Citation: Lilac Al-Safadi, "Interactive Multimedia Teleradiology System," BioMed Research International, vol. 2016, Article ID 4126841, 9 pages, 2016. doi:10.1155/2016/4126841.

controllability of advanced technologies in multimedia—video and audio transmission, image compression and processing, and voice recognition, all in a single application and in real time. The developed system is particularly useful in providing immediate diagnosis for a remote medical care center. The system provides remote consultation in such a way that both the referring physician and radiologist can review the same image and discuss it with each other by the dialog window using various modes.

Problem Definition and Goals

Local healthcare institutions, in particular, primary and secondary care centers, provide lower quality healthcare services because of the lack of experienced staff and adequate technical resources [30]. This means patients have to be transferred to hospitals with appropriate facilities for diagnosis and treatment. These transfers are costly and time-consuming [31].

Traditional, text-only radiology reports are the major, and often only, means of communication between radiologists and their referring clinicians [32]. Although advances in image display and distribution have made some radiology images more readily available to referring physicians, the increase in imaging data generated increases the need for direct involvement of experts in real time [33].

A number of solutions have been provided to connect referring physicians in remote areas with radiologists, as will be described in Section 1.2. However, many physicians are skeptical about the value of remote consultation and remain in favour of face-to-face consultation.

In order to respond to the physicians' concerns, we developed and tested a real-time interactive multimedia teleradiology system. The main goal of MTMS is to serve less well-equipped medical institutions by supporting teleradiology with a number of integrated multimedia tools, in order to improve the quality and efficiency of diagnosis in regular and emergency cases. Our main contribution in this paper is to (1) leverage multimedia technological advances to improve the interaction and achievement of referring physicians, (2) evaluate the performance of a multilayered integration-based architectural design, and (3) quantify referring physicians' perceived value of real-time multimode interaction with radiologists in improving radiologists' satisfaction and in improving their effectiveness.

Background

A number of teleradiology management systems exist for commercial use. XRAYLINE (http://www.xrayline.com/) is an online portal that allows physicians and radiology staff to share medical images and preview online radiology studies. The following services are provided by XRAYLINE: the ability to view images and report online, preview exam results for referred patients, access images at any time from personal computers with a browser and internet connection, download exams, and access local personal archive servers, which can store, forward, query, and retrieve exams from different modalities or other servers.

Miner Miracles Ltd. (http://www.medicexchange.com/) is a company that provides system management, integration, and development for general business and healthcare industries. It provides a management system in digital radiology and teleradiology, security network and maintenance, consultancy, and help desk assistance tracking. Miner Miracles Ltd. provides the following: image viewer software for displaying and manipulating images, a reporting cycle with dictation, and transmission of images.

MxiPACS [34] provides teleradiology management system services. It provides several services such as image viewing and sending of images. The features also include manipulation tools and the facility to download image exams and reports.

These commercial systems are based on the store and forward (S&F) method, which involves sending data (including medical images, lab work, etc.) to the physician, who can assess it at a convenient time. This method does not require both parties to be present at the same time. It is a consultation in an asynchronous mode rather than real-time mode [8].

Various researchers have focused on interactive televideo (ITV) methodology in implementing teleradiology [25–29, 35]. ITV involves video conferencing and more advanced technology. Physicians can be present in primary care on one side and radiologists must be present at the same time on the other side of the encounter. It is also called the real-time method and simulates real-world interaction with patients [8]. However, to our knowledge, no research has evaluated the value of ITV teleradiology systems as perceived by referring physicians. This experimental study is the first to assess the effects of real-time multimode interactive teleradiology to physicians' satisfaction and patient care in Saudi Arabia.

SYSTEM DESCRIPTION

MTMS is designed to test a number of assumptions relevant to physician-radiologist interaction extracted from various research papers.(1)Physicians desire accurate and timely reports over those that are well-organised [36, 37].(2)Real-time consultation between physician and radiologist is essential [38]. (3)Visual, audio, and textual information needs to be accessed synchronously to improve patient care [39].(4)Enhanced personal interaction increases physician satisfaction [38, 40]. This can be achieved through rich multimodal interaction. (5)Multimode interaction increases physician effectiveness in clinical performance [39, 40].(6)Access to previous examinations is needed [38].The online MTMS provides an environment and platform to support referring physicians and clinicians in remote areas or less well-equipped medical care centers (Figure 1). MTMS provides two categories of features: medical case management and user management. The medical case management system provides the following features: establish a medical case, add radiographic images and reports to the medical case, annotate images using text and shapes to highlight interesting areas in real time, provide real-time interaction using various media modes, compress and archive medical cases, view cases with different levels of granularity, search and browse medical cases using advanced search criteria, develop radiology reports and document conversation using voice recognition, assign and unassign medical case to a radiologist in a radiology facility location, and view X-ray images in a special Digital Imaging and Communications in Medicine (DICOM) viewer [41].

Figure 1: MTMS system description.

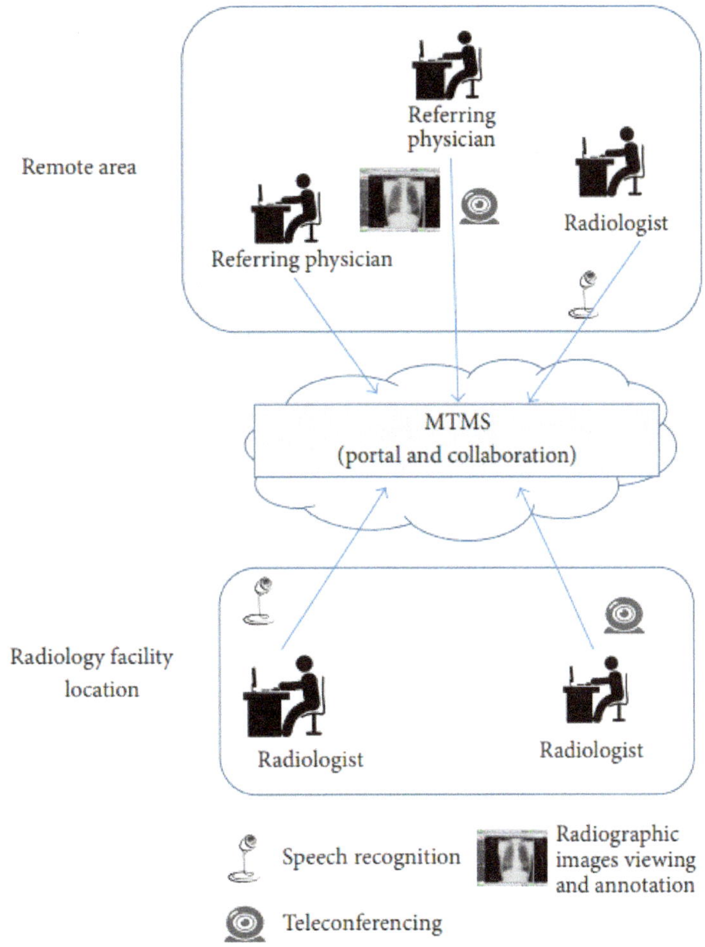

Architectural Design

The architectural design satisfies the functional and nonfunctional system requirements. It establishes the basic structural framework that identifies the major components of a system and communication between these components. This project was developed using a multilayer integration-based architecture (Figure 2). The multilayers are the communication layer, application layer, multimedia tool layers, and user interface layer.

Figure 2: MTMS multilayer integration-based architectural design.

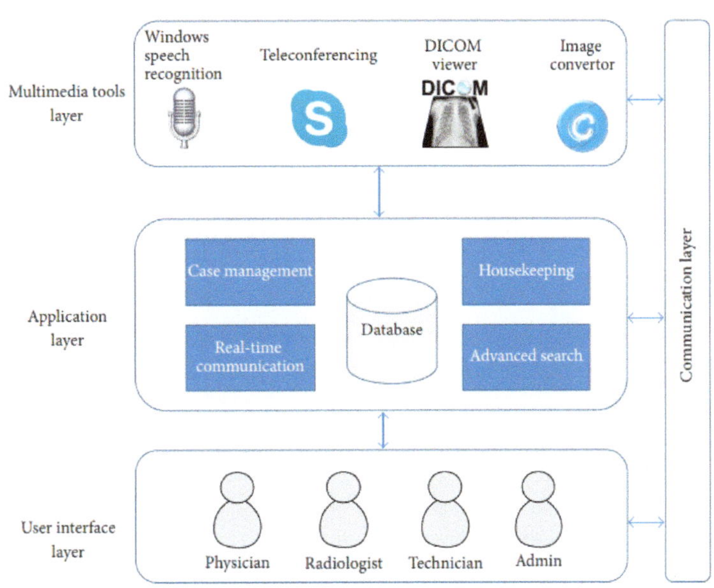

The tool integration architecture helps to optimise the overall functionality of the system by using prebuilt applications or tools across a network. In addition, it allows quick development of the system and delivers a more efficient and accessible application. MTMS integrates four multimedia supporting tools to achieve the goals and objectives of this system.(1)Image converter: software that converts the radiographic images from DICOM format (.dcm) to bitmap format (.bmp) and vice versa. This enables the radiographic images to be transferred, received, and stored in a patient database or other archives.(2)A DICOM viewer: an application to process the radiographic images in DICOM format with high resolution. It enables the radiologist to view the case images in an external DICOM viewer with high resolution imagery and extra features like zoom, print, brightness/contrast control, and so forth.(3)Speech recognition: a software that recognises the voice and converts it to text. It gives the radiologist the opportunity to develop a report automatically and attach it to a medical case using voice and hence reduces the user's keystrokes and the time and effort involved in typing.(4) Teleconferencing: an application with many features like video call, audio call, and instant messaging. It provides the referring physician and the radiologist with a tool for real-time communication so they can discuss medical cases.

Implementation

To experiment and test the introduced concept, a prototype was developed using C# programming language and Microsoft . Net framework 3.5 as part of a graduation project. .NET framework was chosen for its large library and its support for several programming languages, which allows language interoperability. In addition to this, the .NET Framework's Base Class Library provides integration with other outsourced libraries. .NET framework is fully compatible and runs successfully on machines running Microsoft Windows operating systems (Windows XP, Vista, and 7). A Microsoft SQL Server 2008 was used to run the database and store the medical cases.

System integration is about successfully putting together parts of systems or subsystems to work as one unit to perform what the system was intended to do. MTMS joins the functions of a set of subsystems or software through integrating a number of tools to produce a unified system that supports the requirements of the system. MTMS takes the advantages and power of existing tools, which saves time and effort in the implementation phase. MTMS integrates Skype v5.5 (http://www.skype.com/) to gain the advantage of features that Skype provides, such as group teleconferencing and real-time teleconferencing. In addition, it uses MICRODICOM (http://www.microdicom.com/), an image viewer that allows users to manipulate and view radiographic images. The Dicom2 Converter (http://www.barre.nom.fr/medical/dicom2/) converts DICOM images to portable compressed format and vice versa. This is required to integrate the radiographic images in the displayed form and to enable their storage in the database. Microsoft Speech Recognition allows radiologists to record medical reports easily and faster.

Figure 3 shows one of the physician's screens. The screen is composed of four main sections: the radiographic images display area, the patient's information, the case report area, and the case details.

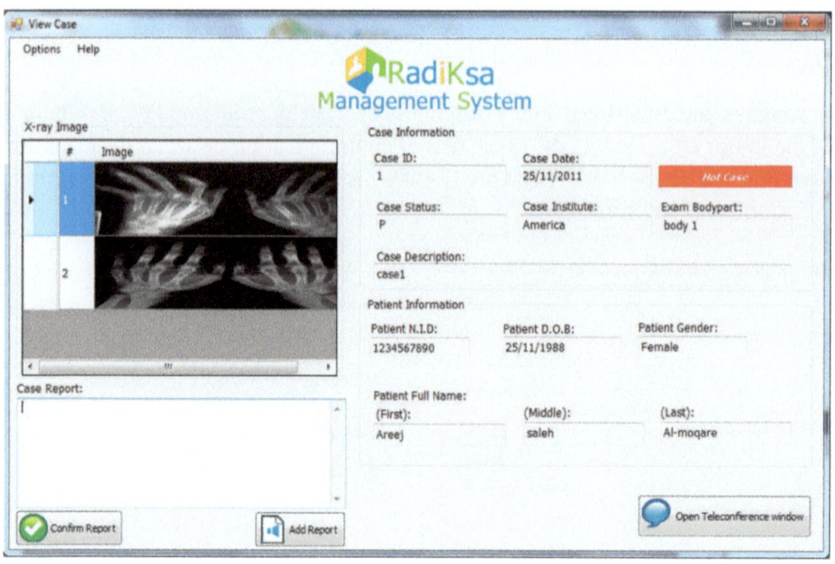

Figure 3: View case screen for physicians—prototype.

TESTING AND RESULTS

A variety of experiments and tests were carried out in Saudi Arabia from June 2014 to January 2015 on the system to explore its functionality and to identify any problems. The experiments were performed to show (1) how the system performs technically and (2) how the end-users perceive the value of the system, in particular, to identify referring physicians' preferences about integrating multimedia tools with teleradiology systems to facilitate real-time and enhanced interaction, and to quantify their perceived value of this system compared with text-based communication alone.

User Interface Testing

A user observation technique was used for user interface testing. This involved watching and listening carefully to users as they worked with the product. Two categories of users participated in the user interface test: eight physicians and three radiologists. One hundred per cent were female with the majority having a range of 3–5 years of experience (73%). Six user observation sessions took place. Users were asked to perform a total of 20 tasks selected to test the functional and nonfunctional system requirements of the system. The following tasks were performed: conduct simple and advanced search for a medical case, retrieve archived medical case, view the medical case at different granularities, add a medical case, upload a number of radiographic images, enter a radiology report, establish real-time interaction using voice, video, and text, and support interaction with annotation tools.

Overall results were acceptable as 90% of the tasks were accomplished within the expected time, with an 18% error rate. Corrective actions were taken to reduce the errors made. The majority of participants viewed each case between one to three times and spent sufficient time on the content. Seventy-eight per cent agreed that the quality of images was satisfactory, 60% agreed that the voice was clear, 65% agreed that the design of the system was consistent and allowed easy navigation, and 63% of the participants thought they could understand the procedure by themselves without any further clarification. The overall familiarity with the system helped in decreasing the time required and errors made in performing tasks.

Performance Testing of Speech Recognition

As regards testing the performance of the speech recognition system, ten radiology reports were tested. Language and size of the report were the only criteria for report selection. On average a report of 350 words was developed in 2.7 minutes and with an average of eight errors, giving 97.8% accuracy. This was quite acceptable compared with the time and effort saved. Software training increases the accuracy of speech recognition results.

User Acceptance Testing

To quantify the referring physicians' perceived value of multimedia technologies and to test the assumptions that referring physicians would value real-time rich interactivity with radiologists, a survey was designed. Physicians were provided with a full description of the system and a link to try the system. They briefly analysed a patient case to initiate a consultation with a radiologist. The patient cases were delivered in two different modes: text-only reports and full integrated mode (text, verbal, image, and real-time interaction). A web-based survey was developed and administered to a test sample of three physicians and then revised. Experts evaluated the survey for clarity and comprehensiveness. The survey included 25 questions and open-ended comments on advantages and disadvantages of the system and difficulties faced while using it. The different sections in the survey covered (1) participants' demographics; (2) physician satisfaction with the multimode real-time interaction; and (3) contribution of multimode real-time interaction to effectiveness questionnaires.

Physicians were asked to rate their agreement concerning their satisfaction and effectiveness by the use of a Likert scale. Assuming 30 participants from five different hospitals in Saudi Arabia, the revised survey was delivered to 150 physicians from a range of specialties via email, with a 20% drop-out calculated rate. The survey was available for 60 days. Missing responses were excluded from analyses, and was calculated based on the actual number of respondents in the sample. Participants' email addresses were pulled from the hospitals' directories. A reminder message was sent by email every week or two to all participants and personal visits were conducted to encourage participation. Seventy-two per cent of physicians completed the survey. The mean age of respondent was 25 (0.5) years, with the majority of them being female (69%). The majority of physicians accessed the system from home (60%).

Ethical Issues

The study request was reviewed by the hospital management who concluded that they did not need special approval as this was nonclinical trial that did not investigate health outcomes. Implied consent was obtained from test participants who completed and returned questionnaires.

Results

Data analyses were performed using Excel 2010 programme. A p value of less than 0.05 was considered significant. Overall, physicians were satisfied with a system that provided real-time multimodal communication with radiologists (3.9 + 0.56). The item that received the highest rank in the satisfaction questionnaire was "multimedia components enhance understanding of a text-based report" (4.23 + 0.9). Physicians also reported high effectiveness for improving patient referral and healthcare delivery. The overall mean effectiveness out of 5-point Likert-type scale was 4.38 (0.42). Additionally, the integrated model of interaction achieved a significantly higher score to the grades of the textonly reports ($p < 0.05$).

The Effect on Effectiveness

Almost 70% of physicians provided positive comments to the qualitative questions related to the effect of real-time multimode interaction on the physicians' effectiveness. According to physicians, the realtime multimedia consultation would significantly improve patient safety and care, decrease their stress in making decisions from a distance, enhance understanding of medical images, improve the quality of interactions with radiologists, and improve patient care as a whole (70%, $n = 72$). The online annotation tools were also reported as a very valuable interaction resource by 82% of physicians ($n = 83$). The integration of annotation tools with real-time video conferencing was very useful in decreasing physicians' anxiety and improving their overall clinical performance. Physician comments included the following: "In the clinic, I found it easier to recall and relate to the annotated image instead of the description in the text-only report" and "MTMS helped me know exactly the medical case I have in hand." In addition, 74% agreed that recording communication for later access was one of the required functions. Figure 4 shows the percentage of physicians who agreed and strongly agreed with each separate item on the positive effect of real-time multimode interaction on effectiveness.

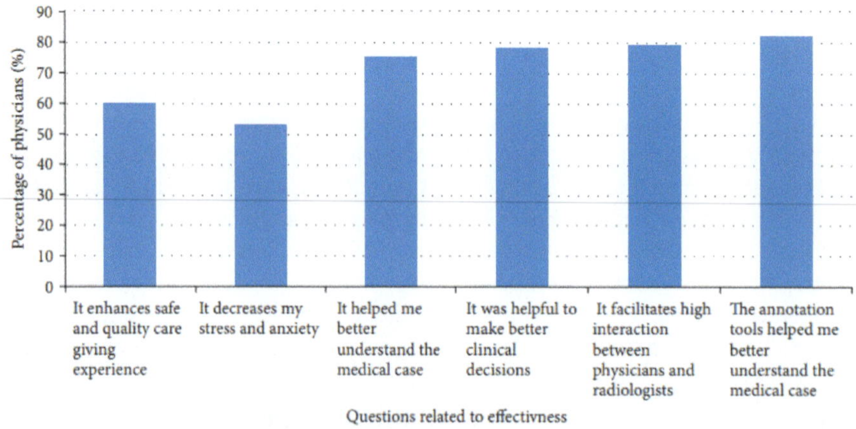

Figure 4: The effect of real-time multimode interaction on effectiveness.

The Effect on Satisfaction

Overall, 75% of physicians provided positive comments to the satisfaction questions. Physicians' satisfaction measurements were based on Konrad et al.'s physicians' satisfaction criteria [42] and included relationships with other health professionals, the availability of resources at work place, satisfaction that comes from doing the job, and satisfaction with being able to make a difference in patients' lives. Physician comments included the following: "MTMS will help in making a difference for patients who live in less developed areas." Figure 5shows the percentages of physicians who agreed and strongly agreed with each separate item on the positive effect of real-time multimode interaction on satisfaction.

Figure 5: The effect of real-time multimode interaction on satisfaction.

Although many physicians were enthusiastic about the idea of real-time multimedia interaction, several also expressed concerns about the time required to download images, the precision of the speech recognition, and the clarity of real-time interactive communication across data networks.

Overall, however, the responses support our design assumptions and the idea that there is value in providing integrated multimedia tools as part of a teleradiology management system that supports real-time interaction with enriched documentation features.

The results of our study suggest that real-time multimedia teleradiology systems have a high perceived value amongst referring physicians and may have the potential for enhancing the practice of referring physicians and improving patient care.

Radiologists' Perspective

Radiologists also reported their experience using a questionnaire. From the radiologist's perspective, the use of real-time multimodal interaction helped provide rich interaction experience with referring physicians. In addition, radiologists have captured 24% potential inappropriate performance by physicians due to misinterpretation of the text-only radiology reports. These were mainly due to insufficient description of the radiographic images in the text reports and overall clarity of received reports. The radiologists, as well, valued the recorded communication for later access and mentioned that this function can be used as a source for learning and research (72%): "Recorded interaction will reinforce the learning process and facilitate transition to practice" and "the best evidence-based reference of consultation received."

DISCUSSION

Because of the limited resources and technologies in medical care units in rural areas, creating real-time access to radiology facility locations using multimedia technologies should be a high priority in terms of enhancing the practice and satisfaction of referring physicians, improving patient care, and emphasising the critical role radiology plays in medical care.

The developed prototype has been designed and implemented for patient treatment to test assumptions relevant to teleradiology. These assumptions were related to the need for (1) real-time consultation between physician and radiologist, (2) access to visual, audio, and textual information synchronously, (3) rich multimodal interaction, and (4) access to previous examinations.

The unified integration of multimedia components in a single computer provides an efficient means to investigate the above assumptions. The software implementation using an integration model of existing off-the-shelf software offers a compact design at a low cost and with ease of use.

Although this project was led by specialists in information technology, the interdisciplinary collaboration between healthcare providers, faculty members, multimedia experts, IT experts, and administrators was a key to the project success.

Experimental tests analysed the technical aspects of the implemented systems and showed that the system could be run with acceptable error. Saving caregivers communication for later access was one of the required functions. Since Skype video calling does not support storage of recorded conversation, other teleconferencing systems will be considered. In addition, in the future, the system will provide access to patients as users to enable them to track their own cases in the system and communicate with their physician at a distance.

The study described physicians' responses to an interactive consultation environment based on the integration of a number of multimedia applications and technologies. The results showed a high level of satisfaction, indicating the effectiveness of the new consultation strategies. The use of real-time interaction decreased physician anxiety, increased physician satisfaction, and improved their ability to succeed in their work. Physicians valued the high interaction and indicated that the interaction and multimedia integration of information can promote safe and high quality care giving experience.

Almost half of the referring physicians (n=46) still think that face-to-face consultation is more effective and preferred to use MTMS as a supplement rather than a replacement for face-to-face consultation. Physicians thought that face-to-face interaction built more trust, clearly shared understanding, and fostered a greater engagement from radiologists. Physician comments included "patient diagnosis is a sensitive task where it cannot tolerate any misinterpretation." Figure 6 shows the percentage of physicians who agreed and strongly agreed on using a real-time interactive multimedia teleradiology system as a substitute for face-to-face consultation. However, with the new technologically savvy generation, the pressure exerted by advances in technology, and radiologist and physician shortages along with patient demand for flexible patient care, the momentum of multimedia technology growth is likely to continue to increase in the future.

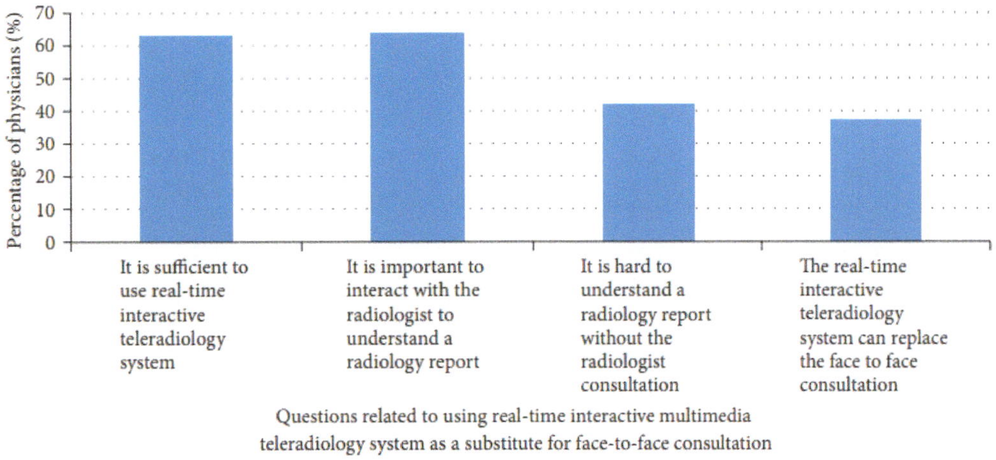

Figure 6: Real-time multimode interactive teleradiology system as a substitute for radiologist consultation.

Limitations

The findings still need to be interpreted and generalised with respect to several limitations. First, more testing should take place on areas such as the overall performance of the system and the quality of images. Second, the participants were physicians in hospitals in the big cities of Saudi Arabia. We need to test the system with participants in rural areas as they represent a group with less advanced medical and technological experience. Third, the study was conducted in an experiment setting where the environment was relatively quiet compared to the hectic, noisy, interrupted, and chaotic context of real clinical communication. In a real clinical setting, it remains unclear to what extend physicians are willing to use advanced communication tools and if the integration of multimedia technologies can contribute to cognitive overload using multiple channels simultaneously. Fourth, we have not reached an answer on how the multimedia components help physicians make fewer errors. Follow-up studies need to support the sustainability of the above preliminary results.

CONCLUSIONS

Real-time interaction is fundamental for healthcare. The use of multimedia with an interactive consultation environment is a valuable strategy that yields a better diagnosis and clinician satisfaction. The creation and delivery of a real-time interactive consultation environment are a complex process that should be carefully designed. An integration-based model allows quick development of the system and delivers a more efficient and accessible application. The design of the system was based on a number of assumptions relevant to physician-radiologist interaction. The results of the experiments support the design assumptions and show that there is value in providing integrated multimedia tools as part of a teleradiology management system to support real-time communication with enriched documentation and interaction features.

Competing Interests

The author declares that they have no competing interests.

ACKNOWLEDGMENTS

This research project was supported by a grant from the Research Center of the Center for Female Scientific and Medical Colleges, Deanship of Scientific Research, King Saud University. Special thanks are due to Heba Khojah, Areej Al-Moqare, and Wojuod Al-Obaied for developing the prototype as part of their undergraduate project.

REFERENCES

1. J. Parker and E. Coiera, "Improving clinical communication: a view from psychology," Journal of the American Medical Informatics Association, vol. 7, no. 5, pp. 453–461, 2000.
2. E. Coiera, "When conversation is better than computation," Journal of the American Medical Informatics Association, vol. 7, no. 3, pp. 277–286, 2000.
3. K. M. Sutcliffe, E. Lewton, and M. M. Rosenthal, "Communication failures: an insidious contributor to medical mishaps," Academic Medicine, vol. 79, no. 2, pp. 186–194, 2004.
4. E. Coiera and V. Tombs, "Communication behaviours in a hospital setting: an observational study," The British Medical Journal, vol. 316, no. 7132, pp. 673–676, 1998.
.
5. L.-A. D. Fitzpatrick, A. J. Melnikas, M. Weathers, and S. W. Kachnowski, "Understanding communication capacity. Communication patterns and ICT usage in clinical settings," Journal of Healthcare Information Management, vol. 22, no. 3, pp. 34–41, 2008.
6. L. Varpio, P. Hall, L. Lingard, and C. Schryer, "Interprofessional communication and medical error: a reframing of research questions and approaches," Academic Medicine, vol. 83, supplement 10, pp. S76–S81, 2008.
7. J. Bezemer, A. Cope, G. Kress, and R. Kneebone, "'Do you have another Johan?' Negotiating meaning in the operating theatre," Applied Linguistics Review, vol. 2, pp. 313–334, 2011.
8. J. Tracy, Telemedicine Technical Assistance Documents, 2011, http://www.nachc.com/client/getting.started.telemedicine.pdf.
9. S. Hosteler, PACS and Teleradiology, Analysis of Market Status and Industry Trends, Miller Freeman, San Francisco, Calif, USA, 1994.
10. L. Alsafadi, "An overview and evaluation of the radiologists lounge, a semantic content-based radiographic images retrieval," Multimedia Tools and Applications, vol. 75, no. 1, pp. 607–625, 2016.
11. Y. Liu, C. Shih, Y. Chang, S. Chang, and J. Wu, "Performance enhancement of a web-based picture archiving and communication system using commercial off-the-shelf server clusters," BioMed Research International, vol. 2014, Article ID 657417, 9 pages, 2014.
12. T. Hachaj, "Real time exploration and management of large medical volumetric datasets on small mobile devices—evaluation of remote volume rendering approach," International Journal of Information Management, vol. 34, no. 3, pp. 336–343, 2014.
13. P. Kumar, A. Vashishtha, and K. Rahmani, "A server based real time system for medical image processing support for doctors analysis," International Journal of Software and Web Sciences, vol. 5, no. 1, pp. 22–26, 2013.
14. J. Thrall, "Teleradiology part 1. History and clinical applications," 2011, http://radiology.rsna.org/content/243/3/613.full.
15. J. M. Clark and A. Paivio, "Dual coding theory and education," Educational Psychology Review, vol. 3, no. 3, pp. 149–210, 1991.
16. A. Paivio, "Mental imagery in associative learning and memory," Psychological Review, vol. 76, no. 3, pp. 241–263, 1969.
17. A. Baddeley and G. Hitch, "Working memory," in The Psychology of Learning and Motivation: Advances in Research and Theory, pp. 8–89, Academic Press, New York, NY, USA, 1974.
18. R. E. Mayer, "Applying the science of learning to medical education," Medical Education, vol. 44, no. 6, pp. 543–549, 2010.
19. R. Mayer, "Cognitive theory of multimedia learning," in The Cambridge Handbook of Multimedia Learning, R. E. Mayer, Ed., pp. 31–48, Cambridge University Press, New York, NY, USA, 2005.
20. A. F. Cardoso, L. Moreli, F. T. M. M. Braga, C. I. Vasques, C. B. Santos, and E. C. Carvalho, "Effect of a video on developing skills in undergraduate nursing students for the management of totally implantable central venous access ports," Nurse Education Today, vol. 32, no. 6, pp. 709–713, 2012. ·
21. N. F. Cook, T. McAloon, P. O'Neill, and R. Beggs, "Impact of a web based interactive simulation game (PULSE) on nursing students' experience and performance in life support training—a pilot study," Nurse Education Today, vol. 32, no. 6, pp. 714–720, 2012.
22. J. Barratt, "A focus group study of the use of video-

recorded simulated objective structured clinical examinations in nurse practitioner education," Nurse Education in Practice, vol. 10, no. 3, pp. 170–175, 2010.

23. F. Paul, "An exploration of student nurses' thoughts and experiences of using a video-recording to assess their performance of cardiopulmonary resuscitation (CPR) during a mock objective structured clinical examination (OSCE)," Nurse Education in Practice, vol. 10, no. 5, pp. 285–290, 2010. ·

24. W. Chen and C.-C. Shih, "Architecture of portable electronic medical records system integrated with streaming media," Journal of Medical Systems, vol. 36, no. 1, pp. 25–31, 2012.

25. S. Han, N. Nijdam, J. Schmid, and N. Kim, "Collaborative telemedicine for interactive multiuser segmentation of volumetric medical images," The Visual Computer, vol. 26, no. 6–8, pp. 639–648, 2010.

26. Y. Kinosada, A. Takada, and M. Hosoba, "Real-time radiology—new concepts for teleradiology,"Computer Methods and Programs in Biomedicine, vol. 66, no. 1, pp. 47–54, 2001.

27. J.-S. Lee, C.-T. Tsai, C.-H. Pen, and H.-C. Lu, "A real time collaboration system for teleradiology consultation," International Journal of Medical Informatics, vol. 72, no. 1–3, pp. 73–79, 2003.

28. H. Evers, A. Mayer, U. Engelmann et al., "Extending a teleradiology system by tools for visualization and volumetric analysis through a plug-in mechanism," International Journal of Medical Informatics, vol. 53, no. 2-3, pp. 265–275, 1999.

29. S. K. Yoo, K. M. Kim, S. M. Jung, K. J. Lee, and N. H. Kim, "Design of multimedia telemedicine system for inter-hospital consultation," in Proceedings of the 26th Annual International Conference of the IEEE Engineering in Medicine and Biology Society (EMBS '04), vol. 2, pp. 3109–3111, San Francisco, Calif, USA, September 2004.

30. J. Simmons, Primary Care Needs New Innovations to Meet Growing Demands, HealthLeadersMedia, Danvers, Mass, USA, 2009.

31. D. D. Tresch, W. M. Simpson Jr., and J. R. Burton, "Relationship of long-term and acute-care facilities: the problem of patient transfer and continuity of care," Journal of the American Geriatrics Society, vol. 33, no. 12, pp. 819–826, 1985.

32. S. S. Naik, A. Hanbidge, and S. R. Wilson, "Radiology reports: examining radiologist and clinician preferences regarding style and content," American Journal of Roentgenology, vol. 176, no. 3, pp. 591–598, 2001.

33. V. R. Iyer, P. F. Hahn, L. S. Blaszkowsky, S. P. Thayer, E. F. Halpern, and M. G. Harisinghani, "Added value of selected images embedded into radiology reports to referring clinicians," Journal of the American College of Radiology, vol. 7, no. 3, pp. 205–210, 2010.

34. SixPACS, SixPACS Teleradiology Management Systems, 2011, https://www.mxipacs.com/docs/RadiologistSupplement.pdf.

35. L. Ling, Y. Dezhong, L. Jianqing, L. Bin, and W. Ling, "A multimedia telemedicine system," in Proceedings of the Engineering in Medicine and Biology 27th Annual Conference, pp. 3746–3748, Shanghai, China, 2005.

36. A. Johnson, J. Ying, J. S. Swan, L. S. Williams, K. E. Applegate, and B. Littenberg, "Improving the quality of radiology reporting: a physician survey to define the target," Journal of the American College of Radiology, vol. 1, no. 7, pp. 497–505, 2004.

37. N. J. Clinger, T. B. Hunter, and B. J. Hillman, "Radiology reporting: attitudes of referring physicians,"Radiology, vol. 169, no. 3, pp. 825–826, 1988.

38. S. Emerson, Interactive Real-Time Ultrasound Telediagnosis, Department of Radiology, University of Tennessee, Memphis, Tenn, USA, 1996.

39. L. Watts and A. Monk, "Telemedical consultation: task characteristics," in Proceedings of the ACM SIGCHI Conference on Human Factors in Computing Systems (CHI '97), pp. 534–535, ACM, 1997.

40. TeamSTEPPS, Team Strategies and Tools to Enhance Performance and Patient Safety, Department of Defense and Agency for Healthcare Research and Quality, 2014.

41. O. Pianykh, Digital Imaging and Communications in Medicine (DICOM): A Practical Introduction and Survival Guide, Springer, New York, NY, USA, 2th edition, 2008.

42. T. Konrad, E. S. Williams, M. Linzer, et al., "Measuring physician job satisfaction in a changing workplace and a challenging environment," Medical Care, vol. 37, no. 11, pp. 1174–1182, 1999.

CHAPTER 4

INTERACTION-AWARE VIDEO COMMUNITY-BASED CONTENT DELIVERY IN WIRELESS MOBILE NETWORKS

Lujie Zhong, Shijie Jia, Youzhong Ma, and Yongxin Zhang

INTRODUCTION

The increase of communication capacities in wireless mobile networks supports the ubiquitous Internet access of mobile users via smart devices (e.g., smart phones and tablet PC) to obtain multimedia services which require high bandwidth [1–7]. As Figure 1 shows, the mobile users make use of multiple network interfaces equipped in smart devices to fetch multimedia content in heterogeneous wireless mobile networks. Video streaming is a popular application, which promotes fast increase of mobile data traffic in the whole world [8]. Provisioning video content to the mobile uses in wireless mobile networks can improve experience of mobile users (e.g., the mobile video can enrich travel of passengers in train or taxi) [9–11]. The multimedia streaming systems mainly employ peer-to-peer (P2P) technologies to address the problems of large-scale deployment [12–15]. In particular, the emerging mobile P2P (MP2P) technologies provide feasible solutions to support the deployment of mobile video streaming system in wireless mobile networks [16–18]. However, the increase in the number of viewers leads to high cost in the management and scheduling of resources, which brings negative effects for the scalability and quality of service (QoS) of mobile video streaming systems.

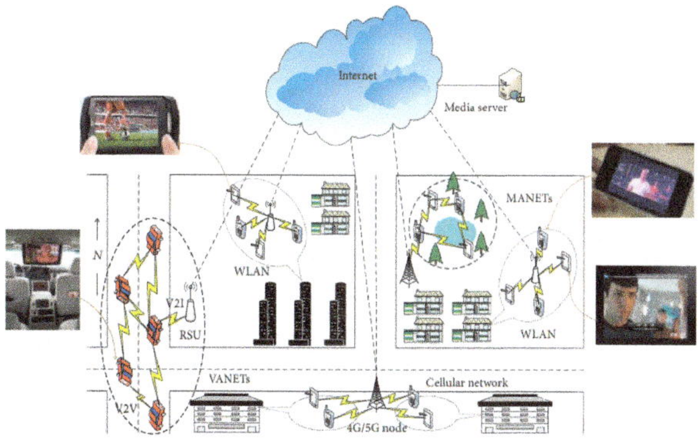

Figure 1: Multimedia streaming services in wireless mobile networks.

The performance of P2P-based resource sharing and peer management determine the QoS and scalability of multimedia streaming systems, so numerous solutions focus on the design of resource sharing and overlay network maintenance. For instance, COME-P2P in [19] groups the mobile nodes into a Chord structure to obtain high performance of resource searching and delivery by making use of the routing information in overlay networks. However, the dynamic peer state causes frequent reconstruction of Chord structure, which increases the maintenance cost of systems. With increasing number of peers, the huge maintenance cost becomes the bottleneck of system scalability. Bethanabhotla et al. proposed a video resource scheduling scheme in wireless networks [20], which supports the dynamic selection of suppliers and adaptively regulates the data transmission rate according to the video quality demand of requesters. However, the adaptive supplier selection leads to high startup delay due to the dynamic distribution of resources. Except for a mass of network bandwidth requirement from high-quality video delivery, the resource redundancy, fragile logical connection, and frequent resource lookup failure in overlay networks also consume the large number of bandwidths. The high-efficiency video content delivery solutions should have optimal distribution and quick lookup for the video resources

Citation: Lujie Zhong, Shijie Jia, Youzhong Ma, and Yongxin Zhang, "Interaction-Aware Video Community-Based Content Delivery in Wireless Mobile Networks," Mobile Information Systems, vol. 2016, Article ID 4047213, 13 pages, 2016. doi:10.1155/2016/4047213

in overlay networks to support green communications for mobile video streaming services.

The virtual community technologies group the users with similar characteristics and define the user behaviors such as search and sharing of resources. The autonomous management of resources in the communities can make the balance between maintenance cost and searching performance of resources to improve the system scalability. For instance, SocialTube captures the common interests between source node and users according to the number of watched videos and groups the users with similar interests into the tree-based communities [21]. However, SocialTube only uses the similarity in the number of requested and stored contents to evaluate the closeness of user relationship, so that the fragile link between users leads to frequent reconstruction of community structure. SAVE in [22] uses two users with common characteristics in watched video content and time period to define the relationship between community members. Although the similar content implies the probability of requesting the same content in the future, the users with common interests still need to use the communication with each other to achieve the resource sharing in multimedia streaming systems. Therefore, an efficient solution which makes use of the interaction behaviors between users to tighten up the relationship between community members and improve searching performance and system scalability should be considered for video sharing in wireless mobile networks.

In this paper, we propose a novel interaction-aware video community-based content delivery (IVCCD) in wireless mobile networks. By the investigation of interaction behaviors between mobile users, IVCCD builds a novel interaction model to find the common characteristics between mobile users. IVCCD employs a partition-based community discovery scheme to group the mobile users with similar interaction behaviors by the iterative refinement for the prepartitioned results according to the serving capacities and contact closeness of mobile users. In order to improve video resource sharing performance, IVCCD formulates a community member management mechanism and a resource sharing scheme that defines member role to achieve the autonomous community maintenance, which optimizes resource distribution and balances searching performance and community maintenance cost. Simulation results based on the two mobility models: random and Gauss-Markov mobility model show how IVCCD achieves much better performance results in comparison with other state-of-the-art solutions.

RELATED WORK

The existing P2P-based multimedia streaming systems make use of the optimization of resource searching and scheduling to improve video sharing performance in recent years. QHWC makes use of caching of video content based on the vehicle disconnectivity and mobility to optimize the resource distribution. QHWC proposed two metrics, LUR and QCR, to ensure high QoS in Internet-based VANETs [23]. Zhou et al. analyze two classes of delayed control information distributions: the class with finite mean and variance and a general class that does not employ any parametric representation in order to understand how the DCI effects the performance of wireless video transmission [24]. The designed distributed video-scheduling scheme realizes the theoretical analysis. COME-P2P in [19] groups the nodes into a DHT structure to obtain the gains of fast resource searching. COME-P2P further makes use of the routing information and multicast path to refine the finger table and routing table by the cross-layer technologies in order to enable smooth video playback. However, COME-P2P relies on the large number of message exchanges to support the update of node state and DHT reconstruction including joining and leaving of nodes. With the increase in the number of nodes, the message overhead brings negative effects for system scalability and wastes mass network bandwidth. Moreover, the dynamic routing and round trip time (RTT) can accurately describe the node mobility, so that it is difficult to achieve the delivery of video resources in near geographical distance. The variation of routing and RTT leads to frequent update of finger table, which further increases the maintenance cost of DHT structure. Bethanabhotla et al. make use of Lyapunov drift plus penalty approach to solve the formulated network utility maximization problem, which achieves the self-adaption in the supplier selection and transmission rate between users and helpers in terms of the user demand for video quality [20]. However, the resource delivery capacities of nodes are dynamic with the change of network topologies in wireless networks. This leads to frequent switchover of link between users and helpers, which increases startup delay of users and influences the playback smoothness. BOSA in [25] assigns the servers in mobile clouds according to the last timeslot information of resource requests and makes use of the first-come-first-served rule to schedule multimedia flows, in order to the impartial use of free time among the servers. However, BOSA neglects the dynamic user demand for the multimedia content, so that it is difficult to achieve impartial scheduling for the server resources.

Recently, the numerous researchers focus on the design of virtual community-based resource sharing solutions. For instance, SAVE in [22] investigates the user switchover behavior between video content and groups the nodes which request the same content into the communities. SAVE builds the connection between communities according to the video content contact in order to obtain high gains of video searching performance. However, the nodes which watch similar video content during the same time period form the communities, which results in the low robustness and scalability of community structure. Doulkeridis et al. make use of hierarchical and partitioning clustering method to group the nodes. The ordinary nodes and super nodes with strong capacities which store the same resources form a community [26]. The super nodes make use of the stored resource index list to speed up the resource lookup process. However, the proposed community discovery method relies on the stored same resources, which leads to fragile relationship between community members. The static community structure is difficult to adapt to the dynamic user demand; namely, the variation of resources stored by the nodes causes frequent reconstruction of community structure, reducing the performance of resource sharing and system scalability. SANE in [27] maps various interest characteristics of users into an interest space where the characteristics of each user are corresponding to an interest vector in the space. The cosine value of two vectors is considered as the closeness level of social relationship. However, the estimation methods based on common interests lead to fragile and changeful user relationship, so that the community structure also is subjected to frequent reconstruction. AMCV in [28] clusters the nodes which store the same video chunk into the community and builds two kinds of connections (static and dynamic connection) to bridge communities according to the common interests of users for the video content, which supports fast resource lookup. However, although the static and dynamic connection can adapt to the change of user interest and help the user to fast fetch desired resources, the increase in the number of communities results in the overload of community broker nodes, reducing the system scalability.

The above community-based solutions have some defects such as fragile member relationship, low scalability, and high maintenance cost of community. In order to address the above problems, an efficient solution should accurately estimate user relationship and build the flexible and scalable community structure to support fast lookup and high-efficiency delivery. We investigate the interaction behaviors among the mobile users to discover the common interests for the video content and obtain the preference of fetching content, which can accurately evaluate the closeness of user relationship and ensure stable community structure and high-efficiency sharing.

IVCCD OVERVIEW

Figure 2 illustrates the design of IVCCD architecture which includes the interaction awareness, community construction, and content delivery. The mobile nodes join the multimedia streaming system by sending request message to the server or overlay networks. The server or the nodes which stores requested video resources in overlay networks return a response message and transmit video data to the request nodes. The request nodes preferentially search and fetch video content from the suppliers in overlay networks in order to reduce the server load. If there are no requested resources in overlay networks, the server provides the initial video content for the request nodes. The built connections between requesters and suppliers are considered as the interaction behaviors between nodes. By the collection and analysis of node interaction behaviors, the system can be aware of interaction range and frequentness of each node to discover the node set with close contact. Based on the results of collection and analysis, IVCCD uses a contact graph to build the interaction model which defines some important parameters used in the community discovery algorithm such as the serving capacities of nodes and closeness between nodes. The community discovery algorithm uses the partition method to obtain initial node sets in terms of node degree and merges and refines these initial sets according to closeness between nodes, where these refined sets are considered as node communities. The member role management defines the roles and task for the community members and formulates the member maintenance scheme. The distribution and sharing of community resource require the members to cooperatively store video resources and formulate the intracommunity and intercommunity resource search algorithms.

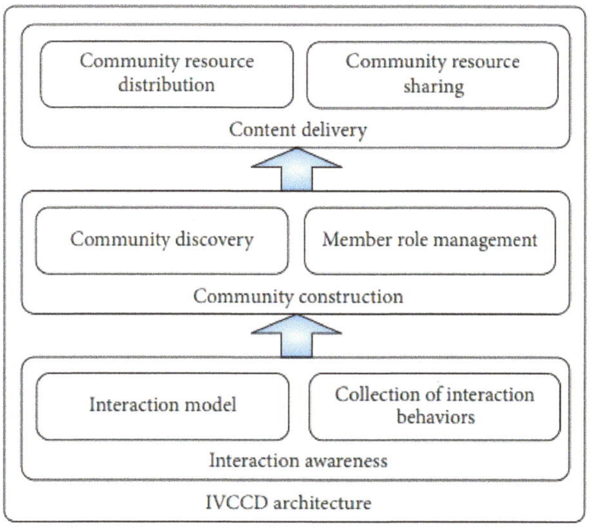

Figure 2: IVCCD architecture.

IVCCD DETAILED DESIGN

The interests for the video content drive the nodes to search the resources in P2P networks. Because the suppliers are watching or have stored the requested video, they can provide corresponding video services for the requesters; namely, the suppliers also are interested in the video content. In fact, the requesters and the suppliers have common interest for current video content and the request-response process between requesters and suppliers is considered as an interaction. The traditional common interest discovery methods rely on the analysis for historical records of watched video content, which difficultly in ensuring accuracy of common interest estimation. The interest-driven interaction not only describes the accurate results of similarity in demand for the video content, but also denotes the close relationship in contact. For instance, if the two nodes have close geographical location, similar demand, and good communication quality, they always keep frequent interaction. The nodes receive the video data from the suppliers and record the information of suppliers. When the nodes quit the system, they send the messages containing the collected information of suppliers and delivery (e.g., transmission delay and packet loss rate (PLR)) to the server. The server uses two tuples R=(requester, supplier) to denote the interaction between nodes. An interaction set $S_R = (R_1, R_2,...)$ is stored at the server side.

Interaction Awareness.

The server makes use of a directed contact graph $G = (V, E)$ to model the node interaction behaviors. $V=(V_1, V_2,..., V_k)$ is a vertex set, where any vertex V_i denotes a node n_i in the system. Any edge e_{ij} in the edge set E denotes the interaction between n_i and n_j. The two nodes which have the edges such as n_i and n_j are neighbor relationship. Any node n_i in the system may repeatedly fetch the video from a supplier; namely, there is the difference for the closeness of contact between nodes. We define the edge weight value w_{eij} to denote the closeness of contact between nodes in terms of the interaction time. The interaction time indicates the transmission time of video data from suppliers to requesters. The connection between nodes is fragile due to the interest change; namely, when the nodes switch the playback content to another video, the data transmission of both communication sides is discontinued. The long interaction time means that the nodes have strong interest for the same video. The estimation value of interaction time between n_i and n_j is defined as

$$w_{e_{ij}} = \arctan\left(\sum_{c=1}^{N_{ij}} l_c\right), \quad l \leq L, \; w_{e_{ij}} \in \left(0, \frac{\pi}{2}\right), \tag{1}$$

where l_c is an interaction time and N_{ij} is the number of interaction between n_i and n_j. w_{eij} also implies the preference of supplier selection of the requester n_i except the contact closeness. For instance, the mobile users preferentially fetch video content from other colleagues in workplace. The degree of each node in G is the total number of in-degree and out-degree due to the directed edge, which represents the interaction range of nodes. The higher the node degree is, the stronger the capacities of resource sharing are. The requesters always want to build the connection with the suppliers which have high-quality delivery capacities, which ensures the watched quality of users. We define serving capacities of each node in terms of the delivery quality of content by the investigation of transmission delay and PLR. Let d_{ji} and r_{ji} denote the average delay and average PLR in the process of data transmission from n_j to n_i, respectively. The serving capacities of n_j are defined as

$$SC_j = \frac{\sum_{c=1}^{N_j} \bar{r}_{jc}}{N_j} \times \log_2\left(1 + \frac{\sum_{c=1}^{N_j} \bar{d}_{jc}}{N_j}\right), \tag{2}$$

where N_j is the number of nodes which receive the data transmission from n_j. The high transmission delay with severe jitter breaks the playback smoothness and the high PLR cause the strong distortion of video screen, reducing the watched quality of users. Further, the low watched quality also results in the fragile connection between nodes; namely, the requesters break current connection and re-search new suppliers. The nodes with strong serving capacities can attract more requesters to fetch the content in order to the better watched quality; namely, they have strong capacities of resource sharing.

Community Construction

The robust and scalable communities not only require close relationship between members, but also need the distinct boundaries to express the difference of intercommunity nodes. We employ a partition method for G to construct the node communities, which includes two steps: firstly, the initial subgraphs are extracted from G according to the node degree; secondly, these subgraphs are combined or partitioned to construct new subgraphs. By the iteration of combination and partition, the refined subgraphs are considered as the node communities. Although there is the probability of interaction for the nodes which do not have edges in G, the frequency of interaction between them is less than that of nodes which have edges.

Therefore, the graph partition-based community structure can obtain accurate clustering results. Firstly, the node n_i which has the maximum value of degree in V is selected as the center node of a new subgraph (n_i). The neighbor nodes of n_i (the nodes have the edges with n_i) are extracted from V and become the members of (n_i). In a similar way, we continue to extract a new subgraph (n_k) from the difference set $V - S(n_i)$. The condition of convergence of the above iteration is that all items in V are partitioned into subgraphs. The nodes with the larger degree have high dissemination capacities, so that the initial subgraphs have better resource sharing performance. However, the partitioned results are limited to the selection of initial subgraph centers. For instance, the degree of noncenter members in (n_i) may be larger than that of center node n_k in $S(n_k)$.

Therefore, the partitioned results need to be refined; namely; the initial subgraphs are further partitioned or combined. Because the subgraphs are adjacent to each other, the combination mainly is to search the incorporable nodes in adjacent subgraphs. For instance, a member n_a in (n_i) finds a neighbor node n_h in $S(n_k)$. If the weight value $weah$ of e_{ah} is larger than w_{ehk} of edge e_{hk} between n_h and n_k, n_h quits from (n_k) and becomes new member in $S(ni)$. When na and nh have two edges eah and eha and nh and nk also have two edges ekh and ehk, we compare the total of $weah$ and $weha$ with that of $wekh$ and $wehk$ to make the decision of combination. If $(weah + weh) > (wekh + w_{ehk})$, n_h leaves $SG(n_k)$ and joins $SG(n_i)$. Otherwise, if $(w_{eah} + w_{eh}) < (w_{ekh} + w_{ehk})$, n_h stays in $SG(n_k)$. With the subgraph combination, if all members in some subgraphs are merged into other subgraphs, namely, these subgraphs only include center nodes, the center nodes are marked as ordinary nodes and wait for the combination by other subgraphs. However, the unlimited combination also leads to the inaccurate results. For instance, after the member na in (n_i) merges n_h, n_h continues to search new nodes in other subgraphs. If this combination process continues, the longest path and member scale in (n_i) keep increasing so that the partitioned results become local optimum. In order to ensure the accuracy of partitioned results and achieve the global optimum, we define the merging node rule to make the decision of merging searched nodes by the comparison of the state of subgraphs before and after merging the nodes. For instance, let $W(SG(n_i))$ and $C(SG(n_i))$ be the initial total of edge weight value and node capacities in $SG(n_i)$, respectively, where $W(\cdot)$ and $C(\cdot)$ are the functions of calculating the total of edge weight value and node capacities. Any member na in (n_i) wants to merge a member nh in other subgraphs. If $W(SG(n_i))/NE(SG(n_i)) \leq W(SG^{(new)}(n_i))/NE(SG^{(new)}(n_i))$ and $C(SG(n_i))/NV(SG(n_i)) \leq C(SG^{(new)}(n_i))/NV(SG^{(new)}(n_i))$, n_h is successfully merged into $SG(n_i)$, where $SG^{(new)}(ni)$ is new subgraph after the combination and $NE(\cdot)$ and $NV(\cdot)$ return the number of edges and nodes in graph, respectively. Otherwise, nh does not become the new member in (n_i) and is marked as the node which is unable to merge by na. In the next process of searching nodes, n_a ignores n_h. $(SG(n_i))/(SG(n_i))$ and $C(SG(n_i))/NV(SG(n_i))$ denote the mean value of edge weight and node capacities in $SG(ni)$, respectively. The defined rule indicates that the new members cannot lead to the decrease in contact closeness and serving capacities for current subgraphs, which ensures the tight relationship and high-quality service provision between members. The convergence condition of combination and partition process for the subgraphs is that all nodes in G are grouped into the subgraphs and the nodes in subgraphs stop to search new nodes in other subgraphs. After the process of combination and partition, the existing subgraphs are considered as the node communities. The pseudocode of the process of community discovery is detailed in Algorithm 1.

```
TG = G; i = 0; j = 0;
/* V is node set in G; |V| returns number of nodes in V; D(·) returns node's degree (in-degree and out-degree). */
while(TG is not NULL && i < NV(G))
  if D(V[i]) is maximum value of degree of nodes in TG
    V[i] and V[i]'s neighbor nodes form a sub-graph SG(V[i]);
    TG = G − SG(V[i]);
  end if
  i++;
end while
/* NB_V[j] is set of V[j]'s neighbor nodes in other sub-graphs; |NB_V[j]| returns number of items in NB_V[j]. */
while(all nodes join into sub-graphs and all nodes stop to search new nodes)
  if (V[j] is not center node)
    for (k = 0; k < |NB_V[j]|; k++)
      if (NB_V[j][k] is not marked by V[j] && NB_V[j][k] meets requirement of becoming new member);
        NB_V[j][k] joins sub-graph of V[j];
      else NB_V[j][k] is marked as unavailable node by V[j];
      end if
    end for
  end if
  j++;
  if (j ≥ |V|)
    j = 0;
  end if
end while
```

Algorithm 1: Process of community discovery.

Content Delivery.

The community management mainly includes the role assignment and cache control of members, which reduces the maintenance cost of members and optimize the distribution of community resources. We define three roles for the community members: ordinary member, broker member, and bridged member.

(1) The ordinary members are responsible for the provision of requested content delivery for the requesters and make the replacement of cached content in terms of the requirement of broker members. When a mobile node joins the system and becomes new community member, the node maintains a connection with any member in current community at least. If the ordinary members quit current communities, they send a message to the neighbor members in current communities.

(2) The center nodes in subgraphs act as the broker members in communities and are responsible for the maintenance of cached resources of members and dissemination of resource request message. The broker members with high degree can achieve the fast and low-cost dissemination of information including resource request and member state in communities, which reduces startup delay and deals with the variation of resource demand of members in real time. When the broker members receive the request messages, they spread the messages to their neighbor members and require these neighbor members to assist the resource searching. When the broker members quit communities, the intracommunity members which have the high node degree become new broker members. The exited broker members require that the neighbor nodes with the maximum degree value maintain the information of their neighbor nodes.

(3) The nodes located in boundary of subgraphs are considered as the bridged members which are responsible for maintaining connections with the neighbor nodes in other communities and forwarding the request messages to other communities. Because the bridged members have the connections with the intercommunity members, they are suitable for becoming the interfaces between communities to achieve the resource sharing.

When the bridged members leave current communities, they send the information of their neighbor nodes to any neighbor node in current communities. When a member ni in any community wants to download a video content, it firstly sends the request messages to the intracommunity neighbor members. If the intracommunity neighbor members of ni store the requested resource, they return the response messages and ni selects the member with the maximum value of serving capacities as the supplier. Otherwise, if the neighbor members of ni do not provide desired resource, ni requests the broker member to assist searching resource by sending a request message containing the information of requested resource and members which have been consulted by ni. The broker member disseminates the request message to the neighbor members and require that these neighbor members continue to spread the request message when they also do not store requested resource. If the broker member finds that there is no resource in current community, it requires that the bridged members assist searching. The bridged members directly forward the request message to the broker members in adjacent communities. If the adjacent communities do not include the requested resource, *ni* directly requests the server to fetch the resource because the lookup resource in the whole overlay network brings high startup delay. The pseudocode of the process of content delivery is detailed in Algorithm 2.

```
/* n_i is request node in a community C_h; n_j is broker member in C_h; n_k is bridged member in C_h. */
n_i sends request messages to neighbor members maintained by n_i
if(n_i receives response messages)
    for(k = 0; k < m; k++)
        estimates serving capacities of member_k by (2);
    end for
    selects member with maximum value of serving capacities as supplier;
else n_i sends request message to n_j;
        n_j forwards message to other members;
        if(n_j receives response messages)
            n_j returns member list to n_i;
        else n_j forward request message to n_k;
            if (n_k successfully receives response from other communities)
                n_k returns list of candidate suppliers to n_i;
                n_i estimates serving capacities by (2) and select supplier;
            else n_k forward request message to server;
            end if
        end if
end if
n_k receives video data from supplier (server);
```

Algorithm 2: Process of content delivery.

With increasing storage capacities of mobile devices, the mobile nodes may carry one or multiple video resources. A key issue is how to make use of storage resource of mobile nodes to support high-efficiency resource sharing. The intracommunity resource lookup can reduce the lookup delay due to the relatively few forwarding nodes. IVCCD employs the local resource lookup strategy in order to avoid the high lookup delay, which reduces the lookup success rate. Therefore, we use a dissemination-aware resource distribution approach to dynamically regulate community resource. After G is divided into multiple communities, the server collects the information of dissemination process of resources. For instance, a member *ni* in any community requests a video content from the server because there are no available resources in all communities. The other requester connects with *ni* and fetches resource; namely, the following members search and select the suppliers in overlay networks. The requesters and suppliers form a tree structure in terms of the video streaming direction; namely, *ni* is the root node of tree and *ni*'s receivers which obtain the video data from *ni* become child nodes of *ni*. The server collects the information of nodes in the above dissemination process and selects the node *nk* with the maximum receivers as the dissemination relay node which is defined as two-tuple $RN = (nk, \text{VID}c)$, where VID*c* denotes the ID of video *c*. We group these relay nodes according to the similarity of watched videos. The similarity between two videos VID*a* and VID*b* is defined as

$$S_{ab} = \frac{|ns_a \cap ns_b|}{\max\left[|ns_a|, |ns_b|\right]}, \tag{3}$$

where n_{sa} and n_{sb} are the sets of nodes which watch VID*a* and VID*b*, respectively, and $|n_{sa} \cap n_{sb}|$ returns the number of intersection between *nsa* and *nsb*. If $S_{ab} > S$, where S is the mean value of similarity of all videos, VID*a* and VID_b are similar in content. Because each video is corresponding to a relay node, there is a relationship between the similar video set and the relay node set. When a member fetches a video from the server, the server requires that the nodes in the corresponding relay node set buffer and spread the requested video, which is beneficial to speeding up the resource dissemination with the help of multiple relay nodes. The relay nodes send the messages containing current resources to the broker members and require the broker members to spread the resource information in communities. If there are members which are interested in pushed resource, these members connect with the intracommunity relay nodes to obtain the resource. Although the resource dissemination messages lead to the increase in the message overhead, the small number of bandwidth consumptions reduces the lookup delay.

TESTING AND TEST RESULTS ANALYSIS

Testing Topology and Scenarios.

We compare the performance of the proposed IVCCD with a state-of-the-art P2Pbased video sharing solution AMCV [28]. The number of video files is 20 and the length of each file is 100 s. IVCCD and AMCV were modeled and implemented in NS-2 where some simulation parameters of the wireless mobile network are listed in Table 1 for the two solutions. Before the simulation, in terms of created 6,000 playback logs for 30 video files, IVCCD analyzes these logs to group 100 mobile nodes into the communities and group the videos with similar content, and 100 mobile users in AMCV randomly request 20 videos and join into the communities corresponding to 20 videos which are same as those of IVCCD.

Table 1: Simulation parameter setting for wireless mobile network

Parameters	Values
Area	$1000 \times 1000\ m^2$
Channel	Channel/WirelessChannel
Network interface	Phy/WirelessPhyExt
MAC interface	Mac/802_11
Number of mobile nodes	500
Mobile speed range of nodes	[1, 20] m/s
Simulation time	500 s
Signal range of mobile nodes	200 m
Default distance between server and nodes	6 hops
Transmission protocol	UDP
Wireless routing protocol	DSR
Bandwidth of server	20 Mb/s
Bandwidth of mobile nodes	10 Mb/s
Transmission rate of video data	128 kb/s

In the process of simulation, we generate 100 playback logs for the 100 community members; namely, they watch diverse video content according to the playback logs where the watched time is 10 random. Moreover, we also create 100 playback logs for the 100 mobile nodes; namely, they randomly request and play video content (join corresponding communities) according to the created playback logs, where the viewing time also is random. 100 mobile nodes join the system following the Poisson distribution from 0 s to 450 s. In IVCCD and AMCV, all community member only store a video file and the mobile nodes delete the local resource and rebuffer new resources when they play new videos.

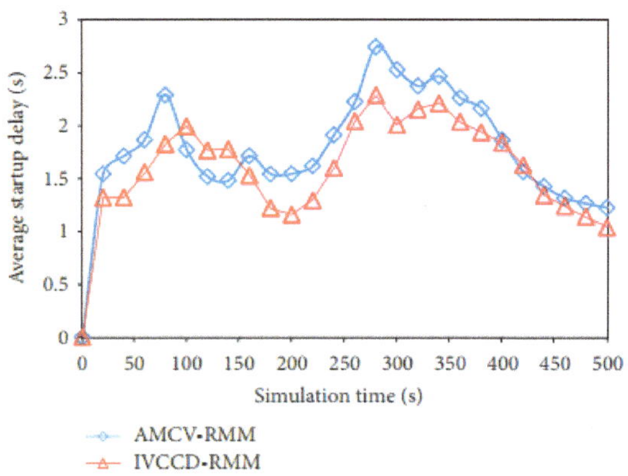

Figure 3: ASD with RMM against simulation time.

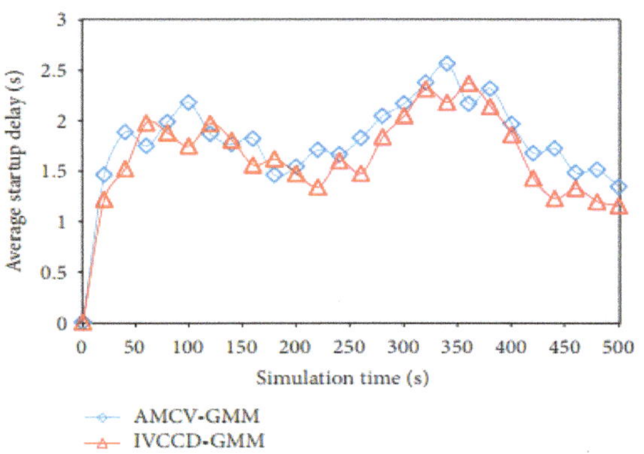

Figure 4: ASD with GMM against simulation time.

On the other hand, we use two mobility models. (1) The first is random mobility model (RMM). Initially, the location, speed, and moving target of mobile nodes are randomly assigned. When the mobile nodes arrive at the assigned target, they keep the movement state following the r-assigned random moving target and speed. (2) The second is GaussMarkov mobility model (GMM) [29]. Initially, the location and moving target of mobile nodes are randomly assigned. The mobile nodes experience the state of acceleration, stable, turn, and deceleration in the process of movement. When the mobile nodes arrive at the assigned target location, they continue to move according to the reassigned target. Because the movement with high speed influences the performance of content delivery such as delay and PLR, the mobile speed range of nodes is set to [1, 20] m/s. The default distance between server and nodes is set to 6 hops in order to ensure the equitable cost of fetching resources and differentiate the access cost for the server and the mobile nodes. In AMCV, PT_b and PTr are set to 0.2 and 0.12, respectively

Performance Evaluation.

The performance of IVCCD is compared with that of AMCV in terms of average startup delay (ASD), packet loss rate (PLR), throughput, video quality, and overlay maintenance cost, respectively. ASD. Let(s) and $t_i(r)$ be the time of sending request message and receiving first video data of a node ni, respectively. (r) − $t(s)$ is considered as the startup delay of ni. The mean value of startup delay of all nodes during a time interval T denotes ASD. Figures 3 and 4 show the performance of ASD of two solutions AMCV and IVCCD in terms of two mobility models: RMM and GMM with the increase in the simulation time, where the time interval T is set to 20 s. As Figure 3 shows, AMCV's ASD results firstly experience a fall after rise from t=0 s to t = 140 s. AMCV's curve also fast increases from t = 160 s to t = 280 s and fast decreases from t = 300 s to t = 500 s. AMCV's ASD results are in the delay range between 1.2 s and 2.75 s and reach the peak value 2.748 at t = 280 s. IVCCD's curve fast increases from t=0 s to t = 100 s and relatively slowly falls with slight fluctuation from t = 100 s to t = 200 s. The red curve also fast rises from t = 220 s to t = 280 s and slowly decreases to roughly 1 s at t = 500 s with slight fluctuation. In Figure 4, the two curves corresponding to the delay results of AMCV and IVCCD experience the two processes of rise and fall. The blue curve has a fall after rise with the fluctuation from t=0 s to t = 180 s, starts to increase from t = 200 s, and decreases from t = 340 s to t = 500 s after reaching the peak value (2.571 s) at t = 340 s. The red curve firstly experiences a fall after rise with the fluctuation from t=0 s to t = 200 s and keeps the fluctuation at high levels. IVCCD's results also have a fall after rise from t = 220 s to t = 500 s and reach the peak value (2.718 s) at t = 360 s. Although IVCCD's results are higher than those of AMCV during initial simulation time, IVCCD's curve maintains lower level than that of AMCV.

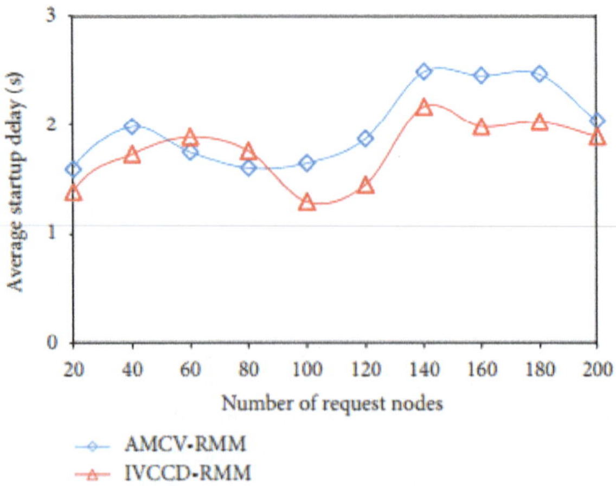

Figure 5: ASD with RMM against number of request nodes.

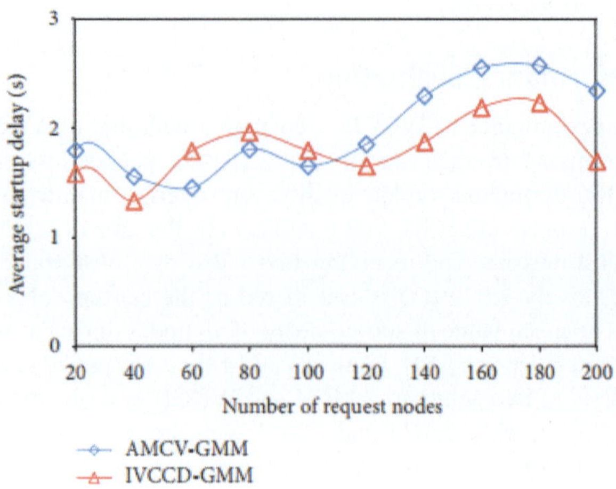

Figure 6: ASD with GMM against number of request nodes.

Figures 5 and 6 show the performance of ASD of AMCV and IVCCD in terms of RMM and GMM with increasing number of nodes. As Figure 5 shows, AMCV's blue curve has two processes of rise and fall with increasing number of request nodes and AMCV's results are in the range (1.55, 2.50). IVCCD's red curve also experiences the two variation process of rise and fall with the fluctuation and IVCCD's results are in the range (1.25, 2.20). In Figure 6, AMCV's blue curve shows a process of rise and fall with the frequent fluctuation and AMCV's results are in the range (1.45, 2.55). IVCCD's results are kept in a stable interval (1.3, 2.2) with the fluctuation. IVCCD's results have both lower values and less fluctuation than those of AMCV

The delay of searching and transmission determines the performance of startup delay. After the construction of communities, AMCV relies on the static and dynamic connections between communities to forward the request message where the dynamic connections are built by the probability of requesting resources of community members. The low accuracy of prediction results leads to the fact that the dynamic connections cannot be built, so that the request messages cannot fast arrive at the suppliers. Moreover, AMCV does not consider the performance of resource delivery between nodes, so that the low delay of data transmission cannot be ensured. On the other hand, if there are no available suppliers in overlay network, the request nodes need to connect with the server to obtain the initial resources. Because the default distance between server and nodes is set to 6 hops, the high data transmission delay also brings negative effects for the startup delay. For instance, AMCV's ASD value reaches 2.29 s at $t = 80$ s and IVCCD's ASD values keep high level from $t = 80$ s to $t = 140$ s. In IVCCD, the request nodes only search the suppliers in current and adjacent communities, which reduces the searching delay. IVCCD makes use of the buffering and dissemination of resources of relay nodes to enlarge the coverage range of requested resources in overlay network, which further reduces the searching delay of resources. Moreover, IVCCD investigates the serving capacities of community members and the requested nodes can select the optimal suppliers to improve the delivery performance. Therefore, IVCCD's ASD results are better than those of AMCV. Packet Loss Rate (PLR). Let N_s and N_r be the number of sent and received packets, respectively. The mean value of ratio between $N_s - N_r$ and Ns during a time interval T is defined as PLR.

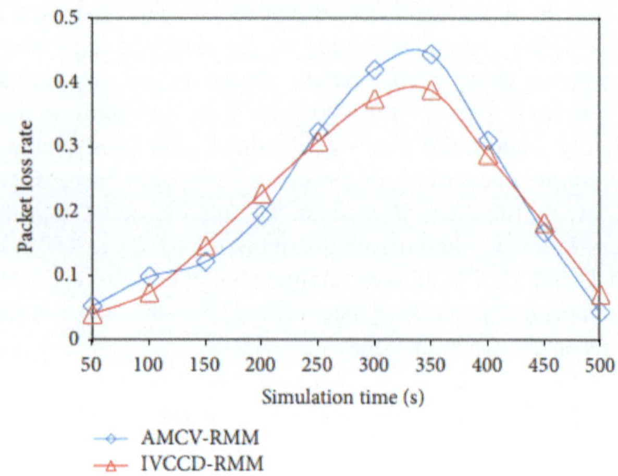

Figure 7: PLR with RMM against simulation time.

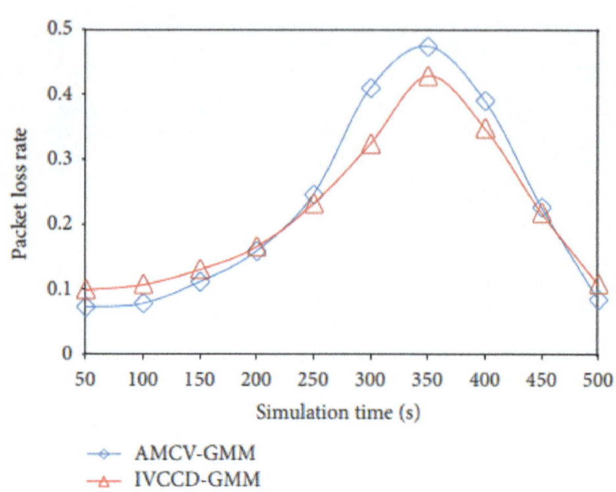

Figure 8: PLR with GMM against simulation time.

Figures 7 and 8 show the PLR performance of AMCV and IVCCD in terms of RMM and GMM with increasing simulation time, where the time interval T is set to 50 s. As Figure 7 shows, the curves of AMCV and IVCCD have similar changing process; namely, they experience fall after fast rise with the increase in the simulation time, where T is set to 50

s. Although IVCCD's curve keeps higher level than that of AMCV from $t = 150$ s to $t = 200$ s, AMCV's results have both larger PLR values and higher increment than those of IVCCD where the curves of AMCV and IVCCD reach the peak value 0.44 and 0.38 at $t = 350$ s, respectively. In Figure 8, the results of AMCV and IVCCD show the trend of fall after rise during the whole simulation time. The curve of IVCCD is higher than that of AMCV from t=0 s to $t = 200$ s, but it has lower increment and peak value than those of AMCV from $t = 250$ s to $t = 500$ s.

Figures 9 and 10 show the PLR performance of AMCV and IVCCD in terms of RMM and GMM with the increase in the number of nodes. As Figure 9 shows, the curves of AMCV and IVCCD also have a rise trend with the increase in the number of request nodes, where T is defined as the time when every 20 request nodes start to search resources. The AMCV results are between [0.03, 0.41] and reach the peak value 0.41 when the number of request nodes is 200. The red curve corresponding to the IVCCD results is between 0.04 and 0.37 and keeps lower levels than that of AMCV.The IVCCD results are roughly 10% lower than those of AMCV. In Figure 10, AMCV's curve experiences the three processes: slow rise and fast and stable increase. IVCCD's results have slow increase and keep uniform rise. Although the IVCCD's curve is higher than that of AMCV during initial stage, IVCCD's results are lower than those of AMCV during the later period of increase in the number of nodes.

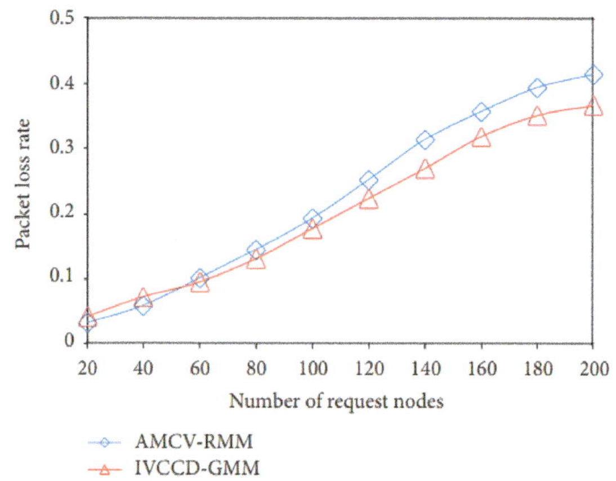

Figure 9: PLR with RMM against number of request nodes.

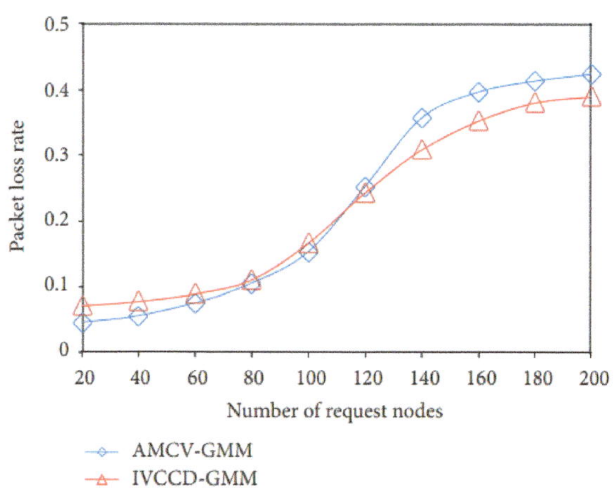

Figure 10: PLR with GMM against number of request nodes.

Initially, because the small number of nodes request videos, the relatively enough network bandwidth can support the high-efficiency delivery; namely, the PLR results of two solutions keep low levels. When the number of request nodes increases, the available network bandwidth is consumed fast so that the PLR results of AMCV and IVCCD fast increase due to the network congestion. Because the request nodes stop the resource searching from $t = 450$ s to $t = 500$ s and some of them have finished video playback, the fast decrease of congestion levels and network traffic lead to fast fall of two curves. On the other hand, AMCV only focus on the efficiency of resource searching and neglect the performance of content delivery. The nodes in AMCV cannot select the optimal suppliers, which leads to the fact that the delivery process of content is subjected to the severe negative influence in wireless mobile network. The high mobility of mobile nodes results in the fast change of geographical distance between two communication parties, which introduces the jitter of delivery performance and increases the probabilities of packet loss. IVCCD investigates the interaction between nodes and the serving capacities of nodes to build the communities. Moreover, the relay nodes can assist spreading resources to multiple communities, which enhances the probabilities of intracommunity delivery. Therefore, the request nodes select optimal suppliers, which ensures high-efficiency data transmission.

Average Throughput. Let Npr and size$p$ be the number and size of packets received in the overlay during a certain time period T, respectively. The ratio between $N_p r$ ×size$p$ and T is defined as the average throughput, where T is set to 20 s.

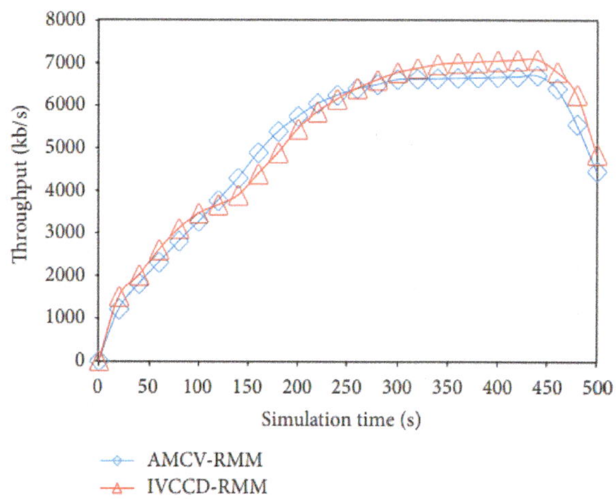

Figure 11: Throughput with RMM against simulation time.

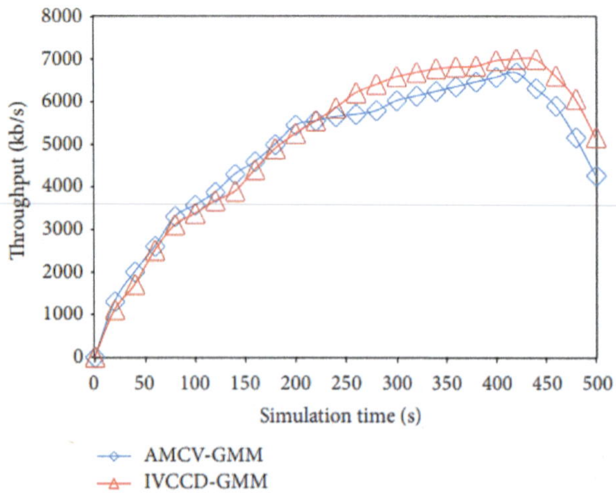

Figure 12: Throughput with GMM against simulation time.

Figures 11 and 12 show the average throughput performance of AMCV and IVCCD in terms of RMM and GMM with increasing simulation time, where the time interval T is set to 20 s. As Figure 11 shows, the curves of average throughput of AMCV and IVCCD have similar changing trend with increasing simulation time. The blue curve corresponding to AMCV's results fast increases from t=0 s to t = 300 s and keeps a slight rise from t = 320 s to t = 440 s. AMCV's results decrease to 4465 kb/s from t = 460 s to t = 500 s. IVCCD's red curve keeps a fast rise from t=0 s to t = 100 s and slowly increases from t = 120 s to t = 140 s. This red curve also fast increases from t = 160 s to t = 440 s and finally decreases to 4842 kb/s at t = 500 s. Although IVCCD's curve is lower than that of AMCV from t = 120 s to t = 240 s, the increment and peak value of IVCCD results are larger than those of AMCV. In Figure 12, the two curves of AMCV and IVCCD also have similar variation process during the whole simulation time. The blue curve fast increases from t=0 s to t = 200 s, keeps slow rise from t = 220 s to t = 420 s, and fast decreases after reaching the peak value at t = 420 s. The red curve also has a fast rise from t=0 s to t = 280 s, keeps slow increase from t = 300 s to t = 440 s, and starts to fall from t = 460 s to t = 500 s. Although IVCCD's results are less than those of AMCV from t=0 s to t = 200 s, IVCCD's curve is higher than that of AMCV and has larger peak value than that of AMCV.

The mobile nodes for two solutions AMCV and IVCCD request and fetch the video content following a Poisson distribution from t=0 s to t = 450 s. The increase in the number of request nodes causes fast rise of network traffic. The two curves corresponding to AMCV and IVCCD fast increase from t=0 s to t = 440 s and rapidly fall from t = 460 s to t = 500 s due to the decrease in the amount of video streaming. Because the high traffic is greater than the available network bandwidth, the generated network congestion leads to high PLR so that the throughput of AMCV and IVCCD keeps slow increase from t = 300 s to t = 440 s. In AMCV, the request nodes randomly select the suppliers, so the delivery performance of video content is subjected to severe influence by the network congestion and mobility of nodes. In IVCCD, the request nodes select the suppliers with maximum serving capacities, which reduce the negative effects by the network congestion and mobility of nodes. Therefore, the delivery performance of IVCCD including average throughput and PLR is better than that of AMCV.

Video Quality. Let EXP Thr and CRT Thr be the average throughput expected from the video delivery and actual throughput measured, respectively. MAX Bit denotes the average bitrate of the video stream and MAX Bit and EXP Thr are set to 128 kb/s according to the simulation settings. We make use of the Peak Signal-to-Noise Ratio (PSNR) to measure the video quality of two solutions in decibels (dB) [30]. The PSNR value is calculated according to

$$\text{PSNR} = 20 \cdot \log_{10}\left(\frac{\text{MAX\_Bit}}{\sqrt{(\text{EXP\_Thr} - \text{CRT\_Thr})^2}}\right) \quad (4)$$

Figures 13 and 14 show the PSNR performance of AMCV and IVCCD in terms of RMM and GMM with increasing number of request nodes. Figure 13 shows PSNR values of AMCV and IVCCD for the single video streaming corresponding to every request node with the increase in the number of request nodes. The two curves of AMCV and IVCCD have a fast fall trend, where AMCV's results are in the range [7, 30] and IVCCD's results are between 8 dB and 28 dB. In Figure 14, AMCV's results fast decrease with the increase in the number of request nodes. However, IVCCD's results keep a stable decrease. Although the IVCCD's results are lower than those of AMCV in the initial phase, IVCCD's bars are higher than those of AMCV in the later stage. PSNR represents the watched quality of users and includes some key impact factors such as throughput and stream bitrate. With the increase in the number of request nodes, the huge traffic triggers the network congestion, which seriously limits the increase of throughput due to high PLR. In other words, PSNR values keep low level with decreasing throughput. In AMCV, the performance of content delivery between request nodes and suppliers is subjected to the influence by the node mobility and network congestion. In IVCCD, the high-efficiency data transmission benefit from the strong serving capacities of suppliers. Therefore, the congestion period time is longer than that of IVCCD and the decrement of AMCV's PSNR values is larger than that of IVCCD.

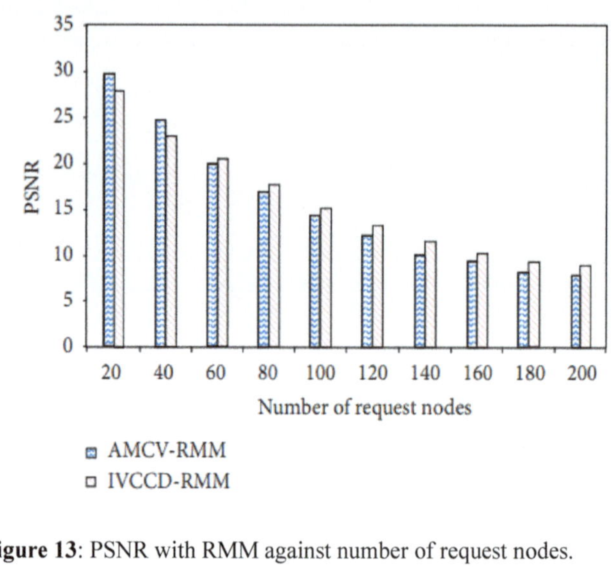

Figure 13: PSNR with RMM against number of request nodes.

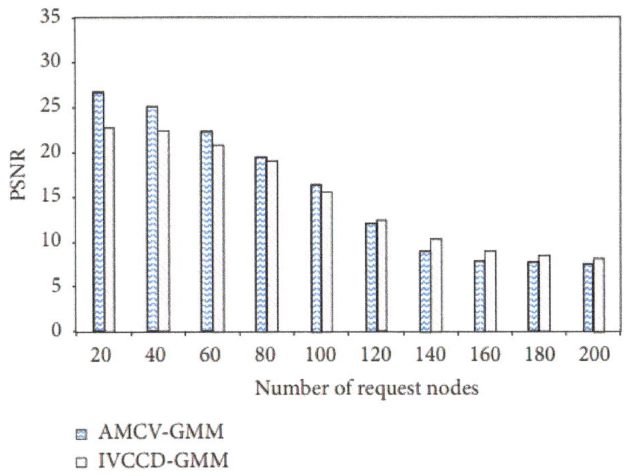

Figure 14: PSNR with GMM against number of request nodes.

Maintenance Overhead. The maintenance cost of overlay topology mainly includes the management of member state, forwarded request message, and interaction between communities. We use the average bandwidth used by the sent messages for maintaining the overlay topology to denote the maintenance overhead. As Figure 15 shows, the two curves of AMCV and IVCCD have fast rise trajectory with the increase in the simulation time. AMCV's blue curve keeps fast rise from t = 50 s to t = 450 s and slightly decreases at t = 500 s. IVCCD's red curve maintains a slow increase from t = 50 s to t = 450 s and finally decreases at t = 500 s. The increment and peak value of AMCV's results are larger than those of IVCCD. In AMCV, the broker members need to forward and handle the messages of requesting resources and member state and maintain the static and dynamic connections with other communities. The increase in the number of request nodes and dynamic connections leads to high load of broker members, which limits the system scalability. Moreover, the frequent change of requested content of community members causes the continuous movement of nodes between communities. The fragile community structure further increases the maintenance cost. However, IVCCD has stable community structure and the dynamic change of requested videos of members cannot cause the community reconstruction. Although the broker members assist spreading resource information in communities and the bridged members maintain the connections with other communities, the range of message dissemination is relatively limited and is low frequency. Therefore, IVCCD's maintenance overhead keeps lower levels than that of AMCV.

CONCLUSION

In this paper, we propose a novel interaction-aware community-based video sharing solution (IVCCD) in wireless mobile networks. IVCCD constructs a directed graph-based interaction model according to the analysis of interaction behaviors between the mobile users. In order to obtain scalable and robust community structure, IVCCD partitions nodes in graph in terms of the node degree and uses the weight values of edges and serving capacities of nodes as refined rules to generate the node community. IVCCD employs a multiple role-based community member management mechanism to balance the community maintenance cost and optimize resource distribution. IVCCD analyzes the resource dissemination process in overlay networks and uses the resource push and prebuffering approach to improve the performance of resource searching. The simulation results based on the two mobility models, random and GaussMarkov mobility model, show how IVCCD has lower average startup delay, less packet loss rate, higher throughput, higher video quality, and lower maintenance overhead than AMCV. The simulation results also show that the mobility is an important influence factor for the performance of multimedia streaming systems. In the future work, we focus on the modeling of mobility of mobile nodes and the evaluation of mobility influence for the performance of multimedia streaming systems. Competing Interests The authors declare that there is no conflict of interests regarding the publication of this paper.

ACKNOWLEDGMENTS

This work was supported in part by the National Natural Science Foundation of China (NSFC) under Grant nos. 61402303, 61501216, 61502219, 61572246, and U1404611, the Project of Beijing Municipal Commission of Education under Grant KM201510028016, the Science and Technology Key Project of Henan province (152102210331 and 152102210332), and Technology Plan Projects (Openness & Cooperation) of Henan province (152106000048).

REFERENCES

1. L. Zhou, H.-C. Chao, and A. V. Vasilakos, "Joint forensicsscheduling strategy for delay-sensitive multimedia applications over heterogeneous networks," IEEE Journal on Selected Areas in Communications, vol. 29, no. 7, pp. 1358–1367, 2011.
2. S. Chen and J. Zhao, "The requirements, challenges, and technologies for 5G of terrestrial mobile telecommunication," IEEE Communications Magazine, vol. 52, no. 5, pp. 36–43, 2014.
3. F. Song, R. Li, and H. Zhou, "Feasibility and issues for establishing network-based carpooling scheme," Pervasive and Mobile Computing, vol. 24, pp. 4–15, 2015.
4. H. Wang, S. Chen, H. Xu, M. Ai, and Y. Shi, "SoftNet: a software defined decentralized mobile network architecture toward 5G," IEEE Network, vol. 29, no. 2, pp. 16–22, 2015.
5. C.-F. Lai, R.-H. Hwang, H.-C. Chao, M. M. Hassan, and A. Alamri, "A buffer-aware HTTP live streaming approach for SDN-enabled 5G wireless networks," IEEE Network, vol. 29, no. 1, pp. 49–55, 2015.
6. C. Xu, T. Liu, J. Guan, H. Zhang, and G.-M. Muntean, "CMTQA: quality-aware adaptive concurrent multipath data transfer in heterogeneous wireless networks," IEEE Transactions on Mobile Computing, vol. 12, no. 11, pp. 2193–2205, 2013.
7. Y. Ye, S. Ci, N. Lin, and Y. Qian, "Cross-layer design for delayand energy-constrained multimedia delivery in mobile terminals," IEEE Wireless Communications, vol. 21, no. 4, pp. 62–69, 2014.
8. Cisco, Cisco Visual Networking Index: Global Mobile Data Traffic Forecast Update, 2012–2017, Cisco, 2013.

9. O. T. Cruces, M. Fiore, and J. M. B. Ordinas, "Cooperative download in vehicular environments," IEEE Transactions on Mobile Computing, vol. 11, no. 4, pp. 663–678, 2012.
10. E. Baccarelli, F. Chiti, N. Cordeschi et al., "Green multimedia wireless sensor networks: distributed intelligent data fusion, in-network processing, and optimized resource management," IEEE Wireless Communications, vol. 21, no. 4, pp. 20–26, 2014.
11. S. Jia, C. Xu, J. Guan, H. Zhang, and G.-M. Muntean, "A novel cooperative content fetching-based strategy to increase the quality of video delivery to mobile users in wireless networks," IEEE Transactions on Broadcasting, vol. 60, no. 2, pp. 370–384, 2014.
12. Y. Zhao, Y. Liu, C. Chen, and J. Zhang, "Enabling P2P one-view multiparty video conferencing," IEEE Transactions on Parallel and Distributed Systems, vol. 25, no. 1, pp. 73–82, 2014.
13. C. Xu, S. Jia, L. Zhong, and G.-M. Muntean, "Socially aware mobile peer-to-peer communications for community multimedia streaming services," IEEE Communications Magazine, vol. 53, no. 10, pp. 150–156, 2015.
14. D. Wu, Y. Liang, J. He, and X. Hei, "Balancing performance and fairness in P2P live video systems," IEEE Transactions on Circuits and Systems for Video Technology, vol. 23, no. 6, pp. 1029–1039, 2013.
15. C.-L. Chang, W.-M. Chen, and C.-H. Hung, "Reliable consideration of P2P-based VoD system with interleaved video frame distribution," IEEE Systems Journal, vol. 8, no. 1, pp. 304–312, 2014.
16. W. Zhang, Z. Li, and Q. Zheng, "SAMP: supporting multisource heterogeneity in mobile P2P IPTV system," IEEE Transactions on Consumer Electronics, vol. 59, no. 4, pp. 772–778, 2013.
17. N. Kumar, J.-H. Lee, and J. J. P. C. Rodrigues, "Intelligent mobile video surveillance system as a Bayesian coalition game in vehicular sensor networks: learning automata approach," IEEE Transactions on Intelligent Transportation Systems, vol. 16, no. 3, pp. 1148–1161, 2015.
18. C. Xu, F. Zhao, J. Guan, H. Zhang, and G.-M. Muntean, "QoEdriven user-centric vod services in urban multihomed P2Pbased vehicular networks," IEEE Transactions on Vehicular Technology, vol. 62, no. 5, pp. 2273–2289, 2013.
19. J.-L. Kuo, C.-H. Shih, C.-Y. Ho, and Y.-C. Chen, "A cross-layer approach for real-time multimedia streaming on wireless peerto-peer ad hoc network,"Ad Hoc Networks, vol. 11, no. 1, pp. 339– 354, 2013.
20. D. Bethanabhotla, G. Caire, and M. J. Neely, "Adaptive video streaming for wireless networks with multiple users and helpers," IEEE Transactions on Communications, vol. 63, no. 1, pp. 268–285, 2015.
21. H. Shen, Z. Li, Y. Lin, and J. Li, "Socialtube: P2P-assisted video sharing in online social networks," IEEE Transactions on Parallel and Distributed Systems, vol. 25, no. 9, pp. 2428–2440, 2014.
22. H. Shen, Y. Lin, and J. Li, "A social-network-aided efficient peer-to-peer live streaming system," IEEE/ACM Transactions on Networking, vol. 23, no. 3, pp. 987–1000, 2015.
23. N. Kumar, S. Zeadally, and J. J. P. C. Rodrigues, "QoS-aware hierarchical web caching scheme for online video streaming applications in internet-based vehicular ad hoc networks," IEEE Transactions on Industrial Electronics, vol. 62, no. 12, pp. 7892– 7900, 2015.
24. L. Zhou, Z. Yang, Y. Wen, and J. J. P. C. Rodrigues, "Distributed wireless video scheduling with delayed control information," IEEE Transactions on Circuits and Systems for Video Technology, vol. 24, no. 5, pp. 889–901, 2014.
25. L. Zhou, Z. Yang, J. J. P. C. Rodrigues, and M. Guizani, "Exploring blind online scheduling for mobile cloud multimedia services," IEEE Wireless Communications, vol. 20, no. 3, pp. 54–61, 2013.
26. C. Doulkeridis, A. Vlachou, K. Nørvag, Y. Kotidis, and M. ° Vazirgiannis, "Efficient search based on content similarity over self-organizing P2P networks," Peer-to-Peer Networking and Applications, vol. 3, no. 1, pp. 67–79, 2010.
27. H. Shen, Y. Lin, and J. Li, "Social connections in user-generated content video systems: analysis and recommendation," IEEE Transactions on Parallel and Distributed Systems, vol. 26, no. 1, pp. 252–261, 2015.
28. C. Xu, S. Jia, L. Zhong, H. Zhang, and G.-M. Muntean, "Antinspired mini-community-based solution for video-on-demand services in wireless mobile networks," IEEE Transactions on Broadcasting, vol. 60, no. 2, pp. 322–335, 2014.
29. D. Perdana and R. F. Sari, "Performance evaluation of corrupted signal caused by random way point and Gauss Markov mobility model on IEEE 1609.4 standards," in Proceedings of the 4th IEEE International Symposium on Next-Generation Electronics (ISNE '15), May 2015.
30. C. Xu, Z. Li, J. Li, H. Zhang, and G.-M. Muntean, "Cross-layer fairness-driven concurrent multipath video delivery over heterogeneous wireless networks," IEEE Transactions on Circuits and Systems for Video Technology, vol. 25, no. 7, pp. 1175–1189, 2015.

CHAPTER 5

VIDEO TRAFFIC FLOW ANALYSIS IN DISTRIBUTED SYSTEM DURING INTERACTIVE SESSION

Soumen Kanrar and Niranjan Kumar Mandal

INTRODUCTION

An interactive video on demand (VOD) system requires smooth data streaming for the user irrespective of geographic location to access on demand video, such as movies, electronic encyclopedia, interactive games, and educational resources from the distributed storage servers through a high-speed network. The number of customer's requests increases exponentially in the local cluster domain. It brings a heavy load to the network system. The consequence is a high rate of customer request drop and huge bandwidth wastage. Next-Generation Network (NGN) provides multimedia services over broadband based networks, which supports high definition DVD quality multimedia data streaming content. The multimedia data streaming services are thus seen to be merging mainly in three areas such as computing, communication, and broadcasting. It has numerous advantages. More exploration for the large-scale deployment of the storage system is still needed. The distributed system hierarchy of multimedia storage has focused on analyzing the system architecture. The distributed system hierarchy of multimedia storage becomes important due to the services supported by the high-speed networks, multimedia storage servers, and distributed multimedia file systems. A customer will be able to request a multimedia stream from anywhere and at any time. In response to a customer's request, local or remote storage system will deliver a high quality digitized multimedia data stream directly to the clients set-top-box over a local distributed network. The local cluster domain may store a complete or a partial set of multimedia data streams. As the overall VOD user population grows, newer local clusters are added to the distributed system, and the network capacities are sized to match the increased user population for that neighborhood. Clearly, it indicates the need for scalability of the distributed system hierarchy of a multimedia storage system. The remote site may be archival in nature, providing a permanent repository for all multimedia streams, or they may act as replicated servers such as mirrored sites. The remote sites may provide service to many user populations. The distributed system itself is a hierarchy of neighborhoods in the geographical region. If a request cannot be served from the local site, it may be directed to other remote sites. A storage container either local or remote has to reserve sufficient I/O and network bandwidths before accepting a customer's request. We define a server channel as the server resource required to deliver a multimedia stream, while guaranteeing a client's continuous playback. In general, the VOD service can be characterized as long lived session with a typical movie on demand service runs for 1 hour to 2 hours. Thus, sufficient storage and I/O bandwidth must be available, and we need a solution that efficiently utilizes the server and network resources. Class based admission control [1] was used in the "video on demand system" to get better performance. However, some level of planning and managing of the resource is required in the Internet-based [2, 3] video on demand to enhance the performance up to an optimum level. In fact, the network I/O bottleneck has been observed in many earlier systems, such as Network Project in Orlando [4] and Microsoft's Tiger Video Fileserver [5]. The multicast facilities of modern communication network [6–8] offer an efficient means of one to many data transmissions. Multicast techniques can also significantly improve the VOD performance by reducing the required network bandwidth greatly, so that the overall network load is reduced. In other ways the multicasting alleviates the workload of the VOD server and improves the system throughput by batching requests [9, 10]. In this paper, we present a new methodology

Citation: Soumen Kanrar and Niranjan Kumar Mandal, "Video Traffic Flow Analysis in Distributed System during Interactive Session," Advances in Multimedia, vol. 2016, Article ID 7829570, 14 pages, 2016. doi:10.1155/2016/7829570

to reduce the traffic load in the "distributed video on demand system" for different types of service request in interactive session. The types of the service requests in interactive session are like fast forward, pause, stop, or move backward. Tewari and Kleinrock [11, 12] have designed a simple queueing model to shape the number of replicas corresponding to the request rate and the driven content. Zhou and Xu [13] have shown the target jointly maximizing the average encoding bit rate in content transfer over the network. The overall average number of content replicas that is minimizing the communication load imbalances the storage servers [14]. The brief content placement for P2P video on demand systems is presented by Suh et al. [15]. Tewari and Kleinrock [11, 12] have designed a simple queueing based model to shape the number of replicas corresponding to the request rate of the content driven. LRU (least recently used) and LRFU (least recently and frequently used) based methods worked efficiently and classified the batches of content with respect to the hit count. They efficiently update the peer cache and proxy server cache in the mesh type network for content replicas [9, 10]. The user initiative huge traffic load to the video on demand network generally follows the Zipf like distribution to analyze the traffic load and shape of the load inside the on demand system [6–8]. Li et al. [16] proposed different types of batching request model. This model integrates both the user activity and the batching model. In this model the user requests are batching and the effect of such batching is captured in a batching model. The user activity includes the various interactive modes like pause, move slowly, move fast, and so forth. The model is unable to describe the user initiative interactive operational mode. The video on demand system requires a uniform model that can be used to determine the requirements of network bandwidth at the user interactive session. The proper bandwidth requirement model at the interactive session gives the trade-off in communication and storage costs for different system resource configurations. This paper is structured as follows. Section 1 presents the brief literature survey for finding the problem in Introduction. We briefly represent the hierarchical architecture of the distributed system and the distributed database storage in Sections 2 and 3. Section 4 presents the session based multiuser model and single-user bandwidth requirement model. Section 5 illustrates the snap of the traffic flow model to this problem. Section 6 presents the parameter's description of the simulation environment and performance evaluation of the system. Section 7 presented broadly the related work on the interactive session and the related domain. The conclusion remark is followed by the references at the end of the document.

DISTRIBUTED ARCHITECTURE

Large-scale VOD system requires the servers to be arranged in a distributed fashion in order to support a large number of concurrent streams. The system architecture is hierarchical, and the local server can handle the requests from specific geographic zone. The local server in the hierarchy takes the requests from the cluster switch; if they cannot handle, then request proceeds for next level. This architecture provides the cost efficiency, reliability, and scalability of servers. Generally, servers are either tree based shaped [9] or graph structured [8]. The graph structured system often offers good quality of service for handling the requests, but the management of request, videos, and streams is complicated in the distributed system. The tree-shaped system can easily manage requests, videos, and streams, but it offers poorer quality of service than the former. In order to evaluate the effectiveness of distribution strategies in such a hierarchy, the authors of [2, 17] investigate how to reduce storage and network costs while taking the customer's behavior into account.

In the distributed system hierarchy of multimedia storage architecture, local proxy servers are installed at strategic locations in the network (closer to the clients). Remote clusters can communicate with the network's distributed storage and with its local proxy servers immediately. Each local cluster server can support a number of customers connected to it through a cluster switch. The customers are connected to the distributed database servers through the cluster switch, which acts as an interface between the client cluster and the database servers. The proxies are used to distribute the storage contained functionality within the network by using the concept of local proxy storage according to Figure 1. If the user cannot be served by the local storage server for any reason, such as a blockage in the local network, or data is not available in the local storage, then the requesting user will be transported to the distributed multimedia storage. By locating the proxy server close to the user, it is expected that there will be significant reductions in the load on the system as a whole [6, 7]. Another advantage of the distributed local proxy video on demand system is that it can be expanded in a horizontal manner for system scalability and evolution. It can start from an initial two-level system (with a centralized multimedia server and one local proxy video server) to a system with as many local proxy servers as needed. The system is incorporated with the distributed multimedia storage system. The distributed system may utilize a lower than average network bandwidth and have a higher system reliability, but at the expense of significant amount of local storage systems.

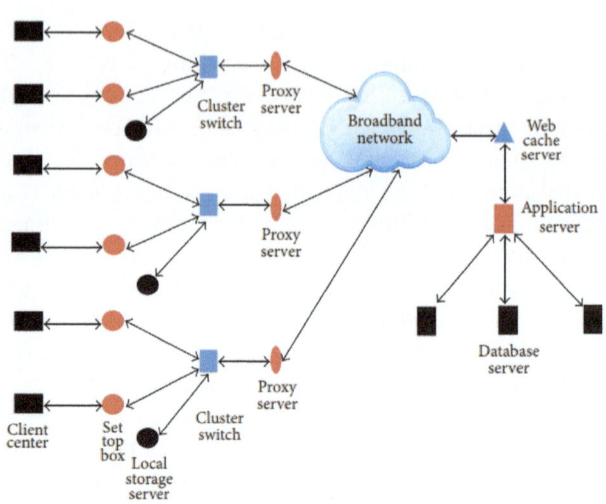

Figure 1: Distributed hierarchy system.

DISTRIBUTED DATABASE SERVER

If the request is not served by the local storage then it will proceed to remote storage. The working structure of distributed storage is presented in Figure 2. The video on demand viewer sends the request simultaneously via the connected network. Here we present streams of request access from the particular video storage site. Initially, all requests from HTTP or HTTPs are forwarded to web cache memory. Now the web cache memory that has the content of the video stream is forwarded directly to the viewer. In case the web cache memory does not have the required content then the request is forwarded to application server in the list of application servers. The application web server is selected from the least loaded application server [4, 6]. The application web server searches the required video stream from a set of the well connected distributed database servers in Figure 2.

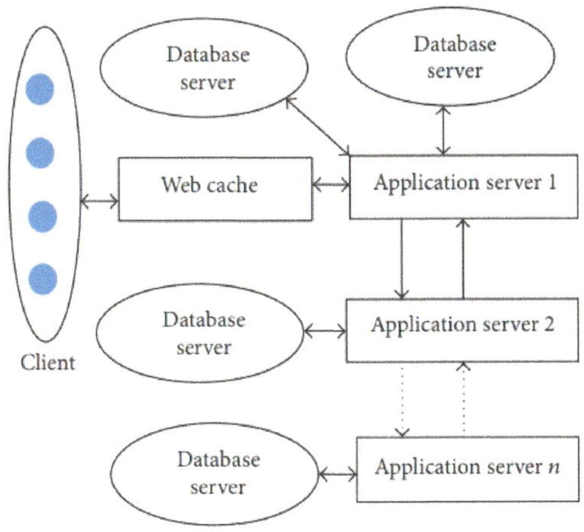

Figure 2: Distributed database server.

In the large-scale video on demand system, bandwidth optimization largely depends on the minimum hop counts in high demand stage or in a specific time or some of the days in a week [9]. The efficiency of the video on demand system depends on the "least recently and frequently used" (LRFU) cache updating policy at each server. LRFU policy is composed of the two dynamically growing cache memory blocks "least recently used" (LRU) and "least frequently used" (LFU) cache memory [9]. The performance of the audio video on demand system purely depends on the efficient cache replacement at the proxy server [10]. The initial submitted request pattern to the web proxy container is approximately presented by the Zif like probability distribution [4, 8].

ANALYTIC STRUCTURE

The required bandwidth varies during the interactive session. Users use various modes of playing operation such as fast forward, skip, pause, and rewind. The required bandwidth continuously varies with the mode of user operation. In general, let p be the initial (prior) probability to select a channel according to the binomial distribution, the total available bandwidth $B_{(\Delta t)}$ (i.e., in the trunk) at session Δt and W is channel required bandwidth at that session, ($p \approx W/B_{(\Delta t)}$). In real time W (assuming) varies according to the user playing mode of operation within (W_{min}, W_{max}) such that ($W_{min} \leq \cdots \leq W_{min} +_{(i)} \leq \cdots \leq W_{max}$) for the ith type of real interactive session; $t(i)$ is the bandwidth demand adjustment function. It initially, Wmax, is assigned to each channel, but in real time when a huge request is coming at a session, the channel is assigned with adjusted bandwidth or otherwise at least Wmin is available. If this is impossible, then the request is buffered to the queue (at the 1st queue of the proxy server or any intermediate router) [18]. For connection, setup Wmin is required and then bandwidth is assigned to the channel according to the user's requirement and the availability of the bandwidth. User requirement or required bandwidth is maximized and subject to condition of availability of the bandwidth from the trunk. During the phase of connection startup to connection closed, the user behavior goes through a number of major interactive sessions in a random fashion. We denote the different mode of operations like fast forward (I^1), play normally (I^2), play slowly or move slowly (I^3), rewind (I^4), pause (I^5), and so forth. So, for the case $I^i \geq I^j$ it seems to be $i \geq j$ according to the bandwidth requirement. Now, there is a possibility of more than one mutually exclusive outcome for each type of interactive operation during any session.

Let e_i for $1 \leq i \leq k$ be k mutually exclusive and exhaustive outcome with the respective probabilities p_i for user mode of operation (Exp i). For example, p_1 is for fast forward, p_2 for play normal, p_3 for play slow, p_4 for rewind, and so forth. If e_1 occurs x_1 times, e_2 occurs x_2 times$\cdots e_k$ occurs x_k times assuming that ei occurs x_i times for $1 \leq i \leq k$. Now, m is the number of independent observations of any customer behavior in a session and then $\sum x_i = m$. So for the Tth customer we get

$$P(X = X_T) = p(x_1, x_2, \ldots, x_k) = C p_1^{x_1} p_2^{x_2} \cdots p_k^{x_k} \tag{1}$$

Here, C is the number of permutations of the events.

so

$$C = \underline{|m} / \underline{|x_1} \underline{|x_2} \underline{|x_3} \cdots \underline{|x_k}$$

Hence

$$p(x_1, x_2, \ldots, x_k) = \frac{\underline{|m}}{\underline{|x_1}\underline{|x_2}\underline{|x_3} \cdots \underline{|x_k}} p_1^{x_1} p_2^{x_2} \cdots p_k^{x_k}$$

$$\text{for, } 0 \leq x_i \leq m, \sum x_i \leq m$$

$$= \frac{\underline{|m}}{\prod_{i=1}^{K} \underline{|x_i}} \prod_{i=1}^{K} p_i^{x_i}. \tag{2}$$

This is true for "single customer" when the allocated bandwidth for that channel is $\geq W_{max}$

So $n \approx_{(\Delta t)} / W_{max}$ and $B_{(\Delta t)}$ is the total bandwidth of the trunk in ideal situation or scenario at session Δt (Exp ii). n is the number of active links for corresponding users. Hence every customer has an independent interactive mode of operational choice.

Session Based Multiuser Model

So, according to function (1) the distribution is

$$P(X_1 \cap X_2 \cap \cdots \cap X_n) = \prod_{T=1}^{n} P(X = X_T) \tag{3}$$

In an interactive session, different bandwidth is required for different service modes like pause, fast forward, rewind, play normally, or play slowly; that is, number of frame downloads by the user node varies, but the frame length is fixed for different interactive session. When the channel is assigned to the user, then at least minimum bandwidth y is assigned to the user for any interactive session. Consider $\Rightarrow W_{min} \leq y \leq W max$. It follows the probability distribution function

$$p_i = \frac{y - W_{min}}{W_{max} - W_{min}} \tag{4}$$

In a session, we get the mixed type distribution by (1), (2), and (3)

$$P(X_1 \cap X_2 \cap \cdots \cap X_n)$$

$$= \prod_{t=1}^{n} \frac{\lfloor m}{\prod_{i=1}^{K} \lfloor x_i} \prod_{i=1}^{K} \left[\int_{W_{min}}^{W_{max}} \left[\frac{y - W_{min}}{W_{max} - W_{min}} \right]^{x_i} dy \right] \tag{5}$$

Here, n is the total number of users in the video on demand system.$m$is the total number of interactive modes used by the particular customer in that session. k is the particular type of modes like pause, move forward, rewind, and so forth and x_i is the number of times in which modes are used by that user in that session.

Single-User Bandwidth Requirement Model

According to Expression (Exp i), i is any type of interactive mode of operation for any individual user. The modes of user operation are like pause, rewind, fast forward, move slowly, and so forth. Let bi be the required bandwidth for particular interactive mode of operation in that session, $W\min \leq b_i \leq W_{max}$, $bi > 0$, $i \in I^{>0}$. If, in a session, there are possible L numbers of interactive modes, then the bandwidth requirement of the user mode of operation satisfies expression

$$W_{min} \leq \max \{b_i\}_{i \in \{1,\ldots,L\}} \approx W. \tag{6}$$

In any interactive mode of operation in a session, there are multiple sub sessions. So the occurrence of that particular interactive sub session is

$$P\left(\frac{(X_i = b_i)}{(X_1 = b_1, \ldots, X_{i-1} = b_{i-1})} \right) \tag{7}$$

To evaluate (7), we require finding out the volume of the solid sphere in k dimension plane such that

$$P\left(\frac{(X_i = b_i)}{(X_1 = b_1, \ldots, X_{i-1} = b_{i-1}, X_{i+1} = b_{i+1}, \ldots, X_k = b_k)} \right) \tag{8}$$

bi is the required bandwidth to continue and maintain the ith type active interactive mode and $c \geq 0$ is the very minimum bandwidth required for other passive interactive user modes of operation at the same session. So the reserved bits for other interactive service connectivity required ($c \approx W_{min}$). So expression (8) becomes

$$P\left(\frac{(X_i = b_i)}{(X_1 = c, \ldots, X_{i-1} = c, X_{i+1} = c, \ldots, X_k = c)} \right) \tag{9}$$

We can assume c as the required reserved bits for other interactive user modes of operation except ith type. In general, the k-dimensional volume of Euclidean ball of radius R in the k-dimensional Euclidean space is defined as $(R) = (\Pi^{k/2} / (k/2 + 1))$ R^k so for even and odd, we get $V_{2k}(R) = (\Pi k / k) R^{2k}$ and $V_{2k+1}(R) = (2^{k+1} \Pi^k / 2k + 1) R^{2k+1}$; here k is the number of interactive modes in a session. Due to interactive mode of user operation at each session, the volume of the sphere is changing. Now we get inequality

$$V_k(R)$$

$$\approx \frac{\Pi^{k/2}}{\lfloor((k/2) + 1)} c^{k-1} (W_{max}) \ll \frac{\Pi^{k/2}}{\lfloor((k/2) + 1)} (W_{max})^k \tag{10}$$

Here, $(x_1, \ldots, _k)$ is a k-dimensional integrand function related to k-dimension volume. If the user is active only in one interactive mode then, in special case, we can consider $(x_1, \ldots, _k) \approx (1)^k = 1$

Expression (9) becomes

$$P\left(\frac{(X_i = b_i)}{(X_1 = b_1, \ldots, X_{i-1} = b_{i-1}, X_{i+1} = b_{i+1}, \ldots, X_k = b_k)}\right)$$
$$\approx \left[\frac{\Pi^{k/2}}{|((k/2)+1)} c^{k-1} (W_{\max})\right]^{-1} \int_{\mathbb{R}^k} dx_1 \cdots dx_k. \tag{11}$$

Here we focused on finding the bandwidth requirement for ith type of user service mode of operation. Since $\int_{R}^{k} dV = \prod_{i=1}^{k}(\int_{-\infty}^{\infty} dxi)$ (Integration by parts), allocated bandwidth for that user holds true with the following expression:

$$x_1 + x_2 + \cdots + x_k \leq W,$$
$$W_{\min} < x_i \leq W_{\max}, \quad 1 \leq i \leq k \tag{12}$$

The interactive sessions are mutually independent for each customer; only one type of interactive session occurs, that is, ith type like pause or watch normally or move forward. If a viewer opens more than one window, for example, one window is paused and another window is using service required except paused, then the service request will be multiplexed to single stream through that dedicated channel that was allocated to that viewer. Expression (11) becomes

$$P\left(\frac{(X_i = b_i)}{(X_1 = b_1, \ldots, X_{i-1} = b_{i-1}, X_{i+1} = b_{i+1}, \ldots, X_k = b_k)}\right) \approx \left[\frac{\Pi^{k/2}}{|((k/2)+1)} c^{k-1} (W_{\max})\right]^{-1}$$
$$\cdot \int_{x_i=0}^{W_{\max}} \cdot \int_{x_{i-1}=0}^{[W-(x_1+\cdots+x_{i-2}+x_i+\cdots+x_k)]} \cdot \int_{x_{i+1}=0}^{[W-(x_1+\cdots+x_i+x_{i+2}+\cdots x_k)]} \cdot \int_{x_k=0}^{[W-(x_1+\cdots+x_i+\cdots+x_{k-1})]} f(x_1, \ldots, x_k)\, dx_k \cdots dx_{i+1} dx_{i-1} dx_i \tag{13}$$

TRAFFIC FLOW MODEL

In distributed local proxy architecture, local proxy servers are installed at strategic locations in the network (closer to the clients). Remote viewer clusters can communicate with the networks of distributed primary storage servers and with its local proxy servers. Each local proxy server supports continuous streaming to the number of customers connected to it through a cluster switch. The customers are also connected to the distributed multimedia storage, that is, databases through the cluster switch and proxy server. This composition acts as an interface between the client cluster and the broadband network. The main idea of distributed video on demand (VOD) local storage (as shown in Figure 1) is to distribute the multimedia data functionality within the user cluster by using the concept of local proxy storage. If the streams cannot be served by the local storage due to reasons, such as blockage at the proxy to pull the required segment or chunk of video objects from the local multimedia storage, or the case of the unavailability of the video clips at the proxy server, then the request will be transported to the distributed database servers. To find the proxy server close to the user, it is expected that there will be significant reductions in the load on the system as a whole [6, 7]. Another advantage of the distributed architecture system is that it can be expanded in a horizontal manner for system scalability and evolution. It can start from an initial two-level system (with a centralized multimedia server and one local storage video server) to a system with as many local servers as needed. Compared with the centralized multimedia server system, the distributed system may utilize a lower than average network bandwidth. It has a higher system reliability, but at the expense of needing a significant amount of local storage to the architecture. The proposed model of the distributed video on demand architecture satisfies the basic requirements of the distributed networks. Let n be the maximum number of customer's requests, serviceable at the proxy server for a user centric cluster. Now Rd is the disk bandwidth and R_p is the client request playback rate including the interactive session at the local storage. Then the stream available at the proxy server will be served to the customer, if the condition still holds true, $n \leq \lfloor R_d/R_p \rfloor$. The request admission control test at the proxy server determines whether the proxy server is able to serve maximum n number of requests. The proposed methodology is used for proxy server. Proxy server has total bandwidth capacity with C ports. Let us have k classes of service requests for interactive operations; each class receives mean rate λ_i to the proxy server for i=1 to k related to different service classes. Service requests are categories of fast forward with one frame, two frames, up to m number of frames, pause, move backward, and so forth. Initially the proxy server port capacities are divided into a number of sections with each section having port capacity C_j, for j=0 to k, and $C_i = Cj$ if $i = j$. The overall proxy port capacity is $C=\sum_{j=0}^{k} Cj$. Initially, each section is assigned with specific category of the service requests. At any interactive session of time $\Delta t$the occupied size of the section of portsCj for j=0 to k can be changed dynamically. It totally depended upon the viewer's choice. So at any session of time Δt, if the request for a particular service class service finds that the specific preassigned section is blocked, then it will search for free port in other sections of the ports. This is mutual shareable port strategy. Request for the section "a" will be admitted to a section "b" with probability

$$p(a,b) = p\left(\frac{(b)}{(a = \text{blocked})}\right) = p_a^b \tag{14}$$

For example, $\sum_{i=0}^{k} pa^{(a+i)\bmod(k+1)} = 1$. So, request generates in viewer cluster and arrives at the connected proxy server with mean Poisson rate. Here the maximum ports occupancy for class i type of service request is Q_i for $i=0$ to k. When a request for class "a" type of service arrives, check whether Q_a ≻ occupancy (C_a). For simplicity we consider port occupancy at the session Δt is $C^{\#}_{a}$ such that occupancy $(C_a) = C^{\#}_{a}$ for $a = 0, 1, \ldots, k$. If so, then a service request of "a" type of service request is admitted to the corresponding "a" section of port with probability p^a_{a}. Now, $p_a^{a} = (Q_a - C^{\#}_{a})/Q_a$. So the request is admitted and updates the port occupancy class as $C^{\#}_{a} = C^{\#}_{a+1}$ at the session Δt. If $Q_a \leq$ occupancy (C_a), then checking continues into other port sections. This happens due to the sectional subnetwork between each proxy to the corresponding local storage in the "distributed video on demand system." This forms a compact topology. To admit the request to the VOD system, checking is continued into the other service section of the port while satisfying the condition $Q_{a+j} \succ$ occupancy (C_{a+j}) for finding free port. If free port is available in the other section then the request is admitted by the proxy server and updates the probability p^{a+j}_{a} for $j = 0, 1, \ldots, k$ according to Lemma 1 and expression (17).

Lemma

Lemma 1. A system will be compact if and only if the execution of any specific event fully depends mutually on other events in compound execution. Proof. In a compact system, the resources are shareable such as channel, link, and port; that is, we prove the converse case; let, $x_1, x_2, \ldots,$ be n mutually dependent events. Here we show that compound execution $(x_1, x_2, x_3, \ldots, _{n-1}, x_n)$ depends on the occurrence of each specific event x_i, that is, $p(x_i)$ for $1 \leq i \leq n$. Now,

$$\begin{aligned} p(x_1, x_2, x_3, \ldots, x_{n-1}, x_n) &= p(x_2, x_3, \ldots, x_{n-1}, x_n) \\ &\cdot p\left(\frac{x_1}{(x_2, x_3, \ldots, x_{n-1}, x_n)}\right) = p(x_3, \ldots, x_{n-1}, x_n) \\ &\cdot p\left(\frac{x_2}{(x_3, \ldots, x_{n-1}, x_n)}\right) \\ &\cdot p\left(\frac{x_1}{(x_2, x_3, \ldots, x_{n-1}, x_n)}\right) = \cdots = p(x_n) \\ &\cdot p\left(\frac{x_{n-1}}{x_n}\right) \\ &\cdot p\left(\frac{x_{n-2}}{(x_n, x_{n-1})}\right) \cdots p\left(\frac{x_1}{(x_2, x_3, \ldots, x_{n-1}, x_n)}\right). \end{aligned} \tag{15}$$

Hence this proves the system is compact.

So according to Lemma 1 and compactness in the local subnetwork of "distributed video on demand system" we get the following expression:

$$\begin{aligned} &p\left(Q_a \leq C^{\#}_{a}, Q_{a+1} \leq C^{\#}_{a+1}, Q_{a+2} \leq C^{\#}_{a+2}, \ldots, Q_{a+j-1} \leq C^{\#}_{a+j-1}, Q_{a+j} \succ C^{\#}_{a+j}\right) \\ &= p\left(Q_{a+1} \leq C^{\#}_{a+1}, Q_{a+2} \leq C^{\#}_{a+2}, \ldots, Q_{a+j-1} \leq C^{\#}_{a+j-1}, Q_{a+j} \succ C^{\#}_{a+j}\right) \\ &\cdot p\left(\frac{(Q_a \leq C^{\#}_{a})}{(Q_{a+1} \leq C^{\#}_{a+1}, Q_{a+2} \leq C^{\#}_{a+2}, \ldots, Q_{a+j-1} \leq C^{\#}_{a+j-1}, Q_{a+j} \succ C^{\#}_{a+j})}\right) \\ &= p\left(Q_{a+j} \succ C^{\#}_{a+j}\right) p\left(\frac{(Q_{a+j-1} \leq C^{\#}_{a+j-1})}{(Q_{a+j} \succ C^{\#}_{a+j})}\right) \\ &\cdot p\left(\frac{(Q_{a+j-2} \leq C^{\#}_{a+j-2})}{(Q_{a+j-1} \leq C^{\#}_{a+j-1}, Q_{a+j} \succ C^{\#}_{a+j})}\right) \cdots p\left(\frac{(Q_a \leq C^{\#}_{a})}{(Q_{a+1} \leq C^{\#}_{a+1}, Q_{a+2} \leq C^{\#}_{a+2}, \ldots, Q_{a+j-1} \leq C^{\#}_{a+j-1}, Q_{a+j} \succ C^{\#}_{a+j})}\right) \\ &= p_a^{a+j} \text{ (say)}. \end{aligned} \tag{16}$$

By reversing the order we get

$$\begin{aligned} &p\left(Q_a \leq C^{\#}_{a}, Q_{a+1} \leq C^{\#}_{a+1}, Q_{a+2} \leq C^{\#}_{a+2}, \ldots, Q_{a+j-1}\right. \\ &\left.\leq C^{\#}_{a+j-1}, Q_{a+j} \succ C^{\#}_{a+j}\right) = p_a^{a+j}. \end{aligned} \tag{17}$$

Now update the occupancy class by $C^{\#}_{a+j} = C^{\#}_{a+j+1}$ for any particular $j = 1, \ldots, k$ according to Figure 3. Otherwise, the service request will not be admitted to the local system. If the request cannot be considered, then it is considered blocked for local networking system and the request is to be forwarded to the remote database server before discarding from the distributed system.

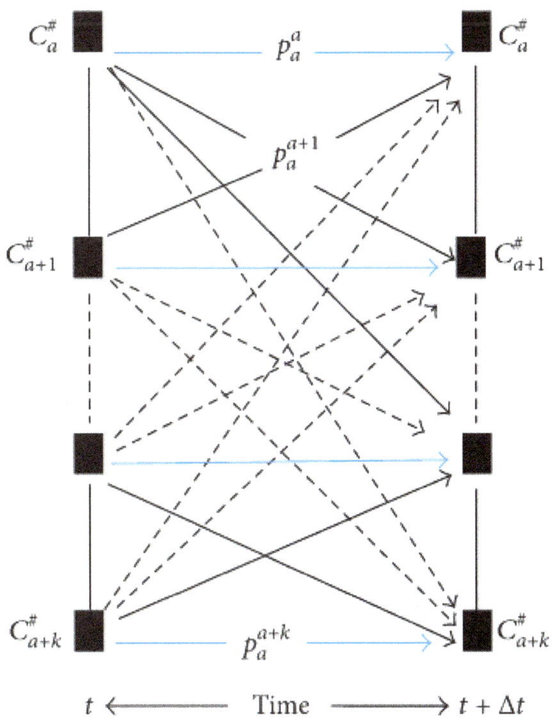

Figure 3: Occupancy transition in a session.

The request is forwarded to retrieve video content from the distributed data storage. The distributed data servers are presented in Figure 2. Let us consider ps as the probability that s out of N video storage servers are active. Active means that the storage server has the required encoded video file, and the end-to-end link is live throughout the streaming at the session Δt. So, we get the expression $p_s = (\ )\ \rho_s\ (1 - \rho)N{-}s$. The event space is {0, 1} with the probability {1/2, 1/2} for ρ. Let $_{(\Delta t)}$ be the aggregate stationary bit rate from the distributed server according to Figure 2 at session Δt. Now, $_{(\Delta t)}$ is the equivalent capacity of networking with respect to bit streaming rate for the whole network according to Figure 1 at session Δt. The value of $_{(\Delta t)}$ is obtained by computing the smallest positive integer k'. k' is the least positive integer number of servers that have the required video objects or chunk of the video stream. If L and$M$are two events such that $M = (_{(\Delta t)} \leq {}_{(\Delta t)})$ and L={At least k' number data storage is currently streaming, out of the N data storage server at session Δt},

$$p\left(\frac{L}{M}\right) = \frac{p(M/L)\,p(L)}{p(M)}$$

$$= \binom{N}{k'+1} \rho^{k'+1} (1-\rho)^{N-k'-1} + \cdots$$

$$+ \binom{N}{k'+r} \rho^{k'+r} (1-\rho)^{N-k'-r} + \cdots \quad (18)$$

for $r \in I^{>0}$. So, $k' \leq N$ is the selected number of minimum database servers from the N number of database servers.

There is at least k' number of servers that have the required segment. Now the search for video segments or stream generated a query and broadcast from the application server towards the database servers. So the optimization problem becomes concentrated to find the value of k'. In the next section, we present the video stream searching procedure to identify the storage location that is the database server IP address.

Session Based Query Matched Algorithm

Algorithm 1 runs at the application server.

```
At t = t_s // t_s is the start time of the
        // session
Var Queue_of_finite_Size : integer
While (t ≠ (t_s + Δt))
{
Initial node {S} // set of data base storage
        // nodes
Boolean matched_node_not_found ← True
Q ← Queue of finite Size
Begin
Q ← push (S) // first in first out
while (match_node_not_found) do
{
    v ← Pop (Q) // pop is queue operation
For each {w} from single hop neighbor of v
   {
   If (query string ∈ w)
   then
       {
       match_node_not_found ← False
       return node ID of w
       exit
       }
   else
   Q ← Push (w) // Push is a queue operation
   } // End for
} // End Inner While
t = t_s + Δt
} // End Outer While
Send("query matched node not found")
        // To application Server
End
Stop
```

Algorithm 1

PERFORMANCE ANALYSES

The simulation parameters are considered according to the real life streaming scenario in distributed architecture. The parameter's values are summarized and presented in Table 1. For simplicity, we have considered that individual occupancy class of customers is contained in equal number of ports at every "sector of the proxy server." A sector of size n ports can be occupied by "occupancy class of customer." The size of "occupancy class of customer" is ($6n$) during the multithreading operation evoked. The traffic arrival rate with different class of the service requests started from 1 Mb/s and ended at 10.5 Mb/s. The number of viewers for each client center is 20. Figures 4–7 present the performance of distributed video on demand system at the local network with respect to analytical methodology.

Table 1: Simulation parameters.

Parameter	Value
Number of viewers per client cluster	20
Number of client clusters	10
Different service request arrival (minimum)	1 Mb/sec
Different service request arrival (maximum)	10.5 Mb/sec
Number of ports for each type service	10
Port access time	140 sec
Number of different service classes	20
Number of application servers	7 to 6
Number of database servers	3 to 5
Simulation time	460 sec
Unified parameter (k/n)	
k number of interactive modes used in a session	
n number of active channels used	
Set 1	0.2 to 1.0 step 0.2
Set 2	0.05 to 0.1 step 0.02

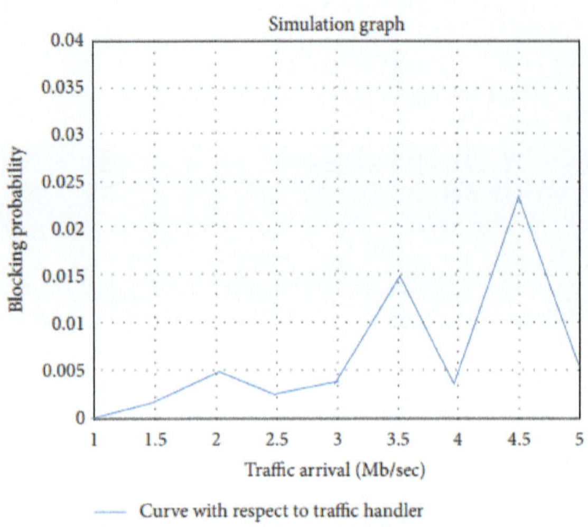

Figure 4: Blocking probability versus arrival rate with respect to incoming service requests.

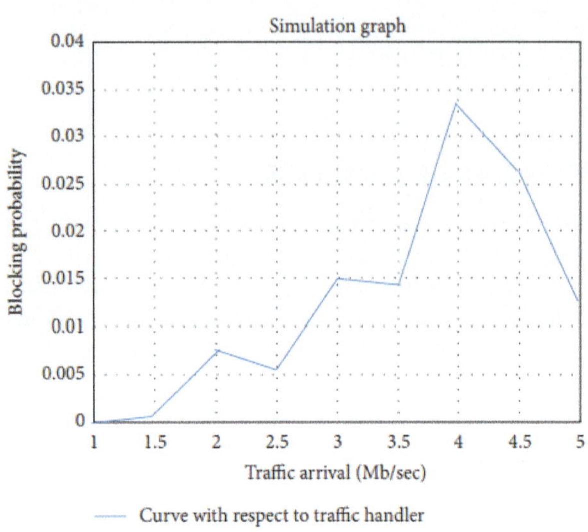

Figure 5: Blocking probability versus arrival rate with respect to the randomly generated probability set.

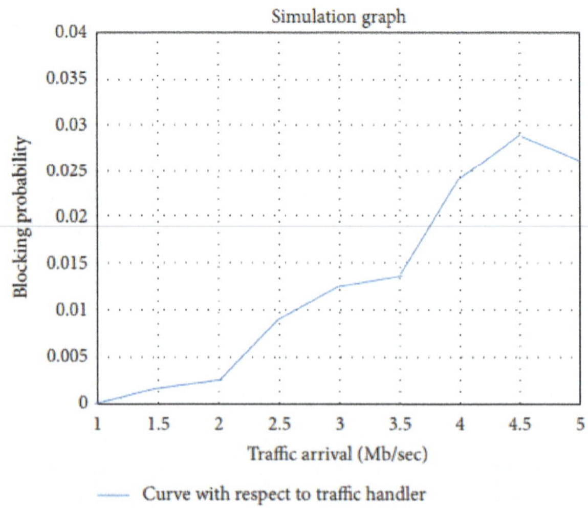

Figure 6: Performance with third probability set.

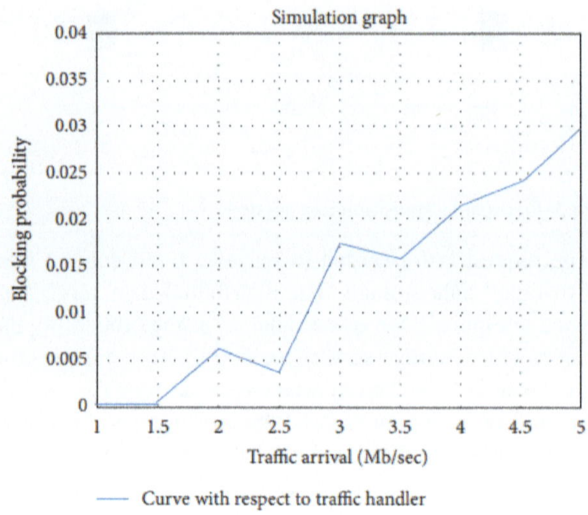

Figure 7: Performance with fourth probability set.

We have considered 1000 trials and mean of the data is presented in the flowing figures. Figure 4 presents the blockage in the "distributed video on demand system" with respect to the incoming "service requests" traffic flows from the 20 clusters towards the proxy server; here the first sector is blocked. The performance of the distributed system at the local network is evaluated with randomly generated probability set (a, b) for the different occupancy class of the service requests. At the first sector, that is, (a = 1) and $2 \leq b \leq 20$, where sector a=1 is blocked. Figure 5 presents the performance of the distributed VOD system with respect to the randomly generated probability set $p(a, b)$ for a=2, $1 \leq b \leq 20$, and $b = \not{2}$; here sector a=2 is blocked. The "request for service" traffic arrival rate to the proxy server varies within 1 Mb/second to 10.5 Mb/second with increment of 0.5 Mb/second. Figure 6 presents the performance of the distributed video on demand system at the proxy server, with respect to the randomly generated probability set (a, b). Now, a=3, $1 \leq b \leq 20$, and $b = \not{3}$; here sector a=3 is blocked. Similarly Figure 7 presents the simulation graph when the sector a=4 is blocked at the proxy server. Figures 8 and 9 present the comparative study of system performance at the proxy server during the pull steam operation for different service requirement. The "pull data operation" draws raw data from every local storage to a connected proxy server in distributed architecture. The service requests are different types of service like fast forward, pause, and move backward. Figures 8 and 9 present the comparative graph at one proxy server. The pull operation retrieves multiplexed raw data stream from local storage to the connected proxy server.The plotted graphs are the system performance with and without proposed methodology of the service request handling. Both the figures have shown when the methodology of traffic handling is not used the blocking at the proxy server of "the distributed video on demand system" increases very rapidly. Figure 8 presents the comparative study of a blocked sector a=3 at the corresponding proxy server. Figure 9 presents the comparative study of a blocked sector a=4 at the corresponding proxy server. Both Figures 8 and 9 show that the blocking rate increases with an exponential growth without using the methodology.

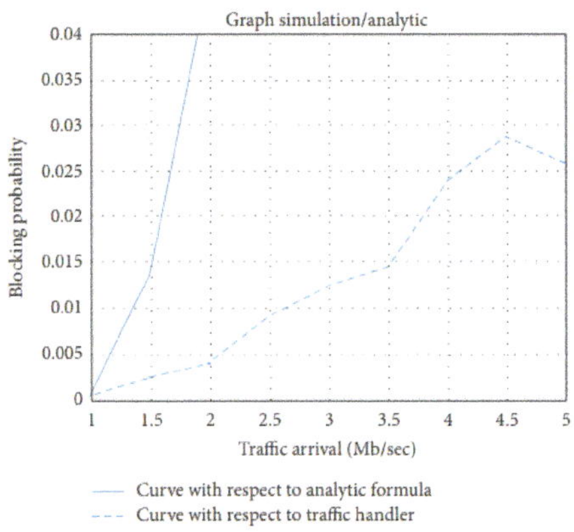

Figure 8: Comparison of service request from local storage with third probability set.

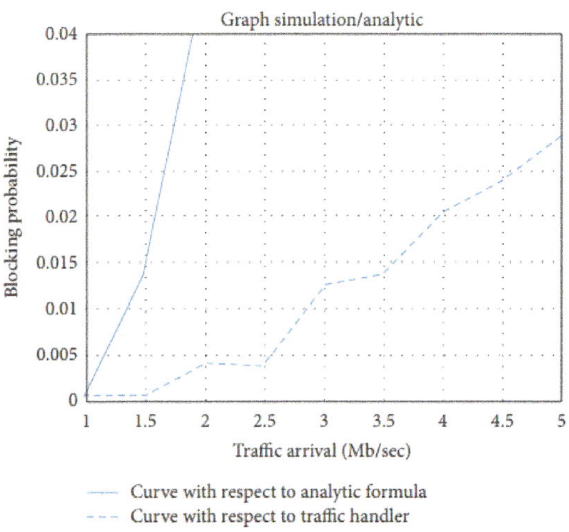

Figure 9: Comparison of request server from local storage with fourth probability set.

When we use methodology, the blocking curve is below the threshold level. Clearly the "service of request" can be handled very efficiently by using the methodology at the proxy server for the distributed VOD system. On the other hand, when the load on the video on demand system decreases, this in turn will increase the overall system performance. The packet loss is clearly reduced efficiently by the methodology which enhances the system performance. In the 2nd part of simulation, we consider distributed database storage that is well connected to the application servers.

The service request is submitted to the proxy server but cannot be served from the connected local server. The service request proceeded further towards the web cache of the distributed database server. The simulation uses the stream search algorithm run at the application server. In the 2nd stage of simulation, we consider seven application servers, and every application server is well connected with three database storage servers according to Figure 2. Similarly, we consider six application servers, and each application server is connected with five data storage servers in the next phase of simulation. We have considered 90% confidence level for acceptance. From Figure 10, we have noticed that 42000 numbers of user service requests well responded from hop count 4. Figure 11 shows that 51000 numbers of user service requests responded from hop count 3. So the balanced storing distribution of the video stream among the database servers reduces the searching cost and hence reduces the delay and packet drop. If we consider a rough estimate to measure the performance metric for the proposed methodology as the sum of the "number of requests served," that is, li multiply the hop counts hi which gives $\sum n\ i{=}1(li * hi)$, the expression gives the following performance metric score value according to Figure 10 that is 368000 and 317000 according to Figure 11. The score value directly depended on the number of computations to search the corresponding stream according to the proposed algorithm. The performance of the system increases as the score value decreases. In the third stage of simulation, we have considered the compact network where the data can be pulled for the user interactive session. The size of the request inside the network grows from 0 to 1000 in one minute that is, 60 seconds presented in the horizontal axis. The vertical axis is the normalized traffic load with respect to maximum bandwidth on demand requirement, and the distributed network provides the amount at a session. We consider the unified demand parameter as ($\approx k/n$) at 90% confidence interval; according to (13) and expression (Exp ii), k is the number of interactive modes used in a session and n is the number of active links for corresponding users. So, n depended upon the size of the network at that session. But, $n{\approx}_{(\Delta t)}/W_{\max} \Rightarrow$ parameters $\approx k(w_{\max})/B_{(\Delta t)}$ and $B_{(\Delta t)}$ is the total bandwidth of the trunk provided in ideal situation or scenario at session Δt.

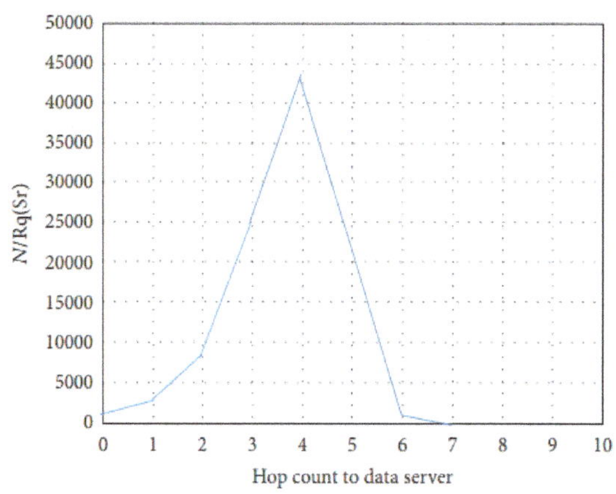

Figure 10: Service request served from database server to application server (orientation 1).

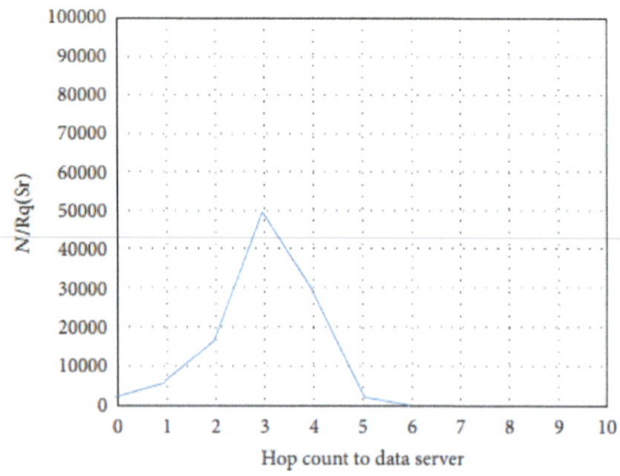

Figure 11: Service request served from database server to application server (orientation 2).

Figures 12 and 13 present the traffic load inside the distributed network for various stages of the user driven interactive session. We observed from the figures that the traffic load increases by the increases over the number of users who operates the user driven interactive mode of operation at any session.The unified demand parameter value increases from 0.2 to 1.0 with the step size 0.2 for a particular session. Figure 13 presents the normalized traffic load at that interactive session, for a number of peer nodes, presented in the distributed system.

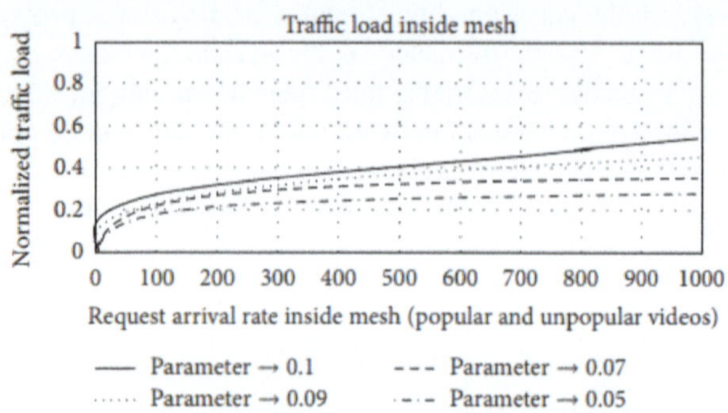

Figure 12: Normalized traffic load in interactive session (lower range of parameters).

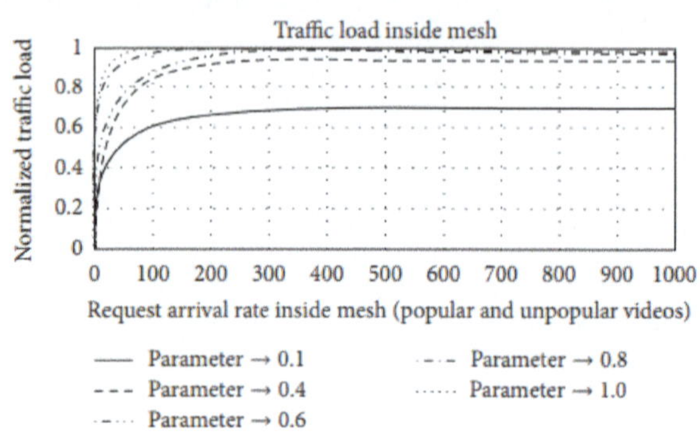

Figure 13: Normalized traffic load in interactive session (higher range of parameters).

The peer node is the representation of local storage or proxy servers or distributed storage in distributed system. Similar type of results is presented in Figure 12 for the unified demand parameter value starting from 0.05 to 0.1 with step size 0.02 for another interactive session with the same set of distributed network environments. In both the cases, we have considered the duration of the interactive session is 60 seconds and 1000 trials.

RELATED WORK

Interactive operation on multimedia systems represents a key technology. It is evolving from viewer demand and research prototypes to commercial deployments. Supporting truly and efficiently interactive multimedia services require smooth providing of personalized, dedicated channels or sessions for each user. For this particular set of services, the user requires complete control over the session and has the freedom to explore the depth of both live and stored archive. Development of these interactive multimedia services requires solving a diverse set of technical problems, many of which are tractable. According to Little and Venkatesh, in the interactive services, virtual VCR capabilities and interfaces to view parallel media streams are the most crucial requirement for video on demand system [19]. The earlier work presented by Paxson and Floyd [20], on Poisson processes for analytic simplicity, and a number of traffic studies have shown that packet interarrivals are not exponentially distributed. In this work, authors considered 24 wide-area traces for investigating a number of wide-area TCP arrival processes. Basically, traces are analyzed: the network, date, duration, and packet (amount). For the analysis purpose tracer considered TCP connection interarrivals, TELNET packet interarrivals, and FTPDATA connection arrivals. The Pareto distribution plays a role both in TELNET packet interarrivals and in the size of FTPDATA burst. Huang et al. [21] mainly focused on the single video stream pull approach. The single peer only redistributes the video stream that it is currently using. This work shows that 95 percentile server bandwidth costs would have been reserved for single peer assisted employment that was instead used. The streaming sessions trace records that were generated by the same Windows Media Player (WMP). Chat application does not consume huge amounts of traffic. This implies that catering to such users can be a promising way of attracting them, especially in low bandwidth environments. The chat traffic uses neither a well defined port nor a well defined protocol, but there exists a wide spectrum of protocols [22]. It is like IRC protocol used by IRC networks or their applet-based user interface equivalents: custom application protocols used by HTML Web chat systems running on top of HTTP. Diot and Gautier [23] describe the design, implementation, and evaluation of MiMaze. MiMaze is the multiplayers game with a distributed architecture using the multicast backbone for carrying IP multicast traffic over the Internet. It describes the design of dedicated transmission control mechanisms. MiMaze used distributed communication architecture based on the IP multicast protocol suite (RTP/UDP/IP). This work analyzed distributed interactive game on the multicast Internet. Zink et al. [24] analyze the content distribution in YouTube. It is realized and conducts a measurement study of YouTube traffic for large university campus network. Based on these measurements, author analyzed the duration and the data rate during streaming sessions. For monitoring the YouTube traffic, a client retrieves a video stream from YouTube. The multithreaded catcher obtains YouTube usage statistics for a particular campus network. Monitoring is done through a two-step process. In the first step, the collected data analyze signaling traffic, that is, HTTP message exchange between the client and the YouTube web server. In the second stage, video streaming is monitored. It is TCP headers of the video data sent from the CDN (content driven network) storage server. The traces are presented as follows: the trace length, user population, and content of local importance on the performance of different distribution architectures. The current tendency in Internet traffic is a shift from web traffic to P2P traffic. Many studies focus on the characterization of P2P traffic analysis [25, 26]. Kim et al. [27] propose a new method to identify current Internet traffic, which is a preliminary but important step toward traffic characterization. The traffic identification method is considered flow grouping in peer-to-peer (P2P) communication architecture. The video traffic is traces by the time-series graph based on the metrics traffic flows, packet, and byte, respectively. Broadband Internet service is popular in many parts of the world. Numbers of research studies have examined the characteristics of such traffic. Maier et al. [28] have considered a common assumption regarding residential traffic. The downstream dominates over the upstream; that is, most bytes are transferred to the local side. Indeed, the considered assumption has shaped and is ingrained in the bandwidth allocations of ADSL (asymmetric digital subscriber line) and cable broadband offerings. In the DSL session characteristics, Maier et al. study with a look at the behavior of the user's DSL sessions (periods of connection to the ISP's network). To trace the traffic, author used HTTP, Bit Torrent, eDonkey, SSL, NNTP, and RTSP protocols.

The performance of traffic monitoring and analysis systems highly depends on the number of flows as well as link utilization and the pattern of packet arrival. Kim et al. [29] examine the characteristics of recent Internet traffic from the perspective of flows. The authors used pipeline based real time traffic monitoring and analysis system architecture. In order to collect IP traffic trace data, authors considered "NG-MON" flow generator simulator and placed at the connection point of the network. The distribution of traffic flow duration and the distribution of the number of packets in flows are presented with the help of TCP and UDP protocols. The simulation result also presented the flow's density. In this work, author used bytes and packets as metrics. In the case of peer-to-peer IPTV communities, Silverston et al. [30] have considered P2P IPTV traffic. It provides useful insights into both transport and packet levels statistical properties of P2P IPTV. It is useful to understand the impact on network nodes and links. The data traffic is collected by peers within the community watching the 2006 FIFA World Cup. The collected data is analyzed on mesh based topological system (PPLive, PPStream, SOPCast, and TVAnts). The tracer plots the (PPLive, PPStream, SOPCast, and TVAnts) traffic with respect to the number of videos downloaded from the neighboring peers with respect to time. The tracer plots the joint probability density function (PDF) of the interpacket time (IPT) and packet size (PS) of the download traffic. The IPT of each packet is the time that elapsed between that packet and the previous one of the same sessions. Loguinov and Radha [31] analyzed the dynamics of a live streaming experiment that has been conducted between a number of unicast dial-up clients, connecting to the Internet through access points, and a backbone video server. The clients streamed low-bit rate MPEG-4 video sequences from the server over paths with a number of distinct Internet routers. The authors have considered client-server based architecture for MPEG-4 streaming on the Internet. The server was fully multithreaded to ensure that the transmissions of chunk video were performed at the target IP. The bit rate of each streaming session provides a quick response to clients' NACK requests. The streaming was implemented in bursts of packets (with the varying burst duration). The author considered six datasets, each collected from the different machine. The plots are mainly distribution of the number of end-to-end hops and average packet loss rates. The author analyzed the dynamics of a large number of TCP web sessions at a busy Internet server. Liang [32] systematically investigates the long term, online, time variable bit-rate (VBR) video traffic prediction. It is the key and complicated component for advanced predictive dynamic bandwidth control and frame allocation. Since in the Internet and other packet/cell switching broad-band networks (such as ATM), VBR video traffic will be a major part of the traffic produced by multimedia as sources, many researchers have focused on VBR video traffic prediction. Liang [32] traced the prediction of video frame by multiresolution learning neural network (NN) based model.

CONCLUSIONS

In this work, we have presented the three-phase simulation for distributed video on demand system for interactive session. The first stage of simulation according to the proposed methodology reduces the blockage at the proxy server for different types of service requests. It efficiently serves from the local server. If the requested video stream is not present at the local storage or the blockage is above some preassigned threshold then the service request proceeds further to distributed databases. The 2nd stage of the simulation results is presented to reduce the search hop counts for the required storage stream in "distributed video on demand system" by using the session based query search algorithm, which runs at the application server. In the third phase we have seen that the bandwidth requirement completely depended upon the number of interactive modes used by the user at any session. Increase in the number of users brings higher use of interactive modes that leads to the high bandwidth requirement at any session. The size of the network brings little impact to this scenario. The size of the network increases linearly, scalable with the number of peers' nodes in the network. The unified demand parameters do not depend upon the size of the network or the number of peer nodes. Furthermore, the single-user bandwidth requirement model for interactive mode at any session does not depend upon the number of peer nodes present in the distributed network. The simulation result also reflects the same scenario.

Competing Interests

The authors Soumen Kanrar and Niranjan Kumar Mandal declare that there is no conflict of interests regarding the publication of the paper.

ACKNOWLEDGMENTS

The authors are grateful to Sharmista Das Kanrar from Bishop Westcott, Ranchi, India.

REFERENCES

1. P. Mundur, A. K. Sood, and R. Simon, "Class-based access control for distributed video-on-demand systems," IEEE Transactions on Circuits and Systems for Video Technology, vol. 15, no. 7, pp. 844–853, 2005.
2. S. Annapu Reddy, "Exploring IP/VOD in P2P swarming systems," in Proceedings of the Conference on Computer Communications (INFOCOM '07), pp. 71–75, Anchorage, Alaska, USA, May 2007.
3. D. Agrawal, M. S. Beigi, C. Bisdikian, and K.-W. Lee, "Planning and managing the IPTV service deployment," in Proceedings of the 10th IFIP/IEEE International Symposium on Integrated Network Management (IM '07), pp. 353–362, Munich, Germany, May 2007.
4. L. Shi, Z. Gu, L. Wei, and Y. Shi, "Quantitative analysis of Zipf's law on web cache," in Parallel and Distributed Processing and Applications, vol. 3758 of Lecture Notes in Computer Science, pp. 845–852, Springer, 2005.
5. G. Hasslinger and O. Hohlfeld, "Efficiency of caches for content distribution on the internet," in Proceedings of the 22nd International IEEE Teletraffic Congress (ITC '10), pp. 1–8, Amsterdam, The Netherlands, September 2010.
6. S. Kanrar, "Analysis and implementation of the large scale video-on-demand system," International Journal of Applied Information Systems, vol. 1, no. 4, pp. 41–49, 2012.
7. S. Kanrar, "Performance of distributed video on demand system for multirate traffic," in Proceedings of the International Conference on Recent Trends in Information Systems (ReTIS '11), pp. 52–56, Kolkata, India, December 2011.
8. S. Kanrar, "Efficient traffic control of VoD system," International Journal of Computer Networks & Communications, vol. 3, no. 5, pp. 95–106, 2011.
9. S. Kanrar and K. N. Mandal, "Dynamic page replacement at the cache memory for the video on demand server," in Advanced Computing, Networking and Informatics—Volume 2, pp. 461–469, Springer, 2014.
10. S. Kanrar and K. N. Mandal, "performance enhancement for audio-video proxy server," in Proceedings of the 3rd International Conference on Frontiers of Intelligent Computing: Theory and Applications (FICTA), 2014, Volume 1, vol. 327 of Advances in Intelligent Systems and Computing, pp. 605–613, Springer, 2015.
11. S. Tewari and L. Kleinrock, "On fairness, optimal download performance and proportional replication in peer-to-peer networks," in Proceedings of the 4th International IFIP-TC6 Networking Conference, Waterloo, Canada, May 2005.
12. S. Tewari and L. Kleinrock, "Proportional replication in peer-to-peer networks," in Proceedings of the Conference on Computer Communications (INFOCOM '06), Barcelona, Spain, 2006.
13. X. Zhou and C.-Z. Xu, "Efficient algorithms of video replication and placement on a cluster of streaming servers," Journal of Network and Computer Applications, vol. 30, no. 2, pp. 515–540, 2007.
14. S. Kanrar and N. K. Mandal, "Optimum storage finding in video on demand system," in Proceedings of the IEEE 2nd International Conference on Signal Processing and Integrated Networks (SPIN '15), pp. 827–830, Noida, India, Feburary 2015.
15. K. Suh, C. Diot, J. Kurose et al., "Push-to-peer video-on-demand system: design and evaluation," IEEE Journal on Selected Areas in Communications, vol. 25, no. 9, pp. 1706–1716, 2007.
16. V. O. K. Li, W. Liao, X. Qiu, and E. W. M. Wong, "Performance model of interactive video-on-demand systems," IEEE Journal on Selected Areas in Communications, vol. 14, no. 6, pp. 1099–1109, 1996.
17. G. M. Lee, C. S. Lee, W. S. Rhee, and J. K. Choi, "Functional architecture for NGN-based personalized IPTV services," IEEE Transactions on Broadcasting, vol. 55, no. 2, 2009.
18. A. Dan, D. Sitaram, and P. Shahabuddin, "Scheduling polices for an on demand video server with batching," in Proceedings of the 2nd ACM International Conference on Multimedia (MULTIMEDIA '94), pp. 15–23, San Francisco, Calif, USA, October 1994.
19. T. D. C. Little and D. Venkatesh, "Prospects for interactive video-on-demand," IEEE MultiMedia, vol. 1, no. 3, pp. 14–24, 1994.
20. V. Paxson and S. Floyd, "Wide area traffic: the failure of Poisson modeling," IEEE/ACM Transactions on Networking, vol. 3, no. 3, pp. 226–244, 1995.
21. C. Huang, J. Li, and W. Keith, "Can internet video-on-demand be profitable?" ACM SIGCOMM Computer Communication Review, vol. 37, no. 4, pp. 133–144, 2007, Proceedings of the Conference on Applications, Technologies, Architectures, and Protocols for Computer Communications (SIGCOMM '07).
22. C. Dewes, A. Wichmann, and A. Feldmann, "An analysis of internet chat systems," in Proceedings of the 3rd ACM SIGCOMM Internet Measurement Conference (IMC '03), pp. 51–64, October 2003.
23. C. Diot and L. Gautier, "A distributed architecture for multiplayer interactive applications on the Internet," IEEE Network, vol. 13, no. 4, pp. 6–15, 1999.
24. M. Zink, K. Suh, Y. Gu, and J. Kurose, "Characteristics of YouTube network traffic at a campus network-measurements, models, and implications," Computer Networks, vol. 53, no. 4, pp. 501–514, 2009.
25. S. Sen and J. Wang, "Analyzing peer-to-peer traffic across large networks," IEEE/ACM Transactions on Networking, vol. 12, no. 2, pp. 219–232, 2004.
26. S. Saroiu, K. P. Gummadi, R. J. Dunn, S. D. Gribble, and H. M. Levy, "An analysis of internet content delivery systems," in Proceedings of the 5th Symposium On Operating Systems Design And Implementation ACM SIGOPS Operating Systems Review (OSDI '02), vol. 36, pp. 315–327, December 2012.
27. M.-S. Kim, Y. J. Won, and J. W.-K. Hong, "Application-level traffic monitoring and an analysis on IP networks," ETRI Journal, vol. 27, no. 1, pp. 22–41, 2005.

28. G. Maier, A. Feldmann, V. Paxson, and M. Allman, "On dominant characteristics of residential broadband internet traffic," in Proceedings of the 9th ACM SIGCOMM Internet Measurement Conference (IMC '09), pp. 90–102, November 2009.
29. M.-S. Kim, Y. J. Won, and J. W. Hong, "Characteristic analysis of internet traffic from the perspective of flows," Computer Communications, vol. 29, no. 10, pp. 1639–1652, 2006.
30. T. Silverston, O. Fourmauxa, A. Bottab et al., "Traffic analysis of peer-to-peer IPTV communities," Computer Networks, vol. 53, no. 4, pp. 470–484, 2008.
31. D. Loguinov and H. Radha, "End-to-end Internet video trafficdynamics: statistical study andanalysis," in Proceedings of the 21st IEEE Annual Joint Conference of the IEEE Computer and Communications Societies (INFOCOM '02), vol. 2, pp. 723–732, New York, NY, USA, 2002.
32. Y. Liang, "Real-time VBR video traffic prediction for dynamic bandwidth allocation," IEEE Transactions on Systems, Man and Cybernetics, Part C: Applications and Reviews, vol. 34, no. 1, pp. 32–47, 2004.

CHAPTER 6

MULTIMEDIA BROADCAST SERVICES IN THE EVOLVED PACKET SYSTEM

Ivaylo Atanasov and Evelina Pencheva

INTRODUCTION

The Evolved Packet System (EPS) is standardized to provide ubiquitous access to multimedia services from any end user device. It encompasses both access network and core network. The multimedia packet core network plays an important role in providing superior user experience from services and applications. It is in charge of provisioning quality of service (QoS) for multimedia bearer services and charging mechanisms.

Multimedia broadcast/multicast service (MBMS) allows data to be transmitted to multiple endpoints. It allows optimizing network resources using a distribution mechanism. The broadcast mode is a unidirectional point-to-multipoint transmission of multimedia data (e.g., text, audio, picture, and video) from a single source entity to all users in a broadcast service area. A broadcast service received by the end user device involves one or more successive broadcast sessions. A broadcast service might, for example, consist of a single ongoing session (e.g., a media stream) or may involve several intermittent sessions over an extended period of time [1, 2]. Examples of content appropriate to a distribution scheme are broadcasting TV channels and distribution of area-based multimedia messaging service including commonly interested traffic, weather, or emergency information. The content provider (broadcast/multicast source) may provide discrete and continuous media, as well as service descriptions and control data. The multimedia content may be provided by a 3rd-party content provider.

The broadcast mode is intended to efficiently use EPS resources. Current research on MBMS covers different aspects related to optimisation of radio technology used for data transmission. Relatively low attention is paid on MBMS third-party control, which allows third-party providers from an IT domain to create applications that use network connections, streaming, messaging, and multimedia.

In this paper, we discuss some model aspects of deployment open access on multimedia message broadcast service in EPS. The open service access allows third-party applications to use broadcast function in the network. The Parlay X Web Services (WS) model provides a high level of abstraction of communication network functions and it facilitates the development of value added applications.

The paper is organized as follows. In Section 2, the related work is presented and the novelty of the proposed approach is highlighted. In Section 3, the broadcast service architecture in EPS is discussed where the Broadcast Multicast Service Centre (BMSC) mediates between third-party applications and the network infrastructure. Next, the Parlay X Message Broadcast WS functionality is analyzed in Section 4. The behavior of BMSC is modeled by formal descriptions of MBMS session state and message broadcast status in Section 5. In Section 6, it is proved that models considering QoS and charging aspects of MBMS are synchronized. The conclusion summarizes the contribution.

RELATED WORK

Research community has studied different architectural aspects of MBMS deployment in next generation networks. In [3], the authors propose service architecture for efficient content delivery based on enhanced MBMS in LTE (Long-Term Evolution), which reduces backhaul traffic. A context-aware architecture for social networking multimedia distribution, which enhances the evolved MBMS systems by adding users' situation knowledge on their assessments and allows

Citation: Ivaylo Atanasov and Evelina Pencheva, "Multimedia Broadcast Services in the Evolved Packet System," International Journal of Digital Multimedia Broadcasting, vol. 2016, Article ID 3154801, 13 pages, 2016. doi:10.1155/2016/3154801.

personalized services delivery over optimized networks, is proposed in [4]. In [5], the authors describe the design and implementation of an open-source virtualized platform that supports both LTE broadcast services and video streaming services and analyze service performance.

The performance of enhanced MBMS in LTE has been thoroughly examined in previous research works. A comparison of multicast/broadcast services support in LTE-advanced and WiMAX IEEE 802.16m is provided in [6]. Challenges in supporting multicast services over LTE with particular attention to resource management, considered as key aspects for efficient provisioning of MBMS services over cellular networks, are analyzed in [7]. In [8], the authors discuss the relationship between LTE evolved MBMS and next generation broadcast television and propose some recommendations aimed at improving efficiency of the respective systems. In [9], the authors present a compact, convenient model for broadcasting in LTE, as well as a set of efficient algorithms to define broadcasting areas and to actually perform content scheduling. A joint multicast/unicast scheduling strategy for MBMS delivery, which improves QoS performance, is proposed in [10]. In [11], the authors propose a method for forming broadcasting area and assignment of content to them so that radio resources are efficiently exploited and user requests satisfied. In [12], a distributed resource allocation scheme is proposed, which includes device-to-device communication broadcasting groups and minimizes interference relationships. In [13], MBMS with inherently low requirement for network resources as a candidate solution for using such resources in a more efficient manner is proposed. High level considerations related to implementation of a session controller, supporting application programming interfaces for message broadcasting/multicasting, can be found in [14].

The proposed solutions have to be implemented by the telecom network operator. We study another multimedia broadcasting issue that has been scarcely addressed so far, namely, third-party control which allows external applications outside the network to control service provisioning. Our research is focused on two standardized technologies whose synergy has not been studied to date. The Parlay X WS is technology aimed at providing a horizontal service architecture which may be shared by different applications. It defines highly abstracted technology neutral application programming interfaces (APIs). Integration of MBMS and Parlay X requires translation of high level interfaces into telecommunication control protocols. The innovative approach to efficient MBMS provisioning requires considering also other advanced network functions such as policy-based quality of service control and flexible charging. We examine how three different functions in EPS, related to multimedia broadcasting, policy and charging control, and third-party control can collaborate and take the advantage of network convergence in provisioning of value added services.

BROADCAST SERVICE ARCHITECTURE IN EPS

Different broadcast business cases may be considered and the relevance of each used case is up to network operators and their relationship with the content owners, agencies, and broadcasters. Used case examples include mobile TV, digital radio, video on demand, electronic magazines and newspapers, and configuration and management of intelligent objects with internet connectivity.

As to 3GPP TS 23.246, the components of the 3GPP solution of MBMS are MBMS bearer service and MBMS user service. The MBMS bearer service enables efficient distribution of content to multiple users while MBMS user service is used by user devices when specific end user applications are activated. The architecture of MBMS for EPS with the proposed third-party control is depicted in Figure 1.

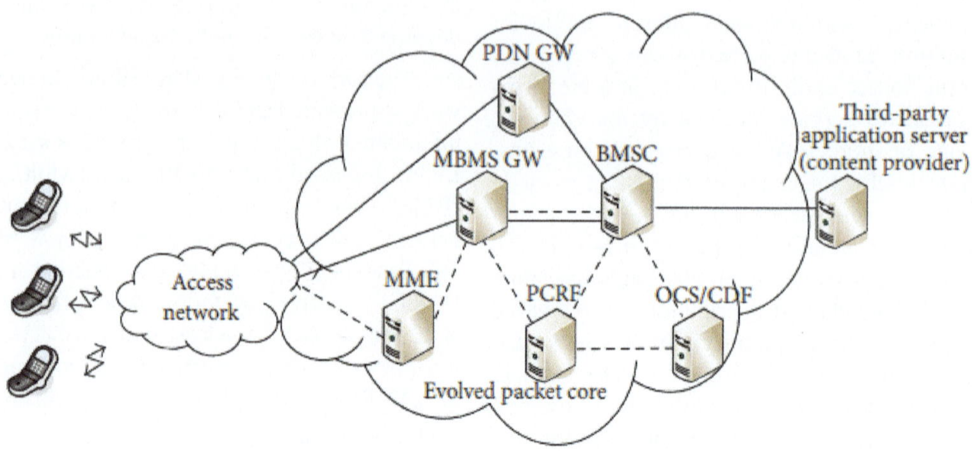

Figure 1: Reference architecture of MBMS for EPS.

The multimedia content that has to be broadcasted is provided by an Application Sever (AS). The MBMS AS may be deployed by network operator or third-party application provider. The Broadcast Multicast Service Centre (BMSC) stores multimedia content to be transmitted, controls the multimedia broadcast service, and interacts with media sources and the end users' devices via Packet Data Network Gateway (PDN GW). It provides interfaces for both signaling and data transfer to the MBMS GW. The MBMS Gateway (GW) distributes the data received from the BMSC to the relevant base stations in the access network. The Mobility Management Entity (MME) communicates with the access network in the concerned area, relaying session control information received by MBMS GW [15].

The end users discover the available MBMS services by service announcement, which provides information about services. Service announcement is used to distribute to users information about MBMS, service activation parameters like IP multicast address, and service start time. Service announcement mechanisms may include short message broadcasting, MBMS broadcasting or multicasting mode, and a push mechanism. Service announcement details may be found in [16].

An MBMS service may contain multiple distinct multimedia streams and it is provided by session setup and termination. Each session is bundled with bearer establishment and release. Signaling procedures related to MBMS session initiation, update, and termination are specified in [15].

In EPS, the network controls QoS parameters for session broadcast MBMS bearer services. QoS Class Identifier, Allocation and Retention Priority, Maximum Bit Rate (MBR), and Guaranteed Bit Rate (GBR) are applicable to MBMS bearer service, where the MBR is set to be equal to the GBR. The QoS management in EPS is provided by means of policy and charging control (PCC) which allows network operator to authorize and control the usage of resources intended for multimedia traffic [17]. PCC ensures that multimedia services are provided with appropriate transport and charging. The Policy and Charging Rule Function (PCRF) encompasses policy control decision and flow based charging control functions. It receives MBMS session information from BMSC as well as information from the access network and makes policy-based decisions about bearer service session, which are then provided to the MBMS GW. The PCC decisions determine the QoS treatment of the bearer traffic.

Both MBMS content provider and MBMS user may be charged for multimedia broadcasting sessions. EPS provides offline and online charging mechanisms [18]. The BMSC contains triggers that generate events for online and offline charging. The Online Charging System (OCS) performs real-time credit control and its functionality includes transaction handlings, online correlation, and management of user account balances. The Charging Data Function (CDF) receives offline charging information from BMSC and creates call detail records.

PARLAY X MESSAGE BROADCAST WEB SERVICE

The Parlay X Message Broadcast WS (MBWS) allows third-party applications to send messages to end user devices in a specific geographical area [19]. It provides APIs for sending a broadcast message to the network, for monitoring the delivery status of a sent broadcast message, and for notifications about the message delivery status.

The sendBroadcastMessage operation is used to send a broadcast message into the designated area(s).

The getBroadcastStatus operation is used by the 3rd-party application to retrieve the status of sent broadcast message. The broadcast status values are as follows:(i)MessageWaiting. The message is still queued and not delivered to the network yet. (ii)Broadcasting. The message is being broadcasted as many as requested in the send operation.(iii)Broadcasted. The message is successfully delivered to network as many as requested.(iv) BroadcastImpossible. This indicates a final state that delivery of broadcast message is impossible due to specific reasons.(v) BroadcastUnknown. The message delivery state is unknown. Figure 2 illustrates the MBMS time line and the message status as seen by 3rd-party application. Thecancel Broadcast Message operation may be used by the third-party application to cancel message broadcasting. The operation affects the subsequent broadcast message delivery.

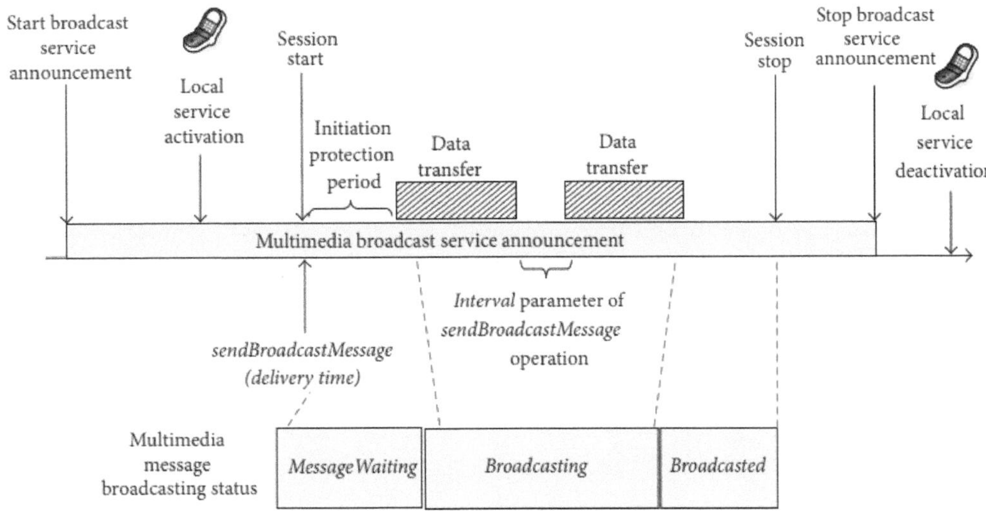

Figure 2: Multimedia broadcast service time line and the parameters ofsendBroadcastMessage operation.

The notifyBroadcastDeliveryReceipt operation is used to notify the third-party application about the delivery status of the message. In order to receive notification the third-party application needs to start notifications using start Delivery Receipt Notification operation. The application may end the receipt of notifications using thestopDeliveryReceiptNotification operation.

We propose a modified model compared to that presented in [19], which is shown in Figure 3. In Null state, there is no message to be broadcasted. As far as the BroadcastUnknown state is of temporary kind it is absorbed by the BroadcastImpossible and Broadcasting states.

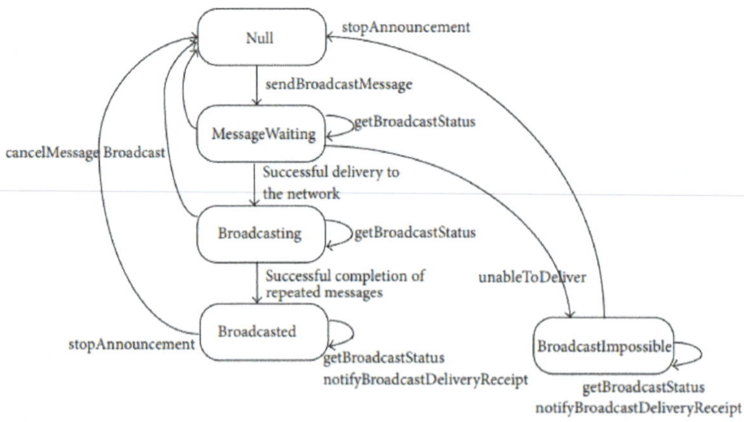

Figure 3: Message broadcast state model.

MODEL ASPECTS OF BROADCAST MULTICAST SERVICE CENTRE

Modeling Views on Message Broadcast

BMSC needs to communicate with the third-party application using the Parlay X MBWS. Toward the network, BMSC has to communicate with MBMS GW to maintain the MBMS session; PCRF to provide information about the MBMS session and to receive notifications about bearers authorized for the session; and CDF to send charging data. Therefore, the BMSC behavior has to be synchronized with the behavior of MBMS GW, PCRF, and CDF, and its view on the MBMS session has to be synchronized with the application view on the state of message broadcast. MBMS GW is in charge of establishment of IP-CAN resources for the MBMS session where IP-CAN stands for Internet Protocol Connectivity Access Network. PCRF controls the QoS that has to be assured for the MBMS session and CDF gathers charging data.

Figure 4 shows the respective state models that have to be synchronized with the BMSC behavior. The BMSC has to transform the MBWS operations and to control the MBMS session appropriately. In practice, the state models of BMSC, MBMS GW, PCRF, and CDF should expose direct correspondence between the transitions and the information they provide; that is, they have to expose equivalent behavior.

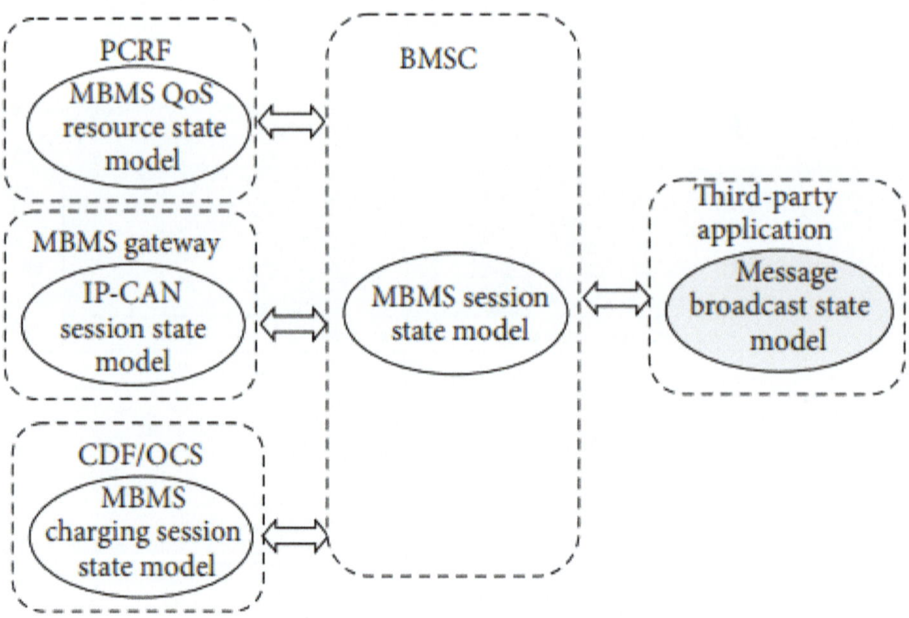

Figure 4: Synchronization of MBMS state models in the network and the 3rd-party application view on the message broadcast state.

The MBMS session state model describes the states of the MBMS session and it is maintained by MBMS GW. The MBMS QoS provisioning requires an MBMS QoS state model reflecting the state of bearer resources allocated by PCRF for the broadcast session. The control protocol used for PCC is Diameter. Similar considerations are applied to the MBMS charging model which holds the states of the MBMS charging session. The control protocol used for charging is also Diameter.

Typical information flows related to multimedia message broadcasting with MBMS session establishment, QoS resource authorization, notification about message broadcast status, and reporting offline charging data are shown in Figure 5.

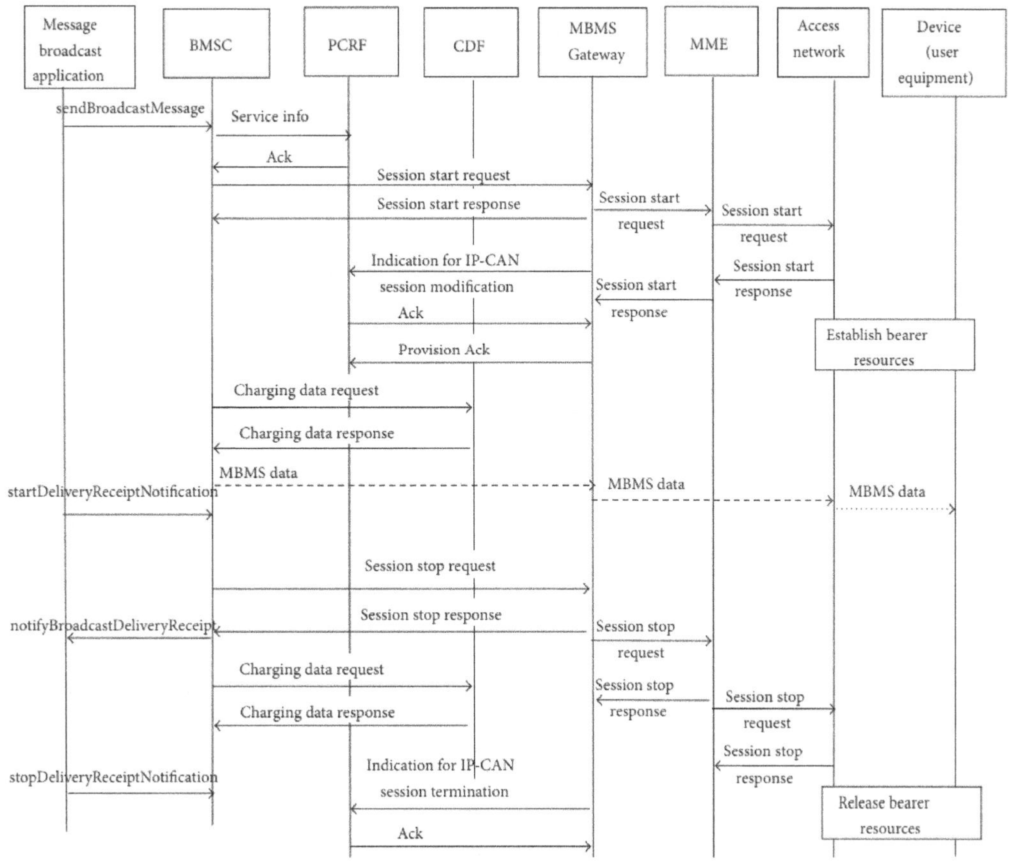

Figure 5: Typical message flow illustrating 3rd-party control of MBMS in the network.

The MB WS can be used for remote management of intelligent devices like smart meters, which are uniquely identified, gather information from their environment, and communicate that information with network applications. Remote entity management provides means for managing device life cycle including software and firmware upgrade and configuration management. With the increasing number of connected devices, the device management becomes cumbersome and costly for the device operator. So, an EPS operator can sell the MBMS to the device operator to keep the fleet updated. The MBMS can deliver all the software and firmware updates as well as configurations needed to manage the devices up to date.

It is a general assumption that IP connectivity is provided to all devices, which means that for each device there is an established default bearer. Let us assume that the device operator makes use of a message broadcast application. By using the application, the device operator sets the target area, where the devices are deployed, and writes a message with configuration data. Then the message broadcast application invokes the MB WS which in turn sends a message delivery operation to the BMSC. Subsequently EPS functional entities supporting MBMS deliver the configuration data to all devices in the target area.

When the message broadcast application invokes sendBroadcastMessage operation the BMSC opens a Diameter session with the PCRF for the multimedia broadcast session and provides the required session information. The BMSC can subscribe to QoS events related to MBMS bearer resources. The BMSC performs the MBMS session start procedure. The MBMS GW in turn indicates to the PCRF that an IP-CAN session modification is required and waits for PCC rules. Based on session information, the PCRF performs session authorization and sends an acknowledgement with the PCC decisions to the MBMS Gateway. The MBMS starts resources reservation in the access network. When the IP-CAN session modification is completed the MBMS GW sends acknowledgement to the PCRF. The BMSC waits for resource authorization and reservation during the initial protection period and the message broadcast status is MessageWaiting. Before starting the MBMS data transfer, the BMSC contacts with the CDF in order to provide charging information. The MBMS content is sent by the BMSC to the MBMS gateway, and then to the respective part of access network. During the MBMS data transfer the message broadcast status is Broadcasting. The broadcasted content is received and decoded by the devices (user equipment) that are authorized to join the MBMS service. Using the message broadcast application and the interfaces of the MBWS, the device operator can subscribe for notifications about message delivery (startDeliveryReceiptNotification operation) and be notified of a broadcast delivery status of a specific area. Once the MBMS data (configuration data) are broadcasted, the BMSC starts the procedure for session termination, which is followed by release of bearer resources authorized for the MBMS session. The BMSC contacts with the CDF to write the charging data. The message broadcast status becomes Broadcasted. ThestopDeliveryReceiptNotification operation is used to end delivery receipt notification. The content provider is charged for the broadcasted content. The PCRF enables also QoS-based charging. The PCC mechanism supports traffic plane event reporting (e.g., bearer lost) which may reflect in charging. In case of active subscription, the PCRF may notify the BMSC about any QoS events occurring during message broadcasting.

In the course of service provisioning, the BMSC needs to maintain in a synchronized manner three state machines describing the MBMS session, QoS resources authorized for the session, and charging session. These state machines have to be synchronized with the application view on the states of the message broadcast.

On receiving an indication about IP-CAN session modification, the PCRF may reject the requested modification (due to overloading in the respective access network or spending credit limits of the content provider in case of online charging). In this case, the PCRF rejects the IP-CAN session modification requested by the MBMS GW and notifies the BMSC about the event during the initial protection period. The message broadcast status becomes BroadcastImpossible. During message waiting or broadcasting, the device operator may decide to cancel message broadcast. In this case, the third-party application invokes thecancelBroadcastMessage operation to request cancelation of the previous sendBroadcastMessage. The BMSC in turn initiates session termination toward the MBMS GW and PCRF, which results in IP-CAN session termination and release of QoS resources.

In the next subsection, we provide formal description of the models representing the view on message broadcast of third-party application, BMSC, MBMS GW, PCRF, and CDF, respectively. This will be used to prove formally that the models are synchronized.

Formal Description of Models Representing Message Broadcast Status.

Let us present the state machines as labeled transition systems (LTS).

Definition 1. A labeled transition system (LTS) is a quadruple (S, Act, $\rightarrow$, $s0$), where S is countable set of states, Act is a countable set of elementary actions, $\rightarrow \subseteq S \times Act \times S$ is a set of transitions, and $s_0 \in S$ is the set of initial states.

Application View on Message Broadcast Status.

The message broadcast status from application point of view may be Null, MessageWaiting, Broadcasting, or Broadcasted. The status is Null when there is no message to be broadcasted. The status is MessageWaiting if the message is waiting to be delivered to the network. The status is Broadcasting or Broadcasted if the MBMS data transfer is ongoing or terminated, respectively. By TApp = (SApp, ActApp, →App, $s0$ App) an LTS representing the 3rd-party view on the message broadcast status is denoted where

(i) S_{App} = {Null, Message Waiting, Broadcasting, Broadcasted, Broadcast Impossible};

(ii) Act_{App} = {sendMessage, getBroadcastStatus, notify Broadcast Delivery Receipt, cancel Message, successful Delivery, unsuccessful Delivery, stop Announcement, unable To Deliver, successful Message Completion};

(iii) $\rightarrow_{App}$ = {Null sendMessage Message Waiting, Message Waiting get BroadcastStatus Message Waiting, Message Waiting unsuccessful Delivery Null, Message Waiting successful Delivery Broadcasting, Message Waiting cancel Message Null, MessageWaiting unable To Deliver BroadcastImpossible, Broadcasting successful MessageCompletion Broadcasted, Broadcasting cancel Message Null, Broadcasting get BroadcastStatus Broadcasting, Broadcasted stop Announcement Null, Broadcasted get Broadcast Status Broadcasted, Broadcasted notify Broadcast Delivery Receipt Broadcasted, Broadcast Impossible getBroadcast Status Broadcast Impossible, Broadcast Impossible notify Broadcast Delivery Receipt Broadcast Impossible, Broadcast Impossible stop Announcement Null};

(iv) s_0^{App} = {Null}.

The get Broadcast Status and notify Broadcast Delivery Receipt operations do not change the session state or message broadcast status.

BMSC Model of MBMS Session.

The simplified BMSC view on the MBMS session states includes the following states. In MBMSIdle state, there is no MBMS session. When the application invokes the sendBroadcastMessage operation, the BMSC sends session information to the PCRF, a session start request to the MBMS GW, and it moves to InitialWaiting state. While being in InitialWaiting state, the BMSC waits for resource authorization and QoS resource reservation. The time delay between a session start indication and actual data should be long enough for the required network actions. When the network is ready to send MBMS data, the BMSC sends charging data and moves to DataTransfer state. In DataTransfer state, MBMS data are transferred to any user equipment which is present. When the MBMS user service determines that there are no more data to send, the BMSC initiates session termination, sends charging data, and moves to MBMSIdle state. In InitialWaiting or DataTransfer state, the BMSC may be notified about any problems related to MBMS bearers and the MBMS session is terminated. It is also possible for third-party application to invoke the cancelBroadcastMessage operation while the BMSC is in InitialWaiting or DataTransfer state, which cancels the MBMS session. By T_{BMSC} = (S_{BMSC}, Act_{BMSC}, →BMSC, s_0^{BMSC}) an LTS representing the BMSC view on the message broadcast status is denoted where

(i) S_{BMSC} = {MBMSIdle, Initial Waiting, Data Transfer};

(ii) Act_{BMSC} = {send Broadcast Message, initial Period, data TransferStop, resource Failed, resource Lost, cancel Broadcast Message};

(iii) $\rightarrow B_{MSC}$ = {MBMSIdle send Broadcast Message Initial Waiting, Initial Waiting initial Period Data Transfer, Initial Waiting resource Failed MBMSIdle, Initial Waiting cancel Broadcast Message MBM SIdle, Data Transfer data Transfer Stop MBM SIdle, Data Transfer resource Lost MBM SIdle}; Data Transfer cancel Broadcast Message MBM SIdle};

(iv) s_0^{BMSC} = {MBMSIdle}. Figure 6 illustrates the MBMS session state machine.

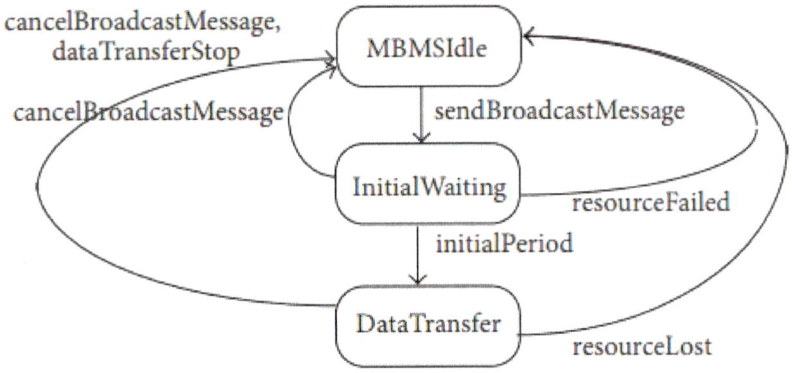

Figure 6: MBMS session state machine.

MBMS GW Model of IP-CAN Session

The MBMS GW view on the IP-CAN session states for the MBMS user service includes the following states. In IPCANIdle state, there is no dedicated IP-CAN session. On receiving session start instructions, the MBMS GW indicates an IP-CAN session modification to the PCRF and moves to WaitForPCCRules state. In WaitForPCCRules state, the MBMS waits for authorization of IP-CAN session modification. Upon receiving the PCC rules, the MBMS GW initiates IP-CAN session establishment in the access network and moves to ResourceReservation state. The MBMS GW moves to SessionActive state after it receives an acknowledgement that the resources in the access network are reserved. The transition to ResourceRelease state occurs when a session stop request is received by the BMSC. In ResourceRelease state, the MBMS waits for the release of IP-CAN bearers. In WaitForTermAck state, the MBMS GW waits for acknowledgement for session termination from PCRF and then moves to the initial IPCANIdle state. In ResourceReservation or SessionActive state, network, the MBMS GW may receive indications from the PCRF that the bearer modification fails or that the bearers are lost. These cause the transition to IPCANIdle state. By $T_{MBMS} = (S_{MBMS}, Act_{MBMS}, \rightarrow_{MBMS}, s^0{}_{MBMS})$ an LTS representing the MBMS GW view on the MBMS IP-CAN session state is denoted where

(i) S_{MBMS} = {IPCANIdle, Wait For PCC Rules, Resource Reservation, Session Active, Resource Release, Wait For Term Ack};

(ii) Act_{MBMS} = {session Start, pcc Rules, ip Can Bearer Establishment, session Stop, session Cancel, ip Can BearerRelease, ip Can Session Term Ack, ip Can Bearer Failed, ip Can Bearer Lost};

(iii) $\rightarrow_{MBMS}$ = {IPCANIdle session Start Wait For PCC Rules, Wait For PCC Rules pcc Rules Resource Reservation, Wait For PCC Rules session Cancel IPCANIdle, Resource Reservation ip Can Bearer Establishment Session Active, Resource Reservation session Cancel IPCANIdle, Resource Reservation ip CanBearer Failed IPCANIdle, Session Active session Cancel Resource Release, Session Active session Stop Resource Release, Session Active ip Can Bearer Lost IPCANIdle, Resource Release ip Can Bearer Release Wait For Term Ack, Wait For Term Ack ip Can Session Term Ack IPCANIdle}; (iv) *s*0 MBMS = {IPCANIdle}

The IP-CAN session state machine is depicted in Figure 7.

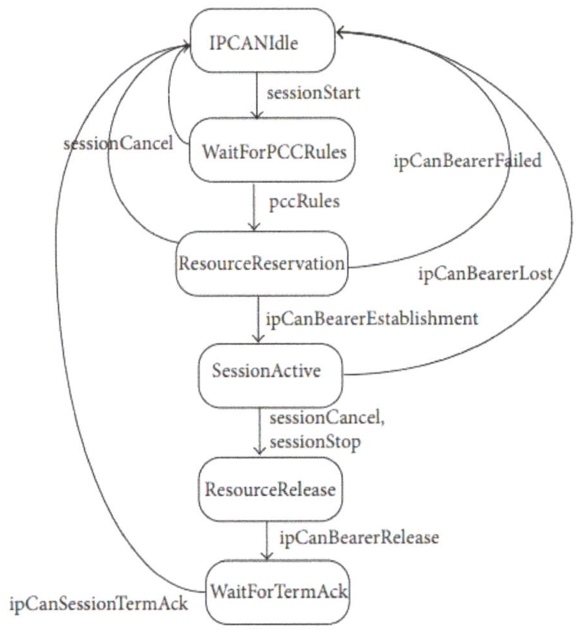

Figure 7: IP-CAN session state machine

PCRF Model of MBMS QoS Resources

The PCRF view on the state of QoS resource intended for MBMS session is as follows. In ResourceNull state, no QoS resources are authorized for the MBMS session. When the BMSC sends session information, the PCRF performs session binding which takes into account the IP-CAN parameters and moves to IPCanSession state storing this information. In IPCanSession state, the PCRF may receive an indication about IP-CAN session modification and correlates appropriate service information with IP-CAN session. In ResourceAuthorizing state, the PCRF makes policy decisions and sends them as PCC rules to the MBMS GW. On receiving provision acknowledgement the PCRF moves to ResourceAuthorized state. The QoS resources for the MBMS session are authorized and reserved, and the MBMS data transfer can start. When the MBMS GW detects that the IP-CAN session termination is required, it sends an indication to the PCRF. In case of subscription, the PCRF may find the PCC rules that require the BMSC to be notified and sends a notification. The QoS resources authorized for the MBMS session are released which causes the transition to ResourceNull state. In ResourceAuthorizing state, the PCRF may decide to reject the IP-CAN session modification. Also, during MBMS data transfer any QoS problems may be reported by the MBMS GW to the PCRF, thus affecting the online charging. In case the MBMS GW reports that all bearer resources authorized for the MBMS session are lost, the PCRF moves to ResourceNull state. By $T_{PCR}F = (S_{PCRF}, Act_{PCRF}, \rightarrow_{PCRF}, s^{0}_{PCR}F)$ an LTS representing the PCRF GW view on the QoS resource state is denoted where

(i) S_{PCRF} = {Resource Null, IP Can Session, Resource Authorizing, Resource Authorized};

(ii) Act_{PCRF} = {sessionInfo, ip Can Session Modification, provision Ack, provision Non Ack, ip Can Session Termination, ip Can Bearer Removed, ip CanSession Cancel};

(iii) $\rightarrow_{PCRF}$ = {Resource Null session Info IP Can Session, IP Can Session ip Can Session Modification Resource Authorizing, IP CanS ession ip Can Session Termination Resource Null, Resource Authorizing provision Ack Resource Authorized, Resource Authorizing

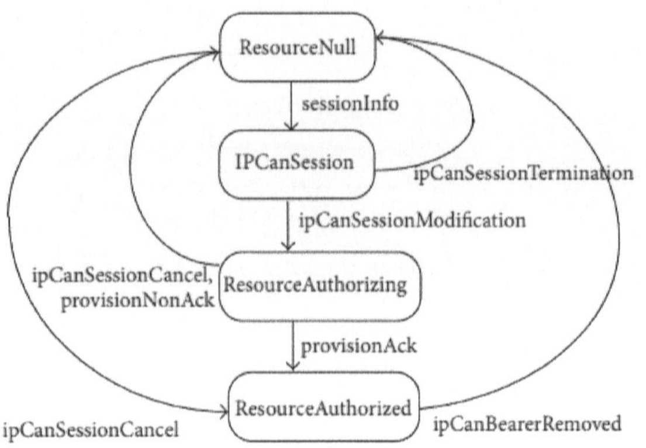

Figure 8: QoS resource state machine.

MBMS Charging Session Model

Both offline and online charging are possible. By applying policy and charging control on MBMS sessions, online charging can reflect the QoS experience during message broadcasting. The BMSC collects charging data such as identification of the content source, type of user service, type of bearer resources used to deliver the content broadcast, and identification of users receiving the service. The BMSC collects also charging data such as session duration, data transfer time, and data volume for mobile users receiving the service through MBMS and/or content providers delivery of the MBMS content. The triggers for charging data are bearer service initiation and termination. In ChargingIdle state, no charging data are gathered. Charging data are provided by the BMSC upon MBMS session initiation, IP-CAN bearer resource establishment/failure, and MBMS session termination. The charging data are sent to the CDF (in case of offline charging) or to the Online Charging System. On receiving charging data related to session start, the charging session moves to $ActiVe_{initial}$ state. In $ActiVe_{initial}$ state, when charging data for IP-CAN session establishment are received, the charging session moves to $ActiVe_{transfer}$ state. The charging data stop instructions may be received due to normal completion of message broadcast, due to some problems in the network, or due to message broadcast cancelation by the third-party application. On receiving charging data stop instructions the charging session moves to ChargingIdle state. By $T_{CS} = (S_{CS}, Act_{CS}, \rightarrow CS, s_0{}^{CS})$ an LTS representing the charging session states is denoted where

(i) S_{CS} = {ChargingIdle, Activeinitial, Activetransfer};

(ii) Act_{CS} = {charging Data Start$_{init}$, charging Data Start$_{interim}$, charging Data Stop$_{normal}$, charging Data Stop$_{canceled}$, charging Data Stop$_{failed}$};

(iii) $\rightarrow_{CS}$ = {ChargingIdle charging Data Start$_{init}$ Active$_{initial}$, Active$_{initial}$ charging Data Start$_{interim}$ Active$_{transfer}$, Active$_{transfer}$ charging Data Stop$_{normal}$ ChargingIdle, Active$_{initial}$ chargingData Stop$_{failed}$ ChargingIdle, Active$_{initial}$ charging DataStop$_{canceled}$ ChargingIdle, Activet$_{ransfer}$ charging Data Stop$_{canceled}$ ChargingIdle Active$_{transfer}$ charging Data Stop$_{failed}$ ChargingIdle};

(iv) $s_0{}^{CS}$ = {ChargingIdle}.

The charging session state machine is depicted in Figure 9.

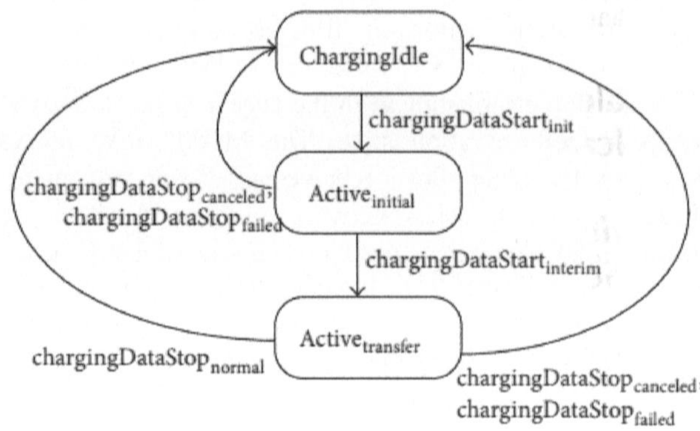

Figure 9: Charging session state machine.

Having formal description of the models representing message broadcast status as seen by both the third-party application and the network, we can prove that these models are synchronized; that is, they expose equivalent behavior.

FORMAL VERIFICATION OF MODELS

Bisimilarity Concept

Intuitively, in terms of observed behavior, two state machines are equivalent if one state machine displays a final result and the other state machine displays the same result. The idea of equivalence is formalized by the concept of bisimilarity [20]. Strong bisimilarity requires existence of homomorphism between transitions in both state machines. In practice, strong bisimilarity puts strong conditions for equivalence which are not always necessary. For example, internal transitions can present actions, which are intrinsic to the system (i.e., not observable). In weak bisimilarity, internal transitions can be ignored. The concept of weak bisimilarity is used to study some model aspects of BMSC. We will use the following notations:

(i) $s \xrightarrow{a} s'$ stands for the transition (s, a, s');

(ii) $s \xrightarrow{a}$ means that $\exists s' : s \xrightarrow{a} s'$;

(iii) $s \overset{\mu}{\Rightarrow} s_n$, where $\mu = a_1, a_2, \ldots, a_n : \exists s_1, s_2, \ldots, s_n$, such that $s \xrightarrow{a_1} s_1 \cdots \xrightarrow{a_n} s_n$;

(iv) $s \overset{\mu}{\Rightarrow}$ means that $\exists s'$, such as $s \overset{\mu}{\Rightarrow} s'$;

(v) $\overset{\hat{\mu}}{\Rightarrow}$ means $\Rightarrow$ if $\mu \equiv \tau$ or $\overset{\mu}{\Rightarrow}$, otherwise,

where τ is one or more internal (invisible) actions.

Definition 2. Two labeled transition systems $T = (S, A, \rightarrow, s_0)$ and $T' = (S', A, \rightarrow', s' 0)$ are weakly bisimilar ($T \sim T'$) if there is a binary relation $U \subseteq S \times S'$ such that if $s_1 U t_1 : s_1 \subseteq S$ and $t_1 \subseteq S'$, then $\forall a \in Act$:

$$\text{(i) } s_1 \overset{a}{\Rightarrow} s_2 \text{ implies } \exists t_2 : t_1 \overset{\hat{a}}{\Rightarrow}' t_2 \text{ and } s_2 U t_2;$$

$$\text{(ii) } t_1 \overset{a}{\Rightarrow}' t_2 \text{ implies } \exists s_2 : s_1 \overset{a}{\Rightarrow} s_2 \text{ and } s_2 U t_2.$$

So in order to prove that considered LTS expose equivalent behavior, it is necessary to identify a relation between their states that satisfies the above conditions.

Equivalence of Models Representing Message Broadcast Status

Behavioral Equivalence between Models of IP-CAN Session and QoS Resources

It can be shown that the MBMS GW model of MBMS session and PCRF model of MBMS QoS resources provide the lower level of abstraction, so we will start with considering the synchronization aspects of these models.

Proposition 3. The labeled transition systems T_{MBMS} and T_{PCR}F are weakly bisimilar.

Proof. To prove the bisimilarity between two labeled transition systems, it has to be proved that there exists a bisimilar relation between their states. By U_{MP} a relation between the states of T_{MBMS} and T_{PCRF} is denoted where

The following homomorphism based on functional mapping may be defined between transitions of T_{MBMS} and T_{PCRF}:

$h_{MP}(\text{sessionStart}) = h_{MP}(\text{sessionInfo})$;
$h_{MP}(\text{pccRule}) = h_{MP}(\text{ipCanSessionModification})$;
$h_{MP}(\text{ipCanBearerEstablishment}) = h_{MP}(\text{provisionAck})$;
$h_{MP}(\text{sessionStop}) = h_{MP}(\text{ipCanSessionTermination})$;
$h_{MP}(\text{sessionCancel}) = h_{MP}(\text{ipCanSessionCancel})$;
$h_{MP}(\text{ipCanBearerFailed}) = h_{MP}(\text{provisionNonAck})$;
$h_{MP}(\text{ipCanBearerLost}) = h_{MP}(\text{ipCanBearerRemoved})$.

The homomorphism between the T_{MBMS} and T_{PCRF} messages shows the action's similarity. Table 1 represents the functional mapping between the transitions in the IP-CAN session state machine and transitions in the QoS resources state machine. Based on the established relation between the states of T_{MBM}S and T_{PCRF}, and on the homomorphism h_{MP} between their transitions, it is proved that $T_{MBMS} \sim T_{PCRF}$; that is, they are weakly bisimilar and expose equivalent behavior.

Table 1: Functional mapping between transitions of T_{MBMS} and T_{PCRF}.

Transitions in T_{MBMS}	Transitions in T_{PCRF}	Event
IPCANIdle sessionStart WaitForPCCRules	ResourceNull sessionInfo IPCanSession	MBMS session initiation
WaitForPCCRules pccRules ResourceReservation	IPCanSession ipCanSessionModification ResourceAuthorizing	IP-CAN session modification request
ResourceReservation ipCanBearerEstablishment SessionActive	ResourceAuthorizing provisionAck ResourceAuthorized	IP-CAN session modification authorization
SessionActive sessionStop ResourceRelease, ResourceRelease ipCanBearerRelease WaitForTermAck, WaitForTermAck ipCanSessionTermAck IPCANIdle	ResourceAuthorized ipCanSessionTermination ResourceNull	MBMS session stop
ResourceReservation ipCanBearerFailed IPCANIdle	ResourceAuthorizing provisionNonAck ResourceNull	IP-CAN session modification authorization fails
SessionActive ipCanBearerLost IPCANIdle	ResourceAuthorized ipCanBearerRemoved ResourceNull	All bearers are lost during data transfer
ResourceReservation sessionCancel IPCANIdle	ResourceAuthorized ipCanSessionCancel ResourceNull	The application cancels the MBMS user service during resource reservation
WaitForPCCRules sessionCancel IPCANIdle	IPCANSession ipCanSessionCancel ResourceNull	The application cancels the MBMS user service during resource authorization
SessionActive sessionCancel ResourceRelease, ResourceRelease ipCanBearerRelease WaitForTermAck, WaitForTermAck ipCanSessionTermAck IPCANIdle	ResourceAuthorized ipCanSessionCancel ResourceNull	The application cancels the MBMS user service during data transfer

Equivalence of Models of MBMS Session, IP-CAN Session, and QoS Resources

A higher level of abstraction on the network resource state for MBMS is provided by the state of MBMS session.

Proposition 4. The labeled transition systems *T*BMSC, *T*MBMS, and *T*PCRF are weakly bisimilar.

Proof. The weak bisimilarity has the property transitivity; that is, as a relation it is transitive. Then, having proved that $T_{MBMS} \sim T_{PCRF}$, it has to be proved that $T_{BMSC} \sim T_{MBMS}$. By U_{BMP} a relation between the states of T_{BMSC}, T_{MBMS}, and T_{PCRF} is denoted where

U_{BMP} = {(MBMSIdle, IpCANIdle), (InitialWaiting, WaitForPCCRules), (DataTransfer, SessionActive)}.

The following homomorphism based on functional mapping may be defined between transitions of T_{BMSC}, T_{MBMS}, and T_{PCRF}:

h_{BMP}(sendBroadcastMessage) = h_{BMP}(sessionzStart) = h_{BMP}(sessionInfo);

h_{BMP}(initialPeriod) = h_{BMP}(pccRule) = h_{BMP}(ipCanSessionModification);

h_{BMP}(dataTransferStop) = h_{BMP}(sessionStop) = h_{BMP}(ipCanSessionTermination);

h_{BMP}(cancel) = h_{BMP}(sessionCancel) = h_{BMP}(ipCanSessionCancel);

h_{BMP}(resourcesFailed) = h_{BMP}(ipCanBearerFailed) = h_{BMP}(provisionNonAck);

h_{BMP}(resourcesLost) = h_{BMP}(ipCanBearerLost) = h_{BMP}(ipCanBearerRemoved).

The functional mapping between the transitions in the MBMS session and IP-CAN state machines represented in Table 2 shows that U_{BMP} is a bisimilar relation. From the homomorphism h_{BMP} and bisimilar property of *U*BMP it follows that $T_{BMSC} \sim T_{MBMS}$. From the bisimulation transitivity it follows that $T_{BMSC} \sim T_{MBMS} \sim T_{PCRF}$. This means that MBMS session state machine, IP-CAN state machine, and the QoS resources state machine are weakly bisimilar.

Table 2: Functional mapping between transitions of *T*BMSC and *T*MBMS.

Transitions in T_{BMSC}	Transitions in T_{MBMS}	Event
MBMSIdle sendBroadcastMessage InitialWaiting	IPCANIdle sessionStart WaitForPCCRules	MBMS session initiation
InitialWaiting initialPeriod DataTransfer	WaitForPCCRules pccRules ResourceReservation, ResourceReservation ipCanBearerEstablishment SessionActive	IP-CAN session modification request IP-CAN session modification authorization
DataTransfer dataTransferStop MBMSIdle	SessionActive sessionStop ResourceRelease, ResourceRelease ipCanBearerRelease WaitForTermAck, WaitForTermAck ipCanSessionTermAck IPCANIdle	MBMS session stop
InitialWaiting resourceFailed MBMSIdle	ResourceReservation ipCanBearerFailed IPCANIdle	IP-CAN session modification authorization fails
DataTransfer resourceLost MBMSIdle	SessionActive ipCanBearerLost IPCANIdle	All bearers are lost during data transfer
InitialWaiting cancelBroadcastMessage MBMSIdle	WaitForPCCRules sessionCancel IPCANIdle ResourceReservation sessionCancel IPCANIdle	The application cancels the MBMS user service during resource reservation
DataTransfer cancelBroadcastMessage MBMSIdle	SessionActive sessionCancel ResourceRelease, ResourceRelease ipCanBearerRelease WaitForTermAck, WaitForTermAck ipCanSessionTermAck IPCANIdle	The application cancels the MBMS user service during resource authorization

Equivalence of Application and Network Models.

The highest level of abstraction on message broadcast status is provided by 3rd-party application. Its view has to be synchronized also with the network resource state and charging session state.

Proposition 5. The labeled transition systems T_{App}, T_{BMSC}, T_{MBMS}, T_{PCRF}, and T_{CS} are weakly bisimilar.

Proof. By U_{ABMPC} a relation between the states of$T_{App'BMSC}$, T_{MBMS}, T_{PCRF}, and T_{CS} is denoted where

*U*ABMPC = {(Null, MBMSIdle, IpCANIdle, ResourceNull, ChargingIdle), (MessageWaiting, InitialWaiting, WaitForPCCRules, IpCanSession, $Active_{initial}$), (Broadcasting, DataTransfer, SessionActive, ResourceAuthorized, $Active_{transfer}$)}

The following homomorphism based on functional mapping may be defined between transitions of T_{App}, T_{BMSC}, T_{MBMS}, T_{PCRF}, and T_{CS}:

h_{ABMPC}(sendMessage) = h_{ABMPC}(sendBroadcastMessage) = h_{ABMPC}(sessionStart) = h_{ABMPC}(sessionInfo) = h_{ABMPC}(sendBroadcastMessage) = h_{ABMPC}(chargingDataStart$_{init}$);

h_{ABMPC}(successfulDelivery) = h_{ABMPCC}(initialPeriod) = h_{ABMPC}(pccRule) = h_{ABMPC}(ipCanSessionModification) = h_{ABMPCC}(chargingDataStart$_{interim}$);

h_{ABMPC}(successfulMessageCompletion) = h_{ABMPC}(dataTransferStop) = h_{ABMPC}(sessionStop) = h_{ABMPC}(ipCanSessionTermination) = h_{ABMPC}(chargingDataStop$_{normal}$);

h_{ABMPC}(cancelMessage) = h_{ABMPC}(cancel) = h_{ABMPC}(sessionCancel) = h_{ABMPC}(ipCanSessionCancel) = h_{ABMPC}(chargingDataStop$_{canceled}$);

h_{ABMPC}(unsuccessfulDelivery) = h_{ABMPC}(resourcesFailed) = h_{ABMPC}(ipCanBearerFailed) = h_{ABMPC}(provisionNonAck) = h_{ABMPC}(chargingDataStop$_{failed}$).

In order to define a weak bisimilar relation between the states of T_{App}, T_{BMSC}, T_{MBMS}, T_{PCRF}, and T_{CS} we establish the valid sequences of ordered transitions from $-\rightarrow_{App}$, $-\rightarrow_{BMSC}$, $-\rightarrow_{MBMS}$, $-\rightarrow_{PCRF}$, and $-\rightarrow_{CS}$ that correspond to U_{ABMPC}. Let $\tau^{App}{}_i \subset \rightarrow_{App}$, where $i \in \{1, \ldots, 6\}$, be the following transition sequences:

$\tau^{App}{}_1$ = (Null sendMessage MessageWaiting);

$\tau^{App}{}_2$ = (MessageWaiting getBroadcastStatus MessageWaiting,
MessageWaiting successfulDelivery
Broadcasting);

$\tau^{App}{}_3$ = (Broadcasting getBroadcastStatus Broadcasting,
Broadcasting successfulMessageCompletion
Broadcasted, Broadcasted getBroadcastStatus Broadcasted,
Broadcasted notifyBroadcastDeliveryReceipt
Broadcasted, Broadcasted stopAnnouncement Null);

$\tau^{App}{}_4$=(MessageWaiting unableToDeliverBroadcastImpossible,
BroadcastImpossible getBroadcastStatus
BroadcastImpossible, BroadcastImpossible
notifyBroadcastDeliveryReceipt BroadcastImpossible,
BroadcastImpossible stopAnnouncement Null);

$\tau^{App}{}_5$ = (MessageWaiting cancelMessage Null);

$\tau^{App}{}_6$ = (Broadcasting cancelMessage Null).

Let $\tau^{BMS}C_i \subset \rightarrow_{BMSC}$, where $i \in \{1, \ldots, 6\}$, be following transition sequences:

τ_1^{BMSC} = (MBMSIdle sendBroadcastMessage InitialWaiting);

τ_2^{BMSC} = (InitialWaiting initialPeriod DataTransfer);

τ_3^{BMSC} = (DataTransfer dataTransferStop MBMSIdle);

τ_4^{BMSC} = (InitialWaiting resourceFailed MBMSIdle);

τ_5^{BMSC} = (InitialWaiting cancelBroadcastMessage MBMSIdle);

τ_6^{BMSC} = (DataTransfer resourceLost MBMSIdle).

Let $\tau^{MBMS}{}_i \subset \rightarrow_{MBMS}$, where $i \in \{1, \ldots, 6\}$, be the following:

$\tau^{MBMS}{}_1$ = (IPCANIdle sessionStart WaitForPCCRules);

$\tau^{MBMS}{}_2$ = (WaitForPCCRules pccRules ResourceReservation,
ResourceReservation ipCanBearerEstablishment
SessionActive);

$\tau^{MBMS}{}_3$ = (SessionActive sessionStop ResourceRelease,
ResourceRelease ipCanBearerRelease WaitForTermAck,
WaitForTermAck ipCanSessionTermAck
IPCANIdle);

$\tau^{MBMS}{}_4$ = (ResourceReservation ipCanBearerFailed
IPCANIdle);

$\tau^{MBMC}{}_5$ = (WaitForPCCRules sessionCancel IPCANIdle,
ResourceReservation sessionCancel IPCANIdle);

$\tau^{MBMS}{}_6$ = (SessionActive ipCanBearerLost IPCANIdle).

Let $\tau^{PCRF}{}_i \subset \rightarrow_{PCRF}$, where $i \in \{1, \ldots, 6\}$, be the following:

τ_1^{PCRF} = (ResourceNull sessionInfo IPCanSession);

τ_2^{PCRF} = (IPCANSession ipCanSessionModification ResourceAuthorizing, ResourceAuthorizing provisionAck ResourceAuthorized);

τ_3^{PCRF} = (ResourceAuthorized ipCanSessionTermination ResourceNull);

τ_4^{PCRF} = (ResourceAuthorizing provisionNonAck ResourceNull);

τ_5^{PCRF} = (IPCANSession ipCanSessionCancel ResourceNull, ResourceAuthorized ipCanSessionCancel ResourceNull);

τ_6^{PCRF} = (ResourceAuthorized ipCanBearerRemoved ResourceNull).

Let $\tau^{CS}{}_i \subset \rightarrow_{CS}$, where $i \in \{1, \ldots, 6\}$, be following transition sequences:

τ_1^{CS} = (ChargingIdle chargingDataStart$_{init}$ Active$_{initial}$);

τ_2^{CS} = (Active$_{initial}$ chargingDataStart$_{interim}$ Active$_{transfer}$);

τ_3^{CS} = (Active$_{transfer}$ chargingDataStop$_{normal}$ ChargingIdle);

τ_4^{CS} = (Active$_{initial}$ chargingDataStop$_{failed}$ ChargingIdle);

τ_5^{CS} = (Active$_{initial}$ chargingDataStop$_{canceled}$ ChargingIdle);

τ_6^{CS} = (Active$_{transfer}$ chargingDataStop$_{canceled}$ ChargingIdle).

Then, based on the defined homomorphism h_{ABMPC} between the actions of T_{App}, T_{BMSC}, T_{MBMS}, T_{PCRF}, and T_{CS}, it follows that for U_{ABMPC} the sequences (τ^{App}_i, τ^{BMSC}_i, τ^{MBMS}_i, τ^{PCRF}_i, τ^{CS}_i) for $i \in \{1, \ldots, 6\}$ agree with Definition 2 for weak bisimilarity. Hence, the state machines that represent the 3rd-party application view on message broadcast, MBMS session, IP-CAN session, QoS resources, and charging session are bisimilar; that is, these state machines expose equivalent behavior.

CONCLUSION

In EPS there are specific features, nodes, and interfaces defined to support broadcasting of content to multiple users simultaneously. Parlay X Message Broadcast WS allows third-party applications to send messages to all mobile terminals in a specific geographical area. The deployment of 3rd-party control on multimedia broadcasting implies more research on synergy between WS APIs and respective communication control protocols.

The paper presents a study on modeling aspects of a network node that mediates between 3rd-party application servers and the evolved packet core of a mobile network. It explores the way the network agnostic WS interfaces collaborate with specific control functionality in order to provide value added multimedia broadcasting services.

The results regard model aspects of the behavior of a Service Capability Server, namely, BMSC, which exposes Parlay X WS interfaces toward applications and "talks" network protocols toward the network. The focus is on collaboration of different functionalities, namely, service control, session management, QoS control, and charging control. In the context of message broadcast, we modeled the states of MBMS session, IP-CAN session, QoS resources, and charging session and showed that these models are synchronized with the 3rd-party application view on message broadcast. The proof is based on functional mapping between the transitions in state machines and the identification of a homomorphism between actions. The concept of weak bisimilarity is used to prove that the state machines expose equivalent behavior. Thus, the novelty of contribution might be summarized as model definitions and proof for bisimilarity.

The utilization of standardized Message Broadcast APIs provides a unified approach for 3rd-party application management and provisioning. It allows development of converged multimedia broadcast applications in a way which is independent of the underlying access technologies.

Conflict of Interests

The authors declare that there is no conflict of interests regarding the publication of this paper.

REFERENCES

1. D. Lecompte and F. Gabin, "Evolved multimedia broadcast/multicast service (eMBMS) in LTE-advanced: overview and Rel-11 enhancements," IEEE Communications Magazine, vol. 50, no. 11, pp. 68–74, 2012.
2. J. Calabuig, J. F. Monserrat, D. Gozálvez, and O. Klemp, "Safety on the roads: LTE alternatives for sending ITS messages," IEEE Vehicular Technology Magazine, vol. 9, no. 4, pp. 61–70, 2014. ·
3. I. Stephanasik, I. Chochliouros, G. Lymperopoulos, and K. Berberidis, "Optimal video delivery in mobile networks using a cache-accelerated multi area eMBMS architecture," in Artificial Intelligence Applications and Innovations, vol. 437 of IFIP Advances in Information and Communication Technology, pp. 13–23, Springer, Berlin, Germany, 2014.
4. F. C. Pinto, N. Carapeto, A. Videira, T. Frazão, and M. Homem, "Context-aware multimedia distribution to mobile social communities," International Journal of Handheld Computing Research, vol. 4, no. 3, pp. 63–92, 2013.
5. C. M. Lentisco, M. Aguayo, L. Bellido, E. Pastor, D. De-Antonio-Monte, and A. G. Bolivar, "A virtualized platform for analyzing LTE broadcast services," in Proceedings of the European Conference on Networks and Communications (EuCNC '15), pp. 512–516, Paris, France, June 2015.
6. J. Calabuig, J. Monserrat, D. Martin-Sacristan, and J. Olmos, "Comparison of multicast/broadcast services in Long Term Evolution Advanced and IEEE 802.16m networks," Wireless Communications and Mobile Computing, vol. 14, no. 7, pp. 717–728, 2014.
7. G. Araniti, M. Condoluci, and A. Molinaro, "Resource management of multicast services over LTE," in Convergence of Broadband, Broadcast, and Cellular Network Technologies, pp. 77–93, IGI Global, 2014.
8. G. K. Walker, J. Wang, C. Lo, X. G. Zhang, and G. Bao, "Relationship between LTE broadcast/eMBMS and next generation broadcast television," IEEE Transactions on Broadcasting, vol. 60, no. 2, pp. 185–192, 2014.
9. F. Malandrino, C. Casetti, C. F. Chiasserini, and S. Zhou, "Real-time scheduling for content broadcasting in LTE," in Proceedings of the IEEE International Symposium on Modelling, Analysis & Simulation of Computer and Telecommunication Systems, pp. 126–131, Paris, France, September 2014.
10. A. de la Fuente, A. G. Armada, and R. P. Leal, "Joint multicast/unicast scheduling with dynamic optimization for LTE multicast service," in Proceedings of the 20th European Wireless Conference (EW '14), pp. 462–467, Barcelona, Spain, May 2014.
11. C. Borgiattino, C. Casetti, C. F. Chiasserini, and F. Malandrino, "Efficient area formation for LTE broadcasting," in Proceedings of the 12th Annual IEEE International Conference on Sensing, Communication, and Networking (SECON '15), pp. 202–210, IEEE, Seattle, Wash, USA, June 2015.
12. C. W. Yeh, M. J. Shih, G. Y. Lin, and H. Y. Wei, "LTE-D broadcast with distributed interference-aware D2D resource allocation," in Proceedings of the 7th International Conference on Ubiquitous and Future Networks (ICUFN '15), pp. 165–170, Sapporo, Japan, July 2015.
13. Y.-H. Xu, C.-O. Chow, M.-L. Tham, and H. Ishii, "An enhanced framework for providing multimedia

broadcast/multicast service over heterogeneous networks," Journal of Zhejiang University Science, vol. 15, no. 1, pp. 63–80, 2014.

14. J. H. Kim, S. K. Kim, and B. S. Lee, "Message service method and message service system," US Patent 8478313 B2, 2013.

15. 3GPP, "Multimedia Broadcast/Multicast Service (MBMS); architecture and functional description," 3GPPTS 23.246, 2015, Release 13.

16. 3GPP, "Multimedia Broadcast/Multicast Service (MBMS); protocols and codecs," 3GPP TS 26.346, 2015, Release 13.

17. 3GPP TS 23.203, "Policy and Charging control architecture," Release 13, v13.5.0, 2015.

18. 3GPP, "Telecommunication management; charging management; charging architecture and principles," 3GPP TS 32.240, 2015, Release 13, v13.0.0.

19. 3GPP, "Open Service Access (OSA); parlay X web services; part 15: message broadcast," 3GPP TS 29.199-15, 2009, Release 9.

20. L. Fuchun, Z. Qiansheng, and C. Xuesong, "Bisimilarity control of decentralized nondeterministic discrete-event systems," in Proceedings of the 33rd Chinese Control Conference (CCC '14), pp. 3898–3903, IEEE, Nanjing, China, July 2014.

CHAPTER 7

A DYNAMIC PROGRAMMING SOLUTION FOR ENERGY-OPTIMAL VIDEO PLAYBACK ON MOBILE DEVICES

Minseok Song and Jinhan Park

INTRODUCTION

The Internet of Things (IoT) allows physical objects to interact and cooperate with one another by exchanging data, and multimedia-related services based on the IoT are now gaining popularity in various applications areas [1]. For example, users of home security systems now see images from cameras on a smartphone, and telemedicine systems allow doctors to monitor a patient's health using video communication.

To support multimedia applications within the IoT, the characteristics of video need to be considered carefully. For example, the amount of data involved requires the use of compression techniques for codecs, but encoding and decoding processes are computationally intensive. Video transmission is a real-time process, which requires continuously periodic decoding to avoid distorted playback. Most importantly, mobile IoT devices have a limited energy budget, making the energy requirements of video transmission an important issue.

An effective way of reducing CPU power consumption is to use a dynamic voltage and frequency scaling (DVFS) technique, which adjusts the operating voltage and frequency of the processor [2–4]. Because the energy dissipated by the CPU scales quadratically with the supply voltage, reducing the voltage saves a lot of energy but also slows program execution, so that an appropriate compromise is always required.

In video playback, frames have to be decoded and rendered at playback rate to avoid a loss of quality. For example, to play a video at 25 frames per second, a frame must be decoded every 40 ms. This decoding process needs to finish within this period, but workload imposed by each frame varies significantly with video content [5–10].

In most previous work on the application of DVFS to videos, the lowest frequency that satisfies the deadline of the decoding time is chosen to reduce power consumption [11], but more energy can be saved by introducing flexibility in timing, by means of buffering techniques: if several frames are decoded in advance, the CPU can operate at lower frequencies on average, but buffering comes with its own costs [12]. Therefore, power saving is only effective with an appropriate frequency selection method subject to buffer constraints, but previous work took no account of this issue.

We propose a new scheme that determines the CPU frequency needed to decode each frame, which minimizes energy consumption while avoiding buffer overrun. We start by developing a video playback and energy model, formulate the energy optimization problem, and go on to use a dynamic programming technique to determine a sequence of frequencies. We finally present experimental results based on measurement of smartphone energy consumption and decoding times.

The rest of this paper is organized as follows. We present related work in Section 2 and the system model in Section 3. We formulate an optimization problem in Section 4, propose a new frequency selection algorithm in Section 5, and extend it in Section 6. We assess our scheme in Section 7 and finally conclude the paper in Section 8.

RELATED WORK

CPU power management has been the subject of a lot of research, and most of the resulting techniques involve either dynamic power management (DPM) or DVFS. DPM puts an idle CPU into sleep mode [13], whereas DVFS reduces the voltage and frequency of an active CPU [2, 4]. DPM is not generally suitable for real-time applications that run

Citation: Minseok Song and Jinhan Park, "A Dynamic Programming Solution for Energy-Optimal Video Playback on Mobile Devices," Mobile Information Systems, vol. 2016, Article ID 1042525, 10 pages, 2016. doi:10.1155/2016/1042525

continuously, because the idle intervals are too short to allow the CPU to enter sleep mode [8]. Therefore, we only review previous works about DVFS only in this section.

DVFS techniques can be classified into interval-based and task-based algorithms [7, 14]. Interval-based schemes monitor the CPU load at intervals and respond by changing the CPU frequency and voltage. A representative scheme is the Linux Ondemand governor, which adjusts frequency periodically based on CPU utilization in the preceding interval [15]. Another scheme is LongRun [16] which varies the frequency to suit the measured utilization. These methods are typically easy to implement but can make inaccurate predictions based on the assumption that loads are similar to recent loads [14].

Task-based schemes can overcome this problem to some extent by classifying tasks into several types to which different frequency selection policies are applied. Ayoub et al. [17] manage frequency and voltage to meet a performance target, expressed as a fraction of maximum system performance. Flautner and Mudge [18] propose a method that chooses a CPU frequency for each task based on its recent computational requirements. Seo et al. [14] present a frequency allocation method to reduce the average response time of tasks. However, all of these methods have been developed for general workloads and therefore may not be suitable for multimedia applications with real-time constraints.

DVFS techniques for real-time systems are generally integrated with real-time scheduling [2–4]. Based on the analysis of worst-case execution times, they select CPU frequencies that satisfy the real-time constraints; but tasks are often complete before their worst-case execution times, so several algorithms incorporate methods of reclaiming the unused time [2, 4]. The CPU starts each period running at a frequency which will meet the worst-case demands and the frequency is then reduced in response to the actual computation requirement.

Several groups have investigated DVFS techniques for video applications [6, 7], in which the key issue is to estimate the computational requirements of successive frames. Most of these techniques predict the workload required to decode a frame from the workloads incurred in decoding previous frames and adjust the CPU frequency. The accuracy of these schemes has been improved by feedback mechanisms, which take previous prediction errors into account [19].

It has been widely observed [5–10] that frame decoding times vary significantly. For example, some of the frames in an MPEG video can take ten times as long to decode as an average frame [20]. That makes it difficult to estimate the computational requirements of successive frames to meet their deadlines [5–7]. Several workload estimation techniques have been proposed for video applications [5–7, 11, 19], and they can be categorized [5] into methods which make use of the relationship between the amount of data in a frame and decoding time and methods which predict decoding times based on recent times and aim to correct prediction errors using a feedback mechanism.

A close relationship between frame size and decoding time has been widely observed [5, 6, 11], especially in videos encoded with MPEG-style compression, and this relationship allows decoding times to be predicted with reasonable confidence. For example, Liu et al. [6] established a linear relationship between frame size and decoding time and used it to predict decoding times, while Yang and Song [11] improved the accuracy of this approach by introducing a logarithmic relationship, and Bavier et al. [21] used it to predict decoding times. Lee et al. [5] introduced particle-filter techniques to further improve the accuracy of this approach for H.264 codecs.

Yuan et al. [8–10] proposed several DVFS techniques in which the CPU speed is adjusted on the basis of a statistical analysis of past workloads. Urunuela et al. [7] developed a history-based DVFS technique, but it is tailored to video kiosks rather than general video players. Choi et al. [22] adopted a hybrid approach in which different DVFS policies are applied depending on the characteristics of each frame. Im and Ha [12] presented DVFS techniques in which buffers were used to reclaim unused CPU time, and Huang et al. [20] introduced a method of predicting decoding times from offline analysis of frame characteristics.

Most of these techniques do not consider the characteristics of video playback, in which some deadline misses and frame skipping are acceptable. Kim et al. [23] presented a DVFS scheme specifically for scalable video coding (SVC) codecs, which makes use of temporal scalability. The scheme put forward by Yang and Song [11] acknowledges the effect of the ratio of deadline miss on energy consumption, but this paper does not provide a satisfactory solution that selects the appropriate frequency while minimizing energy consumption, nor does it examine how buffering affects power consumption.

MODEL

System Model

To support periodic nature of video playback, a video player decodes r frames per second, and so the decoding period of a frame, T^d, is $1/r$. The Notations explain important symbols used in this paper. Suppose that a CPU supports N_f frequency levels and that level k is the frequency $_{fk}$ ($k = 1, \ldots, N_f$). If $k < f_m$, so that $f^N{}_f$ is the highest possible frequency. Let N^d be the number of frames decoded in a video. Let $P^{active}{}_k$ and P^{idle} , respectively, be the active and idle power consumption of the system at frequency level k. We will assume that the decoding time of each frame is known in advance: decoding times can be predicted by an offline analysis of the bitstream of a video [20] or by formulating a relationship between frame size and decoding time [5, 6, 11].This decoding time information can be inserted into the header of a video [20], and we assume that these frames are available to our frequency selection algorithm. Specifically, $d_{j,}$ is the decoding time of frame j at frequency level k.

Video Playback Model.

Frame-level DVFS is appropriate for a media player [5–7, 11], which then selects the frequency which best matches the CPU workload imposed by the current frame, before that frame is decoded. The CPU does not change its frequency until the frame has been decoded. Figure 1 shows our video playback model. The decoding task produces frames at playback rate and passes them to a buffer which stores frames for consumption by a display task, which fetches frames at playback rate. If there was no buffer, then only one frame can be handled by the display task, so the decoder enters sleep state until the frame is consumed by the display task. However, if a number of frames can be stored in the buffer, then decoding can run late, allowing lower frequencies to be selected, but this flexibility is limited by the size of buffer. For example, suppose that the buffer can accommodate N^b frames. If there are already N^b frames in the buffer, then decoding of a new frame must be delayed until the next decoded frame has gone to the display task. For example, consider Figure 1, where $Nb = 4$. If the buffer already contains 4 frames, then the decoder enters sleep state until frame j has been consumed by the display task.

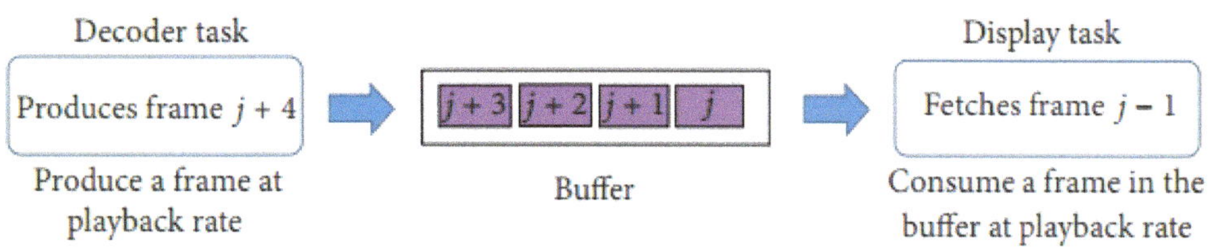

Figure 1: Video playback model.

To explain how this buffering technique can decrease CPU power consumption, consider a CPU with 4 frequency levels of 0.8 GHz, 1.2 GHz 1.6 GHz, and 1.8 GHz. We assume that $T^d = 40$ ms and that the process of a frame requires 36 ms at level 4, 40.5 ms at level 3, 54 ms at level 2, and 81 ms at level 1. If there was no buffer, then frequency level 4 must be chosen for every frame to keep the decoding time within 40 ms, as shown in Figure 2(a). However, if there is a buffer, which contains frames decoded when playback starts, then frequency level 1 can be selected for the first three frames, level 2 for the next two frames, and level 3 for the final frame as shown in Figure 2(b), without violating deadlines.

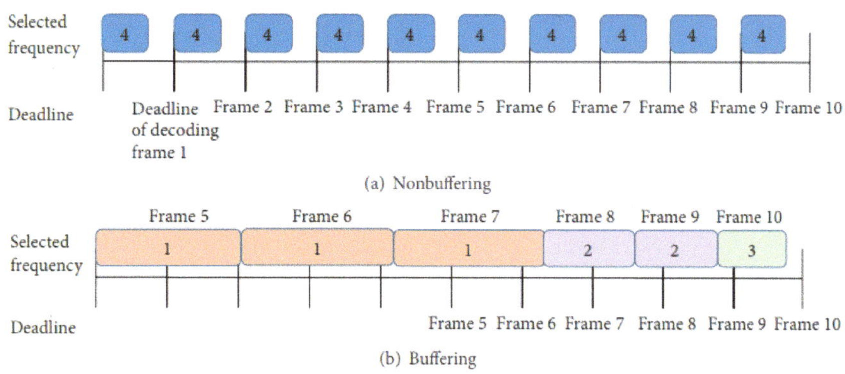

Figure 2: Comparison between buffering and nonbuffering.

PROBLEM FORMULATION

We formulate an optimization problem with a solution which will minimize energy consumption subject to the constraints of buffer size and decoding deadlines. Frame j ($j = 1, \ldots, N^d$) must be decoded before its deadline $Tend\ j$, which is $j^T{}_d$. At $Tend$, frame j leaves the buffer to be displayed on the screen. Let Sj be the frequency level selected for decoding frame j; and let $Tstart\ j$ be the earliest possible time at which the decoding of frame j can start. Because the buffer can contain N^b frames, the decoding of frame j can start at $Tend\ j{-}N^b$ (i.e., ($j-$)), at which frame $j{-}N^b$ can be removed from the buffer and displayed, allowing a new frame to be decoded and stored in the buffer.

Thus, $Tstart\ j$ can be expressed as follows:

$$T_j^{\text{start}} = \begin{cases} 0 & j = 1,\ldots,N^b \\ \left(j-N^b\right)T^d & j = N^b+1,\ldots,N^d \end{cases} \quad (1)$$

Let $T^{over}_{j,k}$ ($j = 1, \ldots, N^{d-1}$) be the length of time by which the decoding of frame j would overrun if frequency level k is chosen, relative to the start time of the next frame T^{start}_{j+1}. The value of $T^{over}_{0,}$ $\forall k$ is initialized to 0. This overrun can be expressed as follows:

$$T_{j,k}^{\text{over}} = \max\left(0, d_{j,k} + T_{j-1,S_{j-1}}^{\text{over}} + T_j^{\text{start}} - T_{j+1}^{\text{start}}\right) \quad (2)$$

If the decoding of frame j indeed finishes after T^{start}_{j+1}, then $Tover\ j,k$ is the time difference between the actual time at which the decoding of frame j finishes (i.e., $d_{j,k} + T^{over}_{j-1},S_{j-1} + T^{start}_{j}$) and T^{start}_{j+1}, when frequency level k is chosen for frame j. Conversely, if time remains after the decoding of frame j, the CPU enters its idle state and remains in this state until T^{start}_{j+1}, when $T^{over}_{j,k}$ is set to 0.

If $T^{over}_{j,} = 0$, then the CPU stays in its idle state for the length of $T^{sleep}_{j,}$, which can be expressed as $T^{start}_{j+1} - (T^{start}_{j} + d_{j,k} + T^{over}_{j-1},S_j)$; otherwise, $T^{sleep}_{j,k}$ is set to 0. The determination of $T^{sleep}_{j,}$ can thus be summarized as follows:

$$T_{j,k}^{\text{sleep}} = \begin{cases} T_{j+1}^{\text{start}} - T_j^{\text{start}} - d_{j,k} - T_{j-1,S_{j-1}}^{\text{over}} & \text{if } T_{j,k}^{\text{over}} = 0 \\ 0 & \text{otherwise.} \end{cases} \quad (3)$$

The energy consumed during the period of $d_{j,k}$ + $T^{sleep}_{j,k}$ while frame j is decoded at frequency level k is written as $E_{j,k}$, which can be expressed as follows:

$$E_{j,k} = d_{j,k}P_k^{active} + T_{j,k}^{sleep}P_k^{idle} \tag{4}$$

At this point, we must introduce a further variable Tdiff j, , which is the difference between the actual time at which the decoding of frame j finishes ($d_{j,k}$ +T^{over}_{j-1},S_{j-1} +T^{start}_j) and T^{start}_j , and this difference can be expressed as follows:

$$T_{j,k}^{diff} = d_{j,k} + T_{j-1,S_{j-1}}^{over} \tag{5}$$

Figure 3 shows the relationship between $T^{over}_{j,}$, $T^{sleep}_{j,k}$, and $T^{diff}_{j,k}$ in a short sequence of frames.

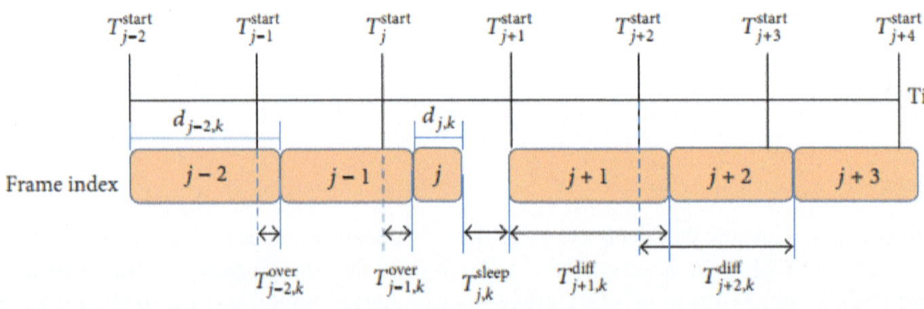

Figure 3: Sequence of frames showing the relationship between $T^{over}_{j,}$, $T^{sleep}_{j,k}$, and $T^{diff}_{j,k}$.

The decoding of frame j must start after T^{start}_j and finish before T^{end} . We can express this period for each frame j (j = 1, . . . , N^d) as T^{round}_j , so that T^{round}_j = T^{end}_j −T^{start}_j . Each frame j must be decoded before its deadline T^{end} , so $T^{diff}_{j,k}$ ≤ T^{round}_j . Our frequency selection policy has to minimize the total energy consumption $\sum^{Nd}_{j=1} Ej,$. We can now formulate this frequency selection problem that determines S_j (j = 1, . . . , Nd) as follows:

$$\text{Minimize} \quad \sum_{j=1}^{N^d} E_{j,S_j} \tag{6}$$

Subject to

$$T_{j,S_j}^{diff} \leq T_j^{round}, \quad \forall j,\ j = 1, \ldots, N^d$$

FREQUENCY ALLOCATION ALGORITHM

Algorithm Concept

We now propose an algorithm to solve the problem using a dynamic programming technique. We will use a resolution of 1 ms for time values such as $T^{diff}_{j,}$. Let Venergy j, be the minimum amount of energy when $T^{diff}_{j,}$ is u milliseconds and frame j is decoded (j = 1, . . . , N^d and u = 1, . . . , T^{round}_j). Let $F_{j,u}$ be the frequency level required to achieve the energy consumption of $V^{energy}_{j,u}$; further, let $V^{over}_{j,}$ u be the corresponding value of $T^{over}_{j,Sj}$ and $V^{diff}_{j,u}$ the value of $T^{diff}_{j-1,Sj}$.

The main idea of the dynamic programming is to construct a table of the optimal energy $V^{energy}_{j,u}$ for each frame j when $T^{diff}_{j,k}$ = u (u = 1, . . . , T^{round}_j), as described in Table 1, where the minimum value in the final row, min$u$=1,...,T^{round}_N ^{d} V^{energy} $N^{d,u}$, represents the amount of energy consumed by the optimal frequency allocation. For this purpose, we first initialize the values of $V^{energy}_{1,}$ and then develop the recurrence relationship between consecutive frames so as to find all the values of $V^{energy}_{j,}$ in the table.

Table 1: Table for the value of $V^{energy}_{j,}$ against $T^{diff}_{j,}$.

Frame number	$T^{diff}_{j,k}$ values				
	1	2	…	$T_j^{round} - 1$	T_j^{round}
1	$V_{1,1}^{energy}$	$V_{1,2}^{energy}$	…	$V_{1,T_1^{round}}^{energy}$	$V_{1,T_1^{round}}^{energy}$
2	$V_{2,1}^{energy}$	$V_{2,2}^{energy}$	…	$V_{2,T_2^{round}}^{energy}$	$V_{2,T_2^{round}}^{energy}$
⋮	⋮	⋮	…	⋮	⋮
N^d	$V_{N^d,1}^{energy}$	$V_{N^d,2}^{energy}$	…	$V_{N^d,T_{N^d-1}^{round}}^{energy}$	$V_{N^d,T_{N^d}^{round}}^{energy}$

We also maintain a two-dimensional array of tuples (Fj,, $V^{\text{diff}}_{j,u}$) which leads to the minimum energy of Venergy j,u as illustrated in Figure 4. Using this array, a backtracking phase starts from frame N^d to frame 1 to select frequency of every frame. For example, Figure 4 shows an array of these tuples when $Nd = 5$ and Tround $j = 10$. Suppose that the third column in the last row has the minimum energy value. Because $V^{\text{diff}}_{j,}$ points to the column index of the previous frame, a sequence of frequencies can be selected as follows: (6, 3, 4, 5, 1). Likewise, our dynamic programming algorithm has three phases: (1) initialization, (2) establishment of recurrence relation, and (3) backtracking.

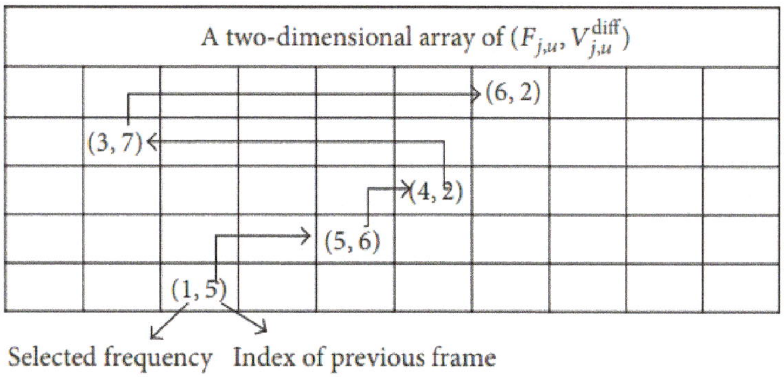

Figure 4: Process of backtracking.

Initialization.

For initialization, consider the following:

(1) $V^{\text{energy}}_{j,u}$, $V^{\text{over}}_{j,u}$, $V^{\text{diff}}_{j,u}$, and $F_{j,u}$ are all initialized to ∞ ($\forall j, u$, $j = 1, \ldots, N^d$ and $u = 1, \ldots, T^{\text{round}}_j$).

(2) $\forall k$, where $d_{1,k} \leq T^{\text{end}}_1$, the values of $T^{\text{over}}_{1,k}$, $T^{\text{sleep}}_{1,k}$, and $E_{1,k}$ are calculated from (2), (3), and (4), respectively. Next, $V^{\text{over}}_{1,d_{1,k}}$ is replaced with $T^{\text{over}}_{1,k}$; then, $V^{\text{energy}}_{1,d_{1,k}}$ is updated to $E_{1,k}$, and $F_{1,d_{1,k}}$ is replaced with frequency level k.

Establishment of Recurrence Relation.

During the recurrence establishment phase, $V^{\text{energy}}_{j,u}$, Fj,u, $V^{\text{diff}}_{j,u}$, and $V^{\text{over}}_{j,u}$ ($j = 2, \ldots, N^d$ and $u = 1, \ldots, T^{\text{round}}_j$) are updated as follows:

(1) For each value of j and u ($j = 2, \ldots, N^d$ and $u = 1, \ldots, T^{\text{round}}_j$), we maintain a two-dimensional array, $A_{j,u}(i, k)$ ($i = 1, \ldots, T^{\text{round}}_{j-1}$ and $k = 1, \ldots, N^f$). The following steps are repeated to find the value of $A_{j,u}(i, k)$, $\forall i, k$ if $V^{\text{energy}}_{j-1,i} \neq \infty$:

(a) Calculate the value of $T^{\text{over}}_{j,k}$ using (2), after replacing $T^{\text{over}}_{j-1,S_{j-1}}$ with $V^{\text{over}}_{j-1,i}$.

(b) Using the resulting value of $T^{\text{over}}_{j,k}$, calculate $T^{\text{sleep}}_{j,k}$ from (3).

(c) Using the resulting value of $T^{\text{sleep}}_{j,k}$, calculate $E_{j,k}$ from (4) and use this value of $E_{j,k}$ to update $A_{\{j,d_{j,k}+V^{\text{over}}_{j-1,i}\}}(i, k)$.

(2) $V^{\text{energy}}_{j,u}$, $F_{j,u}$, $V^{\text{diff}}_{j,u}$, and $V^{\text{over}}_{j,u}$ are updated as follows:

$$V^{\text{energy}}_{j,u} = \min_{i=1,\ldots,T^{\text{round}}_{j-1},\ k=1,\ldots,N^f} \left(V^{\text{energy}}_{j-1,i} + A_{j,u}(i,k)\right),$$

$$F_{j,u} = \arg\min_{k=1,\ldots,N^f} V^{\text{energy}}_{j,u},$$

$$V^{\text{diff}}_{j,u} = \arg\min_{i=1,\ldots,T^{\text{round}}_{j-1}} V^{\text{energy}}_{j,u},$$

$$V^{\text{over}}_{j,u} = \max\left(0, V_{V^{\text{diff}}_{j,u}} + d_{j,F_{j,u}} - T^{\text{start}}_{j+1}\right). \tag{7}$$

Backtracking

We find values of Sj using a backtracking technique as follows:

(1) j is initialized to N^d, and u is set to $\arg\min_{\{u=1,\ldots,T^{\text{round}}_{N^d}\}} V^{\text{energy}}_{N^d,u}$, so that $V^{\text{energy}}_{N^d,u}$ represents the amount of minimum energy consumption.

(2) While $j > 0$, the following procedures are repeated: (1) S_j is set to $F_{j,u}$, (2) $V^{\text{diff}}_{j,u}$ is substituted for u, and (3) j is decremented by 1.

Pseudocode for this frequency selection algorithm (FSA) is presented as Algorithm 1. If T_{ma}x is the maximum round length so that $T_{\text{max}} = \max_{j=2,\ldots,}$ round $_j$, we can easily see from Algorithm 1 that the complexity of FSA is $O(N^d N^f T_{\text{max}})$.

Temporary variables: j, u, i and k;
for $j = 1$ to N^d **do**
  for $u = 1$ to T_j^{round} **do**
    $V_{j,u}^{\text{energy}}, V_{j,u}^{\text{over}}, V_{j,u}^{\text{diff}}$ and $F_{j,u} \leftarrow \infty$;
  end for
end for
for $u = 1$ to T_j^{round} **do**
  for $k = 1$ to N^f **do**
    if $d_{1,k} \le T_1^{\text{end}}$ and $u = d_{1,k}$ **then**
      Calculate $T_{1,k}^{\text{over}}, T_{1,k}^{\text{sleep}}$ and $E_{1,k}$ using (2), (3), and (4), respectively;
      $V_{1,u}^{\text{energy}} \leftarrow E_{1,k}$;
      $F_{1,u} \leftarrow k$;
      $V_{1,u}^{\text{over}} \leftarrow T_{1,k}^{\text{over}}$;
    end if
  end for
end for
for $j = 2$ to N^d **do**
  for $i = 1$ to T_{j-1}^{round} **do**
    for $k = 1$ to N^f **do**
      if $V_{j-1,i}^{\text{energy}} \ne \infty$ **then**
        Calculate the value of $T_{j,k}^{\text{over}}$ from (2) by replacing $T_{j-1,S_{j-1}}^{\text{over}}$ with $V_{j-1,i}^{\text{over}}$;
        $T_{j,k}^{\text{sleep}}$ is calculated from (3) by replacing $T_{j-1,S_{j-1}}^{\text{over}}$ with $V_{j-1,i}^{\text{over}}$;
        $E_{j,k}$ is calculated from (4), and $A_{\{j,d_{j,k}+V_{j-1,i}^{\text{over}}\}}(i,k)$ is updated using this value of $E_{j,k}$;
      end if
    end for
  end for
  $V_{j,u}^{\text{energy}} \leftarrow \min_{\{i=1,\dots,T_{j-1}^{\text{round}} \text{ and } k=1,\dots,N^f\}}(V_{j-1,i}^{\text{energy}} + A_{j,u}(i,k))$;
  $F_{j,u} \leftarrow \arg\min_{\{k=1,\dots,N^f\}} V_{j,u}^{\text{energy}}$;
  $V_{j,u}^{\text{diff}} \leftarrow \arg\min_{\{i=1,\dots,T_{j-1}^{\text{round}}\}} V_{j,u}^{\text{energy}}$;
  $V_{j,u}^{\text{over}} \leftarrow \max(0, V_{V_{j,u}^{\text{diff}}} + d_{j,F_{j,u}} - T_{j+1}^{\text{start}})$;
end for
$j \leftarrow N^d$;
$u \leftarrow \arg\min_{i=1,\dots,T_{N^d}^{\text{round}}} V_{N^d,i}^{\text{energy}}$;
while $j > 0$ **do**
  $S_j \leftarrow F_{j,u}$;
  $u \leftarrow V_{j,u}^{\text{diff}}$;
  $j \leftarrow j - 1$;
end while

Algorithm 1: FSA (frequency selection algorithm).

ALGORITHM EXECUTION

If the frame decoding time is known in advance, then FSA can run without modification. For example, before playback, frequency allocation table during the entire playback can be obtained as a result of algorithm execution. However, since the algorithm complexity depends on the number of frames to be decoded, we divide the algorithm into iterations and limit the number of frames taken by the algorithm to N^l ($N^l < N^d$). Therefore, at the beginning of the mth iteration, the algorithm chooses the frequency for frames between $(m-1)^{+1}$ and mN , which we call FSA-split, as shown in Algorithm 2.

(1) Temporary variables: j, u, i and k;

(2) Input parameter from the previous iteration ($m > 1$): I^{prev}

(3) $I^{prev} \leftarrow \arg\min_{i=1,\dots,T^{round}_{(m-1)N^l}} V^{energy}_{(m-1)N^l,i}$;

(4) **for** $j = (m-1)N^l + 1$ to mN^l **do**

(5) **for** $u = 1$ to T^{round}_j **do**

(6) $V^{energy}_{j,u}$, $V^{over}_{j,u}$, $V^{diff}_{j,u}$ and $F_{j,u} \leftarrow \infty$;

(7) **end for**

(8) **end for**

(9) **for** $u = 1$ to T^{round}_j **do**

(10) **for** $k = 1$ to N^f **do**

(11) **if** $d_{(m-1)N^l+1,k} \leq T^{end}_{(m-1)N^l+1}$ and $u = d_{(m-1)N^l+1,k}$ **then**

(12) **if** $m > 1$ **then**

(13) Calculate $T^{over}_{(m-1)N^l+1,k}$, $T^{sleep}_{(m-1)N^l+1,k}$ and $E_{(m-1)N^l+1,k}$ using (2), (3), and (4), respectively, by replacing $T^{over}_{j-1,S_{j-1}}$ with $V^{over}_{(m-1)N^l,I^{prev}}$;

(14) **else**

(15) Calculate $T^{over}_{(m-1)N^l+1,k}$, $T^{sleep}_{(m-1)N^l+1,k}$ and $E_{(m-1)N^l+1,k}$ using (2), (3), and (4), respectively, by replacing $T^{over}_{j-1,S_{j-1}}$ with 0;

(16) **end if**

(17) $V^{energy}_{(m-1)N^l+1,u} \leftarrow E_{(m-1)N^l+1,k}$;

(18) $F_{(m-1)N^l+1,u} \leftarrow k$;

(19) $V^{over}_{(m-1)N^l+1,u} \leftarrow T^{over}_{(m-1)N^l+1,k}$;

(20) **end if**

(21) **end for**

(22) **end for**

(23) **for** $j = (m-1)N^l + 2$ to mN^l **do**

(24) **for** $i = 1$ to T^{round}_{j-1} **do**

(25) **for** $k = 1$ to N^f **do**

(26) **if** $V^{energy}_{j-1,i} \neq \infty$ **then**

(27) Calculate the value of $T^{over}_{j,k}$ from (2) by replacing $T^{over}_{j-1,S_{j-1}}$ with $V^{over}_{j-1,i}$;

(28) $T^{sleep}_{j,k}$ is calculated from (3) by replacing $T^{over}_{j-1,S_{j-1}}$ with $V^{over}_{j-1,i}$;

(29) $E_{j,k}$ is calculated from (4), and $A_{\{j,d_{j,k}+V^{over}_{j-1,i}\}}(i,k)$ is updated using this value of $E_{j,k}$;

(30) **end if**

(31) **end for**

(32) **end for**

(33) $V^{energy}_{j,u} \leftarrow \min_{\{i=1,\dots,T^{round}_{j-1} \text{ and } k=1,\dots,N^f\}}(V^{energy}_{j-1,i} + A_{j,u}(i,k))$;

(34) $F_{j,u} \leftarrow \arg\min_{\{k=1,\dots,N^f\}} V^{energy}_{j,u}$;

(35) $V^{diff}_{j,u} \leftarrow \arg\min_{\{i=1,\dots,T^{round}_{j-1}\}} V^{energy}_{j,u}$;

(36) $V^{over}_{j,u} \leftarrow \max(0, V_{V^{diff}_{j,u}} + d_{j,F_{j,u}} - T^{start}_{j+1})$;

(37) **end for**

(38) $j \leftarrow mN^l$;

(39) $u \leftarrow \arg\min_{i=1,\dots,T^{round}_{mN^l}} V^{energy}_{mN^l,i}$;

(40) **while** $j > (m-1)N^l$ **do**

(41) $S_j \leftarrow F_{j,u}$;

(42) $u \leftarrow V^{diff}_{(m-1)N^l+j,u}$;

(43) $j \leftarrow j - 1$;

(44) **end while**

Algorithm 2: FSA-split (frequency selection algorithm for the mth iteration).

FSA-split has the following characteristics in comparison with FSA:

(i) FSA-split determines the frequencies of frames between $(m-1)^{+1}$ and mN .

(ii) An initialization part (lines between (9) and (22) in Algorithm 2) takes the length of overrun in the previous iteration ($V^{over}{}_{(m-1)}$,I^{prev}) for the calculation of the parameter values.

Several methods were developed for decoding time estimation, most of which predict future decoding times based on recent measured times [5–7, 11, 19]. The decoding times of the frames in a certain GOP do not change a lot compared with those of its neighboring GOPs [11]. We can therefore predict the decoding times of the next GOP on the basis of those of the current GOP. For example, if Nl is set to the number of frames of a GOP, then the frequency allocation table can be established for the next GOP by passing predicted decoding times of the next GOP to the input parameters of the FSA-split.

EXPERIMENTAL RESULTS

Setup.

We performed simulations to evaluate our schemes using power data and timings obtained experimentally. The power consumption of a Samsung Nexus S smartphone (not just the CPU) was measured, and Table 2 shows its active and idle power values. The time taken to decode video frames was also measured for the two videos in Table 3. We compared our scheme with two other algorithms as follows:

(1) HF always selects the highest frequency, which is equivalent to no DVFS.

(2) LF selects the lowest frequency level which will get each frame decoded in time.

This method is a good heuristic, because CPU frequency can be expected to have a monotonic relationship with energy consumption [4–7, 11].

Table 2: Measured power consumption against frequency of Samsung Nexus S phone.

Frequency (MHz)	1000	800	400	200	100
Active power (mW)	1324	1082	741	557	444
Idle power (mW)	545	527	503	471	420

Table 3: Measured power consumption against frequency of Samsung Nexus S phone.

Type	Title	Resolution	Average bitrate	Playback time	GOP length
Animation	Ice Age 4	352 × 288	736 kb/s	5 minutes	12
Sports	Soccer	352 × 288	199 kb/s	5 minutes	12

Efficacy of FSA.

Table 4 shows how energy consumption depends on the number of frames that are buffered. We see that (1) FSA always shows the best performance, using 13% less energy than LF and 27% less energy than HF on average, and (2) increasing the size of the buffer saves more energy, but this amount of energy saved gradually tails off. In particular, even when $N^b = 1$ so that only one additional buffer is used, FSA uses 11% less energy than LF on average, suggesting that the buffer overhead of FSA is not high.

Table 4: Relative energy consumption of FSA against a number of buffers

Video type	Animation				Sports			
Number of buffers (N^b)	1	2	3	4	1	2	3	4
Energy used relative to HF	68.6%	67.1%	66.9%	66.9%	80%	77.8%	77.3%	77.2%
Energy used relative to LF	84.2%	82.3%	82.1%	82%	93.2%	90.6%	90.1%	89.9%

The results in Table 4 can be attributed to FSA's effective use of the slack times generated by storing decoded frames in the buffer, allowing the CPU to operate at lower frequencies. For example, Table 5 shows the average percentage of the frames in both video clips that are decoded at each frequency; FSA chooses lower frequencies than LF, decreasing energy consumption. FSA chooses the highest frequency (1000 MHz) more often than LF, which increases the idle time, allowing relatively lower frequencies to be chosen than LF. These results suggest that frequency selection has a great effect on energy consumption.

Table 5: Percentage of frames decoded at each frequency

Video type	Animation					Sports				
Frequency (MHz)	100	200	400	800	1000	100	200	400	800	1000
LF	28.5%	3.7%	63.5%	4.3%	0%	0%	9.3%	90.4%	0.2%	0%
FSA (N^b = 1)	72%	0.8%	9.8%	14.8%	2.6%	4.8%	52.7%	31.1%	11.1%	0.3%
FSA (N^b = 2)	75.5%	0%	0.8%	19.9%	3.8%	24.7%	8.6%	27.2%	38.2%	1.3%
FSA (N^b = 3)	75.2%	0%	0.3%	19.7%	4.8%	28.1%	2.1%	21.8%	46.7%	1.3%
FSA (N^b = 4)	75.3%	0%	0.3%	20.0%	4.4%	28.9%	1.1%	18.4%	50.6%	1.1%

Efficacy of FSA-Split

To evaluate the efficacy of FSAsplit, we examined how the values of Nl affect the energy consumption against different values of N^b as tabulated in Table 6. We see that (1) their energy difference is marginal, exhibiting 1.47% difference at maximum, even when N^l is set to 12 which is the GOP size; (2) increasing the value of N^l decreases the energy gap; and (3) increasing the buffer size increases the energy gap even though the difference is negligible. Although FSA exhibits slightly better performance than FSA-split, it takes all frame parameters for algorithm execution, requiring a lot of computation. These results suggest that FSA-split is a practical method of reducing the energy required for video decoding.

Table 6: Percentage energy difference between FSA and FSA-split against different values of ^{Nl}

Video type	Animation					Sports				
N^l	12	24	48	96	192	12	24	48	96	192
N^b = 1	0.88%	0.48%	0.26%	0.14%	0.07%	0.22%	0.11%	0.05%	0.03%	0.02%
N^b = 2	1.26%	0.66%	0.33%	0.17%	0.09%	0.42%	0.21%	0.11%	0.06%	0.03%
N^b = 3	1.40%	0.70%	0.35%	0.18%	0.09%	0.49%	0.24%	0.12%	0.07%	0.04%
N^b = 4	1.47%	0.76%	0.38%	0.20%	0.10%	0.52%	0.24%	0.12%	0.06%	0.04%

CONCLUSIONS

We have proposed a new frequency allocation scheme which minimizes energy consumption while avoiding buffer overrun, using a dynamic programming technique. This scheme establishes recurrence relationship between consecutive frames to construct a table of the minimum energy values required to decode each frame and determines a sequence of frequencies required to decode every frame using a backtracking technique. It was extended to optimize CPU frequencies over a short sequence of frames, which gives a basis for energy-saving video decoding in practice.

Experimental results show that it uses 27% less energy than a processor at the highest frequency on average. In particular, it uses 13% less energy, compared to the widely used heuristic which chooses the lowest frequency to get each frame decoded in time. We believe that these results give a useful guideline for low-power video service by providing the minimum bound on power consumption required for video playback.

NOTATION

r: Playback rate of a video (fps)
N^f: Number of frequency levels supported by a CPU
T^d: Decoding period of a video
f_k: Frequency corresponding to the frequency level k
P_k^{active}: Active power at frequency level k
P_k^{idle}: Idle power at frequency level k
N^b: Number of frames that a display buffer can accommodate
N^d: Number of frames decoded in a video
$d_{j,k}$: Decoding time of frame j at frequency level k
T_j^{end}: Decoding deadline for frame j
T_j^{start}: Earliest possible start time for decoding frame j
T_j^{round}: $T_j^{\text{end}} - T_j^{\text{start}}$
$T_{j,k}^{\text{over}}$: $\max(0, d_{j,k} + T_{j-1,S_{j-1}}^{\text{over}} + T_j^{\text{start}} - T_{j+1}^{\text{start}})$
$T_{j,k}^{\text{sleep}}$: CPU sleep time when frequency level k is chosen for frame j
$E_{j,k}$: Energy consumed during the decoding period for frame j at frequency k
$A_{j,u}(i,k)$: Two-dimensional array for $E_{j,k}$ when $i = T_{j-1,S_j}^{\text{diff}}$, $u = T_{j,k}^{\text{diff}}$, and k is the frequency level chosen for decoding frame j
$T_{j,k}^{\text{diff}}$: Time between completion of decoding frame j and T_j^{start}
S_j: Frequency level selected for decoding frame j
$V_{j,u}^{\text{energy}}$: Minimum energy consumption in decoding frames 1 to j, when $T_{j,k}^{\text{diff}} = u$ ms
$F_{j,u}$: Frequency level selected for decoding frame j to achieve an energy of $V_{j,u}^{\text{energy}}$
$V_{j,u}^{\text{over}}$: Value of T_{j,S_j}^{over} to achieve an energy of $V_{j,u}^{\text{energy}}$
$V_{j,u}^{\text{diff}}$: Value of $T_{j-1,S_j}^{\text{diff}}$ to achieve an energy of $V_{j,u}^{\text{energy}}$
N^l: Number of frames for which frequencies are determined by FSA-split.

COMPETING INTERESTS

The authors declare that they have no competing interests.

ACKNOWLEDGMENTS

This research is supported by Inha University Research Grant.

REFERENCES

1. S. A. Alvi, B. Afzal, G. A. Shah, L. Atzor, and W. Mahmood, "Internet of multimedia things: vision and challenges," Ad Hoc Networks, vol. 33, pp. 87–111, 2015.
2. H. Aydin, P. Mejia-Alvarez, D. Mosse, and R. Melhem, "Dynamic and aggressive scheduling techniques for power-aware real-time systems," in Proceedings of the IEEE Real-Time Systems Symposium, p. 95, London, UK, December 2001.
3. M. Marinoni and G. Buttazzo, "Elastic DVS management in processors with discrete voltage/frequency modes," IEEE Transactions on Industrial Informatics, vol. 3, no. 1, pp. 51–62, 2007.
4. P. Pillai and K. G. Shin, "Real-time dynamic voltage scaling for low-power embedded operating systems," in Proceedings of the ACM Symposium on Operating Systems Principles, pp. 89–102, October 2001.
5. J.-B. Lee, M.-J. Kim, S. Yoon, and E.-Y. Chung, "Application-support particle filter for dynamic voltage scaling of multimedia applications," IEEE Transactions on Computers, vol. 61, no. 9, pp. 1256–1269, 2012.
6. X. Liu, P. Shenoy, and M. D. Corner, "Chameleon: application-level power management," IEEE Transactions on Mobile Computing, vol. 7, no. 8, pp. 995–1010, 2008.
7. R. Urunuela, G. Muller, and J. L. Lawall, "Energy adaptation for multimedia information kiosks," in Proceedings of the 6th ACM and IEEE International Conference on Embedded Software (EMSOFT '06), pp. 223–232, October 2006.
8. W. Yuan and K. Nahrstedt, "Practical voltage scaling for mobile multimedia devices," in Proceedings of the 12th Annual ACM International Conference on Multimedia (MULTIMEDIA '04), pp. 924–931, New York, NY, USA, October 2004.

9. W. Yuan and K. Nahrstedt, "Energy-efficient CPU scheduling for multimedia applications," ACM Transactions on Computer Systems, vol. 24, no. 3, pp. 292–331, 2006.
10. W. Yuan, K. Nahrstedt, S. V. Adve, D. L. Jones, and R. H. Kravets, "GRACE-1: cross-layer adaptation for multimedia quality and battery energy," IEEE Transactions on Mobile Computing, vol. 5, no. 7, pp. 799–815, 2006.
11. A. Yang and M. Song, "Aggressive dynamic voltage scaling for energyaware video playback based on decoding time estimation," in Proceedings of the ACM International Conference on Embedded Software, pp. 1–9, Grenoble, France, October 2009.
12. C. Im and S. Ha, "Dynamic voltage scaling for real-time multi-task scheduling using buffers," in Proceedings of the ACM Conference on Languages, Compilers and Tools for Embedded Systems, pp. 88–94, Washington, DC, USA, June 2004.
13. M. Weiser, B. Welch, A. Demers, and S. Shenker, "Scheduling for reduced CPU energy," in Proceedings of the 1st USENIX Conference on Operating Systems Design and Implementation (OSDI '94), article 2, USENIX Association, 1994.
14. E. Seo, S. Park, J. Kim, and J. Lee, "TSB: a DVS algorithm with quick response for general purpose operating systems," Journal of Systems Architecture, vol. 54, no. 1-2, pp. 1–14, 2008.
15. V. Pallipadi and A. Starikovskiy, "The ondemand governor: past, present, and future," in Proceedings of the Linux Symposium, pp. 223–238, Ottawa, Canada, July 2006.
16. M. Fleischmann, "Longrun power management—dynamic power management for crusoe processors," Tech. Rep., Transmeta, 2001.
17. R. Ayoub, U. Ogras, E. Gorbatov et al., "OS-level power minimization under tight performance constraints in general purpose systems," in Proceedings of the International Symposium on Low Power Electronics and Design (ISLPED '11), pp. 321–326, IEEE, Fukuoka, Japan, August 2011.
18. K. Flautner and T. Mudge, "Vertigo: automatic performance-setting for linux," in Proceedings of the 5th Symposium on Operating Systems Design and Implementation (OSDI '02), pp. 105–116, December 2002.
19. Y. Gu and S. Chakraborty, "A hybrid DVS scheme for interactive 3D games," in Proceedings of the 14th IEEE Real-Time and Embedded Technology and Applications Symposium (RTAS '08), pp. 3–12, St. Louis, Mo, USA, April 2008.
20. Y. Huang, S. Chakraborty, and Y. Wang, "Using offline bitstream analysis for power-aware video decoding in portable devices," in Proceedings of the 13th ACM International Conference on Multimedia (MM '05), pp. 299–302, Singapore, November 2005.
21. A. Bavier, A. Montz, and L. Peterson, "Prediction MPEG decoding time," in Proceedings of the ACM SIGMETRICS Conference, pp. 131–140, Madison, Wis, USA, June 1998.
22. K. Choi, K. Dantu, W.-C. Cheng, and M. Pedram, "Frame-based dynamic voltage and frequency scaling for a MPEG decoder," in Proceedings of the IEEE/ACM International Conference on Computer Aided Design (ICCAD '02), pp. 732–737, ACM, November 2002.
23. E. Kim, H. Jeong, J. Yang, and M. Song, "Balancing energy use against video quality in mobile devices," IEEE Transactions on Consumer Electronics, vol. 60, no. 3, pp. 517–524, 2014.

CHAPTER 8

WIRELESS MULTIMEDIA SENSOR NETWORKS

Vikas Bhandary, Amita Malik, and Sanjay Kumar

INTRODUCTION

A wireless sensor network (WSN) comprises a substantial number of interconnected sensor nodes (SNs) that have the capability to sense the physical environment attributes such as temperature, pressure, humidity, light, and sound and simultaneously interact with each other over the wireless medium. The advancements in various technologies have led to the creation of tiny and low-cost multimedia devices like video cameras and microphones, which can easily be integrated to form a sensor node. These devices are used in special types of wireless sensor networks, called wireless multimedia sensor networks (WMSNs). WMSN is a special type of WSN which can sense and transfer scalar data as well as multimedia data, that is, image, audio, and video streams, in real-time as well as nonreal-time. Usually these networks are more powerful distributed systems [1]. Akyildiz et al. [2] have stated various applications of WMSNs: multimedia surveillance networks, traffic avoidance, enforcement and control systems, industrial process control, environment monitoring, and so forth. Many applications still require intense efforts in various research areas to implement WMSNs more efficiently.

Figure 1 shows the architecture of WMSNs based on the type of node used. WMSN can be classified into various classes: (a) single-tier flat and homogeneous, (b) single-tier clustered and heterogeneous, and (c) multitier heterogeneous. In single-tier flat and homogeneous architecture, sensors with similar physical capabilities are used [2]. A subset of nodes having data processing capability, called multimedia processing hubs, is used. Data processing is done in a distributed fashion. In single-tier clustered and heterogeneous architecture, there are nodes with different physical capabilities, for example, multimedia node and scalar node [2]. Nodes having more capability, processing power, batteries, and so forth are called cluster heads (CHs). The rest of the nodes communicate with CHs, which then process and transfer the information to sink node. The data is stored in the central storage hub. In multitier clustered and heterogeneous architecture, there are multiple layers of nodes with different type and processing tasks at each layer. Data is processed and stored in a distributed fashion.

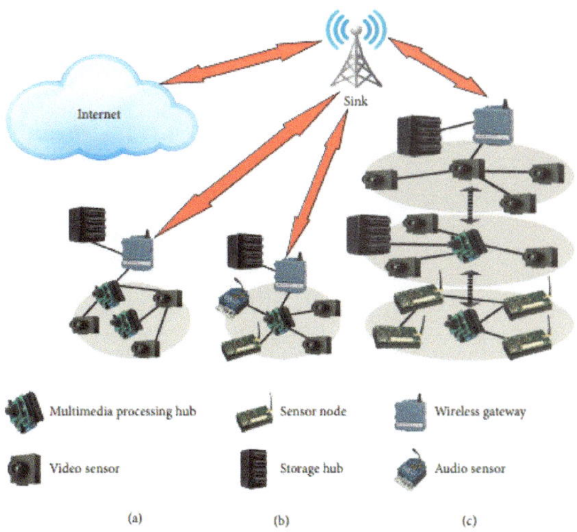

Figure 1: Architecture of WMSNs.

Routing is the most challenging problem in wireless communication system. Only a few survey papers have been published on WMSN routing protocols. A survey presented by Al-Karaki and Kamal [3] included routing protocols for WSN. The authors presented surveyed protocols in taxonomy and a detailed tabular comparison of all the protocols was also included at the end. Akyildiz et al. [2] gave layerwise

---

Citation: Vikas Bhandary, Amita Malik, and Sanjay Kumar, "Wireless Multimedia Sensor Networks" Journal of Engineering, vol. 2016, Article ID 9608757, 27 pages, 2016. doi:10.1155/2016/9608757.

description of WMSN protocols and summarized the open issues of WMSNs. In [4], Förster has summarized various machine learning (ML) techniques which can be used in routing in ad hoc networks. He also discussed the importance of ML techniques and summarized their properties in a table. Misra et al. [5] described layerwise requirements, mechanism, and issues of multimedia streaming in WSN. The paper included QoS based and reliability constrained routing protocols. Saleem et al. [6] presented a paper, which included swarm intelligence (SI) based routing protocols for WSN. The authors briefly explained various SI based energy efficient and QoS based routing protocols. Zungeru et al. [7] did an exhaustive survey of classical and SI based routing protocols for WSN. Detailed analytical and experimental comparison of various QoS based energy efficient and reliable routing protocols was done by the authors. Jayashree et al. [8] classified multipath routing protocols and summarized few QoS based routing protocols. Whereas the authors Ehsan and Hamdaoui [1] performed extensive survey of WMSN, which included detailed classification and analytical comparison based on different criteria and protocol's summary and drawbacks. Guo and Zhang [9] described state-of-the-art SI based routing protocols in WSN. The authors have summed up the performance analysis in a tabular format and have given short description of analysis of network lifetime based on different definitions. Abazeed et al. [10] surveyed different routing protocols for WMSNs. The authors performed the analytical comparison of protocols and also considered simulation scenarios and results of surveyed protocols. Masdari et al. [11] surveyed multipath routing protocols. The protocols were analytically compared and classified based on different criteria. Alanazi and Elleithy [12] have studied real-time QoS routing protocols. The authors classified protocols into probabilistic and deterministic protocols. They performed simulation to analyse various metrics and finally summarized the simulation results. Aswale and Ghorpade [13] surveyed state-of-the-art QoS routing protocols and summarized their analysis in table, including each protocol's strengths and weaknesses, and finally summarized various issues in routing in WMSNs.

At the end, previous works related to ours are condensed in Table 1. The paper presents summarized description and key features of routing protocols, which are classified into different categories based on different characteristics. Further, classification-wise analytical comparison of protocols is done at the end of each class (Tables 2, 3, 4, 5, and 6), in which attributes like characteristics features, suitability for WMSNs, performance metrics, type of network, energy efficiency, and performance results are stated. And in the end, surveyed protocol's characteristics are condensed in Table 7.

Table 1: Previous surveys.

Year of survey	Authors	Characteristics	Time period
2004	Al-Karaki and Kamal [3]	WSN routing	1988–2004
2006	Akyildiz et al. [2]	WMSN survey	1993–2006
2007	Förster [4]	Machine learning based routing	1989–2006
2008	Misra et al. [5]	Multimedia streaming survey	1973–2008
2010	Saleem et al. [6]	SI based routing	1989–2010
2011	Zungeru et al. [7]	Classical and SI based routing	1988–2011
2012	Jayashree et al. [8]	Multipath routing	1993–2011
2012	Ehsan and Hamdaoui [1]	QoS routing	1990–2012
2013	Guo and Zhang [9]	SI based routing	1959–2012
2013	Abazeed et al. [10]	WMSN routing	1998–2011
2013	Masdari et al. [11]	Multipath routing	2003–2012
2015	Alanazi and Elleithy [12]	Real-time QoS routing	2000–2015
2015	Aswale and Ghorpade [13]	QoS routing	1988–2015

Table 2: Latency based routing protocols.

Author [paper]	Year	Characteristics features	Suitability for WMSN	Performance metrics	Type of network	Energy efficiency	Network lifetime	Performance results
Zhou and Wang [20]	2010	HRT	Medium	Delay, Lifetime	Homogeneous	Medium	High	Suitable for small WMSNs
Sohrabi et al. [21]	2000	SRT	Low	Delay	Homogeneous	No	Low	Meets SRT
Akkaya and Younis [23]	2003	SRT	Medium	Delay, RE	Homogeneous	Medium	High	Low throughput
Lu et al. [25]	2002	SRT	Medium	Delay	Homogeneous	No	Low	Outperforms DSR [26] and GF [27]
Karp and Kung [27]	2000	SRT	High	Delay, RE	Homogeneous	Medium	Medium	Outperforms DSR [26] and GF [27]
Chipara et al. [29]	2006	SRT	High	Delay, RE	Homogeneous	Medium	Medium	Outperforms SPEED [28] and EEGR [33]
Ratnaraj et al. [34]	2006	SRT	High	Delay, RE	Homogeneous	Medium	Medium	Outperforms AODV [36] and DSR [26]
Medjiah et al. [38]	2010	SRT	High	RE	Homogeneous	High	Medium	Outperforms GPSR [27]
Xue et al. [37]	2011	SRT	High	Delay, RE	Homogeneous	High	Medium	Outperforms MMSPEED [31] and RAP [25]
Ben-Othman and Yahya [39]	2010	SRT	High	Delay	Homogeneous	High	Medium	Outperforms MCMP [40] and RAP [25]
Li and Kim [15]	2014	(m, k) FRT	High	Delay, RE	Homogeneous	High	Medium	Outperforms SPEED [28]

HRT: hard-real-time, SRT: soft-real-time, FRT: firm-real-time, SD: service differentiation, and RE: residual energy.

Table 3: Multiconstrained routing protocols.

Author [paper]	Year	Characteristics features	Suitability for WMSN	Performance metrics	Type of network	Energy efficiency	Network lifetime	Performance results
Felemban et al. [31]	2006	Multiconstrained	High	Delay and reliability	Homogeneous	High	Low	Outperforms SPEED [28]
Razzaque et al. [41]	2008	Multiconstrained	High	Delay and reliability	Homogeneous	High	High	Outperforms MMSPEED [31] and MCMP [40]
Ahmed and Fisal [42]	2008	Multiconstrained	High	Delay and LQ	Homogeneous	High	Medium	Outperforms MMSPEED [31] and RTPC [43]
Yan et al. [48]	2009	Multiconstrained	High	Delay, PLR	Homogeneous	Medium	Medium	Outperforms SPEED [28] and DD [49]
Shen et al. [44]	2014	Multiconstrained	High	Delay and reliability	Homogeneous	High	High	Outperforms CAQR [45]
Rao et al. [46]	2013	Multiconstrained	High	Delay and reliability	Homogeneous	Medium	Medium	Outperforms VIBE [47]

LR: packet loss ratio; LQ: link quality.

Table 4: SI based routing protocols.

Author [paper]	Year	Characteristics features	Suitability for WMSN	Performance metrics	Type of network	Energy efficiency	Network lifetime	Performance results
Di Caro and Dorigo [14]	1998	Multipath (ACO)	No	Delay	Homogeneous	No	Medium	Slow convergence, high overhead
Rahman et al. [51]	2008	Flat (ACO)	Low	Delay and jitter	Homogeneous	Low	Low	Limited-scalability, high overhead
Sun et al. [53]	2008	Hierarchical (ACO)	Medium	Delay, PLR	Homogeneous	Medium	High	Outperforms Dijkstra and DD [49]
Bi et al. [54]	2010	Hierarchical (ACO)	Medium	Delay	Homogeneous	Medium	High	Outperforms AGRA [55] and M-IAR [51]
Cobo et al. [57]	2010	Hierarchical (ACO)	High	RE, delay, and PDR	Homogeneous	High	High	Outperforms T-ANT [58]
Yu et al. [56]	2011	QoS based (ACO)	High	Delay, PLR, and RBW	Homogeneous	High	High	Limited-scalability
Nayyar et al. [60]	2011	Energy aware (ACO)	High	RE, LB	Homogeneous	Medium	Medium	Outperforms Tiny AODV [36]
Kumar et al. [61]	2014	QoS based (ACO)	High	RBW, RE	Heterogeneous	Medium	Medium	Outperforms EEABR [62]
Liu et al. [63]	2012	QoS based (PSO)	High	Delay, RBW, and jitter	Homogeneous	Medium	Low	Outperforms EEABR [62] and AODV [36]
Huang et al. [64]	2014	Hierarchical (ACO)	Medium	RE, delay, and HC	Homogeneous	Medium	High	Outperforms Dijkstra and IPACR [64]
Förster and Murphys [65]	2007	RL based	Medium	Lifetime, percentage gain over DD	Homogeneous	Medium	High	Outperforms DD [49]
Kotecha and Popat [66]	2007	GA based	Medium	Delay	Homogeneous	Medium	Medium	Outperforms AODV [36] and QoS AODV [67]
Saleem et al. [69]	2012	HBO based	Medium	Routing overhead, PLR, and latency	Homogeneous	Medium	Medium	Outperforms FP-Ant [70], EEABR [62], and AODV [36]
Cai et al. [72]	2015	Hierarchical (HBO)	High	PDR, ESD, and latency	Homogeneous	High	High	Outperforms IEEABR [73], FF-Ant [70], and BeeSensor [69]
Jafarzadeh and Moghaddam [74]	2014	RL	Medium	Delay, PDR, and traffic load	Homogeneous	High	High	Outperforms QoS-AODV [67], RL-QRP [75], and RSSI [76]
Kiani et al. [77]	2015	Hierarchical (RL)	High	Lifetime, PLR	Homogeneous	High	High	Outperforms LEACH [79], HEED-NPF [80], and EECS [81]

ACO: ant colony optimization, PSO: particle swarm optimization, PLR: packet loss ratio, RBW: residual bandwidth, RE: residual energy, HC: hop-count, RL: reinforcement learning, GA: genetic algorithm, HBO: honey bee optimization, PDR: packet delivery ratio, and ESD: energy standard deviation.

Table 5: Flat routing protocols.

Author [paper]	Year	Characteristics features	Suitability for WMSN	Performance metrics	Type of network	Energy efficiency	Network lifetime	Performance results
Lan et al. [82]	2008	Flat	Medium	Delay, RE	Homogeneous	Medium	Low	Outperforms SAR [21]
Nayyar et al. [83]	2011	Flat (Multipath)	Medium	Delay, RE, and RBW	Homogeneous	High	Low	Outperforms AODV [36]

RE: residual energy; RBW: residual bandwidth.

Table 6: Hierarchical routing protocols.

Author [paper]	Year	Characteristics features	Suitability for WMSN	Performance metrics	Type of network	Energy efficiency	Network lifetime	Performance results
Kandris et al. [85]	2011	Hierarchical	Low	RE	Homogeneous	Medium	High	Outperforms TEEN [87]
Lin et al. [88]	2011	Hierarchical	Medium	Delay, LQ	Homogeneous	Medium	High	Outperforms ARCH [89]

RE: residual energy; LQ: link quality.

Table 7: Location based routing protocols.

Author [paper]	Year	Characteristics features	Suitability for WMSN	Performance metrics	Type of network	Energy efficiency	Network lifetime	Performance results
Karp and Kung [27]	2000	Location based	No	Shortest path	Homogeneous	No	Low	Outperforms DSR [26]
Chen et al. [93]	2007	Location based	High	Delay, RE, and RBW	Homogeneous	Medium	Medium	Outperforms GPSR [27]
Shu and Hauswirth [59]	2008	Location based	Low	Shortest path	Homogeneous	Low	Medium	Outperforms GPSR [27] and less throughput
Medjiah et al. [94]	2009	Location based	Low	Shortest path, RE	Homogeneous	Medium	Medium	Outperforms GPSR [27]
Bennis et al. [95]	2013	Location based	High	Shortest path, RE	Homogeneous	High	Medium	Outperforms TPGF [59]
Wang et al. [96]	2015	Location based	High	Delay, RE, and AHC	Homogeneous	High	Medium	Outperforms DGR [93]

RE: residual energy, RBW: residual bandwidth, and AHC: average hop-count.

The remainder of the paper is organized as follows. Section 2 discusses various requirements for WMSN routing protocols. Section 3 discusses various routing techniques, which are classified into various categories. Section 4 summarizes open research issues and Section 5 concludes the paper.

DESIGN REQUIREMENTS FOR WMSN ROUTING

Routing governs the performance of WMSNs in terms of quality of service and energy efficiency. Routing policies accommodate multiple conflicting objectives and constraints, imposed by technologies and user requirements [14]. Real-time multimedia traffic in WMSNs raises many design challenges for routing protocols:(i)QoS Requirements. WMSNs are used in different types of applications. These applications need different requirements. For example, real-time multimedia applications require strictly less end-to-end delay and jitter but high bandwidth and reliability. Various QoS requirements are given below: Latency. End-to-end delay requirements can be classified into soft latency bounded systems, hard delay bounded systems, and firm delay bounded systems. In soft latency bounded systems, the system needs to maintain probabilistic delay guarantee; that is, some delay in packet delivery can be tolerated. But in hard latency bounded system, the system needs to maintain deterministic end-to-end delay, which is also denoted as deadline [15, 16]. The entire system is said to fail, if the system is not able to provide service in the deadline guarantee period. Reliability. It is defined as ability to deliver the data to sink node with minimum packet loss [1, 2]. The unreliability of a system is due to congestion and interference. So it is also regarded as reciprocal of packet loss [1, 2]. Bandwidth. Multimedia traffic requires huge bandwidth. In order to fulfill bandwidth requirements and utilize the resources to its maximum available capacity, routing protocols must employ multipath, multichannel, or stream division method. Jitter. It is defined as the accepted variability of delay between received packets [1]. If the requirement is not met, then it may result in error in audio or video data stream, glitches, and discontinuity. Lifetime. The lifetime of a system is an important factor for deciding the performance of system.(ii)Energy Efficiency [1, 2]. Multimedia sensor nodes are battery constrained devices just like scalar sensor nodes. So energy is one of the major concerns in WMSNs too. Due to network congestion, packet interference, retransmission, and too much concentration on QoS requirements, battery of sensor nodes drains quickly.(iii)Hole Detection [1, 2]. Real-time applications require high bandwidth and low end-to-end delay. As a result, the energy of the routes that are used repeatedly exhausts quickly. This leads to the creation of special scenarios called dynamic holes. An efficient routing protocol must facilitate balanced energy usage in the whole network.(iv)Traffic Classes [1, 2]. Admission control in WMSNs must be based on QoS requirements of the requested service or application as there is a need to provide differentiated service between different applications. Various traffic classes that are defined in [2] are as follows: Real-Time, Loss-Tolerant Multimedia Streams. Usually, this traffic class requires high bandwidth and strict delay bounds. This class includes audio, video stream, multilevel stream, scalar data, and their metadata. Delay-Tolerant, Loss-Tolerant Multimedia Streams. This class includes traffic that is intended for offline storing or processing. This traffic must be transmitted in almost real-time to avoid packet loss. Delay-Tolerant, Loss-Intolerant, Scalar Data. This class includes data from monitoring process and data which are intended for offline storing or processing. The bandwidth requirement is low. Delay-Tolerant, Loss-Tolerant, Scalar Data. This may include any scalar sensor data, non-time critical multimedia snapshot whose bandwidth requirement is low. Real-Time, Loss-Tolerant Scalar Data. This class includes data from monitoring process or loss-tolerant snapshot multimedia. Bandwidth demand is moderate to low. Real-Time, Loss-Intolerant Scalar Data. This class includes data from time critical monitoring process and bandwidth requirement is moderate to low.

WMSN ROUTING TECHNIQUES

Many WMSN routing protocols have been proposed in previous literature. There are many ways to classify routing protocols depending on different parameters. The classes and subclasses are not mutually exclusive as many protocols belong to more than one class or subclass. According to current research trend, categorization of routing protocols is based on number and type of QoS constraints [1]. Hence, QoS based routing protocols are mainly divided into latency constrained and multiconstrained routing protocols [1]. Again, based on deadline delays, latency constrained routing protocols are further classified into protocols providing hard-real-time (HRT), soft-real-time (SRT), and firm-real-time (FRT) QoS guarantees [15, 16]. Another category called "swarm intelligence (SI) based" routing protocol is included in classification. Finally, based on the network structure, routing protocols are further classified into flat routing, hierarchical routing, and location based routing. Classification of different routing protocols for WMSNs is shown in Figure 2.

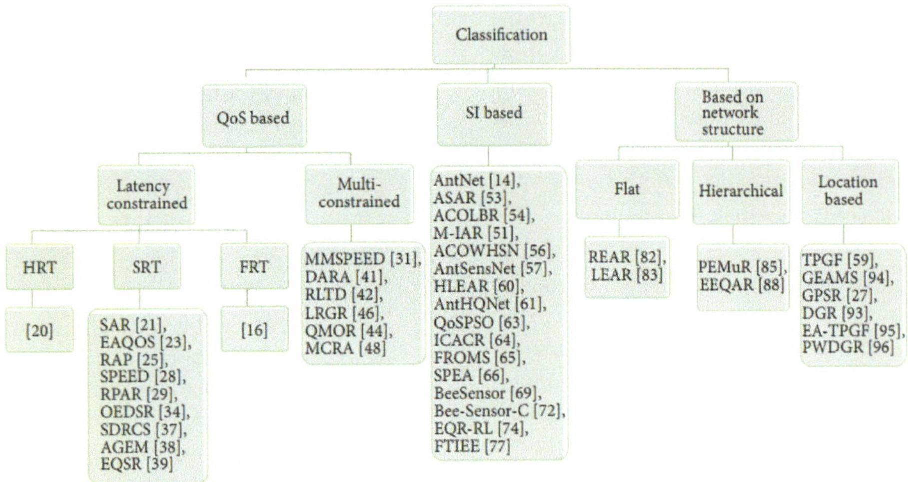

Figure 2: Classification of routing protocols in WMSNs.

QoS Based Routing

In order to guarantee qualitative or quantitative performance parameters, the notion of QoS has been proposed [17]. QoS requirement for WMSNs is a set of constraints like reliability, latency, bandwidth, and jitter. Based on number and type of constraints, QoS based routing protocols are classified into latency constrained and multiconstrained routing protocols.

Latency Based Constrained Routing

In HRT based systems, if packets arrive after the predefined delay deadline, then this is considered as a system failure [15, 16]. But due to lossy links and error-prone medium, it is almost impossible to guarantee HRT in WMSNs. In SRT based systems, some packet missing the delay deadline is tolerable, but a probabilistic delay guarantee is required in order to prevent the system from crashing. There are various protocols that can provide required delay deadline guarantees and deliver the data packets in SRT. In FRT based systems,(m,k)-firm concept is introduced, which demands at least m out of any k consecutive messages must deliver before their delay deadline; otherwise, it is considered as a system failure. Therefore, it is necessary to implement priority based scheduling of stream packets. In [18], distance based Priority (DBP) policy is used to choose between streams. The system maintains DBP state for each stream. DBP is usually calculated at the sink and is used to evaluate the stream not for priority assignment. Recent work in [19] tires to implement cross layer solutions to improve routing.

(1) HRT Based Protocols. The paper [20] proposed delay-constrained routing protocol. The main goal of the protocol is to provide hard real-time delay guarantees and minimize the energy consumption within WMSNs. The proposed algorithm uses global link-state routing algorithm, which needs complete knowledge of network topology in order to compute best possible paths. Global link-state routing algorithms can provide hard real-time delay guarantees. The proposed algorithm is divided into three parts. The first part removes the node with less residual energy from the graphG(V,E), in order to avoid hole problem. The second part uses Dijkstra algorithm in order to find energy efficient routes. Then, the third part ensures that all the paths meet delay upper bound. If a path does not meet delay constraints, then a new path is computed using Dijkstra algorithm and delay as a performance metric.

Key features are as follows:(i)It uses a global state routing algorithm.(ii)It focuses on energy efficiency and QoS.(iii)It computes delay-constrained least energy consumption tree using the Dijkstra algorithm. The proposed protocol guarantees hard-real-time delay bounds. However, the state information exchanged between nodes consumes a huge amount of memory and bandwidth. It is difficult to store and maintain state information in large WMSNs. Therefore, it is only suitable for small WMSNs.

(2) SRT Based Protocols. Sequential assignment routing (SAR) [21] considers both QoS and energy efficiency in route selection process. SAR assigns a priority level to each packet. The main objective of SAR algorithm is to minimize the average weighted QoS metric throughout the lifetime of the network. Weighted QoS metric is computed as the product of additive QoS metric and weight coefficient associated with a priority level. SAR algorithm elects special node called the central node (CN) to perform more sophisticated information processing. It uses Single Winner Election (SWE) algorithm and spanning tree (ST) algorithm. ST algorithm computes a minimum hop spanning tree rooted at CN. Failure recovery in SAR uses a handshaking procedure which enforces table consistency among neighbors. If there is a path failure, then a recomputation procedure is triggered automatically. SNR uses two cooperative signal processing techniques: noncoherent and coherent. Extensive simulation done in [22] shows that SAR has better performance than the minimum metric algorithm.

Key features are as follows:(i)It is a table driven routing protocol.(ii)It is both a QoS based and an energy efficient protocol.(iii)It is a multipath and fault-tolerant routing protocol.The major drawback of SAR is that it is a table driven protocol and hence it is nonscalable. If the number of nodes increases, then the overhead of maintaining the routing table and status information increases drastically [1].

Energy-aware QoS (EAQoS) [23] finds the optimal path to the destination in terms of energy consumption and error rate while meeting the end-to-end delay requirements. EAQoS specifies a queuing model which can handle both nonreal-time and real-time traffic. The implemented queuing model is inspired from class based queuing model [24]. A cost function is associated for each link. This cost function is defined to capture various parameters such as residual energy, transmission energy, and end-to-end delay. EAQoS finds K least cost paths using an extended version of Dijkstra's algorithm. Then, only those paths are chosen that meet the required QoS requirement and maximize network throughput. The cost of each path between nodes is stored. For every discovered path, a tree-like structure is created and total cost of the path between the nodes is recorded. The algorithm terminates when K shortest paths are discovered. If a new path is searched for a particular destination, then only node-disjoint paths are considered. This helps in reducing the congestion over newly found path due to former path.

Key features are as follows:(i)It is a cluster based energy efficient and delay-constrained routing protocol.(ii)It facilitates both real-time and nonreal-time best effort traffic simultaneously.(iii)It ensures guaranteed bandwidth and most energy efficient paths.(iv)The use of node-disjoint paths helps in reducing congestion over the newly found path.EAQoS meets various QoS and energy efficiency requirements. However, EAQoS does not consider MAC and other delays while calculating end-to-end delay and it requires knowledge of the whole network. EAQoS does not treat different real-time traffic separately; therefore, it cannot be used for applications that coexist with other multimedia traffic.

Real-Time Communication Architecture for Large-Scale WSN (RAP) [25] is a priority based, localized routing protocol, which provides soft-real-time delay bounds. RAP introduced a novel packet scheduling policy, Velocity Monotonic Scheduling (VMS) [25]. VMS schedules packets according to their requested velocity. VMS improves deadline miss ratio by giving priority to packets based on requested velocity. VMS is capable of reducing deadline miss ratio by as much as 72.1% [25]. RAP assumes that each node knows its own location, making it location dependent protocol. The combination of VMS and geographic forwarding (GF) makes RAP more scalable and more suitable for multimedia traffic. RAP supports both query oriented and event oriented services. Extensive simulation shows that RAP outperforms DSR [26] and GF [27].

Key features are as follows:(i)It is a location dependent routing protocol, which implements both VMS and GF.(ii)It provides soft-real-time delay bound guarantees.(iii)It provides both query and event based service APIs.(iv)It is a scalable protocol for multimedia applications.There is no need to maintain neighbor database and hence the routing overhead is very little as compared to other classical routing algorithms. RAP uses GF, which can deplete the bandwidth quickly. Also, it does not consider hop-count as routing metric and there is no direct metric to show energy conservation [1].

Stateless Protocol for Real-Time Communication (SPEED) [28] is a stateless, localized, soft-real-time delay bounded protocol, which requires minimum MAC layer support for QoS based routing. Stateless Nondeterministic Geographic Forwarding (SNGF) method is used for routing in SPEED. SNGF maintains desired delivery speed and traffic balance, to reduce the network congestion. MAC layer adaptation of SNGF drops packets in case of congestion. If congestion remains for a long time, then traffic is redirected to a less congested area. SNGF uses four modules.

Beacon Exchange. SNGF uses two extra beacons. One beacon is for delay estimation and the other is for back pressure.

Delay Estimation. Round trip single hop delay for each packet is calculated at the sender's site after receiving ACK.

Neighborhood Feedback Loop (NFL). NFL maintains system performance by maintaining single hop relay speed above a fixed value.

Back Pressure Rerouting. This module is used to reduce congestion in the network.

Key features are as follows:(i)It is an energy efficient and localized routing protocol.(ii)It handles congestion and provides soft-real-time delay bounds.(iii)It avoids the void problem.(iv)It also supports load balancing. SPEED uses nondeterministic geographic forwarding and it maintains only localized database. As a result, the routing overhead is minimized. But SPEED is nonscalable as it uses the idea of per-flow reservation

[1], and its performance degrades when it encounters a large hole and sudden congestion.

Real-time Power-Aware Routing (RPAR) [29] protocol can achieve application specific delay requirements by dynamically adjusting transmission power and other routing metrics. RPAR looks into various serious issues such as network scalability and memory and bandwidth constraints. RPAR have four components: neighborhood manager, delay estimator, forwarding policy, and velocity assignment policy. The neighborhood manager finds eligible forwarding choices that meet both end-to-end delay and energy efficiency requirements. The delay estimator supports real-time multimedia traffic. It further supports two mechanisms: (1) Power Adaptation and (2) neighbor discovery. The delay estimator uses Jacobson's algorithm [30] to estimate contention delay and transmission counts. Jacobson's algorithm computes the retransmission timeout by considering both the average and the estimated variable. RPAR is very good at handling congestion and Holes. RPAR is related to SPEED [28], MMSPED [31], and LAPC [32]. But it is different from these because it integrates power efficiency and supports real-time communication, it handles lossy links, and it employs novel neighborhood management mechanism. Simulation results show that RPAR outperforms SPEED [27] and EEGR [33].

Key features are as follows:(i)It is a power-aware, location dependent, and query based routing protocol.(ii)It can handle holes and congestion.(iii)It is a scalable routing protocol, which can deliver data within delay bounds.(iv)It looks into bandwidth and memory constraints.Neighborhood management and forwarding policy further reduce power consumption. But RPAR's performance degrades when it encounter large holes and sudden congestion.

Optimized energy-delay subnetwork routing (OEDSR) [34] protocol is cluster based and event driven routing protocol where the information from CHs to the base station (BS) is routed in a multihop fashion. OEDSR protocol borrows the idea of an energy-delay metric from OEDR [35]. Routing decision is based on factors such as: available energy, end-to-end delay and distance from BS. The proposed protocol ensures that routes are loop-free. In OEDSR, total numbers of active nodes are reduced by forming a subnetwork with nodes having significant information regarding the event. A temporary header (TH) is selected based on maximum available energy, which calculates and selects required number of CHs. After the selection of CHs, TH broadcasts all the information about CHs and then it becomes a regular node. It does not consider hop-count as one of routing metrics. Simulation results show that OEDSR outperforms AODV [36] and DSR [26].

Key features are as follows:(i)It is a proactive cluster based routing algorithm.(ii)It supports event driven services.(iii)It is multipath and energy efficient and delivers data within delay deadlines.OEDSR minimizes the product of available energy and average end-to-end delay, and it also minimizes the total number of collisions by restricting the number of nodes accessing the channel. OEDSR does not consider hop-count for making routing decisions and average delay is increased if the packets are transmitted between sensor node, THs, and CHs.

Service differentiated real-time communication scheme (SDRCS) [37] is an event driven routing scheme, which implements cross layer functionality in order to route real-time traffic. SDRCS functionally integrates both dynamic forwarding technique and CSMA/CA based prioritization technique [37]. SDRCS uses a novel polling contention period based prioritized MAC. The advantage of the proposed design is that it improves bandwidth utilization even when the total numbers of categories are greater than four. SDRCS also proposes light-weight packet schedulability estimation mechanism, which uses polling contention period and received signal strength based grouping technique. The protocol operation can be categorized in five components: (0) RSS based grouping, (1) admission control, (2) prioritized queuing, (3) real-time MAC, and (4) dynamic forwarding. The grouping mechanism uses RSS to strip the sensor field to layers. Accuracy of distance is maintained using factor called grouping granularity (GRA).

The queuing policy in SDRCS uses per-hop deadline based queues. Every node uses FIFO priority queues for packet scheduling. As shown in Figure 3, per-hop deadline requirements are mapped into N priority levels. Polling contention period based MAC can only provide a limited number of traffic classes. Early deadline miss (EDM) policy is employed in order to drop any unscheduled packets. Simulation results show that SDRCS outperforms MMSPEED [31] and RAP [25], in terms of throughput, on-time delivery ratio, and energy efficiency.

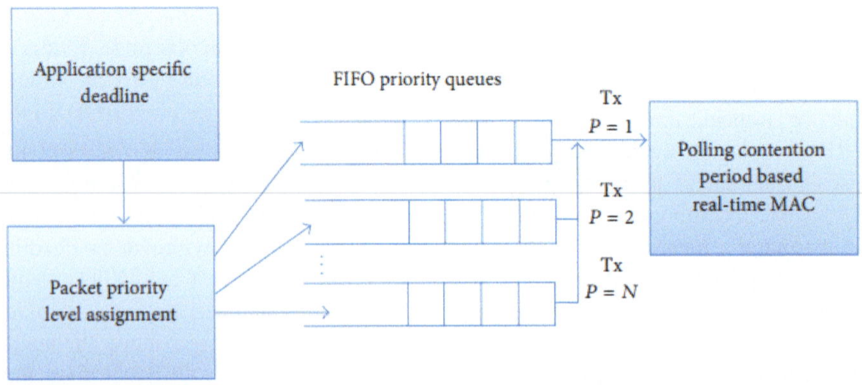

Figure 3: Traffic classification using priority queues.

Key features are as follows:(i)It is an event driven routing protocol.(ii)It requires no extra hardware for localization.(iii)It can adapt to network dynamics (such as channel, void, and channel quality).(iv)It uses cross-layer packet forwarding design for routing multimedia traffic.(v)It can avoid voids very efficiently.SDRCS can avoid false packet drops due to EDM, because it adapts better to change in a network environment.

Adaptive Greedy-Compass Energy-Aware Multipath (AGEM) [38] routing protocol is location based routing protocol for WMSNs which can be considered as an enhanced version of GPSR [27] protocol. AGEM has load-balancing feature to increase the lifetime of the network and to reduce queue size of nodes. It uses adaptive greedy compass policy. Adaptive compass policy selects only a subset of neighbors. Its forwarding policy uses four parameters: remaining energy, hop-count, distance between the current node and its neighbors, and previous history of forwarded packets of the same stream. AGEM protocol has two modes: (1) smart greedy forwarding and (2) walking back forwarding. It is assumed that nodes gather information regarding their position using GPS or by using distributed localization techniques. Each node maintains database containing information regarding one-hop neighbors. Simulation results show that AGEM performs better than GPSR [27], in terms of packet-loss, transmission delay, and energy efficiency.

Key features are as follows:(i)It is a location based, multipath routing protocol, which focuses on load balancing.(ii)It uses adaptive greedy compass policy.(iii)It can be used for both static and mobile sensor networks.(iv)It uses the shortest path which has minimum end-to-end delay.Unlike GPSR [27], data streams in AGEM are routed by different paths; hence, mostly used nodes do not die rapidly because of energy depletion. If network size is low, then mean energy consumption is greater for AGEM as compared to GPSR [27].

Energy efficient and QoS aware multipath routing (EQSR) [39] protocol tries to minimize energy consumption rate to increase the network lifetime. EQSR uses residual energy, available buffer size, and signal-to-noise ratio (SNR) as routing metrics. EQSR increases reliability factor by using XOR-based FEC (forward error correction) technique. As shown in Figure 4, EQSR implements a queuing model, which enables EQSR to handle both real-time and nonreal-time traffic. EQSR discovers node-disjoint paths, which helps in utilizing maximum available network resources. Path discovery phase of EQSR is divided into initialization phase, primary path setup phase, and alternate path setup phase. Each node finds preferred next hop by using the link cost function as defined in [39]. Path discovery phase finds primary and alternate paths. Updated values of metrics are appended on data packets to update previously established paths. This eliminates refreshment overhead.

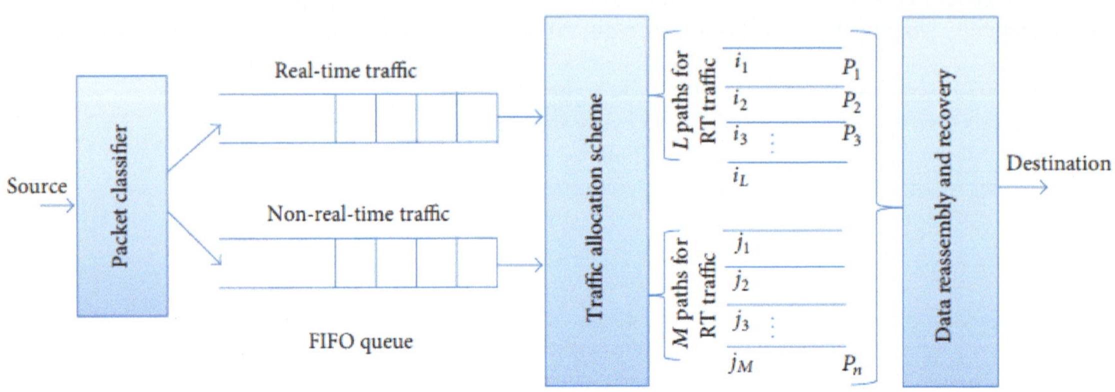

Figure 4: Functional diagram of EQSR.

The segmentation of data packets is done before data transmission, in order to split the data packets into equal sized segments. Then, these segments are scheduled for transmission. Before scheduling process, traffic allocation scheme adds error correction code, which helps in recovering from node failures. Efficient data distribution among the available paths is done using weighted traffic allocation strategy. Simulation results show that EQSR outperforms MCMP [40] and RAP [25].

Key features are as follows:(i)It is an energy efficient multipath routing protocol.(ii)It can handle both real-time and nonreal-time traffic.(iii)It uses FEC codes to increase reliability.EQSR avoids network-wide flooding of route discovery in case of node failures. It also reduces overhead due to route update messages. EQSR uses FEC codes for increasing reliability, but it increases data redundancy.

(3) FRT Based Protocols. The paper [15] defines a real-time fault-tolerant mechanism, which tries to achieve application QoS requirement by utilizing Local Status Indicator (LSI). LSI oversees and assesses the local condition of the nodes and is used to detect network faults. The proposed mechanism enables each node to dynamically adjust its capabilities in order to attenuate performance degradation. As shown in Figure 5, the working of the proposed mechanism is further divided into four submechanisms: (1) neighbor beacon exchange, (2) single hop delay estimation, (3) LSI calculation, and (4) fault recovery mechanisms.

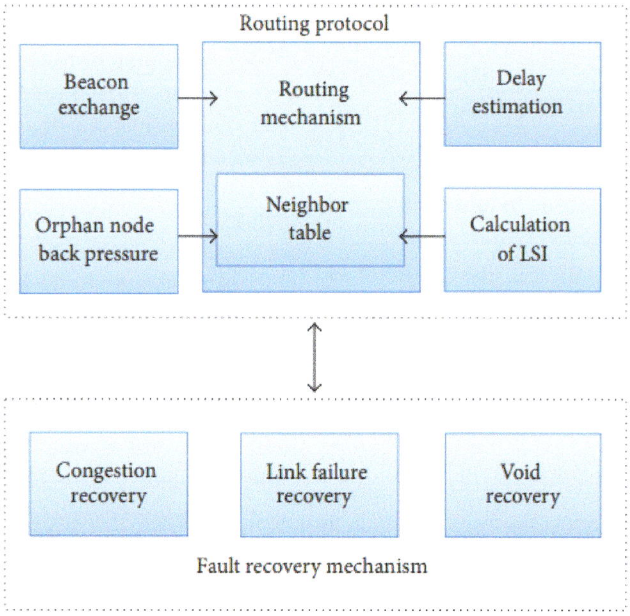

Figure 5: Components of scheme proposed in [11].

In order to share location information among neighbors and to prolong the lifetime of overloaded nodes and of the whole network, periodic beaconing is used. Therefore, the beacon messages contain location information and residual energy of nodes. Three on-demand beacons, single hop delay estimation beacon, stream DBP beacon, and orphan node removal beacon, are used by the proposed mechanism in order to implement different functionalities. At a regular interval, stream DBP beacons are sent by the sink node to source node as a feedback. The value of stream DBP is propagated to the intermediate nodes, which help them in the fault recovery mechanism. The proposed mechanism calculates DBP at the sink node, by using past packet deadline misses. The factor "distance to failure" of a particular node is known after calculating LSI by using , , congestion, and link failure level. After calculating LSI, a node can locally decide to implement recovery mechanisms. The paper [15] proposes a routing protocol, which makes optimal forwarding decisions based on LSI, packet deadline, and remaining power. The proposed protocol implements the mechanism defined in [16]. The protocol has five components: routing mechanism, beacon exchange, orphan node back pressure, delay estimation, and calculation of LSI. Each node maintains a neighbor table, which stores neighbor ID, energy level, estimated delay, expiration time, , deadline, and DBP. The expiration time field is set to standard round trip time (RTT). Simulation results show that the proposed routing protocol outperforms SPEED [28].

Key features are as follows:(i)It is a robust routing protocol, which can fulfill required latency and reliability requirements.(ii)It uses local system evaluation that reduces routing overhead.(iii)It ensures timeliness of the stream transfer by choosing a node with qualified LSI.(iv)It uses fault recovery mechanisms to handle problems like congestion, link failure, and void.(v)Orphan node back pressure prevents void occurrence.The proposed routing protocol efficiently routes stream packets within delay constraints and provides better fault recovery mechanism.

In Table 2, latency constrained routing protocols are compared with each other, where suitability for WMSN for each protocol is based on delay, energy efficiency, network lifetime, and performance of routing protocol.

Multiple QoS-Constrained Routing

Multiple QoS-constrained routing protocols focus not only on latency constraint, but also on other constraints like load balancing, reliability, congestion, bandwidth, and so forth. Many protocols were proposed by researchers in previous literature.

Multipath Multi-SPEED (MMSPEED) [31] is a location based routing protocol, which improves the timeliness and reliability of sensor networks communicating over wireless channels. Reliability requirements are met by using probabilistic multipath forwarding mechanism. The main goals of MMSPEED are as follows: (1) localized packet routing decision making and (2) providing QoS in timeliness and reliability domains. MMSPEED assumes that each node is aware of its location, which makes it more scalable and self-adaptive and removes setup and recovery latency. The virtual isolation of speed layers helps in providing service differentiation. Virtual isolation is maintained by classifying packets according to their speed classes and placing them in priority queues. Probabilistic multipath forwarding mechanism differentiates packets with different requirements. MMSPEED makes proper use of paths without much energy consumption. The back pressure mechanism is employed to remove the void area problem and reduce the incoming traffic. MMSPEED greatly relies on MAC protocol for priority based access to medium depending on speed layer, reliable multicast delivery of packets, and calculation of loss rate and average delay to individual neighbors. MMSPEED relies on EDCF mode of IEEE 802.11e standard.

Key features are as follows:(i)It is a location based and query driven routing protocol.(ii)It focuses on both timeliness and reliability.(iii)It is a multipath routing protocol.(iv)It can solve the void area problem.MMSPEED uses redundant path selection techniques and prevents unnecessary flooding to improve reliability, network lifetime, and load balancing. But MMSPEED does not consider hop-count as one of the routing metrics and it does not consider energy consumption directly. Moreover, the multicast capability of EDCF results in an increment in total size of packets, which in turn increases power consumption.

Distributed aggregate routing algorithm (DARA) [41] is a multisink, multipath, and location aware protocol, which implements the model for achieving multiconstrained QoS (MCQoS). The main goal of [41] is to improve path reliability and delay guarantee while preserving the battery power. MCQoS is a location aware routing scheme which defines three metrics: (1) residual energy, (2) expected sojourn time of packet at the receiving node, and (3) geographic progress towards the destination. It proposes selective greedy forwarding (SGF) to reduce energy consumption and interference [41]. Delay-differentiated packet scheduling (DDPS) reduces packet drop due to deadline failure [36]. DDPS separates queues for time-constrained and non-time-constrained packets in the MAC layer. Further MAC protocol is modified to give higher priority to time-constrained data packets in two levels: (1) internode and (2) intranode. This modification also allows us to control transmission power and save battery and reduce interference. Nodes in DARA algorithm dynamically decide when to broadcast BEACON messages. Simulation results show that DARA outperforms MMSPEED [31] and MCMP [40].

Key features are as follows:(i)It is a fully localized algorithm which means there is no need to maintain any global state information.(ii)It supports both static and dynamic network topologies.(iii)It increases reliability by sending duplicate packets from the source node.(iv)It modifies MAC to give more priority to real-time traffic.DARA reduces energy by using the power control transmission scheme and reducing retransmissions; it also optimizes the trade-off between reliability and delay. But DARA does not provide efficient solution to void problem and it increases routing overhead due to duplicate packet transmission.

Real-time routing protocol with load distribution (RTLD) [42] ensures high packet throughput with minimal packet overhead and prolongs the network lifetime. A novel communication method called "geodirection-cast forwarding" is proposed in [38], which is a combination of both geocast and directional forwarding. It also introduced a mechanism to compute optimal forwarding based on packet reception rate (PRR), remaining power of sensor nodes, and packet velocity over one hop. This optimal forwarding helps in balancing the load of real-time traffic. There are four modules in RTLD: (1) location management, (2) routing management, (3) power management, and (4) neighborhood management. Location management module calculates the location of nodes using the location of predetermined neighbor nodes. The power management module determines the state of the transceiver and the transmission power of sensor nodes. Neighborhood management module discovers a subset of forwarding candidate nodes and maintains a neighbor table of forwarding candidate nodes. Routing management module computes optimal forwarding choices and makes all routing decisions. It further contains submodules: forwarding metrics calculation, forwarding mechanism, and routing problem handler. RTLD outperforms SPEED [28] and RTPC [43].

Key features are as follows:(i)It is a location based routing protocol, which combines geocast forwarding with link quality.(ii)It maximizes the velocity and remaining energy to achieve delay bounds.(iii)It uses neighborhood and power management policies.(iv)It can efficiently detect and bypass holes.(v)It supports query based services and focuses on load balancing. RTLD can deliver data within delay bounds and minimize miss ratio and energy consumption. The only drawback of RTLD is its high cost of deployment.

QoS aware multisink opportunistic routing (QMOR) [44] is an efficient routing protocol, especially designed for delivering real-time multimedia streams on time. The main objective of QMOR is to minimize the energy consumption and meeting the delay and reliability requirements [44]. The use of opportunistic routing scheme enhances the performance of communication by utilizing the broadcast nature of wireless communication. The nodes maintain a forwarder list, which contains a list of nodes that are allowed to forward the broadcasted packets. QMOR focuses on selection and prioritization of the forwarder list to meet application specific QoS requirements.

High level of correlation between video information received from adjacent multimedia sensor nodes results in redundant traffic. QMOR uses a correlation-aware differential coding scheme to reduce redundancy. For reducing redundancy and maximizing energy gains, it is very much important to determine source node and its destination node in the same correlation group. This problem is solved using differential coding-based source and intermediate selection (DCISIS) protocol. Simulation results show that QMOR outperforms CAQR [45].

Key features are as follows:(i)It is a QoS based multisink routing protocol, which implements an opportunistic routing scheme to reduce energy consumption.(ii)It implements priority based forwarding.(iii)It can evaluate expected communication cost.(iv)It meets the reliability and delay requirements.QMOR greatly improves video transmission quality and energy efficiency. But QMOR does not provide service differentiation in heterogeneous networks.

Latency and Reliability-Aware Geographic Routing (LRGR) [46] is a hierarchical routing protocol, which focuses on mobility prediction and energy-aware cluster formation. Each node stores information about two-hop neighbor nodes and adjacency table. Working of LRGR protocol is divided into several rounds. Each round consists of two phases: clustering phase and routing and data transmission phase. Clustering phase is further divided into energy exchange, CH setup, and cluster formation. Cluster maintenance is implemented as required during routing and transmission phase. Energy efficient neighbor discovery protocol (ENDP) is used at MAC layer because it is a low duty beacon-enabled MAC protocol.

In clustering phase, each node broadcasts its residual energy. After energy exchange, sensor nodes calculate average residual energy of their neighbors. The node with a maximum ratio of residual energy/average residual energy becomes CH. For mobility prediction, link expiration time (LET) is calculated, which is computationally less complex. Another factor called linear quality estimation (LQE) is calculated at each sensor node, which is based on previous receptions and transmissions. Both LET and LQE are used by nodes to choose between the CHs. In order to use the most stable path, the main focus is on factors like balanced energy usage, connectivity, position, and congestion. LRGR uses connection reliability metric, forwarding progress metric, and aggregated path metric. Simulation results show that LRGR outperforms VIBE [47].

Key features are as follows:(i)It is a location based hierarchical routing protocol.(ii)It uses energy-aware cluster setup phase.(iii)It uses mobility prediction based clustering, which estimates link quality and improves reliability.(iv) It defines forwarding progress metric to evaluate end-to-end delay and packet loss.LRGR guarantees low latency and maintains a balance between energy efficiency and reliability. But in case of highly mobile environments, LRGR suffers because of limited bandwidth, error-prone wireless channel.

Multiconstrained routing algorithm (MCRA) [48] is based on query-flooding and query driven data delivery models. In MCRA, special messages called "interest" are used to query an event. The MCRA borrows the idea of the logical coordinate system. Logical Coordinate System is a localized approach which calculates the coordinates of nodes using hop-count information. This approach drastically reduces message overhead. Both geographic information based routing and virtual coordinate system based routing algorithms sometimes result in route failure due to inaccurate node coordinate information. MCRA implements message suppression techniques to reduce redundant transmission and retransmission of messages caused by collisions. In MCRA message suppression is done using restraining forwarding and deferring forwarding. Both try to reduce the amount of interests by restraining and deferring forwarding node. Extensive simulation performed in [48] shows that MCRA outperforms agent based DD [49] and SPEED [28].

Key features are as follows:(i)It is a logical location based multiconstrained routing protocol which supports query based services.(ii)It focuses on reliability and energy efficiency.(iii)It implements message suppression techniques to reduce redundant packets.By using the logical location based technique, MCRA reduces routing overhead and it also minimizes redundant messages. But MCRA does not consider reliability and bandwidth.

Multiconstrained routing protocols are analytically compared in Table 3, which contains characteristics features, suitability for WMSNs, performance metrics, type of network, energy efficiency, network lifetime, and performance results of routing protocols.

SI Based Routing Protocols

SI based routing protocols are inspired by the collective behavior of intelligent biological species (e.g., ant colonies). SI based routing protocols simulate the behavior of these species by using mobile software agents. These agents intelligently perform problem solving tasks, in coordination with other agents. Stigmergy plays an important role by supporting communication between the agents, through the environment. SI based routing protocols are scalable, fault tolerant, adaptive, fast, and autonomous. In addition to this, these protocol's operations are modular in nature and they can be executed in parallel. Due to these reasons, SI based routing protocols have become a better alternative to the routing problem. For more than two decades, ant colonies have motivated the design of various novel algorithms [6].

Distributed Stigmergic Control for Communication Networks (AntNet) [14] is an adaptive, distributed, and mobile agent based Monte Carlo system which is used for routing of multimedia traffic. AntNet implements adaptive learning of routing tables using agents called forward ants and backward ants. At fixed intervals forward ants are sent from any network nodes towards a destination to discover feasible, low-cost path. Routing decisions are based on pheromone trails left by ants. QoS Parameters such as residual energy, delay, and bandwidth are used to calculate forwarding probability, which makes the process of exploration adaptable according to traffic distribution. When a forward ant reaches the destination, backward ants are generated. Backward ants update routing tables.

Key features are as follows:(i)It is an adaptive and hybrid routing protocol.(ii)It uses ACO algorithm and reinforcement learning to solve routing problem.(iii)It is a multipath, multiobjective, and multiconstrained routing algorithm.(iv)It is stochastic in nature.(v)It delivers the data in real-time latency constraints.AntNet algorithm provides better throughput as compared to classical routing protocols. But AntNet is very slow as it requires ant agents to reach at the destination without updating routing tables [50] and its routing overhead is very high.

Multimedia-Enabled Improved Adaptive Routing (M-IAR) [51] is an extension of Improved Adaptive Routing (IAR) algorithm [52]. M-IAR is an ant-based flat multihop routing protocol which incorporates some extra multimedia QoS parameters (end-to-end delay and jitter) as compared with IAR. It also supports fault tolerance and self-organization without any need for global route information. Novelty of M-IAR protocol is that it considers the closeness of next-hop neighbors towards the sink but also takes into account the distance of the neighbor from the sender node [46]. This protocol gives a reliable solution as it piggybacks end-to-end acknowledgement packets. M-IAR assumes that each node in the network knows its own position and all other nodes through GPS. In 98% of test cases, M-IAR successfully found the shortest path within the first three route discovery attempts by forward ants [51].

Key features are as follows:(i)It is a localized and ant-based routing protocol.(ii)It is an improved version of IAR algorithm.(iii)It focuses on energy efficiency and end-to-end delay, jitter.(iv)It is self-organized, adaptive, and fault tolerant in nature.M-IAR provides reliable solution and it can be configured for both acknowledgement-based and non-acknowledgement based approach. But M-IAR needs high cost of deployment and it does not concentrate on load balancing between nodes and scalability. Moreover, M-IAR's performance degrades due to hole creation and exponential increase in overhead, in case of high network load.

Ant-based service-aware routing (ASAR) [53] is an ant-based service-aware hierarchical routing protocol for wireless multimedia sensor networks. It facilitates three types of basic services (query driven, data driven, and stream driven). This protocol uses the concept of "pheromone quantization" to improve ant-based optimization algorithm. This quickens the convergence of ASAR. The proposed algorithm is made to run in all CHs. It finds three different routes for each type of services by positive feedback mechanism used in ACO and the results are stored on CHs, respectively. QoS parameters such as delay, packet loss rate, network bandwidth, energy consumption, and network lifetime are used as routing metric. Extensive simulation verified that ASAR performs better than Dijkstra and DD [49]. This algorithm is often used for optimized routing and load balancing in telecommunications and networks.

Key features are as follows:(i)It is a clustered, ant colony optimization based routing protocol.(ii)It supports both query and data driven services.(iii)It uses pheromone quantization to accelerate the convergence of the algorithm and optimize the network resources.(iv)It supports three kinds of services in WMSNs and meets QoS requirements and improves network performance.ASAR converges more quickly and it supports three types of services and meets diverse QoS requirements. But ASAR's performance degrades due to bottleneck problem and repetitive usage of optimal paths [10].

Ant Colony Optimization-based Load-Balancing Routing Algorithm (ACOLBR) [54] is a biologically inspired hierarchical routing algorithm. ACOLBR is further divided into intercluster routing and intracluster routing. Intracluster routing uses minimal spanning tree (MST) algorithm to construct MST with CHs as the root. Intercluster routing finds a path with minimal cost from source node to the destination node and some suboptimal paths using ACO algorithm. ACOLBR enhances the exploring ability of ants by introducing maximum and minimum value of pheromone density values. It also improves transmission efficiency by splitting the stream, when data amount is greater than the path's maximum flow. Simulation results and analysis show that ACOLBR has better adaptability, can achieve load balancing, reduces the end-to-end delay, and prolongs the network lifetime as compared to AGRA [55] and M-IAR [51].

Key features are as follows:(i)It is a swarm-based, hierarchical, and multipath routing protocol.(ii)It focuses on congestion control.(iii)It uses the minimum spanning tree algorithm to create MST.(iv)It has enhanced the exploring ability as compared to other ACO techniques.ACOLBR can recover from path failure by setting pheromone value to zero and then sending an error message to sender. But ACOLBR requires more complex calculations to find optimal route and heavy load results in a bottleneck situation over CHs.

Ant Colony Optimization-Based QoS Routing Algorithm (ACOWMSN) [56] is a reactive routing protocol, which focuses on four QoS metrics. ACOWMSN finds routes which meet application specific QoS requirements. Artificial ants wander around the network in order to find paths which meet the requirements. ACOWMSN uses two types of artificial ants: forward ants and reverse ants. Forwarding ants store information fields like minimum residual energy and cumulative queue delay and packet loss and memory of node visited, in order to evaluate the route in terms of QoS. ACOWMSN protocol finds minimum cost route using heuristics. At each node, next forwarding node is found by calculating the probability. Routing in ACOWMSN is divided into two stages: route discovery and routing confirm. In route discovery stage, forward ants are sent towards the destination node using broadcast or unicast approach. Broadcast approach is used only when current node does not know about the destination node. In routing confirm stage, forward ants are converted into backward ants. Backward ants travel from the destination node to source node. Backward ants update the pheromone table of every intermediate node.

Key features are as follows:(i)It is an ant colony based routing protocol.(ii)It is reactive in nature; therefore, it finds route only when it is needed.(iii)It is adaptable to any change in network conditions.(iv)It is an energy-aware and QoS based routing protocol.ACOWMSN can satisfy bandwidth, delay, and packet loss rate requirements and increase the network lifetime. But in large-scale WMSNs, it is very much difficult to determine the protocol parameters and therefore algorithm converges very slowly.

AntSensNet [57] combines features of both hierarchical network structure and Ant colony optimization based routing. It is specifically designed for WMSNs and hence it meets application specific requirements. It is based on T-ANT [58]. Just like T-ANT [58] algorithm, its operation is split into rounds. Each round is further divided into cluster setup phase and steady phase. It uses special types of agents for cluster setup called cluster ants (CANTS). The node with CANT becomes CH. HELLO packets broadcasted by each node constantly contain information regarding its ID, clustering pheromone value, and its state. The clustering pheromone value decides if the current node is suitable to become CH. A tunable factor called "cluster radius" determines minimum distance between two CH nodes.

Routing tables in AntSensNet are updated in three phases: forward ant phase, backward ant phase, and route maintenance phase. Forward ants are generated if there is no satisfactory route to the sink node. Forward ants carry information regarding routes they travel. The routes are evaluated when they reach the sink node. If the evaluated route does not meet application specific requirements, then forward ants are discarded; otherwise, backward ants are generated in order to update the pheromone values. Backward ants travel the reverse path. Maintenance phase handles the congestion and lost link problems. Figure 6 shows diagram of traffic classifier used by AntSensNet to handle and schedule four different types of traffic classes.

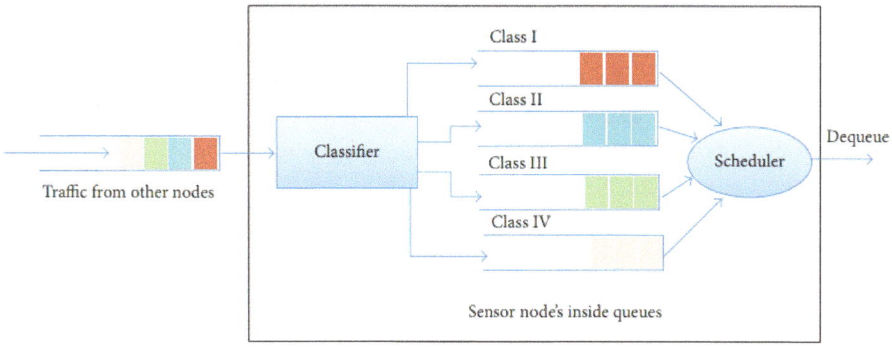

Figure 6: Traffic classification process used in AntSensNet.

Key features are as follows:(i)It is a hybrid routing protocol, and hence it comprises reactive as well as proactive components.(ii)It implements both ACO based routing and clustering.(iii)It supports a power efficient multipath video packet scheduling in order to minimize the distortion in video transmission.(iv)It uses completely distributed clustering algorithm.(v)It can handle different types of traffic classes. AntSensNet can handle congestion problem. It is scalable and multipath and it provides better video quality in terms of distortion as compared to ASAR [53] and TPGF [59].

Hop and load based energy-aware routing protocol (HLEAR) [60] is a swarm-based, reactive, self-organizing routing protocol, which avoids hole and increases network lifetime. HLEAR's main aim is to find completely or partially disjoint path with relative minimum distance. It uses hop-count, rate of forwarding nodes, and residual energy as metric, to find an efficient path for routing multimedia streams. Based on these values, another routing metric β is calculated. Path with the lowest value of β is considered as best path. The protocol operation is further divided into route discovery and path establishment phases. In route discovery phase, RREQ is broadcasted in a controlled manner. When RREQ reaches the sink node, it does not need to analyse path selection, as the path has been already scanned by intermediate nodes. In path establishment phase, destination node sends a route reply message RREP via reverse path. Simulation results show that HLEAR performs better than Tiny AODV in terms of energy efficiency and throughput [60].

Key features are as follows:(i)It is a reactive, swarm-based, and energy efficient routing protocol.(ii)It avoids holes by stopping nodes from taking part in route discovery phase, if their energy is less than 0.5 J.(iii)It finds the minimum distance to destination by finding disjoint paths.(iv)Unlike LEAR, it considers hop-count as routing metric.HLEAR provides better throughput and energy efficiency than Tiny AODV [60], but it cannot handle congestion efficiently due to which its throughput is very low when frame rate is high.

AntHQSeN [61] is a reactive ant-based QoS enabled routing protocol, which works in two phases: (1) route discovery phase and (2) route maintenance phase. The agents called forward ants are created by the source node to find multiple paths to the destination node. They also carry network information in order to evaluate various QoS parameters. AntHQSeN forwards the data packets stochastically. Each forwarding node decides next node based on pheromone values, which makes the protocol adaptable to any change in the network. The route setup phase is completed when destination nodes generate backward ants to update the pheromone tables. Route maintenance phase is activated whenever a node failure occurs. For pheromone calculation, various factors like residual bandwidth, residual energy, and route cost are considered. In AntQHSeN protocol hello ants play a major role in immediate neighbor discovery, exchanging information about the bandwidth, timestamp, energy, and pheromone concentration. Extensive simulation results show that AntQHSeN performs better than AODV [36] and EEABR [62].

Key features are as follows:(i)It is a reactive ant-based routing protocol for heterogeneous sensor network.(ii)It can work fine in both static and dynamic topologies.(iii)It treats multimedia and scalar traffic differently.(iv)It uses a special flag to give an option to use the admission control scheme or not.AntQHSeN provides a more consistent solution due to its reactive route discovery mechanism as compared to EEABR. But AntQHSeN lacks sufficient information at the beginning to find routes. Its setup time is directly proportional to the time needed for convergence of the algorithm. But still the discovered routes are better in terms of quality than those found by AODV [36].

An agent-assisted QoS-based routing (QoS-PSO) [63] is an agent based routing protocol, which focuses on delivering application based QoS services by using practical swarm optimization (PSO) technique. The synthetic QoS parameters are used as parameters of the objective function of PSO. QoS-PSO uses two different types of agents called forward agent and reverse agent in order to find out the optimized route. The synthetic QoS metrics are stored in agents. Forward agent's aim is to find a new route to the destination nodes. If the new route can provide required QoS, then reverse agents are created. All the information stored in forward agents is copied to reverse agents. Reverse agents travel in the reverse direction and update routing tables of all the nodes lying on the newly found path. The algorithm firstly selects the source and destination nodes and uses forward agent and reverse agent to establish a new path to destination. The QoS of each path is evaluated to obtain local best values. Iteration formulae are used to find a new routing path and its QoS is evaluated. If the QoS of a particular path is better, then it is made global best solution. This process is iterated until required values are achieved. After this, global best solution is used to determine the path and update routing table.

Key features are as follows:(i)It is an agent based routing protocol, which uses PSO for optimizing synthetic QoS.(ii)It uses agents which participate in the routing path establishment and maintenance.(iii)It focuses on improving QoS metrics like delay, bandwidth, packet loss, and energy.QoS-PSO shows improvement in QoS metrics by more than 60% and 20%, if compared with AODV [31] and EEABR [57], respectively.

A QoS-aware routing algorithm based on ant-cluster (ICACR) [64] is a hierarchical routing protocol for WMSNs, which integrates clustering and IPACR [64]. IPACR is a flat routing protocol, which outperforms standard ant colony routing algorithm (SACR). The principle disservice of SACR is that it considers the performance of every link between nodes and their neighbors as equivalent and sets the same initial pheromone value. IPACR protocol maintains a neighbor-list, which stores information regarding adjacent nodes. IPACR ensures that there is at least one feasible path. Based on the assumption "if a hello packet arrives earlier at a node, then it can be implied that the path is optimal," the optimality of paths depends on log SEQ. Therefore, IPACR sets more initial pheromone value of nodes with smaller log SEQ. The overall performance of routing protocol depends on the pheromone update procedure followed by forward ants and backward ants.

ICACR uses "divide and conquer" methodology to improve the scalability of the network. The network is divided into a number of clusters. The total number of subnetworks in the original network is one more than the total number of clusters. The additional subnetwork consists of sink node and all the CHs. IPACR protocol finds local optimal paths in each cluster.

Key features are as follows:(i)It is an ant-based hierarchical routing protocol.(ii)It uses IPACR routing in order to find local optimal paths.(iii)It is a multipath routing protocol.(iv) It is a scalable protocol, which can meet QoS requirements for WMSNs.IPACR converges faster than SACR. ICACR is more scalable, energy efficient routing algorithm as compared to IPACR, SACR, and Dijkstra. But if the source node is placed near the sink node, then the performance of ICACR goes down.

Feedback-Enhanced Learning Approach (FROMS) [65] is an in-network protocol which learns by using local information about network topology and tries to converge to optimal routing paths. It assumes that each sensor has to route sensed data to multiple number of sink nodes.

Key features are as follows:(i)It is an intelligent routing algorithm based on reinforcement learning.(ii)It uses local information and optimizes route using feedback mechanism.(iii)It considers equal cost paths to minimize energy consumption.The technique uses three main phases, namely, sink announcement, exploration, and stable data gathering.

In Phase I, each sink broadcasts request message to entire network which contains time to live (TTL), sink ID, and number of hops. When a node receives this message, it verifies if the message has been already received. If entry is already there in routing table and it has less hop-count, received message is not processed. If there is no routing table entry or the entry has more hop-count, routing table is updated and message is broadcasted with decreased TTL and increased hop-count.

In Phase II, all best possible paths are discovered. This phase initiated, when a data packet is received. Fitness function gives the route cost based on single or multiple variables for a set of sinks. The proposed algorithm uses Route Length Estimate (RLE) as metric to decide the fitness of a path, which is equal to total number of hops. Each node organizes the available options for next hop and makes selection task manageable using Path Sharing Tree (PST). Nodes can manage the complex task of data delivery to multiple sinks by using PST. Using PST gives an extra advantage of escaping the path with loops. Updated RLE are shared in form of feedback when the package is rebroadcasted by upstream node. This feedback mechanism results in better decision-making over time. According to selected exploration strategy, Phase II ends and stable data gathering phase starts where sender node starts transmission to set of sinks. Whenever the PST changes Phase II is reinitiated.

FROMS minimizes the energy consumption by considering equal cost paths and switching between them to increase the lifetime of overall network. FORMS is compared with implementation version of directed diffusion [49]. Simulation results show FORMS performs better.

Strength Pareto Evolutionary algorithm (SPEA) [66] uses genetic algorithm (GA) and tries to optimize various QoS parameters such as bandwidth, delay, traffic, and hop-count. GA is best for multiobjective problems where the values to be optimized are more than one. There is no ideal "optimal" solution for such problems. There are sets of solutions, in which improvement in one objective leads to degradation in other objectives. The main objectives of SPEA are to optimize the QoS parameters and provide adaptive route with optimized delay.

Key features are as follows:(i)It is an intelligent routing algorithm based on GA.(ii)It tries to optimize four QoS parameters.(iii)It quickly adapts to changes in network topology.Route discovery in SPEA is carried out at MAC layer of TCP/IP model; therefore, the MAC is redesigned to support the algorithm. To make the process clear, it is designed into two modules: QoS routing module and GA module. Data exchange between the modules is bidirectional. GA generates new routes by combining the existing routes with common node and destination.

QoS routing module on receiving a data transfer request checks for a route to the destination. If route to the destination is not available, then it initiates route discovery procedure by transmitting smart agents. When source node receives RREP, it follows the reverse path and updates the table. When RERR message is received by source node, it uses GA module. Available entries in buffer are used as initial population and fitness function is applied and optimally finds the destination node with desired QoS requirements. If there is no RERR then the buffer is used to find route to destination. The buffer is evaluated periodically to maintain the efficiency of system.

The proposed protocol is compared with AODV [36] and QoS-AODV [67] routing and simulation results show it outperforms both.

Further work done in [68] has proved that using implementation of SPEA and changing the objective functions has increased the performance of system 15 times [68]. The paper has used similar approach and used expected transmission count and delay as objective functions. The expected transmission count (ETX) metric is the expected total number of transmissions. It is calculated using link quality and neighbor link quality. Link quality can be seen as probability that packet originated at node successfully arrives at a subsequent node and neighbor link quality is a measure of quality in opposite direction.

Beesensor [69] is an on-demand SI based reactive, event driven, energy efficient, and scalable routing protocol, which is inspired from behavior of honey bees.

Key features are as follows:(i)It is an intelligent routing algorithm based on Honey bee optimization.(ii)It minimizes the communication and processing cost.(iii)It is energy-aware, scalable, and efficient.Honey bee optimization uses recruitment and agent communication energy efficient foraging and multiflower-site foraging mechanism found in bee colony [69]. There are four types of agents: packers, scouts, foragers, and swarms. Packers are like food storer bees in hive. They receive packets from upper layer and find appropriate forager for them. Scouts explore the network in search of a potential sink node. Foragers play an important role in carrying packets to the sink using predetermined path. They also evaluate the quality of the path and give updates to other foragers. Foragers are piggy-backed in the link layer acknowledgement packets to source node. Foragers wait for certain amount of time at sink node and build a swarm of waiting foragers, which is transported back to source node. The algorithm is divided into four phases: scouting, foraging, swarming and routing loops, and path maintenance.

Scouting is further divided into forward scouting and backward scouting. Packers look for the appropriate forager to transfer an event at a sensor node. If a packer fails to find forager it launches forward scout with source ID, scout ID minimum remaining energy, and number of hops fields in header. This scout is then broadcasted to neighbor. Interested sink converts the forward scout into backward stable. The algorithm maintains three tables: routing table, probability-distribution table, and a forwarding table. Source node maintains routing table and probability-distribution table. Forwarding table is maintained by sink and forwarding nodes. Sink node creates forwarding table entry from the received scout header information and replies with backward scout with same information fields. After discovering the route, foragers transport events to sink node. Packer selects a forager stochastically based on probability-distribution table. Intermediate node does not make routing decisions; next hop is found using path ID.

Swarming encapsulate foragers with identical path ID at sink node. The swarm is routed towards the source node using forward table entries. Swarming also helps in path maintenance. The path becomes invalid when the dance number becomes zero for a particular entry in routing table, which is deleted after some waiting period. Simulation results show that BeeSensor outperforms FP-Ant [70], EEABR [71], and AODV [36].

Bee-Sensor-C [72] is an on-demand event driven multipath routing algorithm based on dynamic clustering scheme and BeeSensor [69]. Bee-Sensor-C reduces the routing overhead and scalability as compared to BeeSensor. It follows multipath construction methodology to increase the overall lifetime of network.

Bee-Sensor-C is divided into three phases: cluster formation, multipath construction, and data transmission. In the second phase, various improvements are made to BeeSensor for finding multipath between CH and relative sink and the path is selected stochastically for data transmission.

BeeSensor is poor in overall performance, when all the nodes near the event need to send data to sink node. Bee-Sensor-C adds a new agent called HiveHeader to bee hive for each sensor. Its major responsibility is to claim the node wants to be cluster head node.

Nodes having information about the cluster join the cluster and the clustering region is called event-subnetwork. Any node can decide to join a cluster based on received signal strength. If a node receives multiple HiveHeader from different node it chooses the node with higher residual energy. The node, which sends the HiveHeader first, becomes the CH node. The node with higher residual energy and closer to event sends HiveHeader earlier and is more likely to become CH node. Each cluster has its TTL; if remaining energy of CH gets lower than 60%, CH selection starts again.

Like BeeSensor [69], Bee-Sensor-C utilizes forward scouts to explore the network. CH broadcasts a forward scout to its neighbors. The scouts are self-destructed when the hop-count is more than H_max, to avoid the communication overhead. Backward scout travels back to CH node using previous hop information in cache. Bee-Sensor-C also modifies the reward mechanism to include the average residual energy factor. When the backward scout arrives at CH with new path, it recruits foragers using "waggle dance" [72]. The simulation results show that Bee-Sensor-C outperforms FF-Ant [70], BeeSensor [69], and IEEABR [73].

EQR-RL [74] is energy-aware QoS routing which uses reinforcement learning. EQR-RL uses control flooding algorithm for updating the latest changes to the network. Each node uses header of its neighbor data packet to maintain up-to-date information about the routes.

Key features are as follows:(i)It is an intelligent dynamic routing algorithm based on reinforcement learning.(ii)It focuses on various QoS requirements like latency hop-count and so forth.(iii)It utilizes data packets to get latest information of neighbors.If a node does not hear any packet from a neighbor, it removes it from its routing table. The routing packet contains neighbor ID, timestamp, number of packets sent, end-to-end delay, and minimum residual energy in route.

When a node sends a packet to its neighbor, it starts the timer to calculate the round trip time. The receiver node finds the next node and updates the receiver address in data packet. After that, it updates minimum residual energy field. The feedback information is piggybacked in the header of data packets.

Exploration strategy provides the trade-off between exploring the low-cost routes and all possible routes. So it uses ε-greedy method for random selection of next hop for exploration [74].

When a node receives a data packet, it accesses various parameters from the packet and compares those parameters with the routing table entries. If it does not find any route, it sends the packet with best effort; otherwise, it selects next hop using roulette wheel. Simulation results show that ERQ-RL outperforms QoS-AODV [36], RL-QRP [75], and RSSI [76].

FTIEE [77] is an intelligent clustering based routing protocol, which aims to reduce energy consumption and make the system more reliable. It focuses on three parameters, namely, network lifetime, packet delay, and delivery. In this routing algorithm, learning and routing phase are realized at the same time, which reduces overall energy and overhead of the system.

Key features are as follows:(i)It is an intelligent cluster based routing algorithm based on reinforcement learning.(ii) It makes system more reliable and reduces packet delay.(iii) It increases the lifetime of system.In this algorithm, any node can act as CH and CH is chosen by election done by means of learning machine. Number of clusters is constant and clusters closer to sink are smaller as compared to the other clusters, size of cluster increases with increase in distance between the clusters and sink. CH nodes have multihop communication to the sink, and sensor nodes do not need to know about the CH.

FTIEE uses Q-learning technique [78] to select the optimal CH node and reduce the cost of CH-sink data transmission to minimum. Each sensor node is independent learning agent and therefore chooses to forward data to neighbor or select itself as CH node. The reward system in protocol is calculated using distance between node and sink and residual energy of node. In simulation, results show that it outperforms LEACH [79], HEED-NPF [80], and EECS [81].

SI based routing protocols are analytically compared in Table 4, which contains characteristics features, suitability for WMSNs, performance metrics, type of network, energy efficiency, network lifetime, and performance results of routing protocols.

Based on Network Structure

Based on network structure, routing protocols are classified into three different categories: (1) flat routing; (2) hierarchical routing; and (3) location based routing.

Flat Routing Protocols

In flat network architecture, all the nodes have the same responsibilities. Flat routing protocols are also called data-centric routing protocol. A BS is responsible for sending requests and queries. However, the sensor nodes can sense the physical environment and transfer the data to BS. Flat routing protocols use data aggregation to reduce redundant data, which ultimately reduces energy consumption. But flat routing protocols are not able to fulfill application specific latency requirements. These protocols suffer due to high routing overhead, delay, congestion, and low versatility.

Real-Time and Energy-Aware Routing (REAR) [82] protocol is a multipath routing algorithm which also reduces energy consumption of links and trades off the relationship of energy and delay. In REAR, metadata is used to find routing paths. Use of metadata stops repeated retransmission of exactly same packets; thus, huge bandwidth is saved. Metadata is used for routing discovery processes. REAR uses Optimized Dijkstra Algorithm which is used to select a link with lowest weight among marked nodes. For QoS determination factors like time delay, bandwidth, and remaining energy are included. In order to guarantee real-time transmission and reduce queue delay, a "classified queue model" is introduced to each node. For link cost evaluation, estimated distance, remaining energy, and queuing delay are used.

Key features are as follows:(i)It is a metadata based routing protocol, which supports query based services.(ii) It focuses on energy efficiency and end-to-end delay.(iii)It uses modified Dijkstra algorithm.(iv)It implements "classified queue model" to reduce queuing delay.REAR reduces repeated retransmissions and energy consumption by using meta-data for route setup. But REAR does not consider reliability and bandwidth requirements. The concept of metadata in streaming applications consumes a lot of energy and bandwidths.

Load Based Energy-Aware Multimedia Routing (LEAR) [83] protocol is a reactive, self-organizing, and energy efficient protocol. LEAR is AODV [49] based protocol. Here active routes refer to the number of routes for different sources in which a node is participating. For route selection, a special factor ("route selection factor β") is calculated by forwarding nodes. If node's power reaches 25% of its total power, then it is labeled as "Swap Node." Swap Nodes do not take part in routing; they transmit packets only in certain critical conditions. So LEAR also has the ability of hole avoidance. LEAR finds disjoint path, if it is available. If disjoint path is not available, then it finds a partial disjoint path. Creating a partial disjoint path increases the hop distance, but it ensures high throughput, reduces congestion, and lowers the latency. This makes LEAR perfectly suitable for routing of multimedia traffic. Simulation results show that "the number of paths selected increases with the increase in the number of multimedia nodes within the event region" [61].

Key features are as follows:(i)It is a reactive, multipath, self-organizing, and event driven routing protocol.(ii)It focuses on energy efficiency, reliability, and load balancing.(iii)It can avoid holes efficiently.(iv)It finds disjoint paths in order to reduce congestion and meet delay bounds.LEAR can find disjoint path while maintaining load balance between the nodes and increase network lifetime. The main drawback of LEAR is that it does not consider delay, reliability, network lifetime, and bandwidth requirements. Table 5 shows comparison of flat routing protocols.

Routing Protocols

Initially, hierarchical protocols were proposed for routing in wired networks [84]. However, they are also suitable for WMSNs. In hierarchical routing protocols, the entire network is divided into different levels. Nodes at different levels have different responsibilities. Generally, the protocol consists of two routing layers only, and data flows from a low level layer to a higher level layer. The nodes with the higher capabilities and responsibilities are known as CHs. Each CH can directly communicate with the BS. The rest of the nodes are called child nodes or cluster members, which associate with CHs to form clusters. Child nodes can only communicate with their CH. The advantages of these protocols over flat routing protocols are as follows: they are more scalable, energy efficient, and reliable. Overall performance of protocol depends on the process of formation of clusters.

Energy efficient and perceived QoS aware video routing (PEMuR) [85] is a novel energy-aware hierarchical routing protocol for WMSNs, which uses intelligent video packet scheduling scheme and predicts the video distortion. It is based on scalable power efficient routing (SHPER) protocol [86]. CHs are further categorized into upper level CHs and lower level CHs. Upper level CHs are near BS and can transmit data directly to the BS. Whereas lower level CHs are far from the BS, distant nodes route their messages to the BS by multihop routing. PEMuR is divided into two phases: (1) initialization phase and (2) steady state phase. The initialization phase starts with the creation of TDMA schedules for all nodes to advertise themselves and calculate relative distances between them. Random numbers of upper and lower CHs are elected by the BS. Non-CH nodes associate with CH having maximum signal strength. In steady state phase, BS elects a node with maximum residual energy in each cluster as CH.

In case of nonavailability of sufficient bandwidth, each sensor node drops video packets to reduce the retransmission rate. The packets to be dropped are chosen wisely in order to minimize overall video distortion using video distortion model [85]. The video distortion is measured in terms of Mean Square Error (MSE). The model also takes into account the random behavior of wireless medium; hence, it can predict video distortion accurately. Simulation result shows PEMuR outperforms TEEN [87].

Key features are as follows:(i)It is an energy-aware hierarchical routing protocol.(ii)It uses an intelligent video scheduling scheme.(iii)It is based on SHPER protocol.(iv) It intelligently handles low bandwidth situation.PEMuR ensures that minimum power is consumed and required QoS is maintained for the transmission of video streams. Also, it can maintain a high level of perceived video quality (PSNR) for uniform and nonuniform energy distributions. But PEMuR is fully dependent on BSs for carrying out the routing process; hence, it is not fully distributed.

Energy efficiency QoS assurance routing (EEQAR) [88] protocol is a hierarchical routing protocol, which implements cellular topology to form clusters. EEQAR uses a QoS trust estimation model, which is based on social network analysis. On a social network, the relationship between two individuals is determined by the trust relationship between them. The concept of social network analysis is used by EEQAR in order to ensure energy efficiency and determine trust relationship. For building trust relationships, distributed metrics are introduced in EEQAR. Direct behavior monitoring and indirect information gathering are used in order to calculate trust value.

Trust value is calculated by calculating various other factors like transmission delay, frame rate, image quality, and audio quality. On the basis of the geographical position of agents and multimedia sensor nodes, the cellular topology is formed. Agent nodes are always deployed in the center of the hexagon. Agents send advertisement messages with their ID, after deployment. Multimedia nodes join agent node with maximum signal strength. If multimedia nodes have no task, then they can go into sleeping mode. But agent nodes must remain awake.

Each node maintains optimization factor table, which stores trust value, energy level, and correlation for each neighbor. The correlation factor estimates correlation between two nodes, which directly affects the fusion process. Each node finds a next forwarding node using optimization factor table. EEQAR operation is divided into various rounds. Where each round is divided into three phases: cluster building, routing probe, and steady state. Cellular clusters are formed in cluster building phase. Intracluster and intercluster routes are built in routing probe phase. Data is collected in steady phase. Simulation results in [88] show that EEQAR outperforms ARCH [89], in terms of delay, energy efficiency, and reliability.

Key features are as follows:(i)It is an energy efficient hierarchical routing protocol.(ii)It uses “data fusion” process in order to reduce unnecessary data transmission.(iii)It uses trust analysis to fulfill application specific QoS requirement.(iv)It uses TDMA at MAC layer to make efficient use of energy resources.EEQAR efficiently improves performance by decreasing delay and energy utilization. But trust relationship is slowly varying and it is not error-free. Direct monitoring increases the energy consumption rate. Table 6 shows comparison of hierarchical routing protocols.

Location Based Routing Protocol

The central idea of location based routing protocols is to exploit the knowledge of location of nodes in order to route data packets. The location of the node can be determined using global positioning system (GPS) or other localization techniques like DVHop [90], Amorphous [91], and so forth.

Few advantages of location based routing protocols over other routing techniques are as follows:(i)Minimized routing overhead.(ii)Efficient bandwidth utilization.(iii)Fully distributed and stateless nature.(iv)Scalable and tolerant to route faults.(v)Less memory and maintenance requirement. However, these routing protocols suffer from “energy hole” problem. Greedy nature of these protocols results in repetitive usage of the same path, if the destination lies in the same region. The batteries of nodes lying on that path drain quickly, resulting in the creation of energy hole. An efficient location based routing protocol must handle and avoid hole problem efficiently.

Greedy Perimeter Stateless Routing (GPSR) [27] is a novel routing protocol, which uses the positions of the router and the destination node to make packet forwarding decisions. GPSR uses two modes: (1) greedy forwarding and (2) perimeter forwarding. GPSR packet headers include a flag to indicate the current forwarding mode of the packet. If a packet reaches a region where greedy forwarding is not possible, GPSR recovers by routing the packet around the perimeter of the region. In perimeter mode GPSR forwards packets using planar graph traversal. Further, a packet can again reenter the greedy forwarding mode if any neighbor is closer to the destination node.

Key features are as follows:(i)It is a location based routing algorithm.(ii)It can detect and avoid the hole problem.(iii)It supports MAC-layer failure feedback.(iv)It uses promiscuous mode.(v)It supports queue traversal.(vi)It implements planarization of graphs.GPSR has a good packet delivery ratio even when the network density is too high. It requires less memory because there is no need to store full knowledge of the network at each node. There is no need for periodic updating of the table. It is an energy efficient routing protocol. End-to-end delay increases when mobility is high, which in turn makes it unsuitable for handling multimedia traffic [92].

Directional Geographic Routing (DGR) [93] protocol is a location based routing protocol, which gives better video transmission quality and prolongs the network lifetime. DGR assumes that any node can send video packets to sink at any instance. It forms multiple application specific disjoint paths to transmit real-time traffic over low bandwidth and unreliable network. Forward error correction (FEC) coding is used in order to make data delivery more reliable. A single real-time video stream is divided into multiple substreams. These substreams are transferred in parallel through disjoint paths, in order to make full utilization of resources. DGR follows the right hand rule to recover from the void problem [27].

Key features are as follows:(i)It is a location based routing protocol.(ii)It uses disjoint paths to optimize bandwidth and energy and reduce delays.(iii)It is a fault-tolerant routing protocol.(iv)It supports various features such as load balancing, fast packet delivery, and good peak signal-to-noise ratio (PSNR).DGR utilizes resources very efficiently, increases the delivery ratio, and reduces end-to-end delay requirements. But DGR is not suitable for WMSNs because it requires additional overhead and hence results in transmission delay in case of fault, and it is impractical to implement for large networks.

Two-phase geographic greedy forwarding (TPGF) [59] routing algorithm overcomes various shortcomings of flat routing protocols. TGPF can be efficiently used in multimedia applications. TGPF avoids "Local Minimum Problem" by adopting face routing (right hand rule) as adopted in GPSR. The Label Based Optimization method is adopted to eliminate path circles and optimize the routing path found by TPGF. It is different from existing geographic routing algorithms as it does not adopt face routing to bypass holes. For hole-bypassing, it follows two approaches: (1) hole-bypassing by computing the planar graph in advance without knowing holes or boundary nodes; (2) hole-bypassing by identifying the holes or boundary node information in advance.

Key features are as follows:(i)It is a location based routing protocol which supports event driven services.(ii)It is a multipath routing protocol.(iii)It implements GF algorithm.(iv)It can bypass holes using two different methods.TPGF provides paths with minimum number of hop-counts, but it requires full knowledge of the network; therefore, it is not a scalable protocol.

Geographic Energy-Aware Multipath Stream-based (GEAMS) [94] routing protocol focuses on load-balancing and minimizing energy consumption. In GEAMS routing protocol, routing decisions are made without global topology knowledge and there is no need for maintenance of topology changes. Here each node stores information about its one-hop neighbors, which is updated by beacon messages. The information includes estimated distance to its neighbors, the distance of neighbor to the sink, data rate of link, and remaining energy. GEAMS uses two policies: (1) Smart Greedy Forwarding and (2) Walking Back Forwarding. Walking Back Forwarding policy is used when there are no neighbors closer to sink. Otherwise, GEAMS uses the Smart Greedy Forwarding policy.

Key features are as follows:(i)It is a geographical multipath routing protocol.(ii)It enforces uniform energy consumption and meets delay requirement.(iii)It works on two policies, Smart Greedy Forwarding and Walking Back Forwarding. (iv)It can detect and avoid hole problems.GEAMS does not require global topology information and its maintenance and it maximizes network lifetime and guarantees QoS requirements. But in sparse network, GEAMS can cause congestion and packet loss.

Energy-Aware TPGF (EA-TPGF) [95] is a routing protocol which is an enhanced version of TPGF [45]. TPGF is a routing protocol, which implements greedy forwarding and step back and mark methods. The first phase in TPGF consists of two methods, greedy forwarding and step back and mark. The greedy forwarding algorithm selects a neighbor closest to the BS as the next node for routing. Step back and mark method is used to handle the situations, when there is not even a single node in the neighborhood that is closer to BS. The second phase of TPGF deals with label based optimizations of path. EA-TPGF defines distance-energy formula, which is used to calculate the score of neighbors; node with minimum value is selected. EA-TPGF also defines the energy cost transmission formula to calculate the cost of energy consumed by the transmitter.

Key features are as follows:(i)It is an enhanced version of TPGF.(ii)It focuses on energy efficiency.(iii)It uses distance-energy formula and energy cost transmission formula to evaluate the path.(iv)It also uses GF algorithm to route the data packets.EA-TPGF routing protocol greatly reduces the energy consumption rate in WMSNs as compared to TPGF. But EA-TPGF increases the average delay of nodes and it always uses the same discovered paths again and again.

Pairwise directional geographical routing (PWDGR) [96] is a multipath routing protocol, which solves the energy bottleneck problem. PWDGR is proposed based on DGR [93]. It makes full use of nodes around the sink. PWDGR finds pairwise nodes around the sink for data transmission. After the data is transferred to pairwise nodes, pairwise node sends data to sink.

Routing in PWDGR is divided into three stages:(I)In first stage video data is collected and packed, and then the data is broadcasted. Broadcasting saves energy and reduces delay. (II)After receiving neighbor nodes check if they are in the cooperative node list. If yes, then they calculate coordinates of the next neighbor node.(III)In the third stage, source cooperative node is selected. Two rules are used to select a source cooperative node: (i) based on cumulative numbers to be selected for cooperative node and (ii) based on distance between ideal point and neighbor node.

Key features are as follows:(i)It is a multipath, location based routing algorithm.(ii)It uses the concept of pairwise nodes to fully utilize the nodes around the sink.(iii)It increases the network lifetime by nearly 70%.(iv)It is reliable and fault tolerant and improves network bandwidth.Use of pairwise nodes in PWDGR around the sink makes full use of nodes within 360° so the energy of nodes around the sink is utilized, to increase the network lifetime. DGR scheme suffers due to energy hole around the sink. If the sink is at the edge of the network, then PWDGR degenerates into DGR algorithm. Also, it increases the delay by 8% as compared to similar protocol DGR.

In Table 7, location based routing protocols are compared with each other, where suitability for WMSN for each protocol is based on delay, energy efficiency, network lifetime, and performance of routing protocol.

In Table 8, aforementioned routing protocols are analytically compared, based on architecture, location awareness, multipath, energy efficiency, real-time nature, congestion control, load balancing, reliability, hole detection/ bypassing, and data delivery model as attributes.

Table 8: Comparison of protocols.

Protocol	Architecture		Location aware	Multipath	Energy efficiency	Real-time	Congestion control	Load balancing	Reliability	Hole detection/bypassin
	Flat	Clustered								
Zhou and Wang [20]	✓				✓	✓				
SAR [21]	✓			✓	✓					
EAQoS [23]		✓			✓	✓				
RAP [25]			✓			✓				
SPEED [28]			✓		✓	✓	✓	✓		✓
RPAR [29]			✓		✓	✓	✓			✓
OEDSR [34]		✓		✓	✓	✓				
SDRC [37]					✓	✓				
AGEM [38]			✓		✓	✓				✓
EQSR [39]				✓	✓				✓	
Li and Kim [16]					✓	✓			✓	
MMSPEED [31]			✓	✓		✓			✓	
DARA [41]			✓	✓	✓	✓			✓	
RLTD [42]			✓	✓	✓	✓		✓		✓
LRGR [46]			✓		✓	✓			✓	
QMOR [44]					✓	✓			✓	
ASAR [53]		✓		✓	✓	✓			✓	
M-IAR [51]			✓		✓					
ACOLBR [54]		✓		✓		✓	✓			✓
AntNet [14]	✓			✓						
ACOWMSN [56]					✓	✓				
AntSensNet [57]		✓		✓	✓	✓	✓	✓		
HLEAR [60]					✓			✓		
AntHQSeN [61]		✓			✓			✓		
QOSPSO [63]					✓	✓				
ICACR [64]		✓			✓	✓				
FROMS [65]	✓									
SPEA [66]	✓				✓					
BeeSensor [69]	✓									
Bee-Sensor-C [72]		✓		✓	✓	✓		✓		
EQR-RL [74]	✓									
FTIEE [77]		✓			✓	✓		✓	✓	
REAR [82]	✓			✓	✓	✓				
LEAR [83]	✓			✓	✓			✓	✓	✓
PEMuR [85]		✓			✓			✓		
EEQAR [88]		✓			✓			✓		
MCRA [48]			✓		✓				✓	
TPGF [59]			✓	✓						✓
GEAMS [94]			✓	✓	✓					✓
GPSR [27]			✓		✓					
DGR [93]			✓		✓	✓				✓
EA-TPGF [95]			✓	✓	✓					✓
PWDGR [96]			✓	✓	✓	✓				

OPEN RESEARCH ISSUES

WMSN has got huge attention in the past few years, but still it is in evolving stage [13]. Research papers [1, 2, 13] have summed up current issues in QoS and energy efficient routing for WSNs and WMSNs. This paper has already mentioned various design requirements. This section is outlining common problems for future exploration.

Selection of Optimal Metrics. QoS routing being the multiobjective problem, it is very difficult to decide between the metrics, because the optimization of one metric leads to degradation of another. So there is need of designing and developing routing protocols which can focus more and more on multiple metrics. The protocols following SI based methodologies like ACO, PSO, RL, and GA are becoming prevalent as they are adaptive and multiobjective in nature.

Cross Layer Functionality. In typical networks, each layer is assigned its functionality and service. One layer can only interact with adjacent layers only. Various factors in wireless communication make layered approach worse, resulting in degradation of overall system performance. For optimal performance, routing protocols in WMSNs share QoS parameters among the layers. Papers [19, 97] propose cross layer solutions for efficient routing.

Multiple Sources and Multiple Sink. In large scale WMSNs, if a single sink is placed there are the chances that the performance of system depletes because of the presence of multiple sources and single sink. Moreover, sink's neighbor nodes get drained much faster and the sink gets isolated. Therefore in real practice, multiple sinks are used, there are some protocols which support multiple source and multiple sinks, but still there is need to make system more efficient.

Duty Cycle Based Routing. Sensors can be in active or in sleep mode; these modes are called duty cycle. Most of the energy is utilized in communication with neighboring nodes. Switching between the states and making the node least idle saves a considerable amount of energy. But to achieve duty cycling in WMSNs is a very complex problem due to volatility of video traffic.

Integration with Other Networks. Sensors sense the environment and transmit the observed data to sink. As shown in Figure 1, sink communicates the data to internet or other network in order to make it useful to the end users. There is need to develop new architecture in order to provide guarantee of QoS, energy efficiency, and other requirements.

Security. Due to various features of WMSNs and unreliable wireless communication channel. WMSNs are always vulnerable to various attacks such as wormhole, sinkhole, and Sybil. Low computation power makes it difficult to implement strong security protocols.

CONCLUSIONS

This paper presents survey of various existing routing protocols for WMSNs, with summarized description and properties of each algorithm. Also, categorywise analytical comparison of protocols is done. QoS routing algorithms can be classified using different metrics but that could make classification more complex so to maintain simplicity, protocols are classified into only main three categories. Tables 2–7 give summarized comparison of protocols based on intrinsic characteristics. Finally, Table 8 gives the overall comparison of all the protocols.

Owing to the increase in applicability of WMSNs, researchers are more inclined to persuade research on WMSN routing protocols, in order to solve various problems in routing in WMSNs. The paper aims to give the introduction to current WMSN routing protocols and improve the understanding of basic concepts. We hope it will encourage them to design an efficient routing protocol.

Competing Interests

The authors declare that they have no competing interests.

REFERENCES

1. S. Ehsan and B. Hamdaoui, "A survey on energy-efficient routing techniques with QoS assurances for wireless multimedia sensor networks," IEEE Communications Surveys and Tutorials, vol. 14, no. 2, pp. 265–278, 2012.
2. I. F. Akyildiz, T. Melodia, and K. R. Chowdhury, "A survey on wireless multimedia sensor networks," Computer Networks, vol. 51, no. 4, pp. 921–960, 2007.
3. J. N. Al-Karaki and A. E. Kamal, "Routing techniques in wireless sensor networks: a survey," IEEE Wireless Communications, vol. 11, no. 6, pp. 6–28, 2004.
4. A. Förster, "Machine learning techniques applied to wireless ad-hoc networks: guide and survey," in Proceedings of the 3rd International Conference on Intelligent Sensors, Sensor Networks and Information (ISSNIP '07), pp. 365–370, Melbourne, Australia, December 2007.
5. S. Misra, M. Reisslein, and G. Xue, "A survey of multimedia streaming in wireless sensor networks," IEEE Communications Surveys and Tutorials, vol. 10, no. 4, pp. 18–39, 2008.
6. M. Saleem, G. A. Di Caro, and M. Farooq, "Swarm intelligence based routing protocol for wireless sensor networks: survey and future directions," Information Sciences, vol. 181, no. 20, pp. 4597–4624, 2011.
7. A. M. Zungeru, L.-M. Ang, and K. P. Seng, "Classical and swarm intelligence based routing protocols for wireless sensor networks: a survey and comparison," Journal of Network and Computer Applications, vol. 35, no. 5, pp. 1508–1536, 2012.
8. A. Jayashree, G. Biradar, and V. Mytri, "Review of multipath routing protocols in wireless multimedia sensor network—a survey," International Journal of Scientific & Engineering Research, vol. 3, no. 7, pp. 1–9, 2012.
9. W. Guo and W. Zhang, "A survey on intelligent routing protocols in wireless sensor networks," Journal of Network and Computer Applications, vol. 38, no. 1, pp. 185–201, 2014.
10. M. Abazeed, N. Faisal, S. Zubair, and A. Ali, "Routing protocols for wireless multimedia sensor network: a survey," Journal of Sensors, vol. 2013, Article ID 469824, 11 pages, 2013.
11. M. Masdari, M. Tanabi, and W. Azarbayjan, "Multipath routing protocols in wireless sensor networks: a survey

and analysis," International Journal of Future Generation Communication and Networking, vol. 6, no. 6, pp. 181–192, 2013.

12. A. Alanazi and K. Elleithy, "Real-time QoS routing protocols in wireless multimedia sensor networks: study and analysis," Sensors, vol. 15, no. 9, pp. 22209–22233, 2015.
13. S. Aswale and V. R. Ghorpade, "Survey of QoS routing protocols in wireless multimedia sensor networks," Journal of Computer Networks and Communications, vol. 2015, Article ID 824619, 29 pages, 2015.
14. G. Di Caro and M. Dorigo, "AntNet: distributed stigmergetic control for communications networks," Journal of Artificial Intelligence Research, vol. 9, pp. 317–365, 1998.
15. B. Li and K.-I. Kim, "A novel real-time scheme for (m, k)-firm streams in wireless sensor networks," Wireless Networks, vol. 20, no. 4, pp. 719–731, 2014.
16. B. Li and K.-I. Kim, "An (m, k)-firm real-time aware fault-tolerant mechanism in wireless sensor networks," International Journal of Distributed Sensor Networks, vol. 2012, Article ID 905740, 12 pages, 2012.
17. S. Chen and K. Nahrstedt, "An overview of quality of service routing for next-generation high-speed networks: problems and solutions," IEEE Network, vol. 12, no. 6, pp. 64–79, 1998.
18. M. Hamdaoui and P. Ramanathan, "A dynamic priority assignment technique for streams with (m, k)-firm deadlines," IEEE Transactions on Computers, vol. 44, no. 12, pp. 1443–1451, 1995.
19. C. Lee, B. Shah, and K.-I. Kim, "An architecture for (m, k)-firm real-time streams in wireless sensor networks," Wireless Networks, vol. 22, no. 1, pp. 69–81, 2016.
20. L. Zhou and J.-X. Wang, "Delay-constrained maximized lifetime routing algorithm in wireless multimedia sensor networks," in Proceedings of the 2nd International Conference on Future Computer and Communication (ICFCC '10), pp. V1215–V1219, IEEE, Wuhan, China, May 2010.
21. K. Sohrabi, J. Gao, V. Ailawadhi, and G. J. Pottie, "Protocols for self-organization of a wireless sensor network," IEEE Personal Communications, vol. 7, no. 5, pp. 16–27, 2000.
22. K. Sohrabi, J. Gao, and V. Ailawadhi, "A self organizing wireless sensor network," in Proceedings of the Annual Allerton Conference on Communication Control and Computing, vol. 37, pp. 1201–1210, 1999.
23. K. Akkaya and M. Younis, "An energy-aware QoS routing protocol for wireless sensor networks," in Proceedings of the 23rd International Conference on Distributed Computing Systems Workshops (ICDCSW '03), pp. 710–715, Providence, RI, USA, May 2003.
24. S. Floyd and V. Jacobson, "Link-sharing and resource management models for packet networks," IEEE/ACM Transactions on Networking, vol. 3, no. 4, pp. 365–386, 1995.
25. C. Lu, B. M. Blum, T. F. Abdelzaher, J. A. Stankovic, and T. He, "RAP: a real-time communication architecture for large-scale wireless sensor networks," in Proceedings of the 8th IEEE Real-Time and Embedded Technology and Applications Symposium (RTAS '02), pp. 55–66, September 2002.
26. D. B. Johnson and D. A. Maltz, "Dynamic source routing in ad hoc wireless networks," in Mobile Computing, T. Imielinski and H. F. Korth, Eds., vol. 353 of The Kluwer International Series in Engineering and Computer Science, pp. 153–181, 1996.
27. B. Karp and H. T. Kung, "GPSR: greedy perimeter stateless routing for wireless networks," in Proceedings of the 6th Annual International Conference on Mobile Computing and Networking (MOBICOM '00), pp. 243–254, August 2000.
28. T. H. T. He, J. A. Stankovic, C. L. C. Lu, and T. Abdelzaher, "SPEED: a stateless protocol for real-time communication in sensor networks," in Proceedings of the 23th IEEE International Conference on Distributed Computing Systems, pp. 46–55, IEEE, May 2003.
29. O. Chipara, Z. He, G. Xing et al., "Real-time power-aware routing in sensor networks," in Proceedings of the 14th IEEE International Workshop on Quality of Service (IWQoS '06), pp. 83–92, New Haven, Conn, USA, June 2006.
30. V. Jacobson, "Congestion avoidance and control," ACM SIGCOMM Computer Communication Review, vol. 18, no. 4, pp. 314–329, 1988.
31. E. Felemban, C.-G. Lee, and E. Ekici, "MMSPEED: multipath multi-SPEED protocol for QoS guarantee of reliability and timeliness in wireless sensor networks," IEEE Transactions on Mobile Computing, vol. 5, no. 6, pp. 738–753, 2006.
32. M. R. Fouad, S. Fahmy, and G. Pandurangan, "Latency-sensitive power control for wireless ad-hoc networks," in Proceedings of the 1st ACM International Workshop on Quality of Service & Security in Wireless and Mobile Networks (Q2SWinet '05), p. 31, 2005.
33. K. Seada, M. Zuniga, A. Helmy, and B. Krishnamachari, "Energy-efficient forwarding strategies for geographic routing in lossy wireless sensor networks," in Proceedings of the 2nd International Conference on Embedded Networked Sensor Systems (SenSys '04), pp. 108–121, November 2004.
34. S. Ratnaraj, S. Jagannathan, and V. Rao, "OEDSR: optimized energy-delay sub-network routing in wireless sensor network," in Proceedings of the IEEE International Conference on Networking, Sensing and Control (ICNSC '06), pp. 330–335, IEEE, April 2006.
35. N. Regatte and S. Jagannathan, "Optimized energy-delay routing in ad hoc wireless networks," in Proceedings of the World Wireless Congress, San Francisco, Calif, USA, 2005.
36. C. E. Perkins and E. M. Royer, "Ad-hoc on-demand distance vector routing," in Proceedings of the 2nd IEEE Workshop on Mobile Computing Systems and Applications (WMCSA '99), pp. 90–100, New Orleans, La, USA, February 1999.

37. Y. Xue, B. Ramamurthy, and M. C. Vuran, "SDRCS: a service-differentiated real-time communication scheme for event sensing in wireless sensor networks," Computer Networks, vol. 55, no. 15, pp. 3287–3302, 2011.

38. S. Medjiah, T. Ahmed, and F. Krief, "AGEM: adaptive greedy-compass energy-aware multipath routing protocol for WMSNs," in Proceedings of the 7th IEEE Consumer Communications and Networking Conference (CCNC '10), pp. 1–6, IEEE, January 2010.

39. J. Ben-Othman and B. Yahya, "Energy efficient and QoS based routing protocol for wireless sensor networks," Journal of Parallel and Distributed Computing, vol. 70, no. 8, pp. 849–857, 2010. View at Zentralblatt MATH

40. X. Huang and Y. Fang, "Multiconstrained QoS multipath routing in wireless sensor networks," Wireless Networks, vol. 14, no. 4, pp. 465–478, 2008.

41. M. A. Razzaque, M. M. Alam, M. Mamun-Or-rashid, and C. S. Hong, "Multi-constrained QoS geographic routing for heterogeneous traffic in sensor networks," IEICE Transactions on Communications, vol. 91, no. 8, pp. 2589–2601, 2008.

42. A. A. Ahmed and N. Fisal, "A real-time routing protocol with load distribution in wireless sensor networks," Computer Communications, vol. 31, no. 14, pp. 3190–3203, 2008.

43. O. Chipara, Z. He, G. Xing, Q. Chen, and X. Wang, "Real-time power control in wireless sensor networks,," Tech. Rep. WUCSE-2005-31, Washington University in St. Louis, St. Louis, Mo, USA, 2005.

44. H. Shen, G. Bai, Z. Tang, and L. Zhao, "QMOR: QoS-aware multi-sink opportunistic routing for wireless multimedia sensor networks," Wireless Personal Communications, vol. 75, no. 2, pp. 1307–1330, 2014.

45. R. Dai, P. Wang, and I. F. Akyildiz, "Correlation-aware QoS routing with differential coding for wireless video sensor networks," IEEE Transactions on Multimedia, vol. 14, no. 5, pp. 1469–1479, 2012.

46. Y. Rao, C. Yuan, Z. Jiang, L. Fu, and J. Zhu, "Latency and reliability-aware geographic routing for mobile wireless sensor networks," Advances in information Sciences and Service Sciences, vol. 5, no. 8, pp. 738–748, 2013.

47. A. Papadopoulos, A. Navarra, J. A. McCann, and C. M. Pinotti, "VIBE: an energy efficient routing protocol for dense and mobile sensor networks," Journal of Network and Computer Applications, vol. 35, no. 4, pp. 1177–1190, 2012.

48. X. Yan, L. Li, and F. J. An, "Multi-constrained routing in wireless multimedia sensor networks," in Proceedings of the International Conference on Wireless Communications & Signal Processing (WCSP ‹09), pp. 1–5, IEEE, November 2009.

49. C. Intanagonwiwat, R. Govindan, D. Estrin, J. Heidemann, and F. Silva, "Directed diffusion for wireless sensor networking," IEEE/ACM Transactions on Networking, vol. 11, no. 1, pp. 2–16, 2003.

50. A. A. A. Radwan, T. M. Mahmoud, and E. H. Hussein, "AntNet-RSLR: a proposed Ant routing protocol for MANETs," in Proceedings of the Saudi International Electronics, Communications and Photonics Conference (SIECPC ‹11), pp. 1–6, Riyadh, Saudi Arabia, April 2011.

51. A. Rahman, R. Ghasemaghaeil, A. El Saddikl, and W. Gueaieb, "M-IAR: biologically inspired routing protocol for wireless multimedia sensor networks," in Proceedings of the Instrumentation and Measurement Technology Conference (IMTC ‹08), pp. 1823–1827, Victoria, Canada, May 2008.

52. R. G. Aghaei, M. A. Rahman, W. Gueaieb, and A. El Saddik, "Ant colony-based reinforcement learning algorithm for routing in wireless sensor networks," in Proceedings of the IEEE Instrumentation & Measurement Technology Conference (IMTC ‹07), 6, p. 1, IEEE, Warsaw, Poland, May 2007.

53. Y. Sun, H. Ma, L. Liu, and Y. Zheng, "ASAR: an ant-based service-aware routing algorithm for multimedia sensor networks," Frontiers of Electrical and Electronic Engineering in China, vol. 3, no. 1, pp. 25–33, 2008.

54. J. Bi, Z. Li, and R. Wang, "An ant colony optimization-based load balancing routing algorithm for wireless multimedia sensor networks," in Proceedings of the IEEE 12th International Conference on Communication Technology (ICCT ‹10), pp. 584–587, Nanjing, China, November 2010.

55. Z. Ke, L. Li, Q. Sun, and N. Chen, "Ant-like game routing algorithm for wireless multimedia sensor networks," in Proceedings of the 4th International Conference on Wireless Communications, Networking and Mobile Computing (WiCOM ‹08), pp. 1–4, Dalian, China, October 2008.

56. X. Yu, J. Luo, and J. Huang, "An ant colony optimization-based QoS routing algorithm for wireless multimedia sensor networks," in Proceedings of the 3rd International Conference on Communication Software and Networks (ICCSN ‹11), pp. 37–41, IEEE, Xi›an, China, May 2011.

57. L. Cobo, A. Quintero, and S. Pierre, "Ant-based routing for wireless multimedia sensor networks using multiple QoS metrics," Computer Networks, vol. 54, no. 17, pp. 2991–3010, 2010.

58. S. Selvakennedy, S. Sinnappan, and Y. Shang, "A biologically-inspired clustering protocol for wireless sensor networks," Computer Communications, vol. 30, no. 14-15, pp. 2786–2801, 2007.

59. L. Shu, Y. Zhang, L. T. Yang, Y. Wang, M. Hauswirth, and N. Xiong, "TPGF: geographic routing in wireless multimedia sensor networks," Telecommunication Systems, vol. 44, no. 1-2, pp. 79–95, 2010.

60. A. Nayyar, F. Bashir, Ubaid-Ur-Rehman, and Z. Hamid, "Intelligent routing protocol for multimedia sensor networks," in Proceedings of the 5th International Conference on Information Technology and Multimedia (ICIM ‹11), pp. 1–6, Kuala Lumpur, Malaysia, November 2011.

61. S. Kumar, M. Dave, and S. Dahiya, "ACO based QoS aware routing for wireless sensor networks with heterogeneous nodes," in Emerging Trends in Computing and Communication, vol. 298 of Lecture

Notes in Electrical Engineering, pp. 157–168, Springer, Berlin, Germany, 2014.

62. T. Camilo, C. Carreto, J. Silva, and F. Boavida, "An energy-efficient ant-based routing algorithm for wireless sensor networks," in Ant Colony Optimization and Swarm Intelligence, vol. 4150 of Lecture Notes in Computer Science, pp. 49–59, Springer, Berlin, Germany, 2006.
63. M. Liu, S. Xu, and S. Sun, "An agent-assisted QoS-based routing algorithm for wireless sensor networks," Journal of Network and Computer Applications, vol. 35, no. 1, pp. 29–36, 2012.
64. H. Huang, X. Cao, R. Wang, and Y. Wen, "A QoS-aware routing algorithm based on ant-cluster in wireless multimedia sensor networks," Science China Information Sciences, vol. 57, no. 10, pp. 1–16, 2014.
65. A. Förster and A. L. Murphy, "FROMS: feedback routing for optimizing multiple sinks in WSN with reinforcement learning," in Proceedings of the 3rd International Conference on Intelligent Sensors, Sensor Networks and Information (ISSNIP ‹07), pp. 371–376, IEEE, Melbourne, Australia, December 2007.
66. K. Kotecha and S. Popat, "Multi objective genetic algorithm based adaptive QoS routing in MANET," in Proceedings of the IEEE Congress on Evolutionary Computation (CEC ‹07), pp. 1423–1428, Singapore, September 2007.
67. I. Gerasimov and R. Simon, "A bandwidth-reservation mechanism for on-demand ad hoc path finding," in Proceedings of the 35th Annual Simulation Symposium, pp. 27–34, 2002.
68. N. Magaia, N. Horta, R. Neves, P. R. Pereira, and M. Correia, "A multi-objective routing algorithm for Wireless Multimedia Sensor Networks," Applied Soft Computing, vol. 30, pp. 104–112, 2015.
69. M. Saleem, I. Ullah, and M. Farooq, "BeeSensor: an energy-efficient and scalable routing protocol for wireless sensor networks," Information Sciences, vol. 200, pp. 38–56, 2012.
70. F. Çelik, A. Zengin, and S. Tuncel, "A survey on swarm intelligence based routing protocols in wireless sensor networks," International Journal of Physical Sciences, vol. 5, no. 14, pp. 2118–2126, 2010.
71. T. C. Camilo, C. Carreto, J. S. Silva, and F. Boavida, "An energy-efficient ant-based routing algorithm for wireless sensor networks," in Ant Colony Optimization and Swarm Intelligence, M. Dorigo, L. M. Gambardella, M. Birattari, A. Martinoli, R. Poli, and T. Stützle, Eds., vol. 4150 of Lecture Notes in Computer Science, pp. 49–59, 2006.
72. X. Cai, Y. Duan, Y. He, J. Yang, and C. Li, "Bee-sensor-C: an energy-efficient and scalable multipath routing protocol for wireless sensor networks," International Journal of Distributed Sensor Networks, vol. 2015, Article ID 976127, 14 pages, 2015.
73. Y.-L. Jin, Y. Zhang, Y. Xue, C. Guo, and L.-N. Xu, "Ant colony optimization routing based on congestion control in WSNs," Journal of Shanghai University (Natural Science Edition), vol. 18, no. 6, pp. 551–554, 2012.
74. S. Z. Jafarzadeh and M. H. Y. Moghaddam, "Design of energy-aware QoS routing protocol in wireless sensor networks using reinforcement learning," in Proceedings of the IEEE 27th Canadian Conference on Electrical and Computer Engineering (CCECE ‹14), pp. 1–5, Toronto, Canada, May 2014.
75. X. Liang, I. Balasingham, and S.-S. Byun, "A reinforcement learning based routing protocol with QoS support for biomedical sensor networks," in Proceedings of the International Symposium on Applied Sciences on Biomedical and Communication Technologies (ISABEL ‹08), pp. 1–5, IEEE, Aalborg, Denmark, October 2008.
76. M. Maalej, S. Cherif, and H. Besbes, "QoS and energy aware cooperative routing protocol for wildfire monitoring wireless sensor networks," The Scientific World Journal, vol. 2013, Article ID 437926, 11 pages, 2013.
77. F. Kiani, E. Amiri, M. Zamani, T. Khodadadi, and A. A. Manaf, "Efficient intelligent energy routing protocol in wireless sensor networks," International Journal of Distributed Sensor Networks, vol. 2015, Article ID 618072, 13 pages, 2015.
78. A. Förster, "Machine learning techniques applied to wireless ad-hoc networks: guide and survey," in Proceedings of the International Conference on Intelligent Sensors, Sensor Networks and Information Processing (ISSNIP ‹07), pp. 365–370, Melbourne, Australia, December 2007.
79. W. R. Heinzelman, A. Chandrakasan, and H. Balakrishnan, "Energy-efficient communication protocol for wireless microsensor networks," in Proceedings of the 33rd Annual Hawaii International Conference on System Sciences, January 2000.
80. H. Taheri, P. Neamatollahi, M. Naghibzadeh, and M.-H. Yaghmaee, "Improving on HEED protocol of wireless sensor networks using non probabilistic approach and fuzzy logic (HEED-NPF)," in Proceedings of the 5th International Symposium on Telecommunications (IST ‹10), pp. 193–198, Tehran, Iran, December 2010.
81. M. Ye, C. Li, G. Chen, and J. Wu, "EECS: an energy efficient clustering scheme in wireless sensor networks," in Proceedings of the 24th IEEE International Performance, Computing, and Communications Conference (IPCCC ‹05), pp. 535–540, IEEE, Phoenix, Ariz, USA, April 2005.
82. Y. Lan, W. Wenjing, and G. Fuxiang, "A real-time and energy aware QoS routing protocol for multimedia wireless sensor networks," in Proceedings of the 7th World Congress on Intelligent Control and Automation (WCICA ‹08), pp. 3304–3309, IEEE, Chongqing, China, June 2008.
83. A. Nayyar, F. Bashir, and Ubaid-Ur-Rehman, "Load based energy aware multimedia routing protocol-(LEAR)," in Proceedings of the 3rd International Conference on Computer Research and Development (ICCRD ‹11), vol. 2, pp. 427–430, Shanghai, China, March 2011.
84. S.-H. Yang, "Routing technologies in WSNs," in Wireless Sensor Networks: Principles, Design and Applications, pp. 101–128, Springer, London, UK, 2014.

85. D. Kandris, M. Tsagkaropoulos, I. Politis, A. Tzes, and S. Kotsopoulos, "Energy efficient and perceived QoS aware video routing over wireless multimedia sensor networks," Ad Hoc Networks, vol. 9, no. 4, pp. 591–607, 2011.

86. D. Kandris, P. Tsioumas, A. Tzes, G. Nikolakopoulos, and D. D. Vergados, "Power conservation through energy efficient routing in wireless sensor networks," Sensors, vol. 9, no. 9, pp. 7320–7342, 2009.

87. A. Manjeshwar and D. P. Agrawal, "TEEN: a routing protocol for enhanced efficiency in wireless sensor networks," in Proceedings of the 15th International Parallel and Distributed Processing Symposium (IPDPS ‹00), pp. 2009–2015, San Francisco, Calif, USA, April 2000.

88. K. Lin, J. J. P. C. Rodrigues, H. Ge, N. Xiong, and X. Liang, "Energy efficiency QoS assurance routing in wireless multimedia sensor networks," IEEE Systems Journal, vol. 5, no. 4, pp. 495–505, 2011.

89. K. Lin, M. Chen, and X. Ge, "Adaptive reliable routing based on cluster hierarchy for wireless multimedia sensor networks," EURASIP Journal on Wireless Communications and Networking, vol. 2010, Article ID 567952, pp. 1–11, 2010.

90. D. Niculescu and B. Nath, "DV based positioning in Ad Hoc networks," Telecommunication Systems, vol. 22, no. 1–4, pp. 267–280, 2003.

91. R. Nagpal, H. Shrobe, and J. Bachrach, "Organizing a global coordinate system from local information on an ad hoc sensor network," in Proceedings of the 2nd International Conference on Information Processing in Sensor Networks (IPSN ‹03), pp. 333–348, Palo Alto, Calif, USA, April 2003.

92. M. A. Zayene, N. Tabbane, and R. Elidoudi, "Performance evaluation of greedy perimeter stateless routing protocol in ad hoc networks," in Proceedings of the 4th International Conference on Computer Sciences and Convergence Information Technology (ICCIT ‹09), pp. 907–912, Seoul, South Korea, November 2009.

93. M. Chen, V. C. M. Leung, S. Mao, and Y. Yuan, "Directional geographical routing for real-time video communications in wireless sensor networks," Computer Communications, vol. 30, no. 17, pp. 3368–3383, 2007.

94. S. Medjiah, T. Ahmed, and F. Krief, "GEAMS: a geographic energy-aware multipath stream-based routing protocol for WMSNs," in Proceedings of the Global Information Infrastructure Symposium (GIIS ‹09), pp. 1–8, Hammamet, Tunisia, June 2009.

95. I. Bennis, O. Zytoune, D. Aboutajdine, and H. Fouchal, "Low energy geographical routing protocol for wireless multimedia sensor networks," in Proceedings of the 9th International Wireless Communications and Mobile Computing Conference (IWCMC ‹13), pp. 585–589, July 2013.

96. J. Wang, Y. Zhang, J. Wang, Y. Ma, and M. Chen, "PWDGR: pair-wise directional geographical routing based on wireless sensor network," IEEE Internet of Things Journal, vol. 2, no. 1, pp. 14–22, 2015.

97. L. Pradittasnee, "Predicting path quality with cross-layer information in multi-hop wireless networks," in Proceedings of the 7th International Conference on Information Technology and Electrical Engineering (ICITEE ‹15), pp. 464–469, IEEE, October 2015.

CHAPTER 9 ENHANCEMENT OF VIDEO STREAMING IN DISTRIBUTED HYBRID ARCHITECTURE

Soumen Kanrar and Niranjan Kumar Mandal

INTRODUCTION

The efficient traffic flow of information is a key element in current technology and business environment. This traffic flow is controlled by a complex network architecture and supported communication infrastructure. High-speed network transport mechanism serves as enabling technologies for new classes of communication service such as multimedia and video on demand. The smooth transport of chunk video objects over the network is a challenging issue. Lots of literature address this issue with various concepts based on content driven network (CDN), pure Peer to Peer network, and hybrid as mix of "CDN and Peer to Peer network" [1]. How to design an efficient P2P VOD system with high utilization of bandwidth and low maintenance cost remains an open challenge [2]. The demand for streaming video over a low bit rate channel is increasing in a fast pace for many applications like the newscast, video conferencing, distance learning, video game, entertainment, and so forth. Some sort of traffic and congestion control, admission control, packet drop, needs to be considered due to the characteristic of the video traffic. However, a major bottleneck is the timely delivery of a large amount of data through a very limited bandwidth. The issue directly involves how efficiently the overlay network adapts to the dynamic topology. The video content is pushed from the origin storage server to the peer nodes in the tree-shaped overlay network. Conceptually tree based overlay network is the address followed by multitree streaming approach tree [3, 4]. Here the topology dynamically changes with the multiple subtrees in place of one single tree [4, 5]. However, the mesh based chunk delivery approach gives the better result for both video on demand and the live video streaming. The latter concepts give better performance as observed in PPlive and Livesky [6]. In mesh shaped overlay network, the peers pull "video objects" from the neighboring peer [7]. The pull operation is done by the buffer map between the peers. To achieve the quality of service, chunk of "video object" delivery delays have to be handled efficiently. Quality of Experience (QoE) is defined in [8] as "the overall acceptability of an application as perceived subjectively by end user." In general, HTTP streaming has a bad QoS (quality of service) but a good QoE (Quality of Experience), because HTTP used reliable mode of transportation. This so happened for QoS (quality of service). The considered parameters are packet loss rate and packet delay and so forth. So it is highly required to enhance HTTP/TCP streaming as a major technology for media transformation [9]. In adaptive bit streaming, the media file is fragmented into small segments or chunks of same duration with the request to some specific time unit [10]. During the adaptive bit streaming, each chunk is decoded independently enabling seamless transport from one quality to another when network conditions are being changed frequently. The playout of a chunk is finished. Video player can start playing the next chunk with a different quality. So, for the adaptive bit streaming, lossy compression is a better option for video on demand [11]. The delay occurs due to the search for a chunk of "video object." On the other side, delay occurs due to the propagation delay and transmission delay from the neighboring peer. So the quality of service mainly depends on fast and correct path search. To find the desired video stream by using the mechanism of minimum hop counts towards the storage peer and to avoid the unnecessary query forwarding as well as to minimize the inter server gossiping during the chunk transfer [12, 13], the major routing protocols for wireless ad hoc networks have traditionally focused on finding paths with minimum hop count (MHC). However, such paths can include slow or lossy links,

Citation: Soumen Kanrar and Niranjan Kumar Mandal, "Enhancement of Video Streaming in Distributed Hybrid Architecture," Advances in Multimedia, vol. 2016, Article ID 5429187, 14 pages, 2016. doi:10.1155/2016/5429187.

leading to poor throughput [14]. The energy efficient routing algorithm in wireless networks typically selects minimum cost multihop paths. But those energy aware routing algorithms select a path with large number of small distance hops in varied power transmission environment [15]. The quality of service depends on the aggregate stationary bit rate which exceeds the minimum threshold level from the viewer perspective [16]. This paper is structured as follows. Section 1 introduces the problem. The basic, video encryption mechanisms have been discussed in this section, followed with video objects formation. Section 2 presents the chunk of video object transfer over the hybrid architecture. Sections 3 and 4 present the required architecture and simulation environment of the problem with conclusion at the end.

(1) Video Traffic Burst in Network. The repeatedly occurring theme relating to traffic transportation in broad-band network and high-speed network is the traffic "burstiness." It is exhibited by the key services such as compressed video and file transfer. Burstiness occurs in the course of traffic flow, due to the presence of several relatively short interarrival time sequences. The peak rate (R_{peak}) is an important requirement parameter used during the connection setup time. The other major traffic descriptors are the mean burst period "b," the average bit rate "m," and utilization factor "γ" which is defined as $\gamma = m/R_{peak}$. The peak rate (R_{peak}) yields the mean bit rate m and the variance σ_2 of the bit rate. The mean of the burst period "b" is used to describe how bursts occur from sender side. It is used to discriminate between different connection setups for streaming from different sources. During multiplexing, it has the same peak and mean bit rate but displays a different behavior. The multiplexer can be modeled as a single queue of length x and N servers each with fixed streaming rate c [17, 18]. The buffer overflow probability for finite buffer size is ε. It can be obtained for given x, c, and N. So the connection setup equivalent bandwidth W for the multiplexed connection is the smallest value of c, for which the buffer overflow probability is smaller than ε. The approximate upper bond of the equivalent bandwidth wi (for single isolated connection) depends upon the parameters (x, R_{peak}, γ, b, and α), where α is the source capacity of streaming. The equivalent bandwidth of the multiplexed connection can be presented as $W=\sum_{i=1}^{N} wi$. As it is considering the approximated upper bound for wi, the equivalent capacity is definitely overestimated. To eliminate the constraint, let us consider a stationary estimation derived from a bufferless fluid flow model. The fluid traffic model gives out with individual traffic units. Instead, it views traffic as a steam of fluid, characterized by a flow rate such as bits per second. The traffic count is replaced by a traffic volume. The bufferless fluid flow model for the stationary approximation exhibits the equivalent bandwidth W. W is selected to ensure that the aggregate stationary bit rate B exceeds W only with the probability smaller than ε. In general expression, it can be presented as $(B > W) \leq \varepsilon$, where B can be determined from the stationary distribution of the number of active sources. B can be modeled by the continuous time Markov chain as it potentially captures traffic burstiness, due to the presence of nonzero autocorrelation in the interarrival time sequence [19].

(2) Video Encryption Mechanisms. Video is the collection of still images. The collected set of still images is well orderly sequenced. The compressing technique is used to compress each individual still image of the collected set of images. Encoding technique is used to encode the image independently according to the sequence in the collected set of images. The Joint Photographic Experts Group (JPEG) format is used to compress the still images of the set of images. The sequences of still images are arranged in increasing order independently and individually. The MPEG-4 is the popular coding scheme that encodes the complete frames of video. The MPEG-4 is a collection of coding tools and maintains simple profiles. The most current implementation for temporal scalability is using H.263, MPEG-4, and secular temporal subband coding [20]. The MJPEG format is the motion JPEG video compressed and encoded using JPEG. Each video signal that carries information contains a definite amount of redundancy. So the video sequence contains redundancy.The aim of the video compression is to remove the redundancy from the video signal. Generally, two types of compression technique exist. One type is the lossless compression technique and the other type of technique is lossy compression technique. The lossless compression technique removes the statistical redundancy that is present in the video signal. When the transported video signal at the received end is reconstructed, it presents an identical copy of the original video. The current available technology supports compressing the video signal up to some modest level only. This is one of the greatest handicap legacies for the lossless compression technique, particularly for the storage and transported video signal over the network.This consumes extra space and bandwidth of the underlay network [21–23]. In lossy compression,

we can compress a huge number of video signals, but the reconstructed video signal at the received side is not identical to the original. The lossy compression meets a given bit rate for the storage and can maintain adaptive bit rate during the transmission of the video signal over the network or the internet. Different CODECs run into the storage as well as at the client sites. So, for adaptive bit streaming, lossy compression is a better option for on demand video streaming. The aim of video source coding is bit rate reduction for storage and transmission. The compression is done by removing the different types of redundancy, spatial, temporal, or frequent. Each image is usually divided into many blocks, each of size 8 pixel × 8 pixels. These 64 pixels are then transformed into frequency-domain representation by using what is called discrete cosine transform (DCT) [24, 25]. The frequency-domain transformation clearly separates out the low-frequency components from high-frequency components. Conceptually, the low-frequency components capture visually important components, whereas the high-frequency components capture visually fewer striking in components. The goal is to represent the low-frequency (or visually more important) coefficients with higher precision or with more bits and the high-frequency (or visually less important) coefficients with lower resolution or with fewer bits. Since the high-frequency coefficients are encoded with fewer bits, some information is lost during compression, and hence this is referred to as "lossy" compression. When inverse DCT (IDCT) is performed on the coefficients to reconstruct the image, it is not exactly the same as the original image but the difference between them is not perceptible to the human eye. The current enhancements in 2D (two-dimensional) video coding are classified mainly into two categories, nonscalable and scalable, respectively [26]. The nonscalable coding, for example, is H.264/AVC (advanced video coding) and H.265/HEVC (high efficiency video coding). The scalable video coding, for example, is H.264/AVC with SVC (scalable video coding) extension. In nonscalable coding bit rate is not reduced, but in scalable coding bit rate is reduced. Generally, H.264/AVC is using an intracoding concept about the prediction of a block inside a frame. Here the neighboring block within the same frame is considered. H.264/AVC provides more flexibility with the blocks of 4×4 samples and blocks of 8×8 samples for transformation. H.264/AVC is using fundamentally advanced intercoding concept for predicting *B*-frames from the set of highly eligible candidates of past and future *B*-frames. H.264/AVC has 10 modes. The modes are eight angular modes, one DC mode, and one planer mode, respectively. The angular prediction interpolates from reference pixels at locations based on the angle. The DC constant value is an average of neighboring pixels (reference samples). Planer is the average of horizontal and vertical prediction. The new key features of H.264/AVC are enhanced motion compression, small block of transform coding, improved deblocking filter, and enhanced coding. H.265/HEVC is the successor to H.264. H.265 is meant to double the compression rates of H.264, allowing for the propagation of 4 K and 8 K content over existing delivery systems. H.265/HEVC used the concepts of frame partitioning "luminance pixels" into coding tree blocks of sample sizes 16 × 16, 32 × 32, and 64 × 64, respectively. It is flexible and smoothly partitioned into multiple variables sized coding blocks. H.265/HEVC is using updated intracoding procedure for merging of small partition of coding trees. A wide range of intraframe predication is used. H.265/HEVC is massively improving the flexibility stricture of transformation which matches the code tree block structure that is 4×4 up to 32 × 32. H.265/HEVC improved the error resilience by using video parameter set (VPS). This concept is used for signaling essential syntax information for the decoding. H.265/HEVC has 35 modes. The modes are 33 angular modes, one DC mode, and one planer mode, respectively [26, 27].

(3) Video Object Formation. The DCT coefficients of each 8 × 8 pixel block are encoded with more bits for highly perceptible low-frequency components and fewer bits for less perceptible high-frequency components. This is achieved in two steps. First step is quantization, which eliminates perceptibly less significant information, and the second step is encoding, which minimizes the number of bits needed for representing the quantized DCT coefficients. Quantization is a technique by which real numbers are mapped into integers within a range, where the integer presents a level or quantum. The mapping is done by rounding a real number up to the nearest higher integer, so some information is lost during this process. At the end of quantization, each 8 × 8 block will be represented by a set of integers, many of which are zeroes because the high-frequency coefficients are usually small, and they end up being mapped to 0. The goal of encoding is to represent the coefficients using as few bits as possible. This is accomplished in two steps. Run length coding (RLC) is used to do the first level of compression. Variable length coding (VLC) does the next level of compression [12, 20]. After quantization, the majority of high-frequency DCT coefficients become zeroes. Run length coding takes advantage of this by coding the high-frequency DCT coefficients before coding the low-frequency DCT coefficients, so that the consecutive number of zeroes is maximized. This is accomplished by scanning the 8 × 8 matrices in a diagonal zigzag manner. Run length coding encodes consecutive identical coefficients by using two numbers. The first number is the "run" (the number that occurs consecutively), and the second number is "length" (the number of consecutive occurrences). Thus, if there is N consecutive zeroes, instead of coding each zero separately, RLC will represent the string of N zeroes as[0, N]. After RLC, there will be a sequence of numbers and VLC encodes these numbers using a minimum number of bits [20]. The technique is to use the minimum number of bits for the most commonly occurring number and use more bits for less common numbers. Since a variable number of bits are used for coding, it is referred to as variable length coding [21, 22]. In video encoding, the order in which frames are coded is not the same as the order in which they are played. Thus, it is not necessarily true that the reference frame for the future frame is the one just before it in the playing sequence. In fact, the video encoder jumps ahead from the currently displayed frame and encodes a future frame and then jumps back to encode the next frame in display order. Sometimes, the video encoder uses two "reference" frames, the currently displayed frame and a future encoded frame to encode the next frame in the display sequence. In this case, the future encoded frame is referred to as *P*-frame ("predicted" frame), and the frame encoded using two reference frames is referred to as *B*-frame ("bidirectionally" predictive frame). However, there is a problem for this approach because an error in one of the frames would propagate through the encoding process for ever. To avoid this problem, the video encoders typically encode one video frame (periodically) using still-image techniques and such frames are referred to as "intraframes" or *I*-frames [28]. A sequence of frames from one *I*-frame to another *I*-frame is referred to as a group of pictures (GOP). A GOP is best represented using a two-dimensional matrix. The order of encoding and the order of display are different for the frames in a GOP. It is transported

over an IP network just like any other type of data transmission [5]. Typically, videos have three types of frames, *I*-frames, *P*-frames, and *B*-frames, where *I*-frames capture most of the information in a scene followed by *P*- frames and *B*-frames, which capture the "deltas" from the original frame (captured in *I*-frame) resulting from motion. Finally, *I*-, *P*-, and *B*-frames are packetized in the encoded format as a sequence of frames, which itself is video objects. When delivery is requested, the chunk delivery of "video object" is done from the storage server to the neighboring requested peer nodes. The MPEG-4 looks after the collection of video objects (VO) [24]. The video object is an entry that the end user is able to manipulate. It is an area, which can be of any shape and may exit for an arbitrary length of time. The instance in which the video object occurs is called the "Video Object Plane" (VOP). In the traditional view, we can say that the VOP is a single frame and a set of frames forming a VO. The VOP is in irregular shape and occupies only a part of a frame.The separate objects are coded independently with different resolutions and qualities. These coding schemes adopt a linear uniform sampling scheme disregarding the varying semantic importance of different frames or segments. The characteristics of video traffic depend on the quality of service (QoS) of video traffic.

(4) Arrangement of Peer Nodes. The hierarchy is created by distributing peer nodes to the different levels as illustrated in Figure 1. The levels are numbered sequentially with the highest level of the hierarchy being level zero (denoted by $L0$). Each level is partitioned into a set of clusters. Each cluster is composed of peer nodes. The size of each cluster varies within k to $3k - 1$, where k is a constant [29]. The cluster is forming with the set of peer nodes. Those are close to each other. Every cluster has one "cluster head." The cluster head also logically belongs to the lower level; that is, a cluster head of level Li logically belongs to level $Li{-}1$. The cluster head has the minimum distance (with respect to hop count) to all other peer nodes in that cluster at the same level. If the size of a set of peer nodes has an upper bond $(2k - 1)$ then during dynamically splitting for cluster formation, the size of the set reaches up to $2k$. This happened, since at least one higherlevel cluster head logically belongs to the lower level. So the set splits into two clusters of size k. The data is transported from one level to another level through the cluster head.

By default, the storage server stayed at the level $L0$, which logically belongs to every level. The choice of a cluster leader is very important during the joining of new peer node to the system at the specific level in the hierarchy. The new peer node required minimum number of query messages for finding its position. During the video chunk transportation, formed multicast tree is overlaid to the hybrid architecture. If there is N number of peer nodes in the hierarch, the number of level is bounded with $\Theta(\log kN)$, where $k>3$ is a constant.

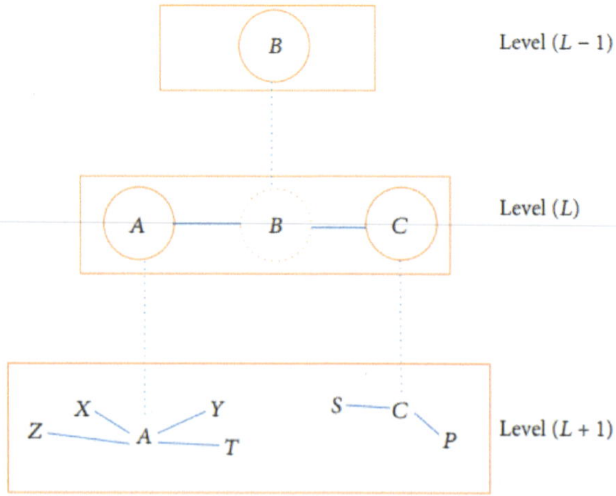

Figure 1: Hierarchal arrangement of peer nodes.

According to Figure 1, *A* and *C* are the cluster heads at the level (*L*). Those cluster heads physically stayed at the level (*L*), but cluster head is logically part of the level ($L - 1$). Set of nodes $\{X, Y, Z, T\}$ are directly communicated with the logical cluster head *A*. Similarly, the set of nodes $\{S, P\}$ are directly communicated with the logical cluster head *C* for exchanging data and information.This type of hierarchal peer nodes distribution efficiently handles the problem regarding the live streaming of media in large P2P network [30]. The multicast tree construction and efficient clustering of peer nodes based on a hierarchy of bounded cluster size are efficiently improving the performance. The neighbors on the levelwise topology can exchange periodic soft state refreshed without generating high volume of control message. The hierarchal architecture successfully reduces the overburden traffic load to the system. The other important advantages include the peer node departure and smooth cluster head section and cost-effective maintenance of the cluster.

CHUNK VIDEO OBJECT TRANSFER OVER HYBRID ARCHITECTURE

Figure 2 presents the physical configuration of the overall structure of the video on demand system. Clusters of viewers are symbolically presented by the viewer node. The cache proxy server is connecting viewer nodes to the next level of peer nodes in the multitier architecture. The cache proxy server is installed at the highest level in reverse order in the proposed model of multitier architecture. The proxy cache servers are not directly connected to each other. They are connected to each other via next level peer nodes.

All the levels including the lowest level, that is, the video storage server, form the multitier mesh shaped architecture. The work of cache proxy server at the highest level is to import the chunk of video objects from next level peer nodes.

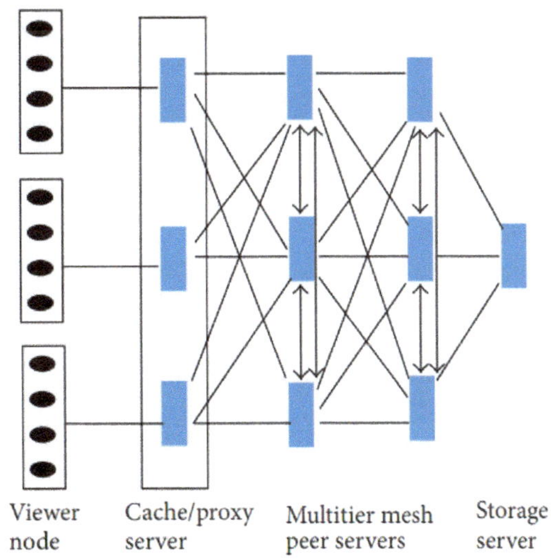

Figure 2: Distributed hybrid architecture.

Figure 3 presents the working mechanism of chunk transfer. The architecture is the composition of local and global network. The cache proxy server is the part of the local as well as the global network. P_1, P_2, P_3,..., are the peer nodes belonging to different level in the multitier architecture. P_N node position is fixed for the main video storage. The initial request tries to serve locally from the local cache proxy server.

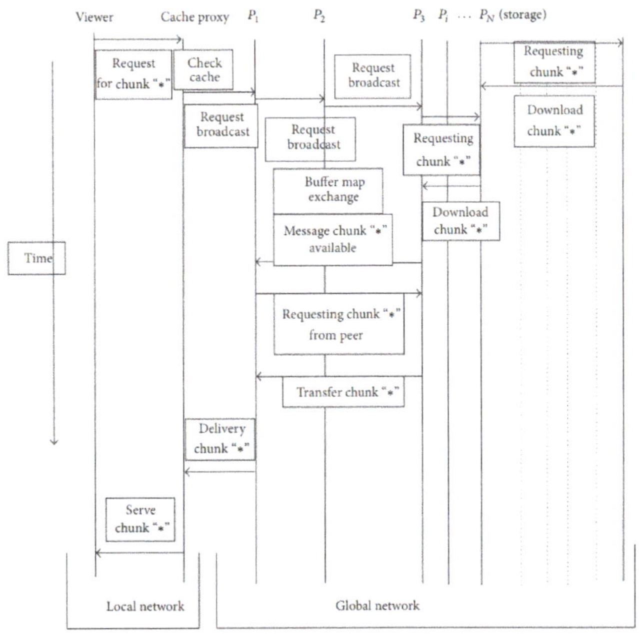

Figure 3: Chunk transfer working mechanism.

If the local proxy server cannot serve the chunk video object, then the request is broadcast to the neighboring peer nodes of the next level. In this fashion, the chunk request is forwarded among the peers. If any of the peer nodes possess the chunk video objects, that also rebroadcast the message chunk availability, then chunk video object is transferred according to the buffer map procedure. This is the mesh push mechanism from the sender peer node and mesh pull from the receiver peer. Now the copy of chunk video object is stored at the local cache proxy server before delivery to the viewer node. The preliminary survey of the literature shows that more than 106 numbers of user's node can concurrently decode the live video streaming within the range of bits rate 400 to 800 Kbps [31]. Current HDMI H.264 video encoders for live streaming and broadcasting use bit rate 250 Kbps to 10 Mbps. Dynamic page replacement at the cache memory of the proxy server can enhance the performance of the video on demand [32] for the "analysis and implementation of large scale video on demand system" [5]. The literatures [33, 34] show that proper cache memory can reduce 50% to 60% of P2P traffic load. Simultaneous viewers are asynchronous; that is, any viewer can access any part of that video at any instance of time. Due to the playback option in video on demand system, a good number of sequential video objects are always available to the media player buffer of the viewers [35–38]. In general, the viewer assesses that video through the cache proxy server. The video objects are a collection of video frames that feed the media player after sequential arranging from the received buffer of the viewer. If the complete video is not available to the cache proxy server, the unavailable part or parts of the chunk block or blocks are imported by the "buffer map via mesh pull approach" according to Figure 3. It uses the multichannel cache proxy server from any numbers of peers at any level in the multitier architecture. The similar buffer map concepts are used in the chunk transfer between the peers in the multitier mesh shaped architecture. The previously proposed video on demand architecture can be classified into some major categories. (i) Closed loop system: the client retrieves the video segments from the server. (ii) Prefix caching assisted periodic broadcast: it is a combined effect of open loop and closed loop system. (iii) Client equipped with set-top box: the set-top box stores locally part of some popular video. (iv) Peer to Peer network used for video on demand system: the video segments are transported through the network according to peer node requirement. In this paper, the proposed "distributed hybrid architecture" is a combination of P2P and mesh type network architecture. The cost of video object's transfer through this structure successfully reduces both cases of static and dynamic environment.

ANALYTIC ARCHITECTURE

Let $C^{\dagger}$ (i) be the equivalent capacity of network at session i. The minimum required bandwidth to ensure the aggregate stationary bit rate approaches $C^{\dagger}$ (i) with the considerable frame loss probability η. The aggregate stationary bit rate is required to approximate the adaptive encoding run at the client side video playback. Aggregate bit rate maintains the video resolution within a certain standard. In a particular session, n is the numbers of links that are active and simultaneously transfer the chunk of video objects from the peer nodes through the proxy servers in the multitier architecture. If the transferring stream or "chunk contents" are presented by the random vector X, for $i = 1. . . n$, $(Xi)=\mu i$ is the mean transferring rate for individual ith viewers, without the loss of generality. We can assume that Xi are the mutually independent random variables. The aggregate content transfer for a particular session is $B = (\sum_{i=1}^{n} Xi)$ and $B_n = \text{var}(X_1 + X_2 + \cdots + X_n)$; this includes the smooth video objects transmission at interactive session like playback, moves forward, and so forth. So far, nothing is assumed about the behavior of Bn for indefinite values of n. According to the Chebyshev inequality for the small positive numbers ε and η (previously assumed), the least number of active links is $k*$ to be found for all n, such that

$$n \succ k^*. \tag{1}$$

$$p\left\{\left(\left|\frac{X_1 + \cdots + X_n}{n} - \frac{B}{n}\right| < \varepsilon\right)\right\} \geq 1 - \frac{B_n}{n^2\varepsilon^2} \tag{2}$$

so

$$B_n/n^2\varepsilon^2 \;<\; \eta \text{ and } \lim_{n\to\infty}(B_n/n^2\varepsilon^2) \;\to\; 0$$

Here η is the approximate frame loss probability in a session. All the individual and shared individual links use the maximum bandwidth to transmit the chunk content. Clearly,

$$\sum_{i=1}^{k^*} \max(E(X_i)) \leq C^{\dagger}_{(i)}$$

Here $C^{\dagger}_{(i)}$ is capacity of the network. Since η is the packet loss or bit loss probability, it maintains the aggregate stationary bit rate streaming which remains the same for the short burst period. Without the loss of generality, all the above inequality holds true for the event$(B > C^{\dagger}_{(i)})$.The probability for the event is

$$\left(B \succ C^{\dagger}_{(i)}\right) \tag{3}$$

so

$$p\left(B \succ C^{\dagger}_{(i)}\right) \leq \eta. \tag{4}$$

We can consider it as

$$p\left(B \leq C^{\dagger}_{(i)}\right) \leq (1 - \eta) \tag{5}$$

The distribution of expression (3) can be obtained from the 2-state Markov chain. For every viewer node, there exists at least one active channel, including the case of broadcasting or multicasting of video data objects from the cache proxy server [32, 39]. It contains the full or part of the required video at any level of the pear nodes in multitier architecture. The video content is fully available to the cache proxy server. The proxy server is the part of mesh architecture, which is placed at the maximum level in hierarchy of the multitier architecture at strategic location. The proxy servers are not the peer server, so there are no interlinks between them. The main reason behind it is for the requirement of security and the billing process for commercial purpose also. The billing servers are installed at the level l_1 that is at level one in multitier architecture. Level zero that is l_0 is the position for video storage server. The proxy cache memory is updated or refreshed by the "least frequency frequently used" concepts [32, 40–42]. $l0$ is the level for video storage server and height level l_{l+1} is for cache proxy server. If λ is the average fraction of full streaming at a session that each of the supplying peers shares or contributes during that session, clearly $0<\lambda<1$. Let N be the total number of peer nodes including the main storage servers in the multitier architecture. Nc is the upload capacity at level 0 of the mesh type Peer to Peer network. Let (l) be the sum of the number of peer nodes at the level $(l + 1)$ and $(0) = N$. Now (l) is the upload capacity of the peers at the level l. So in a balanced state of traffic flow during the smooth chunk video objects transfer at any level depends on just lower-level peer's nodes of the multitier architecture. In a particular session of synchronous chunk transfer, the upload capacity of the peer nodes at level l is equivalent to the product of the average fraction of full streaming with the upload capacity of the participating peers at the level $(l - 1)$. This is expressed by $(l) \approx (l{-}1) \Rightarrow (1) = \lambda N(0) = \lambda Nc$. In real scenario, peer nodes at the higher level (l) get chunk video objects when the lower-level $(l - 1)$ participating peers send the video objects for them. The throughput of the system is contributed by the average fraction of full streaming of participating peer nodes. Some portion of the bandwidth is always used for chunk transfer to peers at the same level (l

− 1) according to Figure 2. So we get the expression $(l) = (l - 1) - (l - 1)$. Dynamic cluster connections are presented in Figure 4. We observe that A, B, and C are the peer nodes at the level $(l-1)$ and D, E, F, and$G$are the peer nodes at the level(l). The dynamic clustering is a logical cluster construction among the peer nodes at every level for the real time requirement at any session. The peer nodes B and C at level $(l - 1)$ exchange the chunk video objects or transfer among themselves. D is the cluster head at level (l) download video chunk from the dynamic cluster head "A" at level $(l - 1)$. Now downloading chunk of video objects from the lower level gives priority over the "chunk video objective" transfers in the same level of multitier architecture in that session. Let us consider that Nl is the number of peer nodes at the level l. To approximate the value Nl by N, the processing is as follows:

$$\begin{aligned} P(l) &= P(l-1) - N(l-1) \quad \text{for } 0 < \lambda < 1 \\ &= [P(l-2) - N(l-2)] - N(l-1) \\ &= P(l-2) - N(l-2) - N(l-1) \\ &= [P(l-3) - N(l-3)] - N(l-2) - N(l-1) \\ &= P(l-3) - N(l-3) - N(l-2) - N(l-1) \\ &= \cdots \\ &= \cdots \\ &= P(0) - N(0) - N(1) - N(2) - \cdots - N(l-1) \\ &= P(0) - N_c - \lambda N_c - \lambda^2 N_c - \cdots - \lambda^{l-1} N_c \\ &= N - N_c\left(1 + \lambda + \lambda^2 + \cdots + \lambda^{l-1}\right) \\ &\approx N - N_c \frac{1-\lambda^l}{1-\lambda}. \end{aligned} \quad (6)$$

Finally, N^l is approximate as $N^l \approx N-((1 - \lambda^l)/(1 - \lambda))$.

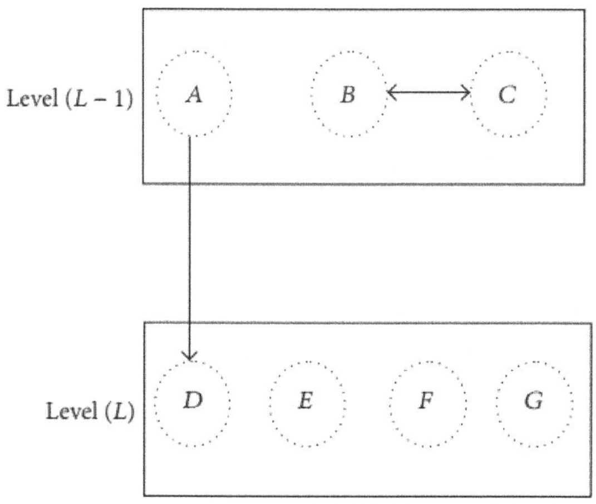

Figure 4: Dynamic cluster connections.

Let us assume that (i) k^l is the probability that at least k^l out of N^l number of peer nodes actively participate in the l level of the multitier architecture at ith session. Active means that the peer node has the required portion of encoded video file and remains live during the chunk video object transfer in that session.

So we get the expression

$$p_{k_l}^{(i)} = \sum_{k=k_l+1}^{N_l} \binom{N_l}{k} \rho^k (1-\rho)^{N_l-k} \quad (7)$$

So during chunk transfer of video objects, the aggregate bit rates depend upon the active participation of the peer nodes at every level $\{l, l-1, l-2, l-3, \ldots, 0\}$. The distribution of B in the expression ((4) and (5)) can be obtained from the multistate Markov chain. $SiLj$ is the sequence of active participation of peer nodes to transfer the chunk of video objects at the session i in the jth level. Since the download capacity at any level depends upon the uploading amount of just the lower level for that session, expression ((4) and (5)) becomes

$$\begin{aligned} p\left(B \le C_{(i)}^{\dagger}\right) &= p\left(S_iL_l, S_iL_{l-1}, S_iL_{l-2}, \ldots, S_iL_0\right) \\ &= p\left(\frac{S_iL_l}{S_iL_{l-1}}\right) p\left(S_iL_{l-1}, S_iL_{l-2}, \ldots, S_iL_0\right) \\ &= p\left(\frac{S_iL_l}{S_iL_{l-1}}\right) p\left(\frac{S_iL_{l-1}}{S_iL_{l-2}}\right) \cdots p\left(S_iL_0\right) \\ &= p_{k_l}^{(i)} p_{k_{l-1}}^{(i)} p_{k_{l-2}}^{(i)} \cdots p_{k_0}^{(i)} = \prod_{j=0}^{l} p_{k_{l-j}}^{(i)}. \end{aligned} \quad (8)$$

Clearly, $(S_iL_0)=1$ for session like session i, by using expression (7), and after reordering the above sequence, we get

$$p\left(B \le C_{(i)}^{\dagger}\right) \approx \prod_{j=l}^{1} \sum_{k=k_j+1}^{N_j} \binom{N_j}{k} \rho^k (1-\rho)^{N_j-k} \quad (9)$$

According to (5), we get

$$\prod_{j=l}^{1} \sum_{k=k_j+1}^{N_j} \binom{N_j}{k} \rho^k (1-\rho)^{N_j-k} \le (1-\eta) \quad (10)$$

Since N_j is the number of peer nodes at the jth level in multitier architecture, in a session k_m is the least required numbers of actively participating peer nodes at the mth level in mesh architecture during smooth transfer of chunk video objective. According to the expression, (10) holds true and inequality (1) becomes $k_l + k_{l-1} + k_{l-2} + \cdots + k_0 \le k^*$:

$$\sum_{j=0}^{l} k_{l-j} \le k^*, \quad (11)$$

where η is controlled by some threshold that depends on the adaptive bit rate for both sides of sender-receiver CODEC. The CODEC runs at the viewer's end and the content transferring peers or proxy server end. To find the optimized cost for transferring the chunk of the video objects, now the issue comes to efficiently finding the video object chunk storage with minimum hop counts in multitier architecture. To keep the value η at the lower level, the problem is to minimize the unnecessary searching packet forwarding and inter server gossiping. We propose the heuristic based path search for finding the chunk container of peer nodes for transferring video objects by using Algorithms 1 and 2. The estimated cost function is used to estimate the distance for possible destination of peer nodes in that particular session. The initial information about the higher-level peers is already available to the proxy server in multitier mesh architecture. For finding the peer, the search path is linear. So the cost of the path is optimized, that is, to avoid the unnecessary query forwarding to minimize the inter server gossiping. The path is considered the route to the farthest number in that session. The root is the proxy server. The distance is measured with the hop counts. In reality, more than one peer's node may contain the required chunk of video objects. So the search path will not be always linear. In the path search computation at a session, some extra additional link exists. So we can express it in form of the expression:

Min {Max d (proxy server, V) + number of duplicate links exist in S | such that V $\in S$, S is the Collection of churn storage peers.}

$$\text{Subject to} \quad \prod_{j=l}^{1} \sum_{k=k_j+1}^{N_j} \binom{N_j}{k} \rho^k (1-\rho)^{N_j-k} \le (1-\eta), \quad 0 < \rho < 1$$

$$\sum_{l=0}^{l} k_l \le k^*,$$

$$k_j < N_j,$$

$$k^* < N. \tag{12}$$

To find the least-cost path that is minimum hop count towards the fastest peer storage is considered. The consisting hashing in the structured overlays for the multitier Peer to Peer network is also being used. The request for the portion of the chunk video object is forwarded through the longest prefix match via Algorithm 2. The consistent hash function [43] is assigned to each node and key by a fixed bit identifier using a base hash function. A node's identifier is chosen by hashing the node IP address, while a key identifier is produced by hashing the key. Here the used term "key" refers to both the original key and its image under the hash functions. Similarly, the term node refers to both the node and its identifier under the hash function. Consistent hashing is assigning key to node. In point to point network, name based consistent hashing maps key onto a node. Both keys and nodes are assigned with an m-bit identifier. For nodes, this identifier is a hash of the node's IP address. For keys, this identifier is a hash of a keyword, such as a file name or query string.

```
Input:   x_s // The Query emits node
         x* // The Query sink node
    Initialize
      Buffer1 ← finite size
      Hop_count (every node) ← (−1) // peers at
                                          // every level
     Begin
    Query initiated from x_s // Proxy server
     If {(x_s.node_id = =x*. node_id) && found (query massage)}
        then
        Hop_count = 0
        Return Hop_count
        Output: chunk present in proxy server
        Exit
        End
     else
for each x ∈ {single hop node from adjutancy list of x_s}
Compute: Query forward to the longest prefix match node x using Algorithm 2.
Buffer1 ← push (x)
while (Bufer1 non empty) do
{
   pop node (v) from Buffer1
      {
       for each w from N_b(v) // select all the
                         //single hop neighbor w of v
         {
          If (Hop_count(w) == (−1)) // peer node yet
                               //not received the query
          then
          Hop_count (w) = Hop_count (v) +1;
     {
     If ((node identifier(w)==node identifier(x*)) && match (keyword_identifier))
     then // peer node having the query stream
     return Hop_count(w);
     Output: chunk present
       else w ∈ N_b(x*) // selected w belongs to
                        // single hop neighbor of x*
          {// heuristic search
          return
          Hop_count (w) +1;
          } // end search
     } // end block
     else
     Output: "Search query stream does not exist in this network".
     } // End for each
     } // End Pop
     } // End While
     End begin
     Stop
```

Algorithm 1: Heuristic Path Search Algorithm, query initiated from the proxy server.

```
Variable:
Prefix: list
L: Array of Record
LPM, M: Record // LPM is longest prefix match
D, D_l, D': Array of Character
R, i, l, A: integer
Initialize
Prefix ← {set of peer nodes}
L [i].length ← {Prefix length of ith distinct length}
L [i].hash ← {Hash table}
D ← {Storage server address}
B ← {Range of the array}// 32 bits for IPv4, 128
                          // bits for IPv6
M ← {Binary string of size R}
Begin
 A = 0;
   while (R ≠ NULL) do
   {
      i = ⌊(A + B)/2⌋;
      l = L[i].length; // longest possible length
      D_l = [(Bit String of D) base 2] ≤ l;
      D' = Assign (Most significant bit of D_l);
      // Index position of the binary string associated
      // to D' in hash table.
      M = Search (D', L [i].hash);
      // search hash table for D'
         If (M = = Null) then B= ⌊(A + B)/2⌋ − 1;
         // search in lower half
         else A = ⌊(A + B)/2⌋; // search in upper half
         if (M ∈ LPM) then break; else continue;
   } // end while
Update: Query forward to (M.address)
End begin
Stop
```

Algorithm 2: Query forward to longest prefix match

Proposition and Algorithm Statement

The hop count between query emitter node for the chunk of video object xs and query matched x^* node (that node has chunk of video objects) is at most $\|x_s - x^*\| \leq \log(n) << (n - 1)$ for $n \geq 2$. n is the size of multitier network and k is the base of the prefix for emitter node.

Proof. Let xs be the query initiative node and let $x*$ be the query matched node. $(k-1)$ is the size of the adjutancy list for a node that has a base prefix k. When the query emits node the same as the query matched node, that is, proxy server, then inequality (13) holds true for the single hop neighbor, and $n \geq 2$:

$$\|x_s - x^*\| \leq \log_k n. \tag{13}$$

When the query is forwarded through the intermediate nodes x_1, x_2,..., starting from the emitter node xs to sink node x^*, the node xs has the adjustable list size $(l_s - 1)$ with base of the prefix l_s, $_{(1)}$ has adjustable list size $(l_1 - 1)$ with base of the prefix l_1, and so on; likewise, $_{(m)}$ has the adjustable list size of $(l_m - 1)$ with the base of the prefix l_m. Query is forwarded by incremental prefix routing. So the path distance is expressed as

$$\|x_s - x^*\| \leq \|x_s - x_{(1)}\| + \|x_{(1)} - x_{(2)}\| + \cdots + \|x_{(k)} - x^*\|. \tag{14}$$

The number of branches maintained at the node x_s is $(l_s - 1)$, the node (1) maintains $(l_1 - 1)$, the number of branches, and so on. Now (m) maintains $(l_m - 1)$, number of branches. As (1) ∈ single hop neighbor of xs, $_{(i+1)}$ ∈ single hop neighbor of $_{(i)}$ and x^* ∈ single hop neighbor of $_{(m)}$. It concludes $\|x_s - (1)\| \approx 1$, $\|x_{(i)} - x_{(i+1)}\| \approx 1, \ldots, \|x_{(k)} - x^*\| \approx 1$. Expression (14) becomes $\|x_s - x^*\| < (n - 1)$.

Algorithms 1 and 2 are developed with the following consideration. The query message is generated from the proxy server. It is bits of a string header of the chunk video objects. There is more than one peer node present in the network.

Those possess the required chunk video objects. The aim of the algorithm is to find the fastest least-cost path towards the desired peer node. The query message is routed to desire peer node via key identification.

SIMULATION RESULTS AND DISCUSSION

The storage server contains the raw file (or coded video). The YUV file is created by decoding the raw file. At first, it is converted to *.m4v file format. Then, we create the mp4 container and simultaneously create the reference videos.The frames are packetized for transport over the network. Here mp4trace command sends the *.mp4 file to the destination peer node through the freely available port except the system port (usually selected ports above 5000) [44]. The transportation of these chunks of video objects, that is, "the sequence of packet frames," is done with RTP/UDP. All this design and implementation of EvalVid-RA, a tool set for rate adaptive VBR (video bit rate) that is added to ns-2, are based on some modification to the EvalVid Version 1.2 tool and the ns-2 interfacing code. The ffmpeg command of EvalVid is used to control rate of some GOP before stabilizing the rate output. The VBR rate controller is set to 600 kbit/s for the individual session. The mesh shaped hybrid multitier architecture, including the cache proxy server, has 10 levels. The higher level l_9 is the cache proxy server and l_0 level is for the video storage server. Levels l_1 to l_8 possess the peer nodes in mesh shaped multitier. Each level has 4 peers that are interconnected. The peers that belong to the same level exchange buffer information to transfer the chunk video objects. The peers at the higher level are connected to lower level peers in unicast; that is, the higher-level peers only download the chunk of video objects from the lower level. In the environment, we consider two types of simulation. In type one, the peers maintain dynamic connection. In dynamic connection, every peer has adjacent list size of 4 and 6. These links are selected from the available 11 links to the peer. The 11 links are orientated as 4 links for the unicast downloading from the lower-level peers, 4 links for the unicast uploading for the higher-level peers, and 3 links for the chunk transfer at the same level of peers. In the second type of simulation, we consider the static links 4 and 6 out of the 11 available links to the peer. In the static link, full content of the video is transferred from the storage server or the intermediate peers through the initial fixed setup links for every session. The link capacity maintains 400 kbps to 800 kbps speed. 400 kbp is the link capacity between the viewers to the cache proxy server. The 800 kbps is the link capacity of the storage server to the next higher server (i.e., billing server). The intermediate level mesh peers maintain the link capacity of 600 kbps. The required parameter values and ranges are summarized in Table 1.

Table 1: Simulation parameters.

Parameter	Values/range
Number of levels in multitier	10
Number of peers at each level	4
Raw video frame rate	30/second
Group of picture length	30 frames
Link capacity	400 kbps to 800 kbps
Number of viewers connected to each proxy	20 (Min)
Number of viewers connected to each proxy	40 (Max)

The confidence interval used in this simulation is 90%. For small prototype evaluation, we restricted the number of viewers connected to proxy server and adjacent list size of peer node. The viewers are connected to each proxy server; minimum is 20 and maximum is 40. The number of viewers connected to the proxy server can grow. The sum-up link capacity of the viewers connected to the proxy server is more than the intermediate link capacity. The simulation result is based on the request initiative from the proxy server, when the viewers submitted his/her requests through the proxy server. In plotting Figures 5– 10, we consider the vertical axis as the number of requests sent (cumulative) for the chunk video objects from the cache proxy server. The horizontal axis is the number of hops to the location of those chunk video objects. The request initiative from the cache proxy server is approximately equal to $100999 \approx 10^6 + 10^3 + 10^1$.

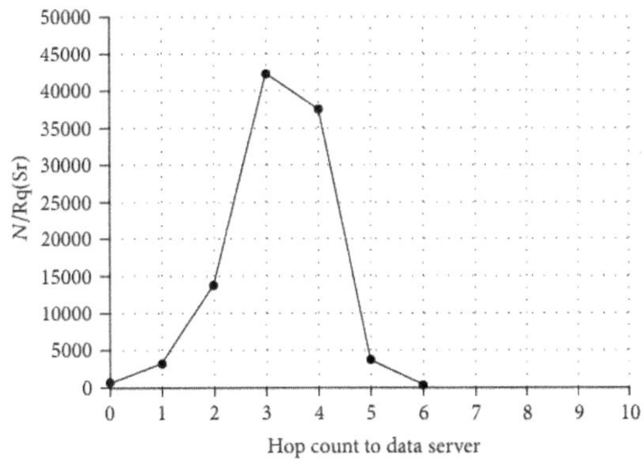

Figure 5: Dynamic adjacent list size (4).

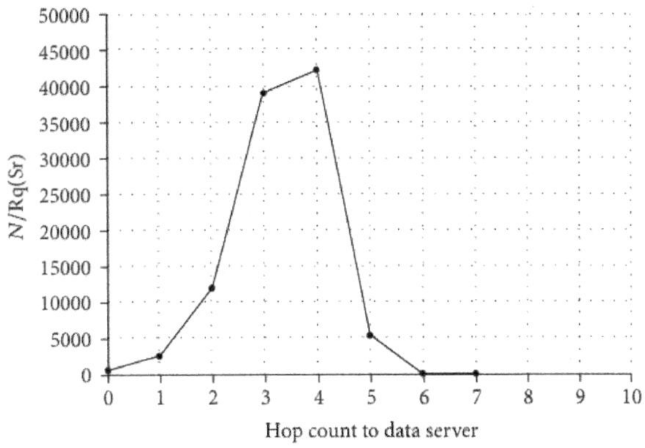

Figure 6: Static adjacent list size (4).

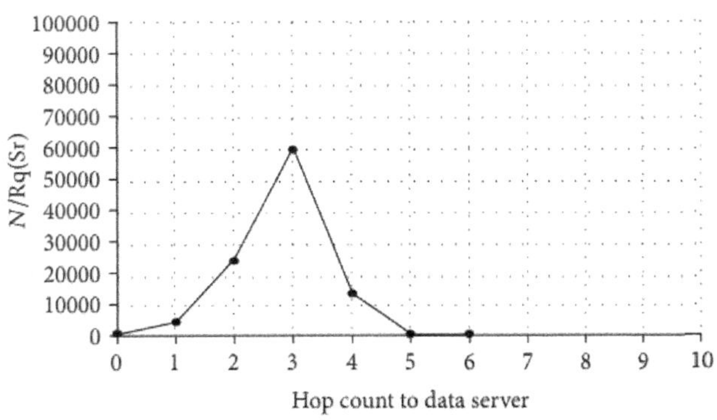

Figure 7: Dynamic adjacent list size (6).

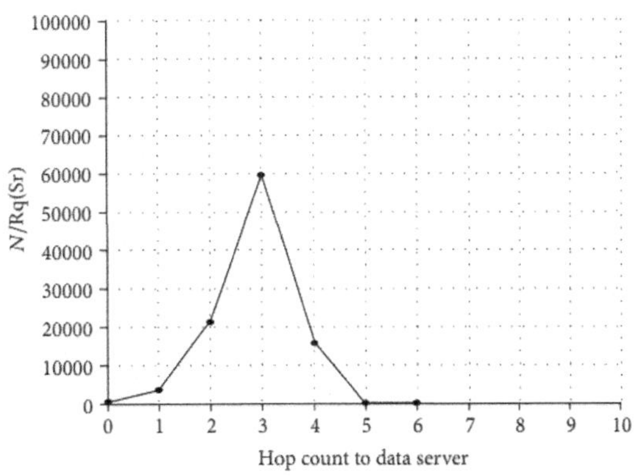

Figure 8: Static adjacent list size (6).

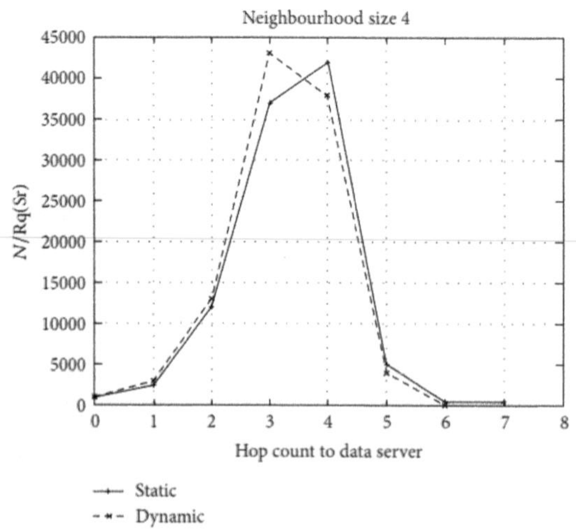

Figure 9: Compare dynamic versus static adjacent list size (4)

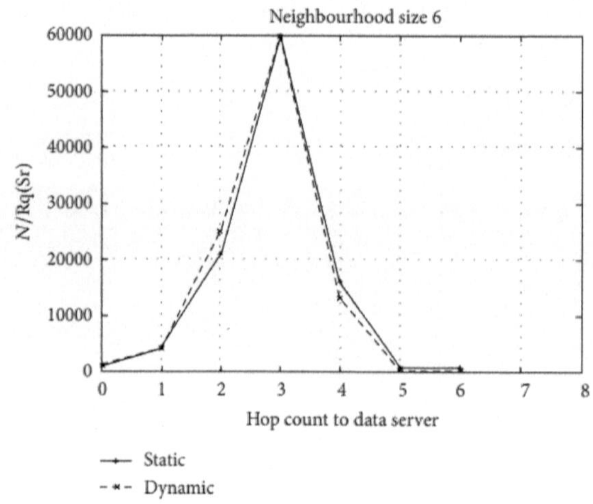

Figure 10: Compare dynamic versus static adjacent list size (6).

Figures 5 and 7 present the simulation result of minimum hop count to the required chunk of the video objects towards the peers or storage server. The peer nodes at *i*th level, for $0 \leq i \leq 9$, maintain dynamic adjacent list sizes 1 to 4 and 1 to 6. Figures 6 and 8 present the simulation result where every peer at every level maintains static adjacent list sizes 4 and 6. To search for destination peers address, we simply start with the longest length hash table and extract the first bits and do a search in the hash table for length entries. If we succeed, we have found the longest prefix match and thus our BMP (best match path); if not, we look at the first length smaller than previous match path (done by the array indexing one position less than the position) and continue the search. The search is forwarded by incremental prefix routing. Keeping $(b - 1)$ hosts at each prefix digit b is the base of the prefix. To minimize the hop count, we consider the number of links at each intermediate node dynamically changing from one to $(b - 1)$. So expression (12) will be always bounded by $\log(N)$, and N is the number of "video objects storage" peer nodes. So $\log(N)$ is the maximum hop to any destination. The comparative simulation results are presented in Figures 9 and 10. The simulation result shows that 43000 numbers of requests were served from the peer at the hop count 3 for the dynamic adjacent list size 4. We have noticed that 40000 numbers of requests were served from the peer at the hop count 3 for static adjacent list size 4.

The chunk size is the same for both the cases. In Figures 9 and 10, we have noticed that the dotted line (dynamic) lies above the nondotted line (static) between the hop count 0 and hop count 3. In the next phase, the nondotted link lies above the dotted line between the hop counts 3 and 7. The longest prefix match with the dynamic adjacent list on the basis of "Heuristic Path Search Algorithm" gives better cost-effective results. The simulation results with the dynamic adjacent list size 4 and static adjacent list size 4 are presented in Figure 9. The simulation result clearly shows that, in dynamic environment with list adjacent size 4, 35×10^2 numbers of video objects serve from the hop count 1. 130×10^2 numbers of video objects serve from hop count 2. 430×10^2 numbers of video objects serve from hop count 3. 370×10^2 numbers of video objects serve from hop count 4. 40×10^2 numbers of video objects serve from hop count 5. Static environment shows that, with adjacent list size 4, 30×10^2 numbers of video objects serve from hop count 1. 120×10^2 numbers of video objects serve from hop count 2. 360×10^2 numbers of video objects serve from hop count 3. 410×10^2 numbers of video objects serve from hop count 4 and 50×10^2 numbers of video objects serve from hop count 5. Here, we consider a rough estimate to measure the cost of video object transfer by using the metrics, such as "number of video objects serves" and hop counts. Cost is the sum of the "number of video objects serves a_m" multiplied by the "hop counts b_m towards the container that possesses the video objects"; that is, $\sum_{m=1}^{n}(am * bm)$. Here m is the hop count towards the chunk video container peer node, and n is an end of hop counts towards the container. The above expression gives the following cost score. Dynamic environment of simulation produced the score 3265×10^2 according to Figure 9. For static environment of simulation, the produced cost score is 3740×10^2 according to Figure 9. Similarly according to simulation the result is presented in Figure 10. That cost score in dynamic environment with adjacent list size 4 is 2840×10^2. The cost score in static environment with adjacent list size 6 is 2880×10^2. The cost score directly depends on the number of computations. The performance of the system increases as the score value decreases, during any stage of transfer of chunk video object through the multitier architecture.

CONCLUSIONS

In this paper, we have shown that the hybrid architecture of Peer to Peer network with mesh type's network enhances the content delivery of video objects. The number of requests generated by the proxy server serves from the distributed chunk video object storage at the various levels of the multitier architecture. The simulation used the static as well as the dynamic growth links at each middle tire containing storage nodes. The result showed the effectiveness of the hybrid architecture over the pure Peer to Peer network. The previous works considered only pure P2P network. The hybrid type's work successfully reduces the cost for the search path; hence it reduces the delay. Another aspect of the work is that it selects the required position of the video objects and supplies it to the desired node in the hybrid multitier architecture, which is the enhancement of previous Peer to Peer type stream data transmission. There is enough scope for further improvement.

Conflict of Interests

The authors Soumen Kanrar and Niranjan Kumar Mandal declare that there is no conflict of interests regarding the publication of the paper.

ACKNOWLEDGMENT

The authors are grateful to Sharmista Das Kanrar from Bishop Westcott, Ranchi, India.

REFERENCES

1. H. Jiang, J. Li, Z. Li, and X. Bai, "Effcient large-scale Content Distribution with Combination of CDN and P2P Networks," International Journal of Hybrid Information Technology, vol. 2, no. 2, 2009.
2. C. Liang, Z. Fu, Y. Liu, and C. W. Wu, "Incentivized peerassisted streaming for on-demand services," IEEE Transactions on Parallel and Distributed Systems, vol. 21, no. 9, pp. 1354–1367, 2010.
3. X. Hei, Y. Liu, and K. Ross, "IPTV over P2P streaming networks: the mesh-pull approach," IEEE Communications Magazine, vol. 46, no. 2, pp. 86–92, 2008.
4. X. Hei, C. Liang, J. Liang, Y. Liu, and K. W. Ross, "A measurement study of a large-scale P2P IPTV system," IEEE Transactions on Multimedia, vol. 9, no. 8, pp. 1672–1687, 2007.
5. S. Kanrar, "Analysis and implementation of the large scale video-on-demand system," International Journal of Applied Information Systems, vol. 1, no. 4, 2012.
6. H. Yin, X. Liu, T. Zhan et al., "Design and deployment of a hybrid CDN-P2P system for live video streaming: experiences with LiveSky," in Proceedings of the 17th ACM International Conference on Multimedia (MM '09), pp. 25–34, ACM, Beijing, China, October 2009.
7. W.-P. K. Yiu, X. Jin, and S.-H. G. Chan, "VMesh: distributed segment storage for peer-to-peer interactive video streaming," IEEE Journal on Selected Areas in Communications, vol. 25, no. 9, pp. 1717–1731, 2007.
8. ITU-T Study Groups, "Definition of Quality of Experience (QoE)," ITU-T SG12, COM12-LS 62-E, TD 109rev2(PLEN/12), Geneva, Switzerland, January 2007, https://www.itu.int/md/ T05-FG.IPTV-IL-0050/en.
9. N. Zong, "Survey and Gap analysis for HTTP streaming standards and implementations," 2010.
10. Q. Wu, "Problem statement for HTTP streaming," 2010.
11. K. D. Singh, Y. Hadjadj-Aoul, and G. Rubino, "Quality of experience estimation for adaptive HTTP/TCP video streaming using H.264/AVC," in Proceedings of the IEEE Consumer Communications and Networking Conference (CCNC '12), pp. 127– 131, Las Vegas, Nev, USA, January 2012.
12. N. Goel, B. Raman, and I. Gupta, "Chaos based joint compression and encryption framework for end-to-end communication systems," Advances in Multimedia, vol. 2014, Article ID 910106, 10 pages, 2014.
13. W. Zeng and S. Lei, "Efficient frequency domain selective scrambling of digital video," IEEE Transactions on Multimedia, vol. 5, no. 1, pp. 118–129, 2003.
14. R. Draves, J. Padhye, and B. Zill, "Comparison of routing metrics for static multi-hop wireless networks," ACM SIGCOMM Computer Communication Review, vol. 34, no. 4, pp. 133–144, 2004.
15. S. Banerjee and A. Misra, "Minimum energy paths for reliable communication in multi-hop wireless networks," in Proceedings of the 3rd ACM International Symposium on Mobile Ad Hoc Networking & Computing (MobiHoc '02), pp. 146–156, ACM, Lausanne, Switzerland, June 2002.
16. S. Kanrar, N. K. Mandal, and S. D. Kanrar, "Session based storage finding in video on demand system," in Proceedings of the 3rd International Symposium on Women in Computing and Informatics (WCI '15), pp. 131–135, Kochi, India, August 2015.
17. A. Erramilli, O. Narayan, and W. Willinger, "Experimental queueing analysis with long-range dependent packet traffic," IEEE/ACM Transactions on Networking, vol. 4, no. 2, pp. 209– 223, 1996.
18. B. Maglaris, D. Anastassiou, P. Sen, G. Karlsson, and

J. D. Robbins, "Performance models of statistical multiplexing in packet video communications," IEEE Transactions on Communications, vol. 36, no. 7, pp. 834–844, 1988.

19. V. S. Frost and B. Melamed, "Traffic modeling for telecommunications networks," IEEE Communication Magazine, vol. 32, no. 3, pp. 70–81, 1994.

20. J. Wen and J. D. Villasenor, "Reversible variable length codes for efficient and robust image and video coding," in Proceedings of the Data Compression Conference (DCC '98), pp. 471–480, IEEE, Snowbird, Utah, USA, April 1998.

21. F. Liu and H. Koenig, "Puzzle—an efficient, compression independent video encryption algorithm," Multimedia Tools and Applications, vol. 73, no. 2, pp. 715–735, 2012.

22. E. Mallika and K. Sivakumar, "Joint video compression and encryption using secure wavelet transformation and entropy coding," International Journal of Computer Science and Mobile Computing, vol. 3, no. 2, pp. 483–489, 2014.

23. C.-P. Wu and C.-C. J. Kuo, "Design of integrated multimedia compression and encryption systems," IEEE Transactions on Multimedia, vol. 7, no. 5, pp. 828–839, 2005.

24. C. Kim and J.-N. Hwang, "Fast and automatic video object segmentation and tracking for content-based applications," IEEE Transactions on Circuits and Systems for Video Technology, vol. 12, no. 2, pp. 122–129, 2002.

25. K. J. Singh and R. Manimegalai, "A survey on joint compression and encryption techniques for video data," Journal of Computer Science, vol. 8, no. 5, pp. 731–736, 2012.

26. M. M. Hannuksela, D. Rusanovskyy, W. Su et al., "Multiviewvideo-plus-depth coding based on the advanced video coding standard," IEEE Transactions on Image Processing, vol. 22, no. 9, pp. 3449–3458, 2013.

27. T. Wiegand and G. J. Sullivan, "Overview of the H.264/AVC video coding standard," IEEE Transactions on Circuits and Systems for Video Technology, vol. 13, no. 7, pp. 560–576, 2003.

28. F. H. P. Fitzek and M. Reisslein, "MPEG-4 and H.263 video traces for network performance evaluation," IEEE Network, vol. 15, no. 6, pp. 40–54, 2002.

29. D. A. Tan, K. A. Hua, and T. Do, "ZIGZAG: an efficient peerto-peer scheme for media streaming," in Proceedings of the 22nd Annual Joint Conference of the IEEE Computer and Communication (INFOCOM '03), vol. 2, pp. 1283–1292, San Francisco, Calif, USA, April 2003.

30. S. Banerjee, B. Bhattacharjee, and C. Kommareddy, "Scalable application layer multicast," in Proceedings of the Conference on Applications, Technologies, Architectures, and Protocols for Computer Communications (SIGCOMM '02), pp. 205–217, 2002.

31. Y. Liu, Y. Guo, and C. Liang, "A survey on peer-to-peer video streaming systems," Peer-to-Peer Networking and Applications, vol. 1, no. 1, pp. 18–28, 2008.

32. S. Kanrar and N. K. Mandal, "Dynamic page replacement at the cache memory for the video on demand server," in Advanced Computing, Networking and Informatics-Volume 2: Wireless Networks and Security Proceedings of the Second International Conference on Advanced Computing, Networking and Informatics (ICACNI-2014), vol. 28 of Smart Innovation, Systems and Technologies, pp. 461–469, Springer, Berlin, Germany, 2014.

33. S. Kanrar and N. K. Mandal, "Optimum storage finding in video on demand system," in Proceedings of the 2nd International Conference on Signal Processing and Integrated Networks (SPIN '15), pp. 827–830, IEEE, Noida, India, Feburary 2015.

34. N. Leibowitz, C. A. Bergman, R. Ben-shaul, and C. A. Shavit, "Are files wrapping network scacheable? Characterizing P2P traffic," in Proceedings of the 7th International WWW Caching Workshop, August 2002.

35. C. Vincenzo, R. Gaeta, R. Loti, and L. Liquori, "Inter connection of large scale unstructured p2p networks: modeling and analysis," in Analytical and Stochastic Modeling Techniques and Applications, vol. 7984, pp. 183–197, Springer, 2013.

36. A. Brocco and I. Baumgart, "A framework for a comprehensive evaluation of ant-inspired peer-to-peer protocols," in Proceedings of the 20th Euromicro International Conference on Parallel, Distributed and Network-Based Processing (PDP '12), pp. 303– 310, IEEE, Garching bei Munchen, Germany, February 2012.

37. J.-S. Li and C.-H. Chao, "An efficient superpeer overlay construction and broadcasting scheme based on perfect difference graph," IEEE Transactions on Parallel and Distributed Systems, vol. 21, no. 5, pp. 594–606, 2010.

38. R. Rodrigues and P. Druschel, "Peer-to-peer systems," Communications of the ACM, vol. 53, no. 10, pp. 72–82, 2010.

39. S. Kanrar, "Performance of distributed video on demand system for multirate traffic," in Proceedings of the International Conference on Recent Trends in Information Systems (ReTIS '11), pp. 52– 56, Kolkata, India, December 2011.

40. S. Kanrar and N. K. Mandal, "Performance enhancement for audio-video proxy server," in Proceedings of the 3rd International Conference on Frontiers of Intelligent Computing: Theory and Applications (FICTA) 2014, vol. 327 of Advances in Intelligent Systems and Computing, pp. 605–613, Springer, Basel, Switzerland, 2015.

41. F. Peng, A. Malatras, B. Hirsbrunner, and M. Courant, "Constructing multi-layer overlays for pervasive environments," in Proceedings of the 8th International Workshop on Mobile P2P Computing (MP2P '12), pp. 1–6, March 2012.

42. S. Tewari and L. Kleinrock, "On fairness, optimal download performance and proportional replication in peer-to-peer networks," in Proceedings of the 4th International IFIP-TC6 Networking Conference, Waterloo, Canada, May 2005.

43. I. Stoica, R. Morris, D. Karger, M. F. Kaashoek, and H. Balakrishnan, "Chord: a scalable peer-to-peer lookup service for internet applications," in Proceedings of the Conference on Applications, Technologies, Architectures, and Protocols for Computer Communications (SIGCOMM '01), pp. 149–160, ACM, San Diego, Calif, USA, August 2001.

44. B. Tan and L. Massoulie, "Optimal content placement for peerto-peer video-on-demand systems," IEEE/ACM Transactions on Networking, vol. 21, no. 2, pp. 566–579, 2013.

CHAPTER 10 NONINTRUSIVE METHOD BASED ON NEURAL NETWORKS FOR VIDEO QUALITY OF EXPERIENCE ASSESSMENT

Diego José Luis Botia Valderrama and Natalia Gaviria Gómez

INTRODUCTION

The assessment of quality in digital video systems is a topic of great interest to the telecommunications companies that hope to increase the quality to their users. The QoE (Quality of Experience) is the degree of user's satisfaction with any kind of multimedia service. This concept has been defined in different ways by various authors. Liu et al. [1] suggested that QoE involves two aspects:(i)The monitoring of the user's experience online.(ii)The service control to ensure that QoS (Quality of Service) can satisfy the user's requirements.

QoE is an extension of QoS, since the former provides information about the services delivery from point of view of the end users. QoE refers to personal preferences of users and so seeks to assess the subjective perception of the received service [2, 3]. However, this perception is influenced, by the network performance in terms of QoS and video encoding parameters. Different methodologies proposed in the literature aim at estimating subjective Quality of Experience, through the assessment of different metrics of video quality generally using objective methods.

In the implementation of digital television platforms (e.g., IPTV and DVB), some important restrictions can affect the management and proper operation of the network. Some of these are(i)the large amount of bandwidth the user should contract,(ii)the limitation of internal buffers in routers and STB (Set Top Box), which can generate problems such as packet loss that are critical on video or audio transmission,(iii) the type of video compression format, which will reduce the channel use without affecting the quality,(iv)other items that should be installed and properly configured, such as the last mile link used and the admission control class used.

Different researches have proposed quality assessment models for video streams and measurement strategies in order to identify the optimal values for each metric guaranteeing the experience of the viewer.

According to Winkler [4], there are projects for QoE assessment: VQEG (Video Quality Experts Group), QoSM (Quality of Service Metrics) from ATIS IPTV Interoperability Forum, and specific metrics such as those oriented to packets, a bitstream, hybrids, and images metrics [5–8]; but these are more complex, and the correlation methods have not yet been applied for real time services assessment. Other works propose a new relationship between KPIs (Key Performance Indexes) with QoE assessment on mobile environments, but it can be applied in other scenarios as fixed broadband networks focused particularly on telecommunications providers [9].

One of the main problems on the estimation of the video subjective quality is the lack of proper estimation or correlation models. These must guarantee results with accuracy but in many cases heavily depend on objective metrics [10–12]. Also, the correlation models in QoE metrics are not accurate and reliable.

According to [13], three strategies were developed to perform the estimation of video quality. The first one is to apply a subjective assessment with a selected group of people; the main drawback of the evaluations is the cost and time. The second one is the objective quality metrics assessment for video, in which the principal disadvantage is the low correlation with regard to subjective quality metrics [14]; in addition, such metrics obviate the network and content parameters. The last one is to use machine learning methods to analyse the objective and subjective assessment but the major drawback is the difficult for configuring and testing;

Citation: Diego José Luis Botia Valderrama and Natalia Gaviria Gómez, "Nonintrusive Method Based on Neural Networks for Video Quality of Experience Assessment," Advances in Multimedia, vol. 2016, Article ID 1730814, 17 pages, 2016. doi:10.1155/2016/1730814.

furthermore, some methods may fail whether a suitable design and optimal parameter selection are not performed.

According to Kuipers et al. [15], the minimum threshold of accepted quality is a MOS (Mean Opinion Score) value of 3.5. The subjective tests (such as MOS) are widely useful in assessing the users satisfaction due to its accuracy; however, the application of them is still very complex due to the high consumption of time and money; therefore, they are impractical for tasks of testing in network devices, and a controlled environment is required is required (in some cases, its implementation are complex).

Also if we want to develop traffic management techniques in real time, it is necessary to find a relationship among them and the objective metrics, measurable by the network equipment.

Objective methods are based on algorithms for the assessment of video quality, making them less complex and, furthermore, can be performed on controlled simulation environments. The objective metrics are supported in mathematical models that approximate themselves to the Human Vision System (HVS) behavior and, therefore, try to estimate as accurately as possible the true QoE. However, the perception of each viewer is highly influenced by the quality of the data network, expressed by the QoS parameters [26]. A lot of proposals for assessing QoE metrics have been created to define the user's experience. ITU-T has carried out standards for some of them [27, 28].

Due to complex factors such as the HVS, different kinds of solutions such as the implementation of machine learning techniques have been proposed. Some of the most used methods are Artificial Neural Network (ANN), fuzzy logic based on rules, neural-fuzzy networks (e.g., ANFIS), support vector machines (SVM), Gaussian processes, and genetic algorithm, among others. Nonintrusive QoE estimation methods for video are mainly based on application layer and network parameters.

Models as artificial neural networks have been little studied for estimation and prediction of video quality. For the evaluation of nonintrusive methods, we decided to employ two methods of machine learning: BPNN feedforward and RNN (Random Neural Network). We assess the output of each system, estimated MOS versus expected MOS. In each case, the fit of the correlation, determined by Pearson and Spearman rank order correlation coefficients, RMSE (Root Mean Square Error), and Outliers Ratio were calculated. The expected MOS was calculated from the VQM (Video Quality Metric), SSIM (Structural Similarity Index Metric), PSNR (Peak Signal Noise Ratio), and QIBF (Quality Index Based Frame) metrics.

This paper presents the key objective and subjective quality metrics and introduces a nonintrusive QoE assessment methodology based on machine learning techniques, showing its main features and functionality. Afterwards, the developed testbed is explained; both results obtained as their analyses are presented. Finally the main conclusions and further works will be shown.

RELATED WORKS

Methods for Quality of Experience Assessment

In spite of all proposals for objective metrics, they are always not close to the human perception, due to the fact that the perception is highly influenced by the performance of the network, defined in terms of QoS parameters. According to [29, 30], the objective metrics are computational models that predict the image quality perceived by any person and can be classified as intrusive and nonintrusive methods, as shown in Figure 1.

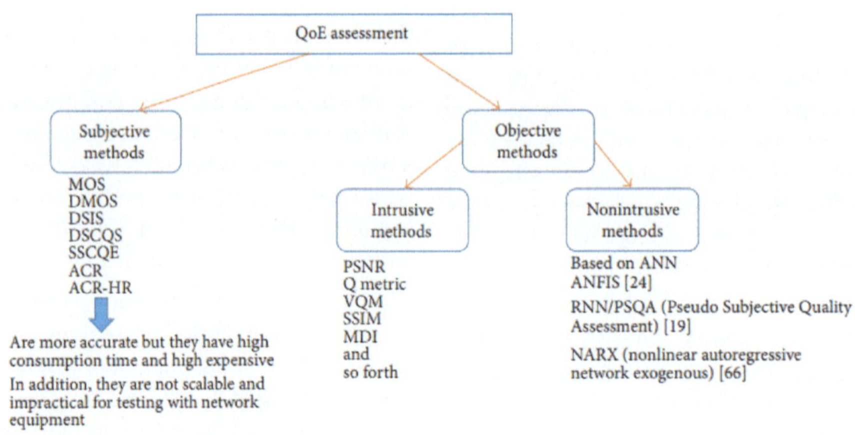

Figure 1: Methods for Quality of Experience assessment.

The Subjective Pseudo Quality Assessment model or PSQA (Pseudo Subjective Quality Assessment) is an example of nonintrusive method (NR). This model uses an RNN (Random Neural Network) [31–33] to learn and recognize the relationship between video and the characteristics of the network with the quality perceived by users.

Initially, for the training process of the RNN, a database is required which contains different sequences to assess the distortions generated by several QoS and coding parameters. Afterwards, the training of the RNN with any video sequence is evaluated in order to validate the MOS measure.

QoE Metrics

PSNR and MSE Metrics

The PSNR (Peak Signal Noise Ratio) and MSE (Mean Square Error) metrics are the most frequently applied ones [11]. They assess the quality of the received video sequence and, thus, can be mapped on a subjective scale PSNR aiming to compare pixel-by-pixel and frame-by-frame the quality of the received image with the source image. It is the most known FR (Full Reference) metric. If we consider frames with a size of $M \times N$ pixels and 8 bits/sample, the PSNR can be calculated using (1) according to [34, 35] as follows:

$$\text{PSNR} = 20 \cdot \log_{10}\left(\frac{255}{\sqrt{(1/(M\times N))\sum_{i=0}^{M-1}\sum_{j=0}^{N-1}\|Y_s(i,j)-Y_d(i,j)\|^2}}\right), \quad (1)$$

where $Y_s(i, j)$ denotes a pixel in the (i, j) position of the original frame and $Y_d(i, j)$ refers to the pixel located at (i, j) position of the frame reconstructed in the receiver side. Around 255 elements are the maximum value that the pixel can take (255 for 8-bit images). The denominator is known as MSE or Mean Square Error, which is the mean square of the differences among the grey level values of the pixels into the pictures or sequences Y_s and Y_d. Since several studies have used this mapping, PSNR is limited by the image content and it is not able to identify artifacts due to packet loss. In addition, the measure does not always correlate with the real user's perception due to the fact that a pixel-by-pixel comparison is carried out without performing an analysis of the image structural elements (e.g., contours or specific distortions introduced by either encoders or transmitting devices on the network or spatial and temporal artifacts). Therefore, some metrics are proposed to generate the extraction and analysis of the features and artifacts into video sequences such as SSIM metric [36].

SSIM Metric.

Assuming that the human visual perception is highly adapted for extracting structures from a scene, SSIM (Structural Similarity Index) calculates the mean, variance, and covariance between the transmitted and received frames [37]. To apply SSIM, three components (luminance, contrast, and structural similarities) are measured and combined into one value called SSIM index ranging between −1 and 1, where a negative or 0 value indicates zero correlation with the original image and 1 means that it is the same image [35]. According to Wang et al. [38], SSIM gives a good approximation of the image distortion due to changes in the measurement of structural information. On the video sequences, this metric considers a wide range of scenes complexity, in terms of movement, spatial details, and color. According to Wang et al. [37], this metric uses a structural distortion measure instead of the error. The above is focused on the human vision system to extract structural information from the visual field and ignored the extraction of errors. Therefore, a calculation of the structural distortion should give a better correlation with subjective metrics. In [39, 40], a simple and effective algorithm was proposed to calculate the SSIM index. Let x be the original signal, $x = \{x_i \mid i = 1, 2, \ldots, N\}$, and let y be the distorted signal, $y = \{y_i \mid i = 1, 2, \ldots, N\}$; the similarity structure index is given by

$$\text{SSIM} = \frac{(2\overline{xy} + C1)(2\sigma_{x,y} + C2)}{\left[(\overline{x})^2 + (\overline{y})^2 + C1\right](\sigma_x^2 + \sigma_y^2 + C2)} \quad (2)$$

where is the mean of x, is the mean of y, and are the variances of x and y, is the covariance of x and y, and $C1$ and $C2$ are constant values. The SSIM value can be defined as

$$\text{SSIM}(x, y) = [l(x, y)]^{\alpha}[c(x, y)]^{\beta}[s(x, y)]^{\gamma}, \quad (3)$$

where $l(x, y)$, $c(x, y)$, and $s(x, y)$ are comparison functions of the luminance, contrast, and structure components, and the parameters α, β, and $\gamma>0$ are constants. SSIM(x, y) is the quality assessment index. For more details see [39].

VQM Metric

The NTIA VQM metric (Video Quality Metric) [39] considers two image inputs, the original and processed video, in which the quality levels are verified through the human vision system and some subjective aspects. This metric divides the image into sequences of space-temporal blocks, measuring elements like blurring, general noise, block distortion, color distortion, and mix among them into a single metric. The score closer to 0 is considered the best possible value. According to Wang [41], this metric shows a good correlation with subjective methods and has also been adopted by ANSI as a standard for the assessment of video quality. In Table 1, the comparative table of the main QoE metrics is summed up, which is used in this work.

Table 1: Comparative table of the main QoE metrics.

Metric	Standard	Class	Estimate	Type
PSNR		Objective	Pixel-by-pixel comparison between reference image and compressed image.	FR
VQM (Video Quality Metric)	NTIA	Objective	Sequences are divided into temporal-space blocks. Calculate the orientation of each block using spatial luminance gradient. Score tends to 0 (best). Assess blurring, global noise, block distortion, and color distortion	RR
SSIM (Structural Similarity Index)		Objective	Find the mean, variance, and covariance within a frame and combine them in a distortion map. Use luminance, contrast, and structure similarity. Use decimal value from 0 to 1 (high correlation with original picture).	FR
MOS	ITU-T P.800	Subjective	Subjective scale from 1 (poor) to 5 (good).	NA

New Mapping QoE Metrics

Zinner et al. [42] proposed a framework for the assessment of the QoE by using streaming video systems. On the other hand, Botia et al. [16] proposed a new mapping among the PSNR, SSIM, VQM, and MOS metrics, shown in Table 2. In our simulations, we calculated the average of each MOS for all video sequences with the value of each FR metric from Table 2 and then we obtained the expected MOS.

Table 2: Mapping among QoE metrics (SSIM, PSNR, VQM, and MOS) [16].

MOS	PSNR (dB)	SSIM	VQM
5 (excellent)	≥37	≥0.93	<1.1
4 (good)	≥31–<37	≥0.85–<0.93	≥1.1–<3.9
3 (fair)	≥25–<31	≥0.75–<0.85	≥3.9–<6.5
2 (poor)	≥20–<25	≥0.55–<0.75	≥6.5–<9
1 (bad)	<20	<0.55	≥9

QIBF Metric

Serral-Garcia et al. [43] propose a framework called PBQAF (Profile Based QoE Assessment Framework). This framework defines three states for frames (correct, altered, and lost) through the analysis of the payload. Moreover, a mapping is performed to generate and associate the quality index. This metric is calculated from payload of the received packets, associated with a PLR (Packet Loss Rate) in particular. Equation (4) shows the quality function to generate the mapping function M:

$$Q(f) = M(\mathrm{PLR}(f)) \tag{4}$$

with PLR(f) being the packet loss rate of the frame f. The mapping function is given by

$$M(x) = 1 - x, \tag{5}$$

where x shows the ratio of lost frames; therefore, when a high packet loss rate is measured, the quality index will be lower and tends to be 0. Thus, the final quality of the video stream into a set of quality values (fx) for particular frames is given by

$$Q_f = \{q(f_1), \ldots, q(f_n)\}, \tag{6}$$

where $f_{1,\ldots,n}$ is the set of all frames in the video stream. From Botia et al. [44], a mapping between QIBF (Quality Index Based Frame) metric and MOS metric is proposed for each frame class $I/P/B$; that is, each frame is equivalent to one class. In (7), the QIBF is given by

$$\mathrm{QIBF}(\mathrm{seq}, \mathrm{nt}) = \sum_{f=1}^{F} \frac{1 - \mathrm{NFL}(f)}{3} - \alpha, \tag{7}$$

where F is the maximum number of frames, seq is the sequence of actual video to be evaluated, nt refers to the class network applied over the transmitted sequence (BestEffort or Diffserv), NFL(f)is the number of frames ($I/P/B$) lost, determined by the set of MPEG images, and α is an adjustment factor set to 0.05, obtained from several developed tests. The factor 1/3 in (7) is defined through 3 classes of frames used in the tests. As NFL(f) ∈ [0, 100], the value of NFL is divided by 100 in order to define NFL(f) ∈ [0, 1] and, therefore, to calculate QIBF(seq, nt) ∈ [0, 1]. Table 3 shows the proposed mapping between quality index and MOS metric, where QIBF(f) ∈ [0, . . . , 1] and, as observed in Table 3, for an index value QIBF(f) > 0.65, a good value for the MOS metric is obtained, indicating a video sequence with a minimum of artifacts.

Table 3: QIBF versus MOS mapping [16].

MOS	QIBF value
5 (excellent)	≥0.85
4 (good)	≥0.65–< 0.85
3 (fair)	≥0.45–< 0.65
2 (poor)	≥0.25–< 0.45
1 (bad)	<0.25

SIMULATION TESTBED

For our test, a testbed is built up to use a simulation software tool NS-2 and the framework Evalvid for assessing a set of video sequences. The results obtained from FR/RR metrics are evaluated to find the possible correlation with subjective metrics using machine learning techniques. In the simulation, we used a selection of different video raw uncompressed sequences in format YUV with color mode or sampling 4: 2: 0, encoded with the ffmpeg and main concept software tools, to adapt them to different bitrates and GOP (Group of Pictures) lengths. Four video sequences were initially assessed with different levels of movement, encoded in the MPEG-4 format, which were adapted to be transmitted by a simulated IP network. Figure 2 illustrates some screenshots of the evaluated videos (News of the Spanish Public TV, Mass, Highway and Winter Tree), converted and encoded at a resolution of 720 × 480 pixels (standard definition) under the NTSC standard, with frame rate of 30 fps. For each video stream, several parameters were combined as length of the GOP (10, 15, and 30), the bit rates recommended by DSL Forum [45] (1.5, 2, 2.5, and 3 Mbps), and packet loss rate for both networks (BestEffort and Diffserv using the congestion control algorithm, WRED), which produced 385 different video sequences for testing [16].

(a) News TVE

(b) Winter tree

(c) Mass

(d) Highway

Figure 2: Screenshots from video sequences assessed.

The generated video traces were adapted to be sent to the data network through the encapsulation of each packet with an MTU (Maximum Transfer Unit) of 1024 bits, using the RTP protocol (Real Time Transport Protocol) with MP4trace software tool. Considering the simulation tool NS-2 and Evalvid framework [46], the sender and receiver trace files that were created, to calculate the sent and received lost frames and packets, delays, and jitters. The above facilitates the analysis of each video sequence for both implemented scenarios (BestEffort and Diffserv data networks). The Evalvid framework also supports PSNR and MOS metrics and has a modular structure, making it easily adaptable to any simulation environment. MSU VQMT software tool [47] allows getting the Y-PSNR, SSIM, and VQM metrics values through the original reference video and received video with distortion. The simulation scenario is composed of a video sender (server for video on demand) and 9 cross-traffic sources, which consist of CBR and On-Off traffic sources. The network is based on dumbell topology [48] (see Figure 3). In our test, we send several video packets over a network with congestion and will be allowed to test the defined QoS scheme (Diffserv with WRED). The MPEG-4 video flow is complete with background On-Off traffic flows, which has an exponential distribution with an average packet size of 1500 bytes, burst time of 50 ms, idle time of 0.01 ms, and sending rate of 1 Mbps [16, 44]. The access network is represented by a video receiver (simulating a last mile with ADSL2), with a bandwidth link of 10 Mbps and several receiving nodes (sink) for cross traffic with a bandwidth of 10 Mbps for each one. Transmission distortions were simulated at different PLR (Packet Loss Rate).The traffic behavior and QoE metrics were tested with several error rates over a link established between the core and edge routers, using a loss model with uniform distribution at rates of 0%, 1%, 5%, and 10% and delay of 5 ms. Tables 4 and 5 show the main parameters used in the simulation and encoding.

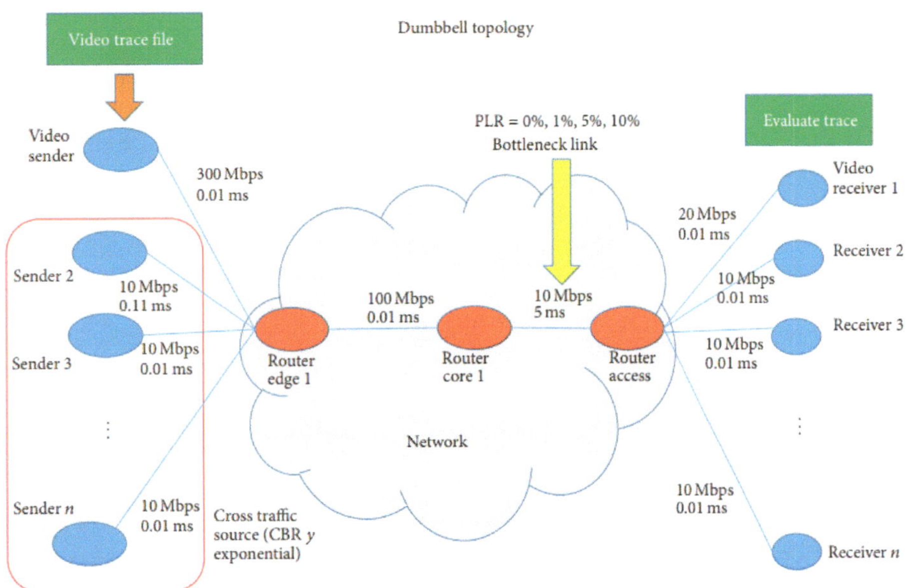

Figure 3: Simulation scenery with NS-2 and Evalvid.

Table 4: Encoder parameters.

GOP length	10, 15, and 30 frames
Frame rate	30 fps
Bitrate	1.5, 2, 2.5, and 3 Mpbs
GOP sequence	IPBBPBBPBBP...
Resolution	NTSC 720 × 480 p
Video color mode	YUV (4:2:0)

Table 5: Simulation parameters.

Bandwidth link	10/100 Mbps
Link delay	0.01 ms–5 ms
Buffer size	50
Tail behavior	DropTail/WRED random early detection
Packet size	1052 bytes (8 bytes UDP and 20 bytes IP)
Max fragment size	1024 bytes
PLR, loss model with uniform distribution	0%, 1%, 5%, and 10% and delay of 5 ms

IMPLEMENTATION OF NONINTRUSIVE METHODS TO ESTIMATE VIDEO QUALITY BY OBJECTIVE AND SUBJECTIVE METRICS

For the evaluation of nonintrusive methods, we decided to use two machine learning methods (BPNN feedforward and Random Neural Network). These methods have been used in different environments described in the next section. To assess the output of each system, we considered the following: estimates MOS versus expected MOS, where the latter is computed through the mapping of PSNR, VQM, SSIM, and QIBF metrics (see Tables 1 and 2). In each case, the correlation adjustment was calculated, determined by the Pearson correlation coefficient and RMSE to estimate the error. The general methodology is presented in Figure 4 [26, 49].

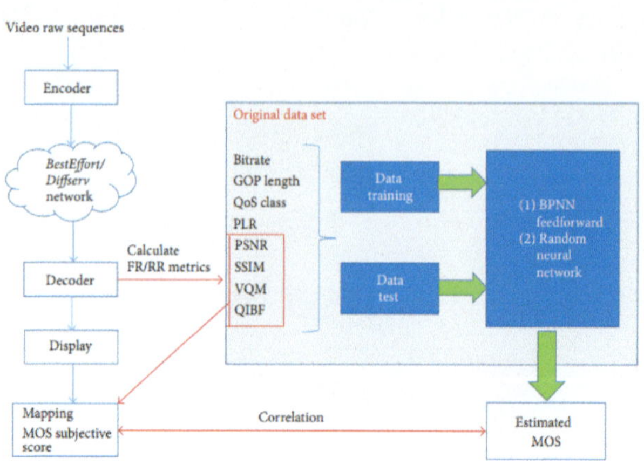

Figure 4: Proposed methodology to estimate the MOS metric using machine learning techniques.

Initially, the video sequences in RAW-format were obtained and they were codified in MPEG-4/AVC-format. Each sequence was sent through an IP-simulated network. The above is based on "BestEffort" and "Diffserv" where each FR/RR metric is calculated and their respective values are mapped. In this manner, average MOS value is obtained by using Tables 2 and 3. Considering the codification values, the kind of QoS network and the obtained FR/RR metrics allow building the input database for training two neural networks. MATLAB software suite was used for BPNN, using the Neural Networks Toolbox. For RNNs case, we used the QoENNR software tool [50]. From 385 different sequences at different configured parameters, around 70% were used as training data and the remaining 30% as test and validation data. Finally, obtaining the estimated MOS value, the correlation is calculated with respect to the average MOS value. The given results of machines learning will be presented and discussed. Table 7 shows a brief state of the art where several papers assess QoE using neural networks as PNN (Probabilistic Neural Network), BPNN (Backpropagation Neural Network), RNN (Random Neural Network), and ANFIS (Adaptive Neurofuzzy Inference System). Works, using a few video sequences, do not show resolutions or codec information and apply low resolutions (for mobile devices). Codec formats more used are H.264 and MPEG-4 AVC. We found that PSNR, SSIM, and VQM metrics are frequently applied and few works use 2 metrics or more. In our case, we were using 5 different metrics and 4 video sequences with motion levels in each scene. Finally, the machine learning based on neural networks (RNN, BPNN, and ANFIs) is used in these works. The results show a good performance of the MOS estimation. However, they are defined by few input parameters, only assessing 1 or 2 video sequences in low resolution(s). They do not compare with other kinds of ANNs and, in most cases, the Pearson correlation coefficient was <0.90.

Case 1 Implementation of a Feedforward Artificial Neural Network with Backpropagation

The ANNs are a paradigm for processing information inspired by the human neural system. Usually, ANNs are composed of a large number of highly interconnected processing elements called neurons, which work together to solve problems [13]. The base is the creation of a neural network also called MLP (Multilayer Perceptron), usually divided into 3 or N-layers. The first layer contains neurons connected to the input vector data; the second layer is called the hidden layer and incudes a set of synapses and a number of weights W_{ij} and some activating functions defined for exciting or inhibiting each neuron, generating a response. According to Rubino et al. [51], if the number of hidden neurons is low, it can have large training and generalization errors due to the underfitting. Otherwise, if there are many neurons in the hidden layer, low training errors may occur, but high generalization errors may appear, causing the undesired effect of overtraining (overfitting) and high variance. The third layer is the output layer directly connected to the hidden layer where data vectors of each estimated output will be obtained. Multiple layers of neurons with nonlinear transfer functions (such as tangential-sigmoid) allow the ANNs learning the linear and nonlinear relationships between the inputs (PLR, GOP, bitrate, QoS class, QIBF, PSNR, SSIM, and VQM) and the desired output vectors (MOS). The structure of Backpropagation Neural Network is shown in Figure 5.

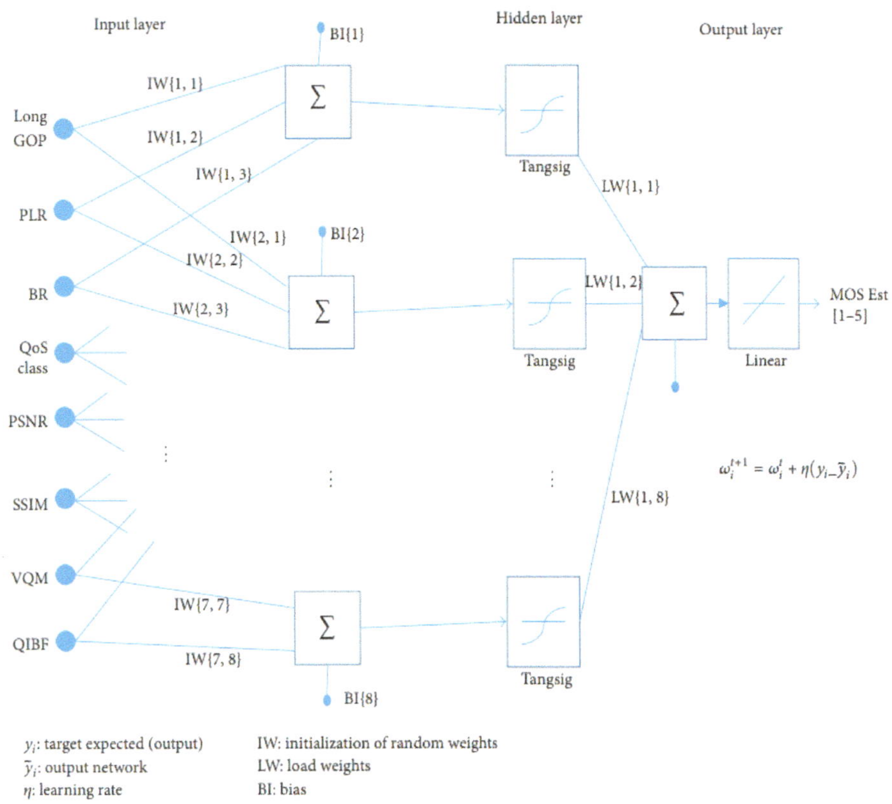

Figure 5: Proposed architecture for estimating MOS through BPNN feedforward.

ANNs type feedforward are the most commonly used ones to perform estimation of subjective metrics. Several works propose different models based on ANN [52–58]. These approaches are generally applied on mobile systems or with low resolutions (QCIF or CIF); furthermore, these works obviate the network parameters or video objective metrics. In most cases, one or two metrics as input to the network are used, and the results from Pearson's autocorrelations almost always are below 0.90. According to Ding et al. [52], the neural network can be used to obtain mapping functions between objective quality assessment and subjective quality assessment indexes. This affirmation allows the understanding of the usefulness of the ANN to analyse the estimated MOS and the proposed model presented in this research. In that case, the network training was carried out through several parameters, which will turn into input variables. As stated, the objective parameters may affect the video quality. After training, an evaluation with a set of test data (96 sequences) will be performed in order to reach the corresponding network validation. The idea is to reach the lowest error and to be able to correlate the estimated MOS by ANN versus the average MOS computed from the objective metrics defined by Tables 1 and 2. For the case of study, we want to build the estimated MOS function, defined by

$$\text{MOS\_Est} = f(x_1, x_2, \ldots, x_n), \tag{8}$$

where $\{x_1, x_2, \ldots, x_n\}$ are the input parameters established by bitrate, packet loss rate, GOP length, QoS class (1 for BestEffort and 2 for Diffserv), SSIM, PSNR, VQM, and QIBF. Like a human being, the ANN system needs a learning phase and another one for validation and testing to establish when the neural network generalized its learning for any data set. For this process, the network is trained through a training algorithm and the lowest possible error is computed through the cost function MSE (Mean Square Error). In that case, we used an iterative gradient descent algorithm or other learning algorithms to achieve convergence to a target value (target), that is, to calculate the minimum training error of the network.

According to Ries et al. [59], in the multilayer network MLP, with a wide variety of nonlinear continuous activation functions on the hidden layers, one of these layers, which contain a largely arbitrary number of neurons, is sufficient to satisfy the property called universal approach. This allowed defining the neural network with a single hidden layer (with 20 neurons) satisfying the outputs (estimated MOS and desired MOS), calculated from the mapping of objective metrics. One of the major drawbacks is to find the right number of hidden neurons due to factors such as the quantity of input/output neurons, the number of training cases, the amount of noise in the output and input, the used architecture, the learning algorithms, and the kind of activation functions in the neurons on the hidden layer. An empirical methodology was performed starting with 16 neurons in the hidden layer equal to twice of input neurons and a new neuron to reach the objective function with the training algorithm Levenberg-Marquardt was added in each training and testing cycle. This is a widely used algorithm to solve the problem of least squares. The proposed BPNN feedforward architecture is shown in Figure 6. In the input and output layer, the neurons have a linear activation function (purelin). In the hidden layer after various tests, the lowest training error was obtained with 20 neurons with function tangent-sigmoid activation (tansig).

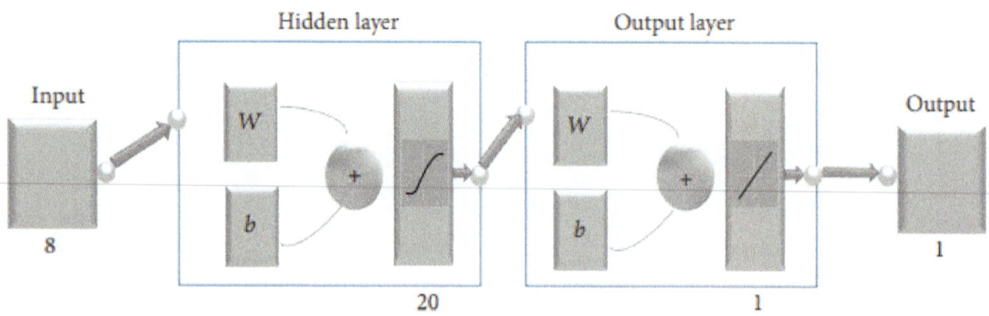

Figure 6: Neural Network feedforward 3-layer architecture.

After performing several iterations and resetting the weights in the training stage, the best performance is obtained as shown in Figure 7.

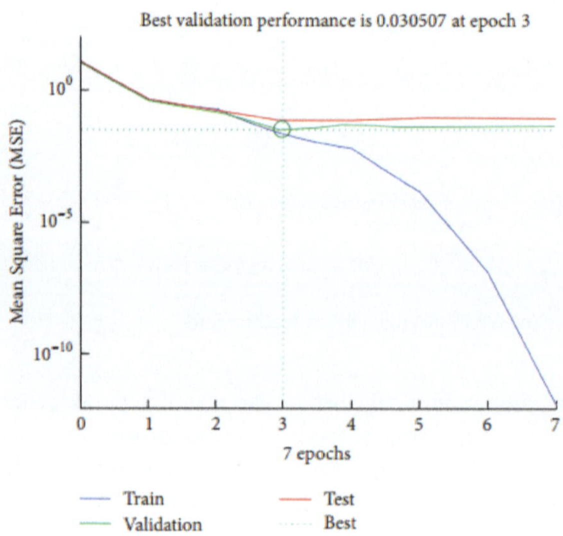

Figure 7: MSE obtained in the training stage.

In Figure 8, the validation stage is illustrated. As shown, a good fit between the output data of the network and the desired MOS is obtained. An analysis of the linear regression between them is performed. The relationship is established between the estimated value by the BPNN (y variable) and desired data (x variable). The representation is given by the following classical linear equation:

$$y = mx + b. \tag{9}$$

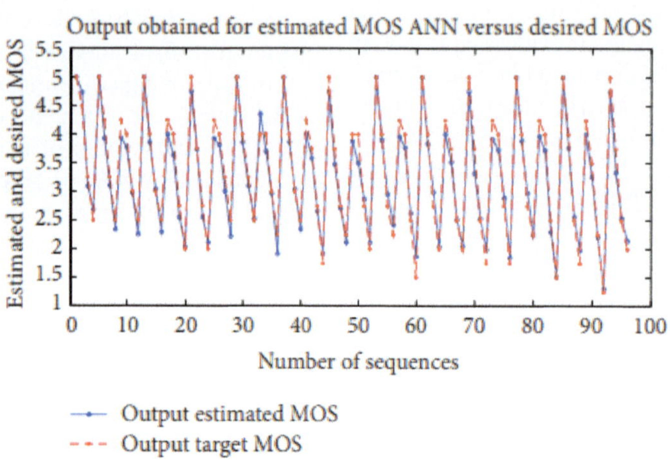

Figure 8: Results of the output, estimated MOS versus desired MOS.

According to Pearson correlation parameter between the estimated MOS by BPNN and the expected MOS, a linear fit of 96.72% and a RMSE of 0.1977 were obtained. Figure 9 shows the output of the correlation obtained. The results establish that the feedforward neural network allowed a good generalization with data used for validation and full linear relationship.

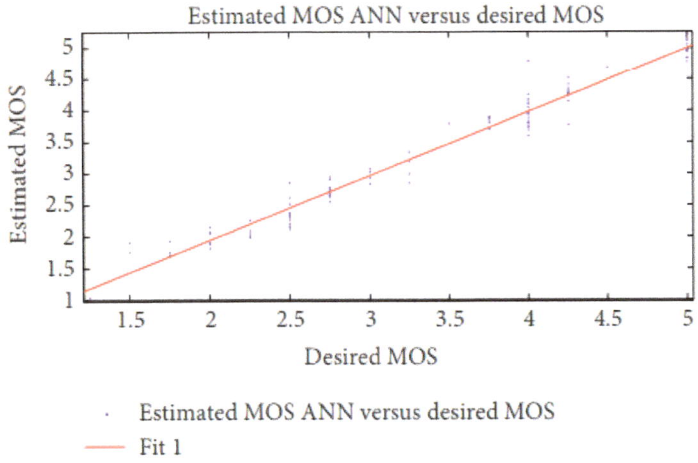

Figure 9: Estimated ANN MOS versus expected MOS.

Implementation of a Random Neural Network (RNN) through PSQA Methodology

This kind of network captures with great accuracy and robustness mapping functions, 1.5 2 2.5 3 3.5 4 4.5 5 1 1.5 2 2.5 3 3.5 4 4.5 5 Desired MOS Estimated MOS Estimated MOS ANN versus desired MOS Estimated MOS ANN versus desired MOS Fit 1 Figure 9: Estimated ANN MOS versus expected MOS. where several parameters are involved. According to Casas et al. [60], such networks have been used on multiple engineering fields, highlighting and solving NP-complete optimization problems, generating textures in images problems, video and image compression algorithms, and classification problems for perceived quality of voice and video over IP, which make them ideal for its application in QoE assess. The RNNs are a cross between neural networks and queuing networks. By definition, RNNs are sets of ANNs formed by a range of interconnected neurons. These neurons exchanged instantly signals which travel from one neuron to another and send signals from and to the environment. Each neuron is associated with an integer random variable associated with a potential. The potential of a neuron i at time t is defined by $_{(t)}$. If the potential of the neuron i is positive, the neuron is excited and randomly sends signals to other neurons or to the environment according to Poisson process of rate r_i. The signals can be positive (+) or negative (−). The RNN has a three-tier architecture. Thus, the set of neurons $R \in \{1, \ldots, N\}$ is split into 3 subsets: the input neuron set, the set of hidden neurons, and the output neurons. An output $Y^{\rightarrow(k)}$ is generated when the input is $X^{\rightarrow(k)}$; therefore, $Y^{\rightarrow(k)}$ = MOSs, for $k = 1, \ldots, K$, the set of weights for step k.

According to Casas et al. [60], it is necessary to apply a methodology to assess the Quality of Experience based on the use of network parameters (probability of packet loss, delay, jitter, etc.) and video parameters (encoding, bitrate, frame rate, GOP length, etc.), which will become input parameters. Based on these criteria, a mapping function between these parameters and subjective quality value defined by the MOS metric can be generated. To perform this task, the author proposes the methodology PSQA (Pseudo Subjective Quality Assessment), which uses the RNNs to learn the mapping between the parameters and perceived quality [51]. This methodology is characterized by its accuracy; it allows generating automatic evaluations in real time which is efficient and can be applied with many kinds of media codec and under different parameters and network conditions. Also, it can be extended for comparison with objective metrics, generating more accurate correlations [61]. The RNN is considered as a supervised learning machine, which uses multimedia and network characteristics and the expected MOS values. If in the training stage a relationship of the input parameters through the objective metrics and the expected output is found, it is possible to estimate and/or predict the subjective values with a higher level of accuracy. Due to the RNNs features, they are perfect to generate good assessments for a wide variation of all parameters that affect the quality [51]. Therefore, it is an accurate model, fast, and with low computational cost. To develop the proposed study case, RNN feedforward 3-layer architecture, proposed by Mohamed and Rubino [61], is implemented. QoE-RNN software tool was used to estimate the MOS value through the use of a RNN. This tool has LGPL license and was developed in the programming language-C [50]. The whole process is presented in Figure 10, where video sequences transmitted over the network are assessed by comparing the target average MOS. Thus, depending on the QoS strategy implemented, the MOS values associated to each objective metrics (PSNR, VQM, SSIM, and QIBF) are set and are defined by $MOSo_{bj}$ and so the average MOS (MOS_p) that is the target value of the RNN is calculated. MOS_p is expressed as shown in the following equation [26]:

$$MOS_p = \sum_{i=1}^{N} \frac{MOS_{obj}}{N} \tag{10}$$

where MOS_{obj} refers to the MOS for each objective metric and N is the total of samples.

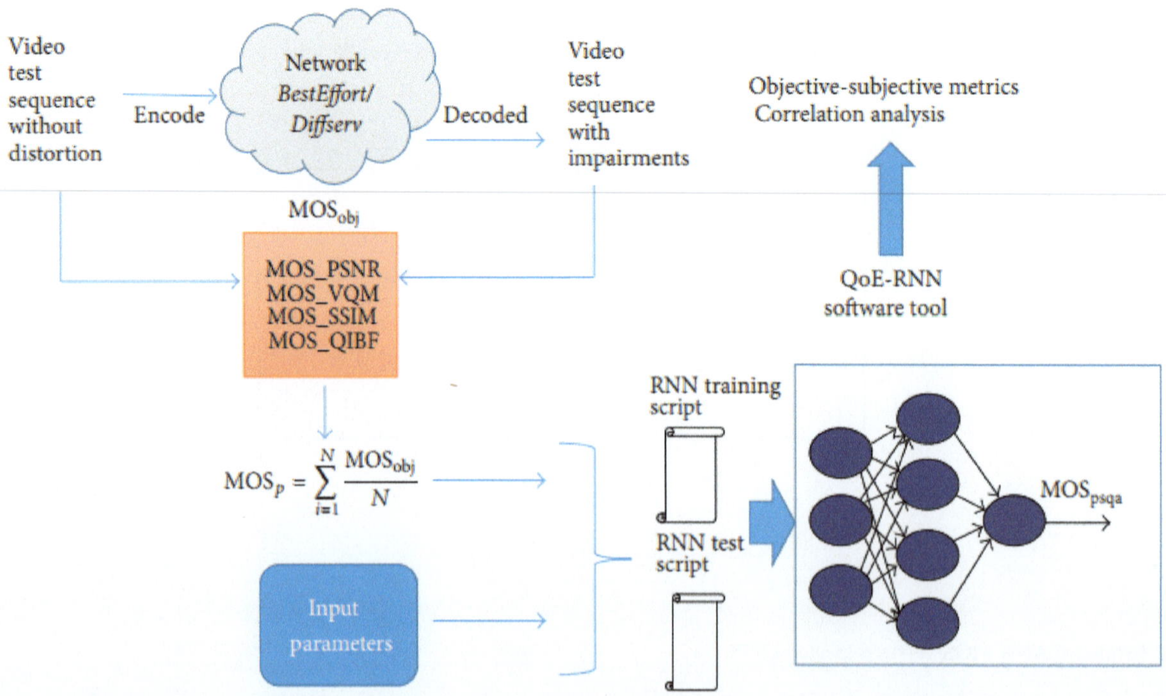

$$MOS_p = \sum_{i=1}^{N} \frac{MOS_{obj}}{N}$$

Figure 10: Employed methodology for the implementation of PSQA with the RNN

The input parameters are chosen and, with the MOS_{psqa} obtained from the network, the corresponding correlation analysis is performed. The number of boundary iterations is 2000 and the network topology is defined by 9 input neurons, 10 neurons in the hidden layer, and one output neuron. In different conducted tests, the best fit is achieved with 10 neurons in the hidden layer. Using MATLAB, an analysis of the linear correlation between the expected MOS and MOS_{psqa} is performed. A good linear fit is found by the Pearson coefficient R^2 at 0.9812 and RMSE at 0.1412. In Figure 11, this correlation is shown.

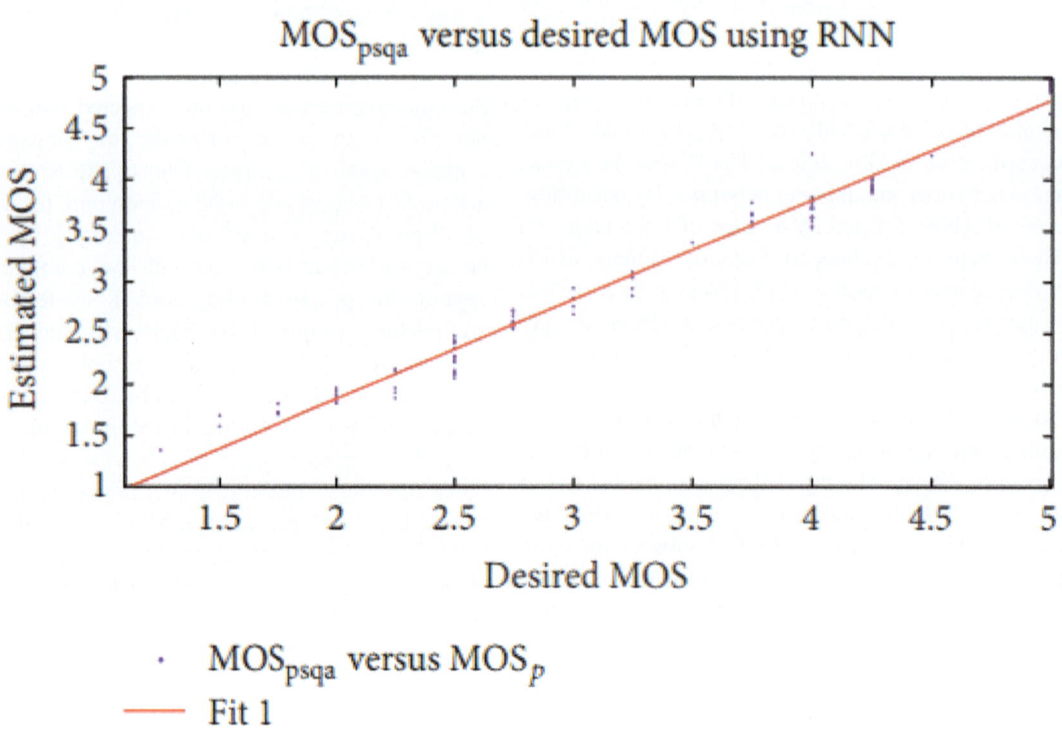

Figure 11: Correlation between MOS_{psqa} and MOS expected through the RNN.

The general summary of all correlations obtained from each study case is presented in Table 6.

Table 6: General overview of the correlations obtained for the study cases.

Correlation	PCC	SROCC	RMSE	OR
Y-PSNR versus MOS BPNN	0.9303	0.9713	0.2882	0.5833
VQM versus MOS BPNN	0.9412	0.9707	0.2647	0.1979
SSIM versus MOS BPNN	0.9446	0.9733	0.257	0.1483
QIBF versus MOS BPNN	0.937	0.9711	0.2739	0.1562
Y-PSNR versus MOS_{psqa}	0.9698	0.9873	0.1796	0.5833
VQM versus MOS_{psqa}	0.9645	0.9900	0.1948	0.1666
SSIM versus MOS_{psqa}	0.9497	0.9889	0.2319	0.1354
QIBF versus MOS_{psqa}	0.9254	0.9853	0.2824	0.1354

Note: PCC (Pearson correlation coefficient) for prediction accuracy.
SROCC (Spearman rank order correlation coefficient) for monotonicity.
RMSE (Root Mean Square Error) for correlation quality assessment.
OR (Outlier Ratio) for consistence.

Table 7: Papers with machine learning methods for assessing QoE.

Paper	# video sequences	Resolution	Code c	SSIM	VQM	PSRN	MSE	BR	FR	PLR	Q value (decodificables frames rate)	QP	Playout interruptions	Delay	Jitter	BW	MLBS	GOP	Machine learning	Assess MOS/DMOS?	Correlation performance PCC	SROCC	RMSE	OR
He et al. [17], 2012	1	QCIF	MPEG4			X				X				X	X		X		Probabilistic Neural Network (PNN)	Yes	0.9286	No	No	No
Kipli et al. [18], 2012	N/D	No data	No data	X		X	X												BPNN	Yes	0.891	No	No	No
Singh et al. [19], 2012	4	HD-720p	H.264							X		X	X	X					RNN	Yes	No	No	0.37	No
Lia et al. [20], 2011	4	No data	No data																BPNN	No	No	No	No	No
Khan at al. [21], 2010	6	QCIF	H.264					X	X								X		ANFIS	Yes	0.8717	No	0.2812	No
Du et al. [22], 2009	1	SD	No data			X				X				X	X	X	X		BPNN	Yes	No	No	No	No
Piamrat et al. [23], 2009	1	No data	H.264			X				X							X		PSQA with RNN	Yes	No	No	No	No
Khan et al. [24], 2008	3	CIF	MPEG4					X	X	X	X					X			ANFIS	Yes	$R = 0.8056$ for MOS predicted versus MOS Measure and $R = 0.9229$ for Q predicted versus Q measure	No	RMSE = 0.1846 for MOS predicted versus MOS measure and RMSE = 0.06234 for Q predicted versus Q measure	No
Rubino et al. [25], 2004	Only VoIP	No data	No data							X							X		RNN	No	No	No	No	No

BR: bitrate, FR: frame rate, PLR: Packet Loss Rate, QP: Quantization Parameter, BW: bandwidth, MLBS: Mean Loss Burst Size, GOP: Group of Pictures, PCC: Pearson correlation coefficient, SROCC: Spearman rank order correlation coefficient, RMSE: Root Mean Square Error, and OR: Outlier Ratio.

The performance of perceptual quality metrics depends on its correlation with the results of objective metrics. Thus, the accuracy in the estimation of subjective metrics with respect to issues such as prediction accuracy, monotonicity, and consistency is evaluated.This guarantees a high reliability in the subjective assessment of video quality over a range of video test sequences with different artifacts. The assessment methods are proposed by the Video Quality Experts Group (VQEG) [62]. Four statistical measurements are applied to evaluate the video quality metrics performance: Pearson correlation coefficient (PCC), Spearman's rank order correlation coefficient (SROCC), Mean Square Error (RMSE), and Outlier Ratio (OR) [63, 64]. As shown in the results of Table 6, the correlations between MOS_{psqa} metrics were certainly good with objective metrics, with high Spearman coefficient proving high linear trend in all cases. The generalization was very high and we noted the consistency, accuracy, and monotonicity results. In the simulations performed, we observed that the VQM, SSIM, and QIBF metrics are highly correlated and are close to the users' perception (established by the MOS metric). For all cases, the correlation reached values higher than 90%, and the correlation between the objective and subjective metrics in each case presents an excellent linear behavior. Accordingly, the metrics as VQM, SSIM, and QIBF are largely related to the subjectivity established by MOS. Also it was observed that the results of the BPNN feedforward indicate a good generalization for estimated MOS against every assessed objective metrics, although it was slightly higher for applying the RNN. The RNN with PSQA provides a better correlation with the predicted values for MOS. The strategy generated by the nonintrusive model based on machine learning methods was shown to be accurate and highly flexible. It allows the estimation of subjective MOS values by relating them with FR (Full Reference) and RR (Reduced Reference) chosen for the research.

CONCLUSION

In this work, we obtained excellent correlation values between the objective and subjective QoE metrics through the use of nonintrusive methods. The accuracy, consistency, and monotonicity were validated with the analysis of Pearson's and Spearman's correlations, outliers rate, and RMSE (Roots Mean Square Error). One of the main limitations of the objective and subjective methods is the lack of complete methodologies to analyze the accuracy of QoE. Therefore, this problem was addressed in order to propose a new methodology that allows finding new correlations between objective and subjective metrics. To improve the analysis, the machine learning techniques were proposed through backpropagation artificial neural networks and Random Neural Networks to enhance the approach of the estimation of human perception. In different performed simulations, we observed that VQM, SSIM, and QIBF metrics are highly correlated and are close to the user perception (determined by the MOS metric). Unlike previous works, we developed a general correlation model which uses network and coding parameters applied to several video sequences. Analyzing the results from learning machines, the BPNNs and RNNs generated high correlations with objective metrics, obtaining PCC values higher than 90% and low error rates. The consistency of correlations between the metrics through outliers was calculated with low values. We conclude that the application of nonintrusive methods allows us to generate more accurate approaches to human perception. In addition, telecommunications providers can use this methodology for estimating the QoE of users and improve their data network architectures and/or global settings on their platforms, optimize the QoS, and employ better encoding mechanisms. The development of new models for the assessment of QoE is a top research topic according to the state of the art. The topics that are being currently working include

(i) development of new objective metrics, which are easy to apply and can be mapped accurately to the true perception of the viewer,

(ii) the close relationship of all QoS factors which affect the QoE,

(iii) new transmission strategies over highly congested data networks that can have a greater impact on transmission environments for streaming video over the internet which affect the user experience on the multimedia content over the next generation mobile devices,

(iv) the application of new kinds of video codecs specifically aimed at HD (H.265/MPEG-DASH, Dynamic Adaptive Streaming over HTTP) [65],

(v) the application of different methodologies based on machine learning techniques especially those related to artificial neural networks, neurofuzzy networks, support vector machines, and genetic algorithms.

CONFLICT OF INTERESTS

The authors declare that there is no conflict of interests regarding the publication of this paper.

ACKNOWLEDGMENT

This research was developed as part of the macroproject "System of Experimental Interactive Television" for the Research and Innovation Center (Regional Alliance of Applied ICTArtica) with code 1115-470-22055 and project no. RC584 funded by Colciencias and MinTIC.

REFERENCES

1. L.-Y. Liu, W.-A. Zhou, and J.-D. Song, "The research of quality of experience evaluation method in pervasive computing environment," in Proceedings of the 1st International Symposium on Pervasive Computing and Applications, pp. 178–182, IEEE, Urumqi, China, August 2006.

2. S. Mohseni, "Driving Quality of Experience in mobile content value chain," in Proceedings of the 4th IEEE International Conference on Digital Ecosystems and Technologies (DEST '10), pp. 320–325, Dubai, United Arab Emirates, April 2010.

3. A. Devlic, P. Kamaraju, P. Lungaro, Z. Segall, and K. Tollmar, "Towards QoE-aware adaptive video streaming," in Proceedings of the IEEE/ACM International Symposium on Quality of Service, Portland, Ore, USA, February 2015, http://people.kth.se/~devlic/publications/IWQoS15.pdf.

4. S. Winkler, "Standardizing quality measurement for video services," IEEE COMSOC MMTC E-Letter, vol. 4, no. 9, 2009.

5. S. Winkler, "Video quality measurement standards—current status and trends," in Proceedings of the 7th International Conference on Information, Communications and Signal Processing (ICICS '09), Macau, China, December 2009.

6. K. Seshadrinathan and A. C. Bovik, "Motion tuned spatiotemporal quality assessment of natural videos," IEEE Transactions on Image Processing, vol. 19, no. 2, pp. 335–350, 2010.

7. H. R. Sheikh and A. C. Bovik, "Image information and visual quality," IEEE Transactions on Image Processing, vol. 15, no. 2, pp. 430–444, 2006.

8. A. K. Moorthy and A. C. Bovik, "A motion compensated approach to video quality assessment," in Proceedings of the 43rd Asilomar Conference on Signals, Systems and Computers, pp. 872–875, Pacific Grove, Calif, USA, November 2009.

9. K. Radhakrishnan and L. Hadi, "A study on QoS of VoIP networks: a random neural network (RNN) approach," in Proceedings of the Spring Simulation Multiconference (SpringSim '10), Society for Computer Simulation International, Orlando, Fla, USA, April 2010.

10. S. Winkler and P. Mohandas, "The evolution of video quality measurement: from psnr to hybrid metrics," IEEE Transactions on Broadcasting, vol. 54, no. 3, pp. 660–668, 2008.

11. F. Boavida, E. Cerqueira, R. Chodorek et al., "Benchmarking the quality of experience of video streaming and multimedia search services: the content network of excellence," in Proceedings of the

23rd National Symposium of Telecommunications and Teleinformatics (KSTiT '08), Institute of Telecommunication and Electrical Technologies of University of Technology and Life Sciences, Bydgoszcz, Poland, September 2008.

12. P. Casas, A. Sackl, R. Schatz, L. Janowski, J. Turk, and R. Irmer, "On the quest for new KPIs in mobile networks: the impact of throughput fluctuations on QoE," in Proceedings of the IEEE International Conference on Communication Workshop (ICCW '15), pp. 1705–1710, London, UK, June 2015.
13. M. Ries and J. R. Kubanek, "Video Quality Estimation for mobile streaming applications with neural networks," in Proceedings of the Measurement of Speech and Audio Quality in Networks Workshop (MESAQIN '06), Prague, Czech Republic, June 2006.
14. O. Nemethova, M. Ries, E. Siffel, and M. Rupp, "Quality assessment for H.264 coded low rate and low resolution video sequences," in Proceedings of the IASTED International Conference on Communications, Internet and Information Technology (CIIT '04), pp. 136–140, St. Thomas, Virgin Islands, November 2004.
15. D. Kuipers, R. Kooij, D. Vleeshauwer, and K. Brunnstrom, "Techniques for measuring quality of experience," in Wired/Wireless Internet Communications, vol. 6074 of Lecture Notes in Computer Science, pp. 216–227, Springer, Berlin, Germany, 2010.
16. D. Botia, N. Gaviria, D. Jimenez, and J. M. Men ´ endez, "An ´ approach to correlation of QoE metrics applied to VoD service on IPTV using a diffserv network," in Proceedings of the 4th IEEE Latin-American Conference on Communications (IEEE LATINCOM '12), Cuenca, Ecuador, November 2012.
17. Y. He, C. Wang, H. Long, and K. Zheng, "PNN-based QoE measuring model for video applications over LTE system," in Proceedings of the 7th International ICST Conference on Communications and Networking in China (CHINACOM '12), pp. 58–62, Kunming, China, August 2012.
18. K. Kipli, M. Muhammad, S. Masra, N. Zamhari, K. Lias, and D. Azra, "Performance of Levenberg-Marquardt backpropagation for full reference hybrid image quality metrics," in Proceedings of International Conference of Muti-Conference of Engineers and Computer Scientists (IMECS '12), Hong Kong, March 2012.
19. K. D. Singh, Y. Hadjadj-Aoul, and G. Rubino, "Quality of experience estimation for adaptive Http/Tcp video streaming using H.264/AVC," in Proceedings of the 9th Anual IEEE Consumer Communications and Networking Conf. Multimedia and Entertaiment Networking and Services (CCNC '12), pp. 127– 131, Las Vegas, Nev, USA, January 2012.
20. Q. Lia, J. Yangb, L. He, and S. Fan, "Reduced-reference video quality assessment based on bp neural network model for packet networks," Energy Procedia, vol. 13, pp. 8056–8062, 2011, Proceedings of the International Conference on Energy Systems and Electric Power (ESEP '11).
21. A. Khan, L. Sun, E. Ifeachor, J.-O. Fajardo, F. Liberal, and H. Koumaras, "Video quality prediction models based on video content dynamics for H.264 video over UMTS networks," International Journal of Digital Multimedia Broadcasting, vol. 2010, Article ID 608138, 17 pages, 2010.
22. H. Du, C. Guo, Y. Liu, and Y. Liu, "Research on relationship between QoE and QoS based on BP neural network," in Proceedings of the IEEE International Conference on Network Infrastructure and Digital Content (IC-NIDC '09), pp. 312–315, Beijing, China, November 2009.
23. K. Piamrat, C. Viho, A. Ksentini, and J.-M. Bonnin, "Quality of experience measurements for video streaming over wireless networks," in Proceedings of the 6th International Conference on Information Technology: New Generations (ITNG '09), pp. 1184–1189, IEEE, Las Vegas, Nev, USA, April 2009.
24. A. Khan, L. Sun, and E. Ifeachor, "An ANFIS-based hybrid video quality prediction model for video streaming over wireless networks," in Proceedings of the 2nd International Conference on Next Generation Mobile Applications, Services, and Technologies (NGMAST '08), pp. 357–362, Cardiff, Wales, September 2008.
25. G. Rubino and M. Varela, "A new approach for the prediction of end-to—end performance of multimedia streams," in Proceedings of the International Conference on Quantitative Evaluation of Systems (QUEST '04), pp. 110–119, IEEE CS Press, University of Twente, Enschede, The Netherlands, September 2004.
26. P. Goudarzi, "A no-reference low-complexity QoE measurement algorithm for H.264 video transmission systems," Scientia Iranica Transactions: Computer Science & Engineering and Electrical Engineering, vol. 20, no. 3, pp. 721–729, 2013.
27. ITU-T, "Subjective video quality assessment methods for multimedia applications," Recommendation P.910, International Telecommunication Union, Geneva, Switzerland, 1999.
28. ITU-T, Recommendation, QoE Requirements in Consideration of Service Billing for IPTV Service, UIT-T FG-IPTV, International Telecommunication Union, Geneva, Switzerland, 2006.
29. P. Casas, P. Belzarena, I. Irigaray, and D. Guerra, "A user perspective for end-to-end quality of service evaluation in multimedia networks," in Proceedings of the 4th International IFIP/ACM Latin American Conference on Networking (LANC '07), San Jose, Costa Rica, 2007. ´
30. P. Casas, P. Belzarena, and S. Vaton, "End-2-end evaluation of IP multimedia services, a user perceived quality of service approach," in Proceedings of the 18th ITC Specialist Seminar on Quality of Experience (ITEC '08), Karlskrona, Sweden, May 2008.
31. R. Immich, P. Borges, E. Cerqueira, and M. Curado, "QoEdriven video delivery improvement using packet loss prediction," International Journal of Parallel, Emergent and Distributed Systems—Smart Communications in Network Technologies, vol. 30, no. 6, pp. 478–493, 2015.

32. M. Kailash and D. Padma, "An overview of quality of service measurement and optimization for voice over internet protocol implementation," International Journal of Advances in Engineering & Technology, vol. 8, no. 1, pp. 2053–2063, 2015.

33. S. Timotheou, "The random neural network: a survey," The Computer Journal, vol. 53, no. 3, pp. 251–267, 2010.

34. K. Kilkki, "Next generation internet and QoE," in Presentation at EuroFGI IA.7.6 Workshop on Socio-Economic Issues of NGI, Santander, Spain, June 2007.

35. ITU. FG-IPTV.DOC-0814, Quality of Experience Requirements for IPTV Services, 2007.

36. E. Cerqueira, L. Veloso, M. Curado, and E. Monteiro, Quality Level Control for Multi-User Sessions in Future Generation Networks, University of Coimbra INESC Porto, Coimbra, Portugal, 2008.

37. Z. Wang, A. C. Bovik, H. R. Sheikh, and E. P. Simoncelli, "Image quality assessment: from error visibility to structural similarity," IEEE Transactions on Image Processing, vol. 13, no. 4, pp. 600– 612, 2004.

38. D. Wang, W. Ding, Y. Man, and L. Cui, "A joint image quality assessment method based on global phase coherence and structural similarity," in Proceedings of the 3rd International Congress on Image and Signal Processing (CISP '10), vol. 5, pp. 2307–2311, IEEE, Yantai, China, October 2010.

39. M. Vranje˘s, S. Rimac-Drlje, and D. Zagar, "Objective video qual- ˇ ity metrics," in Proceedings of the 49th International Symposium ELMAR, Faculty of Electrical Engineering, University of Osijek, Zadar, Croatia, September 2007.

40. Z. Wang and A. C. Bovik, "A universal image quality index," IEEE Signal Processing Letters, vol. 9, no. 3, pp. 81–84, 2002.

41. Y. Wang, Survey of Objective Video Quality Measurements, EMC Corporation, Hopkinton, Mass, USA, 2004, ftp://ftp.cs.wpi .edu/pub/techreports/pdf/06-02.pdf.

42. T. Zinner, O. Abboud, O. Hohlfeld, T. Hossfeld, and P. TrainGia, "Towards QoE management for scalable video streaming," in Proceedings of the 21st ITC Specialist Seminar on Multimedia Applications Traffic, Performance and QoE, Miyazaki, Japan, March 2010.

43. R. Serral-Garcia, Y. Lu, M. Yannuzzi, X. Masip-Bruin, and F. Kuipers, Packet Loss Based Quality of Experience of Multimedia Video Flows, Crente de Recerca d'Arquitectures Avancades de Xarxes (Politencic University of Cataluna), Spain ˜ , Delft University of Technology, Delft, The Netherlands, 2009, http:// personals.ac.upc.edu/rserral/research/techreports/psnr mos .pdf.

44. D. Botia, N. Gaviria, J. Botia, D. Jimenez, and J. M. Men ′ endez, ′ "Improved the quality of experience assessment with quality index based frames over IPTV network," in Proceedings of the 2nd International Conference on Information and Communication Technologies and Applications (ICTA '12), Orlando, Fla, USA, 2012.

45. DSL Forum, "Triple play services quality of experience requierements and machanism," Working Text WT-126 version 0.5, 2006.

46. J. Klaue, B. Rathke, and A. Wolisz, "EvalVid—a framework for video transmission and quality evaluation," in Proceedings of the 13th International Conference on Modelling Techniques and Tools for Computer Performance Evaluation, pp. 255–272, Urbana, Ill, USA, September 2003.

47. D. Vatolin, "MSU Video Metric Quality Tool," MSU Graphics and media Lab, 2012, http://compression.ru/video/quality measure/video measurement tool en.html, Rusia.

48. P. Subramanya, K. Vinayaka, H. Gururaj, and B. Ramesh, "Performance evaluation of high speed TCP variants in dumbbell network," IOSR Journal of Computer Engineering, vol. 16, no. 2, pp. 49–53, 2014.

49. D. Botia, N. Gaviria, D. Jimenez, and J. M. Men ′ endez, "Strate- ′ gies for improving the QoE assessment over iTV platforms based on QoS metrics," in Proceedings of the IEEE International Symposium on Multimedia (ISM '12), pp. 483–484, Irvine, Calif, USA, December 2012.

50. QoE-RNN Tool, 2011, http://code.google.com/p/qoe-rnn/.

51. G. Rubino, M. Varela, and J.-M. Bonnin, "Controlling multimedia QoS in the future home network using the PSQA metric," The Computer Journal, vol. 49, no. 2, pp. 137–155, 2006.

52. W. Ding, Y. Tong, Q. Zhang, and D. Yang, "Image and video quality assessment using neural network and SVM," Tsinghua Science and Technology, vol. 13, no. 1, pp. 112–116, 2008.

53. A. Bouzerdoum, A. Havstad, and A. Beghdadi, "Image quality assessment using a neural network approach," in Proceedings of the 4th IEEE International Symposium on Signal Processing and Information Technology, pp. 330–333, Rome, Italy, December 2004.

54. J. Choe, K. Lee, and C. Lee, "No-reference video quality measurement using neural networks," in Proceedings of the 16th International Conference on Digital Signal Processing (DSP '09), pp. 1–4, IEEE, Santorini-Hellas, Greece, July 2009.

55. X. Zhang, L. Wu, Y. Fang, and H. Jiang, "A study of FR video quality assessment of real time video stream," International Journal of Advanced Computer Science and Applications, vol. 3, no. 6, 2012.

56. C.-H. Kung, W.-S. Yang, C.-Y. Huan, and C.-M. Kung, "Investigation of the image quality assessment using neural networks and structure similarty," in Proceedings of the International Symposium on Computer Science, vol. 2, no. 1, p. 219, August 2010.

57. C. Wang, X. Jiang, F. Meng, and Y. Wang, "Quality assessment for MPEG-2 video streams using a neural network model," in Proceedings of the IEEE 13th International Conference on Communication Technology (ICCT '11), pp. 868–872, IEEE, Jinan, China, September 2011.

58. P. Reichl, S. Egger, S. Moller et al., "Towards a comprehensive framework for QOE and user behavior

modelling," in Proceedings of the 17th International Workshop on Quality of Multimedia Experience (QoMEX '15), pp. 1–6, IEEE, Pylos-Nestoras, Greece, May 2015.

59. M. Ries, J. Kubanek, and M. Rupp, "Video quality estimation for mobile streaming applications with neural networks," in Proceedings of the Measurement of Speech and Audio Quality in Networks Workshop (MESAQIN '06), Prague, Czech Republic, June 2006.

60. P. Casas, D. Guerra, and I. Bayarres, "Perceived Quality of Service in Voice and Video Services over IP," School of Engineering, Universidad de la Republica, End of career project, Electrical ´ Engineering—Plan 97, Telecommunications, Uruguay, 2005.

61. S. Mohamed and G. Rubino, "A study of real-time packet video quality using random neural networks," IEEE Transactions on Circuits and Systems for Video Technology, vol. 12, no. 12, pp. 1071–1083, 2002.

62. VQEG, "Video Quality Experts Group, Final Report from the VQEG on the validation of Objective Models of Video Quality Assessment, Phase II," 2003, http://www.its.bldrdoc.gov/vqeg/ vqeg-home.aspx.

63. S. Winkler, Digital Video Quality—Vision, Models and Metrics, John Wiley & Sons, 2005.

64. A. Bath, I. Richardson, and S. Kannangara, A New Perceptual Quality Metric for Compressed Video, The Robert Gordon University, Aberdeen, Scotland, 2007.

65. M. Alreshoodi, J. Woods, and I. K. Musa, "Optimising the delivery of Scalable H.264 Video stream by QoS/QoE correlation," in Proceedings of the IEEE International Conference on Consumer Electronics (ICCE '15), pp. 253–254, IEEE, Las Vegas, Nev, USA, January 2015.

66. A. Kuwadekar and K. Al-Begain, "User centric quality of experience testing for video on demand over IMS," in Proceedings of the 1st International Conference on Computational Intelligence, Communication Systems and Networks (CICSYN '09), pp. 497– 504, Indore, India, July 2009.

CHAPTER 11

DEVELOPMENT AND EVALUATION OF GAME-BASED LEARNING SYSTEM USING THE MICROSOFT KINECT SENSOR

Chih-Hsiao Tsai, Yin-Hao Kuo, Kuo-Chung Chu, Jung-Chuan Yen

INTRODUCTION

Natural user interfaces (NUIs) provide a great potential to facilitate new ways of computer enhanced learning; these have the potential to enhance classroom interactions, by increasing learners' participation, facilitating the teachers' presentations, and creating opportunities for discussion [1]. Learning with virtual objects integrated into realistic interactive technology has produced a novel digital learning type [2] in recent years and has become a controversial discussion topic in e-learning research. However, to guide learners to learn scientific knowledge quickly and efficiently, integrating innovative technology into scientific learning activities without causing any distraction from learning is a crucial research topic.

Physically interactive and augmented reality is increasingly used; ARCS model and game-based learning requirements for digital learning applications have become critical. Learners can learn effectively when they use multimedia-assisted learning systems, which motivates them to focus on the information presented and effectively retain the information. Lu and Yao stated that presenting abstract material using multimedia enables learners to clearly understand the material, and audio and visual displays allow learners to interact with the material [3]. Although a teacher's professional education seems to play a vital role in the teaching process, innovative instructional designs that differ from traditional teaching designs must be developed. The education mode must be changed from "technology-adapted instruction" to "instruction-adapted technology" [4]. Most learners demonstrate difficulty with reasoning and the conversion of shape and space in elementary school mathematics education, causing learning achievement in this unit to be lower than that in other units [5]. However, spatial ability plays a crucial role in learning geometry [6].

The National Council of Teachers of Mathematics [7] suggested that geometry helps students to analyze the characteristics of geometric shapes as well as to use visualization, spatial reasoning, and geometric modeling to solve problems. Van Hiele [8] described a theory of mathematical education, the development of geometric thought, to enhance the achievement of learning and to promote learner comprehension. Van Hiele suggested five teaching phases in designing teaching methods and materials step by step. This model of teaching phases was used as the fundamental theoretical framework for this study. Game-based learning (GBL) is an instructional method that incorporates educational content or learning principles into video games to engage learners. The use of this method in the field of natural science and technology has increasingly been an object of study in recent years. Learning through digital games not only increases motivation, active learning, and

Citation: Chih-Hsiao Tsai, Yin-Hao Kuo, Kuo-Chung Chu, and Jung-Chuan Yen,Development and Evaluation of Game-Based Learning System Using the Microsoft Kinect Sensor,International Journal of Distributed Sensor Networks July 2015 11: 498560, first published on July 12, 2015 doi:10.1155/2015/498560

individual learning opportunities, but also reduces the learning pressure experienced by learners.

The primary focus of this study was on developing and evaluating a cubic net interactive system using the Kinect sensor for enhancing learners' spatial ability. We developed courseware for interactive learning using an interactive cubic net system and applied it in a lesson on space geometry at an elementary school. The content of the system was based on the geometric learning theory, and real-time three-dimensional (3D) objects were used to provide various viewing angle controls. A qualitative analysis was also performed to evaluate the learners' interaction with the Kinect sensor design through observation records, video recording, and structural interviews.

This paper is structured as follows: The foundations for the development of the research are discussed in the subsequent section; the research methodology is then presented in Section 3, with full details on the system development and the instruments and procedures used; the results are then presented, with a thorough description of the system usability, in Section 4; and finally, the results are discussed and the conclusion is presented in Section 5.

RELATED WORK

ARCS Model

According to Keller's ARCS model of motivation design [9, 10], he found possible ways to supplement the learning process with motivation. There are four major steps for learners to become and remain motivated in the learning process: attention, relevance, confidence, and satisfaction (details in Table 1 [11]). The first two steps can be considered the backbone of the ARCS theory, the latter steps relying upon the former. In accordance with the theory, attention refers to the interest displayed by the learners in taking in the concepts or ideas being taught. Relevance to consider in the process must be established by using language and examples that the learners are familiar with. Confidence focuses on establishing positive expectation for achieving success among learners. The last aspect of this model is satisfaction, in which learners must obtain satisfaction or reward from learning experience. Feedback and reinforcement are important elements and when the learners appreciate the result, they will be motivated to learn. However, ARCS model cannot explain how information processing elements are integrated with the learning process or how these elements interact with motivation. Designers should increase motivation and germane cognitive load to enhance learning effectiveness [12]. This paper focuses on knowing, understanding the implementation of ARCS motivational model in teaching and learning process, understanding the precise definition of kinesthetic pedagogical practices learning, the approaches in the implementation, the advantages and disadvantages of kinesthetic pedagogical practices learning, and finally the implication in the teaching and learning experience. Following Keller's ARCS model of motivation, we design our game with four key components: interactivity (attention), representation and story (relevance), rules and goals (confidence), and consequences (satisfaction).

Table 1 ARCS motivational theory and game components.

Step	Description	Component	Game component
Attention	Arouse and sustain a learner's curiosity and interest.	Perceptual arousal Inquiry arousal Variability	Interactivity
Relevance	Link a learner's needs, interests, and motives.	Goal orientation Motive matching Familiarity	Representation and story
Confidence	Develop positive expectations for achieving success.	Performance requirements Success opportunities Personal control	Rules and goals
Satisfaction	Provide reinforcement and reward for learners.	Intrinsic reinforcement Extrinsic rewards Equity	Consequences

Bishop [11] referred to the power of spatial ability in assisting learners in visual and figural representation and in introducing complex abstractions in mathematics. Piaget and Inhelder [13] determined that children initially recognize various objects through the sense of touch alone and then develop and use certain primitive relationships (topological space). Contrary to the historical development of geometry, which began with the treatment of straight lines, angles, distances, and plane figures, children begin by observing the topological rather than the metric properties of objects (projective space and Euclidean space). Lohman and Kyllonen [14] determined that spatial abilities include spatial visualization, spatial perception, spatial orientation, spatial imagination, and spatial translation and transformation. We focused on the spatial visualization skill, which is the ability to mentally manipulate complex spatial two-dimensional and 3D figures. Van Hiele describes a theory of mathematics education, Development of Geometric Thought [15], to enhance the achievement of learning and to promote learners' comprehension. Van Hiele suggested five teaching phases to design teaching methods and materials step by step (see Table 2).

Table 2 The model of the Development of Geometric Thought [15].

Level	Phases of learning	Description
Level 0 visualization	Inquiry/information	Teacher learns what prior knowledge the students have about the topic. Students learn what direction further study will take.
Level 1 analysis	Directed orientation	Students explore the topic of study through materials that the teacher has carefully sequenced.
Level 2 informal deduction	Explication	Building on their previous experiences, students express and exchange their emerging views about the structures that have been observed.
Level 3 formal deduction	Free orientation	The student encounters more complex tasks—tasks with many steps, tasks that can be completed in several ways, and open-ended tasks.
Level 4 rigor	Integration	The students review and summarize what they have learned with the goal of forming an overview of the new network of objects and relations.

The Kinect Sensor

The Kinect sensor for Windows functions as a computer's eyes and ears, and the sensor provides the capacity to use those functions. To access the Kinect data using nonproprietary software, the USB communication had to be reverse-engineered. The basic parts of the Kinect device are (Figure 1)

(i) video camera (color stream) that delivers the color stream data with the combination of three basic color components red, green, and blue (RGB);

(ii) IR cameras (depth stream) composed of an IR projector and a monochrome CMOS sensor, which captures video data under any ambient light conditions;

(iii) microphones (audio stream) which consist of a four-element, linear microphone array to capture audio data at a 24-bit resolution.

(iv) tilt motor (direction and angle control) that allows us to adjust it at any vertical angle between 27 and −27 degrees according to learners' height.

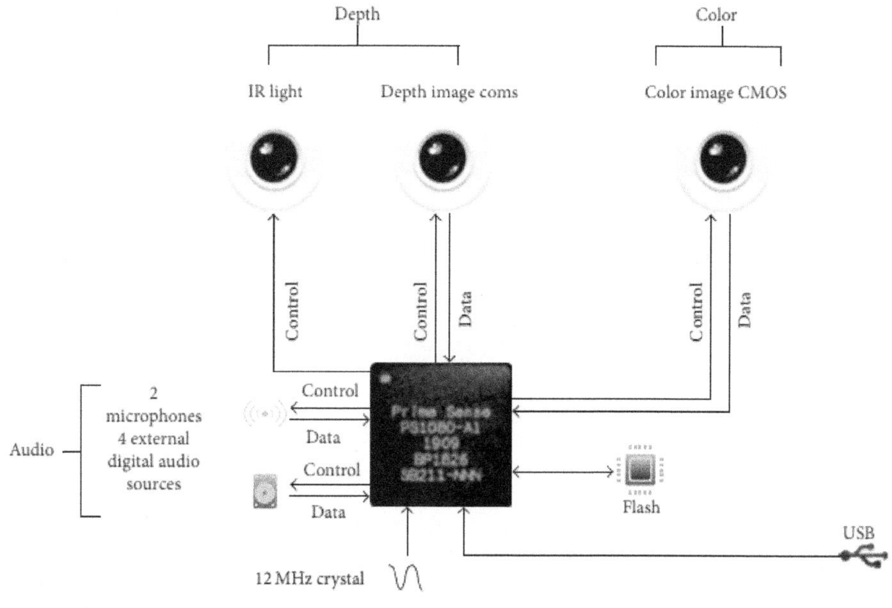

Figure 1 Recommended design of Primesense chip. (Reference: Traumabot blog.)

The Kinect sensor receives the information stream (e.g., video, depth, or audio stream) and delivers it to the natural user interface library. We used the application interface (API) to control all of the functions of the Kinect sensor, such as hand tracking, skeleton tracking [16], speech commands, and face tracking. The OpenNI (natural interaction) organization provides a framework and application programming interface (API) for dealing with devices like Kinect. OpenNI addresses a range of devices including visual and audio devices as shown in Figure 2.

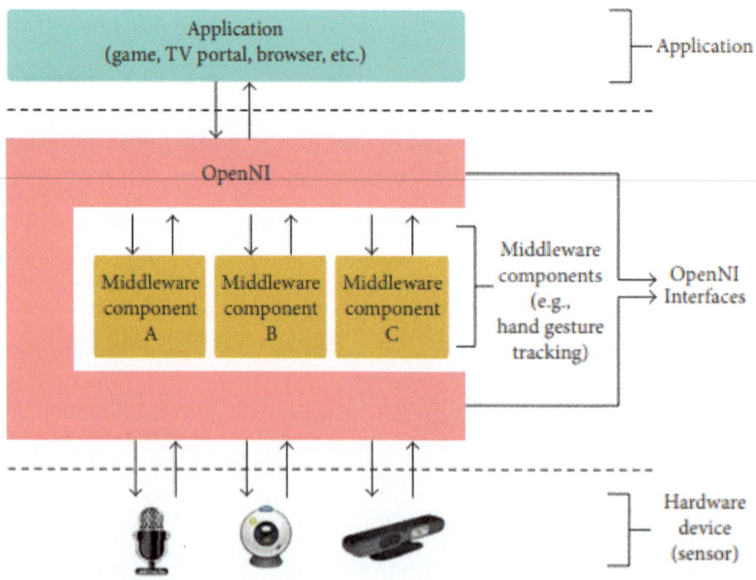

Figure 2 OpenNI middleware provides natural interaction tracking functionality. (Reference: Microsoft Wiki.)

Game-Based Learning

Game-based learning (GBL) is a specific term used in instructional strategy or activities associated with applications that have defined learning outcomes. As an emergent learning process, GBL is designed to balance subject matter with gameplay and to help players retain and apply the subject matter to the real world [17]. GBL typically uses video-game technology, scoring strategies, interactive interfaces, flexibility courses, and real-time feedback to engage learners in learning. GBL not only makes learning meaningful, but also creates a mental model that motivates the participants [18].

Because information and communication technology has rapidly developed, computer and simulation games have become popular leisure activities in daily life. Some scholars assert that computer games are natural and necessary elements in student learning and that they should be integrated into instructional design as well as learning environments [17]. Scholars also believe that the concept of "learning-by-playing," which helps students overcome the boredom of classroom learning, applies to playing computer games [19]. However, weaknesses and drawbacks in the implementation of GBL remain: (a) GBL requires substantial preparation and effort, and (b) the subjects and content are usually predefined and fixed. As Clark and Mayer [20] noted in their review of e-learning, a well-designed system can help generate the content of an entertaining scenario that corresponds to the learning subject. In other words, a game-based e-learning system enables simple and efficient preparation of learning applications. Figure 3 shows the key component game cycle that is triggered by game characteristics and instructional content come together to bring about learning outcomes [21].

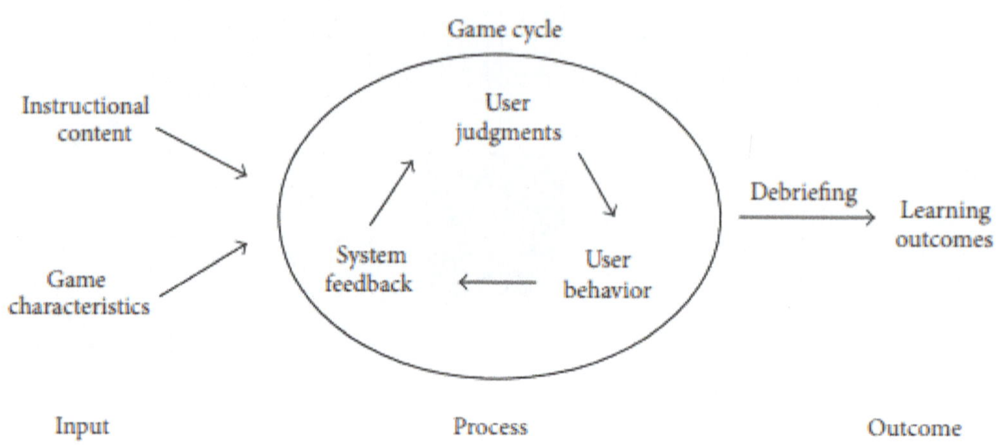

Figure 3 Input-Process-Outcome Game Model.

Input-Process-Outcome Game Model includes three parts. The first is input phase; the objective is to design an instructional content that incorporates characteristics of games. The second is process phase; these features trigger a cycle that includes user judgments (enjoyment or interest), user behaviors, and system feedback. Finally is outcome phase; this shows the learning achievement and learning outcomes.

METHOD

Teaching Materials

To develop material using the Kinect sensor, various programming frameworks, such as the OpenNI architecture, which was used to control the Kinect sensor, and the OpenTK architecture, which was used to provide a cross platform library, must be surveyed. The system architecture is shown in Figure 4.

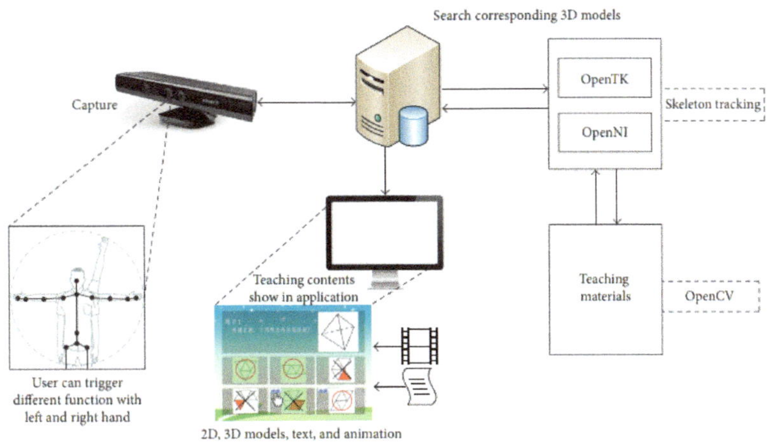

Figure 4 The system architecture.

Using the Kinect sensor to present questions and interactive games and including a hand-mouse function (joints tracked by the Primesense NITE middleware skeleton tracking algorithm) enable learners to learn the geometric learning theory and relevant information (shown in Figure 5). We provided three types of learning models.

(i) Shapes and space: a questions' and answers' game where you can recognize the properties of geometric shapes. There are different levels of difficulty and random questions. Student stands in front of the screen and operate with both hands to select, confirm, and check the answer.

(ii) Drawing and visualization: we generate a random visualization shape, so that student uses the right hand as a brush to draw the same shape. After that, the system compares drawing shape with the answer and informs the teaching contents for student.

(iii) Skeleton interactive model: a questions' and answers' game where you can recognize the properties of unfolding and reconstructing polyhedron. Student needs to imagine a classic open problem whether the surface of every polyhedron can be cut along some of its edges and unfolded into the plane without overlap and operate with both hands to select, confirm, and check the answer.

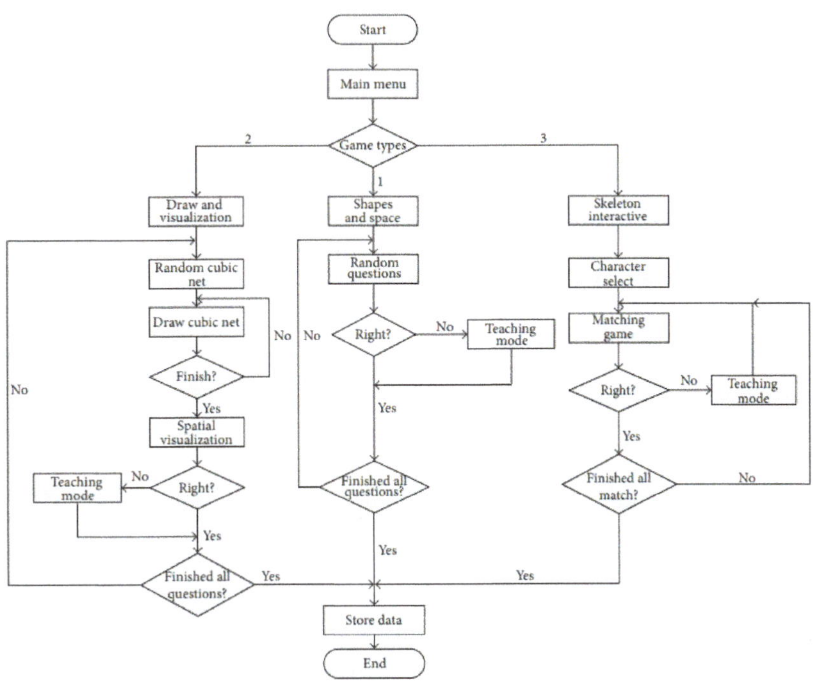

Figure 5 Kinect sensor-assisted learning system process.

Experiment Participants

The subjects included three classes and total of 146 students participated from the University in Northern Taiwan that study natural sciences course in general education. They were assigned into two groups randomly. The experimental group, including seventy-two students, was received the bodily-kinesthetic intelligence materials developed by Kinect technology (3D objects, related information, and interaction) for learning the concepts of spatial visualization skills, while the control group with seventy-four students was received the simulation-based materials devised by flash animation technology that consisted of the same learning materials as those used by the experimental group. All of students were taught by the same instructor who had taught the natural sciences course for more than 10 years.

Research Tools

The research tools used in this study included the learning achievement tests and the questionnaire for measuring the system usability for surveying the students' acceptance in learning system.

(i) The achievement test sheets were developed based on the content of the "spatial visualization" by three experienced instructors (teaching more than a decade) in this field. The pretest was composed of 20 multiple-choice items designed to evaluate the learners' prior knowledge about the course unit "knowing the spatial visualization in Taiwan" before the learning activity, 5 points for each item, out of 100 points. The posttest followed the same structure and aimed to evaluate the learners' ability. The test scope of the posttest was the learning materials of the learning activity and the perfect score was 100.

(ii) The questionnaire of System Usability Scale (SUS) [22] was administered to evaluate system usability. It is a Likert scale used to assess system usability, learnability, and users' subjective satisfaction concerning specific aspects of the interactive interface. In addition, we included an adjective scale to rate our SUS (Figure 6). The SUS was highly reliable (alpha = 0.91) and useful in a wide range of interface types [23]. The SUS was intended to measure only perceived ease-of-use; however, Lewis and Sauro [24] demonstrated that it provides a global measure of system satisfaction and subscales of usability (Items 1, 2, 3, 5, 6, 7, 8, and 9) and learnability (Items 4 and 10) (the summed score contributions of the usability and learnability items were multiplied by 3.125 and 12.5, resp.).

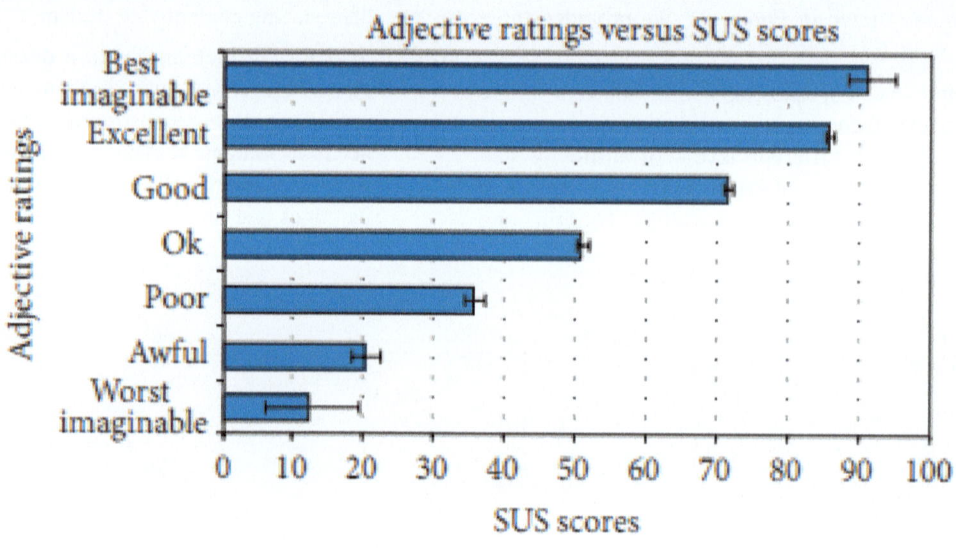

Figure 6 Mean score ratings corresponding to the seven adjective ratings.

PROCEDURES

Before the experiment, students completed a two-unit course on the basic knowledge of spatial visualization. Instruction consisted of 4 hours over a period of 2 weeks. For each unit, both groups completed learning activities that included readings, videos, field observations, and classroom discussion. At the beginning of the learning activity, students in the experimental and control groups took the pretest simultaneously. The purpose of pretest was to find out the equivalence of the two groups in their abilities and readiness before the treatment.

Afterward, students in the experimental group learned with the bodily-kinesthetic intelligence materials developed by this study employing Kinect technology for the unit "spatial visualization." Learners were allowed to manipulate the Kinect sensor aforementioned to immersion interaction with the 3D virtual objects and understand the knowledge related to them. On the other hand, those in the control group learned with the simulation-based materials developed by flash animation technology for learning the concepts through 2D animation and diagrams. The duration of the experimental instruction was 2 weeks. After the learning activity, the students took the achievement posttest and completed the questionnaire of SUS. All the learning activities were video-recorded for later observation and further analysis. Figure 7 shows the procedure of the experiment.

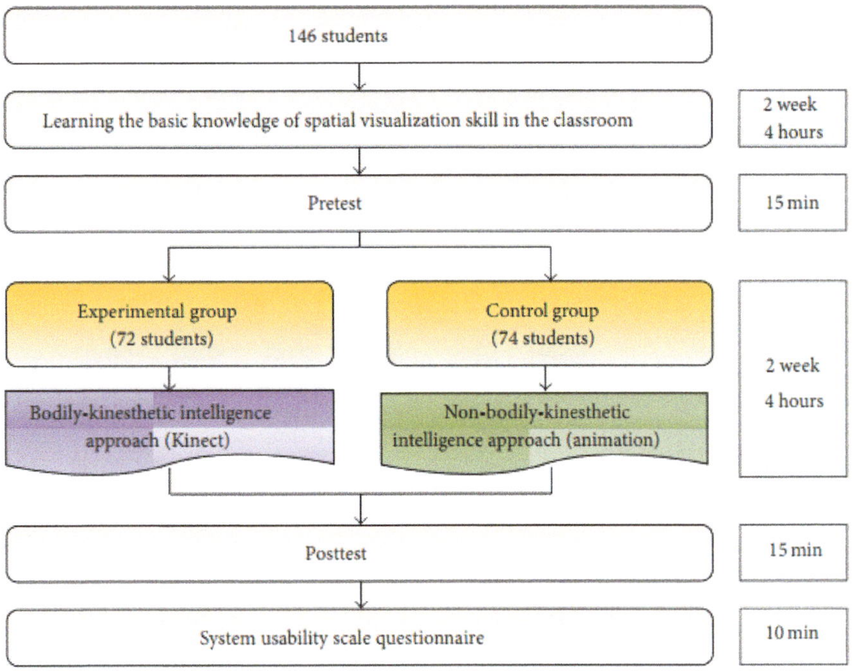

Figure 7 Procedures of the experimental design.

EVALUATION RESULTS

One-way ANCOVA was conducted to examine the research questions. The significance level was set at 0.05. The effects on learning performance and system usability toward natural science learning are analyzed in the following sections. Originally, the mean scores and standard deviation of the pretests and posttests of both groups are shown in Table 3.

Table 3 The mean scores and standard deviation of pretest, posttest of learning achievement.

Learning approach	N	Pretest		Posttest	
		M	SD	M	SD
Bodily-kinesthetic intelligence (Kinect)	72	52.61	11.96	83.19	11.29
Non-bodily-kinesthetic intelligence (animation)	74	51.23	13.27	77.48	12.72

The purpose of this study was to examine the effectiveness of the different learning approach in terms of improving the students' learning achievement. After the learning activity, one-way ANCOVA was adopted for the analyses, in which the posttest scores were the dependent variable, the pretest scores were the covariate, and the type of using authentic technology was the fixed factor. As can be seen from analysis of covariance (ANCOVA) of the posttest score, the mean value and standard deviations of the posttest score were 83.19 and 11.29 for the Kinect group and 77.48 and 12.72 for the animation group. That is, students who learned with the Bodily-kinesthetic intelligence (Kinect) showed significantly better learning achievements than those who learned with the non-bodily-kinesthetic intelligence (animation) when exploring spatial visualization skills knowledge of natural science.

The participants operated the system and completed the SUS questionnaire. The mean score of the SUS was 71.73 (SD = 13.06) for the Kinect group and 73.17 (SD = 12.85) for the animation group. According to the adjective rating score, the assisted learning system in this study lies between "good" and "excellent." We discussed opinions on the interactive learning system with the participants after they operated the system and completed the SUS. The participants generally agreed that the interactive learning system increased their interest in the concept and made them aware of various things.

Figure 8 lists the student distribution regarding system usability, which indicates that most of the learners agreed that the Kinect-based support system is satisfactory and also suggested that the system is helpful for learning. Figure 9 shows the student distribution regarding the two-factor orthogonal structure, usability and learnability. The scores indicate that high usability is not highly consistent with high learnability. However, usability plays a vital role in the initial adoption or rejection of a technology, and learners believed that the system can facilitate learning.

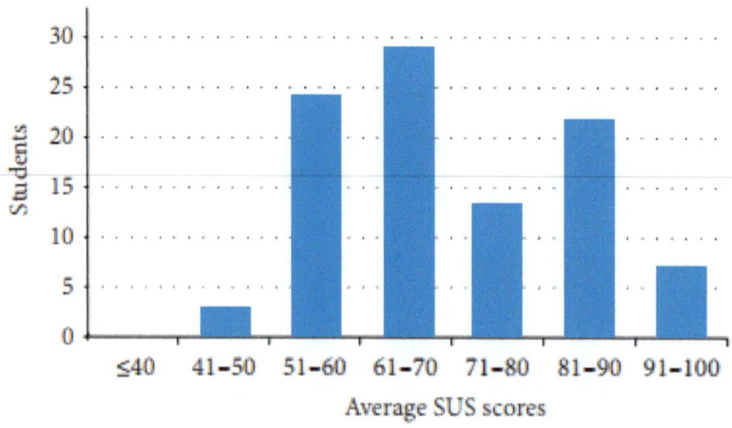

Figure 8 Distribution of SUS scores.

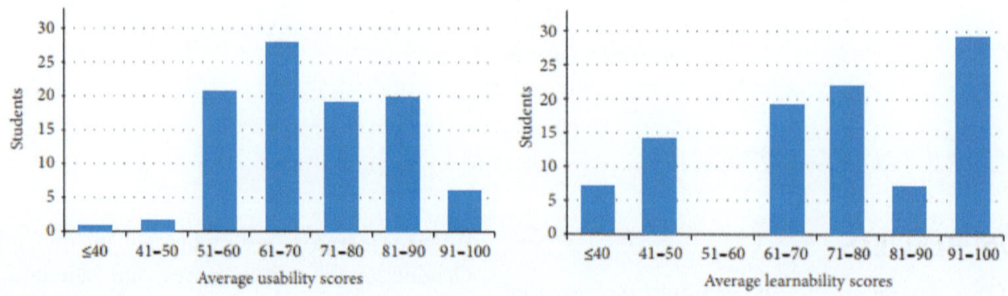

Figure 9 Distribution of usability scores and distribution of learnability scores.

Regarding the analysis of the scale, we further discuss the mean, usability, and learnability scores that can help improve the system. Hence, we summarize the following reasons that may affect system satisfaction:

(i) the control and learning interfaces were not sufficiently smooth;

(ii) the materials could not be displayed properly because of the angle and distance, which may confuse learners' operation.

CONCLUSION

In this paper, we presented the results of the learning achievement and system usability of a bodily-kinesthetic intelligence assisted learning system using the Kinect sensor. Regarding the SUS questionnaire, most learners highly appreciated employing the Kinect sensor to present the teaching materials and considered the material to be interesting, easy to control and play with, and simple to operate using the interactive functions. The learners also reported that teaching by employing an interactive system enhanced their motivation to learn and was helpful for learning spatial visualization skills. Several parts of the system must still be improved. A small portion of the learners reported that the learning system performed undesirably in response to speed during interactive operation. The buttons should be clearly defined, the cubit net knowledge should be highlighted, and proper instructions should be provided to ensure that the learners are focused on learning the knowledge expressed in the teaching materials. We conclude that the Kinect sensor-assisted learning system promotes the development of students' spatial visualization skills and encourages them to become active learners. This is a case study for exploratory purposes; it will be more efficient to test the effect of Kinect on the game-based learning class with a larger sample size in the future and compare between the results before and after using the sensor. Furthermore, instructors need to improve Kinect's graphical interface which may increase the efficiency of the feedback.

Conflict of Interests

The authors declare that there is no conflict of interests regarding the publication of this paper.

ACKNOWLEDGMENT

The funding of this study was supported by the Ministry of Science and Technology of Taiwan under Grant MOST 101-2511-S-147-001-.

REFERENCES

1. M. A. M. Echeverr´ıa, P. C. Santana-Mancilla, H. F. Q. Carrillo, and E. A. F. Enciso, "Natural user interfaces to teach math on higher education," Procedia—Social and Behavioral Sciences, vol. 106, pp. 1883–1889, 2013.

2. S. C. Lin, K. H. Chen, W. C. Hsieh, W. T. Lee, and K. C. Huang, "Somatosensory interaction in digital

game-based learning for Taiwanese classical poems," in Proceedings of the Global Chinese Conference Computers in Education, pp. 187–194, 2012.

3. C. C. Lu and N. D. Yao, "The application and introspection of information education in elementary-school curriculum," Elementary Education, vol. 42, no. 6, pp. 19–24, 2002.
4. Y. T. Sung, K. E. Chang, and H. T. Hou, "Technology-instruction integration: learning form America's experience and reflecting on Taiwan's development," Bulletin of Educational Research, vol. 51, no. 1, pp. 31–62, 2005.
5. H. W. Wang and Y. Y. Wang, "A study of developing a gamebased courseware for cubic net," Elementary Education, vol. 49, no. 1, pp. 30–40, 2008.
6. G. H. Wheatley, "Spatial sense and mathematics learning," The Arithmetic Teacher, vol. 37, no. 6, pp. 10–11, 1990.
7. National Council of Teachers of Mathematics, Principles and Standards for School Mathematics, National Council of Teachers of Mathematics, Reston, Va, USA, 2000.
8. P. M. Van Hiele, Structure and Insight: a Theory of Mathematics Education, Academic Press, Orlando, Fla, USA, 1986.
9. J. M. Keller, "Use of the ARCS model of motivation in teacher training," IDD&E Working Paper 10, 1983.
10. J. M. Keller, "Using the ARCS motivational process in computer-based instruction and distance education," New Directions for Teaching and Learning, vol. 1999, no. 78, pp. 37–47, 1999.
11. A. J. Bishop, "Review of research on visualization in mathematics education," Focus on Learning Problems in Mathematics, vol. 11, no. 1, pp. 7–16, 1989.
12. J.-C. Woo, "Digital game-based learning supports student motivation, cognitive success, and performance outcomes," Journal of Educational Technology & Society, vol. 17, no. 3, pp. 291–307, 2014.
13. J. Piaget and B. Inhelder, The Child's Conception of Space, Norton, New York, NY, USA, 1967.
14. D. F. Lohman and P. C. Kyllonen, "Individual differences in solution strategy on spatial and change," in Psychology: A Study of Science, S. Koch, Ed., vol. 3, pp. 423–475, McGraw Hill, New York, NY, USA, 1984.
15. M. L. Crowley, "The van hiele model of the development of geomemc thought," in Learning and Teaching Gemretry , K-12, 1987 Yearbook of the National C ouncil of Teachers of Mathematics, M. M. Lindquist, Ed., National Council af Teachers af Mathematics, Reston, Va, USA, 1987.
16. A. Kar, "Skeletal tracking using microsoft kinect," Methodology, vol. 1, pp. 1–11, 2010.
17. M. Prensky, Digital Game-Based Learning, McGraw-Hill, New York, NY, USA, 2001.
18. J. Chumbley and M. Griffiths, "Affect and the computer game player: the effect of gender, personality, and game reinforcement structure on affective responses to computer game-play," CyberPsychology & Behavior, vol. 9, no. 3, pp. 308–316, 2006.
19. S. I. de Freitas, "Using games and simulations for supporting learning," Learning, Media and Technology, vol. 31, no. 4, pp. 343–358, 2006.
20. R. C. Clark and R. E. Mayer, E-Learning and the Science of Instruction, Pfeiffer, San Francisco, Calif, USA, 2003.
21. R. Garris, R. Ahlers, and J. E. Driskell, "Games, motivation, and learning: a research and practice model," Simulation & Gaming, vol. 33, no. 4, pp. 441–467, 2002.
22. J. Brooke, System Usability Scale (SUS): A Quick-and-Dirty Method of System Evaluation User Information, Digital Equipment, Reading, UK, 1986.
23. A. Bongor, P. Kortum, and J. Miller, "Determining what individual SUS scores mean: adding an adjective rating scale," Journal of Usability Studies, vol. 4, no. 3, pp. 114–123, 2009.
24. J. R. Lewis and J. Sauro, "The factor structure of the system usability scale," in Human Centered Design, vol. 5619 of Lecture Notes in Computer Science, pp. 94–103, 2009.

CHAPTER 12 FPGA-AWARE SCHEDULING STRATEGIES AT HYPERVISOR LEVEL IN CLOUD ENVIRONMENTS

Julio Proaño Orellana, Blanca Caminero, Carmen Carrión, Luis Tomas, Selome Kostentinos Tesfatsion, and Johan Tordsson

INTRODUCTION

Nowadays, the processing computational resources have shown an important change to achieve a balance between performance and power consumption. Devices such as GPUs and FPGAs among others are integrated as specialized processing elements into cloud environments to extend the capacity of the cloud.

FPGAs are commercial off-the-shelf reconfigurable silicon devices that achieve hardware-like performance with software-like flexibility. These are facts of great interest in the context of cloud computing. Cloud mainly leverages virtualization technology (i.e., virtual machines) to manage resources of a data center. Thus, providers can share the physical resources between clients.

In this context, resource scheduling is a critical issue that can contribute to increasing the benefits of cloud platforms. On one hand, depending on how many resources are allocated to different users' requests for service, more or fewer requests can be serviced while fulfilling their SLA. This fact impacts the benefits obtained by the cloud provider. On the other hand, additional advantages can exist, such as achieving a positive effect on the data center energy consumption. The combination of both implies getting a better Return on Investment (ROI) from the infrastructure which is crucial when serving Software as a Service (SaaS) requests with QoS requirements. Typically, a SaaS user issues a request for a specific service, with particular QoS-related constraints (i.e., a deadline). The user does not need to be aware of which type and how many resources are required to get its response. The system must be able to allocate and schedule the necessary resources (both in quantity and type) to serve this request.

This paper addresses the scheduling of jobs within a cloud infrastructure which is composed of heterogeneous physical nodes (with and without FPGA accelerators) from a hierarchical point of view. In this structure the two levels of scheduling are(1)the Cluster Level Scheduler (CLS), to decide the type of node where the virtual machine (VM) that will serve the request will be deployed,(2)the Node Level Scheduler (NLS), to decide which one of the VMs allocated to the node will get the use of the accelerators (FPGAs in particular) available in a node.

The problem of high-level scheduling among physical nodes, referred to as CLS, has previously been addressed by the authors in [1, 2]. Now, this work focuses on the impact of different scheduling strategies within a physical node with FPGA resources, which are applied at the hypervisor level. In a nutshell, the main contributions of the paper are the following:(i)to extend the hypervisor functionality to support dynamic control of FPGA devices as cloud computational resources,(ii)to propose a novel FPGA-aware Node Level Scheduler (NLS) metric aimed at QoS provision while reducing energy consumption,(iii)to present a novel fine-grained FPGA-aware Node Level Scheduler,(iv)to evaluate the Node Level Scheduler proposals in a real testbed, comparing them to some simple scheduler techniques.

This paper is structured as follows. Sections 1 and 2 introduce and motivate the problem being tackled. Section3 reviews literature related to the topic of the paper. The

Citation: Julio Proaño Orellana, Blanca Caminero, Carmen Carrión, Luis Tomas, Selome Kostentinos Tesfatsion, and Johan Tordsson, "FP-GA-Aware Scheduling Strategies at Hypervisor Level in Cloud Environments," Scientific Programming, vol. 2016, Article ID 4670271, 12 pages, 2016. doi:10.1155/2016/4670271.

framework where the presented research has been carried out is outlined in Section 4. Next, Section 5 provides the details on how accelerators (and in particular, FPGAs) are included into the scheduling strategies, and the additional fine-grained level of scheduling is introduced in Section 6. The evaluation of results are presented in Section 7. Finally, Section 8 provides some concluding remarks.

BACKGROUND AND MOTIVATION

During the last few years, cloud computing has consolidated as a paradigm that enables a flexible and on-demand use of IT resources at different levels (infrastructure, platform, or software) as a service. Typical cloud providers support their service by means of massive data centers (usually spread around the globe), while cloud users get access to the resources with a pay-per-use model. This is referred to as a public cloud model. The cloud computing paradigm can also be applied within an organization, leading to the private cloud deployment model. Resources are pooled and shared among the different organization user groups to meet their demands on IT resources. In either case (public or private), cloud computing platforms are composed of pools of computing, storage, and networking resources that are made available as a service to their users. Service Level Agreements (SLAs) are established between providers and users, to specify the conditions of the service, both from technical (availability, Quality of Service,) and formal (cost of the service, penalties in case of contract breach,) points of view.

Many challenges exist in this model that turn out to be the focus of many research projects, such as efficient resource management [3], security and privacy concerns [4], or standardization [5], just to name a few of them. In particular, some kind of orchestration is needed in order to allocate the adequate resources to every user request [6]. As it has been pointed out before, cloud providers face the following dilemma: admitting more users into the system would lead to more incomes, but if the available resources are not enough for fulfilling the established SLAs, penalizations will cut benefits down. Thus, care must be taken when admitting more users into the system.

From another point of view, data center's energy consumption is nowadays a big concern. Energy costs are a major contributor to a data center's Total Cost of Ownership (TCO) [7]. Thus, strategies to improve data center's efficiency are the topic of many research efforts, such as adjusting the voltage supplied to servers according to their workload [8] or even creating specific hardware designs [9]. One strategy that can provide benefits regarding energy consumption as well as performance in data centers is the integration of accelerators as specialized resources within the cloud infrastructure [10], such as General Purpose Graphics Processing Units (GPGPUs) or Field Programmable Gate Arrays (FPGAs).

FPGAs allow cloud computing data centers to scale up in a more efficient way than using just conventional processors [11]. It is interesting to note that the initiatives towards building exascale systems with low-energy consumption driven by the European Union (EU) are based on the integration of FPGAs with ARM processors [12].

However, using heterogeneous resources in cloud environments is still an open challenge, as illustrated by the work presented by Microsoft in [13]. Frequently, cloud applications which are running on VMs with a fixed amount of hardware resources including accelerators do not use the same number of them all the time due to their features. Thus, a proper scheduling strategy might help to optimize the utilization of these resources.

Moreover, different applications could benefit from the FPGA over time, depending on their degree of compliance with QoS requirements. To achieve this objective, the FPGA should be properly shared among competing service requests.

RELATED WORK

Incorporation of FPGAs in the cloud context is a relatively new area of research. So, the Catapult project [13] led by Microsoft represents the first detailed investigation of applying FPGAs within an enterprise-level data center application. In this case, FPGA-accelerated nodes are used for the Bing web search engine. Results show great improvements in both the latency and the throughput of the service.

Nevertheless, FPGA-aware scheduling in a cloud environment is still at initial stages. Integrating FPGAs as first class computational resources to provide cloud service demands novel high-level programming models to simplify the development of software applications, maximizing communication to FPGAs, and the development of efficient FPGA-aware scheduling algorithms.

One crucial step to efficiently run applications across heterogeneous hardware is to provide optimized versions of computational kernels (as BLAS routines or FFT) [14]. OpenCL [15], VIVADO [16], and Lime [17] are high-level programming models focused on reducing the time-to-market in the designing process.

In addition, providing FPGAs as cloud computing resources demands virtualization support in hardware with near-native performance. Open source interface frameworks have recently emerged (RIFFA [18], DyRACT [19]) that enable FPGA designs to be accessed through an abstracted software API on the host with communication throughput between the host and FPGA close to the limits of modern PCIe interfaces.

Moreover, efficient resource managements and scheduling algorithms are open key challenges to providing FPGA cloud services. The scheduling of jobs faces a multiobjective optimization problem in the process of assigning jobs to a pool of limited resources. Resource management and scheduling have been a hot research topic in a cloud context, and many approaches have been proposed to place the VMs to physical CPU hosts. A survey of the most recent proposals about metaheuristic scheduling solutions for cloud can be found in [20].

In this context, cloud-centric integration of FPGAs frameworks is developed in [11, 21] by extending the open source cloud management system OpenStack [22]. The systems support the on-demand deployment of a user designed custom hardware while maintaining the cloud computing benefits of scalability and flexibility. The bitstream of the application is considered as a special VM image. So, FPGAs are eligible as computational resources by the clients.

Another recent related work presents a framework that integrates FPGAs in a standard server with virtualized resource management and communication [23]. The resource management selects the smallest reconfigurable FPGA area able to attend the request. If no one is found, the user request is rejected, and the request can be processed in software. As an application case study, they built a MapReduce accelerator for word counting and preliminary results are evaluated about integrating FPGA devices in the cloud using partial reconfiguration.

At some points, the systems mentioned above can be complementary to the work presented in this paper because all of them focusing on supporting FPGAs as computational cloud devices. But in contrast, in our case FPGAs are not visible to the clients. The idea is to provide a QoS Software as a Service by making efficient use of FPGA-aware scheduling algorithms. Our work focuses on developing a cloud management framework able to scale up and down FPGA devices in a dynamical way.

HIERARCHICAL SCHEDULER ARCHITECTURE OVERVIEW

In previous works [1, 2] the problem of integrating FPGAs into a cloud was faced by "HECCO" (Heterogeneous Cloud Computing) architecture. In those approaches, every node of the cloud system is composed of one or more CPUs with a certain number of cores each and zero or more accelerators. Frequently, the number of accelerators available within a node is lower than the number of CPU cores available. Therefore, they must be shared between clients. HECCO enables the provision of IaaS and SaaS services with Quality of Service (QoS) requirements.

In this work, the proposal architecture leveraged the use of accelerators to (a) finish job tasks within a particular time frame in order to fulfill their QoS requirements, expressed as Service Level Objectives (SLO) within a Service Level Agreement (SLA), and (b) reduce the energy footprint of cloud data centers.

The whole picture of the framework is depicted in Figure 1. It is organized into several layers:(i)The Management Layer is responsible for receiving client requests and selecting the most suitable node to allocate their applications. Each request is defined by a template in which parameters such as the type of service and the utilization time are defined. This layer is composed of the Heterogeneous Cloud Computing (HECCO), which includes the Cluster Level Scheduler (CLS). As outlined above, it provides the "intelligence" to fulfill the QoS requirements expressed by clients within their SLAs. In particular, the CLS implements a series of mechanisms that are mainly aimed at allocating every request to the most appropriate resource (i.e., a node with or without accelerators). Its decision is based on the client's SLA and the availability of the resources. More details on the management layer can be found in [2].(ii)The Deployment Layer, which receives instructions from the management layer, is responsible for performing actions such as the creation and monitoring of the whole virtual environment. It has a complete view of the cloud and is composed of the Virtual Infrastructure Manager (VIM). The VIM is a centralized data center manager that allows to build and manage the cloud environment.(iii)The Hypervisor Layer provides the control of the physical resources. This layer has a local view of the system and is composed of a hypervisor, which is responsible for the supervision of the VMs and resources for each node. This layer also contains a Node Level Scheduler (NLS) that is responsible for sharing the local resources within a node. In this case, the scheduling's decision is focused on the management of the use of the accelerators within each node, in order to get the most out of them. More details about this element are provided in Section 5.

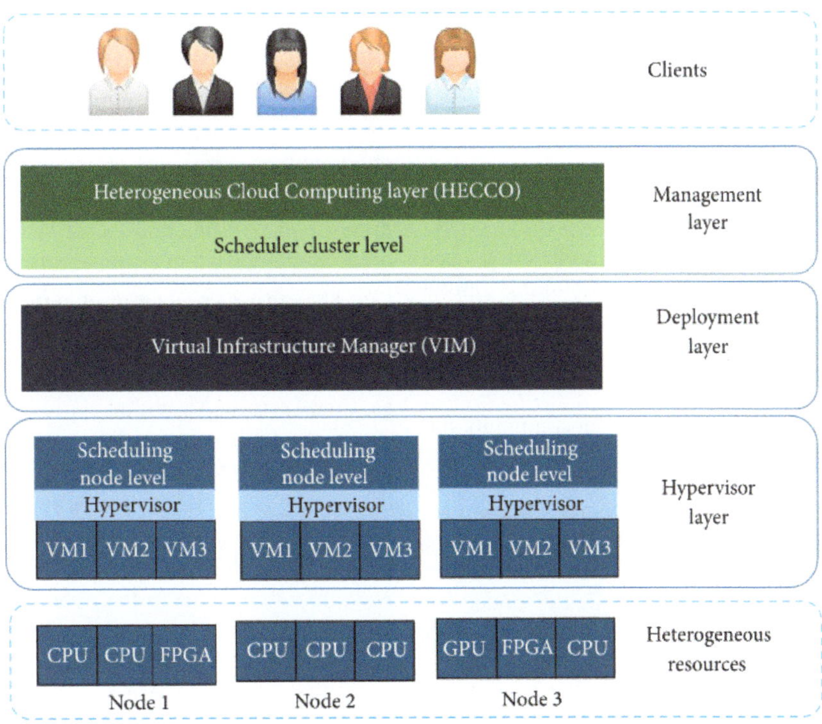

Figure 1: Architecture overview.

Figure 2 depicts the two different levels of scheduling. First, the CLS receives the tasks and selects the most suitable node to allocate each of them, following the strategies proposed in [2]. Second, the NLS manages the tasks allocated to a specific node.

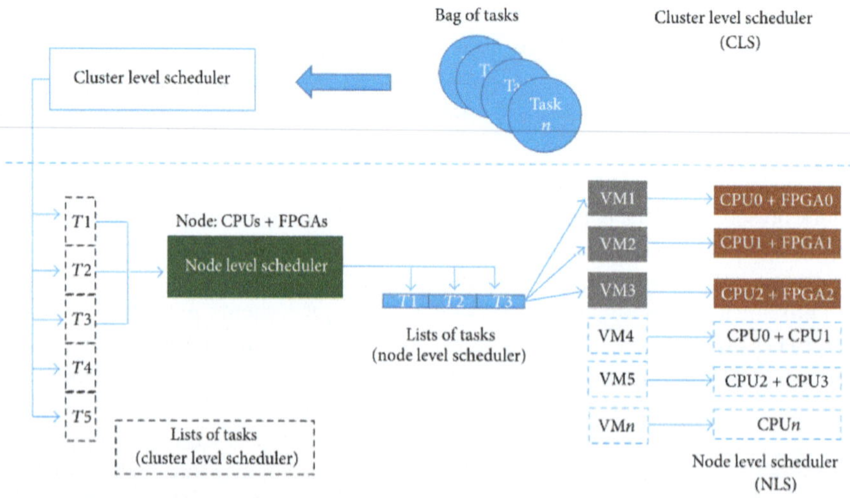

Figure 2: Different scheduling levels.

More precisely, it selects the task which is going to receive the accelerator and for how long, by certain metrics.

In other words, given the fact that there may be more virtual machines allocated to a node than accelerators available, which virtual machine will deserve the use of an accelerator? In the rest of this work, some insight will be given on this issue.

NODE LEVEL SCHEDULING

In this section we will focus on the dynamic scheduling strategy for allocated jobs within a node and timing-related indicators, such as a deadline. This deadline is related to when the job must have finished in order to deem its SLA as fulfilled.

The main objective of the node level scheduling strategy is twofold: first, to meet application SLOs and second, to consume as less energy as possible. To achieve this multiobjective, the scheduling algorithm is aware of the properties of the physical nodes and due to the good performance and low-cost energy offered by the FPGAs, the scheduling maximizes their utilization.

Basically, the algorithm uses a heuristic process for assigning the physical resources inside the node (FPGAs and CPUs) to the virtual machines that will be deployed at each point of time. It is worth to mention that the use of this simple algorithm avoids the overhead of the system. Recall that the NLS is implemented within the hypervisor and should be able to run with minimal computational resources.

In other words, a matching is done between computational resources and tasks (deployed as VMs) minimizing the computational impact. On one side, the scheduler algorithm has as input a list of tasks (), assigned by the CLS algorithm, with all the nonattended job requests that have been received in the node (see Figure 2). On the other side, each time a computational virtual resource is released in the node, the scheduler is notified and a matching process is done. Then, a resource driven algorithm selects the best candidates to match resources according to some efficient metric. This scheduling is called a coarse-grained scheduling because FPGA resources are busy (not available for allocation) until the end of an assigned task.

In addition, in this paper, a multiobjective metric is proposed and computed as the fraction of the computational work of a task and the deadline or time available to finish it up in order to fulfill the SLA.

Therefore, the multiobjective metric measures the computational workload demanded on the node over the time; that is, it provides a measure of the computational stress. And it is a fact that the higher the computational requirements, the more the energy consumption. That is why the task with most demanding requirements is matched to an FPGA resource. In other words, the algorithm matches the most demanding job according to this criterion to the VM with FPGA accelerators.

The computational work parameter involved in the metric reflects the workload that must process the VM. Then, we need to apply some criteria to calculate this value. For example, in our experiments with multimedia applications this parameter is computed as the number of video frames to be processed. Other examples are data-encryption services, where this parameter could be the size of the data that will be encrypted, or social network analysis services, where it could be the number of tweets stored in a log file. Techniques such as application profiling and using data from previous executions are frequently used to estimate this value.

The other parameter used in the metric is the deadline that is established by the client in the SLA.

To sum up, the node level scheduling process works as follows (see Algorithm 1): First, the selected metric is computed for each task. Next, the scheduler sorts all tasks based on that metric and the FPGA is assigned to the most demanding task. This process is repeated every time the FPGA becomes available. To achieve this goal, the status of the FPGA is periodically monitored. This synchronization process is an important issue in the overall scheduling process. Thus, some implementation details will be explained in the next subsection. The algorithm is aware of the heterogeneity of the node, because the most demanding task is executed in a VM deployed with FPGA resources.

Require: Task_i, $i = 1, 2, \ldots, K$: Task T_i to be executed in the local node
$\text{List}_{\text{Task}}$ = Set of tasks
$\text{metric}(\text{Task}_i)$: function which computes the metric for task Task_i
$\text{include}(\text{Task}_i, \text{List}_{\text{Task}})$: function which includes Task_i in $\text{List}_{\text{Task}}$
$\text{rank}(\text{List}_{\text{Task}})$: function which sorts $\text{List}_{\text{Task}}$ according to the selected metric
$\text{top}(\text{List}_{\text{Task}})$: function which extracts the first VM from $\text{List}_{\text{Task}}$

loop
  Wait until FPGA_status == Free
  for each $\text{Task}_i / i \in 1 \cdots N$ **do**
    $\text{Task}_i.\text{metric} = \text{metric}(\text{Task}_i)$
    $\text{include}(\text{Task}_i, \text{List}_{\text{Task}})$
    $\text{rank}(\text{List}_{\text{Task}})$
  end for
  $\text{VM}_{\text{first}} = \text{top}(\text{List}_{\text{Task}})$
  attach FPGA to VM_{first}
end loop

Algorithm 1: Node level scheduling algorithm.

Implementation Details

FPGAs are physically plugged into computing nodes via the PCI express bus. The communication between VMs and the FPGAs is made through the Intel Virtualization Technology for Directed I/O (VT-d) [24], which is an extension of the Intel Virtualization Technology. It allows a direct exchange of data between I/O devices and VMs.

As pointed out above, a strategy able to control the communication between the Node Level Scheduler (NLS) and the VMs currently running in the node is required. So, an FPGA synchronization service has been developed which consists of an exchange of status messages between the NLS and every VM deployed in the node. The full node information is wrapped into a "JSON" [25] data structure because it is easy to parse. The NLS is implemented as a daemon. It is constantly listening to the status information from the VMs currently deployed at the node. Each VM also has a daemon, which is periodically monitoring the status of the FPGA (whether an FPGA is attached to the VM or not). Besides, the VMs periodically send their identification and the progress of the running applications through an UDP socket connection to the NLS. If a VM is using an FPGA, its status is also forwarded to the scheduler by means of updating a "status file."

Figure 3 depicts the process of reassigning the FPGA to different VMs. In this example, the FPGA is initially attached to VM1. Then, when computation on the FPGA ends, VM1 updates the status of the FPGA as "free." As a result, the NLS learns this state and gets aware of the fact that the reassignment process can be made safely. At this point the NLS can detach the FPGA from the current VM and attach it to another VM (i.e., the one in the head of the list of pending requests) through the hypervisor. The VM which finds an FPGA attached to it (VM2, in this case) immediately uses it and updates its status accordingly.

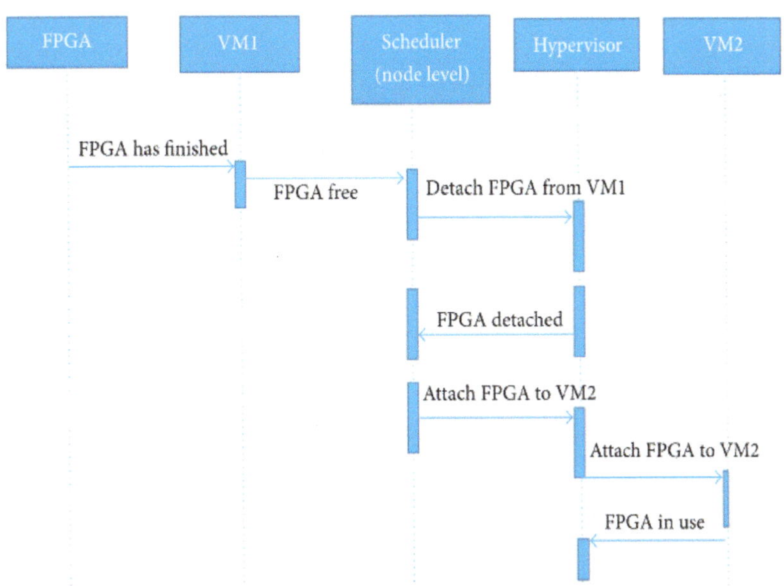

Figure 3: FPGA synchronization service example.

We use KVM [26] as hypervisor. It enables the management of the FPGA because it supports hot-plug devices with VT-d. So, it is a must that the underlying hardware supports VT-d. The NLS uses the "device_add" [27] command to attach the FPGA to a particular VM. Also, when the FPGA has fulfilled a request, the NLS uses "device_del" [27] to release the FPGA.

The NLS is not only focused on the FPGA assignment, it also considers the CPUs. In this case, the NLS matches VMs to physical CPUs using First-Fit criteria. Moreover, the scheduler uses the "taskset" [28] linux command to set the CPU affinity of a running process given its identification (PID). So, each VM has a PID and the CPU affinity "bonds" this process to the first available CPU. This is made in order to avoid swapping when a VM is assigned to different cores along time. Finally, due to the complexity of coding FPGAs, the RIFFA framework offered by Jacobsen and Kastner in [18] has been used to develop the hardware acceleration design.

In Section 7.3 the evaluation of this strategy is shown.

FINE-GRAINED STRATEGY

In the previous section, the Node Level Scheduler decides to assign the FPGA to a VM and the FPGA is not released until the end of the task running in that VM. But it might be the case that the task does not need to be accelerated during its whole runtime in order to fulfill its deadline. Moreover, it might occur that other tasks (which initially was not placed at the head of the list due to the value of its metric) would depend on the use of the FPGA to fulfill its deadline. Thus, reconsidering the allocation of the FPGA with a finer granularity could improve the number of fulfilled SLAs and, consequently, improve the system ROI. Under this context, a strategy which consists of dividing each task into smaller subtasks (called "chunks") has been explored. A trade-off between the execution time of a chunk and the frequency of checkpoints must be taken into account to decide the size of a chunk. The rationale is to reschedule the FPGA more often, so that more tasks can potentially benefit from the acceleration and power efficiency of the FPGA.

More precisely, all the chunks have the same requirements of computational workload, but different deadline restrictions. Figure 4 shows how a task with size and deadline is divided into three chunks, with sizes and deadline . Chunk size is set according to the characteristics of the application that implements the task. This can be a certain amount of data to be processed or any other application relevant parameter. As an example, for the video processing service, the chunk size is set as a certain number of video frames to process.

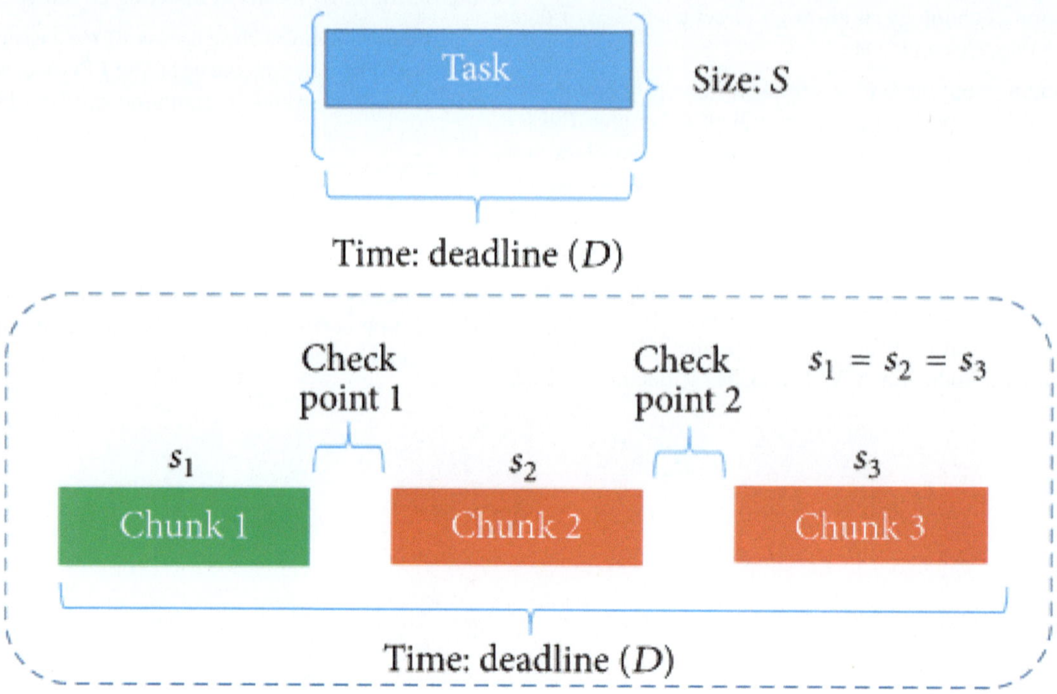

Figure 4: Division of a task to chunks.

Thus, Node Level Scheduler decisions on the use of the FPGA are taken every time and a VM finishes the processing of a chunk (see check point in Figure 4). In the current implementation, this is done every minute. The Node Level Scheduler selects the best candidate VM and attaches the FPGA to it as is depicted in Figure 5. The process is similar as in the previous case but now communication and scheduling are done at the chunk level. It is worth to notice that the application is completely independent and parallelizable. What it means is that the application receives a group of data as input and when the task has been finished the system sends the result as output. For acceleration process a wrapper function is used to map the application that will use CPU and FPGA at the same time because it is different than the one who is only running over a CPU. All the VMs of a node can take advantages of the FPGA's features and the whole node can keep the performance while the energy consumption is reduced.

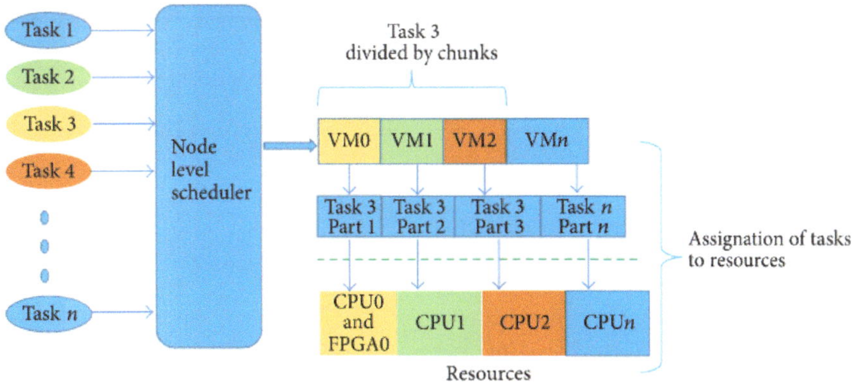

Figure 5: Scheduler by chunks.

In Section 7.3, some experiments are made showing the necessity to adopt a balanced criteria for all requests due to the fact that FIFO leads to lack of efficiency.

EVALUATION

To evaluate the impact of the scheduling algorithms proposed in this paper some experiments have been carried out on a Heterogeneous Cloud Computing testbed environment, with a real application case study. Details on the platform, application, and workload are given next, prior to explaining some evaluation results.

All the experiments have been run on a real testbed, depicted in Figure 6.

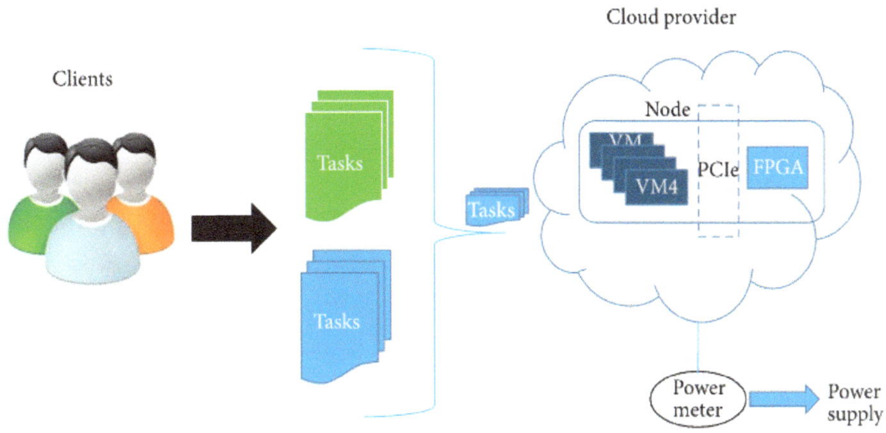

Figure 6: Cloud computing experimental testbed.

Hardware is composed of an Intel Core i5 with 6 Gb of DRAM and an FPGA Virtex 6 by Xilinx (a ML605 Evaluation Kit, based on the powerful XC6VLX-240T-1FFG1156 [29]).

Additionally, as a way to measure the energy the testbed includes a power consumption monitor node. More precisely, the WattsUp PRO [30] power meter has been used. This device aims to provide an independent managed and accessed power data collecting mechanism. This device must be positioned between the computing node power supply and the main power plug, as shown in Figure 6. The output data can be recorded into a file according to a predefined interval or when particular events occur (i.e., when the power consumption exceeds a threshold previously configured). In our experiments, the monitoring frequency has been setup to one sample per second.

Application

As real use case application an Image Convolution Software (ICS) is used as a service provided by cloud. This application consists on convolving an image with a filter or kernel (integer value) in both directions horizontal and vertical. This technique can be applied also to process sequences of video. Different type of filters can be used depending on the target. For our experiments we use a Sobel filter to process a sequence of video. This video is an AVI file with resolution. The application has two versions, the first one runs over a CPU and the another one over a combination between CPU and FPGA.

Workload

In order to generate a realistic cloud workload we have run the real ICS application and monitored its behavior. Thus, for every test, a bag of tasks (20) was created. Each of these requests are defined by two parameters: the deadline of the task and the number of videos to process (which relates to the amount of data to be processed by the task). There are two types of service requests, depending on how demanding their deadline. The first type of requests is based on more relaxed deadline requirements (referred to as soft requirements, SR), while the second type of requests exhibits a more demanding deadline (referred to as high requirements, HR).

The HR requests are more challenging than SR because they require to fulfill stricter deadlines and specific resources such as FPGAs to ensure the QoS-related SLOs.

To set up the deadline of each service request, we have previously characterized the application. Basically, the Sobel filter application has been run on the cloud using different computational resources for different video sequences. In this step, the number of frames, the power consumption, and the time have been stored. Thus, we have got the profile of each video stream. Then, the deadline is assigned to each input request as a random value between the execution times obtained in the profile with a margin of tolerance. For instance, for a video stream composed of three chunks the deadline could be a random value between 450 and 480 seconds while for nine chunks, the values are between 1400 and 1430.

To emulate the behavior of cloud clients, the input requests rate follows a Poisson distribution. The is the arrival time of the next requests and it was tuned for this concrete scenario to avoid an early saturation.

Moreover, three types of bags of tasks have been created, depending on the ratio between SR and HR requests. Note that the same input request rate has been used for the different types of bags of task, only the deadline of the requests has been modified, in order to get a fair comparison of the scheduling algorithms under evaluation. In particular, workloads include 10%, 25%, and 50% of HR requests.

Evaluation for Coarse-Grained Scheduling

To carry out a performance evaluation of the novel multiobjective metric proposed in Section 5 hereinafter called Highest-Job-First (HJF), QoS compliance and energy consumption are taken into account. Moreover, for the sake of comparison both a random (RND) (with none consideration for QoS requirements) and an Earliest-Deadline-First (EDF) scheduling algorithm (the VM with closest deadline gets the FPGA use, independently of the amount of data to be processed) have also been implemented.

In order to understand the behavior of the whole system we have selected several groups of metrics.

The first one describes the behavior of the whole system. It is composed of the total energy used for the system to process a bag of tasks (energy-to-solution [31]).

The second group is relative to SLA compliance, the percentage of SLA fulfilled successfully, and the average energy invested per fulfilled SLA.

And the last one is focused on application performance, namely, the average number of frames successfully processed per unit of time (fps).

Table 1 shows energy consumed by the system. Results show that the HJF and EDF metrics reduce the energy-to-solution for all the type of bags of tasks with respect to the RND baseline algorithm.

Table 1: Energy (KJoules) for different scheduling criteria.

% HR request	FPGA assignation criteria		
	RND	EDF	HJF
10%	648	638	614
25%	653	638	616
50%	657	639	634

Hence, from these results we can point out that the FPGA-aware Node Level Scheduler should use a QoS-aware metric.

Nevertheless, before getting a clue time an energy-to-solution should be analyzed together with the number of SLAs fulfilled. Table 2 shows the percentage of fulfilled SLAs for the different scheduling techniques. Results show that HJF gets more fulfilled SLA for all the input workloads.

Table 2: Percentage of fulfilled SLAs for different scheduling criteria.

% HR requests	FPGA assignation criteria		
	RND	EDF	HJF
10%	85%	85%	90%
25%	75%	80%	85%
50%	60%	65%	70%

Figure 7 shows the cost per SLA measured as the energy consumed. In all the cases, the cost per SLA increases with the percentage of high requirements. These result from the fact that some unlucky scheduling decisions can affect in a quite negative way the future tasks. The allocation of the FPGA to the most demanding task will change the state of the FPGA to nonfree for a period of time. Then, if the physical node receives a quite demanding task over this period of time, as no preemption of task is possible, the new request only can run in CPU resources. This can lead to a nonfulfilled SLA. Finally, regarding the performance as is shown in Figure 8the amount of frames per second keeps an acceptable level even when more demanding requests are processed. So, in the next section we will evaluate our solution (fine-grained scheduling see Section 6) to address this problem.

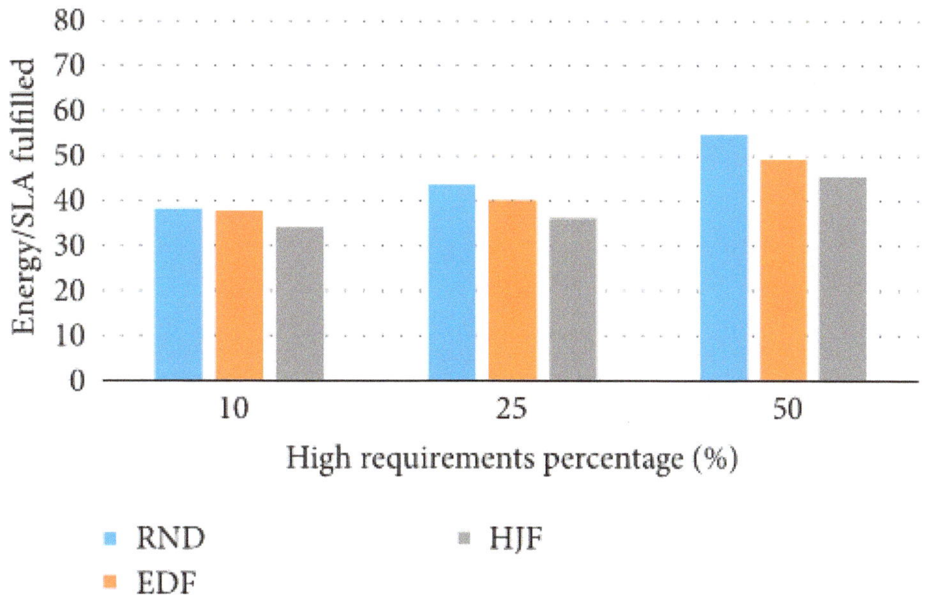

Figure 7: Energy (KJoules) per number of fulfilled SLAs.

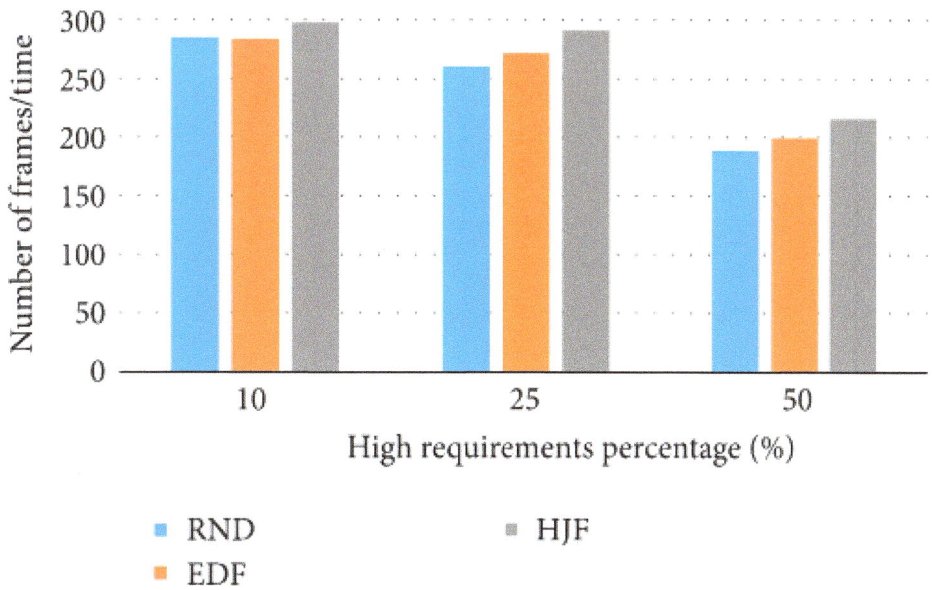

Figure 8: Number of successfully processed frames per second.

Evaluation for Fine-Grained Scheduling

In this section the fine-grained scheduling strategy proposed in Section 6 will be evaluated. Evaluation conditions are the same as detailed in Section 7. Recall that now the task is subdivided into chunks and the FPGA assignation mechanism is job-aware.

Table 3 shows that the energy tends to rise with the percentage of high requirements requests (these metrics present the same behavior as in previous evaluation). However, the energy per SLA fulfilled decreases 35% for the HJF scheduling strategy in comparison with the other strategies (RND, EDF) (see Figure 9). Results also show that the energy relative to the number of fulfilled SLAs tends to decrease which means a save of effective energy. Thus, the combination of both an FPGA as an accelerator and an efficient scheduling strategy allows the system to save energy. The reason is the system's selection of the most suitable resources for each request and the speedup of the FPGA with lower energy impact. On the other hand, the percentage of fulfilled SLAs (see Table 4) shows a slightly upward trend (20%) for the HJF scheduling with 50% of high requirements. What it means is that the system is able to keep an acceptable ratio of SLA fulfilled.

Table 3: Energy (KJoules) for different scheduling criteria (fine-grained).

% HR requests	FPGA assignation criteria		
	RND	EDF	HJF
10%	686	665	626
25%	694	699	646
50%	774	772	696

Table 4: Percentage of SLAs fulfilled for different FPGA assignation criteria (fine-grained).

% HR requests	FPGA assignation criteria		
	RND	EDF	HJF
10%	90%	95%	95%
25%	80%	80%	85%
50%	55%	70%	75%

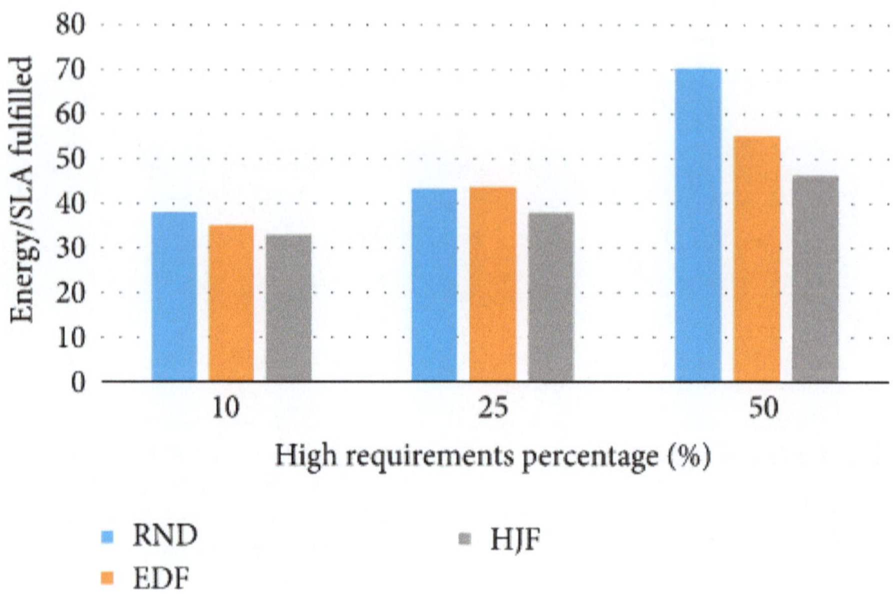

Figure 9: Energy (KJoules) per number of fulfilled SLAs (fine-grained).

Figure 10 shows the performance of the system in terms of the number of processed frames per second. The use of the proposed HJF strategy clearly outperforms the RND and obtains similar results to the EDF. However, as shown before, this is achieved with a lower energy consumption for the HJF metric.

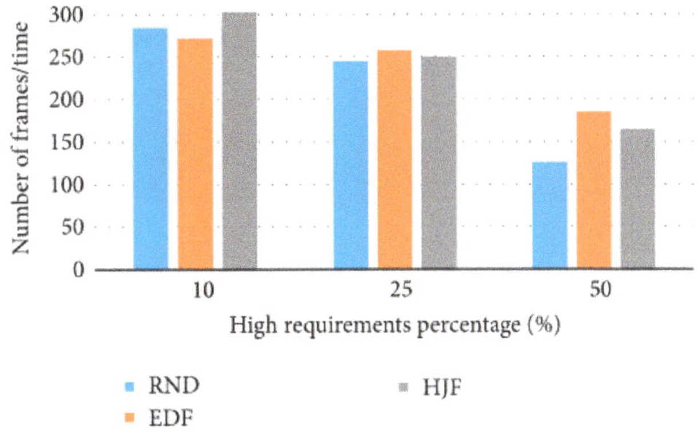

Figure 10: Number of successfully processed frames per second (fine-grained).

Fine-Grained Scheduling Optimization

The last strategy presented above raises the following concern: when we check with a certain frequency which VM needs most the FPGA in order to fulfill its requirements, why not to check also if the deadline is past? In case the deadline of the task had arrived, the VM would be killed. In this way, no task keeps running after its deadline, savings on energy.

When a SLA is violated, apart from penalties, some amount of energy is wasted because the system uses the resources to run a task that will not successfully end before its deadline. The system behavior shows that keeping VMs alive has a direct effect on the total energy and number of SLA fulfilled. Now, an optimized scheduling, where VMs running a request whose SLA has been violated are killed, is analyzed.

In this scenario, even though the scheduling and communication issues are the same as before, energy consumption for all the FPGA assignation strategies is reduced as shown in Table 5.

Table 5: Energy (KJoules) for different scheduling criteria (optimized fine-grained).

% HR requests	FPGA assignation criteria		
	RND	EDF	HJF
10%	678	649	597
25%	638	619	611
50%	637	563	586

On the other hand, if we consider the effective energy per fulfilled SLA, 40% of consumed energy is saved (see Figure 11). In addition, the percentage of successfully fulfilled SLAs is 15% better for HJF (see Table 6). Finally, Figure 12 shows an increase of 20% of frames per second for HJF in the most demanding scenario (50% of high requirements).

Table 6: Percentage of SLAs fulfilled for different FPGA assignation criteria (optimized fine-grained).

% HR requests	FPGA assignation criteria		
	RND	EDF	HJF
10%	90%	95%	100%
25%	80%	85%	90%
50%	65%	70%	85%

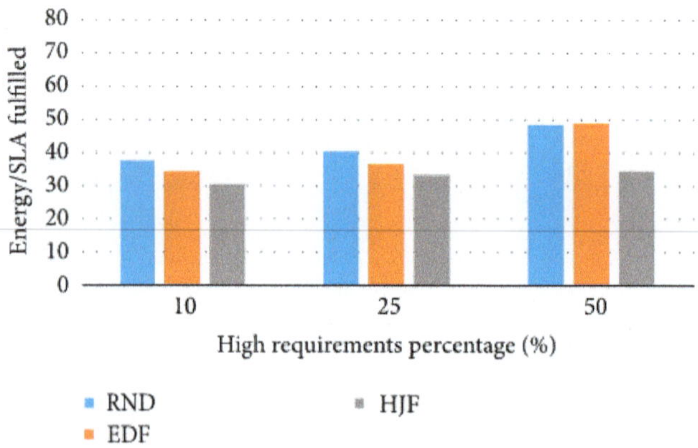

Figure 11: Energy (KJoules) per number of SLAs fulfilled (optimized fine-grained).

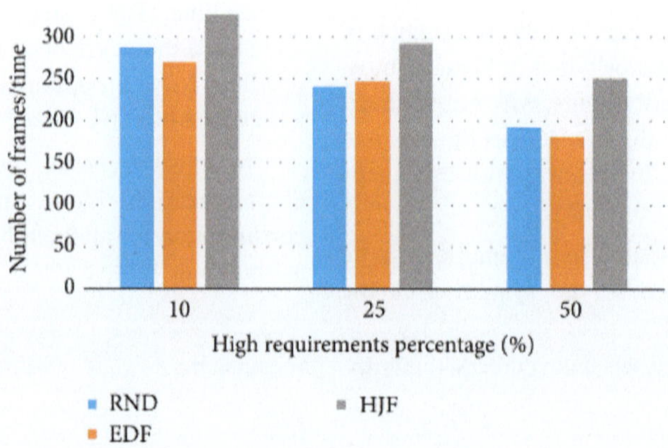

Figure 12: Number of successfully processed frames per second (optimized fine-grained).

To sum up, releasing the resources involved in the execution of a task when its deadline is due improves the percentage of fulfilled SLAs and increases the performance of the cloud system while reducing the energy waste. A comparison summary of the node level scheduling impact is presented in Table 7.

Table 7: Summary of tests.

% of high requirements	Scheduling strategy	FPGA assignation criteria	% of fulfilled SLAs	Energy/fulfilled SLA	Frames processed per second
10%	Coarse-grained	RND	85	38	285
		EDF	85	37	283
		HJF	90	34	300
	Fine-grained	RND	90	38	284
		EDF	95	35	271
		HJF	95	32	302
	Optimized fine-grained	RND	90	37	286
		EDF	95	34	268
		HJF	*100*	*30*	*326*
25%	Coarse-grained	RND	75	43	260
		EDF	80	39	271
		HJF	85	36	291
	Fine-grained	RND	80	43	244
		EDF	80	43	257
		HJF	85	38	249
	Optimized fine-grained	RND	80	48	240
		EDF	85	48	245
		HJF	*90*	*34*	*292*
50%	Coarse-grained	RND	60	54	188
		EDF	65	49	198
		HJF	70	45	215
	Fine-grained	RND	55	70	126
		EDF	70	55	184
		HJF	75	46	164
	Optimized fine-grained	RND	65	48	192
		EDF	70	48	180
		HJF	*85*	*34*	*250*

Figure 13 shows the number of frames unsuccessfully processed due to the SLA violation occurring. However, the number of frames unsuccessfully processed decreases significantly for the optimized fine-grained strategy because it allows taking advantage of killing the VMs when their deadline is achieved.

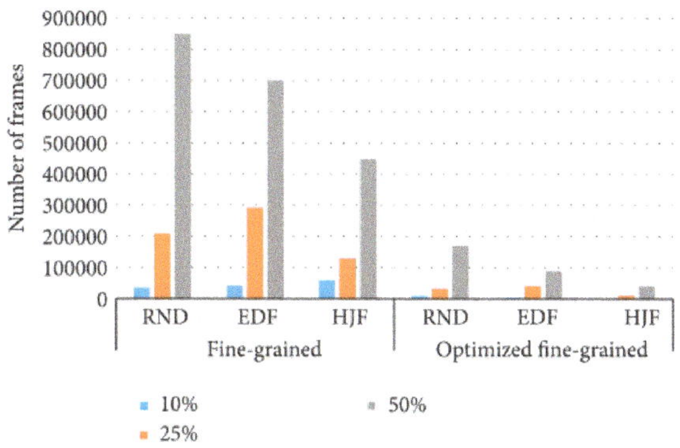

Figure 13: Number of processed frames belonging to unsuccessful SLAs (wasted).

Evaluation Summary

Table 7 summarizes the different results when applying the different FPGA assignation strategies and scheduling techniques. It can be seen that for all the cases, the proposed HJF policy obtains the best performance, in terms of SLA fulfillment and energy consumption. Moreover, the configuration that yields the best results is combining HJF policy with the optimized fine-grained assignation strategy. Recall that for "fulfilled SLAs" and "Frames processed per second," the greater is better, while for "Energy/fulfilled SLA" the lower is better.

CONCLUSIONS AND FUTURE WORK

We have presented a hierarchical scheduler framework to manage heterogeneous resources within a SaaS cloud environment. This framework is responsible for selecting on-demand the most suitable resources for a service while keeping a balance between performance and power consumption. The key of the framework is to maximize the number of fulfilled SLAs saving energy by making efficient use of FPGA devices. Thus, we have proposed a novel dynamic scheduling metric which considers a combination of the workload of a task, its remaining time to complete the task, and the deadline. In addition, a fine-grained accelerator-aware scheduling has been developed and improved by releasing the resources associated with a task as soon as the system realizes its SLA is not going to be fulfilled.

The proposed techniques have been compared with some well-known scheduling strategies such as Earliest-Deadline-First and Random. Experiments carried out over a real testbed indicate that the proposed metric together with the optimized fine-grained scheduling strategy increases the performance of the system even when more demanding requirements are involved. Moreover, these techniques save 23% of the total energy while the percentage of fulfilled SLAs is 85% under the most demanding workload conditions. This can be explained by the fact that FPGAs (as a accelerators) have a great ratio performance/power consumption for certain type of applications. Thus, a proper use of these devices can be turned into benefits for clients and providers.

The efficiency of this approach can be further improved by using more sophisticated strategies such as machine learning algorithms. Also, as a future work we will include the memory and network metrics as variables to optimize the use of the computational resources.

Competing Interests

The authors declare that there are no competing interests regarding the publication of this paper.

ACKNOWLEDGMENTS

This work was supported by the Spanish Government under Grant TIN2015-66972-C5-2-R (MINECO/FEDER) and by Ecuadorian Government under the SENESCYT Scholarships Project.

REFERENCES

1. J. P. Orellana, M. B. Caminero, and C. Carrión, "On the provision of SaaS-level quality of service within heterogeneous private clouds," in Proceedings of the 7th IEEE/ACM International Conference on Utility and Cloud Computing (UCC '14), pp. 146–155, IEEE, London, UK, December 2014.
2. J. Proaño, C. Carrión, and B. Caminero, "Towards a green, QoS-enabled heterogeneous cloud infrastructure," in Proceedings of the 25th Heterogeneity in Computing Workshop in Conjunction with International Parallel and Distributed Processing Symposium (HCW-IPDPS ‹16), IEEE, Chicago, Ill, USA, May 2016.
3. PANACEA: Proactive autonomic management of cloud resources, 2016, http://www.panacea-cloud.eu/.
4. Microsoft Research: Cloud Security & Cryptography, April 2016, http://research.microsoft.com/en-us/projects/cryptocloud/.
5. The Cloud Standards Wiki, http://cloud-standards.org/.
6. R. Ranjan, B. Benatallah, S. Dustdar, and M. P. Papazoglou, "Cloud resource orchestration programming: overview, issues, and directions," IEEE Internet Computing, vol. 19, no. 5, pp. 46–56, 2015.
7. Q. Zhang and W. Shi, "Energy-efficient workload placement in enterprise datacenters," Computer, vol. 49, no. 2, pp. 46–52, 2016.
8. T. Guérout, T. Monteil, G. Da Costa, R. Neves Calheiros, R. Buyya, and M. Alexandru, "Energy-aware simulation with DVFS," Simulation Modelling Practice and Theory, vol. 39, pp. 76–91, 2013.
9. Open Compute Project, http://www.opencompute.org/.
10. R. Buyya, C. Vecchiola, and S. T. Selvi, Mastering Cloud Computing: Foundations and Applications Programming, Morgan Kaufmann, 1st edition, 2013.
11. F. Chen, Y. Shan, Y. Zhang et al., "Enabling fpgas in the cloud," in Proceedings of the 11th ACM International Conference on Computing Frontiers (CF ‹14), Cagliari, Italy, May 2014.

12. T. Trader, EU Projects Unite on Heterogeneous ARM-Based Exascale Prototype, 2016, http://www.hpcwire.com/2016/02/24/eu-projects-unite-exascale-prototype.

13. A. Putnam, A. M. Caulfield, E. S. Chung et al., "A reconfigurable fabric for accelerating large-scale datacenter services," in Proceedings of the ACM/IEEE 41st International Symposium on Computer Architecture (ISCA ‹14), pp. 13–24, IEEE, Minneapolis, Minn, USA, June 2014.

14. C. Augonnet, S. Thibault, R. Namyst, and P.-A. Wacrenier, "StarPU: A unified platform for task scheduling on heterogeneous multicore architectures," Concurrency Computation Practice and Experience, vol. 23, no. 2, pp. 187–198, 2011.

15. OpenCL, The Open Standard for Parallel Programming of Heterogeneous Systems, April 2016, http://www.khronos.org/opencl/.

16. Vivado, Vivado Design Suite, April 2016, http://www.xilinx.com/products/design-tools/vivado/.

17. J. Auerbach, D. F. Bacon, P. Cheng, and R. Rabbah, "Lime: a java-compatible and synthesizable language for heterogeneous architectures," in Proceedings of the ACM International Conference on Object Oriented Programming Systems Languages and Applications (OOPSLA ‹10), pp. 89–108, Reno, Nev, USA, 2010.

18. M. Jacobsen and R. Kastner, "RIFFA 2.0: a reusable integration framework for FPGA accelerators," inProceedings of the 23rd International Conference on Field Programmable Logic and Applications (FPL ‹13), pp. 1–8, IEEE, Porto, Portugal, September 2013.

19. K. Vipin and S. A. Fahmy, "DyRACT: a partial reconfiguration enabled accelerator and test platform," inProceedings of the 24th International Conference on Field Programmable Logic and Applications (FPL ‹14), pp. 1–7, IEEE, Munich, Germany, September 2014.

20. C.-W. Tsai and J. J. P. C. Rodrigues, "Metaheuristic scheduling for cloud: a survey," IEEE Systems Journal, vol. 8, no. 1, pp. 279–291, 2014.

21. S. Byma, J. G. Steffan, H. Bannazadeh, A. Leon-Garcia, and P. Chow, "FPGAs in the cloud: booting virtualized hardware accelerators with OpenStack," in Proceedings of the 22nd IEEE International Symposium on Field-Programmable Custom Computing Machines (FCCM ‹14), pp. 109–116, Boston, Mass, USA, May 2014.

22. OpenStack, Open source software for building private and public clouds, April 2016, https://www.openstack.org/.

23. S. A. Fahmy, K. Vipin, and S. Shreejith, "Virtualized FPGA accelerators for efficient cloud computing," inProceedings of the IEEE 7th International Conference on Cloud Computing Technology and Science (CloudCom ‹15), pp. 430–435, Vancouver, Canada, November 2015.

24. Intel, Intel Virtualization Technology of Directed I/O, Architecture Specification, Rev. 2.2, 2014, http://www.intel.com/content/www/us/en/embedded/technology/virtualization/vt-directed-io-spec.html.

25. D. Crockford, "The application/JSON media type for JavaScript object notation (JSON)," 2006.

26. KVM, Kernel Based Virtual Machine (KVM), 2008, http://www.linux-kvm.org/.

27. WeidongHan, How to assign devices with vt-d in kvm, 2009, http://www.linux-kvm.org/index.php?title=How_to_assign_devices_with_VT-d_in_KVM&action=info.

28. R. M. Love, Taskset, 2004, http://linux.die.net/man/1/taskset.

29. Xilinx ML605, Virtex-6 FPGA ML605 Evaluation Kit, March 2016, http://www.xilinx.com/publications/prod_mktg/ml605_product_brief.pdf.

30. PowerMeterStore, Power Meter Store, March 2016, http://www.powermeterstore.com/p1206/watts_up_pro.php.

31. R. da Rosa Righi, C. A. da Costa, V. F. Rodrigues, and G. Rostirolla, "Joint-analysis of performance and energy consumption when enabling cloud elasticity for synchronous HPC applications," Concurrency and Computation: Practice and Experience, vol. 28, no. 5, pp. 1548–1571, 2016.

CHAPTER 13

AN IMPROVED PARTICLE SWARM OPTIMIZATION ALGORITHM USED FOR BP NEURAL NETWORK AND MULTIMEDIA COURSE-WARE EVALUATION

Tianhua Liu, and Shoulin Yin

Keywords: BP neural network PSO Adaptive acceleration factor Adaptive inertia weight Multimedia evaluation model

INTRODUCTION

Chaos phenomenon is a random phenomenon in a certain system. Modeling, prediction and control of chaotic system has become a hot topic. The state of chaos system builds the model of chaos. Its methods include global prediction, locality predication and adaptive prediction. Neural network is an effective tool for approximation and modeling of nonlinear system. It not only achieves global prediction, but realizes the local prediction. Many researchers have studied the model of chaos using neural network [5, 6, 12].

Wang et al. [10] employed linear matrix inequality and particle swarm optimization based on cellular neural networks. Among these templates obtained by using linear matrix inequality, it utilized the PSO to carry out the optimization parameters. (Jiang et al., 2014) represented that fault diagnosis based on fuzzy neural network and chaos theory could solve uncertain problem essentially, moreover, it was easy to understand and the system features was easy to maintain. Therefore, it was an effective method to diagnose complex system. Wang et al. [10] proposed a hybrid method comprising a chaos synchronization (CS)-based detection scheme and an extension neural network classification algorithm for power quality monitoring and analysis. The new method could detect minor changes in signals of the power systems. Chatzinakos et al. [1] proposed that a member of a time series could be optimally expressed as a deterministic function of the d past series values, where d is the dimension of the system. A new algorithm was for the estimation of the dimension of chaotic dynamical systems using neural networks and robust location estimate. Therefore, this article uses the BP neural network prediction model which has strong of ability of nonlinear fitting. But this model has the slow convergence speed and low prediction accuracy.

PSO is an effective global optimization algorithm which generates swarm intelligence optimization search by cooperation and competition between particles in the group. So we adopt PSO algorithm to optimize BP neural network. The algorithm divides particles into two parts according to the fitness value. Fitness value can measure the particles mass. By comparing the fitness value of individual particle and average fitness value of particle group, it can distinguishes the merits of particle mass. Also it reasonably adjusts the global searching ability and self-learning ability, social learning ability which is conducive to the rapid convergence of particle swarm. Using particle swarm algorithm optimizes initial weight and threshold of BP neural network. We can get better initial weight and threshold and pass it to the BP neural network. BP neural network will train and predict it. First, PSO uses improved adaptive acceleration factor and improved adaptive inertia weight to improve the initial weight value and threshold value of BP neural network. Second, This paper's new algorithm uses improved PSO to optimize BP neural network's initial weight value and threshold value. Finally, we conduct experiments to verify its feasibility. The follows are the structures of this paper. Section 2 is some basic knowledge about BP neural network and phase-space reconstruction. Section3 is multimedia course-ware evaluation model based

Citation: Tianhua Liu, Shoulin Yin, An improved particle swarm optimization algorithm used for BP neural network and multimedia course-ware evaluation, DOI: 10.1007/s11042-016-3776-5.

on BP neural network. Section 4 introduces the PSO algorithm. Section 5 represents the improved scheme. Section 6 makes simulation and analysis. The conclusions are drawn in section 7.

BP NEURAL NETWORK AND PHASE-SPACE RECONSTRUCTION

Phase-space reconstruction [3, 9] is foundation of chaos theory. Setting X is the observed chaotic time series. x(t), t = 1,2,3……n. Based on Takens theory, it conducts phase-space reconstruction. In the state space, after reconstructing the state vector can be shown as:

$$X_i\left(x_i, x_{i+\omega}, \ldots\ldots, x_{i+(m-1)\omega}\right)^T, i = 1, 2, 3\ldots\ldots M$$

$M = n-(m-1)\omega$ is the number of phase point in phase space. ω is delay time. m is the number of embedded dimension. Takens found a suitable m, $m \geq 2d+1$, d is the dimensions of the power system, which can recover attractor. In the reconstruction space R^m, prime mover system maintain differential homeomorphism, thus it lays a solid theoretical basis for the prediction of chaotic time series.

In essence, prediction of chaotic time series is a reverse problem, it re-factors dynamic model of system through the state of dynamic system. The BP neural network [2, 13] has strong ability of nonlinear fitting, which is a good method to construct chaotic time series nonlinear prediction model. Typical three layer BP neural network is composed of input layer, hidden layer and output layer. Its main principle is that BP neural network transmits error and rectifies the error at the same time to adjust the weights and threshold of network and realize or approximate the input and output mapping relationship. Using three layers BP neural network to predict chaotic time series, the number of input layer neurons can select m which is equal to embedded dimension. The number of hidden layer neurons mostly relies on experience to choose, here it isp. Output layer neuron number is 1. and $f. R^m \rightarrow R^1$. The function of BP neural network is Sigmoid, its output is linear unit.

The input of hidden layer nodes is:

$$S_j = \sum_{i=1}^{m} w_{ij}x_i - \theta_j, j = 1, 2, \ldots\ldots, p$$

Where x_i state vector. w_{ij} is connecting weight between input layer and hidden layer. θ_j is threshold of hidden layer nodes.

The output of hidden layer nodes is:

$$b_j = \frac{1}{1 + e^{\theta_j - \sum_{i=1}^{m} w_{ij}x_i + \theta_j}}, j = 1, 2, \ldots\ldots, p$$

The input of output layer nodes is:

$$L = \sum_{j=1}^{p} v_j b_j - \gamma$$

Where v_j is connecting weight between output layer and hidden layer. γ is threshold of output layer nodes.

The output of output layer nodes is:

$$x_{i+1} = \frac{1}{1 + e^{\gamma - \sum_{j=1}^{p} v_j b_i}}$$

Inputting the chaos time series and training the BP neural network, it will get trained network, and then makes predictions. Before starting work, however, each layer connection weights and threshold values of the BP neural network are randomly initialized, which can reduce the convergence speed and accuracy of BP neural network and makes it easy to fall into local minimum value. Using PSO algorithm can optimize the initial weights and thresholds, the optimized initial weights and thresholds ensure that the BP neural network has better convergence speed and higher prediction precision. BP neural network structure is as Fig. 1.

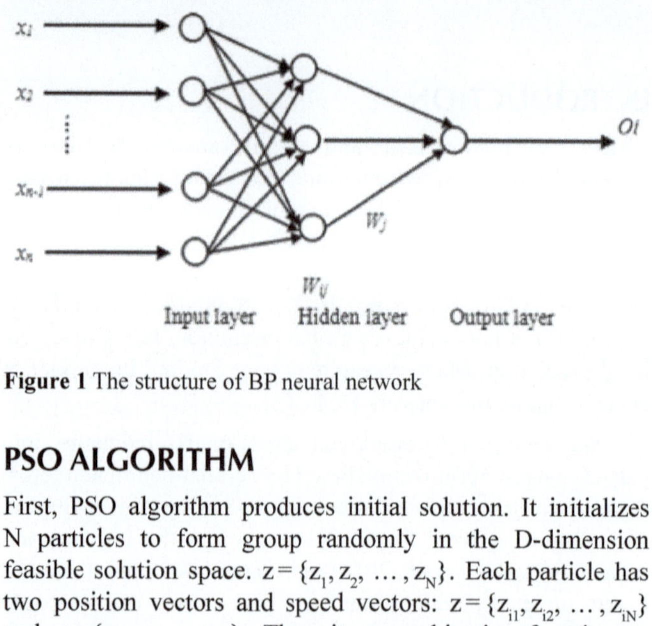

Figure 1 The structure of BP neural network

PSO ALGORITHM

First, PSO algorithm produces initial solution. It initializes N particles to form group randomly in the D-dimension feasible solution space. $z = \{z_1, z_2, \ldots, z_N\}$. Each particle has two position vectors and speed vectors: $z = \{z_{i1}, z_{i2}, \ldots, z_{iN}\}$ and $v = \{v_{i1}, v_{i2}, \ldots v_{iN}\}$. Then it uses objective function to calculate fitness value of particles and iteratively searches in the S-dimension solution space. When iterating algorithm, particle will track two extreme value (one is the best solution p_{id} searched by particle itself , one is the best solution p_{gd} searched by group) to update itself. Every particle updates its speed and position by the following:

$$v_{id}(t+1) = \eta v_{id}(t) + a_1 r_1 \left[p_{id} - z_{id}(t)\right] + a_2 r_2 \left[p_{gd} - z_{id}(t)\right] \tag{1}$$

$$z_{id}(t+1) = z_{id}(t) + v_{id}(t+1) \tag{2}$$

Where η is weight. a_1 and a_2 are acceleration constant. $0 \leq r_1, r_2 \leq 1$ are random number. $v_{id}(t+1)$ is i-th particle's d-dimension speed in the t + 1-th iteration.

Linear descend inertia weight η is:

$$\eta = \eta_{\max} - \frac{\eta_{\max} - \eta_{\min}}{iter_{\max}} \times \text{iter} \tag{3}$$

Where iter is current iteration's number. $iter_{max}$ is maximum iteration's number. η_{max} is initial inertia weight value. η_{min} is final inertia weight value.

η changing completely dependents on the iter and $iter_{max}$. In later iterations, its convergence rate is slow. It is difficult to jump out of local optimal solution. Since the particles are based on their own experience and the experience of all the particles in the optimal solution direction, under the larger study factor, particle is likely to miss the optimal solution, so that the convergence is slow. In addition, when the algorithm starts convergence, all the particles search solution in the direction of optimal solution. Particles in the group tend to accordance and lose the diversity of solution which reduces the convergence speed and accuracy of algorithm.

MULTIMEDIA COURSE-WARE EVALUATION MODEL BASED ON BP NEURAL NETWORK

Multimedia course-ware is a huge nonlinear system, the relation of influence factors is very complex. Course-ware evaluation, however, is based on a large number of "experience" of original data, so BP network can better meet the needs of evaluation and represent the intrinsic essence of the course-ware. The following will introduce the process of evaluating.

When evaluating the quality of multimedia course-ware, the qualitative index information will be quantitatively conducted and transformed into input vector of neural network $T=\{t_1, t_2, \ldots, t_n\}$. Comprehensive evaluation value obtained by expert will be conducted Fuzzy processing and it will get Y={μS1,μS2,...,μSn} Y={μS1,μS2,...,μSn} as the output of neural network. Then it uses enough sample set to train network, through repeated iteration, gets stable training results. At this time, weight value W_{ij} and threshold θ is the correct expression through adaptive learning. And the training results will regarded as knowledge base to evaluate the multimedia course-ware.

- Step1. Determining learning parameters. Supposing expected minimum error value is err_{goal}, maximum iteration is max_{epoch}. Learning rate of amending the weight is lr ranging from 0.01 to 0.7.
- Step2. Network initialization. Using smaller random number initializes the network weights W_{ij} and V_{jk}, threshold value θ_j and r_k.
- Step3. Inputting training set. Supposing input vector of k samples is $t^k=(T^k_1,T^k_2,\ldots,T^k_n)^T$ and output vector of expected value is $y^k=(Y^k_1,Y^k_2,\ldots,Y^k_n)^T$.
- Step4. Calculating network output of each layer. Using $t^k=(T^k_1,T^k_2,\ldots,T^k_n)^T$ W_{ij} and θ_j calculates each neuron of middle layer input $U_j = \sum_{i=1}^{n} W_{ij} t_i + \theta_j$. Then it adopts activation function $f(x)=1/(1+e^{-x})$ to calculate the real output ($H_j=f(U_j)$) of each neuron in middle layer. And it will compute the input value $S_k = \sum_{j=1}^{p} V_{jk} H_j + r_k$ (p is node number of hidden layers) in the output layer and the corresponding output values $O_k=f(S_k)$.
- Step5. Calculating training error. It calculates the error of output layer weights $\delta_k=(O_k-y_k)\cdot(1-O_k)\cdot O_k$ and the error of middle layer weights $\sigma_j = H_j \cdot (1-H_j) \cdot \sum_{k=1}^{q} \delta_k V_{jk}$ (q is output layer node number).
- Step6. Correcting weights and thresholds of output layer and hidden layer. a is weight adjustment parameters, $0<a<1$; η is learning coefficient, $0<\eta<1$.
- $V_{jk}=V_{jk}+a\delta_k H_j$, $r_k=r_k+a\delta_k$, $W_{ji}=W_{ji}+\eta\sigma_j t_i$, $\theta_j=\theta_j+\eta\sigma_j$
- Step7. Entering the next learning mode. Return step3 to iterate. Until the error is less than the set minimum error value err_{goal} or leaning number is more than max_{epoch}, the training stops. And evaluation model is built.

IMPROVED PSO ALGORITHM

Improved PSO based on chaos

Chaotic time series has randomness, ergodicity and regularity. Tang et al. [8] combines particle swarm optimization algorithm with chaos and multi-agent system, it is applied to reactive power optimization of power system. It synthesizes advantages of the swarm search of PSO and the intelligent search of agents. She et al. [7] represents that dynamic chaos particle swarm optimization is the improvement of the standard PSO algorithm, is used to optimize the multi-objective optimized mathematical model of elevator configuration. So this paper proposes a new PSO algorithm based on chaos. In this scheme, it uses adaptive control particle's search capability ω and learning ability c_1, c_2 to jump out of local optimum. Algorithm adopts typical Logistic chaotic time series.

$$x_{i+1} = \mu x_i(1-x_i),\ \mu = 4 \tag{4}$$

The algorithm divides particles into two parts according to the fitness value. Fitness value can measure the particles mass. By comparing the fitness value of individual particle and average fitness value of particle group, it can distinguishes the merits of particle mass. Also it reasonably adjusts the ω and c_1, c_2 which is conducive to the rapid convergence of particle swarm.

$$\begin{cases} \omega = \omega_0 + k_1 \cdot \mu \cdot x(1-x) \\ c = c_{10} - k_2 \cdot \mu \cdot x(1-x), f > f_{avg} \\ c_2 = c_{20} + k_3 \cdot \mu \cdot x(1-x) \end{cases} \tag{5}$$

$$\begin{cases} \omega = \omega_0 + k_1 \cdot \mu \cdot x(1-x) \\ c = c_{10} - k_2 \cdot \mu \cdot x(1-x), f > f_{avg} \\ c_2 = c_{20} + k_3 \cdot \mu \cdot x(1-x) \end{cases} \tag{6}$$

Where $0<\omega_0<1$, $1<c_{10}<2$, $1<c_{20}<2$, $0<k_1,k_2,k_3<1$ $\mu=4$. $0<x<1$, f is i-th particle's fitness value. f_{avg} is all particles' average fitness value.

When $f>f_{avg}$, particle's quality is poor. Equation (5) reduces self-learning ability c_1 by enhancing global searching ability ω and social learning ability c_2. So the particle's quality will be improved. When $f<f_{avg}$, particle's quality is better. Equation (6) reduces social learning ability $c_2$by enhancing global searching ability$\omega$and self-learning ability c_1. So it will protect particles with better quality and solution diversity.

Improved PSO for BP neural network

Using particle swarm algorithm optimizes initial weight and threshold of BP neural network. We can get better initial weight and threshold and pass it to the BP neural network. BP neural network will train and predict it. The detailed processes are as following:

- Step1. Initializing particle swarm parameters, population size, iteration number, learning factor, range of speed and position.
- Step2. Building the topological structure of BP neural network, generating particle swarm and initializing the particle's position and speed randomly.

$$z_i = \{z_{i1}, z_{i2}, \cdots, z_{is}\}, v_i = \{z_{i1}, z_{i2}, \cdots, z_{is}\}, i = 1, 2 \cdots s = R \times s_1 + s + s_2 \tag{7}$$

Where s is dimension of the particle, R is input layer node number. s_1 is hidden layer node number. s_2 is output layer node number.

- Step3. Calculating fitness value of particle, the fitness value of i-th particle is:

$$f(i) = \sum_{i=1}^{n} \left(y_k - y_k\right)^2, i = 1, 2, \ldots, N \tag{8}$$

Where n is training sample number, N is population size.

We calculate fitness value of each particle and set the current position as the optimal positionp_{id}, set the optimal particle in the population as the global optimal position p_{gd}.

- Step4. Using [4, 11] to update ω, c_1, c_2 and [5, 12] to update position and speed of particle. After the above process, we calculate the fitness value of new particle. Then we update the individual extremum and group extremum according to the fitness value.
- Step5. When the iteration number is less than maximum iteration number, return to step4, otherwise exit the particle optimization algorithm. We get the optimal particle and pass it to the connection weight and threshold of BP neural network.

SIMULATION EXPERIMENTS AND ANALYSIS

Example1

Under the MATLAB platform, we make experiments to compare improved PSO and PSO. We select 800 data to analysis (for the reason that at 400 s, it changes movement direction, we re-record its values at 401 s). In the simulation experiments, we suppose that prediction performance index is error e, root mean square error E_{rmse} and relative error err, y is target value, y^y^is prediction value.

$$e = y_k - y_k \tag{9}$$

$$E_{rmse} = \left(\frac{1}{N}\sum_{k=1}^{N} \left(y_k - y_k\right)^2\right)^{1/2} \tag{10}$$

$$err = \left[\sum_{i=1}^{N} \left(y_i - y_i\right)^2\right] / \left[\sum_{i=1}^{N} y_1^2\right] \tag{11}$$

For the traditional PSO, we set the training number 800, learning rate 0.01, population size 30, evolutional generation 100, accelerated factor $c_1=c_2=2$. The range of position and speed is [−5,5] and [−1,1] respectively.

For the improved PSO, we set training number 800, learning rate 0.01, population size 30, evolutional generation 100, $c_{10}=c_{20}=1.6$, $k_1=0.3$, $k_2=k_3=0.5$. Range of inertia weight and accelerating factor is [0.2,0.9] and [1.2,2.4] respectively. Range of particle position and speed is [−5,5] and [−1,1] respectively. We use these data to make experiments and get Figs. 2 and 3.

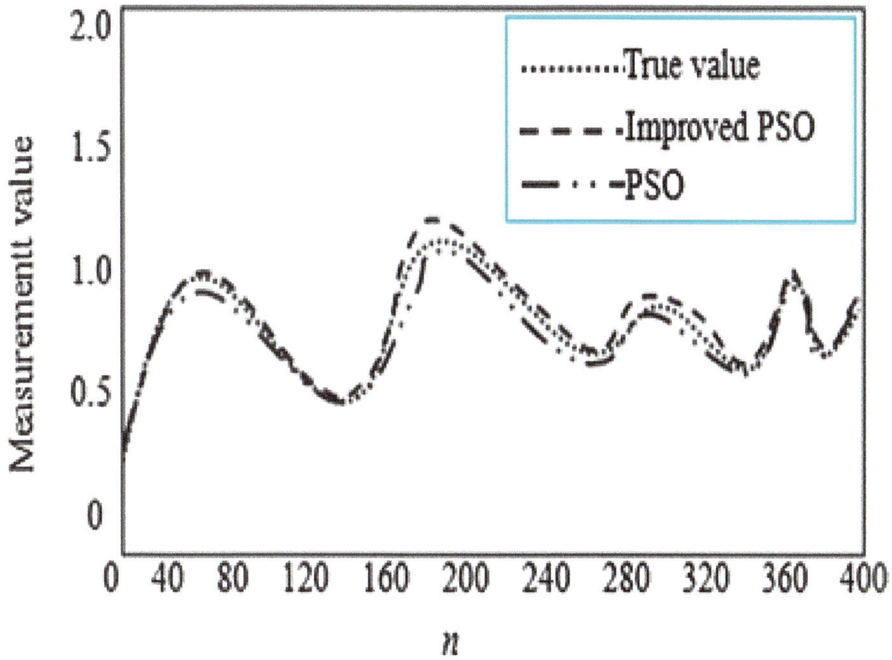

Figure 2 Measurement value n ≤ 400

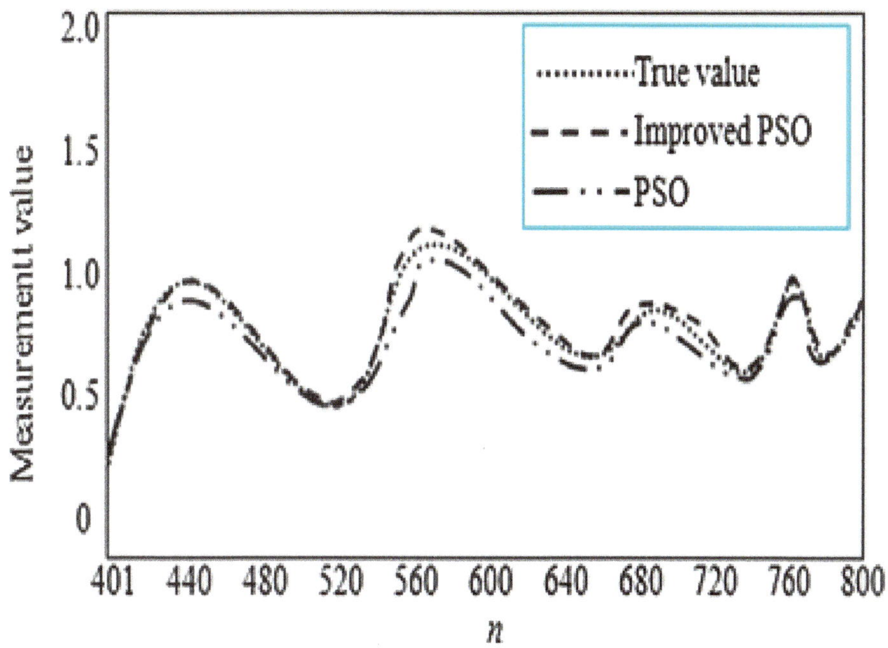

Figure 3 Measurement value 400 ≤ n ≤ 800

From Figs. 2 and 3, we can know that the improved PSO is much closer to the true value. We select the same experiments parameter. The convergence speed of improved PSO is faster than PSO algorithm.

Figs. 4 and 5 are the prediction error. The error of improved PSO is small than PSO algorithm. The smaller the fitness value is, the better the quality of the particles is (as Figs. 6 and 7). The initial weight and threshold are more conducive to the BP neural network training. BP neural network has fast convergence with good initial weight and threshold. It will improve the prediction accuracy and reduce the BP neural network to fall into a minimal value. From the above results, we can conclude that improved PSO is conducive to globally optimized solution.

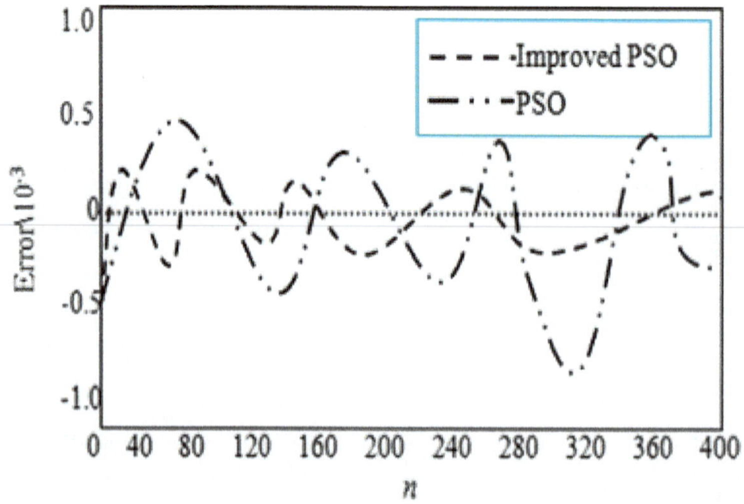

Figure 4 Error n ≤ 400

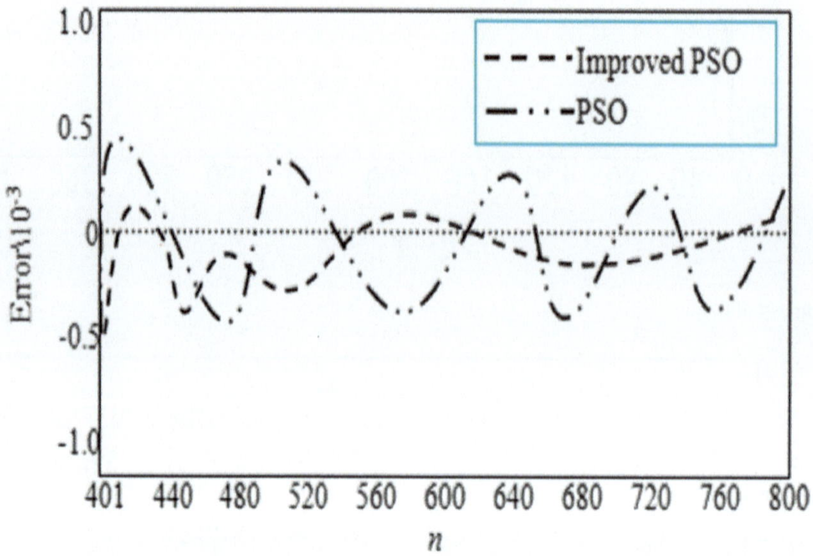

Figure 5 Error 400 ≤ n ≤ 800

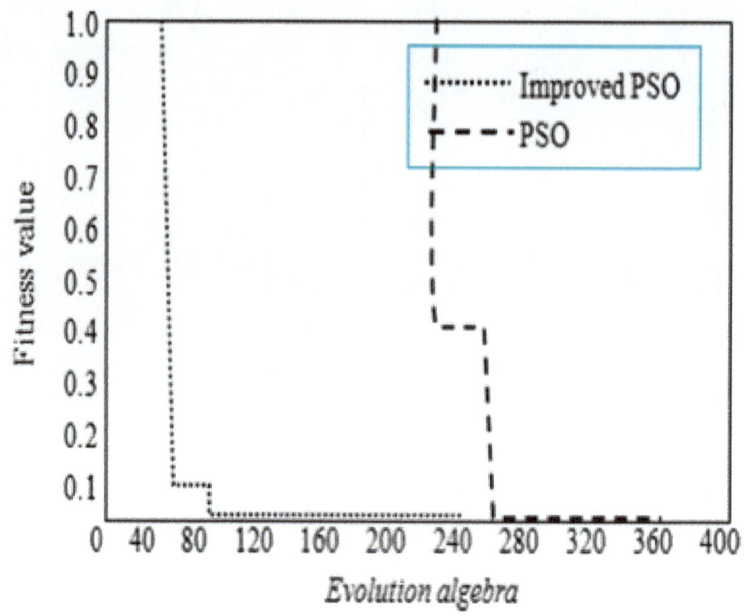

Figure 6 Fitness value n ≤ 400

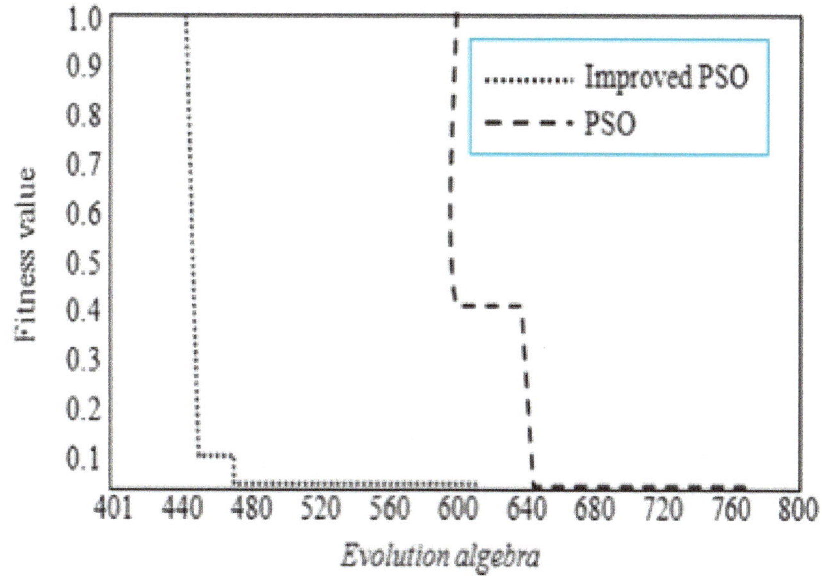

Figure 7 Fitness value 400 ≤ n ≤ 800

Also we use PSO and improved PSO to predict chaotic system (Lorenz) at the same condition of physical. We get figs. 8 and 9. From this two figures, we can obtain that improved PSO are very precise prediction and has low error than PSO method.

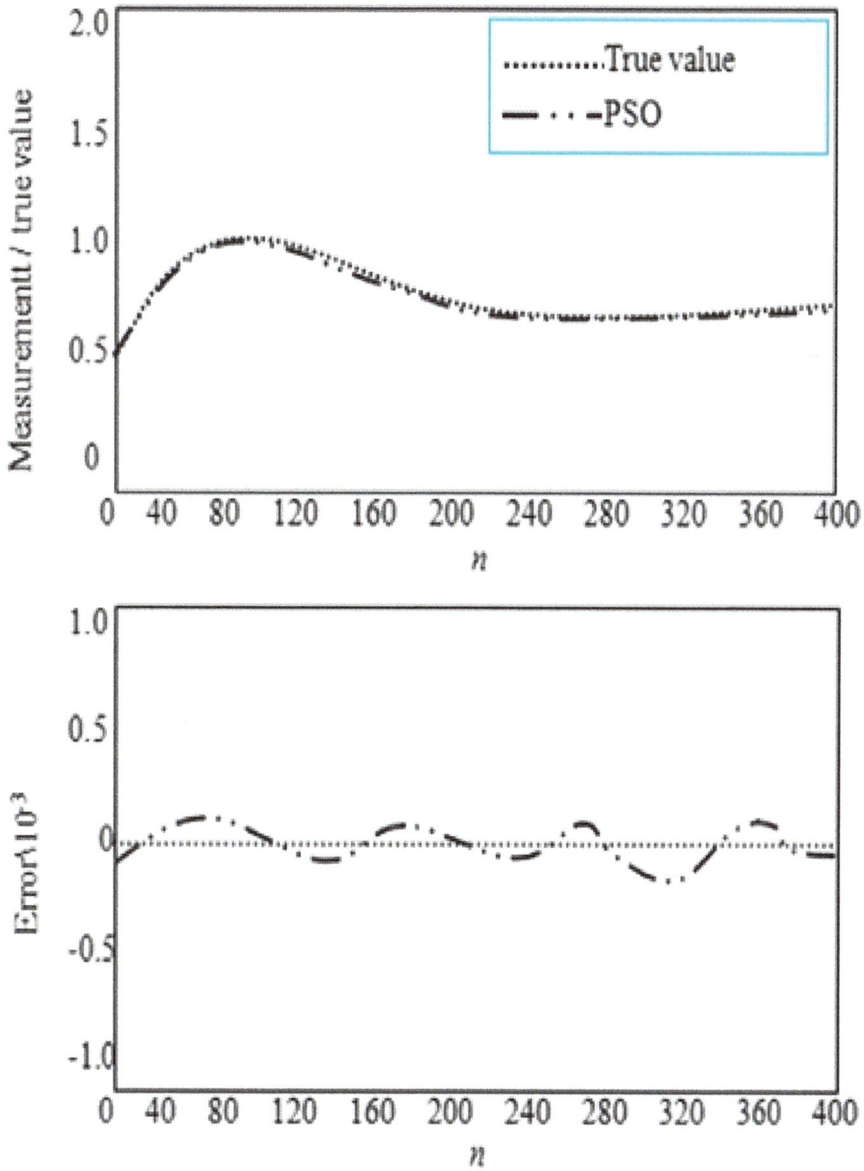

Figure 8 PSO prediction and its error

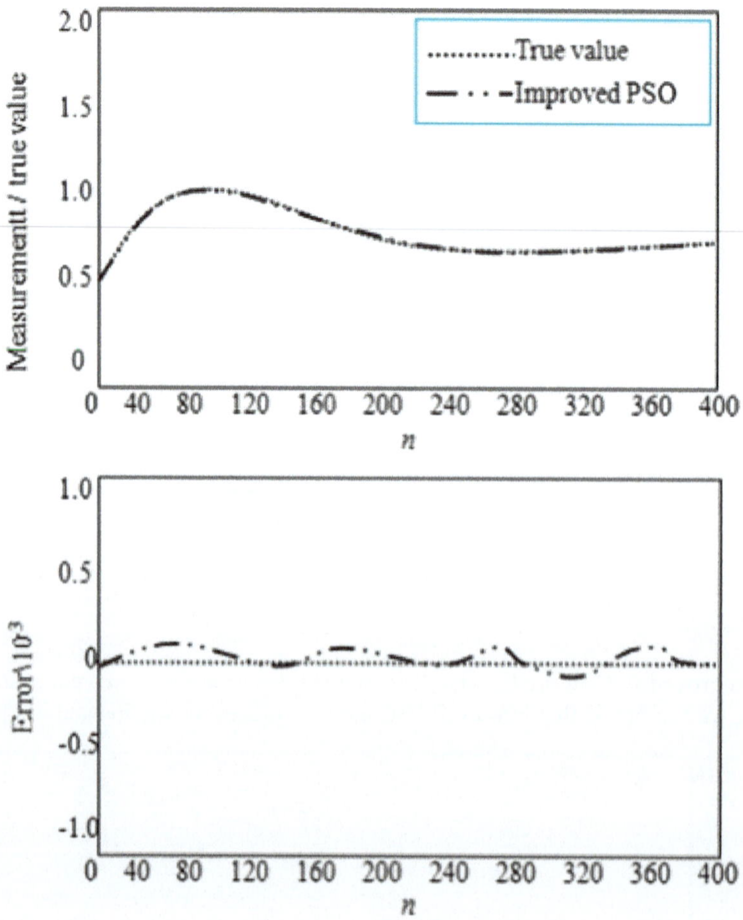

Figure 9 Improved PSO prediction and its error

Example 2 Selecting fifteen typical course-wares as the evaluation objects. Experts give evaluation interval for index effectiveness and course-ware integrated level for each course-ware. The evaluation basis is as follows: bad [0,0.55], pass [0.55,0.7], good [0.7,0.85], excellent [0.85,1]. We get a sample data as Table 1. And it calculates Y={μS1,μS2,…,μSn} Y={μS1,μS2,…,μSn} as output data represented in Table 2. The former 10 data is as training set and the later 5 data is as testing set.

Table 1 Sample input data

Sample	**Index set**										
	t_1	t_2	t_3	t_4	t_5	t_6	t_7	t_8	t_9	t_{10}	t_{11}
T1	0.95	0.88	0.91	0.95	0.84	0.91	0.94	0.98	0.87	0.84	0.96
T2	0.82	0.95	0.94	0.83	0.84	0.87	0.91	0.95	0.97	0.86	0.89
T3	0.84	0.87	0.77	0.78	0.94	0.85	0.90	0.91	0.97	0.86	0.88
T4	0.76	0.72	0.64	0.84	0.82	0.78	0.81	0.87	0.89	0.86	0.85
T5	0.89	0.92	0.81	0.75	0.56	0.64	0.89	0.84	0.82	0.80	0.73
T6	0.58	0.47	0.75	0.55	0.57	0.45	0.34	0.54	0.60	0.65	0.79
T7	0.25	0.34	0.40	0.28	0.17	0.64	0.35	0.44	0.48	0.68	0.65
T8	0.64	0.61	0.44	0.48	0.32	0.94	0.85	0.56	0.65	0.85	0.48
T9	0.74	0.67	0.65	0.77	0.79	0.80	0.79	0.69	0.76	0.78	0.82
T10	0.87	0.78	0.83	0.85	0.76	0.89	0.91	0.81	0.87	0.85	0.82
T11	0.84	0.89	0.86	0.82	0.91	0.84	0.87	0.95	0.88	0.76	0.79
T12	0.67	0.77	0.74	0.84	0.68	0.62	0.65	0.74	0.89	0.62	0.65
T13	0.73	0.84	0.71	0.77	0.92	0.85	0.70	0.91	0.90	0.91	0.88
T14	0.49	0.55	0.59	0.63	0.57	0.48	0.34	0.84	0.71	0.64	0.53
T15	0.65	0.74	0.67	0.84	0.85	0.83	0.89	0.92	0.55	0.86	0.61

Table 2 Sample output data

Sample output	**Group evaluation value (v v)**	**Fuzzy set**				**Evaluation degree**
		μS1μS1	μS2μS2	μS3μS3	μS4μS4	
Y1	0.94	0	0	0	1.0	excellent
Y2	0.87	0	0	0.3	0.7	excellent
Y3	0.81	0	0	0.7	0.3	good
Y4	0.75	0	0.3	0.7	0	good
Y5	0.79	0	0	1.0	0	good
Y6	0.54	0.5	0.5	0	0	pass
Y7	0.38	1.0	0	0	0	bad
Y8	0.67	0	0.6	0.4	0	pass
Y9	0.82	0	0	0.6	0.4	good
Y10	0.84	0	0	0.5	0.5	good
Y11	0.81	0	0	0.7	0.3	good
Y12	0.73	0	0.2	0.8	0	good
Y13	0.81	0	0	0.7	0.3	good
Y14	0.52	0.8	0.2	0	0	bad
Y15	0.82	0	0	0.8	0.2	good

Table 2. shows that network training is successful, the error is small, and it can accurately evaluate the quality of multimedia course-ware for students.

CONCLUSIONS

This paper's aim is to perfect the convergence speed, accuracy of algorithm and to solve the problem with Local minimum shortage and slow convergence speed in BP neural network. Also we finally build multimedia course-ware evaluation model based on the improved PSO. First, we give a detailed explanation on BP neural network and phase-space reconstruction. Multimedia course-ware evaluation model based on BP neural network is further illustrated. Then we propose improved PSO to optimize the initial weight and threshold value. Compared with the traditional PSO, the convergence speed of improved PSO becomes faster. It will add the probability of jumping out of local optimal solution and it is conducive to find the global optimal solution. This paper makes experiments with chaos system to verify the superiority of improved PSO. The new scheme improves convergence speed and prediction accuracy and reduces the probability of falling into local value with BP neural network. Multimedia course-ware evaluation model is well improved, which is conducive to valuating multimedia course-ware in some universities. In the future, we will study the advanced PSO algorithm based on this paper's method to solve the accuracy and convergence speed problem.

ACKNOWLEDGMENTS

Foundation item: The National Nature Science Foundation of China (No.: 6097011). Authors are grateful to the Software College Shenyang Normal University, Government of China for financial support to carry out this work.

REFERENCES

1. Chatzinakos C, Tsouros C (2015) Estimation of the dimension of chaotic dynamical systems using neural networks and robust location estimate [J]. Simul Model Pract Theory 51:149–156
2. Du, W. (2015) Research on Evaluation of Enterprise Performance Based on BP Neural Network Improved by Levenberg-marquardt Algorithm [C]// International Conference on Automation, Mechanical Control and Computational Engineering. Atlantis Press, 2015
3. Han L, Romero CE, Yao Z (2015) Wind power forecasting based on principle component phase space reconstruction [J]. Renew Energy 81:737–744
4. Jiang YL, Shao YX Fault diagnosis of rolling bearing based on fuzzy neural network and chaos theory [J]. Vibroeng PROCEDIA 4:211–216
5. Jinkun L, Yi G. (2014) Neural network based adaptive dynamic surface control for flexible-joint robots[C]// Control Conference (CCC), 33rd Chinese IEEE, 2014: 8764–8768
6. Liu B, Che Y, Cui X, et al. (2015) Synchronization of Light-Emitting Diodes Networks via Adaptive Neural Network Control [C]//2015 International Symposium on Computers & Informatics. Atlantis Press
7. She K, Ma LZ, Wan JR, et al. (2015) Application of Dynamic Chaos PSO Algorithm in Elevator Configuration [C]. Appl Mech Mater 734:548–553
8. Tang X, Zhang H, Cui Y, et al. (2014) A novel reactive power optimization solution using improved chaos PSO based on multi-agent architecture [J]. Int Trans Electr Energy Syst 24(5):609–622
9. Wan L, Zhu YQ, Deng XC (2015) Analysis on phase space reconstruction and chaotic characteristic of element concentration series of gold deposit [J]. Analysis 5:6

10. Wang Z, Li L (2014) Image Edge Detection Based on Cellular Neural Network and Particle Swarm Optimization [J]. Trans. Computer Sci Technol 3(1)
11. Wang MH, Yau HT (2014) New Power Quality Analysis Method Based on Chaos Synchronization and Extension Neural Network [J]. Energy 7(10):6340–6357
12. Yoshida H, Murakami T, Liuc Z. (2015) High-Speed and Highly Secure Pseudo-Random Number Generator based on Chaos Neural Network [J]. New Trends on System Science and Engineering: Proceedings of ICSSE 2015, 276: 224
13. Zhang Y, Gao X, Katayama S (2015) Weld appearance prediction with BP neural network improved by genetic algorithm during disk laser welding [J]. J Manuf Syst 34:53–59

CHAPTER 14

INTERACTIVE VIDEO SEARCH TOOLS: A DETAILED ANALYSIS OF THE VIDEO BROWSER SHOWDOWN 2015

Claudiu Cobarzan, Klaus Schoeffmann, Werner Bailer, Wolfgang Hurst, Adam Blazek, Jakub Lokoc, Stefanos Vrochidis, Kai Uwe Barthel, Luca Rossetto

Keywords: Exploratory search Video browsing Video retrieval

INTRODUCTION

The *Video Browser Showdown (VBS)*, also known as Video Search Showcase, is an interactive video search competition where participating teams try to answer ad-hoc queries in a shared video data set as fast as possible. Typical efforts in video retrieval focus mainly on indexing and machine-based search performance, for example, by measuring precision and recall with a test data set. With video getting omnipresent in regular consumers lives, it becomes increasingly important though to also include the user into the search process. The VBS is an annual workshop at the International Conference on MultiMedia Modeling (MMM) with that goal in mind.

Researchers in the multimedia community agree that content-based image and video retrieval approaches should have a stronger focus on the user behind the retrieval application [13, 45,50]. Instead of pursuing rather small improvements in the field of content-based indexing and retrieval, video search tools should aim at better integration of the human into the search process, focusing on interactive video retrieval [8, 9, 18, 19] rather than automatic querying.

Therefore, the main goal of the Video Browser Showdown is to push research on interactive video search tools. Interactive video search follows the idea of strong user integration with sophisticated content interaction [47] and aims at providing a powerful alternative to the common video retrieval approach [46]. It is known as the interactive process of video content exploration with browsing means, such as content navigation [21], summarization [1], on-demand querying [48], and interactive inspection of querying results or filtered content [17]. Contrarily to typical video retrieval, such interactive video browsing tools give more control to the user and provide flexible search features, instead of focusing on the *query-and-browse-results* approach. Hence, even if the performance of content analysis is not optimal, there is a chance that the user could compensate shortcomings through ingenious use of available features. This is important since it has been shown that user can give good performances even with very simple tools, e.g. a simple HTML5 video player [10, 12, 42, 44].

Other interesting approaches include using additional capturing devices such as the Kinect sensor in conjunction with human action video search [32], exercise learning in the field of healthcare [20] or interactive systems for video search [7]. In [7] for example, an interactive system for human action video search based on the dynamic shape volumes is developed – the user can create video queries by posing any number of actions in front of a Kinect sensor. Of course, there are many other relevant and related tools in the fields of interactive video search, video interaction, and multimedia search, which are however out of the scope of this paper. The interested reader is referred to other surveys in this field, such as [34, 46, 47].

In this paper we provide an overview of the participating tools along with a detailed analysis of the results. Our observations highlight different aspects of the performance and

---

Citation: Claudiu Cobârzan, Klaus Schoeffmann, Werner Bailer, Wolfgang Hürst, Adam Blažek, Jakub Lokoč, Stefanos Vrochidis, Kai Uwe Barthel, Luca Rossetto, Interactive video search tools: a detailed analysis of the video browser showdown 2015, DOI: 10.1007/s11042-016-3661-2.

provide insight into better interface development for interactive video search. Details of the data set and the participating tools are presented, as well as their achieved performance in terms of score and search time. Further, we reflect on the achieved results so far, give detailed insights on the reasons why specific tools and methods worked better or worse, and subsume the experience and observations from the perspective of the organisers. Based on this, we make several proposals for highly promising approaches to be used with future iterations of this interactive video retrieval competition.

The remainder of the paper is organized as follows. Section 2 gives a short description of the competition. Section 3 makes an overview of both the presented tasks and of the obtained results. Section 4 provides short descriptions of the participating tools. A detailed analysis of the results for visual expert rounds is presented in Section 5. The results for the textual expert round are presented in Section 6 and the ones for the novice round in Section 7. A short historical overview over the last rounds of the Video Browser Showdown together with some advice on developing interactive video search tools are given in Section 8. Section 9 concludes the paper and highlights the most important observations stemming from the competition.

VIDEO BROWSER SHOWDOWN 2015

VBS 2015 was the fourth iteration of the Video Browser Showdown and took place in Sydney, Australia, in January 2015, held together with the International Conference on MultiMedia Modeling 2015 (MMM 2015). Nine teams participated in the competition and performed ten visual known-item search tasks (*Expert Run 1*), six textual known-item search tasks (*Expert Run 2*), as well as four visual and two textual known-item search tasks with non-expert users (*Novice Run*). The shared data set consisted of 153 video files containing about 100 hours of video content in PAL resolution (720 ×576@25p) from various BBC programs, and was a subset of the MediaEval 2013 Search & Hyperlinking data set [15]. The size of the data set was about 32 GB; the videos were stored in webm file format and encoded with the VP8 video codec, and the Ogg Vorbis audio codec. The data were made available to the participants about two months before the event.

During the event, users interactively try to solve search tasks with the participating tools; first in a closed expert session with the developers of a respective tool, then in a public novice session with volunteers from the audience – typically experts in the field of multimedia. Search tasks are so-called known-item search tasks where users search for information that they are familiar with. For the last two years [41] visual and textual queries were used. These are clips or textual descriptions of 20-seconds long target segments in a moderately large shared data set (100 hours at VBS 2015), which are randomly selected on site. After a clip or the text for a task is presented, participants have to find it in the database. They are presented through a PC connected to a projector, which runs the *VBS Server* that presents target segments (1) through playback of the corresponding clip for visual tasks, and (2) through presentation of a static textual description of the clip – collaboratively created by the organizers – for textual queries. After presentation of the visual or textual description, the VBS Server is responsible for collecting and checking the results found by the participants and for calculating the achieved*score* for each team.

The tools of all teams are connected to the VBS Server, and send information about found segments (frame numbers or frame ranges) to the server via HTTP requests. The server checks if the segment was found in the correct video and at the correct position and computes a score for the team, according to a formula that considers the search time (typically a value between 4 and 8 minutes) and the number of previously submitted wrong results for the search task (see [2, 42]). According to these parameters a team can get up to 100 points for a correct solved task, and in worst case zero points for a wrong or unanswered task. The scores are summed up and the total score of each session is used to determine the winner of the session. Finally, the team with the maximum grand total score is selected as the final winner of the competition. VBS 2015 used three sessions: (1) a visual expert's session, (2) a textual expert's session, and (3) a visual novice's session.

In order to focus on the interactive aspects of search and avoid focusing too much on the automatic retrieval aspects, restrictions are imposed. Retrieval tools that only use text queries without any other interaction feature are therefore not allowed. However, participants may perform textual filtering of visual concepts, or navigate through a tree of textual classifications/concepts, for example. Moreover, the Video Browser Showdown wants to foster simple tools and, therefore, perform a novice session where volunteers from the audience use the tools of the experts/developers to solve the search tasks and by doing so test the usability in an implicit way.

In 2015, the focus of the competition has further moved towards dealing with realistically sized content collections. Thus, the tasks using only single videos, that were present in the 2013 and 2014 editions, have been discontinued, and the data set has been scaled up, from about 40 hours in 2014 to about 100 hours. The competition started with expert tasks in which visual and textual queries had to be solved. Then the audience was invited to join in and the tools were presented to allow the participants to understand how the tools are used by the experts. In the next sessions members of the audience ("novices") took over for visual and text queries, and operated the tools themselves.

Each task in each of the three sessions (visual/textual expert run, novice run) aimed at finding a 20 seconds query video, where the excerpt does not necessarily start and stop at shot or scene boundaries. For visual queries, the video clip is played once (with sound) on a large, shared screen in the room. For textual queries, experts created descriptions of the contents of the clips, which were displayed on the shared screen and read to the participants. Participants were given a maximum time limit of eight minutes to find the target sequence in the corresponding video data (note that in the 2013 and 2014 competitions, the search in single videos was limited to three minutes, while the archive tasks in the 2014 competition had a limit of six minutes).

The systems of all participating teams were organized to face the moderator and the shared screen, which was used for presenting the query videos and the current scores of all teams via the VBS server. Figure 1 shows the setup of the VBS session at MMM2015. The participating systems were connected to an HTTP-based communication server over a dedicated Wi-Fi private network. This server computed the performance scores for each tool and each task accordingly. Each tool provided a submission feature that could be used by the participant to send the current position in the video (i.e., the frame number or segment) to the server. The server checked the submitted frame number for correctness and computed a score for the corresponding tool and task based on the submission time and the number of false submissions. The following formulas were used to compute the score skisik for tool *k* and task *i*, where mkimik is the number of submissions by tool *k* for task *i* and pkipik is the penalty due to wrong submissions:

$$s_i^k = \frac{100 - 50\frac{t}{T_{max}}}{p_i^k} \quad (1)$$

$$p_i^k = \begin{cases} 1, & \text{if } m_i^k \leq 1 \\ m_i^k - 1, & \text{otherwise.} \end{cases} \quad (2)$$

Figure 1 Teams competing during the VBS 2015 competition

The overall score S^k for tool *k* is simply the sum of the scores of all tasks of the three sessions. Equations (1) and (2) were designed in order avoid trial-and-error approaches: participants submitting several wrong results get significantly fewer points than participants submitting just one correct result. Additionally, the linear decrease of the score over time should motivate the teams to find the target sequence as fast as possible.

The hardware for the competition was not normalized; all participating teams were free to use the equipment best supporting the requirements and efficiency of their video browsers. The teams used notebook computers or tablets, depending on the respective browsing approaches.

VBS2015 EVALUATION OVERVIEW

The current section aims to give a general overview of the competition's tasks and results and to point towards some of the most interesting conclusions. A detailed analysis and discussion of the results which focuses on the different tasks types follows in Section 5.

Overview of the rounds and of presented tasks

As already mentioned in Section 2, the competition focused on two types of tasks, namely visual and textual tasks.

Expert run 1

In Table 1, an overview of the 10 target clips of the visual expert round (*Expert Run 1*) is presented as a series of temporally uniformly sampled frames captured at a two seconds interval. This should help readers to understand how the presented clips looked like. As visible in Table 1, some target clips showed quickly changing actions (e.g. tasks 1, 3, 6, 7, 8), only a few tasks - in particular 2 and 10 - showed scenes of longer duration, which are more distinct but proved hard to find.

Table 1 Overview of the presented video targets for the visual experts round

	Frame capture at									
Task no.	0s	2s	4s	6s	8s	10s	12s	14s	16s	18s
1										
2										
3										
4										
5										
6										
7										
8										
9										
10										

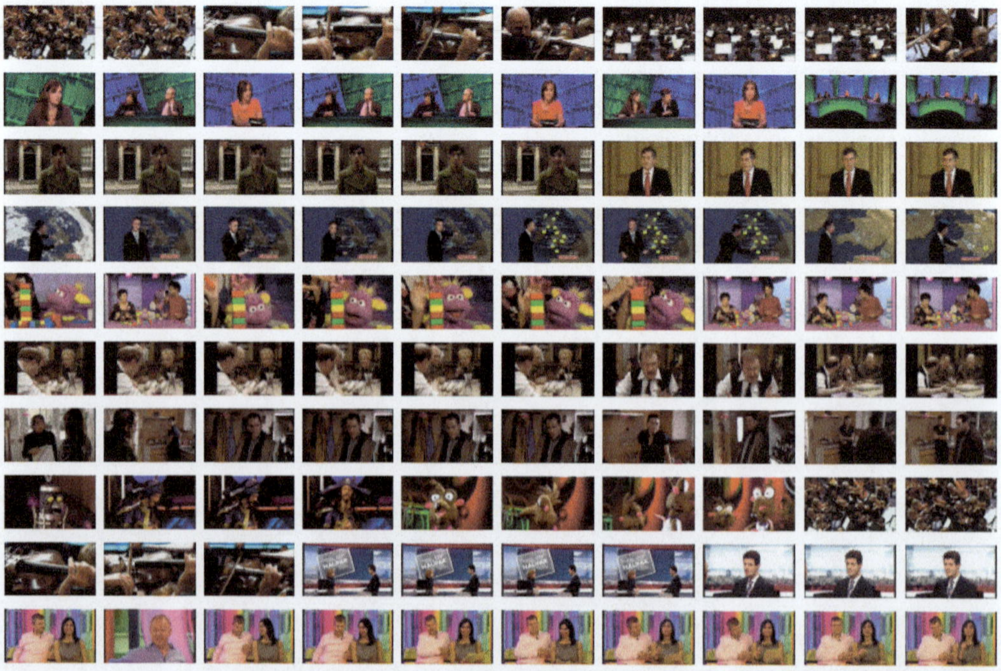

Expert run 2

The textual descriptions that the participants were provided with during the competition's textual expert round (*Expert Run 2*) can be read in Table 2.

Table 2 Descriptions of the target segments provided for the text experts session

Task no.	Description
1	Panel of four participants with bluish background on the top ("COMEDIANS" displayed on their desk below) being asked a quiz question about a Russian exclave (i.e., separated region) in Europe, after the question is asked close-ups of the people are shown.
2	A man on a meadow (green grass in background), standing next to an ultralight aircraft and getting into a red and black overall.
3	A group of mostly kids practicing Karate moves indoors (in white clothes), including close-ups of a blond young woman talking to a girl, and shots showing the instructor, a bald man with glasses.
4	A prairie scenery with a hill on the left and mountains in the background, an old man with a black suit and hat walking slowly up the hill. He is first seen from behind, then a close-up of the man is shown. Then a close-up shot of a running wolf in the grass is shown.
5	A red/brown coloured map of Europe, with Alsace and the city of Strasbourg highlighted, showing also the surrounding countries (e.g., Germany, France). Then black/white shots of soldiers marching in a city (for several seconds). During the whole sequence a female sign language interpreter is visible in the lower right.
6	A BBC Four trailer, starting with a colourful huge bookshelf, then showing a sequence of countryside shots, and in each of them a yellow/gold glowing path showing music notes is appearing.

Table 3 shows an overview of the 6 target scenes described by Table 2 also as a sequence of temporally uniformly sampled frames at a two seconds interval. The difficulty with the textual tasks is the fact that the searchers have no idea about the actual visual presentation of the scene.

Table 3 Overview of the described video targets for the text experts round

	Frame capture at									
no.	0s	2s	4s	6s	8s	10s	12s	14s	16s	18s

Novice run

As already mentioned, the novice round that followed the visual and textual expert rounds, consisted of a total of six tasks, out of which four were visual tasks and two were textual tasks. They were presented as two sequences of two visual tasks followed by a textual task. Those tasks were extracted from the same pools as the tasks of the previous visual and text rounds and were in no way different.

The overview of the visual tasks (Task 1, Task 2, Task 4, Task 5) and that of the textual tasks (Task 3, Task 6) is shown in Table 4, while Table 5 gives the descriptions of the two textual tasks (Task 3 and Task 6 respectively).

Table 4 Overview of the presented and described video targets for the novices round

	Frame capture at									
Task no.	0s	2s	4s	6s	8s	10s	12s	14s	16s	18s
1										
2										
3										
4										
5										
6										

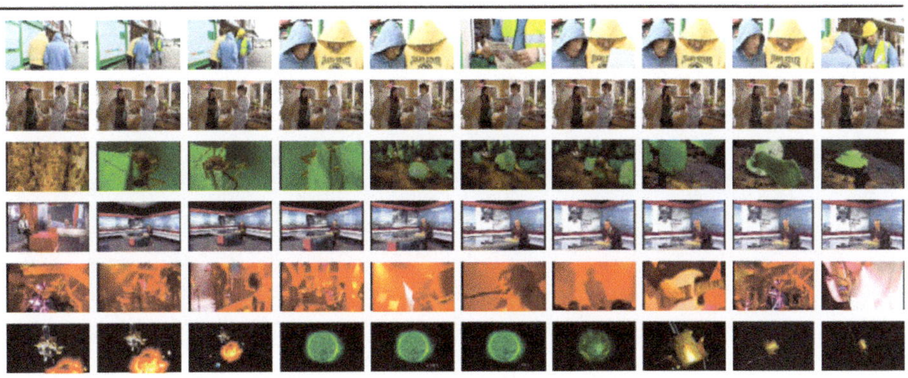

Table 5 Descriptions of the target segments provided for the text novices tasks

Task	Description
3	First a close-up of a beehive with many bees, then close-up shots of ants cutting and carrying large green leaves.
6	Piece about the ESA Ulysses mission, showing an image of the sun and the probe left above it, while zooming out it is explained how it orbits around the sun.
	The next shot shows the sun centered in a greenish hue ("STEREO" image). The flyby of a rendered model of the probe is shown.

Overview of results

In the following we present the results of the competition rounds. An overview of the final scores over all these rounds is presented in Fig. 2 while the overall submission times for the successful submissions within the competition across all tasks are shown in Fig. 3. The average number of submissions per round and team is shown in Fig. 4. The acronyms in all three figures' legends identify the tools of the participating teams: HTW (Germany), IMOTION (Switzerland-Belgium-Turkey), NII-UIT (Vietnam - Japan), SIRET (Czech Republic), UU (The Netherlands), VERGE (Greece-UK). Detailed descriptions of those tools are available in Section 4, while the interested readers might consider the corresponding references in the Reference list for additional details.

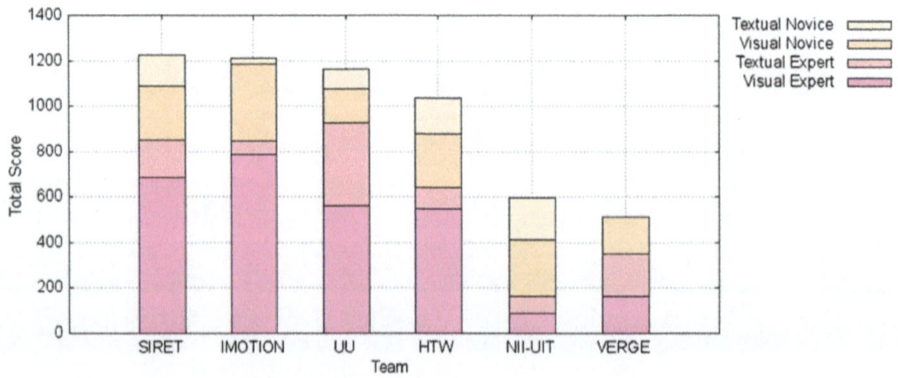

Figure 2 Total score of teams in the VBS 2015 competition

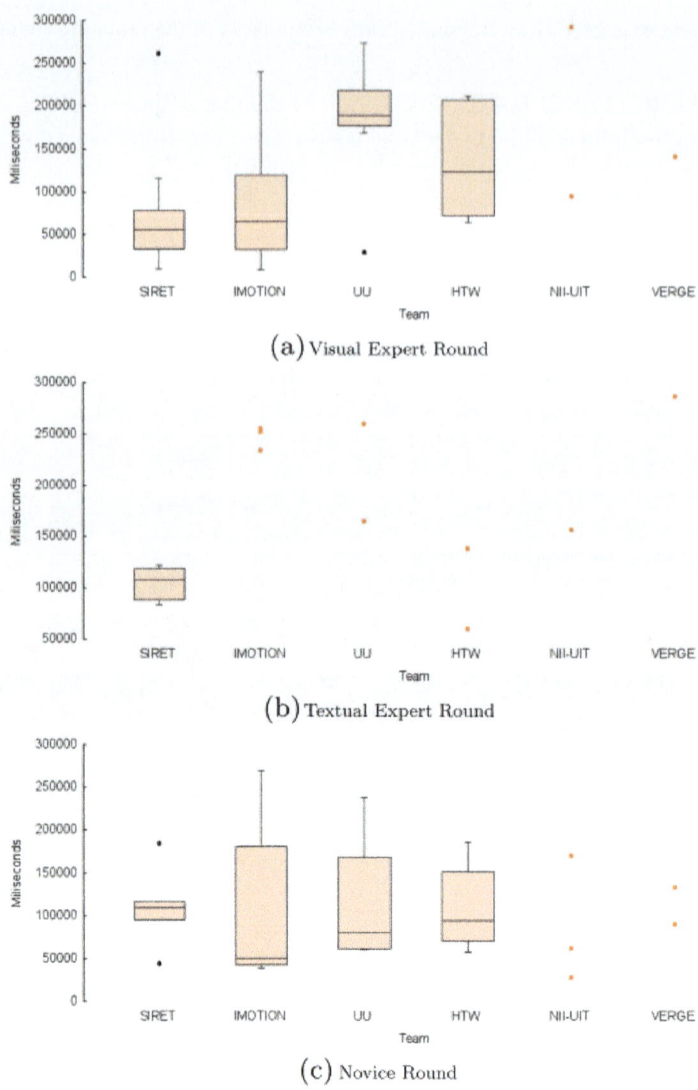

Figure 3 Box plot of the submission time per team in the VBS 2015 competition, based on correct submissions

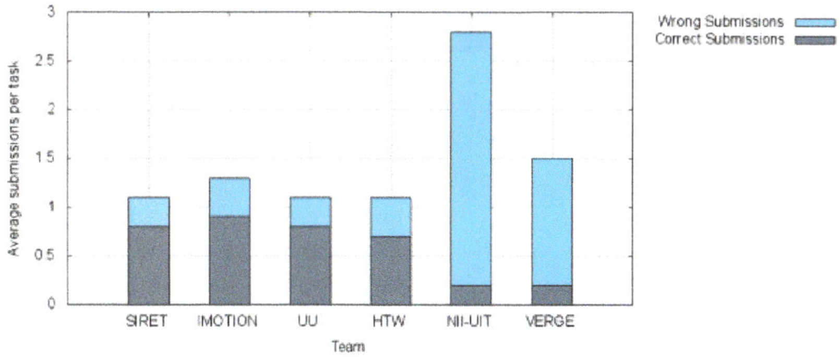

(a) **Average number of submissions for the Visual Expert Round**

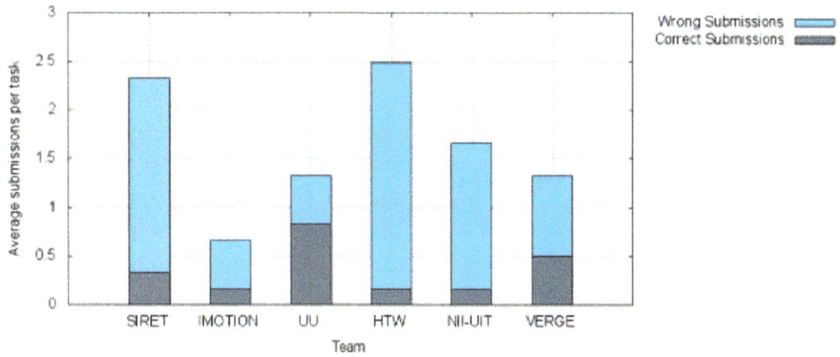

(b) **Average number of submissions for the Textual Expert Round**

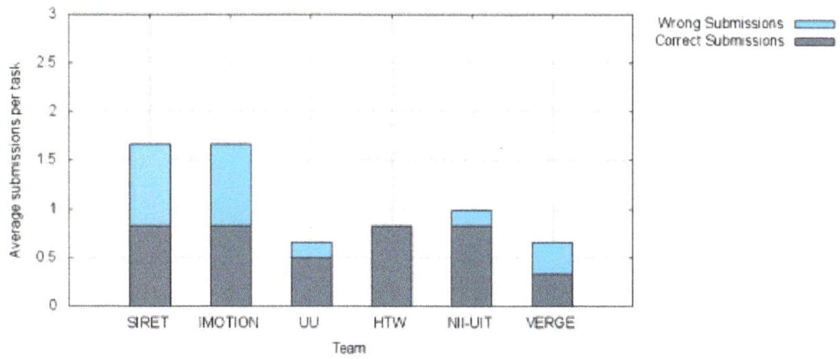

(c) **Average number of submissions for the Novice Round**

Figure 4 Average number of submissions (correct and wrong) in the VBS 2015 competition

Out of the nine participating teams [3, 5, 11, 22, 27, 35, 37, 39, 51], six managed to score points during the competition. Further analysis of the logs showed that one of the three non-scoring teams managed to solve one of the tasks but submitted its data using a wrong format.

Some interesting aspects can be observed when looking at both Figs. 2 and 3:

- The three top ranking teams (SIRET, IMOTION and UU) together with the forth (HTW) show the most uniform increases in terms of scored points across the visual expert and novice rounds (Fig. 2). In the case of the text expert round, only the UU and NII-UIT teams show this pattern. Overall the achievements during the novice round were over those in the text expert round.
- In the case of the NII-UIT team, the best scoring round was that of the novices (it actually won the round) during which the team climbed up to rank 5.
- The slowest of the participants (Fig. 2) was by far the UU team which was almost 2 times slower than the for-last participant in terms of speed - the HTW team. Since the UU team presented a tool designed for human computation this does not come as a surprise. What comes as a surprise is the excellent score they achieved - rank 3 overall. Also, it is interesting to note that the UU team was slowest during the visual expert round and got faster during the text expert and novice rounds with the additional note, that during the novice round only half of the targets were found (two visual and one textual targets).
- When comparing the three rounds, visual expert, textual expert and novice, the difference in speed, when it comes to finding the correct target, is not that big as when comparing experts and novices. The novices are a little bit slower except in the case of UU team, where the novices actually seem to perform faster then the experts. Unfortunately, due to the small number of novice tasks we are not able to generalize on whether this has to do with the actual tasks being presented, or this is because the novices just exploited the tools close to their full potential, as they had no false expectations. Also, as already mentioned, it is important to note that in most cases, the participants in the novice round were actually experts from the other participating teams which tested the "competition's" tools.

- From the scoring point of view we see two team clusters: one that scored over 1000 points (SIRET, IMOTION, UU and HTW) and one that score under 600 (NII-UIT and VERGE), while from the time point of view, all the teams with the exception of the UU team, had similar overall completion times for their successful submissions.

We have performed a one-way ANOVA to determine if the successful submission times for the visual experts round was different for the participating teams. Each of the IMOTION, SIRET and UU teams had one outlier. The search time was normally distributed for all interfaces, as assessed by Shapiro-Wilk's test ($p > .05$). There was homogeneity of variances, as assessed by Levene's test for equality of variances ($p = .92$). The search time was statistically significantly different between the interfaces, $F(5, 30) = 3.045$, $p < .05$.

SCORING VIDEO SEARCH TOOLS IN VBS2015

IMOTION

The IMOTION system [39] is a sketch and example-based video retrieval system. It is based on a content-based video retrieval engine called Cineast [38] that focuses on *Query-by-Sketch* and also supports *Query-by-Example* and *motion queries*.

In IMOTION, a user can specify a query by means of a sketch that may include edge information, color information, motion information, or any combination of these, or provide sample images or sample video snippets as query input. It uses multiple low-level features such as color- and edge histograms for retrieval.

The IMOTION system extends the set of features by high level visual features such as state-of-the-art convolutional neural network object detectors and motion descriptors. All feature vectors along with meta-data are stored in the database and information retrieval system ADAM [16] which is built upon PostgreSQL and is capable of performing efficient vector space retrieval together with Boolean retrieval.

The browser-based user interface, which is optimized to be usable with touch screen devices, pen tablets as well as a mouse, provides a sketching canvas as well as thumbnail previews of the retrieved results.

Figure 5 shows an example query with corresponding results. The results are grouped by row, each row containing shots which are similar to the query by a different measure such as colors, edges, motion or semantics. The topmost row shows the combination of these individual result lists whereas the influence of each category can be adjusted by sliders which change the combination in real time. The UI also offers a video capture functionality to collect reference frames using a webcam which then could be used during retrieval. Video capturing was successfully used during the visual tasks where images from the webcam were used as queries directly after cropping. In certain cases, the images were modified using the sketching functionality. For the textual challenges, only sketches were used.

Figure 5 Screenshot of the IMOTION system

SIRET

The SIRET system [5] is a new version of the Signature-based Video Browser tool (SBVB) [33] that was successfully introduced at the Video Browser Showdown in 2014. The tool combines two orthogonal approaches – efficient filtering using simple color-based sketches and enhanced presentation/browsing of the results. Both the filtering and the browsing parts of the application received various adjustments. Nonetheless, the overall concept utilizing position-color feature signatures [30, 40] was preserved, because representation of key-frames by the feature signatures enables effective and efficient location of searched key-frames. The concept relies on the *Query-by-Sketch* approach, where simple sketches representing memorized color stimuli can be quickly defined by positioning colored circles (see the right side of Fig. 6). The tool enables users to define either one sketch or two time-ordered sketches. In case when two sketches are specified, the tool searches for clips having matching key-frames in this particular order. The two searched key-frames have to be within a user specified time window. The retrieval model was described in more detail in [6]. The current enhanced version of the tool also considers the complexity of the key-frames to automatically adjust settings of the retrieval model.

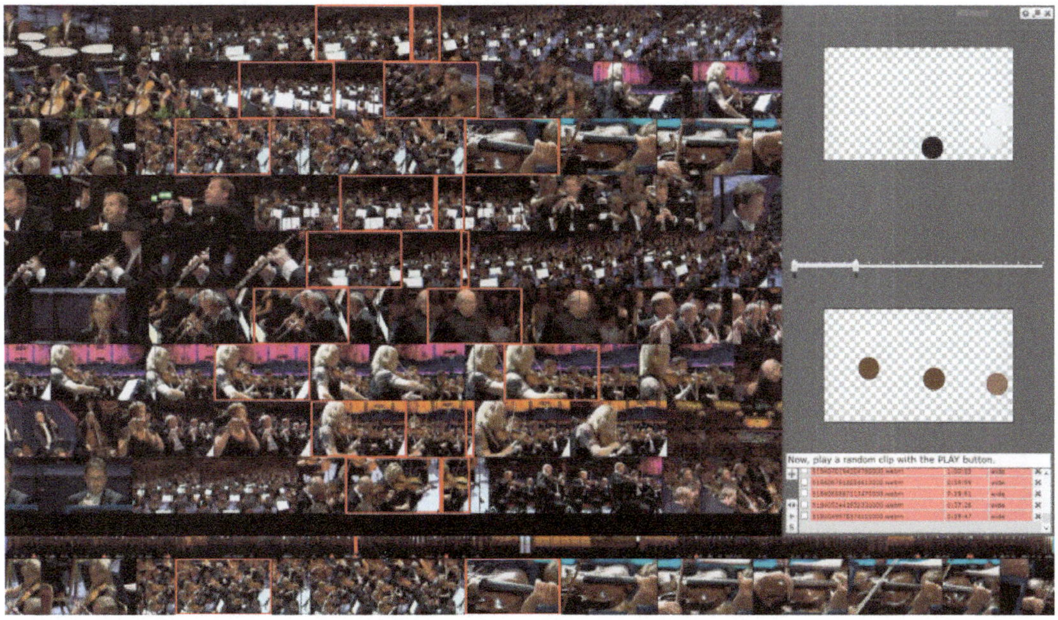

Figure 6 Screenshot of the SBVB tool in action

Every query sketch adjustment is projected to the results area (see the left side of Fig. 6) immediately thanks to the efficient retrieval model employed which is based on position-color feature signatures. Each row represents one matched scene delimited by the matched key-frames (marked with red margin) and accompanied by a few preceding and following key-frames from the video clip. Any displayed scene can be selected as either positive or negative example for additional filtering. Alternatively, particular colored circles might be picked from displayed key-frames to the sketches similarly to picking up a color with the eyedropper tool. Regarding the video-level exploration, users may exclude a particular video from the search or contrary, focus on a single video. Especially the later mentioned feature often led to success as its appropriate usage can significantly increase results relevancy. When exploring a single video, users may find useful the extended results row (see the bottom of Fig. 6) enriched with Interactive Navigation Summary [43] displaying (in this case, 5 dominant colors of each key-frame).

HTW

The HTW system [3] is a map-based browsing system for visually searching video clips in large collections. Based on ImageMap [4], it allows the user to navigate through a hierarchical-pyramid structure in which related scenes are arranged close to each other. An extended version of Image Map can be viewed online at www.picsbuffet.com. The interaction is similar to map services like Google Maps: a view port revealing only a small portion of the entire map at a specific level. Zooming in (or out) shows more (or less) similar scenes from lower (or higher) levels. Dragging the view shows related images from the same level. While the hierarchical-pyramid of all scenes in the data set ("Map of Scenes") has been precomputed to avoid performance issues, the map for a single video is generated on the fly and can therefore be filtered or altered based on the actions of the user.

The HTW-Berlin video browsing interface is divided into three parts: the browsing area on the left, the search result area in the middle and the search input area on the right.

Generally the user starts with a sketch and maybe some adjustments to the brightness/contrast and saturation of the input. In the meanwhile the tool updates all views in real-time and presents the best match as a paused video frame on the bottom right of the interface (Fig. 7). The "Map of Scenes" jumps to a position where the frame of the video is located and other similar looking scenes are displayed in the result tab. If the detected scene is not the right one, the user can use the Image Map to find related scenes and start a new search query by clicking them. All views are updated again and the sketch gets replaced by the selected frame. Upon finding the right scene it is suggested to check the "Video Map" for multiple look-alike alternatives and use the "Video Sequence" to verify the correct adjacent key frames.

Figure 7 Screenshot of the HTW-Berlin tool

In case the content of a scene is described as text or verbally, less or no visual information may be available, making a search nearly unfeasible. Usually the user still has an idea how the scene might look like. With the help of ImageMap it is possible to quickly navigate and check potential key frames.

UU

The UU system [27] excludes all kinds of video analysis and machine-based query processing and relies exclusively on interaction design and human browsing abilities. Past research has demonstrated that a good and efficient interaction design can have a significant impact on search performance [24, 49] – especially when searching in single video files or small data sets. This claim is supported by previous years' VBS results, for example, the baseline study presented in [42].

Assuming that a simplistic design will increase search performance, all data is presented in a storyboard layout, i.e., a temporarily sorted arrangement of thumbnail images representing frames extracted from the videos. Considering that no video analysis is applied, these thumbnails have to be extracted at a low step size. Here, one second is used, resulting in about 360,000 single thumbnails for the approximately 100 hours of video. It is obvious that browsing such a huge amount of images in a short time is only possible if the related system is optimized for speed and the search task at hand. Figure 8 illustrates the related design decisions. Targeting a tablet as device with 9 inch screen size, and based on previous research about optimal images sizes for storyboards on mobiles [25, 26], 625 images are represented on one screen (cf. Fig. 8a). In order to better identify scenes, thumbnails are arranged not in the common left/right-then-top/down order but a mixture of up/down-left/right directions (cf. Fig. 8b). With 625 thumbnails on one screen and a total amount of about 360,000 thumbnails, more than 550 screens have to be visually inspected if the whole database has to be browsed. In order to speed up this process and considering related research results [23], interaction is simplified and restricted to up/down motions (i.e., storyboards of all files are represented horizontally; cf. Fig. 8c) and navigation is limited to discrete jumps between single screens or video files (cf. Fig. 8d).

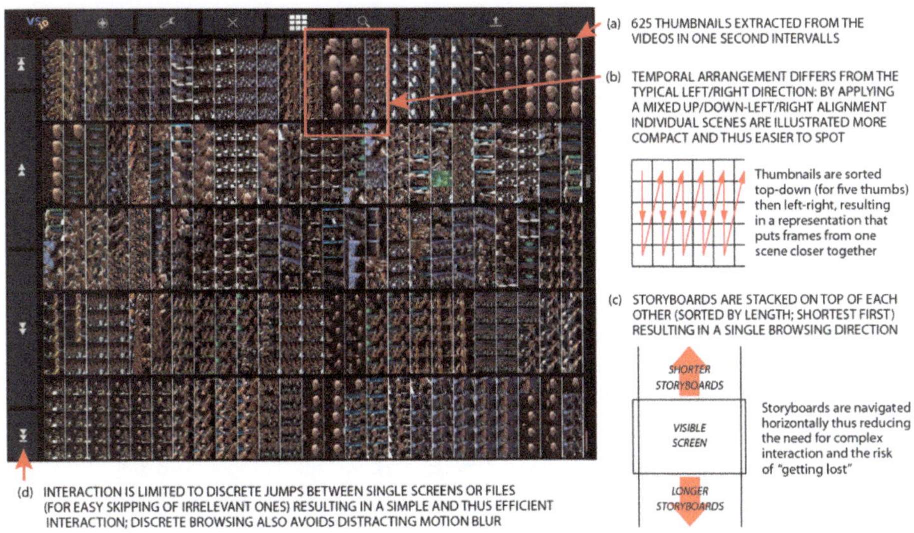

Figure 8 UU's interface for purely human-based video browsing

VERGE

The VERGE system [35] is an interactive retrieval system that combines advanced retrieval functionalities with a user-friendly interface, and supports the submission of queries and the accumulation of relevant retrieval results. The following indexing and retrieval modules are integrated in the developed search application: a) Visual Similarity Search Module based on K-Nearest Neighbour search operating on an index of lower-dimensional PCA-projected VLAD vectors [28]; b) High Level Concept Detection for predefined concepts by training Support vector machines with annotated data and five local descriptors (e.g. SIFT, RGB-SIFT, SURF, ORB etc), which are compacted and aggregated using PCA and encoding; the output of the trained models is combined by means of late fusion (averaging); c) Hierarchical Clustering incorporating a generalized agglomerative hierarchical clustering process [29], which provides a structured hierarchical view of the video keyframes.

The aforementioned modules allow the user to search through a collection of images and/or video keyframes. However, in the case of a video collection, it is essential that the videos are preprocessed in order to be indexed in smaller segments and semantic information should be extracted. The modules that are applied for segmenting videos are: a) Shot Segmentation; and b) Scene Segmentation. All the modules are incorporated into a friendly user interface (Fig. 9) in order to aid the user to interact with the system, discover and retrieve the desired video clip.

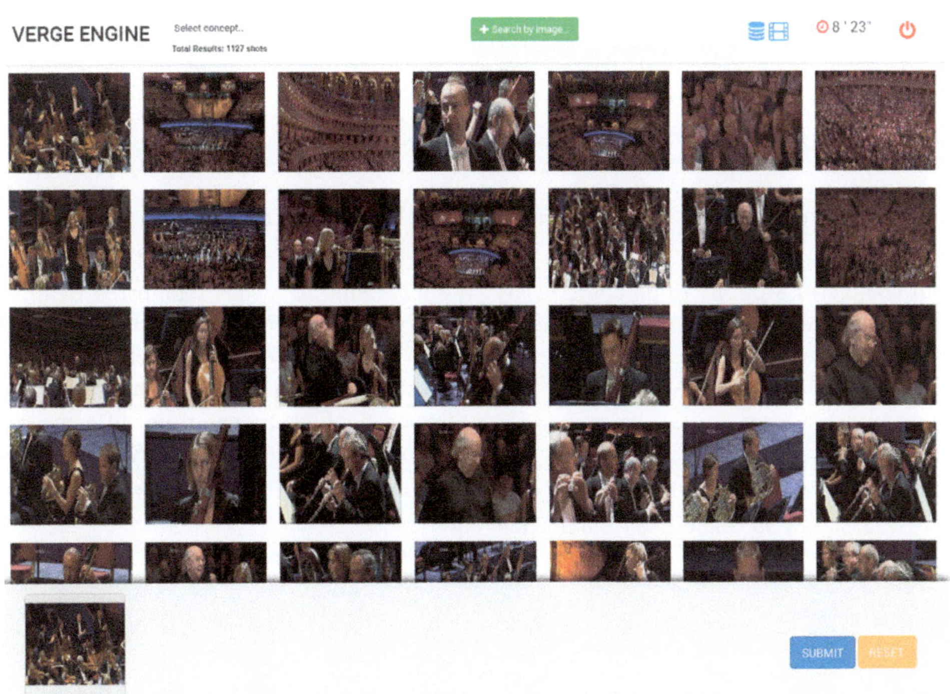

Figure 9 VERGE video retrieval engine interface

EVALUATION DETAILS ON VISUAL EXPERTS TASKS

Search time and achieved points

The breakdown of the final scores per task as well as the information regarding the time needed for the completion of each successful submission are presented in Figs. 10 and 11.

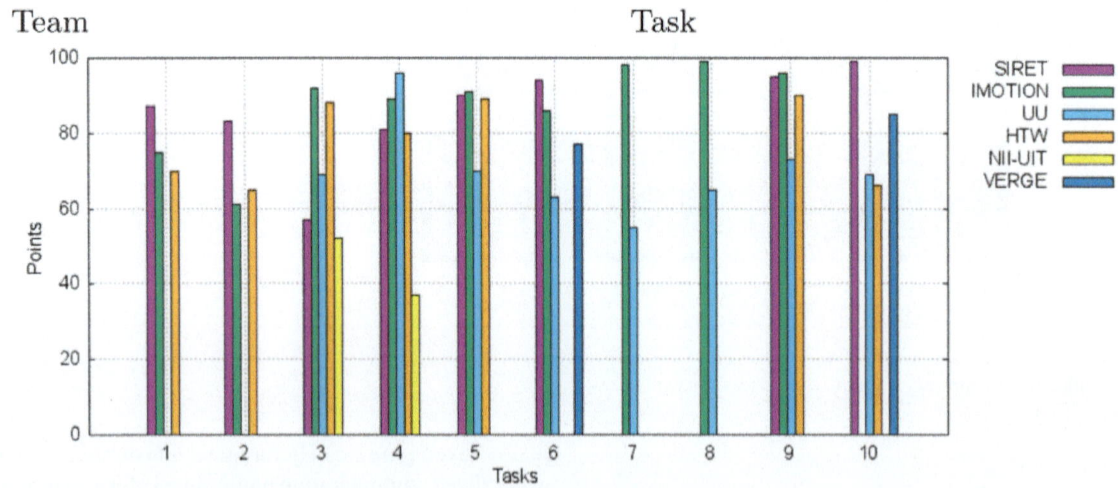

Figure 10 Breakdown per individual tasks of the scores for the visual experts round

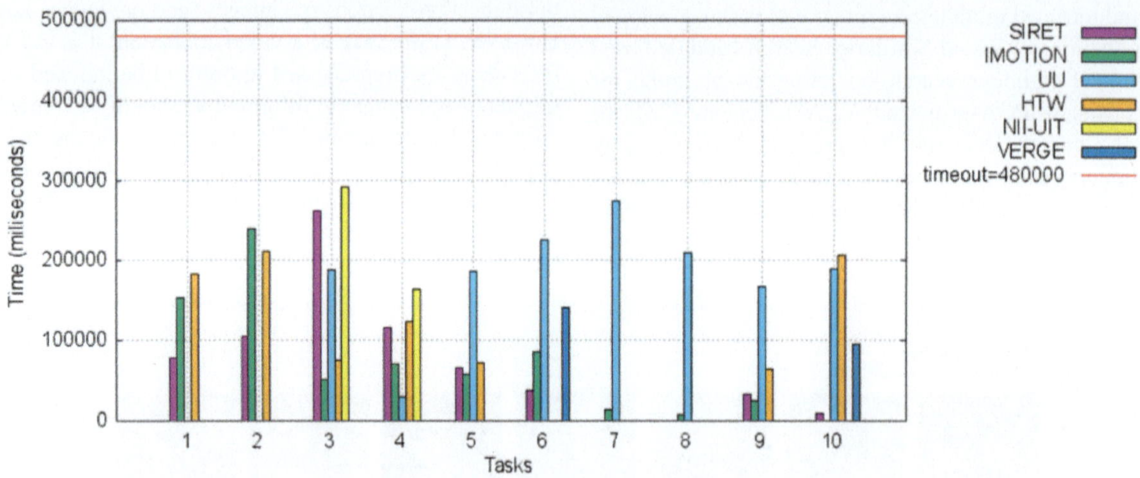

Figure 11 Breakdown per individual tasks of the time needed for the successful submissions for the visual experts round

The SIRET team completed 8 out of 10 proposed tasks, while the IMOTION team successfully completed 9 of the 10 tasks. The UU and HTW teams completed 7 tasks while the NII-UIT and VERGE teams completed 2 tasks each.

From Table 6 we can see that these two teams (in particular NII-UIT) submitted many wrong results, which however were quite visually similar to the targets. The frames for all the false submissions are shown in Table 6 as thumbnails with red contour. It can be seen that, most of the times, the visual similarity when compared with the target scenes is very high (see both Tables 1 and 7 - the thumbnails with the green contour). This is because the majority of the tools concentrated on the visual features, which in cases of similar/identical looking frames from different segments/shots does not suffice for correctly identifying the target scene. In those cases, additional information like for example the audio track, is needed.

Table 6 Frames submitted during the visual experts round (wrong submissions have red contours; right submissions have green contours)

Table 7 Frames submitted by the participant teams during the textual experts round (wrong submissions have red contours; right submissions have green contours)

A closer examination of Fig. 11 hints towards some interesting aspects:

- The IMOTION team had a slow start during the first 2 tasks, but then submitted the correct target scene very quick for the next 7 tasks. In fact they were the quickest for task number 3, 5, 7, 8 and 9.
- The same slow start during the first tasks can be seen in the case of the other teams: SIRET, HTW and UU. This might be due to an accommodation phase in which the teams got accustomed to the competition spirit as well as with the responsiveness of the various tools' features under the on-site conditions.
- In the case of the three teams that successfully completed the first two tasks IMOTION, SIRET and HTW, the time needed to complete the tasks actually increases: this can be explained either by the fact that the target scene is located "deep" within the archive and more time is needed for investigation, or by the fact that they tried to apply for the second round the same strategy they employed for the first one and failed.
- For the UU team which had a tool that relied heavily on human computation, the time needed to successfully find a target scene shows the lowest variance with the exception of task 4 in which actually the UU team was the fastest (this might be due to the positioning of the target scene at the very beginning of the video and the navigation model employed).
- The tasks 3, 4 and 6 were successfully completed by 5 teams; in the case of tasks 3 and 4 by the same teams configuration: IMOTION, SIRET, UU, HTW and NII-UIT. The tasks 5, 9 and 10 were completed by 4 teams, tasks 1 and 2 by 3 teams while tasks 7 and 8 were completed by only 2 teams: IMOTION and UU. While in the case of IMOTION it seems that the internals have played the most important role, since the team was fastest for exactly those two "difficult" tasks, in the case of UU it seems to be raw human power that had been rewarded - in the case of task 7 the UU team had the slowest completion time over all tasks (not in comparison with the other teams though).

Erroneous Submissions

It is interesting to note that the IMOTION and UU teams always identified the correct files, while the HTW and SIRET teams each had 1, and 2 wrongly identified files respectively, but in all 3 cases the correct file was later identified. The UU team achieved the best ratio for correct submissions vs. wrong submissions with 8 correct submissions to 3 wrong submissions.

The distances in terms of frame numbers from the submitted segment center to the target segment center for both right and false submissions are presented in Fig. 12 (Fig. 12a for right/successful submissions and Fig. 12b for false submissions within the correct file). Negative values in both sub-figures, represent submissions in the first half of the target segment or frames leading up to the target segment, while positive values represent submissions in the second half of the target segment or frames past the target segment up to the end of the video.

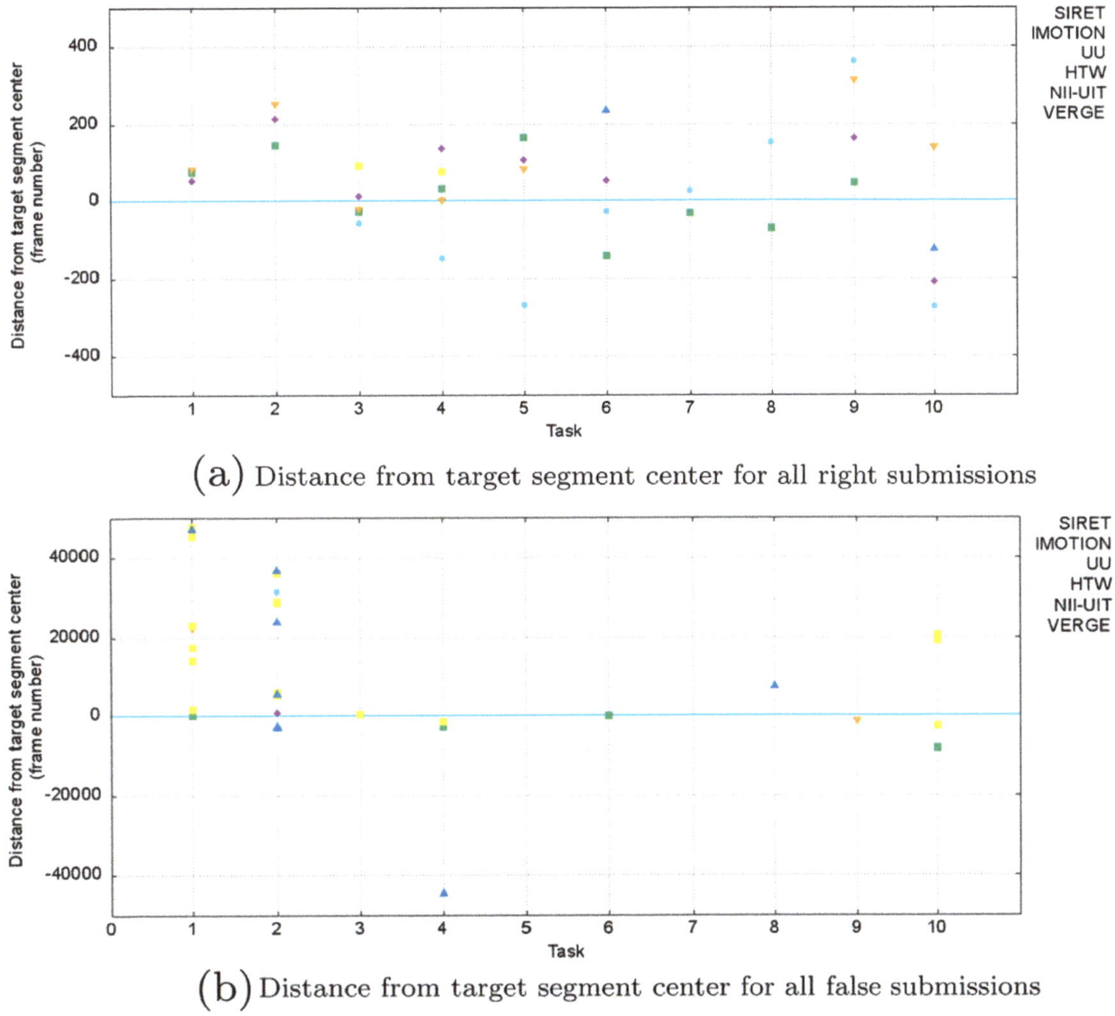

Figure 12 Breakdown per tasks for teams' submissions distances from target segment center for visual experts session

In the case of the successful submissions (see Fig. 12a) a greater number of submissions have been issued with frames from the second half of the target segment (positive values), although there is also a significant number of submissions from the first half. In the case of the false submissions (Fig. 12b) most of them are made by indicating frames/segments past the target segment and later in the video.

The actual frames sent for validation by the participating teams, for all the successful submissions, can be seen in Table 6 as thumbnails with green contour (in the case of the IMOTION team which sent a frame range, as permitted by the competition rules, we have chosen the central frame of the sent segment).

Evaluation details on textual experts tasks

The final scores at the end of the text round are also shown in Fig. 2. This proved to be the most challenging round of the competition. From the nine participating teams, only the UU team managed to score more than 50 % of the possible points for the session, with 367 points out of 600, while VERGE and SIRET scored close to 33 % with 188 and 166 points respectively. The performance of the UU team is particularly surprising since it employed only human computation and only static small thumbnails (no audio or video playback capabilities). Those results show there is still enough room for improvement in this area.

Figures 13 and 14 show the breakdown of the final scores per task as well as the information regarding the time needed for the completion of each successful submission for the tasks in the text experts' round.

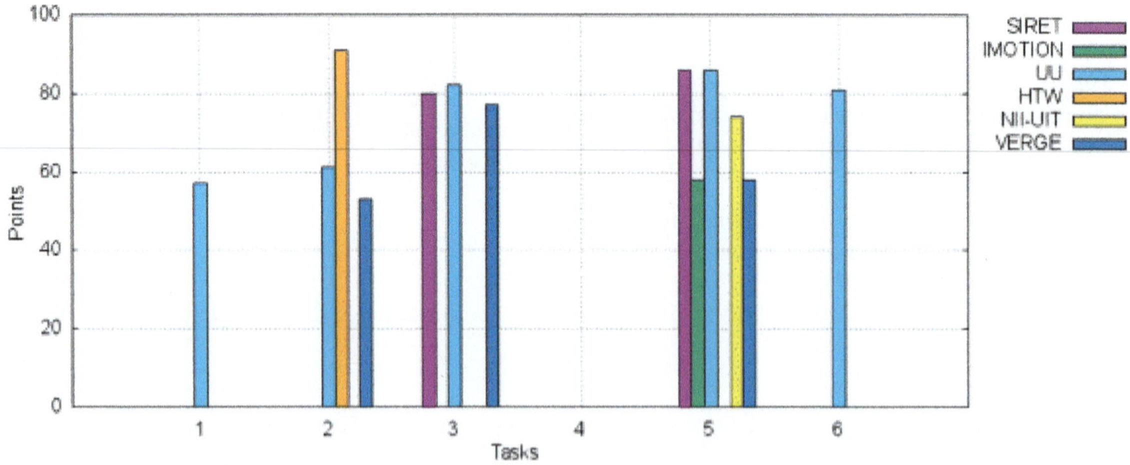

Figure 13 Breakdown per individual tasks of the scores for the text experts round

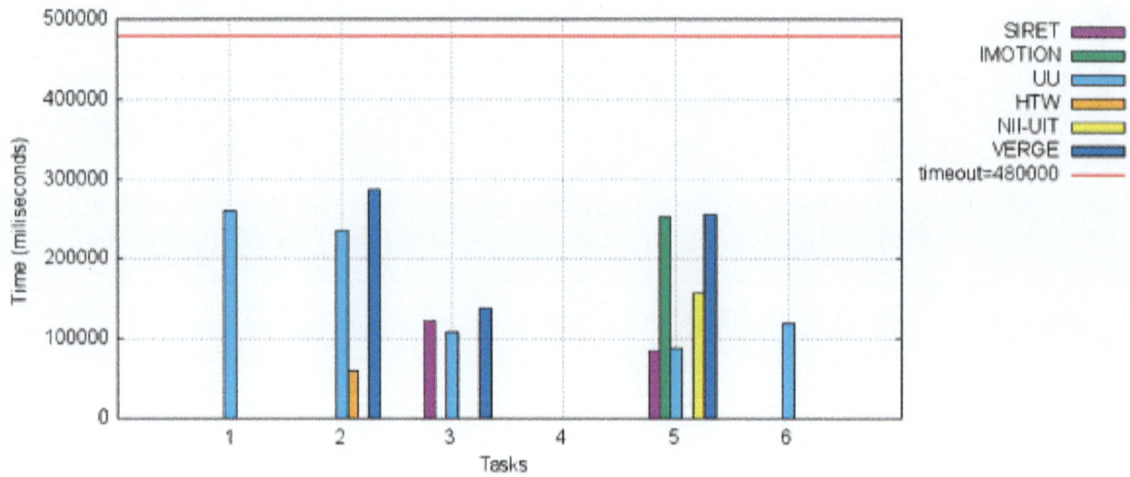

Figure 14 Breakdown per individual tasks of the time needed for the successful submissions for the text experts round

Regarding task completion, no team managed to solve Task 4, while Task 1 and Task 6 were solved only by the UU team. Task 2 and Task 3 were successfully solved by 3 teams, while Task 5 seams to have been the easiest, with 5 teams solving it. All teams scored over 50 % of the available points per task (more than 50 points) and as in the case of the visual round, no successful submission was made past the 5 minutes mark.

EVALUATION DETAILS ON THE NOVICE TASKS

Figure 2 also shows the scores obtained by each of the participating teams for the visual and text tasks of the novice round. With four visual tasks and two text tasks, the maximum possible scores were 400 for the visual and 200 for the text tasks. This gave an overall of 600 possible points for the novice round, as much as the text expert round.

IMOTION obtained the highest score for the visual novice (340 points, close to the maximum of 400), but the lowest score (28 points from the maximum of 200) for the text novice. NII-UIT, HTW, SIRET, VERGE and UU also scored high in the visual novice tasks. For the text novice tasks, NII-UIT, HTW and SIRET obtained the highest scores, with NII-UIT scoring a surprisingly high score of 181 points. The UU team also managed to score 90 points while, as already mentioned, IMOTION were last in this category with only 28 points. VERGE scored no points for the text tasks in the novice round, which is very surprising, since their concept-based search tool seems to be particularly well suited for novices.

The breakdown per tasks of the scores for the novice round as well as the time needed for the correct submissions are shown in Figs. 15, and 16 respectively. The scores obtained for all 4 visual tasks (Task 1, Task 2, Task 4, Task 5) were high and very high for all the novices - all scored over 60 points. This was true also for the 2 text tasks (Task 3 and Task 6), with the 2 notable exceptions of the IMOTION and SIRET teams in the case of Task 6 for which both achieved under 50 points. When looking at the time needed for submitting a correct answer as shown in Fig. 16, it can be seen that it was way under half of the maximal available time in most of the cases.

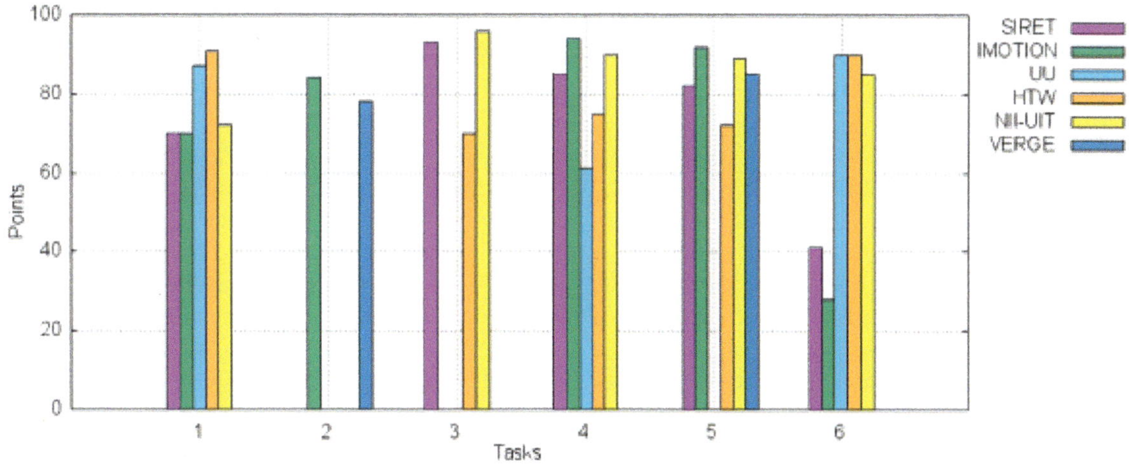

Figure 15 Breakdown per individual tasks of the scores for the novices round for both visual and textual tasks

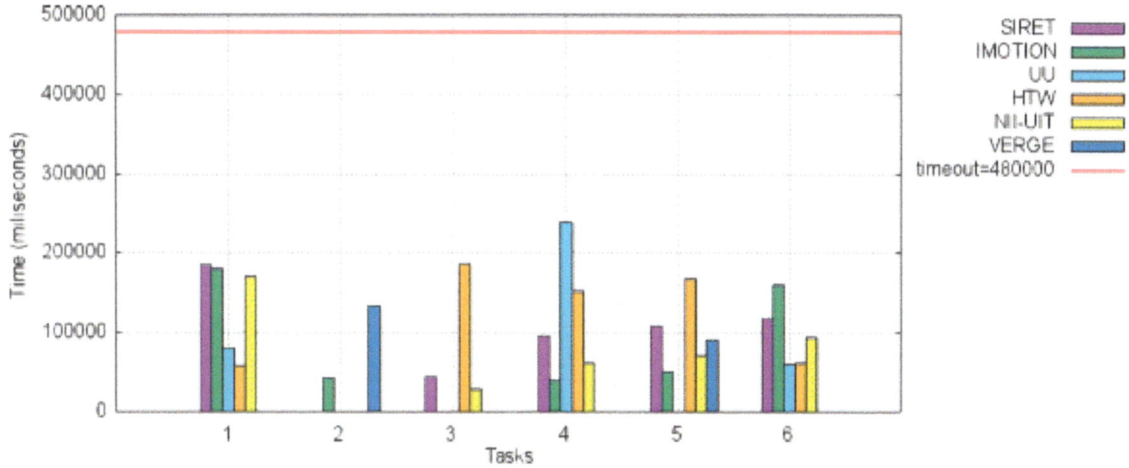

Figure 16 Breakdown per individual tasks of the time needed for the successful submissions for novice round for both visual and textual tasks

Overall, as also seen from Fig. 4c which presents the average number of submissions (wrong as well as correct) per team for the novice round, the participants seemed more than cautious when submitting frames for validation. In fact the novice round had overall the smallest number of wrong submissions when compared with both expert rounds. We have two possible non-exclusive explanations for this:

- it was the final round which was to decide the winner in a very tight competition and the participants were over-cautious;
- the majority of the"novices" were in fact members of the participating teams testing the "competition's" tools under their colleagues close supervision and they did not want to "sabotage" their winning chances by making wrong submissions and by this achieving a low score. At that point we want to mention that the novice session in general is kind of problematic for the final analysis, as it may distort the results. Therefore, we might want to skip it in future iterations of the VBS.

A closer inspection revealed that there is no difference between the two types of tasks (visual vs. text) from the outcome of submissions point of view. It can be seen though, that Task 6 seemed more difficult since it had overall the largest number of false submissions in both the right and wrong files. It has also been a textual task. The unusual large number of submissions for Task 6 when compared to the other five previous tasks could be also explained by the fact that it was the last task and by an all-or-nothing approach from some of the participants. In fact, the winner of the competition was decided by novices during this last task, when SIRET overcame IMOTION, after three false submissions for each team: two vs. one from a wrong file for SIRET when compared to IMOTION. The difference was made by the speed of the submissions, with SIRET being twice as fast as IMOTION for this particular task with 117049 ms vs. 268769 ms.

DEVELOPMENT OF INTERACTIVE VIDEO SEARCH TOOLS

VBS sessions happen to be indeed interactive and VBS 2015 was not an exception. Participants are exploring tools of other teams and the audience often discuss the approaches during breaks etc. It is thus natural to adapt and perhaps enhance a well-performing feature introduced by some other participant. Thanks to the gradual improvements, a tool winning the competition one year would probably fail without further development the next year. Several teams participated steadily for the last few years, each year improving their tools, adding modalities, features or ever reworking their concepts from scratch. We may ask then, are there any trends that we can distinguish? Can we find a common feature that is sooner or later incorporated by almost every team? And lastly, can we derive guides or best practices for developing such interactive video search tool?

In the following paragraphs, we track the evolution of the tools which had won VBS in one of the previous years, namely teams AAU (2012), NII-UIT (2013) and SIRET (2014 and 2015).

NII-UIT established themselves in 2013 by actually winning VBS [31]. The tool utilized filtering by prior-detected concepts and visual content, a grid of dominant color more precisely. The results were presented with a coarse-to-fine hierarchical refinement approach. In 2014 they came up with quite a similar tool with one important enhancement – a user could define a sequence of patterns, i.e., define two sets of filters and search for clips having two matching scenes in the same order [36]. Finally, in 2015 they additionally focused on face and upper body concepts together with audio filters and replaced the grid of dominant colors with less rigid free-drawing canvas [37].

The tool which was introduced by SIRET team in 2014 [33] appeared quite different. Instead of complex processing pipelines, such as state-of-the-art concept detectors etc., the authors employed only one feature capturing color distribution of key-frames (so called *feature signatures*) together with convenient sketch drawings (apparently, NII-UIT adapted sketch drawings later on). Surprisingly it was enough to win the VBS that year. Note that similarly to NII-UIT's tool, users were allowed to specify two consecutive sketches to improve the filtering power which seemed to be quite effective. Changes introduced to the tool in 2015 [5] were rather subtle, focusing the browsing part of the tool, such as compacting static scenes in order to save space etc.

The list of winners of previous VBS competitions is completed by AAU tool from 2012 [14] which is somewhat similar to the most recent UU's application, both exhibiting surprisingly powerful human computation potential. In this case, the videos are simply scanned in parallel during the search time without any prior content analysis.

Overlooking all the various approaches, we can identify three main techniques appearing repetitively:

- Content-based filtering may be based on either high-level concepts or low-level features. In particular, most of the participants used some kind of color-based filtering and although their filtering power decreases steadily as the dataset size increases, they seem to remain quite effective. Also, temporal filtering (e.g., two content sketches that focus two neighboring segments in a video) seem to be quite effective, because static approaches (focusing on a single image only) do not work well with the sheer amount of frames.
- Browsing is perhaps a crucial part that cannot be avoided. In many cases, the number of relevant results is simply too large to fit one screen and users need an effective and convenient way to browse through the results.
- As users do so, they will probably encounter scenes quite similar to the searched one which may be used as a query for additional similarity search. By giving the search engine either positive or negative examples users can rapidly navigate themselves towards the target if an appropriate similarity model is employed. Note that regarding the textual tasks, we face the problem of proper initialization of this similarity search loop.

At this moment, we do not see a single approach, feature or concept that is clearly outperforming the others. We believe, though, that a successful interactive video search tool has to incorporate all the three techniques mentioned above.

It is of course hard to predict the future in this challenging field. However, we can assume that future systems will also strongly rely on color-based filtering (e.g., color maps such as used by the system described in Section 4.3), on concept-based filtering (e.g., visual semantic concepts detected with deep learning approaches), on temporal filtering as well as on improved content visualization with several techniques, for example with hierarchical refinement of similar results. Since the VBS plans to increase the size of the data set every year, we believe that in the long run the biggest challenge will be the efficient handling of the large amount of content, i.e., content descriptors and indexes, and providing a highly responsive interactive system that allows for iterative refinement.

CONCLUSIONS

In the context of the discussion that follows, we would like to highlight the fact that all target segments for the three rounds, were randomly generated from the 154 files totaling over 100 hour of video material that formed the competition dataset. Approximately 10% of the cues had also textual description assigned by the organizers. From within those two pools, the target videos for the competition rounds were randomly chosen: ten targets for the visual expert round, six targets for the text expert round and six targets for the novice round (four targets for visual tasks and two targets for text tasks).

The case of the novice round differs a little bit from the two expert rounds, because the visual and textual tasks were mixed and not consecutive. Also, because of time constraints, the organizers were able to allow only six novice tasks out of which four were visual (Task 1, Task 2, Task 4 and Task 5) and two were textual tasks (Task 3 and Task 6).

Some interesting facts emerge when looking and comparing the figures presenting the breakdowns per individual tasks of the scores and of the times needed for the correct submissions for the three rounds:

- The visual tasks in the novice round achieved the best overall scores across all teams when compared with the visual tasks in the visual expert round.
- the text tasks in the novice round (2 tasks) achieved comparable results with the best performances across the 6 tasks in the text expert round.
- The completion time in the case of the visual and text tasks in the novice round is comparable with the completion time in the case of the visual and text expert rounds. The main difference is that the advantage that the SIRET, IMOTION and sometimes UU teams had in the expert rounds, is much reduced in the case of the novice round.
- The novice round brought the best performance for the NII-UIT team in both scored points and speed. Actually for the first text task in the novice round, the NII-UIT team achieved the best score and had the fastest correct submission.

It is also interesting to have a closer look at the frames being submitted across the three competition rounds, both the ones of the correct submissions as well as the ones of the wrong submissions (both from the correct and wrong files) and to compare them with the uniform sampled frames of the video targets. The tables in question are Table 1, Table 1 and Table 4 for the overview of the target videos and Tables 6 and 7 for the correct submitted frames as well as for the wrong submitted frames. Some interesting observations can be made:

- Within each of the scenes used as targets in the visual expert round there are multiple highly similar images (this is also apparent in Table 1 as well as Tables 3 and 4 which display overviews of the 20 seconds long target scenes while using 2 second granularity for each image). Because of the granularity used in the figures, not all the details are visible, from here the difference in terms of actually submitted frames.
- The scenes are very diverse including indoor and outdoor shots as well as overlays of computer generated content spread across TV reporting, TV series, TV documentaries.

The best results were obtained by tools that employed some form of sketching for an query-by-example approach, as in the case of the SIRET and IMOTION teams, or that made heavy use of browsing, like in the case of the UU team which had an approach centered on human computation. All those tools had effectively put the user in the center of their approaches to an interactive multimedia retrieval system and had tried to exploit its mental and physical capacities to their fullest in order to solve the proposed tasks. The results of the text tasks during both the expert and novice rounds show that there is still a lot of room for improvement and that in this particular case further research is needed.

ACKNOWLEDGMENTS

Open access funding provided by University of Klagenfurt.

The authors would like to thank all the colleagues that participated in the development of the VBS2015 tools, the colleagues that took part in the VBS2015 competition as well as the colleagues that took time to read and make observations on draft versions of this paper: Laszlo Böszörmenyi, Marco A. Hudelist, Anastasia Moumtzidou , Vasileios Mezaris, Ioannis Kompatsiaris, Rob van de Werken, Nico Hezel, Radek Mackowiak, Ivan Giangreco, Claudiu Tănase, Heiko Schuldt.

The video content used for VBS is programme material under the copyright of the British Broadcasting Corporation (BBC), kindly provided for research use in the context of VBS.

This work was funded by the Federal Ministry for Transport, Innovation and Technology (bmvit) and Austrian Science Fund (FWF): TRP 273-N15 and the European Regional Development Fund and the Carinthian Economic Promotion Fund (KWF), supported by Lakeside Labs GmbH, Klagenfurt, Austria.

The research leading to these results has received funding from the European Union's Seventh Framework Programme (FP7/2007-2013) under grant agreement no. 610370, ICoSOLE ("Immersive Coverage of Spatially Outspread Live Events", http://www.icosole.eu).

This research has been supported by Charles University Grant Agency project 1134316.

REFERENCES

1. Adams B, Greenhill S, Venkatesh S (2012) Towards a video browser for the digital native. In: ICMEW'12. doi:10.1109/ICMEW.2012.29, pp 127–132
2. Bailer W, Schoeffmann K, Ahlström D, Weiss W, Del Fabro M, Mei T (2013) Interactive evaluation of video browsing tools. In: Li S, Saddik A, Wang M, Sebe N, Yan S, Hong R, Gurrin C (eds) Advances in multimedia modeling, lecture notes in computer science. doi:10.1007/978-3-642-35725-1_8, vol 7732. Springer, Berlin Heidelberg, pp 81–91
3. Barthel KU, Hezel N, Mackowiak R (2015) Graph-based browsing for large video collections. In: He X, Luo S, Tao D, Xu C, Yang J, Hasan M (eds) MultiMedia modeling, lecture notes in computer science. doi:10.1007/978-3-319-14442-9_25, vol 8936. Springer International Publishing, pp 237–242
4. Barthel KU, Hezel N, Mackowiak R (2015) Graph-based browsing for large video collections. In: Proceedings of multimedia modeling - 21st international conference, MMM 2015. Part II. doi:10.1007/978-3-319-14442-9_21. Sydney, pp 237–242
5. Blažek A, Lokoč J, Matzner F, Skopal T (2015) Enhanced signature-based video browser. In: Proceedings of multimedia modeling - 21st international conference, MMM 2015. Part II. Sydney, pp 243–248
6. Blažek A, Lokoč J, Skopal T (2014) Video retrieval with feature signature sketches. In: Proceedings of similarity search and applications - 7th international conference, SISAP 2014. Los Cabos, pp 25– 36
7. Chen HM, Cheng WH, Hu MC, Lin YC, Hsieh YH (2013) Human action search based on dynamic shape volumes. In: Li S, Saddik AE, Wang M, Mei T, Sebe N, Yan S, Hong R, Gurrin C (eds) MultiMedia modeling, lecture notes in computer science, vol 7733. Springer International Publishing, pp 99–109
8. Christel M, Huang C, Moraveji N, Papernick N (2004) Exploiting multiple modalities for interactive video retrieval. In: ICASSP'04. doi:10.1109/ICASSP.2004.1326724, vol 3, pp iii–1032
9. Christel MG, Yan R (2007) Merging storyboard strategies and automatic retrieval for improving interactive video search. In: CIVR'07. doi:10.1145/1282280.1282351. ACM, New York, pp 486–493
10. Cobârzan C (2014) Evaluating interactive search in videos with image and textual description defined target scenes. In: IEEE international conference on multimedia and expo workshops (ICMEW), 2014. IEEE, pp 1–6
11. Cobârzan C, Del Fabro M, Schoeffmann K (2015) Collaborative browsing and search in video archives with mobile clients. In: He X, Luo S, Tao D, Xu C, Yang J, Hasan M (eds) MultiMedia modeling, lecture notes in computer science, vol 8936. Springer International Publishing, pp 266– 271
12. Cobârzan C, Schoeffmann K (2014) How do users search with basic html5 video players? In: Gurrin C, Hopfgartner F, Hurst W, Johansen H, Lee H, O'Connor N (eds) MultiMedia modeling, lecture notes in computer

science, vol 8326. Springer International Publishing, pp 109–120

13. Datta R, Joshi D, Li J, Wang JZ (2008) Image retrieval: ideas, influences, and trends of the new age. ACM Comput Surv 40(2):5:1–5:60. doi:10.1145/1348246.1348248CrossRef
14. Del Fabro M, Boszormenyi L (2012) Aau video browser: Non-sequential hierarchical video browsing without content analysis. In: Schoeffmann K, Merialdo B, Hauptmann AG, Ngo CW, Andreopoulos Y, Breiteneder C (eds) MultiMedia modeling, lecture notes in computer science, vol 7131. Springer International Publishing, pp 639–641
15. Eskevich M, Aly R, Chen S, Jones GJF (2013) The search and hyperlinking task at mediaeval 2013. In: Proc. of MediaEval Workshop, pp 18–19
16. Giangreco I, Al Kabary I, Schuldt H (2014) Adam-a database and information retrieval system for big multimedia collections. In: IEEE international congress on big data (bigdata congress), 2014. IEEE, pp 406–413
17. Girgensohn A, Shipman F, Wilcox L (2011) Adaptive clustering and interactive visualizations to support the selection of video clips. In: ICMR '11. doi:10.1145/1991996.1992030. ACM, New York, pp 34:1–34:8
18. Hopfgartner F (2007) Understanding video retrieval. VDM Verlag
19. Hopfgartner F, Urban J, Villa R, Jose JM (2007) Simulated testing of an adaptive multimedia information retrieval system. In: CBMI'07, pp 328–335
20. Hu MC, Chen CW, Cheng WH, Chang CH, Lai JH, Wu JL (2015) Real-time human movement retrieval and assessment with kinect sensor. IEEE Trans Cybern 45(4):742–753. doi:10.1109/TCYB.2014.2335540CrossRef
21. Huber J, Steimle J, Mühlhäuser M (2010) Toward more efficient user interfaces for mobile video browsing: an in-depth exploration of the design space. In: MM'10. doi:10.1145/1873951.1873999. New York, pp 341–350
22. Hudelist MA, Xu Q (2015) The multi-stripe video browser for tablets. In: He X, Luo S, Tao D, Xu C, Yang J, Hasan M (eds) MultiMedia modeling, lecture notes in computer science, vol 8936. Springer International Publishing, pp 272–277
23. Hürst W, Darzentas D (2012) Quantity versus quality: The role of layout and interaction complexity in thumbnail-based video retrieval interfaces. In: Proceedings of the 2Nd ACM international conference on multimedia retrieval, ICMR '12. doi:10.1145/2324796.2324849. ACM, New York, pp 45:1–45:8
24. Hürst W, Hoet M (2015) Sliders versus storyboards – investigating interaction design for mobile video browsing. In: He X, Luo S, Tao D, Xu C, Yang J, Hasan M (eds) MultiMedia modeling, lecture notes in computer science. doi:10.1007/978-3-319-14442-9_11, vol 8936. Springer International Publishing, pp 123–134
25. Hürst W, Snoek C, Spoel WJ, Tomin M (2011) Size matters! How thumbnail number, size, and motion influence mobile video retrieval. In: Lee KT, Tsai WH, Liao HY, Chen T, Hsieh JW, Tseng CC (eds) Advances in multimedia modeling, lecture notes in computer science. doi:10.1007/978-3-642-17829-0_22, vol 6524. Springer Berlin Heidelberg, pp 230–240
26. Hürst W, Snoek CG, Spoel WJ, Tomin M (2010) Keep moving!: Revisiting thumbnails for mobile video retrieval. In: Proceedings of the international conference on multimedia, MM '10. doi:10.1145/1873951.1874124. ACM, New York, pp 963–966
27. Hürst W, van de Werken R, Hoet M (2015) A storyboard-based interface for mobile video browsing. In: He X, Luo S, Tao D, Xu C, Yang J, Hasan M (eds) MultiMedia modeling, lecture notes in computer science. doi:10.1007/978-3-319-14442-9_25, vol 8936. Springer International Publishing, pp 261–265
28. Jegou H, Douze M, Schmid C, P, P (2010) Aggregating local descriptors into a compact image representation. In: IEEE conference on computer vision and pattern recognition (CVPR), 2010. doi:10.1109/CVPR.2010.5540039. IEEE, pp 3304–3311
29. Johnson S (1967) Hierarchical clustering schemes. Psychometrika 2(2):241–254CrossRef
30. Kruliš M, Lokoč J, Skopal T (2013) Efficient extraction of feature signatures using multi-gpu architecture. In: MMM (2), pp 446–456
31. Le DD, Lam V, Ngo TD, Tran VQ, Nguyen VH, Duong DA, Satoh S (2013) Nii-uit-vbs: a video browsing tool for known item search. In: Li S, Saddik AE, Wang M, Mei T, Sebe N, Yan S, Hong R, Gurrin C (eds) MultiMedia modeling, lecture notes in computer science, vol 7733. Springer International Publishing, pp 547–549
32. Lin YC, Hu MC, Cheng WH, Hsieh YH, Chen HM (2012) Actions speak louder than words: Searching human action video based on body movement. In: Proceedings of the international conference on multimedia, MM '12. doi:10.1145/2393347.2396432. ACM, New York, pp 1261–1262
33. Lokoč J, Blažek A, Skopal T (2014) Signature-based video browser. In: Gurrin C, Hopfgartner F, Hürst W, Johansen H, Lee H, O'Connor N (eds) MultiMedia modeling, lecture notes in computer science, vol 8326. Springer International Publishing, pp 415–418
34. Mei T, Rui Y, Li S, Tian Q (2014) Multimedia search reranking: a literature survey. ACM Comput Surv 46(3):38:1–38:38. doi:10.1145/2536798CrossRef
35. Moumtzidou A, Avgerinakis K, Apostolidis E, Markatopoulou F, Apostolidis K, Mironidis T, Vrochidis S, Mezaris V, Kompatsiaris Y, Patras I (2015) Verge: a multimodal interactive video search engine. In: He X, Luo S, Tao D, Xu C, Yang J, Hasan M (eds) MultiMedia modeling, lecture notes in computer science. doi:10.1007/978-3-319-14442-9_25, vol 8936. Springer International Publishing
36. Ngo TD, Nguyen VH, Lam V, Phan S, Le DD, Duong DA, Satoh S (2014) Nii-uit: a tool for known item search by sequential pattern. In: Gurrin C, Hopfgartner F, Hurst W, Johansen H, Lee H, O'Connor N (eds) MultiMedia modeling, lecture notes in computer science, vol 8326.

Springer International Publishing, pp 419–422

37. Ngo TD, Nguyen VT, Nguyen VH, Le DD, Duong Duc A, Satoh S (2015) Nii-uit browser:a multimodal video search system. In: He X, Luo S, Tao D, Xu C, Yang J, Hasan M (eds) MultiMedia modeling, lecture notes in computer science, vol 8936. Springer International Publishing, pp 278–281
38. Rossetto L, Giangreco I, Schuldt H (2014) Cineast: A multi-feature sketch-based video retrieval engine. In: IEEE international symposium on multimedia (ISM), 2014. IEEE, pp 18–23
39. Rossetto L, Giangreco I, Schuldt H, Dupont S, Seddati O, Sezgin M, Sahillioglu Y (2015) Imotion - a content-based video retrieval engine. In: He X, Luo S, Tao D, Xu C, Yang J, Hasan M (eds) MultiMedia modeling, lecture notes in computer science, vol 8936. Springer International Publishing , pp 261–265
40. Rubner Y, Tomasi C (2001) Perceptual metrics for image database navigation. Kluwer Academic Publishers, NorwellCrossRefMATH
41. Schoeffmann K (2014) A user-centric media retrieval competition: The video browser showdown 2012-2014. IEEE MultiMedia 21(4):8–13. doi:10.1109/MMUL.2014.56CrossRef
42. Schoeffmann K, Ahlström D, Bailer W, Cobârzan C, Hopfgartner F, McGuinness K, Gurrin C, Frisson C, Le DD, Del Fabro M, Bai H, Weiss W (2014) The video browser showdown: a live evaluation of interactive video search tools. IJMIR 3(2):113–127. doi:10.1007/s13735-013-0050-8
43. Schoeffmann K, Boeszoermenyi L (2009) Video browsing using interactive navigation summaries. In: 7th international workshop on content-based multimedia indexing, 2009. CBMI '09, pp 243–248
44. Schoeffmann K, Cobarzan C (2013) An evaluation of interactive search with modern video players. In: IEEE international conference on multimedia and expo workshops (ICMEW), 2013. IEEE, pp 1–4
45. Schoeffmann K, Hopfgartner F (2015) Interactive video search. In: Proceedings of the 23rd annual ACM conference on multimedia conference (MM '15). doi:10.1145/2733373.2807417. ACM, New York, pp 1321–1322
46. Schoeffmann K, Hopfgartner F, Marques O, Boeszoermenyi L, Jose JM (2010) Video browsing interfaces and applications: a review. SPIE Rev 1(1):018004. doi:10.1117/6.0000005. http://link.aip.org/link/?SV2/1/018004/1
47. Schoeffmann K, Hudelist MA, Huber J (2015) Video interaction tools: a survey of recent work. ACM Comput Surv 1–36. Accepted for publication
48. Schoeffmann K, Taschwer M, Boeszoermenyi L (2010) The video explorer: a tool for navigation and searching within a single video based on fast content analysis. In: MMSys'10. doi:10.1145/1730836.1730867. ACM, pp 247–258
49. Sun Q, Hürst W (2008) Video browsing on handheld devices - interface designs for the next generation of mobile video players. IEEE Multimedia 15(3):76–83. doi:http://doi.ieeecomputersociety.org/10.1109/MMUL.2008.66CrossRef
50. Worring M, Sajda P, Santini S, Shamma DA, Smeaton AF, Yang Q (2012) Where is the user in multimedia retrieval? IEEE MultiMedia 19(4):6–10. doi:10.1109/MMUL.2012.53CrossRef
51. Zhang Z, Albatal R, Gurrin C, Smeaton Alan F (2015) Interactive known-item search using semantic textual and colour modalities. In: He X, Luo S, Tao D, Xu C, Yang J, Hasan M (eds) MultiMedia modeling, lecture notes in computer science, vol 8936. Springer International Publishing, pp 282–286

CHAPTER 15

A MULTIMEDIA SYSTEM FOR BREATH REGULATION AND RELAXATION

Wen-Ching Liao, Han-Hong Lin, He-Lin Ruo and Po-Hsiang Hsu

INTRODUCTION

Recently, mental stress is becoming one of the major factors causing illness. Health problems caused by stress include hypertension, cardiovascular diseases, increased likelihood of infections and depression [1-3]. To release stress multiple relaxation techniques have been developed over hundreds of years, including yoga, meditation, qi-kung, tai-chi, etc. in eastern culture society. Also in modern psychophysiology, relaxation techniques like autogenic training, diaphragmatic breathing, mindfulness, etc. are also developed [4]. Among those relaxation techniques breath regulation usually plays an essential role. Researchers demonstrated that breath regulation is beneficial for reducing blood pressure [5, 6] and focusing the mind for optimal performance [6]. Over the past decades, computing technologies have been utilized to support breath regulation in multiple applications. For instance, Moraveji proposed peripheral paced respiration, which integrated breath pacing application in the operating system, to slow down user breath during information work [7]. Yu proposed a multimedia biofeedback system for abdominal breath learning [8]. Park et al. designed multiple modes of breath induction to facilitate relaxation and other mental function promotion [9]. Most of these studies tend to influence user breath through providing respiratory guidance for users to follow, and turned their breath slow and deep eventually. However, human breath actually involves randomness between each cycle of inhalation and exhalation. Even in calm status, there exit correlation plus random variation between each breath. Breath features like breath period, breathing depth, and the inhalation/exhalation ratio varies spontaneously. In fact, a range of studies has shown that healthy breathing is characterized by complex variability consisting of considerable structured variability and some random variability [10-13]. Forced breath pacing though mechanically changes user breath, the subjective feeling of relaxation may not be promoted [14]. Therefore, pure guiding style of breath regulation may not be suitable when applied for relaxation.

Figure 1. The relaxation system appearance

Citation: Wen-Ching Liao, Han-Hong Lin, He-Lin Ruo and Po-Hsiang Hsu, "A Multimedia System for Breath Regulation and Relaxation" International Journal of Advanced Computer Science and Applications(ijacsa), 6(12), 2015. http://dx.doi.org/10.14569/IJACSA.2015.061208 - See more at: http://thesai.org/Publications/ViewPaper?Volume=6&Issue=12&Code=ijacsa&SerialNo=8#sthash.8Cd5uG5z.dpuf

In the breath interaction module of our relaxation system, we propose a target-based breath regulation. Unlike traditional pure breath guiding, in which the guiding multimedia is unrelated to user breath and the user is required to breathe following the guide during the entire process of the breath regulation, the visual or aural feedback reflects user breath in the target-based breath regulation. The user is asked to achieve some feedback target through his or her breathing. For instance, if the visual feedback of user breath is a flower, which opens and closes to reflect inhaling and exhaling. The instruction given to the user may be "Let the flower open to the maximum and close to the minimum through your breathing". After giving the instruction to the user, we can influence users' breathing pattern differently through manage the underlying signal mapping mechanism. The mechanism mapping the breath signal to the visual/aural multimedia feedback can be designed to slow down and deepen user breaths as we expected. The difference between this target-based breath regulation and common pure breath pacing is that user breath is less constrained. Target achievement timing is loosely stipulated. Tension and discomfort caused by forced breath pacing reduce while the influence on breath can still be achieved because of the attempt to accomplish the given target. Except proposing novel form of breath regulation, we integrate newly developed noncontact breath detection technique, special reflection mechanism, and bio-signal monitoring to implement a relaxation system. Following, we first illustrate the construction of the system in Section II. Then we detailed the proposed breath interaction mechanism and a preliminary experiment conducted in Section III. In Section IV, a formal experiment is introduced. The experiment procedure designed to investigate the effects of three forms of breath regulation - pure guiding mode, target-based mode, and free breathing mode, which means no multimedia feedback is involved, is demonstrated. The experiment results are also reported and illustrated. In Section V, the analysis and comparisons of physiology changes are demonstrated. Subjective reports when experiencing these three modes are also discussed. Finally, conclusions and acknowledgements are represented in Section VI and Section VII.

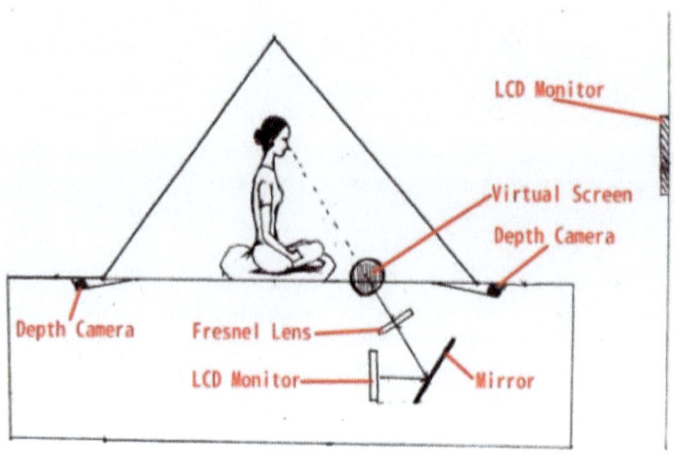

Figure 2. The platform design diagram

SYSTEM DESIGN

System Structure

The reason we have the opportunity to implement this multimedia system is because of a collaborative project with a professional music company. The system will be settled at a realistic music store for long term commercial exhibition after this study. Therefore, sometimes the reason of the appearance selection is partially due to the artistic sensation, not entirely for the technical reasons. To deliver the isolated and stable visual sensation, the appearance of this system is specially designed in the shape of a pyramid. Copper tubes are used to construct the pyramid shape frame (Fig. 1). Construction of the system is illustrated in Fig. 2. A user is required to sit at a specified position under the pyramid so that his or her respiration can be detected correctly. Two depth cameras are placed in the front and in the back of the user to detect respiration [15], in the meantime, a blood volume pulse (BVP) sensor and a skin conductance response (SCR) sensor are integrated in a sphere (Fig. 3). The sphere is put aside the seat and meant to be hold by the user when using this system. There are two monitors in this system. One is embedded in the wall in front of the user, showing immediate detected biosignals including breaths, heart rate, and SCR (Fig. 4). The other one is under the user's sitting ground displaying a metaphor (i.e. a lotus in our design). Displayed metaphor image is reflected by a mirror and projected through a Fresnel lens so that only people sitting at the specified position under the pyramid can have a clear view of it [16] (Fig. 2). Because the background of the metaphor image is removed and the special optical effect of the Fresnel lens, this projected metaphor looks floating in the air in front of the user.

Sensors

Respiration Sensor

In the past, the respiratory inductive plethysmography (RIP) sensor is usually the choice of the respiration sensor, and it is widely used in respiration related researches. Although the bound feeling while using RIP makes the user uncomfortable, traditional noncontact respiration detection techniques are too expensive and related settings are complicated. For instance, optoelectronic plethysmography requires the user being attached with multiple light-reflecting markers.

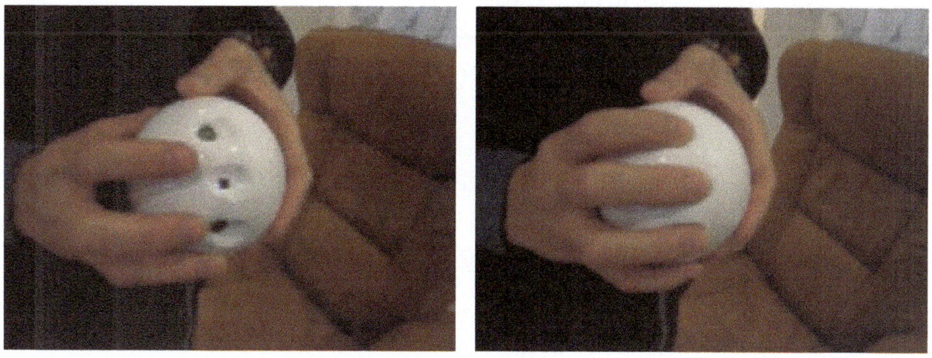

Figure 3. The remade sphere shape sensor of heart rate and skin conductance

Until recently, a novel respiration detection method using depth camera is proposed [15]. The emitter mounted in the depth camera emits infrared (IR) light beams and the depth sensor reads the IR beams reflected back to the sensor. The reflected beams are converted into depth information measuring the distance between an object and the sensor. Since we put two depth cameras in front and in back of the user. We can obtain the distance from the front side of the user to the front depth camera and the distance at the back side. Then, given the distance between two depth cameras, we can obtain the thickness of the user torso. Therefore, the respiratory signal (respiratory rate and depth) can be measured through the thickness changes as a result of breathing. This depth information based detecting method is not only cheap but also simple to operate. The only device needed are depth cameras and no other miscellaneous gadget is required. Therefore, we choose this technique as our respiration detection method. Another advantage of using depth cameras as the respiration sensor is that we can observe the fluctuation at chest and at belly separately. With this information, we can provide user more concrete visual feedback when practicing diaphragmatic breathing (Fig. 4). Diaphragmatic breathing, also known as abdominal breathing, is a well-known breathing technique which activates parasympathetic nervous system (PNS) and induces relaxation [18]. It will be recommended to the users when using this relaxation system in our experiment.

Heart Rate and Skin Conductance Sensors

The bio-sensor adopted is the peripheral device of WildDivine, which includes a photoplethysmograph (PPG) sensor and two electrodes so that user's BVP and SCR can be detected [17]. In order to provide comfortable and naturalistic sensor interface, we specially embedded the bio-sensor into a sphere ball with pits for easy contact (Fig. 3).

Biofeedback Medium

There are two forms of visual feedback in this system. The first one is the bio-signal monitoring shown on the screen in front of the user (Fig. 4). Signals shown in the order: left up, left down, right up, and right down, are respectively chest breath, belly breath, heartbeat, and SCR. There is a rectangle mask composed of blue and green regions in the middle window. This mask uses blue region to cover the chest part and green region to cover the belly part. A user can adjust the position of this mask and the covering range of the blue and green regions by mouse clicks. This enables identifying the proportion of the abdominal breath. Besides, the SCR curve at the right down window also indicates the relaxing extent of the user.

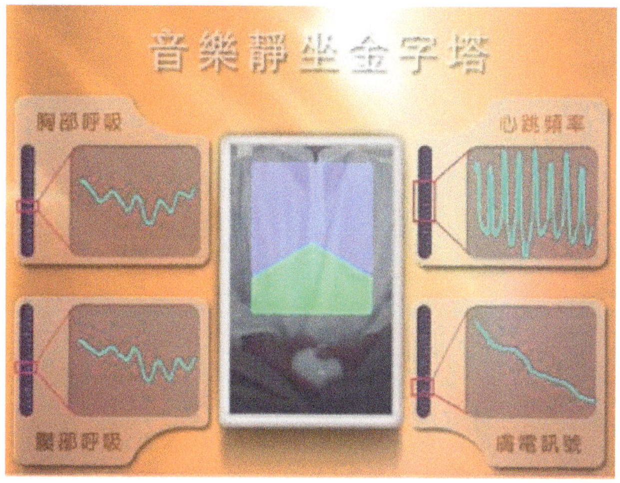

Figure 4. Bio-signal monitoring

The second form of visual feedback is a metaphor (it is a lotus in our application) projected by the reflection mechanism beneath the sitting ground. The user sitting at the specific position so that he or she can have a special visual effect that the projected metaphor seems floating in the air. The projected metaphor is replaceable, and we choose a lotus as the metaphor of breath in our application because that a lotus is widely used in eastern culture to symbolize a pure, peaceful and clear mental state. Later in the experiment, the lotus is designed to open and close to imply inhalation and exhalation of the user respectively.

BREATH INTERACTION

The Mapping Mechanism

Traditionally, to influence user breath, users are required to breathe following visual or aural guidance, which is unrelated to their breath. However, pure guiding style of breath regulation though mechanically slow down and deepen user breath, it also induces tension due to unnatural paced breathing. Therefore, we propose the concept of target-based breath regulation. The target-based breath regulation reflects user breath with the visual or aural multimedia. Users are required to achieve some feedback target through their breathing. Hence, the underlying mapping mechanism which maps breath signal to the feedback multimedia content can affect the result of breathing pattern. To verity that managing the underlying mapping mechanism can effectively affect the breathing pattern of the user a preliminary experiment is conducted. In this preliminary experiment we use a variable circle to symbolize user breath. The circle expands when the user breathes in and shrinks when breathing out. Two mapping mechanism are designed. The first one, named local-mapping mode, maps the extremes of the circle variation to the local extremes of the breath signal. The second one, named global-mapping mode, maps the extremes of the circle variation to the global extremes of the breath signal. Details are described below. We first generate n circle images with the radiuses ranging from 1 to n. Then we index these circle images from 1 to n orderly so that the bigger the index is the bigger the circle is.

Assume the breath signal is f(t) and the corresponding index of the circle image displayed is g(t). Then we let

$$g(t) = \frac{f(t) - \min(f(t))}{\max(f(t)) - \min(f(t))} \times n$$

where $max(f(t))$ is the local maximum and $min(f(t))$ is the local minimum in local-mapping mode, and they are global extremes in the global-mapping mode. An example of mapping illustration using n=300 and breathing depth signal ranging from 5mm to 20 mm is shown in Fig. 5. In the local-mapping mode, the extremes are obtained in the period from immediate sampling time t to 15 seconds backward t-15. The reason 15 seconds are specified is that we hope to find the extremes in at least one complete breath cycle, and normally people breathe with the frequency higher than 4 times per minute, which means the breath period should be lower than 15 seconds. In the global-mapping mode, the extremes are found in the period from t=0 to immediate time t.

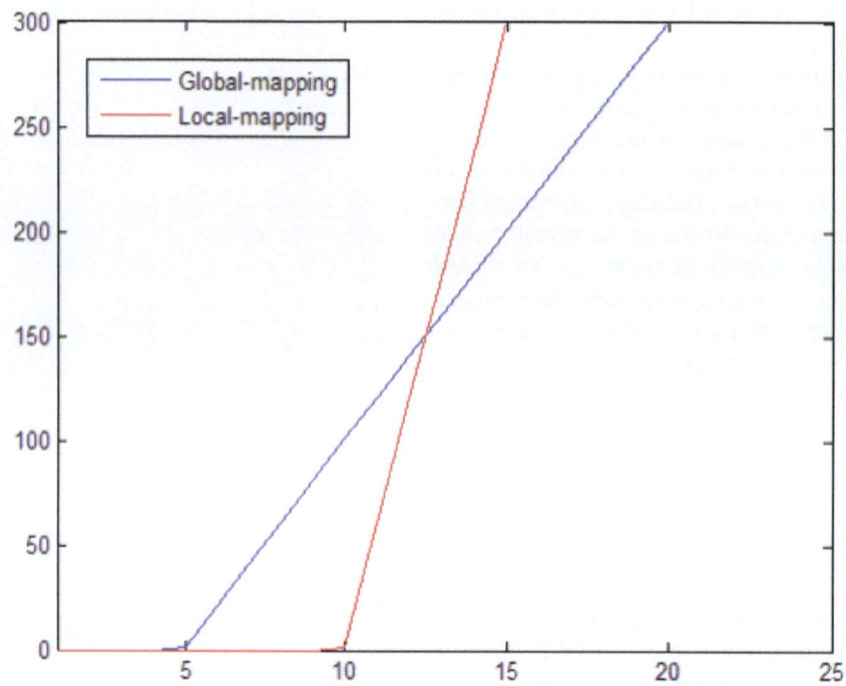

Figure 5. An example of mapping of the breathing depth and the corresponding image index

Preliminary Experiment

We recruit 12 labmates (5 females) as experiment participants. Each participant was required to proceed 3 trials of abdominal breathing practices. Each trial lasts 3 minutes and total 9 minutes for a participant. For all participants, the first trial is free breathing without multimedia. For 6 of the participants the second trial is the local-mapping mode and the third trial is the global-mapping mode. For the other 6 participants the order of the second and the third trial is reversed. Experiment results show that breathing patterns are significantly different in these three modes (Fig. 6, Fig. 7).

A one-way repeated measure analysis of variance (ANOVA) was conducted to evaluate the average breathing depth and frequency among three modes. The results indicated a significant difference in breathing depth (N=12, $F(2, 10) = 10.29$, $p=0.004$). Follow up pairwise paired t-test comparisons also showed significant difference in breathing depth ($p<0.05$) but not in breathing frequency.

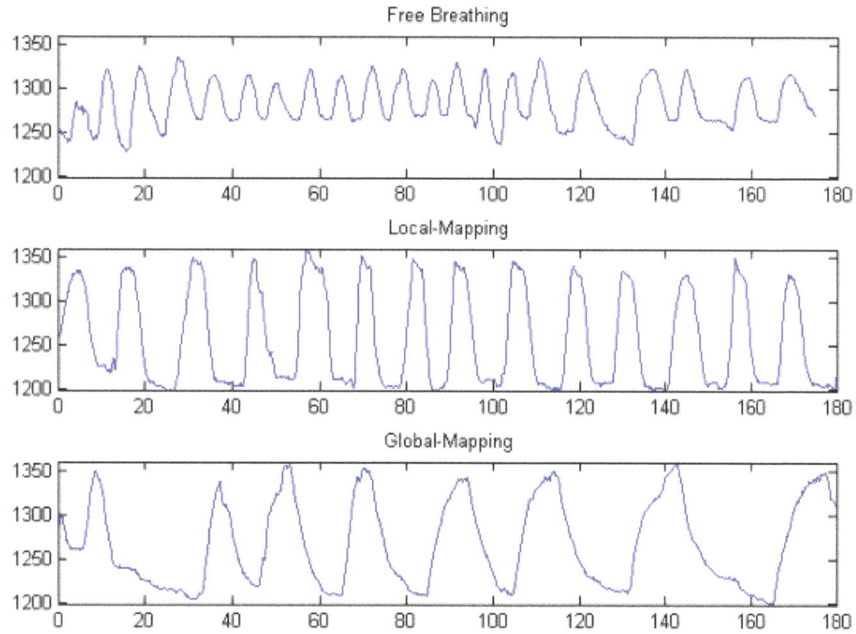

Figure 6. Three breathing patterns in the preliminary experiment: Free breathing mode, Local-Mapping mode, and Global-Mapping mode

There was significant increase in breathing depth when multimedia feedback was used, and the increase in global mapping mode is even higher than that in the local-mapping mode. However, the result of ANOVA conducted to compare breathing frequency showed no significant difference. Follow up pairwise paired t-test comparisons showed that the breathing frequency in global-mapping mode was significant lower than those in the other two modes. But there was no significant difference between the free breathing mode and the local-mapping mode (Fig. 7). According to the research of McCaul et al. in 1979, slowing respiration rate reduced physiological arousal and self-reported anxiety [19]. Although the global-mapping mode performed better in deepening and slowing down user breath, subjects reported that achieving the given target, which was to maximize and minimize the lotus through their breathing, was harder in the global-mapping mode. Some of the participants even feel uncomfortable tension instead of relaxation. To compromise on the effect of slow and deepen user breath and the subjective feeling of tension due to over required effort. We choose the local-mapping mode as our design of the underlying mapping mechanism of the breath regulation. It can effectively deep and slow user breath while the multimedia feedback target provided for the user can be achieved without causing uncomfortable tension instead. In our formal experiment, we compare it with the traditional pure guiding mode and the free breathing mode.

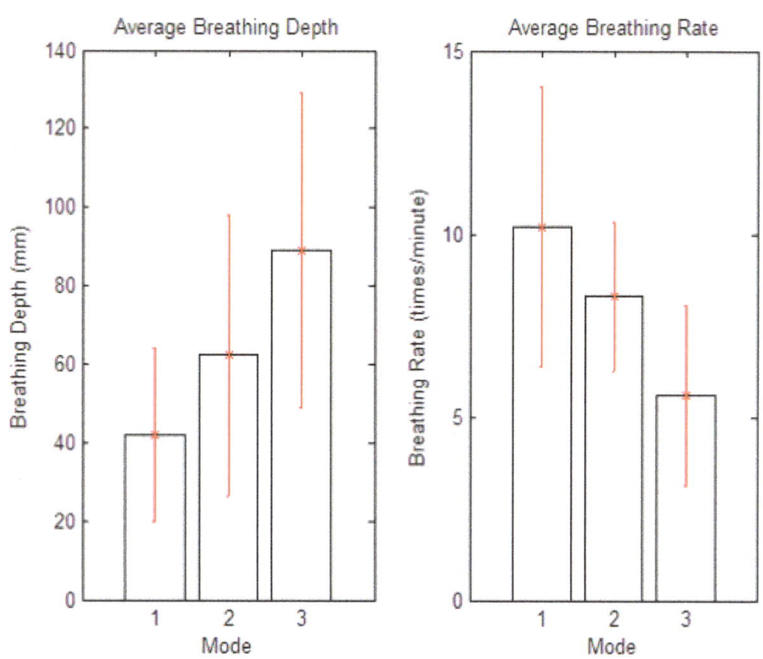

Figure 7. Comparison of average breathing depth and frequency in three modes. The number 1 to 3 in x-axis represent free breathing mode, local-mapping mode, and global-mapping mode respectively

EXPERIMENT

Among several relaxation techniques, deep breathing or diaphragmatic breathing (DB) is an easy and intuitive evidence-based method for stress management [18]. DB addresses the autonomic nervous system (ANS) imbalance that arises after exposure to a stressor and activation of the sympathetic 'fight-or-flight' response. As DB activates the parasympathetic ANS branch, action of the sympathetic branch becomes inhibited which leads to a calmer, more relaxed state. Generally, the chest part fluctuates more obviously than the belly part when breathing normally. When practicing DB, the primary motion should be changed to the abdominal part. The aim of the experiment is to investigate the effects of slowing and deepening user's abdominal breath in three different forms of breath regulation. We also compare the induced tension of the user when using the proposed target-based breath regulation and the common pure guiding style of breath regulation. Following, we describe three modes of breath regulation in the experiment, the experiment procedure, and the analysis of the experiment results.

Three Modes of Breath Regulation

In Mode-I, the free breathing mode, the user was required to close eyes and practice DB comfortably. No multimedia assistance was adopted. In Mode-II, the pure guiding mode, a lotus used as the metaphor for breathing guided user's respiration. At first, the system detected the user's initial respiration frequency, then the lotus started to open and close at the same frequency (e.g. 14 times per minute). After the frequency synchronization, the user was told to follow the visual guide and practice DB. If the user paced their breathing to the guidance well, the guiding frequency decreased eventually (e.g. 13 times per minute). In Mode-III, the local-mapping mode, the lotus reflected user breathing. It opened and closed corresponding to the inhalation and exhalation. The underlying mapping mechanism has been detailed in the last section. The users were told that the lotus variation reflected their breathing, and they were instructed to breathe to make the lotus open to the maximum and close to the minimum.

Participants

We recruited subjects in our laboratory without considering rigorous demography. Total 17 subjects participated in this experiment, including 12 males and 5 females with ages ranging from 21 to 38. Three of them had ever learned abdominal breathing before the experiment while others were not familiar with it.

Experiment Procedure

Every subject was first taught how to correctly proceed DB. Then they ran through these three modes of trials in a random order, five minutes for each trial. Between two trials, there was a two minute rest for users to answer some feedback questions. Total time cost was about 20 minutes. At the beginning of each trial the user was instructed to sit properly and hold the biosignal sensor fitly. When bio-signals including breathing, heart rate, and skin conductance were correctly shown on the screen (Fig.4), the trial began.

After entire three modes of trials, a five minutes interview was conducted to further realize the user experience of using this system.

Experiment Results

Recorded bio-signals include breath, BVP, and SCR. They were analyzed and transformed into five bio-signal features including breathing depth, breathing frequency, belly breath proportion, heart rate, and SCR. The averaged bio-features in three modes are shown in Fig. 8. We ran a one way ANOVA to investigate the difference of these three modes in each biosignal feature, but there was no overall significant difference found (Breathing Depth: $F=2.48$, $p=0.095$, Breathing Frequency: $F=1.78$, $p=0.18$, Belly Breath Proportion: $F=1.35$, $p=0.27$, Heart Rate: $F=0.59$, $p=0.56$, SCR: $F=0.05$, $p=0.95$). To further investigate the effects of the two types of multimedia-assisted breath regulation, we conducted paired ttests to compare the bio-signal features in Mode-II and ModeIII to those in Mode-I respectively. The results show that the breathing depth in Mode-II and Mode-III is higher than that in Mode-I (Mode-I vs. Mode-II: $p=0.03$, Mode-I vs. Mode-III: $p=0.009$), however, there is no significant difference between Mode-II and Mode-III ($p=0.353$). In respect of breathing frequency, Mode-III is significantly slower than Mode-I ($p=0.001$), and other comparisons of Mode-II vs. Mode-I and Mode-II vs. Mode-III show no significant difference (Mode-II vs. Mode-I: $p=0.195$, Mode-II vs. Mode-III: $p=0.107$).

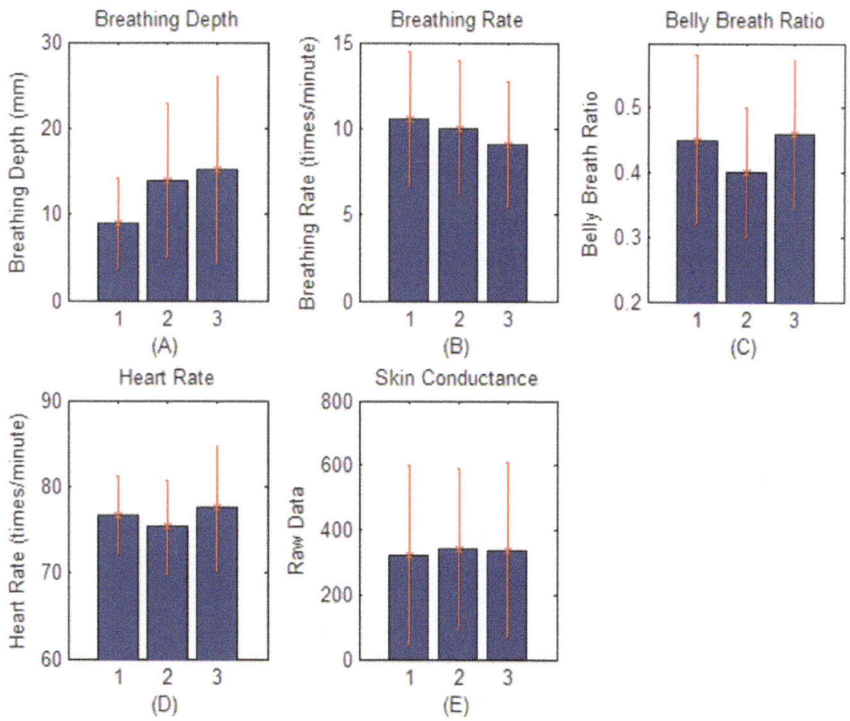

Figure 8. Bio-signal features of three modes. (A) Breathing Depth (B) Breathing Rate (C) Belly Breath Proportion (D) Heart Rate (E) Skin Conductance Response

These results indicate that multimedia-assisted breath regulation effectively deepen user breath, and that Mode-III, the local-mapping mode, can also slow down user breath significantly. In respect of the belly breath proportion, which means the proportion of belly fluctuation among entire breath fluctuation involving chest and belly fluctuation, Mode-III and Mode-I are not significant different (p=0.47), but Mode-II is significantly lower than Mode-I (p=0.035). It means users breathe with fewer belly part and more chest part in the pure guiding mode. The reason for this result will be discussed later. Other comparisons in heart rate and SCR show few differences. To realize the variation of each bio-signal feature in time, we also calculate averages per minute for each feature (Fig. 9).

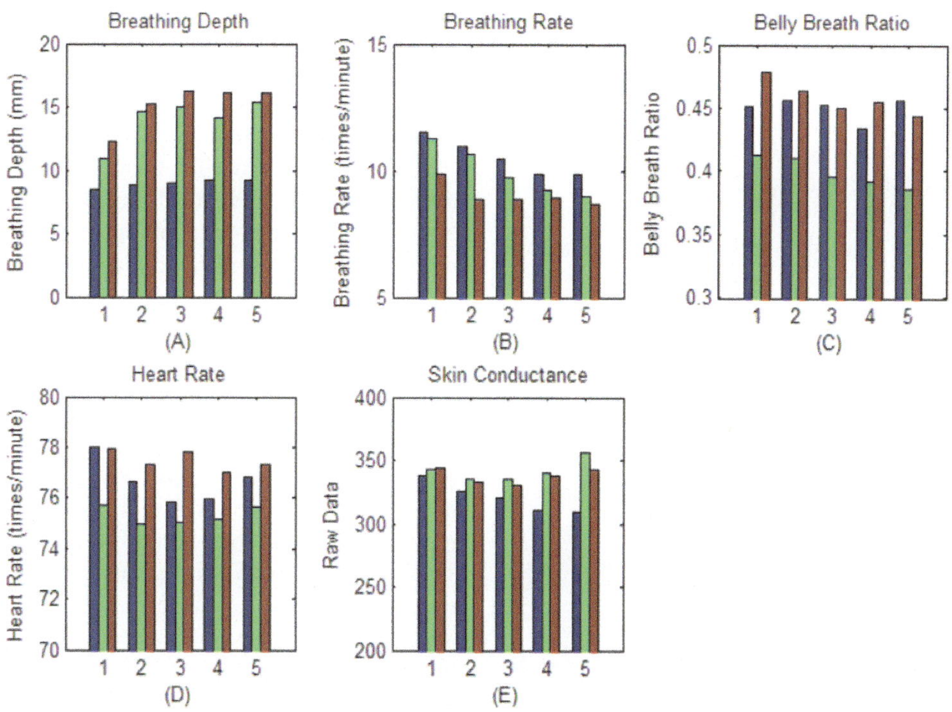

Figure 9. Bio-signal features during five minutes experience process. (A) Breathing Depth (B) Breathing Rate (C) Belly Breath Proportion (D) Heart Rate (E) Skin Conductance Response. The unit of x-axis is minute and three bars at each minute indicate the results of Mode-I, Mode-II and Mode-III from left to right. (Blue: Mode-I, Green: Mode-II, and Red: Mode-III)

This figure shows that the average breathing depth remains relatively stable for Mode-I during entire five minutes process, and a raising trend is shown in Mode-II and Mode-III (see Figure 6(A)). This shows multimedia-assisted breath regulation deepen user breath eventually. In respect of breathing frequency, the decreasing trends are shown in three modes, and the breathing frequency in Mode-III is relatively lower than those in the other two modes. This indicates that there is a trend users slow down their breath rate naturally during practicing DB, and that the local-mapping mode may slow down user breath more rapidly and significantly. When discussing about belly breath proportion, compared with other features, this feature shows fewer variation during the entire process. Fig. 9(C) shows that proportions of Mode-I and Mode-III are similar, and Mode-II is with the especially lower proportion from beginning the end. Finally, in respects of other bio-features - heart rate and SCR, there is few difference in three modes is observed.

DISCUSSION

Bio-signal Feature Observation

The experiment result indicated that multimedia guidance or feedback indeed facilitated deepening abdominal breathing when practicing DB. The visual guidance (Mode-II) or visual feedback (Mode-III) of respiration reminded users of staying in the process of breath regulation so that their breathing depth continuously increased during the entire process of the trials (Fig.9 (A)(B)). The overall effect increased the amount of oxygen exchange and slowed down the breathing rate, which was beneficial for relaxation [19]. Among three modes of trials, the effect of slowing and deepening breathing of Mode-III is better than that of Mode-II. Some users reported that following the breath guidance in Mode-II caused mental tension because of worrying about falling behind the guidance. In contrast, the lotus reflected user respiration in Mode-III. Although users were given a target that to maximize and minimize the lotus through their breathing, they can accomplish the target at their own paces without rushing. The tension caused in Mode-II may also be the reason that the belly breath ratio of Mode-II is specially lower. According to user feedback, people reflected that they tended to breathe with more chest part forgetting to proceed DB when they focused on following the guidance. To sum up, the localmapping mode of breath regulation, proposed based on the concept of target-based method, effectively slow and deepen user breath when practicing DB, in the meantime, eliminate the drawback of causing mental tension as in traditional pure guiding style method. The experiment results in perspective of breathing depth and frequency fulfilled our expectation, but there was some unexpected features observed. For instance, the averaged SCR decreased at first in three modes but increased in the end of the trials in Mode-II and Mode-III (Fig.9 (C)). In Mode-II the phenomenon may be easier to explain. The guiding frequency of the pure guiding mode decreased as long as the user can still catch up with the guidance. Therefore, in the end of the trial the frequency had become so slow that to breathe following the guidance become uncomfortable. This even induced the raise in SCR. However, the reason for the phenomenon in Mode-III is not clear. The explanation may be similar. In the local-mapping mode, the mechanism mapping the respiratory signal to the opening state of the lotus maps the local extremes of the respiratory signal to the most and the least opening state of the lotus. Once the user increased their breathing depth, they had to remain or rise their breathing depth so that they can achieve the next target. Therefore, in the end of the trials, they may also suffer from uncomfortableness due to the attempt of achieving too deep breathing. This should be noticed and be further improved in the next design of mapping mechanism.

User Feedback

After experiencing three modes of trials, some participants reported that they can concentrate on breath regulation better when eyes were closed in the free breathing mode (Mode-I), and others thought it more interesting to have a visual feedback. They reported that the visual feedback was advantageous for reducing wandering minds and calming down. In the pure guiding mode (Mode-II), some participants thought it difficult to follow the guidance. Others can follow the guiding rhythm and become comparably more concentrative. The reason why the guiding rhythm is hard to follow may be that we simply activate the opening and closing of the lotus by a sinusoidal wave with different frequencies. So the length of the inhaling and exhaling periods are equal, which is usually not the case our voluntary respiration is. This reminds us that a customized ratio of inhalation and exhalation should be considered in a pure guiding style of breath regulation in the future. In the local-mapping mode (Mode-III), most of people tested the accuracy of the lotus response at first. Sometimes participants thought the reflection inaccurate. We found the reason for that was the inappropriate locating of the respiration detection mask. Looking at a loosely controlled lotus certainly bothered users. However, for most cases of correct breath detection, participants favor this mode because of the connection between their breathing and the motion of the lotus. It made them feel more relaxed and immersive in the process of breath regulation. Those feedback suggest that the interaction form through real time visualization of respiration may be beneficial and suitable when applied in the relaxation application. There are also user feedbacks about other components in this relaxation system. Most of users thought that the bio-signal feedback on the wall (Fig. 4), was assistive for identifying whether they breathe primarily with the abdominal part. Besides, the reflected image of the lotus also interested multiple users. They like the design of visual feedback and the immersive visual effect created by that.

CONCLUSION

In this paper, we integrate the non-contact breath detection technique, the bio-signal sensors and the specially designed reflection mechanism to construct a multimedia system for breath regulation and relaxation. A novel form of breath regulation named target-based breath regulation is proposed. This concept is between the pure guiding style and the pure reflecting style of breath regulation. Through managing the underlying mapping mechanism we can variously affect the breathing pattern of the user. A preliminary experiment was conducted to prove the concept. Finally, two forms of multimedia-assisted breath regulation were adopted in the formal experiment to investigate the effects of the pure guiding mode and the local-mapping mode on breathing depth and frequency and the subjective experiences. Quantified analysis of bio-signal features was conducted and the results were discussed. Experiment results show that the local-mapping mode is actually beneficial for slowing and deepening user breathing, in the meantime, reduces the drawback of inducing mental tension, which is usually the case in the common pure guiding style of breath regulation. At the end, some user feedbacks from interviews were discussed and essential factors worth noticing for constructing a breath-based application for relaxation in the future were suggested.

ACKNOWLEDGEMENTS

We gratefully acknowledge the support and comments from the editor and the reviewers, respectively. This work is in part supported by grants from Ministry of Science and Technology of Taiwan under NSC 104-2627-E-002-001.

REFERENCES

1. Steptoe, A., "Invited review: The links between stress and illness." Journal of Psychosomatic Research, 35(6), pp. 633-644, 1991.
2. Schubert, C., Lambertz, M., Nelesen, R., Bardwell, W., Choi, J.-B., and Dimsdale, J., "Effects of stress on heart rate complexity-a comparison between short-term and chronic stress." Biological Psychology, 80(3), pp. 325-332, 2009.
3. Tsigos, C., and Chrousos, G.-P., "Hypothalamic-pituitary-adrenal axis, neuroendocrine factors and stress. " Journal of Psychosomatic Research, 53, pp. 865-871, 2002.
4. Varvogli, Liza, and Christina Darviri. "Stress Management Techniques: evidence-based procedures that reduce stress and promote health." Health Science Journal, 5(2), pp.74-89, 2011.
5. Grossman, E., Grossman, A., Schein, M., Zimlichman, R., Gavish, B., "Breathing-control lowers blood pressure." Journal of Human Hypertension, 15(4), pp. 263-269, 2001.
6. Ley, R., "The Modification of Breathing Behavior: Pavlovian and Operant Control in Emotion and Cognition." Behavior Modification. 23(3), pp.441-479, 1999.
7. Moraveiji, N.,Olson, B., Nguyen, T., Saadat, M., Khalighi, Y., Pea, R., Heer, J., "Peripheral Paced Respiration: Influencing User Physiology during Information Work." The 24th ACM User Interface Software and Technology (UIST) Symposium. Pp.423-427, 2011.
8. Yu, M.-C., Chen, J.-S., Chang, K.-J., Hsu, S.-C., Lee, M.-S., Hung, Y. - P., "i-m-Breath: The Effect of Multimedia Biofeedback on Learning Abdominal Breath." Multimedia Modaling (MMM), pp.548-558, 2011.
9. Park, S.-H., Jang, D.-G., Son, D.-H., Zhu, W., Hahn, M.-S., "A biofeedback-based breathing induction system."The 3rd International Conference on Bioinformatics and Biomedical Engineering (ICBBE), pp.1-4, 2009.
10. Donaldson, G. C., "The chaotic behaviour of resting human respiration." Respiration Physiology, vol. 88, pp. 313–321, 1992.
11. Hughson, R. L., Yamamoto, Y., & Fortrat, J. O., "Is the pattern of breathing at rest chaotic? A test of Lyapunov exponent." Advances in Experimental Medicine and Biology, vol.393, pp.15-19, 1995.
12. Small, M., Judd, K., Lowe, M., & Stick, S., "Is breathing in infants chaotic? Dimension estimates for respiratory patterns during quiet sleep." Journal of Applied Physiology, vol. 86, pp. 359–376, 1999.
13. Wysocki, M., Fiamma, M.-N., Straus, C., Poon, C.-S., & Similowski, T., "Chaotic dynamics of resting ventilatory flow in humans assessed through noise titration." Respiratory Physiology & Neurobiology, vol. 153, pp. 54–65, 2006.
14. Vlemincx, Elke, Ilse Van Diest, and Omer Van den Bergh. "Imposing respiratory variability patterns." Applied psychophysiology and biofeedback, 37(3), pp.153-160, 2012.
15. Yu, M.-C., Liou, J.-L., Kuo, S.-W., Lee, M.-S., Hung, Y.-P.: Noncontact Respiratory Measurement of Volume Change Using Depth Camera. In: Proc. of IEEE EMBC, 2371-2374 (2012)
16. Chan, L.-W., Chuang, Y.-F., Yu, M.-C., Chao, Y.-L., Lee, M.-S., Hung, Y.-P., Hsu, J.: Gesture-based Interaction for a Magic Crystal Ball. In: Proc. of the ACM VRST. 157-164 (2007)
17. WildDivine. Finger sensor "The Iom"
18. online.. Available: http://www.wilddivine.com/
19. Varvogli, L., Darviri, C., "Stress Management Techniques: evidencebased procedures that reduce stress and promote health," Health Sci J, vol. 5, pp. 74-89, 2011.
20. McCaul, K., Solomon, S., Holmes, D.: Effects of Paced Respiration and Expectations on Physiological and Psychological Responses to Threat. In: Journal of Personality and Social Psychology, vol. 37(4), pp. 564-571, 1979.

CHAPTER 16 INTELLIGENT MULTIMEDIA SYSTEM FOR UBIQUITOUS CLOUD COMPUTING

Abhilash Sreeramaneni , Hyungjin Im , Won Min Kang , Chan Koh and Jong Hyuk Park,

Keywords: Context-based intelligent multimedia system; mobile users; ubiquitous cloud computing; K-means clustering; mobile-cloud offloading system; context-aware decision; pervasive cloud computing

INTRODUCTION

Over the last decade, Internet usage around the world has been increasing day by day. Internet users daily browse billions of multimedia webpages and face difficulties in finding the content in which they are interested. Ubiquitous computing plays a vital role in smart devices (*i.e.*, smartphones, iPads, tablets, *etc.*) by providing strong data networks (3G/4G) for mobile users to access fast Internet anywhere at any time. As mentioned above, mobile cloud computing has grown in popularity for many reasons, such that today smart devices are hampered by limitations, e.g., memory space, CPU usage, and battery life, when compared to notebooks and desktops [1]. A question thus arises: How can we diminish the above challenges for mobile users so that they can acquire their desired contents from several multimedia applications [2]? To date, recommended lists have been provided only for videos [3], to list the video's classification, description tags, watching history, and clips sharing in websites from end-users [4]. This paper concentrates on providing real-time notifications for mobile user applications about their desired multimedia contents. Moreover, these recommendation results are not implicit and stable for mobile users. Many websites are commercially driven because search engines based on keywords remember users' favorite videos on mobile applications. Several recommendation algorithms are successfully developed and exploited only for videos. For example, Google and AdWords services are based on context-based filtering (CB), and in recent years Amazon and Taboo have attained success by introducing collaborative filtering (CF) recommender systems to make browsing more user-friendly. The fundamental idea is to ensure that highly popular contents are distributed across a large group of common users, but that less popular contents will never be recommended to the users. One of the world-famous social networking websites, Facebook, has a recommendation system based on social network filtering (SNF) according to space links, content forwards, user concerns, and user interactions. Almost all of the existing recommendation algorithms consider two essential components: content recommender and contextual information, (e.g., time and location). Maximum contextual information is collected in a ubiquitous environment, according to the user interests. Due to inexorable computations, a real-time recommendation cannot be guaranteed in the existing algorithms. In this paper "a context-based intelligent multimedia system (CIMS) for ubiquitous cloud computing" is proposed, with cost-effective mechanisms (*i.e.*, recommendation, distribution, and offloading). The main idea of this paper is to reduce the computing percentage and storage complexities and extend the battery life for smartphones through a mobile cloud offloading system, which decides whether to offload actions to/from the cloud servers. Context-aware decision-making (CAD) takes advantage of different historical benchmarks, based on context, to produce offloading decisions for lessening energy consumption, response time, and other criteria [1]. The rest of

Citation: Abhilash Sreeramaneni, Hyungjin Im, Won Min Kang, Chan Koh and Jong Hyuk Park, Intelligent Multimedia System for Ubiquitous Cloud Computing, doi:10.3390/info6020228.

the paper is structured as follows. Section 2 discuss the related works, and Section 3illustrates our proposed framework, "context-based intelligent multimedia system (CIMS) for ubiquitous cloud computing" and its design. Finally, we conclude and outline future work in Section 4.

RELATED WORK

In this section, we discuss the core technologies for CIMS, existing research, and system considerations. The core technologies include a recommendation system, mobile cloud offloading systems, and mobile energy modeling.

Core Technologies

Recommendation System

Recommendation systems concentrate on particular domains, e.g., Google News, Amazon and YouTube users. CB recommendation [5] considers similarities based on content titles, tags, or descriptions, while CF-based recommendation [6,7] focuses on user proceedings such as content browsing history and prominence. A CF system requires ample information about the history and feedback from users. Context-aware recommendation furnishes constant information without examining the user context (*i.e.*, location, time, and network). As a matter of fact, user interests differ depending on context (*i.e.*, location, time, and emotion), so context-aware recommendation conveys the sensed information to smartphones and takes a long time to aid the user and select his/her contents of interest [3]. Graph-based recommendation [8] is mostly used to reduce the memory usage in cloud servers by mapping similarities between a group of users' data (context and multimedia contents); these systems are important algorithms for a recommender system.

Mobile Cloud Offloading Systems

In the early years, mobile cloud offloading became popular [1,9,10,11]. MAUI [9] is designed by Microsoft for Windows phones; it recognizes that the best way to offload is by stating the current context (*i.e.*, energy consumption, CPU utilization, and network conditions) of a mobile at runtime. ThinkAir [10] is like MAUI, but the script of offloading methods is added by the builder. Clone cloud [11] is specially designed for the Android offloading system. As a matter of fact, mobile applications offload information continuously if a network is available, and this does not check the energy consumption. Kwon and Tilevich [12] found that offloading minimizes higher energy consumption by using checkpoints.

Energy Model

For a decade numerous energy consumption models have been presented for mobile devices [13,14,15,16,17]. Three important energy consumption components are categorized: (i) computation; (ii) communications; and (iii) display. In this paper, we contemplate the multimedia contents' energy consumption, because it is directly affected by contexts and its remaining behaviors are static. Many energy models consider the different states of network interface and utilize the energy consumption levels [13,14]. This serves a useful purpose as an adjustable power model, because it considers the dependence between mobile hardware and power models [15]. These energy models never take different network conditions into consideration. Rahmati and Zhong consider the benefits of retransmission when any transferring data has failed over the same network [16]. Mittal *et al.* examine signal strength, which is a key function for communication energy [17].

System Considerations

This subsection explains the system considerations of ubiquitous computing.

Computing Management:

To address the resource constraints of smartphones, mobile cloud computing has emerged to meet the demands for intensive computing tasks. In the coming years immense usage of cloud servers will lead to computation and database concerns; to overcome these issues, our research uses K-means clustering in our system.

Real-Time Recommendation:

Generally mobile users expect to find exact information in real time. User context and content data interests vary day by day. A cloud server executes a distribution process to control users' data similarities without collisions and provide accurate notifications to mobile user applications in real time.

Energy Saving:

Most smartphones continuously offload data when they are connected to a network; this process leads to high energy consumption. We consider a mobile cloud offloading system for mobile devices, with the aims of a short response time and lower energy consumption with the aid of a customized CAD. Using real-time notification is another way to lessen the energy consumption and computing costs for mobile users.

CIMS: CONTEXT-BASED INTELLIGENT MULTI-MEDIA SYSTEM

In this section, we present an architecture of CIMS with mechanisms such as recommendation, distribution, offloading, and design of the systems. We discuss a service scenario and efficiency analyses for CIMS in detail.

Architecture of CIMS

Figure 1 represents our proposed CIMS Architecture in Mobile Cloud Computing. As aforementioned, smart devices with limited resources acquire needed information from a cloud via the Internet. To reduce computing and storage concerns for mobile users, we perform computation in cloud servers and send notifications to user applications in real time. We consider user specifications in order to collect user context and multimedia contents of interest, and to identify similarities between users. After installing the application, users should perform authorized authentication (*i.e.*, email, password) and fill in his/her content fields of interest; when the user starts browsing, all this data is stored in a cloud database. By collecting a user's information (as stated in his/her profile) in a cloud server, it is easy to match up similarities between a user's context and content data. The following sections explain the recommendation system, distribution process, and offloading mechanisms to lessen the computation cost, energy consumption, and memory size for mobile users and cloud servers.

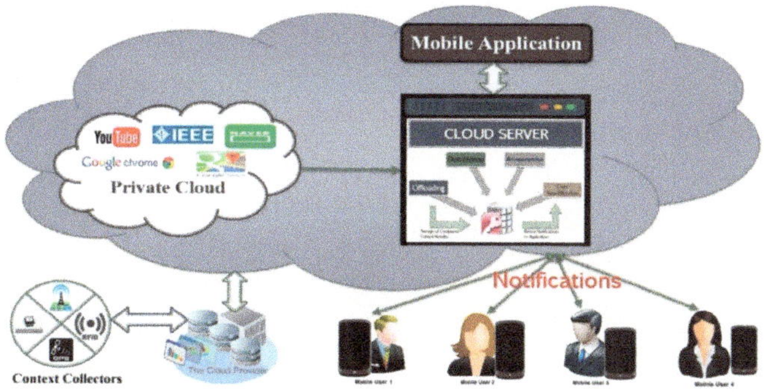

Figure 1: CIMS in Mobile Cloud Computing Architecture.

Design of Recommendation System

The proposed system, CIMS, is composed of a recommendation system. The dominant role behind the recommendation system is to reduce computing tasks in the mobile framework by using pervasive cloud computing. Usually mobile users depend on implicit and complete behavior models; for this we obtain a recommendation system, which includes four functions as illustrated in Figure 2: (1) User's Context and Content Data Collector, (2) Context Data Clustering, (3) Content Data Clustering, and (4) Clique Profiles Collector. All these functions are processed in the cloud server. A cloud server has several user profiles, which manage the user's privacy and data (*i.e.*, context and multimedia contents). The user's Context and Content Data Collector collects data from the database and divides the user's data (context and content) for clustering evaluation process to finally form several groups of user profiles according to their similarities (between context and content) (Figure 2). The cloud server performs recommendation processing by collecting data stated in user profiles and executing a clustering function according to the users' relationships and similarities in context and content data. These processes minimize the storage constraints for the cloud server, offer updates to a user profile if such data is available, and impart notifications without a mobile user's interactions, according to context entities (*i.e.*, location, time, network type, and user's interests). Finally, the recommendation system forms several groups of user profiles based on their similarities in context and multimedia contents and transmits the results to a distribution process to give real-time notifications for mobile user applications. The four major recommendation system functions are described as follows:

User's Context and Content Data Collector

The user's context collectors (*i.e.*, sensors, General packet radio service (GPRS), Radio-frequency identification (RFID), *etc.*) gathers the user information and transmits the context data (*i.e.*, network types, time, and location) to the cloud server. The user's contents of interest (*i.e.*, audio, video files, documents) are collected from user profiles (*i.e.*, Gmail, Yahoo, Hotmail, *etc.*) at the initial stage of application and continue to be updated according to the user's browsing history. The recommendation system collects context and content data from a highly secure cloud database according to user profiles. We think it is worthwhile to develop a notification technique for mobile user applications because users spent a lot of time surfing for their interests on the Internet, and this leads to high computation and energy concerns. Our goal is to reduce computation and energy consumption for smart devices; we achieve these constraints by sending updated notifications to a mobile user's application in real time according to his/her profile interests. Due to the daily increase of similarities in a user's interest and context types, computing will lessen quickly. To minimize the diverse challenges for recommendation systems, we perform a clustering procedure to reduce the computing load at cloud servers. User profiles and their data (*i.e.*, context and multimedia contents) collection are updated simultaneously to keep the recommendation process fresh at the server side.

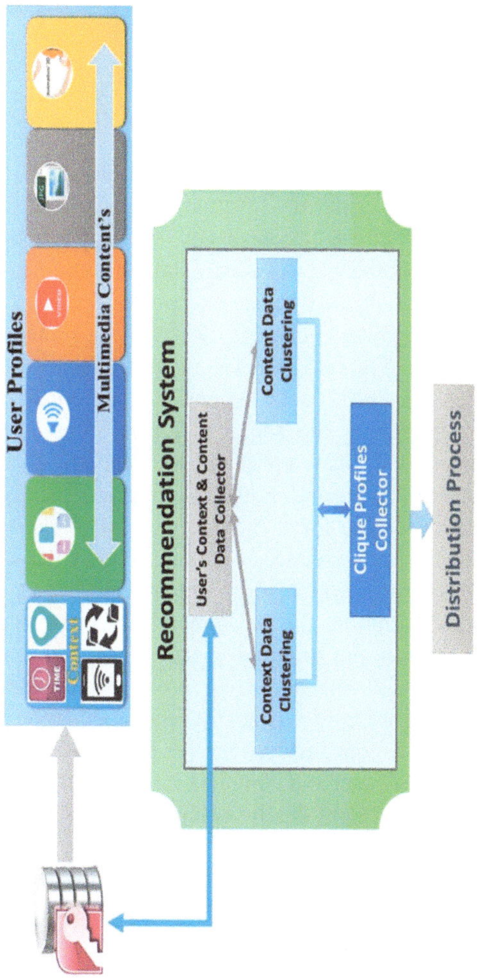

Figure 2: Design of Recommendation System.

Context Data Clustering

As aforementioned, ubiquitous computing relies on precise context data to provide an accurate service to users. Studying users' context (*i.e.*, network types, time and location) is significant. For example: consider YouTube, a famous entertainment application with billions of users enjoying their favorite music and videos at any one time. In this context several users have similarities in accessing the same video clip or music album on either a particular network (3G/4G, Wi-Fi), or at a particular time or location. We use these context similarities to cluster and form several groups of users based on their similarities. Through research studies considering examples like the above, we perform a clustering method on context data to notify the user automatically only if there is any update relevant to the user's interests, according to their context entities. As said before, to obtain an exact recommendation system, we use cluster algorithms for user satisfaction. In our paper we perform the K-means clustering operation shown in Figure 3:

(1) User profiles are divided into s chunks; each truck includes the profile of different users. We compare user profile context data (time, location, and network type) to find parallel context between profiles.

(2) K-means clustering algorithm collects the user's content information (browsed content (BC), keywords, and content-type) and again matches the user profiles to obtain content similarities.

(3) Next it will match user profiles by both context and content; finally, the results are stored in clique profiles with their similarities.

(4) If any user does not find similarities, his/her profile will be stored in clique profiles for future use.

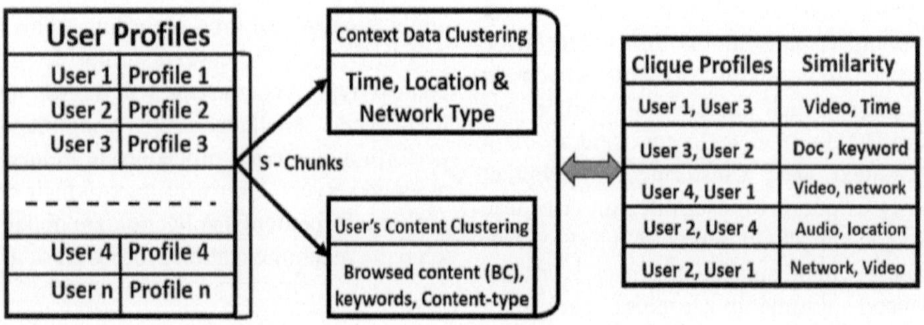

Figure 3: User's Context & Content Clustering.

Content Data Clustering

User's profiles are exploited by the recommendation system to find user content similarities. Multimedia content applications retrieve the user's favorite contents by browsing history, audio, video files, documents, keywords, *etc.* In addition, several user groups are formed based on similarities with content illustrations (browsed content, keywords, content type). For instance, in Figure 3, the second row shows similarities between user 3 and 2 with keywords. This means users 2 and 3 are searching the same document in a multimedia application. Our system considers the similarities in a set of user profiles and sends notifications automatically if any updates are available for their related research. This feature lessens the storage concerns for cloud servers (by not saving an individual profile with his/her contents of interest). Relying on content illustration, the recommendation system requires little computation and provides exact information. Naturally, a user's interests change according to context and old profiles produce a lot of noise throughout the recommendation process; to control these concerns we merge the context clustering (Figure 3) to get exact and complete information according to the user profile. We do this by placing the group of users in one truck and performing K-means clustering on user's data (context and content). Based on clustering, the data cloud server collects a group of users' information with shared interests or other features in common; this method helps the application providers to make implicit recommendations for users.

Clique Profile Collector

Users usually browse multimedia content applications (*i.e.*, YouTube, IEEE, Naver, *etc.*) for their favorite content; many users have highly similar interests in the resources. By considering similar resources (*i.e.*, browsing history, audio video files, documents, *etc.*), research studies find users with highly similar behavior. The recommendation system uses a Clique Profiles Collector to achieve better performance and reduce the storage and computing complexities for the cloud server, based on the similarities between several users. Moreover, users' clustering data (context and content) is replaced by the Clique Profiles Collector to remove the collisions between several groups of user profiles and also give exact results for individuals as well as for groups of users. For example, a person is searching for a job opportunities with his/her user ID and his friend (or another authorized user with similar interests) is browsing the same website. First the recommendation system considers individual histories (context and content data) and performs matching with several user profiles; if any match exists it will store the similar data (content and context) in a group with several users, and send notifications only if there is any update regarding the user's interests. In cases where the user does not match with another user, his/her profile will be stored in clique profiles for future use. This approach reduces the computing cost for the cloud server. After performing the recommendation process, results are directed towards the distribution process, which performs real-time recommendation process.

Service Scenario of CIMS

This section explains the general process and core mechanisms of our proposed system (CIMS) with defined functions shown in Table 1.

Table 1: Explanation of terms

Terms	Explanation
MU	Mobile User
APP	Application
CS	Cloud Server
OFF	Offloading
DB	Data Base
RS	Recommendation System
DP	Distribution Process
RR	Real-Time Recommendation

CIMS General Process

Figure 4 illustrates the general process of CIMS.

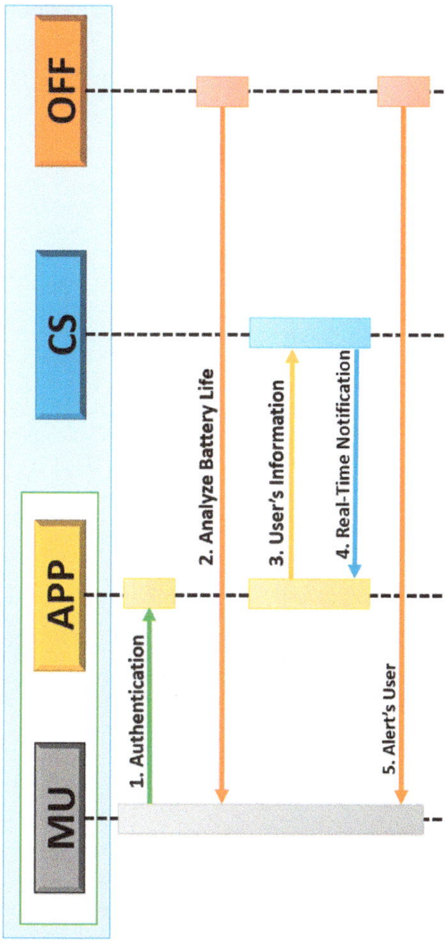

Figure 4: General process of CIMS.

Step 1 MU→APP: Authentication

After installation of the application, the mobile user performs authentication with his/her personal username and password.

Step 2 OFF→MU: Analyze the Battery Life

An offloading process analyzes the battery life of the user's mobile by using an energy model and allows the application to store user information to the cloud only if battery life is efficient.

Step 3 APP→CS: User Information

The user application collects information (*i.e.*, context and multimedia contents) and stores it on the cloud server database.

Step 4 CS→APP: Real-Time Notification

With all users' data, the cloud server performs its core operations to post updated notifications to a mobile user's application in real time.

Step 5 OFF→MU: Alerts the User

The offloading system alerts the user while downloading large contents, to lessen the energy consumption based on the user context.

Core Mechanisms of CUM System

Figure 5 demonstrates the core mechanisms of our system (CIMS). After obtaining the user's information, the cloud server uses the recommendation system to generalize about users' similarities based on context and content information. The distribution system obtains the similarities between attributes to provide real-time notifications to mobile users.

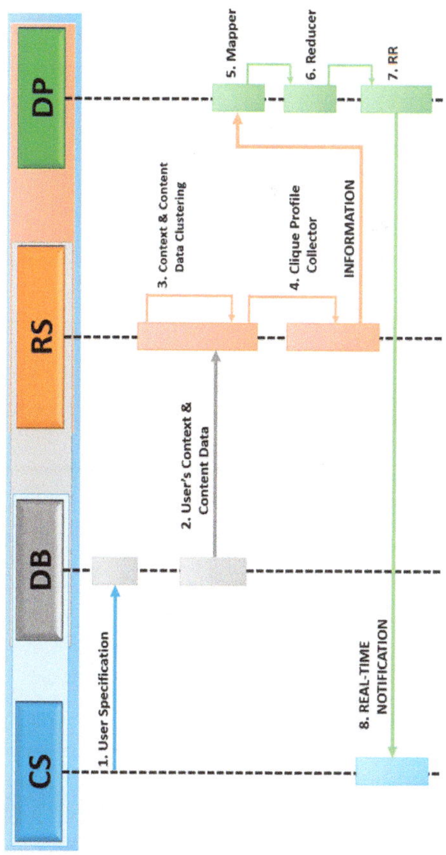

Figure 5: Core Mechanisms of CIMS.

Step 1 CS→DB: User Specification

The application requests the user to enter fields of interests, because without basic information it is very difficult for the server to analyze the user's interests at this initial stage. Along with the user's interests, his/her browsing data (*i.e.*, context, multimedia contents) are stored to the cloud database.

Step 2 DB→RS: User's Context and Content Data

A cloud database containing many users' profiles with their context data and multimedia contents of interest is processed by the recommendation system.

Step 3 RS: Context and Content Data Clustering

K-means clustering first finds similarities in context and then proceeds for content information between many users.

Step 4 RS: Clique Profile Collector

A clustering process is performed between the context and multimedia contents of users' data to form several groups of users based on their similarities.

Step 5 RS→DP: Mapper

Obtain Clique Profile information from RS for cluster mapping. Then the mapper computes user similarities based on attributes, arranges the user profiles according to high similarities, and organizes them into one cluster.

Step 6 DP: Reducer

The reducer performs similarly to the mapper, but to deepen the search it considers *K* clusters by mixing the *KS* profiles. If any similarities are found it will merge them; otherwise it updates the cluster.

Step 7 DP: Real-Time Recommendation (RR)

This can be obtained by analyzing user behavior in cloud-based clustering.

Step 8 DP→CS: Real-Time Notification

Recommendation rules (Figure 8) help the cloud server to convey notifications to mobile users' applications in real time by matching the user context in order.

Distribution Process for CIMS Service

After obtaining recommendation results, the distribution process performs real-time recommendation (*i.e.*, time, location, and network) and automatically returns favorite notifications to the applications according to user profiles, as shown in Figure 6. By having these recommendation rules, we ensure that user needs are met in real time. To reduce the burden for the recommendation system we include a profile partition using cluster mapping and a reducer to merge user profiles with similar interests in both context and multimedia contents. These functions reduce the computation and give real-time notifications to the mobile user. Clustering mappers are prompted as in Figure 7, to process the partition profiles.

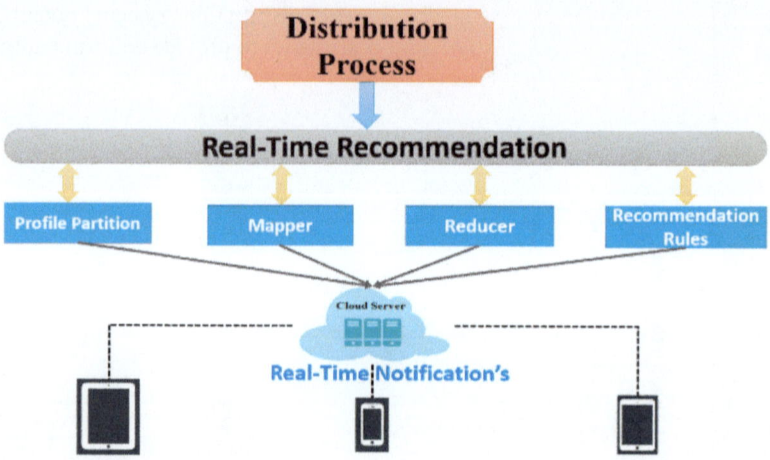

Figure 6: Distribution Process Design.

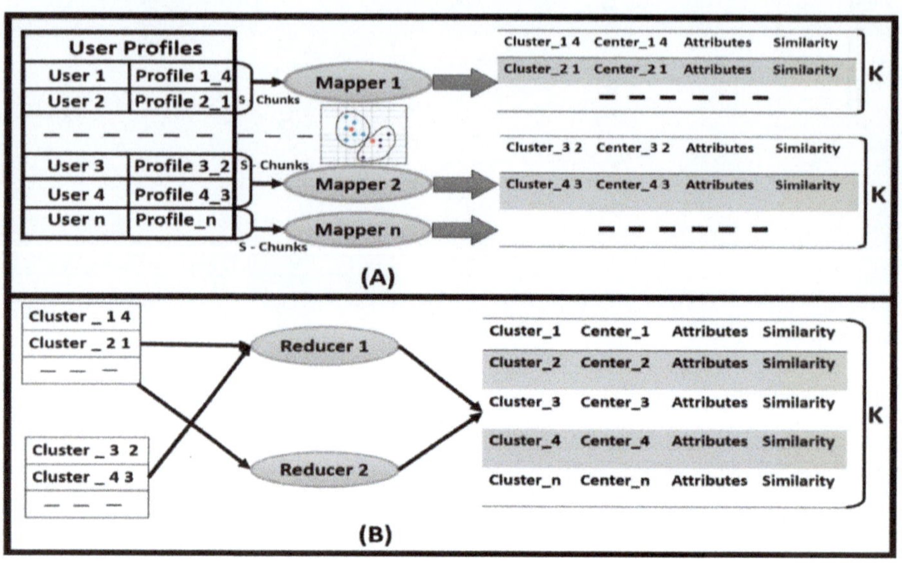

Figure 7: K-Means Clustering Mapper & Reducer.

Mapper

To compute similarities in attributes between user profiles at chunk-s, we employ a mapper in the distribution system to find the central point of *K* clusters, as shown in Figure 7A. For example, if many users in YouTube search for their favorite music, based on attributes (*i.e.*, key words, browsing history, location, time and network type) application stores the information on the cloud server in the user's profile. The mapper computes the similarities between users based on attributes and arranges the user profiles linked by close similarities into one cluster. To minimize the memory size requirements, we re-choose the cluster central point *K* and compare it with old clusters; if no matches exist, the mapper ends the task. Otherwise it updates the central point *K* cluster to give surety and stability to the cluster.

Reducer

The reducer is the final phase for lessening memory size in cloud servers. A mapper with a central profile acquires the K-clustering means of similarities by using profile attributes (*i.e.*, key words, browsing history, location, time, and network type). In the distribution system, after processing with the mapper, the reducer intermixes the KS profiles into single *K* clusters, as shown in Figure 7B. The reducer performs similarly to the mapper; taking a step in advance, it builds *K*clusters by mixing the KS profiles, because user profile attributes with similarities are merged directly. Otherwise the reducer does the same job as the mapper, stabilizing the K-means clustering through iteration.

Real-Time Recommendation

Real-time recommendation can be obtained by analyzing user behavior in cloud-based clustering. Example recommendation rules are shown in Figure 8. The cloud-server notifies the user when new updates are available. For example, users often access the Google map application to reach their office, but the next day bus timings might have changed. Our real-time recommendation helps the user to get the notification in real time and thus choose another way to reach the office. The rules help the application server to convey the information at the right time by achieving the rules one by one in order by matching the user contexts. As we discussed before, the user context and interests change from day to day, so we should keep on updating recommendation rules to improve the real-time process.

Recommendation Rules:

Context Rule:

```
Rule-cxt: context(?s)^hasaccessnetwork(?s, ?net-type)^Swrld:equal(?net, "wifi")^hasdevicetype(?s,?dt)^swrld(?dt, "smartphone")^hasaccesstime(?s, ?t)^swrld:greaterthan(?t, "15:00")^swrld:greaterthan(?t, "24:00") ^haslocation (?s, ?loc) ^swrld:greaterthan(?loc, "1m")->viewcluster(?s,cxt)
```

Content Rule:

```
Rule-ctnt: content(?s)^hastype (?s, ?type)^Swrld:frequency(?s, "audio")^haspixels (?s, ?pi) ^Swrld:scale(?size, "width,height") hasresolution (?s, ?res) ^Swrld:greaterorequal(^res, "360p")^hasalphabets(?s, ?alpha) ^Swrld:type(?s, "doc,pdf")->viewcluster(?s,ctnt)
```

Recommending Rule:

```
Rule-recc: recommending(?s)^hascontext(?s.?context)^swrld:similar(?context,m)^haskeywords(?s,?key) ^haskey_1(?key,?key_1)^swrld:similar(?Key_1, "cloud") ^haskey_2(?key,?key_2)^swrld:similar(?Key_1, "IOS")^haskey_3(?key,?key_3) ^swrld:similar(?Key_3, "push")^hassimilar(?s,?sim)^swrlb:similar(?sim,1) ->recommendation(?s,recc)
```

Figure 8: Recommendation Rules.

Offloading System

Mobile cloud computing appears to lessen the resource constrains of smart devices, but it suffers from continuously offloading actions as long as network is available. The process of offloading between the smart phone and the cloud server is shown in Figure 9, which consists of three components: energy model, user profiler, and context-aware decision (CAD). We detail each component in the following subsections.

User's Profiles

Several aspects underlying user profiles are required to process the offloading decisions. We assess four important contexts: (1) Network Signal—periodically collects the latest network signal (*i.e.*, Wi-Fi, 3G/4G); (2) Transmission rate—by transmitting dummy data to/from cloud server, we measure the transmission time and energy estimation; (3) Time—by partitioning the 24 hours into time slots and recording the opportunities for offloading; (4) Location—obtaining a user's geographical location by GPS every half an hour.

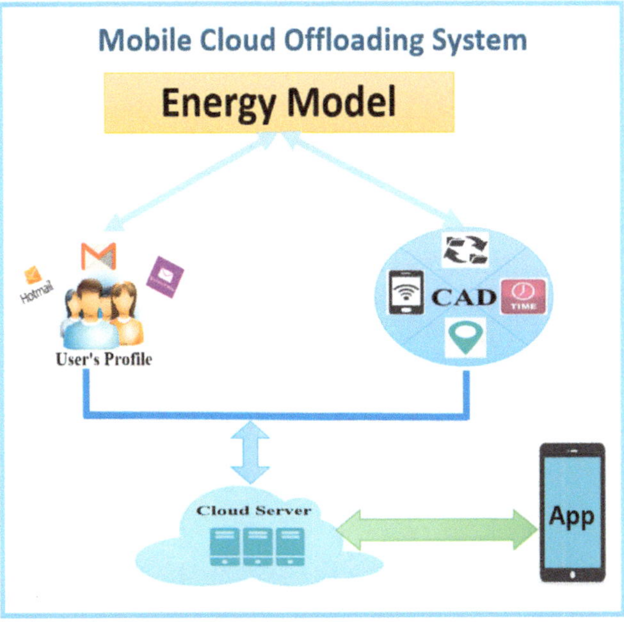

Figure 9: Mobile Cloud Offloading System Design.

Context-Aware Decision (CAD)

Considering the existing research on offloading systems, we strongly believe that power saving does not always happen while offloading to the cloud. For example, if a mobile performs offload computation, especially on a 3G/4G network, the transmission energy may be greater than consumption energy. However, a context-aware decision engine is deployed to lessen the energy consumption. We assess four important contexts—network signal, transmission rate, time, and location—in a CAD engine to measure a user's regular behaviors, *i.e.* the places a user regularly visits at the same time, particularly on weekdays, thus accessing the same network conditions and applications. For example, user might go to the office Monday–Friday, 9 a.m. to 5 p.m., and go to the park on weekends from 5 p.m. to 8 p.m. Generally the wireless network (Wi-Fi) in an office will be sufficient for offloading computation, and power consumption does not matter. However, for a user in the park, a wireless network (3G/4G) is not as good as an office network.

Based on users' past context data, CAD executes the offloading process. Before calling up users' data, CAD checks the present user's context. If it is good enough, it will carry on; otherwise, it utilizes past execution costs.

Energy Model

Once the process of recommendation system, distribution process, and offloading mechanisms is executed, the costs including computing time, energy consumption, and time are recorded in a secure database in the cloud server. Our energy model estimates energy consumption using the above costs based on network signal, transmission rate, location, and time. We store all these context data in the user profile on the cloud sever. A CAD engine with context rules (Figure 8) uses all this contextual information to perform offloading computation on a mobile device and returns the standard performance to the cloud. Another important point to bear in mind so as to avoid null results is that CAD requests information from the user at the initial stage.

Efficiency Analyses of CIMS

This section presents the efficiency of our proposed system, CIMS, and presents a comparative analysis with existing research models. We compare and analyze the recommendation and offloading systems, presented in Section 2.1 [1,3,6] with our proposed system. We obtain the following considerations for comparison analysis: computing process, data-base management, real-time processing, and power consumption. Table 2 shows the analysis results.

Table 2: Analyses of performance.

Performance	CIMS	[1]	[3]	[6]
Computing Process	⊙	X	Δ	Δ
Data-Base Management	⊙	X	Δ	X
Real-time Processing	⊙	⊙	⊙	X
Power Consumption	⊙	Δ	X	X

(⊙: Good, Δ: Moderate, X: Weak.)

Computing Process

A resource-constrained mobile device refers to a cloud server over the Internet that is used to simplify the computing process. An offloading engine [1] deploys a mobile and uses the CAD algorithm for offloading to cloud servers. The existing literature only considers video applications [3,6]. The recommendation system [3] considers video sharing websites that collect user context, relationship, and profiles to generate multimedia recommendation rules. The recommendation system created by Go *et al.* studies three user behaviors: favorites, uploads, and viewing of videos in YouTube [6]. The proposed system conveys real time notifications to mobile user by obtaining the users' profile, contexts, multimedia contents of interest, and attributes. The offloading engine in the cloud server performs offloading actions to/from the mobile user, based on the user's context. The above factors are included in our system without user interaction via cloud computing, which reduces the high computation task for a smartphone.

Database Management

Database management refers to how to reduce the database concerns in cloud servers in the upcoming years. Mo *et al.* [3] utilized user profiles to find content similarities between users; several communities were formed based on access patterns and content descriptions were mapped and clustering algorithms performed to obtain users' similarities in content. Existing literature does not consider database management in the cloud server [1,6]. Our system performs K-means clustering on user profiles and procures similarities between user contexts and multimedia contents, and then we use a clique profile collector to acquire groups of user profiles with features in common. We use a reducer to deepen the search based on arranging highly similar user profiles into one cluster to reduce storage concerns for cloud servers.

Real-Time Processing

Real-time processing is a must and should guarantee the quality of the user experience. Our proposed system and mobile cloud offloading engine [1] perform similar actions, by notifying the user according to their contexts. A new user request is accepted by the real-time component and returns recommendation lists to the user [3]. The component translates the request into recommendation rules on the basis of keywords and user context and then searches for user favorites according to those rules. By contrast, the proposed system makes it easier for the user, by collecting the user's information and sending absolute notifications related to the mobile user's profile to his/her applications in real time, from the cloud server. We employ the reducer in a distribution process to avoid collisions between several user profiles and impart absolute information in real time, based on the recommendation rules in Figure 8.

Power Consumption

Most smartphones with many multimedia applications continuously perform offloading actions when connected to a network, which leads to high power consumption. A mobile cloud offloading system [1], on the other hand, decides whether to offload from cloud servers and evaluates the CAD algorithm for low power consumption. The existing literature does not review power consumption in smartphones [3,6]. However, in our system downloading as well as offloading are performed via the cloud server, relying on CAD with a user's context to reduce the power consumption for mobile users. Therefore, the proposed system has better availability in ubiquitous cloud computing than the previously proposed schemes.

CONCLUSIONS

In this paper we proposed CIMS as a method of automatically sending notifications to mobile users according to their profiles in real time. We analyze three kinds of user behaviors—user contexts, contents of interest, and clique profiles in the recommendation system, to reduce the storage and computation complexities for mobile users. Our energy model, with context-aware decision (CAD), uses the transmission rate, network signal location, and time to make better mobile cloud offloading decisions. Existing research [3,6] does not consider real-time notifications and energy saving for smartphone users. Our system evaluates user profiles to obtain the similarities between users' contexts, contents of interest, and attributes, using K-means clustering to lessen the storage burdens in the cloud server. The distribution process controls users' data similarities without collisions and provides accurate notification to the mobile user in real time. Our mobile cloud offloading system is flexible and supports different optimization criteria, by minimizing the response time and energy consumption. Comparative analysis (Table 2) shows that our proposed system provides higher quality multimedia information to mobile users than present systems.

In future work, we will modify the pattern of clustering and distribution processes to reduce the storage constraints for the cloud server and develop efficiency in providing real-time notifications. Moreover, we are looking into additional user contexts that may further improve the decision accuracy of CAD. Another important goal is designing a cache for multimedia systems to reduce computation pressures in the cloud server.

ACKNOWLEDGMENTS

This research was supported by the MSIP (Ministry of Science, ICT and Future Planning) of Korea, under the ITRC (Information Technology Research Center) support program (IITP-2015-H8501-15-1014) supervised by the IITP (Institute for Information & Communications Technology Promotion).

AUTHOR CONTRIBUTIONS

Abhilash Sreeramaneni: Main writing and also designing the total system; Won Min Kang and Hyungjin Im: Design of the total system; Chan Koh: Research on related works, analyzing and improving the proposed system; Jong Hyuk Park: Total supervision of the paperwork, review, and comments, *etc.* All authors have read and approved the final manuscript.

CONFLICTS OF INTEREST

The authors declare no conflict of interest.

REFERENCES

1. Lin, T.-Y.; Lin, T.-A.; Hsu, C.-H.; King, C.-T. Context-Aware Decision Engine for Mobile Cloud Offloading. In Proceedings of the 2013 IEEE Wireless Communications and Networking Conference Workshops (WCNCW), Shanghai, China, 7–10 April 2013; pp. 111–116.
2. Chang, K.-D.; Chen, C.-Y.; Chen, J.-L.; Chao, H.-C. Challenges to next generation services in IP multimedia subsystem. *J. Inf. Process. Syst.* 2010, *6*, 129–146.
3. Mo, Y.; Chen, J.; Xie, X.; Luo, C.; Yang, L.T. Cloud-based Mobile multimedia recommendation system with user behavior information. *IEEE Syst. J.* 2014, *8*, 184–193.
4. Lai, C.-F.; Huang, Y.-M.; Chao, H.-C. DLNA-based multimedia sharing system for OSGI framework with extension to P2P network. *IEEE Syst. J.* 2010, *4*, 262–270.
5. Li, L.; Wang, D.; Li, T.; Knox, D.; Padmanabhan, B. SCENE: A scalable two-stage personalized news recommendation system. In Proceedings of the 34th International ACM SIGIR Conference on Research and Development in Information Retrieval, SIGIR'11, Beijing, China, 29–29 July 2011; pp. 125–134.
6. Go, G.; Yang, J.; Park, H.; Han, S. Using online media sharing behavior as implicit feedback for collaborative filtering. In Proceedings of the 2010 IEEE Second International Conference on Social Computing (SocialCom), Minneapolis, MN, USA, 20–22 August 2010; pp. 439–445.
7. Chan, N.N.; Gaaloul, W.; Tata, S. Collaborative filtering technique for web service recommendation based on user-operation combination. In *On the Move to Meaningful Internet Systems: OTM 2010*; Meersman, R., Dillon, T., Herrero, P., Eds.; Springer: Berlin/Heidelberg, Germany, 2010; Part 1; Volume 6426, pp. 222–239.
8. Baluja, S.; Seth, R.; Sivakumar, D.; Jing, Y.; Yagnik, J.; Kumar, S.; Ravichandran, D.; Aly, M. Video suggestion and discovery for YouTube: Taking random walks through the view graph. In Proceedings of the 17th International Conference on World Wide Web, Beijing, China, 21–25 April 2008; pp. 895–904.
9. Cuervo, E.; Balasubramanian, A.; Cho, D.; Wolman, A.; Saroiu, S.; Chandra, R.; Bahl, P. Maui: Making smartphones last longer with code offload. In Proceedings of the 8th International Conference on Mobile Systems, Applications, and Services (MobiSys'10), San Francisco, CA, USA, 15–18 June 2010; pp. 49–62.
10. Kosta, S.; Aucinas, A.; Hui, P.; Mortier, R.; Zhang, X. ThinkAir: Dynamic resource allocation and parallel execution in the cloud for mobile code offloading. In Proceedings of the IEEE INFOCOM, Orlando, FL, USA, 25–30 March 2012; pp. 945–953.
11. Chun, B.; Naik, M.; Ihm, S.; Patti, A.; Maniatis, P. Clonecloud: Elastic execution between mobile device and cloud. In Proceedings of the 6th European Conference on Computer Systems (EuroSys'11), Salzburg, Austria, 10–13 April 2011; pp. 301–314.
12. Kwon, Y.; Tilevich, E. Energy-efficient and fault-tolerant distributed mobile execution. In Proceedings of the 2012 IEEE 32nd International Conference on Distributed Computing Systems (ICDCS'12), Macau, China, 18–21 June 2012; pp. 586–595.
13. Perrucci, G.; Fitzek, F.; Widmer, J. Survey on energy consumption entities on the smartphone platform. In Proceedings of the 2011 IEEE 73rd Vehicular Technology Conference (VTC Spring'11), Yokohama, Japan, 15–18 May 2011; pp. 1–6.
14. Zhang, L.; Tiwana, B.; Qian, Z.; Wang, Z.; Dick, R.; Mao, Z.; Yang, L. Accurate online power estimation and automatic battery behavior based power model generation for smartphones. In Proceedings of the IEEE/ACM/IFIP International Conference on Hardware/Software Codesign and System Synthesis (CODES/ISSS'10), Scottsdale, AZ, USA, 24–29 October 2010; pp. 105–114.
15. Dong, M.; Zhong, L. Self-constructive high-rate system energy modeling for battery-powered mobile systems. In Proceedings of the 9th International Conference on Mobile Systems, Applications, and Services (MobiSys'11), Washington, DC, USA, 28 June–1 July

2011; pp. 335–348.

16. Rahmati, A.; Zhong, L. Context-based network estimation for energy-efficient ubiquitous wireless connectivity. *IEEE Trans. Mobile Comput.* 2011, *10*, 54–66.

17. Mittal, R.; Kansal, A.; Chandra, R. Empowering developers to estimate app energy consumption. In Proceedings of the Annual International Conference on Mobile Computing and Networking (Mobicom'12), Istanbul, Turkey, 22–26 August 2012; pp. 317–328.

CHAPTER 17 ERROR AND CONGESTION RESILIENT VIDEO STREAMING OVER BROADBAND WIRELESS

Laith Al-Jobouri, Ismail A. Ali, Martin Fleury and Mohammed Ghanbari

Keywords: Broadband wireless, access network congestion, data partitioning, multimedia networking, packet scheduling

INTRODUCTION

Despite increases in capacity, broadband wireless systems still suffer from limitations in bandwidth capacity [1], leading to congestion at a base-station's (BS's) output buffer to its mobile stations (MSs). To reduce the risk of buffer overflow, this paper proposes a customized packet-scheduling regime for data-partitioned video streams. However, taking measures to reduce the impact of congestion at a BS buffer is only one part of the story of how to achieve resilient video streaming over wireless links, which are prone to error bursts [2], leading to a lack of synchronization between video encoders and decoders. In fact, the proposed packet-scheduling regime takes place within the context of a video streaming system that makes use of two measures to counteract the impact of errors: (1) source-coded error resilience [3], *i.e.*, within the video codec, in the form of data partitioning [4]; and (2) channel-coded adaptive Forward Error Correction (FEC) combined with error-control signaling [5]. However, these measures are powerless against packet drops through buffer overflow. Unfortunately, due to the predictive nature of video coding [6], most packet losses also have an effect that extends in time until the decoder is reset (intra refreshed).

One source-coded error resilience scheme, data partitioning, in its current form, is vulnerable to congestion due to the number of small packets that are produced. Data partitioning, which is a form of layered error resilience, can provide graceful degradation of video quality and, as such, has found an application in mobile video streaming [4]. In an H.264/Advanced Video Coding (AVC) codec [7], when data partitioning is enabled, every slice is divided into three separate partitions: partition-A has the most important data, including motion vectors (MVs); partition-B contains intra coefficients; and partition-C contains inter coefficients, the least important data in terms of reconstructing a video frame at the decoder. These data are packed into three types of Network Abstraction Layer units (NALUs) output by the codec. The importance of each NALU-bearing packet is identified in the NALU header. Though it is possible to aggregate (or segment) NALUs [8] before encapsulation in Internet Protocol (IP)/User Datagram Protocol (UDP)/Real-time Transport Protocol (RTP) packets, when data partitioning is in use, this would be to neglect the advantages of retaining smaller partition-A and -B bearing packets because smaller packets have a lower probability of channel error. Therefore, in this paper each NALU is assigned to its own packet, prior to the addition of network protocol headers.

To reduce the risk of buffer overflow for data-partitioned video streams, this paper proposes a packet-scheduling method, which can work in addition to other channel error protection methods, one of which is the adaptive rateless channel coding that is described in Section 2. Packet-scheduling schemes, which are referred to in Section 3, act irrespective of physical-layer (PHY-layer) data scheduling and may be independent of the data-link Medium Access Control (MAC) sub-layer

Citation: Laith Al-Jobouri, Ismail A. Ali, Martin Fleury, and Mohammed Ghanbari, Error and Congestion Resilient Video Streaming over Broadband Wireless, doi:10.3390/computers4020113

(though some other schemes do indeed intervene at the MAC sub-layer). The proposed packet-scheduling method works by smoothing the packet-scheduling times across one or more video frame intervals, according to allowable latency. Packets are allocated a scheduling time for output to a BS buffer in proportion to their size.

As such, the scheduling method is relatively simple to implement, which is one of its attractions owing to the need to reduce latency for interactive services such as mobile video-conferencing and video telephony. In the paper, the potential value of the application-layer (AL) scheduling approach is demonstrated in simulations that take account of PHY-layer packetization and scheduling. The paper also comments on video-content-dependent packetization issues as an aid to others planning AL packet scheduling or video-smoothing algorithms [9]. Alongside the scheduling regime, the paper also presents the gains from employing adaptive FEC as opposed to statically determining the redundancy overhead. In fact, adaptive rateless FEC is a significant feature of the proposed scheme. For codec-dependent aspects of the scheme, the reader is referred to [10] by the authors.

In general, the contribution of this paper is that a resilient video streaming scheme needs to consider both error resilience and congestion resilience, as error resilience alone is unable to protect against packet drops before the wireless channel is even reached. Section 2 describes the design decisions made by the authors in arriving at the video streaming system, such as the decision to employ rateless channel coding, which at the application layer of the protocol stack has largely superseded [11] fixed rate codes, especially those codes with high decoding complexity. Section 3 of the paper critically reviews recent work on packet scheduling, especially for use in multimedia applications. Section 4 details the methodology of both the error resilience and the congestion resilience aspects of the video streaming scheme. This is followed in Section 5 by an evaluation of selected aspects of the proposed scheme, as simulated for a Worldwide Interoperability for Microwave Access (WiMAX) wireless link, especially the performance of adaptive, rateless coding and the video-content response for packet scheduling. Finally, Section 6 draws some conclusions about the proposed video-streaming scheme.

ACHIEVING ERROR RESILIENCE: DESIGN DECISIONS

Robust unicast communication can be achieved by two means of error control [12,13]: (1) Automatic Repeat ReQuest (ARQ) and (2) FEC. ARQ allows a higher video data throughput than FEC provided there is a feedback channel and provided the channel is not inherently error prone. ARQs are also much simpler to process than FEC. However, as in the example of this paper, ARQ and FEC are not mutually exclusive: they can be employed together.

In best-effort wired networks, in order to add reliability to an unreliable protocol such as UDP, ARQ at the application layer can be achieved by Acknowledgments (ACKs), assuming the ACK latency does not impact upon the video display rate [14]. For example, in [15] the transmitter keeps a buffer of packets containing video frames, some of which have been transmitted but not acknowledged and others of which have yet to be transmitted. The transmitter must ensure that the buffer occupancy level does not exceed the potential transmission delay. Cyclic Redundancy Checks (CRCs) are required (and assumed in this paper) to detect errors, if the data has not already been so checked at the transport layer. For example, the UDP-Lite protocol [16] allows, when desired, data with errors to be passed up the protocol stack. UDP Lite is a possible implementation route for the ARQ/FEC system in this paper, allowing data to be corrected at the receiver rather than lost to the wireless receiver.

In a broadband wireless link designed for multimedia traffic such as the WiMAX link of this paper, a communication frame [17] is divided into two sub-frames: the first from the base station to mobile stations and the second from mobile stations to use for communication with the base station. Therefore, a natural way of delivering an AL ACK is by placing it in the return sub-frame, as we do in this paper. Notice that WiMAX also permits data-link layer ACKs and, alternatively, even a form of hybrid ACKs to be turned on on a per-link basis. However, switching ACKs on at the MAC sub-layer may result in arbitrary delays that are beyond the control of a multimedia application, which is why they were not enabled in this paper's evaluations. Instead AL ACKs were sparingly utilized, namely just once per packet. Soft ACKs can also counter the problem of arbitrary delays resulting from data-link ACKs by limiting the delay to a maximum [18], but there is a risk of poor-quality video. To reduce that problem, the source coding rate [19] can be varied according to the potential delay. However, in designing our system, it was simpler to implement AL ACKs.

To avoid the problem of delay and possible resource consumption by ACKs, FEC-based approaches transmit source-coded data with additional redundant parity data. Traditional fixed-rate channel codes cannot dynamically adapt to changing channel conditions easily, while rateless codes, with changing ratios of redundant to information data, can now adapt in a graduated fashion. However, to enable adaptation, Hybrid-ARQ (H-ARQ), e.g., as in [20], becomes necessary. In Type II H-ARQ, the transmitter only retransmits the necessary redundant data to increase the probability that the received data can now be reconstructed. In this paper, Type II H-ARQ is used. Moreover, as previously mentioned, to limit the impact of ARQs on latency, only one request for additional FEC is permitted.

Adaptive FEC with hybrid H-ARQ is still possible with fixed rate codes, but some other means of rate adaptation is required such as code puncturing [21] (the removal of parity bits) or code extension (the addition of parity bits resulting in a slower code rate). Unfortunately, some codes, for example Reed-Solomon (RS), are known to consume battery power [22], caused ultimately by their asymptotic (decoding) complexity which is $O(k^3)$ for the Gaussian elimination algorithm and $O(k^2)$ for the Berlekamp-Massey algorithm, where k is the number of information symbols. Therefore, due to their computational complexity, fixed-rate codes were avoided by us. Instead, Raptor codes [23], the variety of rateless code employed herein, have linear complexity both for encoding and decoding. They permit decoding if any k encoded symbols successfully arrive at the decoder. Usually, a small percentage (approximately 5%–10%) of additional encoded symbols are transmitted for successful recovery, but in the case of the requirement for additional encoded symbols, these additional symbols can be generated by the rateless encoder, in what has been called the fountain approach [24].

Raptor codes are one of a number of concatenated codes, e.g., the Turbo-Fountain code [25], which historically were developed to reinforce Luby Transform (LT) codes [26] when it was pointed out that LT codes had high error floors [27]. High error floors imply that the risk of decoder failure does not fall away as the channel conditions improve; instead, the risk remains at the same level as for lower Signal-to-Noise Ratios (SNRs). In order to achieve this, linear-time decoding iterative belief-propagation algorithms are necessary, which can be applied both to Raptor's outer code, a variant of Low-Density Parity Check (LDPC), and to the LT inner code. Furthermore, a systematic Raptor code can be achieved by initially applying the inverse of the inner code to the first *k*symbols prior to the outer coding step, which operates on the first *k* information symbols and an additional set of redundant symbols. Systematic channel codes separate the redundant coding data from the information data, allowing the information data to be passed directly to the decoder if no errors are detected (usually by means of CRCs). However, finding the inverse via Gaussian elimination increases the time complexity. Notice that in practice [28], Raptor codes, despite their low theoretical time complexity, are only computationally effective if an appropriate outer code is chosen, originally LDPC and latterly two concatenated LDPC-like codes.

In a traditional packet erasure rateless coding scheme, if PHY-layer correction fails due to checksum detection [29], then a packet becomes an erasure to be corrected by the rateless code at the application layer. However in our paper, upon PHY-layer correction failure, packets are not marked as erased but their data are passed to the application layer for Raptor code correction. This is possible because, in our paper, the information symbol is no longer an erased packet but a data block within a packet (intra-packet). (Notice that in the Multimedia Broadcast Multicast Service (MBMS) implementation of rateless codes [30], blocks are in general inter packet, not intra packet. However, this arrangement has the potential to increase the organizational overhead and the latency of the decoding process.) For a real-time multimedia application, intra-packet symbols have the additional advantage that there is no longer a requirement to wait for *k* packets to successfully arrive; *k* data blocks within a packet can arrive. In a procedure introduced in [31], each data block is assigned a checksum. If the checksum calculation fails, that block is then marked as an erasure. As an alternative, also in [31], each block can be given a confidence value based on the log-likelihood ratio (LLR) of the bits within it. Thus, the reduced risk of decoder failure is traded off both against lower latency and also the reduced efficiency of the code. The latter is due to the risk of declaring as erased blocks that are actually valid. In our intra-packet scheme, the data block is reduced to the size of a single byte, which has the advantage that the risk of decoding failure (see next paragraph) from shortage of data symbols within a packet is reduced. However, this raises the issue of CRCs, as the overhead would be too much if each byte were to be protected by a CRC. Therefore, a hybrid scheme is more suitable, in which blocks of bytes are assumed to be protected by a single CRC and marked as erasures if the CRC fails.

In a Raptor code for the inner LT code, even in an error-free channel, there is a small probability that the decoding will fail. However, that probability converges to zero in polynomial time in the number of input symbols [32] and a similar analysis applies to an outer LDPC [33]. In this paper, the probability of decoder failure is modeled statistically by the following equation from [34]:

$$\begin{aligned} P_f(m,k) &= 1 && \text{if } m < k \\ &= 0.85 \times 0.567^{m-k} && \text{if } m \geq k \end{aligned} \qquad (1)$$

where Pf(m,k) is the decode failure probability of the code with *k* source symbols if *m* symbols have been successfully received (and $1-P_f$ is naturally the success probability). Notice that for $k > 200$ [34] the model of Equation (1) almost ideally models the performance of the code. This implies that, if block symbols are used, approximately 200 blocks should be received before reasonable behavior takes place. Therefore, we require packets of at least 200 bytes in our scheme.

In summary, the resulting video communication system used by us over a WiMAX link has protection at several layers of the protocol stack. Data randomization is applied at the PHY layer to avoid runs of 1 s or Os. Subsequently, one of WiMAX's modulation and coding schemes is selected. Mobile WiMAX offers modulation by one of Binary Phase-Shift Keying (BPSK), Quadrature Phase-Shift Keying (QPSK), 16-Quadrature Amplitude Modulation (QAM), or 64-QAM in descending order of robustness. The mandatory convolutional coding rate is selected from 1/2, 2/3, 3/4, and 5/6 in ascending order of protection. There are other WiMAX PHY-layer protection options such as Turbo coding or PHY-layer H-ARQ which were not configured in the simulation experiments of Section 5. Thus, bit-level FEC protection is first applied at the PHY layer and additional FEC is applied in our scheme at the application layer by means of a rateless channel coder. However, unlike conventional block-based AL channel coding, a variant of packet-level channel coding, we used intra-packet byte-level rateless channel coding. By selecting this form of application-layer channel coding, we were able to use adaptive rateless coding enabled by means of a simple, low-latency H-ARQ mechanism.

RELATED WORK

Rateless Code for Video Streaming

Prior usage of AL Raptor coding, especially that in various wireless standards [35], such as DVB-H and 3rd Generation Partnership Project (3GPP)'s Multimedia Broadcast Multicast Service (MBMS), has been multicast [36] without feedback, rather than unicast with feedback as herein. Moreover, unlike herein, it has been deployed in the standards with block-level symbols that can extend across packets rather than intra-packet as herein, resulting in longer repair latencies if and when the blocks extend over many packets.

Data-partitioned video streams were first protected by a form of Raptor codes in [37], which paper from the current author also demonstrated that data partitioning has the least overhead of H.264/AVC error resilience methods. Since then, the idea was taken up in [38] providing an application to DVB-H and comparing with random linear codes (RLC). It was demonstrated that this form of AL-FEC is effective at lower data rates when compared to H.264/AVC without data partitioning. RLC were competitive with rateless coding in terms of error protection. However, as the information data length increases, the need to employ a Gaussian elimination (rather than belief propagation) decoding algorithm causes the computational complexity and, hence decoding latency, to increase as $O(n^3)$ rather than $O(n)$ for Raptor codes. In [39], RLC were applied in the same form as [37] had already used for Raptor codes, that is with expanded windows code (called Growth codes in [37]) to provide scalable channel coding. However, in [39], the protection was not applied to data-partitioned video but by prioritizing the different H.264/AVC slice types. Finally, there is a summary of the previous investigations of [38,39] in [40]. The current contribution does not pursue the ideas originally developed by us in [37] because we seek herein to show that the complication of expanding window or growth codes may be unnecessary for data-partitioned video streaming.

In our paper, adaptive provision of redundant rateless code results in reduced channel coding overhead. It is possible that if further advantage of cross-layer communication could be made then the overhead of rateless coding can be reduced still further. For example in [41,42], the amount of rateless data was jointly determined by the modulation and coding scheme (MCS) at the PHY layer. It is possible that adaptation according to the wireless channel state could be combined with adaptation according to the PHY-layer MCS mode in a future cross-layer scheme.

Packet Scheduling for Video

In [43], the authors combined scheduling at the transmitter with control of playout speed at the receiver, across a time-varying wireless link. This proposal required video-content-dependent decisions with the aim of maximizing video quality at the receiver. Decisions were driven by a Markov process informed by the motion activity of the transmitted video frames. In the scenario of [43], the scheduler discards late packets and catches up with delayed playout during poor wireless channel conditions. The receiver adapts its playout rate (the rate video frames are displayed at), slowing it down when playing video with low motion and, hence, low coding complexity occurs. The aim was to avoid playout interruptions, which are thought to be less disconcerting to the viewer than small slowdowns in the playout rate. The authors concluded their research by identifying the need for practical heuristics that reduce the complexity of their proposed schemes due to the need to inspect the content type, which remains a problem for real-time operation and is the specific problem our simplified scheme seeks to address.

The optimal scheduling decision is again computed through a Markov process in [44]. However, the authors of [44] are aware that burst errors are a threat and, in particular, may disrupt feedback signals. Therefore, modeling is designed to take into account incomplete information about the receiver's state. The end result is improved video quality but delays to video packet transmission during poor channel states. In this early work, the impact on playout delay was not taken into account and the authors also acknowledge the need to develop heuristic decision-guiding rules.

In [45], the video content is taken into account to vary the packet scheduling decision at the transmitter. Inspection of the video content does imply an increase in end-to-end delay, as does the need to await protocol acknowledgments. The position of a packet's data within a Group-of-Pictures (GOP) weights its importance to the playout process and, hence, determines its transmission schedule deadline. Similarly, the texture- and motion-complexity governed scheduling decisions when adapting the packet transmission order. Simplified wireless conditions were assumed to test the scheme. However, the authors note that channel coding is insufficient in itself during "bursty" error conditions, requiring intelligent ARQs and/or packet scheduling. The result of packet scheduling was improved objective video and a more even distribution of temporal distortion. Data partitioning was also turned on in some of the evaluation tests but with the Moving Picture Experts Group (MPEG)-4 part 2 form of data partitioning, in which each video packet is internally divided between shape/motion data and less important texture data.

The work in [46] is aimed at IEEE 802.11 Wireless Local Area Networks (WLANs) running the Distributed Coordination Function (DCF) at the MAC layer, *i.e.*, retransmitting data packets that are lost. By determining the importance of the video data within a packet, differing retry limits occur. The codec includes the importance of the video data as side information with the video data. However, to achieve significant gains in video quality requires cross-layer intervention in the wireless protocol stack as well as modification of the video codec. Research in [47] introduced another scheduling scheme that relies on video content side information placed in advance within the bitstream by the encoder. It is designed in a practical fashion for a multi-user, Time Division Multiple Access (TDMA) wireless environment such as High Speed Downlink Packet Access (HSPDA).

Long Term Evolution (LTE) leaves the choice of packet scheduler to the vendor, resulting in many research proposals [48]. These are system-level schedulers, of which [49] combines the popular proportional fair algorithm with a higher-level scheduler that allocates the amount of data that each real-time flow can send within one time epoch.

METHODOLOGY

The error and congestion resilient video streaming scheme is demonstrated for IEEE 802.16, which is the standardized version of WiMAX wireless broadband technology [50]. WiMAX continues to be rolled out in parts of the world that do not benefit from existing wired infrastructures or cellular networks. WiMAX is also cost effective in rural and suburban areas in some developed countries. It is designed to provide effective transmission at a cell's edge by the allocation to a mobile user of sub-channels with separated frequencies to reduce co-channel interference. The transition to the higher data rates of IEEE 802.16 m [51] indicates the technological route by which WiMAX will respond to the technological advances of its competitors, especially LTE. However, we modeled version IEEE 802.16e-2005 (mobile WiMAX), of which IEEE 802.16-2009 is an improved version [52], as this is backwards compatible with fixed WiMAX (IEEE Project P802.16d), which still remains the most widely deployed version of WiMAX. Time Division Duplex (TDD) (Figure 1) and effective scheduling of time slots between MSs through TDMA (not to be confused with AL packet scheduling as described in this paper) increases spectral efficiency. Figure 2 provides a closer look at the frame and sub-frame structure within which are contained per-MS data bursts. (For simplicity, the MS to BS sub-frame structure is illustrated.) Within each data burst are WiMAX packets, which at the MAC sub-layer are called Protocol Data Units (PDUs) and consist of a MAC header, MAC Service Data Unit (MSDU), and a CRC, as shown in Figure 3. An MSDU corresponds to a packet passed to the MAC layer from higher layers in the protocol stack, most immediately from the transport layer. It consists of an IP packet with typical IP/UDP/RTP headers attached, though, in practice, packet header compression is normally employed over wireless links in order to reduce the heard overhead. The payload of this network packet will contain an NALU and additional rateless channel coding data added at the application layer, as described below.

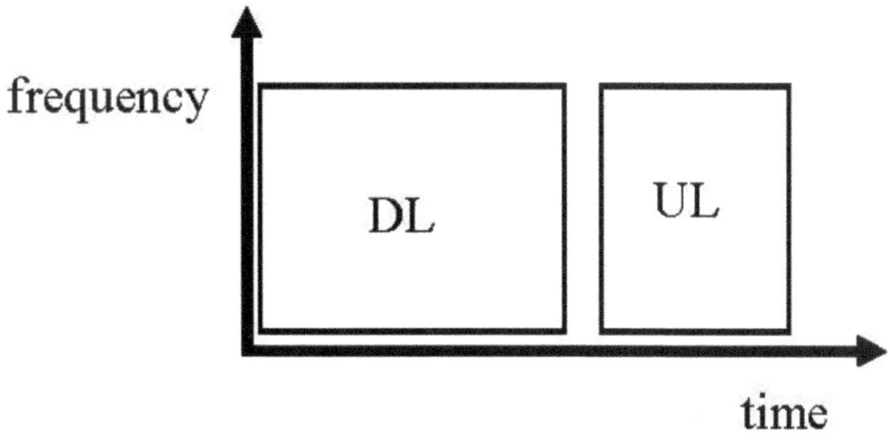

Figure 1: Worldwide Interoperability for Microwave Access (WiMAX) frame divided into two sub-frames separated by a guard interval, namely the downlink (DL) sub-frame from a base-station (BS) to mobile stations (MSs), and an uplink (UL) sub-frame following in time from the MSs to the BS. The time direction consists of successive Orthogonal Frequency-Division Multiple Access (OFDMA) symbols, while the frequency direction is assigned to data bursts on a per-MS basis (OFDMA is a refinement of Orthogonal Frequency Division Multiplexing (OFDM) that in mobile WiMAX allows more flexible sub-channelization in the frequency dimension). (Additional preamble, burst mapping, and ranging signaling is also present. For more details refer to [50].)

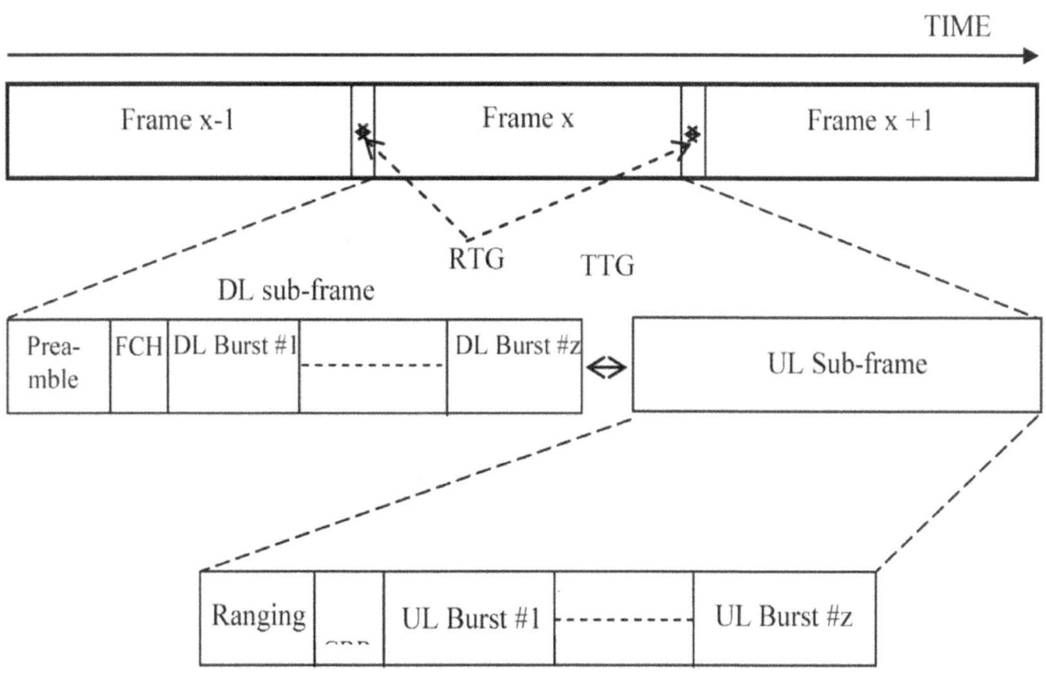

Figure 2: Sub-frame structure showing per-MS data bursts (numbered from 1 to z). (FCH = frame control header, RTG = receive/transmit transition gap, TTG = transmit/receive transition gap.)

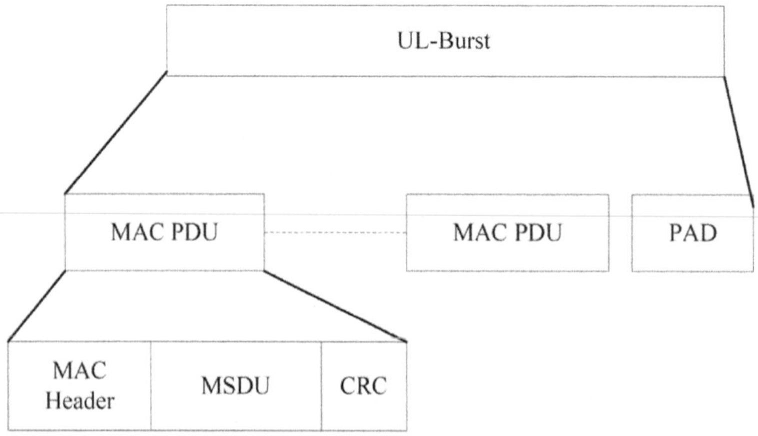

Figure 3: WiMAX burst structure showing MAC Service Data Unit (MSDU) packets. The DL-Burst is similar, except that there are additional headers included prior to the MAC PDUs. (PAD = padding, as the PDU size is variable.)

As a whole, the WiMAX video-streaming scheme, Figure 4, comprises three components: (1) source-coded data partitioning of the video bitstream; (2) adaptive rateless channel coding; and (3) AL packet scheduling. This Section now describes these three components. As analyzed in Section 1, the first two of these are error resilience measures, while the third, supports congestion resilience. Therefore, the following description of the methodology is split into error resilience and congestion resilience. The error-resilience description includes the way that the source packets (NALUs) are mapped to the underlying broadband wireless MAC and PHY layers.

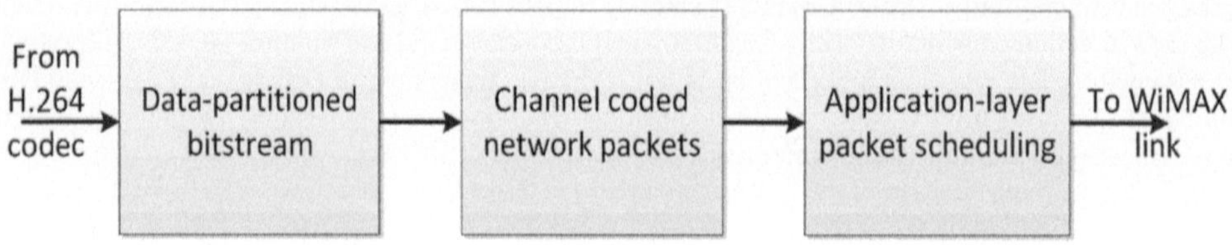

Figure 4: Overview of video-streaming scheme.

Error Resilience

As previously remarked, data-partitioned H.264/AVC compressed video can be an effective means of placing more important data (as far as video decoding is concerned) in smaller, less error-prone packets in a wireless channel, provided low-quality video (quantization parameter (QP) greater than 30) is not transmitted, as then the less important packets diminish in size. As is common in mobile video communication, in this paper an IPPPP… frame coding structure is employed, that is an intra-coded (I)-frame followed thereafter by predictively-coded (P)-frames. Notice that bi-predictively-coded (B)-slices are not permitted in the H.264/AVC Baseline profile, aimed at reducing the complexity of bi-predictive coding on mobile devices. Random Intra Macroblock Refresh (RIMR) (forcibly embedding a given percentage of randomly placed intra-coded macroblocks (MBs) in a P-frame) was turned on to counteract spatio-temporal error propagation that would otherwise occur in the absence of I-frames. The advantages of omitting periodic intra-coded I-frames for wireless communication are reviewed in [53]. Figure 5 illustrates the standard frame structure of a codec (called a Group of Pictures or GOP). In the common wireless transmission frame structure, P-frames take the place of the B-frames implying that all prediction is in the forward direction from one P-frame to the next. Moreover, the final I-frame in a GOP is also replaced by a P-frame, as I-frames are now not the means of re-setting the decoder in the event of error corruption or frame drops. The sequence of P-frames now extends to the end of the video sequence or stream. RIMR is employed by us to gradually re-set the decoding process, which implies that there will always be intra-coded MBs within each frame.

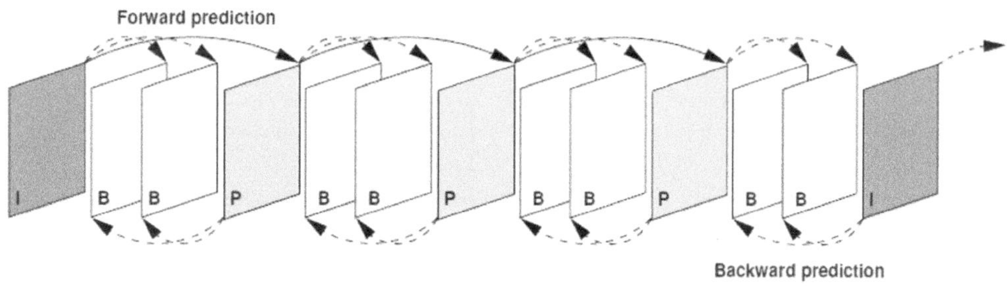

Figure 5: Standard frame structure within a codec.

When data partitioning is enabled, every slice within a video frame (Figure 6) is divided into up to three separate partitions and each partition is encapsulated in either of type 2 to type-4 NALUs (refer to Figure 7). Partition-A, carried in an NALU of type 2, comprises the MB addresses and types, their MVs, and QPs. If any MBs in the frames are intra-coded, their frequency-transform coefficients are packed into a type-3 NALU or partition-B. Partition-C contains the transform coefficients of the motion-compensated inter-coded MBs and is carried in an NALU of type-4. (Partition-B and partition-C also contain Coded Block Patterns (CBPs), compact maps indicating which blocks within each MB contain non-zero coefficients.) Figure 8 illustrates the overall process from the point of view of the H.264/AVC codec processing the raw video data input from a camera. A compressed video stream is output from the Video Coding Layer (VCL) after applying the normal redundancy reduction steps [6] including motion estimation and compensation, transform coding, quantization and entropy coding, which result in a compressed bit-stream. As these steps take place on a per-MB basis, it is possible to separate groups of MBs into slices, which in Figure 6are formed from geometrically adjacent MBs, selected in raster scan order. The data-partition step separates out the per-MB data by function, e.g., all MVs of the MBs within a slice are separated out. The data-partition step subsequently assigns that data to the appropriate data-partition type. Notice that in Figure 8, one of the slices has no partition-B data, because there are no intra-coded MBs within it. That situation may arise if RIMR MBs do not fall within the slice and also because the encoder does not select any MBs for intra coding, as might happen if an occluded object prevents a prediction match being found. The other two slices have MBs that are spatially-coded (intra-coded). Once partitioning has taken place, the data partitions are allocated to a NALU of the appropriate type at what is termed the NAL of the codec. The FEC redundant data (Raptor code data) are also included (refer to Figure 9) within the packet payload along with checksums. If additional FEC data are requested over the uplink, that data also is included in the packet payload. As NALU aggregation was not enabled, each NALU is assigned to a separate network packet as its payload. Additionally, it is important to notice that, for our experiments, each video frame formed a single slice.

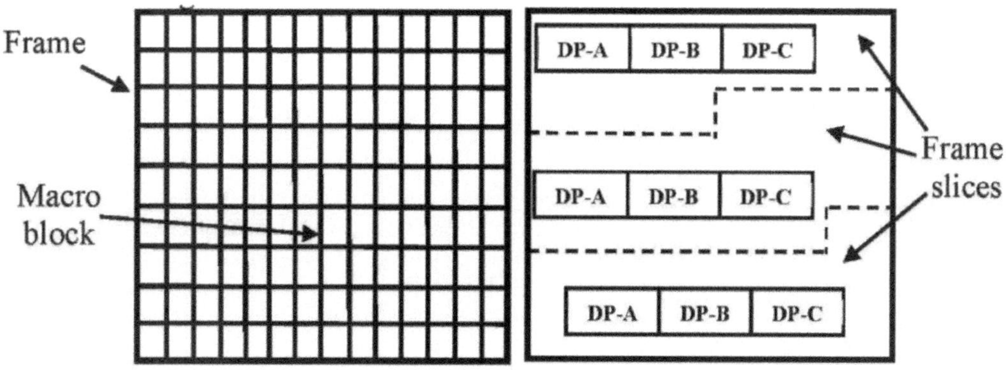

Figure 6: Decomposing a video frame into partitions within slices.

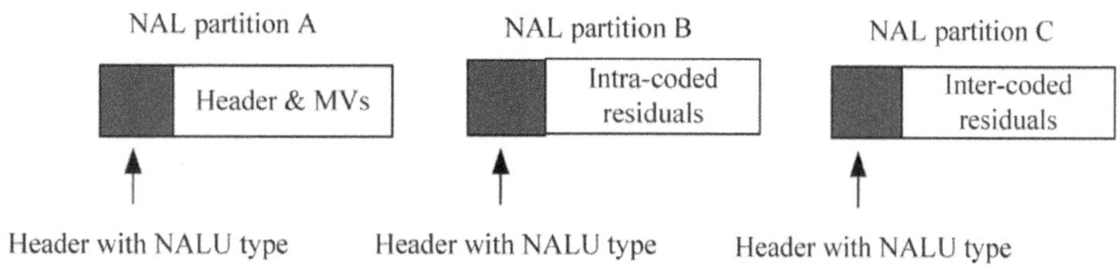

Figure 7: H.264/AVC data partitioning in which the partitions of a single slice are assigned to three NAL units (types 2 to 4). As described in the text, the relative size of the partitions varies with the QP setting of the encoder and is not fixed, as shown in the schematic representation of this figure.

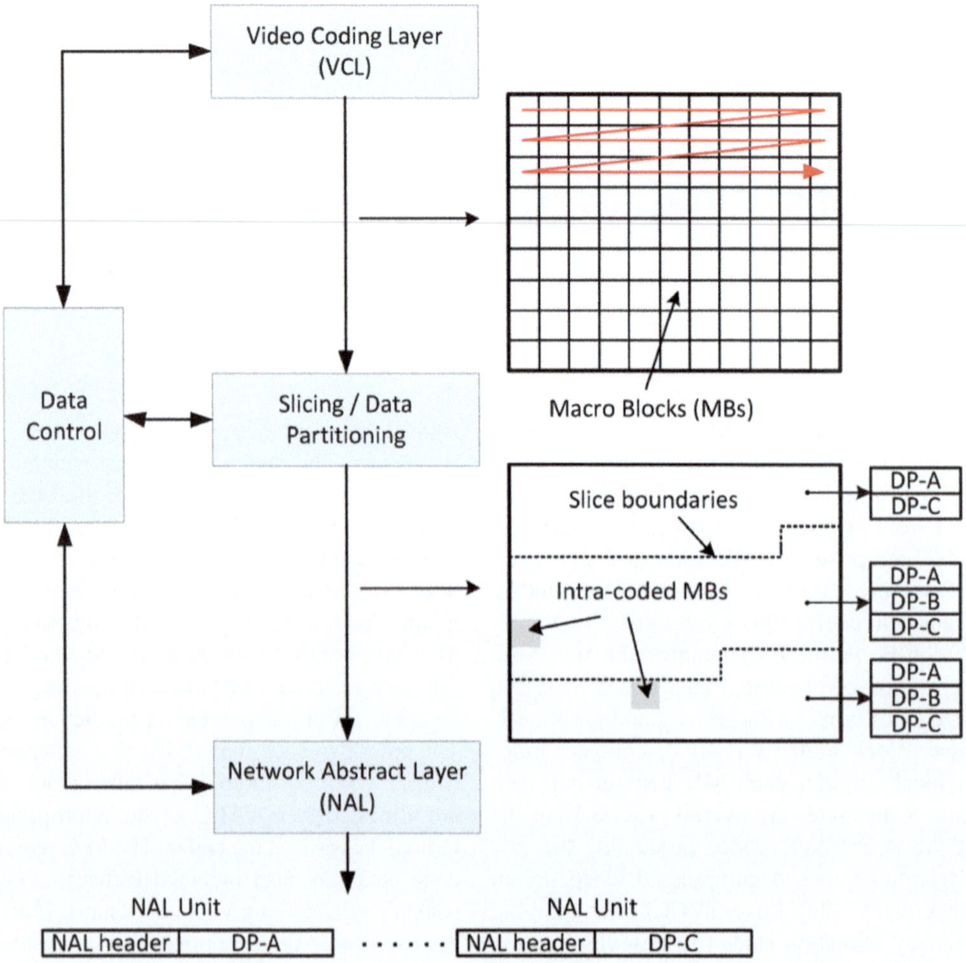

Figure 8: H.264/ Advanced Video Coding (AVC) data flow for combined slicing with data partitioning.

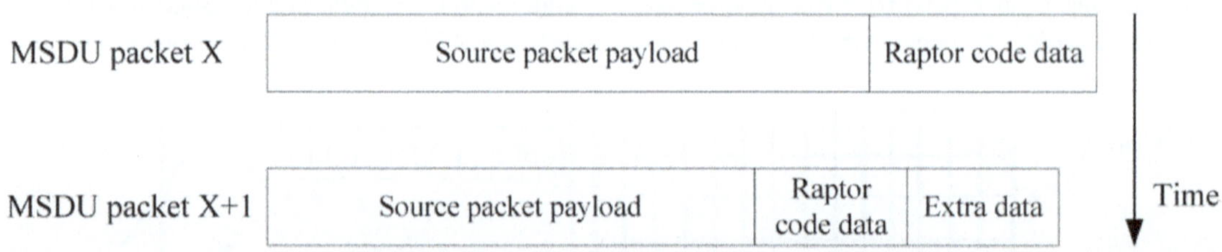

Figure 9: WiMAX packets (MSDUs) from BS to an MS containing video source data from higher layers with additional application-layer-forward error correction (AL-FEC) added by the streaming application. Packet x + 1 contains additional piggybacked AL-FEC data requested to aid in recovery. The Raptor code data overhead is adapted to channel conditions. The amount of code data added is schematic only, as in practice around 5% would be present. Not shown are possible cyclic redundancy checks (CRCs) added by the application and Internet Protocol (IP)/User Datagram Protocol (UDP)/Real-time Transport Protocol (RTP) headers that would also be present in the source packet payload in addition to the Network Abstraction Layer units (NALU).

Reconstruction of the other partitions is dependent on the survival of partition-A, though that partition remains independent of the other partitions. Constrained Intra-Prediction (CIP) [54] (Ref. [54] introduces standardized intra CIP while proposing non-standard inter-CIP) was set in order to make partition-B independent of partition-C. When only partition-A survives, its motion vectors can then be employed in error concealment at the decoder using motion copy. When partition-A and partition-B survive, then error concealment can combine texture information from partition-B when available, as well as intra concealment when possible. When partition-A and partition-C survive, to reconstruct it requires partially discarding partition-C data reliant on missing partition-B MBs and then reconstructing either of them using partition-A MVs or partition-A with partition-C texture data, when it is available.

The relative size of the data-partition packets is determined by the quality of the video, which in turn is governed by the QP of the MBs. The QP is set in the configuration file of the H.264/ AVC codec, prior to compression. Figure 10 is a comparison between the relative sizes of the partitions according to QP for the two diverse reference video clips used later in Section 5. For the purposes of assessing the impact of the QP, Variable Bit-Rate (VBR) was encoded in Section 5.1's evaluation. In VBR video, the QP remains constant in order to preserve video quality. However, many broadcasters prefer Constant Bit-Rate (CBR) video, as it allows transmission bandwidth and storage to be predicted. Transmission jitter is also reduced. For that reason, CBR video is tested in Section 5.2, though the QP value may vary a little [55] in order to maintain a constant bit-rate.

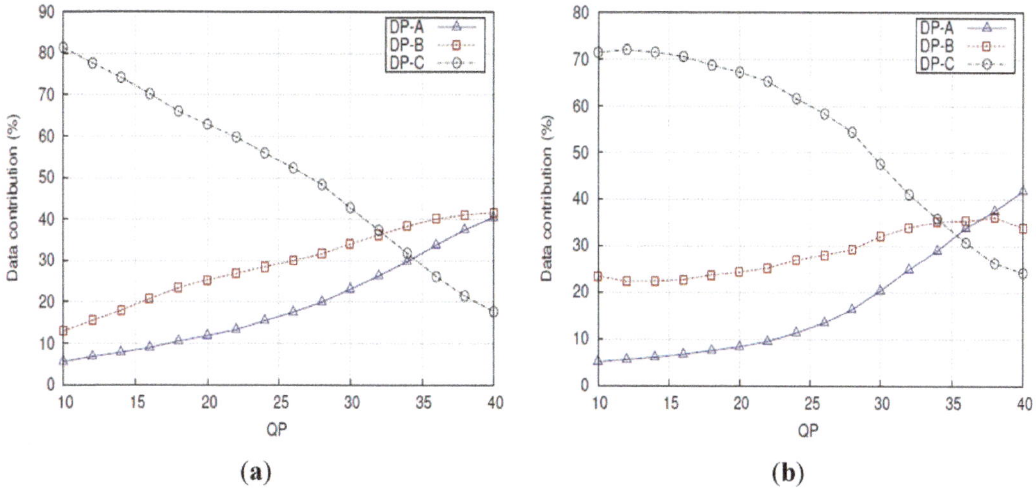

Figure 10: Percentage contributions of data partitions (DPs) A, B and C over a range of QPs for (**a**) *Paris* and (**b**) *Stefan* video clips.

Rateless Raptor code is an effective form of FEC that provides protection to the data partitioned video stream with reduced computational complexity and capacity approaching overhead. Rate adaptation of AL FEC is performed in order to match wireless channel conditions. The code was applied at the level of bytes within a packet in the interests of reduced latency rather than at the usual packet level. Thus, the byte forms the block symbol size and only bytes passing the CRC at the PHY layer are accepted at the application layer channel decoder. The probability of channel byte loss (*BL*) serves to predict the amount of redundant data to be added to the payload. In implementation, *BL* is found through measurement of channel conditions, which is mandatory anyway in a WiMAX mobile station. If the original packet length is *L*, then the redundant data is given simply by

$$R = L \times BL + (L \times BL^2) + (L \times BL^3)\ldots = L/(1 - BL) - L \tag{2}$$

which is arrived at by adding successively smaller additions of redundant data, based on taking the previous amount of redundant data multiplied by *BL*. The statistical model of Equation (1) in Section 2 was utilized to determine the Raptor code failure probability.

Packets with "piggybacked" repair data are also sent. Suppose a packet cannot be decoded despite the provision of redundant data. It is implied from Equation (1) that if less k symbols (bytes) in the payload are successfully received, a further $k - m + e$ redundant bytes can then be sent to reduce the risk of failure. This reduced risk arises because of the exponential decay of the risk that is evident from Equation (1), which gives rise to Raptor code's low error probability floor. In practice, $e = 4$, reduces the probability of failure to decode to 8.7%. Only one retransmission over a WiMAX link is allowed to avoid further increasing latency. If that retransmission fails to allow reconstruction, that packet is abandoned.

Congestion Resilience

With respect to congestion resilience, consider Figure 11 in which a single video frame has been assigned equal bit length slices. The geometric space taken up by any slice is dependent on the coding complexity of the content. Shaded MBs in Figure 11 represent intra-coded MBs. Each slice was further partitioned in source coding space into up to three partitions. As mentioned already, it is possible that partition-B may occasionally be absent (the top slice in Figure 11) if no RIMR MBs are allocated to a slice and if no naturally intra-coded MBs are assigned to the slice by the encoder. (Naturally encoded intra MBs are inserted if an encoder can find no matching MB in a reference frame or as a way of improving the quality.) Similarly, it is possible that if, for example, an extremely high bit rate was allocated to the stream, partition C might not be present, as the encoder could afford the luxury of encoding all MBs with intra coding. However, the simple packet scheduling scheme for data-partitioned streams is independent of source-coding allocations of partitions and slices.

Figure 11: Example video frame from *Stefan* split into equal bit length slices, showing each slice partitioned into up to three data partitions (DPs) (A, B, C).

Figure 12 demonstrates the results of two alternative packet scheduling regimes. A frame interval is shown, which is 1/30 s at 30 frame/s. In the default case, scheduling is at equal intervals in time. We are aware that packet scheduling may never follow this ideal regime in a processor even with a real-time operating system present. However, the regime acts as a point of comparison. In the simple scheduling scheme proposed, packets are allocated a scheduling point according to their relative size within a frame's (or multiple frames') compressed size. Thus, for any one packet indexed as *j* with length lj, its scheduling time allocation is:

$$t_{alloc}^{j} = \frac{l^j}{\sum_{i=1}^{n} l^i} f \tag{3}$$

where *f* is the fixed frame interval, and there are *n* packets in that frame. The denominator of Equation (3) sums the lengths of the packets within frame *j* and allocates a time interval relative to its size (numerator of Equation (3)) relative to the total length of the packets within frame *j*.

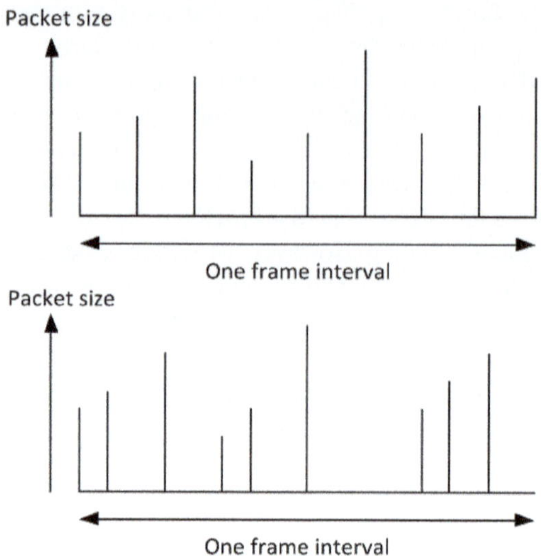

Figure 12: Example of packet scheduling regimes: (**top**) Equally spaced in time; (**bottom**) Packet ordering preserved but scheduling time allocated according to packet size.

The proposed scheduling method obviously preserves the original average bitrate, though there is a single video-frame latency while the frame's packet sizes are assessed and the scheduling takes place. In [56], it is pointed out that IEEE 802.21 Media Independent Handover (MIH) services (IEEE 802.21 WG, 2008) provide a general framework for cross-layer signaling that can be used to achieve the scheduling. In IEEE 802.21, a layer 2.5 is inserted between the level 2 link layer and the level 3 network layer. Upper-layer services, known as MIH users or MIHU communicate through this middleware to the lower layer protocols. For mobile WiMAX and later versions of WiMAX, another WiMAX-specific set of standardized communication primitives exists as IEEE 802.16 g.

Figure 13 identifies the place that AL packet scheduling takes place with the processing cycle and also summarizes the processing cycle as a whole. After compression through the video codec, rateless channel coding is applied at the application layer on an intra-packet basis at the byte level. A simple form of application-layer H-ARQ serves to operate the adaptive form of channel coding. AL packet scheduling now takes place for the source packets. After packetization at the upper protocol stack layers, the PHY layer is responsible for a series of protection measures already mostly described. Data interleaving of each PHY FEC block in an OFDM-based system acts to map adjacent bits across non-adjacent sub-carriers. As previously stated, PHY layer H-ARQ was not enabled in the evaluation of Section 5.

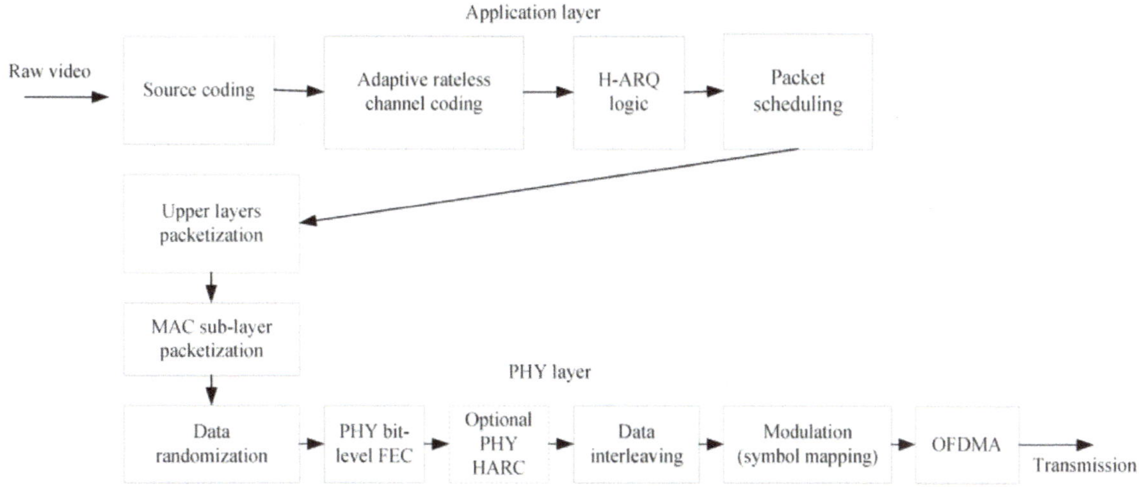

Figure 13: Overview of protection measures and packet handling across the upper and WiMAX protocol stack layers.

EVALUATION

This section begins by describing the simulation model for the evaluations, while the later two sections concentrate on aspects of error resiliency and congestion resiliency.

Simulation Model

To model video communication over WiMAX, the well-known ns-2 simulator [57] was combined with a module from the Chang Gung University, Taiwan [58] that has turned out to be an effective way of modeling IEEE 802.16e's behavior. In the evaluation, transmission over WiMAX was carefully modeled. The IEEE 802.16e TDD frame length was set to 5 ms, as previously remarked, because only this value is supported in the WiMAX Forum simplification of the standard (In fact, a frame size of 20 ms benefits video streaming [59] because there is more time to transfer enough data.). The raw downlink data rate of 10.67 Mbps results from the use of one of the mandatory WiMAX modulation and coding modes [50] for a TDD downlink/uplink sub-frame ratio of 3:1, namely 16-QAM at ½ rate. The WiMAX BS was assigned more bandwidth capacity than the uplink to allow the BS to respond to multiple MSs. All buffers were set to 50 packets and all packets were directed to WiMAX's real-time Polling System (rtPS) class of service.

Apart from video streaming to a WiMAX MS, three other MSs received continuous CBR data, Figure 14, with two receiving at 1 kbps, and one at 840 kbps. A typical low bitrate parametric speech codec such as a Linear Prediction Coding (LPC) vocoder operates from 1.2 kbps to 4.8 kbps, close to the lowest rate of these two signals. The G.711 vocoder for high-quality Voice-over-IP (VOIP) has a typical data rate of 87 kbps, implying that the larger of these signals is equivalent to ten such speech signals. Packet size was set at 1 kB, the WiMAX maximum transport unit. It is these streams that inject cross-traffic into the scenario modeled and provide any congestion experienced in the experiments by the video stream.

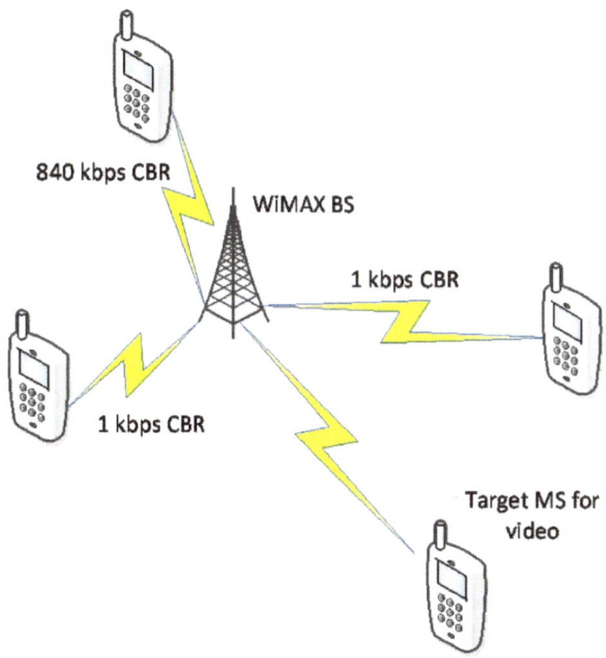

Figure 14: Scenario for evaluation experiments.

To model adverse channel conditions across the WiMAX link, "bursty" errors (time correlated errors) were modeled by a Gilbert-Elliott two-state hidden Markov model [60]. This channel model was introduced into the ns-2 simulator. The Gilbert-Elliott channel model itself is a two-state Markov chain. It is based on good and bad states, the probabilities of these states, and the probabilities of the transition states between them. In the bad state, losses happen with higher probability, whereas in the good state, losses happen with lower probability. P_{GG} refers to the probability of being in the good state and P_{GB} is the probability of a transition from the good state to the bad state. P_{BB} is likewise the probability of being in the bad state and transitioning back to the same bad state. P_{BG} refers to the probability of a transition from the bad to good state. $P_{GG}(P_{BB})$ can be interpreted as the probability of remaining in the good (bad) state, given that the previous state was good (bad). Conversely, P_{GB} represents the probability that, given that the previous state was good, a transition is made from the good to the bad state. By the law of total probability, all probabilities sum to one (certainty). Therefore, we have $P_{GG} + P_{GB} = 1$, resulting in Equation (4). A similar argument for the bad state leads to Equation (6).

$$P_{GG} = 1 - P_{GB} \tag{4}$$

$$P_{BB} = 1 - P_{BG} \tag{5}$$

For the stochastic process to remain stationary in time,

$$\pi_G P_{GB} = \pi_B P_{BG} \tag{6}$$

where πG and πB are the steady state probabilities of being in a good or bad state respectively. The law of total probability πB=1−πG again applies. Substituting this expression for πB into Equation (6) easily leads to:

$$\pi_G = \frac{P_{BG}}{P_{BG} + P_{GB}} \tag{7}$$

Similarly, πG=1−πB. Substituting this expression for πG into Equation (6) easily leads to:

$$\pi_B = \frac{P_{GB}}{P_{BG} + P_{GB}} \tag{8}$$

Thus the average loss rate produced by the Gilbert-Elliott channel model is

$$L = p_G . \pi_G + p_B \pi_B \tag{9}$$

where p_G and p_B are the error rates of the good and bad states respectively.

To model the effect of slow fading [61] at the packet-level, as the Gilbert-Elliott model's parameters, the P_{GG} was set to 0.96, $P_{BB} = 0.95$, $p_G = 0.01$ and $p_B = 0.02$. Additionally, it is still possible for a packet not to be dropped in the channel but nonetheless be corrupted through the effect of fast fading (or other sources of noise and interference). This byte-level corruption was modelled by the second Gilbert-Elliott model, with the same parameters (applied at the byte level) as that of the packet-level model except that p_B (now probability of byte loss) was increased to 0.165. Effectively, this second model emulates fast fading between good and bad conditions. Notice that the packet drops caused by the channel model are not the packet losses resulting from buffer overflow in the congestion experiments.

Error Resilience

This section concentrates on the impact of the Gilbert-Elliott channel model rather than any packet losses from buffer overflow. As previously outlined, there are two types of channel packet errors: those caused by error bursts of sufficient intensity in which complete packets are dropped and those bursts errors resulting in the corruption of packets. As previously mentioned, in the event of a failure to decode a corrupt packet, a repair is attempted by an ARQ request for additional rateless data if an attempt at decoding fails. If the additional redundant data still fails in allowing successful packet recovery, that packet is then also regarded as dropped. If not, it is regarded as corrupted but suffers from the additional delay required to request redundant data. Upon receiving that additional data, the packet's data is then decoded again.

For this set of experiments, two different video traces were employed for input to ns2 in the WiMAX downlink tests. The first one was the *Paris* sequence (also used in the congestion resilience experiments). The second one was *Football* (high temporal coding complexity) sequence. Both sequences had Variable BitRate (VBR) encoded in Common Intermediate Format (CIF) (352 × 288 pixels/frame) at 30 frame/s.

The RIMR level was set to 5% in the IPPP.... GOP structure (where I is an I-frame followed by all P-frames denoted as PPP...). In these experiments, a single slice per frame was allocated.

The experiments determined the effect of changing the percentage of redundant rateless data or alternatively adopting the adaptive scheme, which initially calculates the amount of redundant data sent through Equation (2). To make a comparison with the adaptive scheme, fixed amounts, 5% or 10%, of redundant data were added to the packets prior to transmission over the WiMAX link.

In Figure 15, it is apparent that increasing the redundancy from 5% to 10% and then changing to the adaptive scheme of Section 4.1 has an effect on packet drops, which impacts video quality, as FEC cannot be applied to dropped packets. However, video content has little impact even though *Football* is much more active than *Paris*. In contrast, QP has a significant impact because the reduction in size of partition C packets as the QP is lowered (refer back to Figure 10) results in a reduction in the number of larger packets.

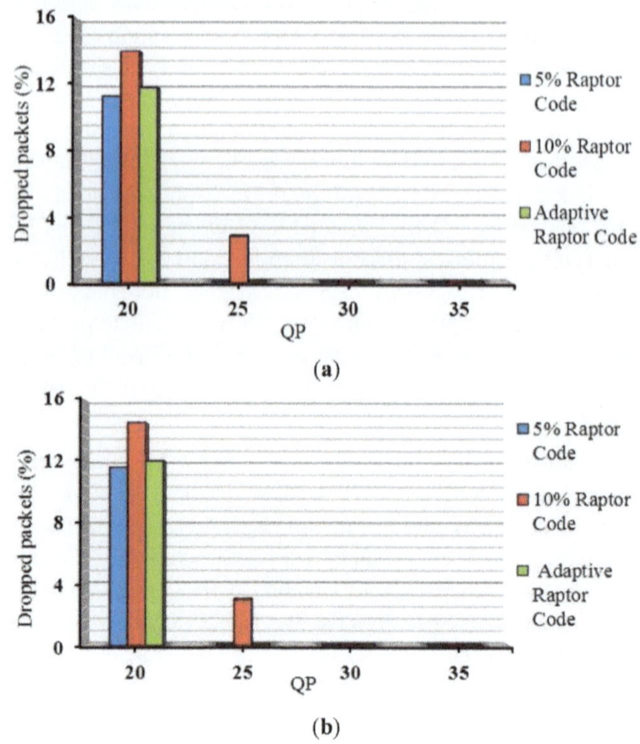

Figure 15: Dropped packets (%) for streaming (**a**) *Football* and (**b**) *Paris* with 5%, 10% and adaptive redundant data.

Comparing the number of corrupted packets in Figure 16, one sees a dramatic increase in their number, with only 5% redundant data but their elimination with adaptive FEC. Thus, for adaptive FEC, the mean delay of corrupted packets (the mean delay including retransmission of all corrupted packets) is zero because there are no corrupted packets. However, in Figure 17 the reconstructed objective video quality, Peak Signal-to-Noise Ratio (PSNR), for 5% and adaptive redundant data is much the same. There is, of course, a penalty from not adapting the redundancy rate according to the channel conditions, because the total delay in retransmitting the corrupted packets (Figure 18), would build up if only 5% rateless coding was applied, leading to larger start-up buffers and discouraging interactive video applications. The higher percentage of dropped packets at low QP (high broadcast quality) and larger packet sizes leads to unacceptable video quality, with the redundant 10% data leading to a drop in quality at QP = 25.

There are small variations in the mean end-to-end packet delays across the QPs (Figure 18 and Figure 19), whose variations are influenced by packet sizes and their propagation times. Therefore, adaptive rateless coding reduces delay considerably over using 5% redundant data but achieves better video quality than when using 10% redundant data. Naturally, delay is an important issue in a real-time service, as it governs buffering provision, enables interactive applications, and if not checked can lead to freeze frame effects.

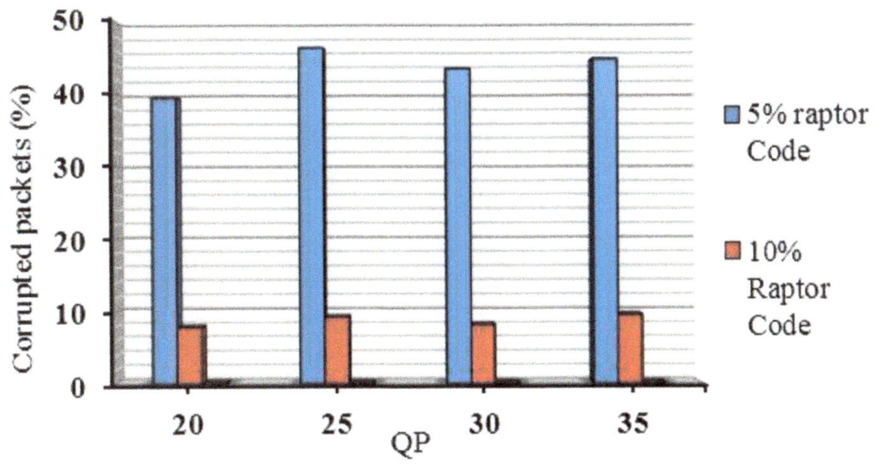

(a)

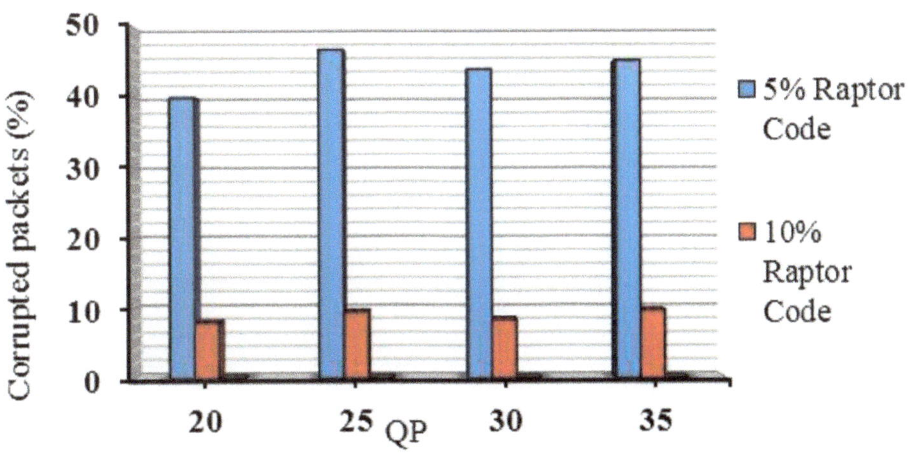

(b)

Figure 16: Corrupted packets (%) for streaming (**a**) Football and (**b**) Paris with 5%, 10% and adaptive redundant data.

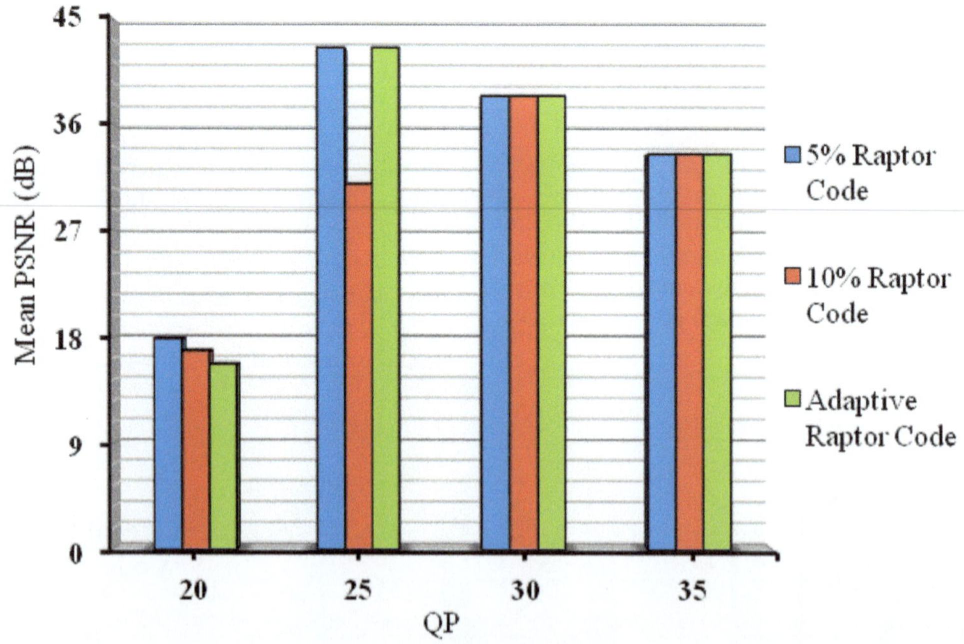

(a)

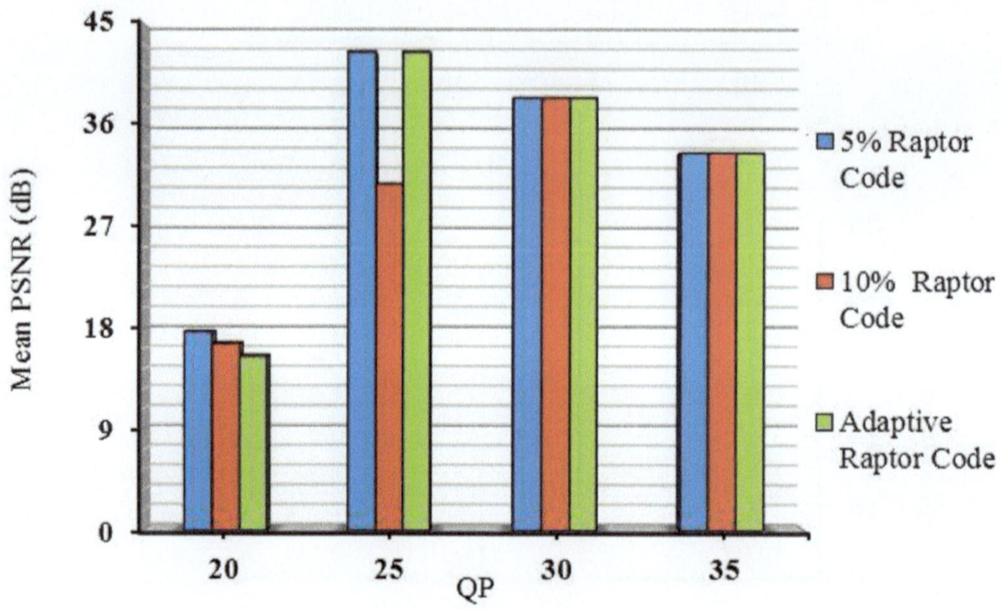

(b)

Figure 17: Mean Peak Signal-to-Noise Ratio (PSNR) (dB) for streaming (**a**) *Football* and (**b**) *Paris,* with 5%, 10% and adaptive redundant data.

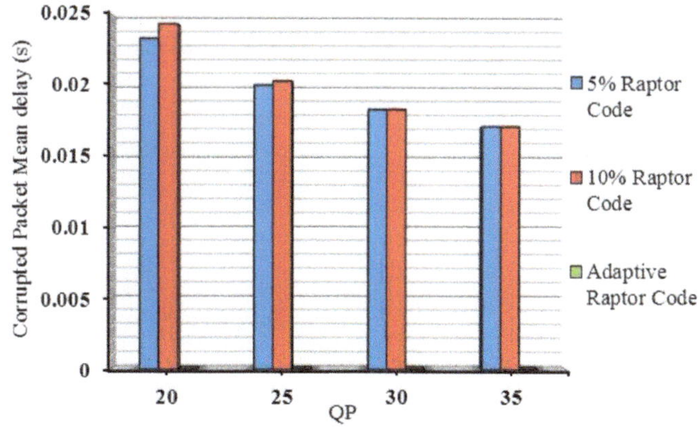

(a)

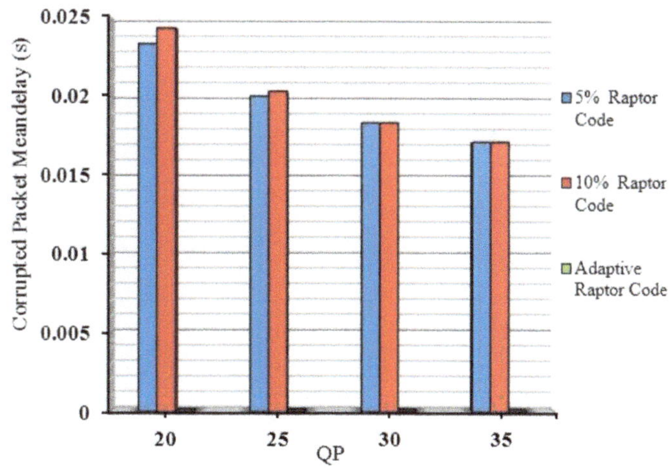

(b)

Figure 18: Corrupted packet mean delay (s) for streaming (**a**) *Football* and (**b**) *Paris,* with 5%, 10% and adaptive redundant data.

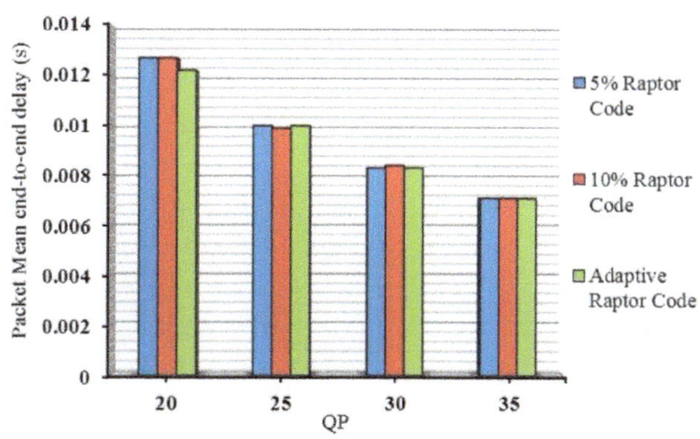

(a)

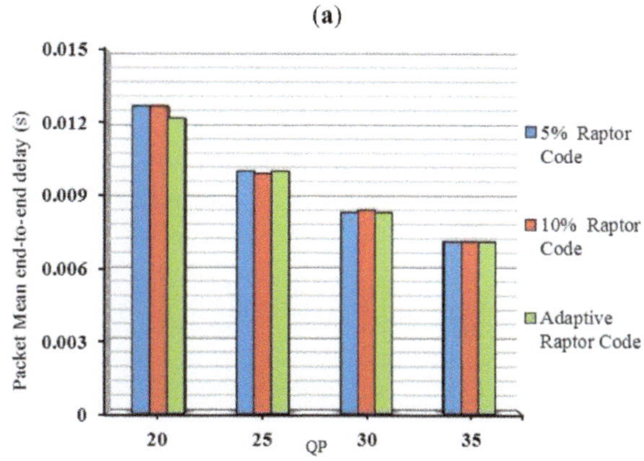

(b)

Figure 19: Packet mean delay (s) for streaming (**a**) *Football* and (**b**) *Paris* with 5%, 10% and adaptive redundant data.

Congestion Resilience

Figure 20 and Figure 21 show the packet size distribution as a result of coding the two test video clips, *Paris* and *Stefan*, with CIF at 30 frame/s. The sequences were this time coded with a CBR target of 500 kbps. In this distribution, 5.6% intra-coded MBs were randomly added to each frame, equivalent to one row of MBs in CIF. (In the Joint Model (JM) reference software of H.264/AVC used, this results in a gradual decoding refresh within 18 frames, because there is no replication of previously allocated random MB positions in successive frames.) From Figure 20 for *Paris*, about 63% of packets are moderately sized, with 11% relatively large. The remaining 26% are small. The average absolute length of motion vectors in the *Stefan* sequence is 5.5, while for *Paris*, it is only 2.2, implying that there is much more motion activity in *Stefan*. Partially as a result, the more active *Stefan* sequence has fewer smaller packets (Figure 21), than *Paris* at this bitrate.

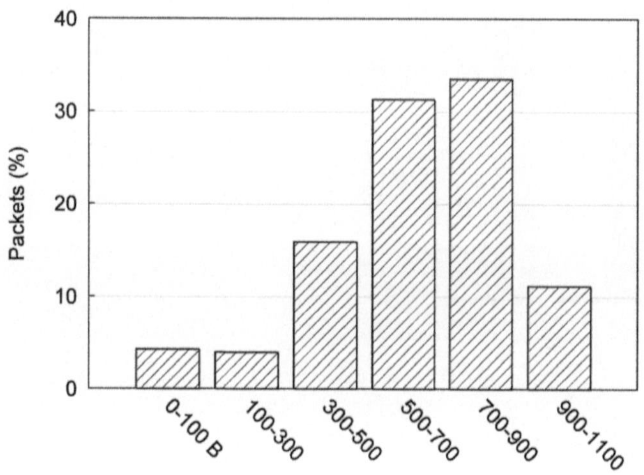

Figure 20: Packet size (bytes) distribution for Paris CIF@30 Hz, coded at a Constant Bit-Rate (CBR) of 500 kbps, with 5.6% Random Intra Macroblock Refresh (RIMR).

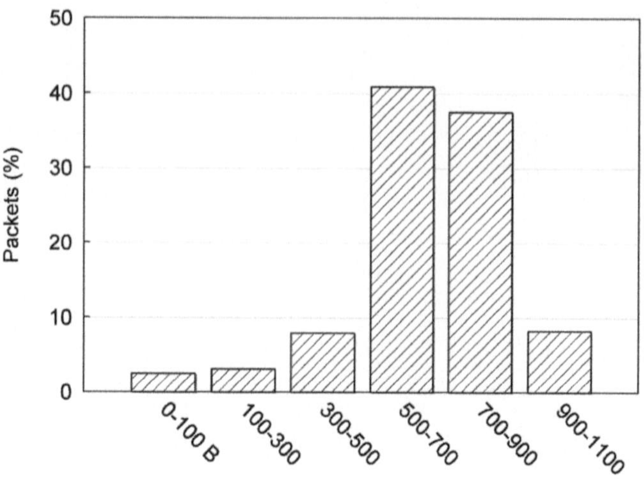

Figure 21: Packet size (bytes) distribution for *Stefan* CIF@30 Hz, coded at a CBR of 500 kbps, with 5.6% RIMR.

Figure 22 and Figure 23 present the result of streaming *Paris* and *Stefan* respectively across the WiMAX link, before and prior to turning on the congesting sources mentioned at about frame number 125. During this period, approximately 2% of the CBR stream packets are dropped through buffer overflow. From the figures, it is apparent that there is a content-dependent effect, as the more active sequence, *Stefan*, does not benefit from the scheme as much as *Paris* does. The reason for this is apparent from looking back at the packet size histograms of Figure 20 and Figure 21. As *Stefan's* packet sizes are predominantly in the range 500–900 B, they are more likely to pose a risk of overflow at the WiMAX BS output buffer. However, for both types of content there is a positive gain from turning on the packet scheduling and, in the case of *Paris*, there is a very definite gain in video quality, which remains stable.

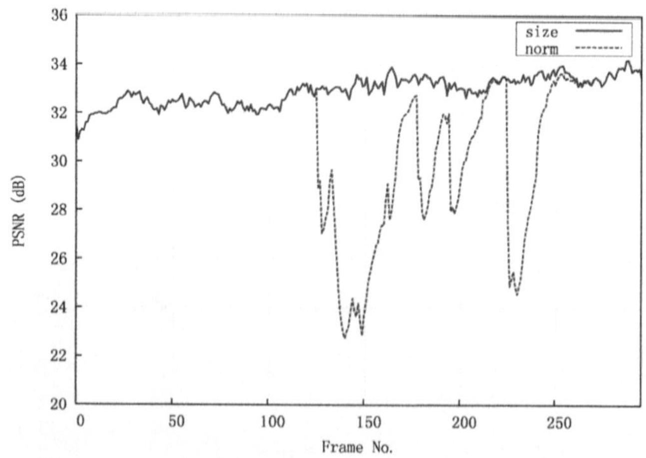

Figure 22: Objective video quality for *Paris* when using both scheduling approaches, by "size" and the equispaced "norm".

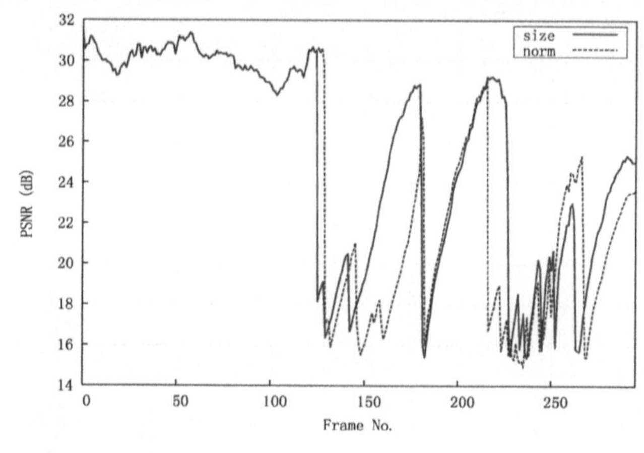

Figure 23: Objective video quality for *Stefan* when using both scheduling approaches, by "size" and the equi-spaced "norm".

CONCLUSIONS AND DISCUSSION OF FUTURE WORK

Because of the way research is commissioned, it is sometimes not apparent that wireless links suffer not just from an increased level of errors but that the problems of congestion at the input to the wireless channel does not go away either. The errors tend not to be isolated but are correlated as bursts. This paper proposes a scheme that is both error resilient and congestion resilient. The error resilience scheme is multi-faceted as it includes adaptive rateless coding, ARQ error control, and source-coded data partitioning.

The proposed sized-based scheduling solution, specialized to data-partitioned video streams, will certainly benefit the types of content favored by mobile viewers according to quality-of-experience studies, which are studio scenes with limited motion activity. Active sports clips, especially those with small balls, are less attractive but may become more so as the move to higher resolutions on mobile devices continues (e.g., full Video Graphics Array (VGA) format (640 × 480 pixels/frame at 30 Hz) for streaming in Apple's FaceTime). However, in that case the problem of packet scheduling regimes may become more acute. Future work will require a robust investigation of appropriate packet scheduling for congested broadband links for a range of content genres.

High Performance Video Coding (HEVC) [62] emerged as a successor to H.264/AVC during the period of this research. Broadly, HEVC refines and extends the structure of H.264/AVC rather than radically departing from it. However, very few error-resilience tools were included in HEVC, in part because some of these, such as Flexible Macroblock Ordering, were reportedly [63] rarely used in commercial applications. However, this situation provides an opportunity for researchers themselves to add data partitioning to the HEVC source code. Another likely reason why few error resilience tools were built into HEVC is that a full implementation is likely to be computationally demanding, including data partitioning coming at a cost of some other feature of the code. In contrast, direct and efficient implementation of Raptor code has become easier to accomplish with the development of RaptorQ [64], a systematic version of Raptor code software. However, inclusion of such code in a commercial product is subject to a patent in many jurisdictions even if it may be available for educational and research purposes. Such issues do not fall within the scope of this article, though in terms of future research, increased opportunities of confirming the error-correcting performance of Raptor codes now exist. The inner LT code of Raptor is a late decoding type of coding scheme, as sufficient symbols need to be collected before decoding can commence. If network coding is permitted, Switched Code [65] is then a low-latency form of rateless code that is worthy of investigation by us for multimedia applications, as it permits early decoding of packets. Another area for future work is in error resilience. For example, intra-refresh provision in [66] is varied according to an estimate of the rate-distortion trade-off that takes into account expected errors over a wireless channel.

AUTHOR CONTRIBUTIONS

Laith Al-Jobouri and Ismail A. Ali were chiefly responsible for the experimental contributions in this paper, whereas Martin Fleury contributed the theoretical development and was responsible for the presentation of this paper. Mohammed Ghanbari supervised the overall direction of this research. All authors have read an approved the final manuscript.

CONFLICTS OF INTEREST

The authors declare no conflict of interest.

REFERENCES

1. Oyman, O.; Foerster, J.; Tcha, Y.J.; Lee, S.C. Towards enhanced mobile video services over WiMAX and LTE. *IEEE Commun. Mag.* 2010, *48*, 68–76.
2. Liang, Y.J.; Apostolopoulos, J.G.; Girod, B. Analysis of packet loss for compressed video: Effect of burst losses and correlation between error frames. *IEEE Trans. Circuits Syst. Video Technol.* 2008, *18*, 861–874.
3. Fleury, M.; Moiron, S.; Ghanbari, M. Innovations in video error resilience and concealment. *Recent Pat. Signal Process.* 2011, *1*, 1–11.
4. Stockhammer, T.; Bystrom, M. H.264/AVC data partitioning for mobile video communication. In Proceedings of the IEEE International Conference on Image Processing, Singapore, 24–27 October 2004; pp. 545–548.
5. Al-Jobouri, L.; Fleury, M.; Ghanbari, M. Protecting H.264/AVC data-partitioned video streams over broadband WiMAX. *Adv. Multimed.* 2012.
6. Ghanbari, M. *Standard Codecs: Image Compression to Advanced Video Coding*; IET: London, UK, 2003.
7. Wiegand, T.; Sullivan, G.J.; Bjontegaard, G.; Luthra, A. Overview of the H.264/AVC video coding standard. *IEEE Trans. Circuits Syst. Video Technol.* 2003, *13*, 560–576.
8. Ferré, P.; Doufexi, A.; Chung-How, J.; Nix, A.R.; Bull, D.R. Robust video transmission over wireless LANs. *IEEE Trans. Veh. Technol.* 2008, *57*, 2596–2602.
9. Jammeh, E.; Fleury, M.; Ghanbari, M. Smoothing transcoded MPEG-1 video streams for Internet transmission. *IEEE Proc. Vis. Image Signal Process.* 2004, *151*, 298–306.
10. Al-Jobouri, L.; Fleury, M.; Ghanbari, M. Engineering wireless broadband access to IPTV. *J. Vis. Commun. Image Represent.* 2014, *25*, 1493–1506.
11. Declercq, D.; Fossorier, M.; Biglieri, E. *Channel Coding: Theory, Algorithms, and Applications*; Academic Press: Boston, MA, USA, 2014.
12. Wicker, S.B. *Error Control Systems*; Prentice-Hall: Engelwood Cliffs, NJ, USA, 1995.
13. Lin, S.; Costello, D.J. *Error Control Coding*, 2nd ed.; Pearson Prentice Hall: Upper Saddle River, NJ, USA, 2004.
14. Girod, B.; Färber, N. Wireless video. In *Compressed Video over Networks*; Sun, M.T., Reibman, A.R., Eds.; Marcel Dekker: New York, NY, USA, 2001; pp. 465–512.
15. Khansari, M.; Jalali, A.; Dubois, E. Low bit-rate video transmission over fading channels. For wireless microcellular system. *IEEE Trans. Circuits Syst. Video Technol.* 1996, *6*, 1–11.
16. Larzon, L.A.; Degermark, M.; Pink, S.; Jonsson, L.E.; Fairhurst, G. The Lightweight User Datagram Protocol (UDP-Lite). RFC 3828. Available online: http://www.hjp.at/doc/rfc/rfc3828.html (accessed on 17 April 2015).
17. Andrews, J.G.; Ghosh, A.; Muhamed, R. *Fundamentals of WiMAX: Understanding Broadband Wireless Networking*; Prentice Hall: Upper Saddle River, NJ, USA, 2007.
18. Heron, A.; MacDonald, N. Video transmission over a radio link using H.261 and DECT. In Proceedings of the International Conference on Image Processing and Its Applications, Maastricht, The Netherland, 7–9 April 1992; pp. 621–624.

19. Hsu, C.; Ortega, A.; Khansari, M. Rate control for robust video transmission over burst-error channels. *IEEE J. Sel. Areas Commun.* 1999, *17*, 756–773.

20. Joe, I. An adaptive hybrid ARQ scheme with concatenated FEC codes for wireless ATM. In Proceedings of the 3rd Annual ACM/IEEE International Conference on Mobile Computing and Networking, Budapest, Hungary, 26–30 September 1997; pp. 131–138.

21. Kallel, S.; Haccoun, D. Generalized Type II Hybrid ARQ scheme using punctured convolutional coding. *IEEE Trans. Commun.* 1990, *38*, 1938–1946.

22. Lettieri, P.; Fragouli, C.; Srivastava, M.B. Low power error control for wireless links. In Proceedings of the 3rd Annual ACM/IEEE International Conference on Mobile Computing and Networking, Budapest, Hungary, 26–30 September 1997; pp. 139–150.

23. Shokorallahi, A. Raptor codes. *IEEE Trans. Inf. Theory* 2006, *52*, 2551–2567.

24. Byers, J.; Luby, M.; Mitzenbacher, M.; Rege, A. A Digital Fountain approach to reliable distribution of bulk data. In Proceedings of the ACM SIGCOMM, Seattle, WA, USA, 2–4 September 1998; pp. 56–67.

25. Jenkăc, H.; Hagenauer, J.; Mayer, T. The Turbo-Fountain. *Eur. Trans. Telecomm. (ETT)* 2006, *17*, 337–346.

26. Luby, M. LT codes. In Proceedings of 2013 IEEE 54th Annual Symposium on Foundations of Computer Science, Berkeley, CA, USA, 26–29 October 2013; pp. 271–280.

27. Palanki, R.; Yedidia, J.S. Rateless codes on noisy channels. In Proceedings of the IEEE International Symposium of Information Theory, Chicago, IL, USA, 27 June–2 July 2004.

28. Nguyen, T. An Investigation of Coding Complexity and Coding Rate Performance of Raptor Codes. Master's Thesis, University of Concordia, Montreal, QC, Canada, 2011.

29. Bonello, N.; Chen, S.; Hanzo, L. Myths and realities of rateless coding. *IEEE Commun. Mag.*2011, *49*, 143–151.

30. Afzal, J.; Stockhammer, T.; Gasiba, T.; Xui, W. Video streaming over MBMS: A system design approach. *J. Multimed.* 2006, *1*, 25–35.

31. Jenkăc, H.; Mayer, T.; Stockhammer, T.; Xu, W. Soft decoding of LT-codes for wireless broadcast. In Proceedings of the IST Mobile Summit, Dresden, Germany, 19–23 June 2005.

32. Karp, R.; Luby, M.; Shokorallahi, A. Finite length analysis of LT codes. In Proceedings of IEEE International Symposium of Information Theory, Chicago, IL, USA, 27 June–2 July 2004.

33. Di, C.; Proietti, D.; Telatar, E.; Richardson, T.; Urbanke, R. Finite-length analysis of low-density parity-check codes on the binary erasure channel. *IEEE Trans. Inf. Theory* 2002, *48*, 1570–1579.

34. Luby, M.; Gasiba, T.; Stockhammer, T.; Watson, M. Reliable multimedia download delivery in cellular broadcast networks. *IEEE Trans. Broadcast.* 2007, *53*, 235–246.

35. Luby, M.; Stockhammer, T.; Watson, M. Application layer FEC in IPTV services. *IEEE Commun. Mag.* 2008, *46*, 95–101.

36. Hepsaydir, E.; Witvoet, E.; Binucci, N.; Jadhav, S. Enhanced MBMS in UMTS networks and Raptor codes. In Proceedings of the IEEE International Symposium on Personal, Indoor, and Mobile Radio Communications, Athens, Greece, 3–7 September 2007; pp. 1–5.

37. Rouzbeh, R.; Fleury, M.; Altaf, M.; Sammak, H.; Ghanbari, M. H.264 video streaming with data partitioning and growth codes. In Proceedings of the IEEE International Conference on Image Processing, Cairo, Egypt, 7–10 November 2009; pp. 909–912.

38. Nazir, S.; Stanković, V.; Vukobratović, D. Unequal error protection for data partitioned H.264/AVC video streaming with raptor and random linear codes for DVB-H networks. In Proceedings of the IEEE International Conference on Multimedia and Expo, Barcelona, Spain, 11–15 July 2011; pp. 1–6.

39. Nazir, S.; Stanković, V.; Vukobratović, D. Scalable broadcasting of sliced H.264/AVC over DVB-H network. In Proceedings of the IEEE International Conference on Networks, Singapore, 14–16 December 2011; pp. 36–40.

40. Nazir, S.; Vukobratović, D.; Stanković, V.; Andonović, I.; Nybom, K.; Grönroos, S. Unequal error protection for data partitioned H.264/AVC video broadcasting. *Multimed. Tools Appl.*2014.

41. Sgardoni, V.; Bull, D.R.; Nix, A.R. Spectrum efficient cross-layer adaptation of Raptor codes for video multicasting over mobile broadband networks. *Pervasive Mob. Comput.* 2014. in press.

42. Sgardoni, V.; Nix, A.R. Raptor code-aware link adaptation for spectrally efficient unicast video streaming over mobile broadband networks. *IEEE Trans. Mob. Comput.* 2015, *14*, 401–415.

43. Li, Y.; Markopoulou, A.; Apostolopoulos, J.; Bambos, N. Content-aware playout and packet scheduling for video streaming over wireless links. *IEEE Trans. Multimed.* 2008, *10*, 885–895.

44. Tian, D.; Li, X.; Al-Regib, L.G.; Altunbasak, B.; Jackson, J.R. Optimal packet scheduling for wireless video streaming with error-prone feedback. In Proceedings of the IEEE Wireless Communications and Networking Conference, Atlanta, GA, USA, 21–25 March 2004; pp. 1287–1292.

45. Kang, S.H.; Zakhor, A. Packet scheduling algorithm for wireless video streaming. In Proceedings of the International Packet Video Workshop, Pittsburgh, PA, USA, 24–26 April 2002.

46. Chen, C.M.; Lin, C.W.; Chen, Y.C. Packet scheduling for video streaming over wireless with content-aware packet retry limit. In Proceedings of the IEEE 8th Workshop on Multimedia Signal Processing, Victoria, Canada, 3–6 October 2006; pp. 409–414.

47. Liebl, G.; Kalman, M.; Girod, B. Deadline-aware scheduling for wireless video streaming. In Proceedings of the IEEE International Conference on Multimedia and Expo, Amsterdam, The Netherlands, 6–8 July 2005.

48. Capozzi, F.; Piro, G.; Grieco, L.A.; Boggia, G.; Camarda,

P. Downlink packet scheduling in LTE cellular networks: Key design issues and a survey. *IEEE Commun. Surv. Tutor.* 2013, *15*, 678–700.

49. Piro, G.; Grieco, L.A.; Boggia, G.; Fortunat, R.; Camarda, P. Two-level downlink scheduling for real-time multimedia services in LTE networks. *IEEE Trans. Multimed.* 2011, *13*, 1052–1065.

50. Nuaymi, L. *WiMAX: Technology for Broadband Wireless Access*; John Wiley & Sons: Chichester, UK, 2007.

51. Ahmadi, S. *Mobile WiMAX: A Systems Approach to Understanding IEEE 802.16 m Radio Access Technology*; Academic Press: Burlington, MA, USA, 2011.

52. *IEEE Std., 802.16-2009, IEEE Standard for Local and Metropolitan Area Networks—Part 16: Air Interface for Broadband Wireless Access Systems*; IEEE Computer Society: New York, NY, USA, 2009.

53. Fleury, M.; Ali, I.A.; Ghanbari, M. Video intra coding for compression and error resilience: A review. *Recent Pat. Signal Process.* 2014, *4*, 32–43.

54. Dhondt, Y.; Mys, S.; Vermeirsch, K.; van de Walle, R. Constrained Inter Prediction: Removing dependencies between different data partitions. In Proceedings of the Advanced Concepts for Intelligent Visual Systems, Delft, The Netherlands, 28–31 August 2007; pp. 720–731.

55. Bing, B. *HD and 3D Broadband Video Networking*; Artech House: Norwood, MA, USA, 2010.

56. Neves, P.; Sargneto, S.; Pentikousis, K.; Fontes, F. WiMAX cross-layer system for next generation heterogeneous environments. In *WiMAX, New Developments*; Dalal, U.D.D., Kosta, Y.P., Eds.; In-Tech: Vukovar, Croatia, 2009; pp. 357–376.

57. Issariwakul, T.; Hossain, E. *An Introduction to the ns-2 Simulator*, 2nd ed.; Springer Verlag: Berlin, Germany, 2012.

58. Tsai, F.C.D.; Chen, J.; Chang, C.W.; Lien, W.J.; Hung, C.H.; Sum, J.H. The design and implementation of WiMAX module for ns-2 simulator. In Proceedings of the Workshop on ns2: The IP Network Simulator, Pisa, Italy, 10 October 2006.

59. Al-Jobouri, L.; Fleury, M.; Al-Majeed, S.S.; Ghanbari, M. Effective video transport over WiMAX with data partitioning and rateless coding. In Proceedings of the 2010 IEEE 10th International Conference on Computer and Information Technology (CIT), Bradford, UK, 29 June–1 July 2010; pp. 767–772.

60. Jiao, Ch.; Schwiebert, L.; Xu, B. On modeling the packet error statistics in bursty channels. In Proceedings of the IEEE Conference on Local Computer Networks, Tampa, FL, USA, 6–8 November 2002; pp. 534–541.

61. Goldsmith, A. *Wireless Communications*; Cambridge University Press: Cambridge, UK, 2005.

62. Sullivan, G.J.; Ohm, J.R.; Han, W.J.; Wiegand, T. Overview of the High Efficiency Video Coding (HEVC) standard. *IEEE Trans. Circuits Syst. Video Technol.* 2012, *22*, 1648–1667.

63. Schierl, T.; Hannuksela, M.M.; Wang, Y.K.; Wenger, S. System layer integration of High Efficiency Video Coding. *IEEE Trans. Circuits Syst. Video Technol.* 2012, *22*, 1871–1884.

64. Luby, M.; Shokrollahi, A.; Watson, M.; Stockhammer, T.; Minder, L. RaptorQ forward error correction scheme for object delivery. RFC 6330. Available online: http://www.rfc-editor.org/info/rfc6330 (accessed on 17 April 2015).

65. Kadi, N.; Al Agha, K. New degree distribution to improve LT-code in network coding for broadcasting in ad-hoc wireless networks. In Proceedings of the IEEE International Symposium on Personal Indoor and Mobile Radio Communications, Istanbul, Turkey, 26–29 September 2010; pp. 1853–1857.

66. Zhao, P.; Liu, Y.; Liu, J.; Ci, S.; Yao, R. SSIM-based error-resilient rate-distortion optimization of H.264/AVC video coding for wireless streaming. *Signal Process. Image Commun.* 2014, *20*, 303–315.

INDEX

J

K

L

M

N

O

P

Q

R

S

T

U

V

W